AESTHETICS AND THE PHILOSOPHY OF CRITICISM

AESTHETICS
AND THE
PHILOSOPHY
OF
CRITICISM

EDITED BY

Marvin Levich

REED COLLEGE

RANDOM HOUSE

NEW YORK

To Laurie

PREFACE

Since it is customary for the editor of an anthology to identify and justify the nature of his project, it is only fair that the reader should know of the considerations that affected the business of selection. The reader may find, of course, that whatever value he assigns to the anthology is different from that envisaged by the editor. I am tempted to say "is *urged* to find," because the book will, I hope, serve a wide variety of objectives.

The many problems in aesthetics are understood more easily and the adequacy of their solutions appraised more responsibly when aesthetics is approached by way of criticism. This is not to say that the literature of criticism illuminates everything in aesthetics but rather that the study of criticism can clarify some otherwise baffling questions about the arts. Although it is not always obvious, philosophers do talk about the vocabulary and conceptual apparatus that critics invoke in their study of the arts, and attention to that apparatus should enhance our understanding of aesthetics and provide a basis for evaluating its findings.

In addition, the concurrent study of aesthetics and criticism could raise some questions about the fairness of the bad press that aesthetics has suffered at the hands of professional philosophers and critics in recent years. Some of the charges of sterility and obscurity are no doubt warranted; aesthetics does abound in vague generalities and elegant epigrams. Too, some of the decline in its intellectual prestige can be put down to aesthetics' monocular concern with its own business when a look out of the other eye would have found much in the literature of criticism to clarify and reduce the scope of needlessly extravagant generalizations. Of course many philosophers have begun with the problems of description and evaluation as they are suggested in criticism, but they have sometimes couched their discussions in a vocabulary which makes it difficult to locate the source of their puzzlement and easy to disparage the results.

The charge of intellectual sterility sometimes cites the irrelevance of aesthetics to the enlightened conduct of criticism. Exclusive talk about problems *in* aesthetics can lend credence to the indictment; the picture is of a discipline chewing its intellectual tail, generating problems *de novo* and resolving them on arbitrary grounds of ingenuity or elegance of expression. Students may conclude (mine sometimes have) that doing aesthetics is simply learning and re-membering what aestheticians have said.

This impression of aesthetics is, I think, caricature, and there are many ways to correct it. While discussing aesthetics and criticism together is not a novel departure, it should dispel the notion that aesthetics spontaneously generates and then digests its own subject matter.

The themes which determine the overall organization of this anthology were selected because they are characteristic of recurrent problems in aesthetics and because, when arranged in an obvious sequence, they seemed to exhibit a fairly coherent and orderly chain of analysis. This discussion of tragedy as a kind of style, for example, seemed to follow naturally the previous section where general issues of stylistic attribution were raised. In the same way, the discussion of the nature and intellectual warrant of critical judgment seemed to follow naturally previous sections which examined a variety of such judgments in some detail.

Of course, the readings do not exhaust the problems of aesthetics. That would be hard to do while providing for any of them dis-cussions of reasonable clarity and substance. They should suggest what aesthetics is like and how its problems can be located and discussed.

I have tried also to include groups of essays that were not only interesting in their own right but exhibited the nature of philosophical debate. Although the two are not ultimately separable, it is at least as important for the student to learn about and to master the strategy of philosophical argument as it is for him to learn that such and such philosopher said this or that. I think the essays by Professors Tomas, Sibley, and Cohen in Section III have the special merit of illustrating this strategy.

The connection between aesthetics and criticism is pointed up by introducing each section with one or more critical essays which use the concepts and vocabulary that are investigated in the essays in philosophy which follow them. For example, the notion of period-style is discussed in the context of alternative definitions of the baroque, and an entry into other problems of style is provided by particular disagreements about the tragic character of *Death of a Salesman*. This sequence should enable the reader to determine whether the philosophical mill has refined the grist or simply ground it away.

The sections, with the exception of the final two, are supplied with introductions. (Those two are concerned with the nature of critical judgment and the role of definition and are, I think, implicitly introduced by everything that comes before.) The purpose of these introductions is not to identify everything of importance but to discuss, sometimes in detail, a particular problem germane to the section. The objective was to cast as much light as possible by reducing the focus of attention. The discussions naturally reveal my prejudices, but I could not find the *modus operandi* that would permit both clarification of issues and a position of strict neutrality. I urge, in all candor, any instructor who finds the introductions confused, mistaken, or prejudiced to ignore them and go directly to the selections.

Acknowledgments

My special thanks go to the following: Professor William Halewood allowed me to exploit his knowledge of the seventeenth century in preparing the section on style. Professor Herbert Kamins of San Fernando Valley State College challenged my thinking about aesthetics with his uncompromising standards of philosophic rigor. Professor Hugo Bedau of Reed College was an untiring and exacting partner in discussion and insisted at appropriate intervals that I should finish.

Professor Morton Levine of Vassar was always available for instruction in the mysteries of art-history and generously encouraged me to think that even anthropologists might benefit from this project. Professor Warren Susman of Rutgers University was critic and friend. I owe him a debt which can neither be expressed nor repaid.

CONTENTS

V: The Nature and Uses of Critical Judgment   483

VI: The Nature and Uses of Definition 557

I

The Form and Content of a Work of Art

INTRODUCTION

This section deals with a protean and central term of critical vocabulary—*form*. It takes on an almost bewildering variety of senses and the essays following will illustrate some of them.

"Form" sometimes has the use of identifying elements of pattern or structure in works of art. In this sense, it is cognate with "formal" and distinguishes for patterned material between the pattern, which it denominates, and the material, which relative to the pattern, becomes "content" (cf. the essays by Brooks and Levich).

"Form" sometimes designates *particular* structures of organization and is defined by the effect associated with the specific structure in question. For instance, "spatial" form is a special ordering of language that has the effect of presenting bodies and/or events in their spatial relations and as perceived in a moment of time (cf. the essay by Frank).

"Form" may take on evaluative force and describe effects regarded appropriate to the different arts. Previously structure, it becomes an aesthetic boundary the transgression of which insures the failure of an art-work. Thus in one classic statement, the form of the visual arts is spatial and that of the narrative arts is temporal. And to say of a poem that it depicts properties of bodies in space, or of a painting that it narrates the sequential order of events, is to cite violations of form sufficient for condemning either as a work of art (cf. Lessing).

"Form" is a term of evaluation also identifying a property whose presence or absence in a work of art uniquely determines aesthetic value. The difference is that, in the last sense, a good work of art is not simply one conforming to the appropriate form. It must have something else, that which Lessing and others have called "beauty." For Lessing, form is the necessary condition of a good work of art; Bell changes the sense and makes it necessary and sufficient (cf. Bell).

These differences suggest the difficulty of making general statements about the role of form in discussions of works of art and of making wholesale evaluations of its force and suitability. It suggests, at least, the merit of postponing wholesale evaluations unless and until specific investigations establish the required generality of meaning.

The essays that follow should suggest further the importance of discriminating between the nature of "form," and like terms, as *used* and as *described* by critics. They are frequently different and it is often a mistake, therefore, to equate them or to construe their use in terms of their description.

The discussion of form and content, as I present it in a later paper, is addressed exclusively to the analysis of what critics have said about them and their relation. The remarks there are almost entirely negative, but this is not to say that the terms themselves should be read out of the critical vocabulary. What *is* required is a fairer statement of their point and justification. Despite the quasi-descriptive character allotted to the form-content relationship by critics describing and justifying its nature, its use by critics is, I think, almost entirely strategic.

When the critic says that form and content are completely inseparable in poetry, unlike their relation in the language of assertion, he is saying, in effect, that poetry is different from science, and that the critical instruments for its understanding and evaluation are similarly different. First, he is using the distinction to counter the view that the canons of meaning, truth, and falsity that apply to the special sciences apply equally well to the understanding of poems or the evaluation of their aesthetic merit.

In addition, the notion that form and content are inseparable is frequently invoked to counter particularly simple-minded interpretations of poetry. Suppose someone contends, for example, that Milton's *Paradise Lost* is no better than the hymn "I Walk in the Garden Alone" because, relative to God, both express the same body of information and feeling. It would be silly to waste a sophisticated battery of literary distinctions on such a person. He wouldn't understand them. It is simpler and more efficient to say, "But poetry is *both* form and content. What is expressed affects, and is affected by, the manner of expression. You have paid attention only to what is expressed. You have missed the *whole* poem."

Of course the same reply, if taken seriously within the profession of literary criticism, would have the force of denying to any reading of poetry its intellectual authority. There is no interpretation of a poem in which the poem is not considered in its separable constituents. No reading of a poem is identical with the poem itself, and every reading extracts from it an aspect for analysis. But since advocates of the form-content relation usually maintain that the meaning of a poem is determined by the nature of the language in which it is expressed, and, conversely, that any formulation of its meaning or any description of its language not identical with the poem is, in principle, false, it follows that anything said about a poem must always be false. However, the very critics who advocate this view of poetry do say what they think is true about a particular poem and do dispute other critics for saying what is false. And in neither case do the critics in question invoke their statement about the form-content relation as a way of warranting their claims or denying those of their opponents. Accordingly the form-content distinction is not used as a criterion for determining the adequacy of professional readings of poetry but as a convenient device for discounting, without undue expenditure of labor or argument, readings that are unprofessional.

As a result, the strategic role of the form-content distinction is one thing, its abstract statement is another. And to automatically export any doubts that we have from the latter to the former is gratuitous and misleading.

Whatever the special merit of these remarks they suggest one advantage of working with criticism and aesthetics; we have to study together *statements about* and *uses of* a critical vocabulary. Otherwise, we run the risk of distorting, oversimplifying, or neglecting significant features of the working vocabulary of art-criticism.

Joseph Frank

SPATIAL FORM IN
MODERN LITERATURE*

INTRODUCTION

Lessing's *Laokoön*, André Gide once remarked, is one of those books it is good to reiterate or contradict every thirty years. Despite this excellent advice, neither of these attitudes toward *Laokoön* has been adopted by modern writers. Lessing's attempt to define the limits of literature and the plastic arts has become a dead issue—one to which respectful reference is occasionally made, but which rarely seems to have any fecundating influence on esthetic thinking. This was comprehensible in the nineteenth century, with its passion for historicism; but it is not so easy to understand at present when so many writers on esthetic problems are occupied with questions of form. To a historian of literature or the plastic arts, Lessing's effort to define the unalterable laws of these mediums may well have seemed quixotic; but modern critics, no longer overawed by the bugbear of historical method, have begun to take up again the problems he tried to solve.

Lessing's own solution to these problems seems, at first glance, to have litttle relation to modern esthetic thinking. The literary school against which the arguments of *Laokoön* were directed—the school

---

* From the *Sewanee Review*, Spring, Summer, Autumn, 1945. Reprinted with some revisions by permission of the author.

of pictorial poetry—has long since ceased to interest the modern sensibility. Many of Lessing's conclusions grew out of a now-anti-quated archeology, whose discoveries, to make matters worse, he knew mainly at second-hand. But it was precisely his attempt to rise above history, to define the unalterable laws of esthetic perception rather than to attack or defend any particular school, which gives his work the perennial freshness to which André Gide alluded. The validity of his theories does not depend on their relationship to the literary movements of his time, or on the extent of his first-hand acquaintanceship with the artworks of antiquity. It is thus always possible to consider them apart from these circumstances, and to use them in the analysis of later developments.

In *Laokoön* Lessing fuses two distinct currents of thought, both of great importance in the cultural history of his time. The arche-ological researches of his contemporary Winckelmann had stimu-lated a passionate interest in Greek culture among the Germans. Lessing went back to Homer, Aristotle and the Greek tragedians, and using his first-hand knowlege attacked the distorted critical theories, supposedly based on classical authority, which had filtered into France through Italian commentators and had then taken hold in Germany. At the same time Locke and the empirical school of English philosophy had given a new impulse to esthetic speculation. For Locke tried to solve the problem of knowledge by breaking down complex ideas into simple elements of sensation, and then examining the operations of the mind to see how these sensations were combined to form ideas.

This method was soon taken over by estheticians; and the focus of interest shifted from external prescriptions for beauty to an analysis of esthetic perception. Writers like Shaftesbury, Hogarth, Hutche-son and Burke, to mention only a few, concerned themselves with the precise character and combination of impressions that gave esthetic pleasure to the sensibility, and Lessing's friend and critical ally Mendelssohn popularized this method of dealing with esthetic problems in Germany. *Laokoön*, as a result, stands at the confluence of these two intellectual currents. Lessing analyzes the laws of esthetic perception; shows how they prescribe necessary limitations to literature and the plastic arts; and then demonstrates how Greek writers and painters, especially his cherished Homer, created master-pieces by obeying these laws.

Lessing's argument starts from the simple observation that literature and the plastic arts, working through different sensuous mediums, must differ in the fundamental laws governing their creation. "If it is true," Lessing wrote, "that painting and poetry in their imitations make use of entirely different means or symbols—the first, namely, of form and color in space, the second of articulated sounds in time—if these symbols indisputably require a suitable relation to the thing symbolized, then it is clear that symbols arranged in juxtaposition can only express subjects of which the wholes or parts exist in juxtaposition; while consecutive symbols can only express subjects of which the wholes or parts are themselves consecutive."

Lessing did not originate this formulation, which has a long and complicated history; but he is the first to use it systematically as an instrument of critical analysis. Form in the plastic arts, according to Lessing, is necessarily spatial because the visible aspect of objects can best be presented juxtaposed in an instant of time. Literature, on the other hand, makes use of language, composed of a succession of words proceeding through time; and it follows that literary form, to harmonize with the essential quality of its medium, must be based primarily on some form of narrative sequence. Lessing used this argument to attack two artistic genres highly popular in his day: pictorial poetry and allegorical painting. The pictorial poet tried to paint with words; the allegorical painter to tell a story in visible images. Both were doomed to fail because their aims were in contradiction with the fundamental properties of their mediums. No matter how accurate and vivid a verbal description might be, Lessing argued, it could not give the unified impression of a visible object. No matter how skillfully figures might be chosen and arranged, a painting or piece of sculpture could not successfully set forth the various stages of an action.

As Lessing develops his argument, he attempts to prove that the Greeks, with an unfailing sense of esthetic propriety, respected the limits imposed on different art mediums by the conditions of human perception. The importance of Lessing's distinction, however, does not depend on these ramifications of his argument, nor even on his specific critical judgments. Various critics have quarreled with one or another of these judgments, in the belief that this would undermine Lessing's position; but such a notion is based on a misunderstanding of *Laokoön*'s importance in the history of esthetic theory. It is quite possible to use Lessing's insights solely as instruments of analysis, without proceeding to judge the value of individual works by how closely they adhere to the norms he laid down. And unless this is done, as a matter of fact, the real meaning of *Laokoön* cannot be understood; for what Lessing offered was not a new set of norms but a new approach to esthetic form.

The conception of esthetic form inherited by the eighteenth century from the Renaissance was a purely external one. Classical literature—or what was known of it—was presumed to have reached perfection, and later writers could do little better than imitate its example. A horde of commentators and critics had deduced certain rules from the classical masterpieces (rules like the Aristotelian unities, of which Aristotle had never heard), and modern writers were warned to obey these rules if they wished to appeal to a cultivated public. Gradually, these rules came to be regarded as an immutable mold into which the material of a literary work had to be poured: the form of a work was nothing but the technical arrangement dictated by the rules. Such a superficial and mechanical notion of esthetic form, however, led to serious perversions of taste— Shakespeare was considered a barbarian even by so sophisticated a writer as Voltaire, and Pope found it necessary in translating Homer to do a good deal of editing. Lessing's point of view, breaking sharply with this external conception of form, marks out the road for esthetic speculation to follow in the future.

For Lessing, as we have seen, esthetic form is not an external arrangement provided by a set of traditional rules. Rather, it is the relation between the sensuous nature of the art medium and the conditions of human perceptions. The "natural man" of the eighteenth century was not to be bound by traditional political forms but was to create them in accordance with his own nature. Similarly, art was to create its own forms out of itself rather than accepting them ready-made from the practice of the past. Criticism, instead of prescribing rules of art, explored the necessary laws by which art governs itself. No longer was esthetic form confused with mere externals of technique, or felt as a straitjacket into which the artist, willy-nilly, had to force his creative ideas. Form issued spontaneously from the organization of the art work as it presented itself to perception. Time and space were the two extremes defining the limits of literature and the plastic arts in their relation to sensuous perception; and it is possible, following Lessing's example, to trace the evolution of art forms by their oscillations between these two poles.

The purpose of the present essay is to apply Lessing's method to modern literature—to trace the evolution of form in modern poetry and, more particularly, in the novel. The first two sections will try to show that modern literature, exemplified by such writers as T. S. Eliot, Ezra Pound, Marcel Proust and James Joyce, is moving in the direction of spatial form. This means that the reader is ideally intended to apprehend their work spatially, in a moment of time, rather than as a sequence. So far as the novel is concerned, this tendency receives an original development in Djuna Barnes's remarkable book *Nightwood*, which has never received the critical attention it deserves. The third section [here omitted] will deal with *Nightwood* in detail, analyzing its form and explaining its meaning. Finally, since changes in esthetic form always involve major changes in the sensibility of a particular cultural period, an effort will be made to outline the spiritual attitudes that have led to the predominance of spatial form.

I. MODERN POETRY

Modern Anglo-American poetry received its initial impetus from the Imagist movement of the years directly preceding and following the first World War. Imagism was important not so much for any actual poetry written by Imagist poets—no one knew quite what an Imagist poet was—but rather because it opened the way for later developments by its clean break with sentimental Victorian verbiage. The critical writings of Ezra Pound, the leading theoretician of Imagism, are an astonishing farrago of keen esthetic perceptions thrown in among a series of boyishly naughty remarks whose chief purpose is to *épater le bourgeois*. But Pound's definition of the image, perhaps the keenest of his perceptions, is of fundamental importance for any discussion of modern literary form.

"An image," Pound wrote, "is that which presents an intellectual and emotional complex in an instant of time." The implications of this definition should be noted—an image is defined not as a pictorial reproduction, but as a unification of disparate ideas and emotions into a complex presented spatially in an instant of time. Such a complex does not proceed discursively, according to the laws of language, but strikes the reader's sensibility with an instantaneous impact. Pound stresses this aspect by adding, in a later passage, that only the instantaneous presentation of such complexes gives "that sense of sudden liberation; that sense of freedom from time limits and space limits; that sense of sudden growth, which we experience in the presence of the greatest works of art."

At the very outset, therefore, modern poetry advocates a poetic method in direct contradiction to Lessing's analysis of language. And if we compare Pound's definition of the image with Eliot's description of the psychology of the poetic process, we can see clearly how profoundly this conception has influenced our modern idea of the nature of poetry. For Eliot, the distinctive quality of a poetic sensibility is its capacity to form new wholes, to fuse seemingly disparate experiences into an organic unity. The ordinary man, Eliot writes, "falls in love, or reads Spinoza, and these two experiences have nothing to do with each other, or with the noise of the typewriter or the smell of cooking; in the mind of the poet these experiences are always forming new wholes." Pound had attempted to define the image in terms of its esthetic attributes; Eliot, in this passage, is describing its psychological origin; but the result in a poem is the same in both cases.

Such a view of the nature of poetry immediately gave rise to numerous problems. How was more than one image to be included in a poem? If the chief value of an image was its capacity to present an intellectual and emotional complex simultaneously, to link up images in a sequence would clearly destroy most of their efficacy. Or was the poem itself one vast image, whose individual components were to be apprehended as a unity? But then it would be necessary to undermine the inherent consecutiveness of language, frustrating the reader's normal expectation of a sequence and forcing him to perceive the elements of the poem juxtaposed in space rather than unrolling in time.

This is precisely what Eliot and Pound attempted in their major works. Both poets, in their earlier work, still retained some elements of conventional structure. Their poems were looked upon as daring and revolutionary chiefly because of technical matters, like the loosening of metrical pattern and the handling of subjects ordinarily considered non-poetic. Perhaps this is less true of Eliot than of Pound, especially the Eliot of the more complex early works like *Prufrock, Gerontion* and *Portrait of a Lady;* but even here, although the sections of the poem are not governed by syntactical logic, the skeleton of an implied narrative structure is always present. The reader of *Prufrock* is swept up in a narrative movement from the very first lines:

> Let us go then, you and I,
> When the evening . . .

And the reader, accompanying Prufrock, finally arrives at their mutual destination:

> In the room the women come and go
> Talking of Michelangelo.

At this point the poem becomes a series of more or less isolated fragments, each stating some aspect of Prufrock's emotional dilemma. But the fragments are now localized and focused on a specific set of circumstances, and the reader can organize them by referring to the implied sitution. The same method is employed in *Portrait of a Lady*, while in *Gerontion* the reader is specifically told that he has been reading the "thoughts of a dry brain in a dry season"—the stream-of-consciousness of "an old man in a dry month, being read to by a boy, waiting for the rain." In both poems there is a perceptible framework around which the seemingly disconnected passages of the poem can be organized. This was one reason why Pound's *Mauberly* and Eliot's early work were first regarded, not as forerunners of a new poetic form, but as latter-day *vers de société* —witty, disillusioned, with a somewhat brittle charm, but lacking that quality of "high seriousness" which Matthew Arnold had chosen as the touchstone of poetic excellence. These poems were considered unusual mainly because *vers de société* had long fallen out of fashion, but there was little difficulty in accepting them as an entertaining departure from the grand style of the nineteenth century.

In the *Cantos* and *The Waste Land*, however, it should have been clear that a radical transformation was taking place in esthetic structure; but this transformation has been touched on only peripherally by modern critics. R. P. Blackmur comes closest to the central problem while analyzing what he calls Pound's "anecdotal" method. The special form of the *Cantos*, Blackmur explains, "is that of the anecdote begun in one place, taken up in one or more other places, and finished, if at all, in still another. This deliberate disconnectedness, this art of a thing continually alluding to itself, continually breaking off short, is the method by which the *Cantos* tie themselves together. So soon as the reader's mind is concerted with the material of the poem, Mr. Pound deliberately disconcerts it, either by introducing fresh and disjunct material or by reverting to old and, apparently, equally disjunct material."

Blackmur's remarks apply equally well to *The Waste Land*, where syntactical sequence is given up for a structure depending on the perception of relationships between disconnected word-groups. To be properly understood, these word-groups must be juxtaposed with one another and perceived simultaneously. Only when this is done can they be adequately grasped; for while they follow one another in time their meaning does not depend on this temporal relationship. The one difficulty of these poems, which no amount of textual exegesis can wholly overcome, is the internal conflict between the time-logic of language and the space-logic implicit in the modern conception of the nature of poetry.

Esthetic form in modern poetry, then, is based on a space-logic that demands a complete re-orientation in the reader's attitude towards language. Since the primary reference of any word-group is to something inside the poem itself, language in modern poetry is really reflexive. The meaning-relationship is completed only by the simultaneous perception in space of word-groups which, when read consecutively in time, have no comprehensible relation to each other. Instead of the instinctive and immediate reference of words and word-groups to the objects or events they symbolize, and the construction of meaning from the sequence of these references, modern poetry asks its readers to suspend the process of individual reference temporarily until the entire pattern of internal references can be apprehended as a unity.

It would not be difficult to trace this conception of poetic form back to Mallarmé's ambition to create a language of "absence" rather than of presence—a language in which words negated their objects instead of designating them; nor should one overlook the evident formal analogies between *The Waste Land* and the *Cantos* and Mallarmé's *Un Coup de Dés*. Mallarmé, indeed, dislocated the temporality of language far more radically than either Eliot or Pound have ever done; and his experience with *Un Coup de Dés* showed that this ambition of modern poetry has a necessary limit. If pursued with Mallarmé's relentlessness, it culminates in the self-negation of language and the creation of a hybrid pictographic "poem" that can only be considered a fascinating historical curiosity. Nonetheless, this conception of esthetic form, which may be formulated as the principle of reflexive reference, has left its traces on all of modern poetry. And the principle of reflexive reference is the link connecting the esthetic development of modern poetry with similar experiments in the modern novel.

II. FLAUBERT AND JOYCE

For a study of esthetic form in the modern novel, Flaubert's famous county fair scene in *Madame Bovary* is a convenient point of departure. This scene has been justly praised for its mordant caricature of bourgeois pomposity, its portrayal—unusually sympathetic for Flaubert—of the bewildered old servant, and its burlesque of the pseudo-romantic rhetoric by which Rodolphe woos the sentimental Emma. At present, however, it is enough to notice the method by which Flaubert handles the scene—a method we might as well call cinematographic since this analogy comes immediately to mind.

As Flaubert sets the scene, there is action going on simultaneously at three levels; and the physical position of each level is a fair index to its spiritual significance. On the lowest plane, there is the surging, jostling mob in the street, mingling with the livestock brought to the exhibitions. Raised slightly above the street by a platform are the speech-making officials, bombastically reeling off platitudes to the attentive multitudes. And on the highest level of all, from a window overlooking the spectacle, Rodolphe and Emma are watching the proceedings and carrying on their amorous conversation in phrases as stilted as those regaling the crowds. Albert Thibaudet has compared this scene to the medieval mystery play, in which various related actions occur simultaneously on different stage levels; but this acute comparison refers to Flaubert's intention rather than to his method. "Everything should sound simultaneously," Flaubert later wrote, in commenting on this scene; "one should hear the bellowing of cattle, the whisperings of the lovers, and the rhetoric of the officials all at the same time."

But since language proceeds in time, it is impossible to approach this simultaneity of perception except by breaking up temporal sequence. And this is exactly what Flaubert does. He dissolves sequence by cutting back and forth between the various levels of action in a slowly-rising crescendo until—at the climax of the scene

—Rodolphe's Chateaubriandesque phrases are read at almost the same moment as the names of prize winners for raising the best pigs. Flaubert takes care to underline this satiric similarity by exposition as well as by juxtaposition—as if afraid the reflexive relations of the two actions would not be grasped: "From magnetism, by slow degrees, Rodolphe had arrived at affinities, and while M. le Président was citing Cincinnatus at his plow, Diocletian planting his cabbages and the emperors of China ushering in the new year with sowing-festivals, the young man was explaining to the young woman that these irresistible attractions sprang from some anterior existence."

This scene illustrates, on a small scale, what we meant by the spatialization of form in a novel. For the duration of the scene, at least, the time-flow of the narrative is halted; attention is fixed on the interplay of relationships within the limited time-area. These relationships are juxtaposed independently of the progress of the narrative, and the full significance of the scene is given only by the reflexive relations among the units of meaning. In Flaubert's scene, however, the unit of meaning is not, as in modern poetry, a word-group or a fragment of an anecdote; it is the totality of each level of action taken as an integer. The unit is so large that each integer can be read with an illusion of complete understanding, yet with a total unawareness of the "dialectic of platitude" (Thibaudet) interweaving all levels and finally linking them together with devastating irony.

In other words, the adoption of spatial form in Pound and Eliot resulted in the disappearance of coherent sequence after a few lines; but the novel, with its larger unit of meaning, can preserve coherent sequence within the unit of meaning and break up only the time-flow of narrative. (Because of this difference readers of modern poetry are practically forced to read reflexively to get any literal sense, while readers of a novel like *Nightwood,* for example, are led to expect narrative sequence by the deceptive normality of language sequence within the unit of meaning.) But this does not affect the parallel between esthetic form in modern poetry and the form of Flaubert's scene. Both can be properly understood only when their units of meaning are apprehended reflexively in an instant of time.

Flaubert's scene, although interesting in itself, is of minor importance to his novel as a whole and is skillfully blended back into the main narrative structure after fulfilling its satiric function. But

Flaubert's method was taken over by James Joyce, and applied on a gigantic scale in the composition of *Ulysses*. Joyce composed his novel of a vast number of references and cross-references that relate to each other independently of the time-sequence of the narrative. These references must be connected by the reader and viewed as a whole before the book fits together into any meaningful pattern. Ultimately, if we are to believe Stuart Gilbert, these systems of references form a complete picture of practically everything under the sun, from the stages of man's life and the organs of the human body to the colors of the spectrum. But these structures are far more important for Joyce, as Harry Levin has remarked, than they could ever possibly be for the reader. And while students of Joyce, fascinated by his erudition, have usually applied themselves to exegesis, our problem is to inquire into the perceptual form of his novel.

Joyce's most obvious intention in *Ulysses* is to give the reader a picture of Dublin seen as a whole—to re-create the sights and sounds, the people and places, of a typical Dublin day, much as Flaubert had recreated his provincial county fair. And like Flaubert, Joyce wanted his depiction to have the same unified impact, the same sense of simultaneous activity occurring in different places. Joyce, as a matter of fact, frequently makes use of the same method as Flaubert—cutting back and forth between different actions occurring at the same time—and usually does so to obtain the same ironic effect. But Joyce faced the problem of creating this impression of simultaneity for the life of a whole teeming city, and of maintaining it—or rather of strengthening it—through hundreds of pages that must be read as a sequence. To meet this problem Joyce was forced to go far beyond what Flaubert had done. Flaubert had still maintained a clear-cut narrative line except in the county fair scene; but Joyce breaks up his narrative and transforms the very structure of his novel into an instrument of his esthetic intention.

Joyce conceived *Ulysses* as a modern epic. And in the epic, as Stephen Dedalus tells us in *The Portrait of the Artist as a Young Man*, "the personality of the artist, at first sight a cry or a cadence and then a fluid and lambent narrative, finally refines itself out of existence, impersonlizes itself, so to speak . . . the artist, like the God of creation, remains within or beyond or above his handiwork, invisible, refined out of existence, indifferent, paring his fingernails." The epic is thus synonymous for Joyce with the complete self-effacement of the author; and with his usual uncompromising rigor Joyce carries this implication further than anyone had dared before.

He assumes—what is obviously not true—that all his readers are Dubliners, intimately acquainted with Dublin life and the personal history of his characters. This allows him to refrain from giving any direct information about his characters and thus betraying the presence of an omniscient author. What Joyce does, instead, is to present the elements of his narrative—the relations between Stephen and his family, between Bloom and his wife, between Stephen and Bloom and the Dedalus family—in fragments, as they are thrown out unexplained in the course of casual conversation, or as they lie embedded in the various strata of symbolic reference. The same is true of all the allusions to Dublin life and history, and to the external events of the twenty-four hours during which the novel takes place. In other words, all the factual background summarized for the reader in an ordinary novel must here be reconstructed from fragments, sometimes hundreds of pages apart, scattered through the book. As a result, the reader is forced to read *Ulysses* in exactly the same manner as he reads modern poetry, that is, by continually fitting fragments together and keeping allusions in mind until, by reflexive reference, he can link them to their complements.

Joyce intended, in this way, to build up in the reader's mind a sense of Dublin as a totality, including all the relations of the characters to one another and all the events which enter their consciousness. The reader ideally acquires this sense and he progresses through the novel, connecting allusions and references spatially and gradually becoming aware of the pattern of relationships. At the conclusion it might almost be said that Joyce literally wanted the reader to become a Dubliner. For this is what Joyce demands: that the reader have at hand the same instinctive knowledge of Dublin life, the same sense of Dublin as a huge, surrounding organism, which the Dubliner possesses as a birthright. It is such knowledge which, at any one moment of time, gives the latter a knowledge of Dublin's past and present as a whole; and it is only such knowledge that would enable the reader, like the characters, to place all the references in their proper context. This, it should be realized, is the equivalent of saying that Joyce cannot be read—he can only be reread. A knowledge of the whole is essential to an understanding of any part; but unless one is a Dubliner such knowledge can be obtained only after the book has been read, when all the references are fitted into their proper place and grasped as a unity. The burdens placed on the reader by this method of composition may well seem insuperable. Nonetheless, in his unbelievably laborious fragmentation of narrative structure, Joyce proceeded on the assumption that a unified spatial apprehension of his work would ultimately be possible.

III. PROUST

In a far more subtle manner than with either Joyce or Flaubert, the same principle of composition is at work in Marcel Proust. Since Proust himself tells us that his novel will have imprinted on it "a form which usually remains invisible, the form of Time," it may seem strange to speak of Proust in connection with spatial form. He has almost invariably been considered the novelist of time *par excellence;* the literary interpreter of that Bergsonian "real time" intuited by the sensibility, as distinguished from the abstract, chronological time of the conceptual intelligence. To stop at this point, however, is to miss what Proust himself considered the deepest significance of his work.

While oppressed and obsessed by a sense of the ineluctability of time and the evanescence of human life, Proust was suddenly visited by certain quasi-mystical experiences (described in detail in the last volume of his book, *Le Temps Retrouvé*). These experiences provided him with a spiritual technique for transcending time, and thus enabled him to escape from time's domination. Proust believed that these transcendent, extra-temporal moments contained a clue to the ultimate nature of reality, and, by writing a novel, he wished to translate these moments to the level of esthetic form. But no ordinary narrative, which tried to convey their meaning indirectly through exposition and description, could really do them justice. For Proust desired, through the medium of his novel, to communicate to the reader the full impact of these moments as he had felt them himself.

To define the method by which this is accomplished, we must first understand clearly the precise nature of the Proustian revelation. Each such experience, Proust tells us, is marked by a feeling that "the permanent essence of things, usually concealed, is set free and our true self, which had long seemed dead but was not dead in other ways, awakes, takes on fresh life as it receives the celestial nourishment brought to it." This celestial nourishment consists of some sound, or odor, or other sensory stimulus, "sensed anew, simultaneously in the present and the past."

But why should these moments seem so overwhelmingly valuable that Proust calls them celestial? Because, Proust observes, his imagination could only operate on the past; the material presented to his imagination thus lacked any sensuous immediacy. At certain moments, however, the physical sensations of the past came flooding back to fuse with the present; and in these moments, Proust believed that he grasped a reality "real without being of the present moment, ideal but not abstract." Only in these moments did he attain his most cherished ambition—"to seize, isolate, immobilize for the duration of a lightning flash" what otherwise he could not apprehend, "namely: a fragment of time in its pure state." For a person experiencing this moment, Proust adds, the word "death" no longer has meaning. "Situated outside the scope of time, what could he fear from the future?"

The significance of this experience, though obscurely hinted at throughout the book, is made explicit only in the concluding pages which describe the final appearance of the narrator at the reception of the Princesse de Guermantes. And the narrator decides to dedicate the remainder of his life to re-creating these experiences in a work of art. This work will differ essentially from all others because it will be rooted in a vision of reality refracted through an extra-temporal perspective. This decision, however, should not be confused with the Renaissance view of art as the guarantor of immortality, nor with the late nineteenth-century cult of art for art's sake (though Proust has obvious affinities with both traditions, and particularly with the latter). It was not the creation of a work of art *per se* that filled Proust with a sense of fulfilling a prophetic mission; it was the creation of a work of art that should stand as a monument to his *personal* conquest of time. His own novel was to be at once the vehicle through which he conveyed his vision, and the concrete substance of that vision expressed in a form that compelled the world (the reader) to re-experience its exact effect on Proust's own sensibility.

The prototype of this method, like the analysis of the revelatory moment, occurs during the reception at the Princesse de Guermantes. The narrator had spent years in a sanatorium and had lost touch almost completely with the fashionable world of the earlier volumes; now he comes out of his seclusion to attend the reception. The result is that he finds himself bewildered by the changes in social position, and the even more striking changes in character and personality, among his former friends. No doubt these pages paint a striking picture of the invasion of French society by the upper bourgeoisie, and the gradual breakdown of all social and moral standards caused by the first World War; but as the narrator takes great pains to tell us, this is far from being the most important theme of this section of the book.

Of much greater consequence is that, almost with the force of a blow, these changes jolt the narrator into a consciousness of the passage of time. He tries painfully to recognize old friends under the masks which, as he feels, the years have welded to them. And when a young man addresses him respectfully instead of familiarly, he realizes suddenly that, without being aware of it, he too has assumed a mask—the mask of an elderly gentleman. The narrator now begins to understand that, in order to become conscious of time, it had been necessary for him to absent himself from his accustomed environment (or in other words, from the stream of time acting on that environment) and then to plunge back into the stream after a lapse of years. In so doing, he found himself presented with two images—the world as he had formerly known it, and the world, transformed by time, that he now saw before him. When these two images are juxtaposed, the narrator discovers that the passage of time is suddenly experienced through its visible effects.

Habit is a universal soporific which ordinarily conceals the passage of time from those who have gone their accustomed ways. At any one moment of time the changes are so minute as to be imperceptible. "Other people," Proust writes, "never cease to change places in relation to ourselves. In the imperceptible, but eternal march of the world, we regard them as motionless in a moment of vision, too short for us to perceive the motion that is sweeping them on. But we have only to select in our memory two pictures taken of them at different moments, close enough together however for them not to have altered in themselves—perceptibly, that is to say—and the difference between the two pictures is a measure of the displacement that they have undergone in relation to us." By comparing these two images in a moment of time, the passage of time can be experienced concretely, through the impact of its visible effects on the sensibility. And this discovery provides the narrator with a method which, in T. S. Eliot's phrase, is an "objective correlative" to the visionary apprehension of the fragment of "pure time" intuited in the revelatory moment.

When the narrator discovers this method of communicating his experience of the revelatory moment, he decides, as we have already said, to incorporate it in a novel. But the novel the narrator determines to write has just been finished by the reader; its form is controlled by the method that the narrator has outlined in its concluding pages. The reader, in other words, is substituted for the narrator, and is placed by the author throughout the book in the same position as the narrator occupies before his own experience at the reception of the Princesse de Guermantes. This is done by the discontinuous presentation of character—a simple device which, nevertheless, is the clue to the form of Proust's vast structure.

Every reader soon notices that Proust does not follow any of his characters through the whole course of his novel. Instead, they appear and re-appear in various stages of their lives. Hundreds of pages sometimes go by between the time they are last seen and the time they re-appear; and when they do turn up again, the passage of time has invariably changed them in some decisive way. Rather than being submerged in the stream of time and intuiting a character progressively, in a continuous line of development, the reader is confronted with various snapshots of the characters "motionless in a moment of vision" taken at different stages in their lives; and in juxtaposing these images, he experiences the effects of the passage of time exactly as the narrator had done. As Proust had promised, therefore, he does stamp his novel indelibly with the form of time; but we are now in a position to understand exactly what he meant by this engagement.

To experience the passage of time, Proust learned it was necessary to rise above its flow and to grasp both past and present simultaneously in a moment of what he called "pure time." But "pure time," obviously, is not time at all—it is perception in a moment of time, that is to say, space. And, by the discontinuous presentation of character, Proust forces the reader to juxtapose disparate images of his characters spatially, in a moment of time, so that the experience of time's passage is communicated directly to their sensibility. Ramon Fernandez has acutely stressed this point in some remarks on Proust and Bergson. "Much attention has been given to the importance of time in Proust's work," he writes, "but perhaps it has not been sufficiently noted that he gives time the value and characteristics of space . . . in affirming that the different parts of time reciprocally exclude and remain external to each other." And he adds that while Proust's method of making contact with his *durée* is quite Bergsonian (that is, springing from the interpenetration of the past with the present), "the reactions of his intelligence on his sensibility, which determine the trajectory of his work, would orient him rather toward a *spatialisation* of time and memory."

There is a striking analogy here between Proust's method and that of his beloved Impressionist painters; but this analogy goes far deeper than the usual comments about the "impressionism" of Proust's style. The Impressionist painters juxtaposed pure tones on the canvas, instead of mixing them on the palette, in order to leave the blending of colors to the eye of the spectator. Similarly, Proust gives us what might be called pure views of his characters—views of them "motionless in a moment of vision" in various phases of their lives—and allows the sensibility of the reader to fuse these views into a unity. Each view must be apprehended by the reader as a unit; and Proust's purpose is only achieved when these units of meaning are referred to each other reflexively in a moment of time. As with Joyce and the modern poets, spatial form is also the structural scaffolding of Proust's labyrinthine masterpiece.

Gotthold Ephraim Lessing

LAOCOÖN*

II

Whether it be fable or history that Love prompted the first attempt in the plastic arts, it is at least certain that she was never weary of lending her guiding hand to the ancient masters. For if painting, as the art which imitates bodies on plane surfaces, is now generally practised with an unlimited range of subject, certainly the wise Greek set her much straiter bounds, and confined her solely to the imitation of beautiful bodies. His artist portrayed nothing but the beautiful; even the ordinary beautiful, beauty of inferior kinds, was for him only an occasional theme, an exercise, a recreation. In his work the perfection of the subject itself must give delight; he was too great to demand of those who beheld it that they should content themselves with the bare, cold pleasure arising from a well-caught likeness or from the daring of a clever effort; in his art nothing was dearer to him, and to his thinking nothing nobler, than the ultimate purpose of art.

"Who will wish to paint you, when no one wishes to see you?" says an old epigrammatist concerning an extremely misshapen man. Many a more modern artist would say, "Be you as misshapen as is possible, I will paint you nevertheless. Though, indeed, no one may wish to see you, people will still wish to see my picture; not in so

* From the book *Laocoön* by Gotthold Ephraim Lessing, translated by W. A. Steel. Everyman's Library. Reprinted by permission of E. P. Dutton & Co., Inc., and J. M. Dent & Sons, Ltd. (London).

far as it represents you, but in so far as it is a demonstration of my art, which knows how to make so good a likeness of such a monster."

To be sure, with pitiful dexterities that are not ennobled by the worth of their subjects, the propensity to such rank boasting is too natural for the Greeks to have escaped without their Pauson, their Pyreicus. They had them; but they did strict justice upon them. Pauson, who confined himself entirely to the beauty of vulgar things and whose lower taste delighted most in the faulty and ugly in human shape, lived in the most sordid poverty. And Pyreicus, who painted, with all the diligence of a Dutch artist, nothing but barbers' shops, filthy factories, donkeys and cabbages, as if that kind of thing had so much charm in Nature and were so rarely to be seen, got the nickname of the rhyparograph, the dirt-painter, although the luxurious rich weighed his works against gold, to help out their merit by this imaginary value.

The magistrates themselves consider it not unworthy of their attention to keep the artist by force in his proper sphere. The law of the Thebans, which commanded him in his imitation to add to beauty, and forbade under penalties the exaggeration of the ugly, is well known. It was no law against the bungler, as it is usually, and even by Junius, considered. It condemned the Greek "Ghezzi"; the unworthy artifice of achieving likeness by exaggeration of the uglier parts of the original: in a word, caricature.

Indeed, it was direct from the spirit of the Beautiful that the law of the Hellanodiken proceeded. Every Olympian victor received a statue; but only to the three-times victor was an Iconian statue awarded. Of mediocre portraits there ought not to be too many amongst works of art. For although even a portrait admits of an ideal, still the likeness must be the first consideration; it is the ideal of a certain man, not the ideal of a man.

We laugh when we hear that with the ancients even the arts were subject to municipal laws. But we are not always right when we laugh. Unquestionably the laws must not usurp power over the sciences, for the ultimate purposes of the sciences is truth. Truth is a necessity of the soul; and it is nothing but tyranny to offer her the slightest violence in satisfying this essential need. The ultimate purpose of the arts, on the other hand, is pleasure, and pleasure can be dispensed with. So, of course, it may depend on the law-giver what kind of pleasure, and in what measure any kind of it, he will permit.

The plastic arts in particular, beyond the unfailing influence they exert on the character of a nation, are capable of an effect that demands the close supervision of the law. When beautiful men fashioned beautiful statues, these in their turn affected them and the State had beautiful statues in part to thank for beautiful citizens. With us the tender imaginative power of mothers appears to express itself only in monsters.

From this point of view I believe that in certain ancient legends, which men cast aside without hesitation as lies, something of truth may be recognised. The mothers of Aristomenes, of Aristodamas, of Alexander the Great, of Scipio, of Augustus, of Galerius, all dreamed in their pregnancy that they had to do with a serpent. The serpent was a symbol of deity, and the beautiful statues and pictures of a Bacchus, an Apollo, a Mercury and a Hercules were seldom without a serpent. The honest women had by day feasted their eyes on the god, and the bewildering dream called up the image of the reptile. Thus I save the dream, and surrender the interpretation which the pride of their sons and the shamelessness of flatterers gave it. For there must certainly be a reason why the adulterous phantasy was never anything but a serpent.

Here, however, I am going off the line. I merely wished to establish the fact that with the ancients beauty was the supreme law of the plastic arts. And this being established, it necessarily follows that all else after which also the plastic arts might strive, if it were inconsistent with beauty must wholly yield to her, and if it were consistent with beauty must at least be subordinate.

I will dwell a little longer on *expression*. There are passions and degrees of passion which express themselves in the countenance by the most hideous grimaces, and put the whole frame into such violent postures that all the beautiful lines are lost which define it in a quieter condition. From these, therefore, the ancient artists either abstained wholly or reduced them to lower degrees in which they were capable of a measure of beauty. Rage and despair disfigured none of their works. I dare maintain that they never depicted a Fury.

Wrath they reduced to sternness: with the poet it was an angry Jupiter who sent forth his lightnings; with the artist the god was calmly grave.

Lamentation was toned down to sadness. And where this softening could not take place, where lamentation would have been just as deforming as belittling—what then did Timanthes? His picture of Iphigenia's sacrifice, in which he imparted to all the company the peculiar degree of sadness befitting them individually, but veiled the father's face, which should have shown the supreme degree, is well known, and many nice things have been said about it. He had, says one, so exhausted himself in sorrowful countenances that he despaired of being able to give the father one yet more grief-stricken. He confessed thereby, says another, that the pain of a father in such events is beyond all expression. I, for my part, see here neither the impotence of the artist nor the impotence of art. With the degree of emotion the traces of it are correspondingly heightened in the countenance; the highest degree is accompanied by the most decided traces of all, and nothing is easier for the artist than to exhibit them. But Timanthes knew the limits which the Graces set to his art. He knew that such misery as fell to Agamemnon's lot as a father expresses itself by distortions which are at all times ugly. So far as beauty and dignity could be united with the expression of sorrow, so far he carried it. He might have been willing to omit the ugliness had he been willing to mitigate the sorrow; but as his composition did not admit of both, what else remained to him but to veil it? What he dared not paint he left to be guessed. In a word, this veiling was a sacrifice which the artist offered to Beauty. It is an example, not how one should force expression beyond the bounds of art, but rather how one must subject it to the first law of art, the law of Beauty.

And if we now refer this to the Laocoön, the motive for which I am looking becomes evident. The master was striving after the highest beauty, under the given circumstances of bodily pain. This, in its full deforming violence, it was not, possible to unite with that. He was obliged, therefore, to abate, to lower it, to tone down cries to sighing; not because cries betrayed an ignoble soul, but because they disfigure the face in an unpleasing manner. Let one only, in imagination, open wide the mouth in Laocoön, and judge! Let him shriek, and see! It was a form that inspired pity because it showed beauty and pain together; now it has become an ugly, a loathsome form, from which one gladly turns away one's face, because the aspect of pain excites discomfort without the beauty of the suffering subject changing this discomfort into the sweet feeling of compassion.

The mere wide opening of the mouth—apart from the fact that

the other parts of the face are thereby violently and unpleasantly
distorted—is a blot in painting and a fault in sculpture which has
the most untoward effect possible. Montfaucon showed little taste
when he passed off an old, bearded head with widespread mouth
for an oracle-pronouncing Jupiter. Must a god shriek when he un-
veils the future? Would a pleasing contour of the mouth make his
speech suspicious? I do not even believe Valerius, that Ajax in the
imaginary picture of Timanthes should have cried aloud. Far inferior artists, in times when art was already degraded, never once
allow the wildest barbarians, when, under the victor's sword, terror
and mortal anguish seize them, to open the mouth to shrieking
point.

Certain it is that this reduction of extremest physical pain to a
lower degree of feeling is apparent in several works of ancient art.
The suffering Hercules in the poisoned garment, from the hand of
an unknown ancient master, was not the Sophoclean who shrieked
so horribly that the Locrian cliffs and the Euboean headlands re-
sounded. It was more sad than wild. The Philoctetes of Pythagoras
Leontinus appeared to impart his pain to the beholder, an effect
which the slightest trace of the horrible would have prevented.
Some may ask where I have learnt that this master made a statue of
Philoctetes? From a passage of Pliny which ought not to have
awaited my emendation, so manifestly forged or garbled is it.

III

But, as we have already seen, Art in these later days has been
assigned far wider boundaries. Let her imitative hand, folks say,
stretch out to the whole visible Nature, of which the Beautiful is
only a small part. Let fidelity and truth of expression be her first
law, and as Nature herself at all times sacrifices beauty to higher
purposes, so also must the artist subordinate it to his general aim and
yield to it no further than fidelity of expression permits. Enough,
if by truth and faithful expression an ugliness of Nature be transformed into a beauty of Art.

Granted that one would willingly, to begin with, leave these
conceptions uncontested in their worth or worthlessness, ought
not other considerations quite independent of them to be examined
—namely, why the artist is obliged to set bounds to expression and
never to choose for it the supreme moment of an action?

The fact that the material limits of Art confine her imitative effort to one single moment will, I believe, lead us to similar conclusions.

If the artist can never, in presence of ever-changing Nature, choose and use more than one single moment, and the painter in particular can use this single moment only from one point of vision; if, again, their works are made not merely to be seen, but to be considered, to be long and repeatedly contemplated, then it is certain that that single moment, and the single viewpoint of that moment, can never be chosen too significantly. Now that alone is significant and fruitful which gives free play to the imagination. The more we see, the more must we be able to add by thinking. The more we add thereto by thinking, so much the more can we believe ourselves to see. In the whole gamut of an emotion, however, there is no moment less advantageous than its topmost note. Beyond it there is nothing further, and to show us the uttermost is to tie the wings of fancy and oblige her, as she cannot rise above the sensuous impression, to busy herself with weaker pictures below it, the visible fullness of expression acting as a frontier which she dare not transgress. When, therefore, Laocoön sighs, the imagination can hear him shriek; but if he shrieks, then she cannot mount a step higher from this representation, nor, again, descend a step lower without seeing him in a more tolerable and consequently more uninteresting condition. She hears him only groan, or she sees him already dead.

Further. As this single moment receives from Art an unchangeable continuance, it must not express anything which thought is obliged to consider transitory. All phenomena of whose very essence, according to our conceptions, it is that they break out suddenly and as suddenly vanish, that what they are they can be only for a moment—all such phenomena, whether agreeable or terrible, do, by the permanence which Art bestows, put on an aspect so abhorrent to Nature that at every repeated view of them the impression becomes weaker, until at last the whole thing inspires us with horror or loathing. La Mettrie, who had himself painted and engraved as a second Democritus, laughs only the first time that one sees him. View him often, and from a philosopher he becomes a fool, and the laugh becomes a grin. So, too, with cries. The violent pain which presses out the cry either speedily relaxes or it destroys the sufferer. If, again, the most patient and resolute man cries aloud, still he does not cry out without intermission. And just this

unintermitting aspect in the material imitations of Art it is which
would make his cries an effeminate or a childish weakness. This at
least the artist of the Laocoön had to avoid, if cries had not been
themselves damaging to beauty, and if even it had been permitted
to his art to depict suffering without beauty....

I V

Glancing at the reasons adduced why the artist of the Laocoön was
obliged to observe restraint in the expression of physical pain, I find
that they are entirely drawn from the peculiar nature of Art and its
necessary limits and requirements. Hardly, therefore, could any one
of them be made applicable to poetry.

Without inquiring here how far the poet can succeed in depicting
physical beauty, so much at least is undeniable, that, as the whole
immeasurable realm of perfection lies open to his imitative skill, this
visible veil, under which perfection becomes beauty, can be only
one of the smallest means by which he undertakes to interest us in
his subject. Often he neglects this means entirely, being assured that
if his hero has won our good-will, then his nobler qualities either so
engage us that we do not think at all of the bodily harm, or, if we
think of it, so prepossess us that we do, on their very account, attribute to him, if not a beautiful one, yet at any rate one that is not
uncomely. At least, with every single line which is not expressly
intended for the eye he will still take this sense into consideration.
When Virgil's Laocoön cries aloud, to whom does it occur then
that a wide mouth is needful for a cry, and that this must be ugly?
Enough, that *clamores horrendos ad sidera tollit* is an excellent feature for the hearing, whatever it might be for the vision. Whoso-
ever demands here a beautiful picture, for him the poet has entirely
failed of his intention.

In the next place, nothing requires the poet to concentrate his
picture on one single moment. He takes up each of his actions, as
he likes, from its very origin and conducts it through all possible
modifications to its final close. Every one of these modifications,
which would cost the artist an entire separate canvas or marble-
block, costs the poet a single line; and if this line, taken in itself,
would have misled the hearer's imagination, it was either so prepared for by what preceded, or so modified and supplemented by
what followed, that it loses its separate impression, and in its proper

connection produces the most admirable effect in the world. Were it therefore actually unbecoming to a man to cry out in the extremity of pain, what damage can this trifling and transient impropriety do in our eyes to one whose other virtues have already taken us captive? Virgil's Laocoön shrieks aloud, but this shrieking Laocoön we already know and love as the wisest of patriots and the most affectionate of fathers. We refer his cries not to his character but purely to his unendurable suffering. It is this alone we hear in his cries, and the poet could make it sensible to us only through them. Who shall blame him then, and not much rather confess that, if the artist does well not to permit Laocoön to cry aloud, the poet does equally well in permitting him? . . .

XVI

But I will turn to the foundations and try to argue the matter from first principles.

My conclusion is this. If it is true that painting employs in its imitations quite other means or signs than poetry employs, the former—that is to say, figures and colours in space—but the latter articulate sounds in time; as, unquestionably, the signs used must have a definite relation to the thing signified, it follows that signs arranged together side by side can express only subjects which, or the various parts of which, exist thus side by side, whilst signs which suceed each other can express only subjects which, or the various parts of which, succeed each other.

Subjects which, or the various parts of which, exist side by side, may be called *bodies*. Consequently, bodies with their visible properties form the proper subjects of painting.

Subjects which or the various parts of which succeed each other may in general be called *actions*. Consequently, actions form the proper subjects of poetry.

Yet all bodies exist not in space alone, but also in time. They continue, and may appear differently at every moment and stand in different relations. Every one of these momentary appearances and combinations is the effect of one preceding and can be the cause of one following, and accordingly be likewise the central point of an action. Consequently, painting can also imitate actions, but only by way of suggestion through bodies.

On the other hand, actions cannot subsist for themselves, but must attach to certain things or persons. Now in so far as these things are bodies or are regarded as bodies, poetry too depicts bodies, but only by way of suggestion through actions.

Painting, in her co-existing compositions, can use only one single moment of the action, and must therefore choose the most pregnant, from which what precedes and follows will be most easily apprehended.

Just in the same manner poetry also can use, in her continuous imitations, only one single property of the bodies, and must therefore choose that one which calls up the most living picture of the body on that side from which she is regarding it. Here, indeed, we find the origin of the rule which insists on the unity and consistency of descriptive epithets, and on economy in the delineations of bodily subjects.

This is a dry chain of reasoning, and I should put less trust in it if I did not find it completely confirmed by Homer's practice, or if, rather, it were not Homer's practice itself which had led me to it. Only by these principles can the great manner of the Greeks be settled and explained, and its rightness established against the opposite manner of so many modern poets, who would emulate the painter in a department where they must necessarily be outdone by him.

Homer, I find, paints nothing but continuous actions, and all bodies, all single things, he paints only by their share in those actions, and in general only by one feature. What wonder, then, that the painter, where Homer himself paints, finds little or nothing for him to do, his harvest arising only there where the story brings together a multitude of beautiful bodies, in beautiful attitudes, in a place favourable to art, the poet himself painting these bodies, attitudes, places, just as little as he chooses? Let the reader run through the whole succession of pictures piece by piece, as Caylus suggests, and he will discover in every one of them evidence for our contention. . . .

XVII

But, some will object, the signs or characters which poetry employs are not solely such as succeed each other; they may be also arbitrary; and, as arbitrary signs, they are certainly capable of representing bodies just as they exist in space. We find instances of this in Homer himself, for we have only to remember his Shield of Achilles in order to have the most decisive example in how detailed and yet poetical a manner some single thing can be depicted, with its various parts side by side.

I will reply to this twofold objection. I call it twofold, because a just conclusion must prevail even without examples, and, on the other hand, the example of Homer weighs with me even if I know not how to justify it by any argument. It is true, as the signs of speech are arbitrary, so it is perfectly possible that by it we can make the parts of a body follow each other just as truly as in actuality they are found existing side by side. Only this is a property of speech and its signs in general, but not in so far as it suits best the purposes of poetry. The poet is not concerned merely to be intelligible, his representations should not merely be clear and plain, though this may satisfy the prose writer. He desires rather to make the ideas awakened by him within us living things, so that for the moment we realise the true sensuous impressions of the objects he describes, and cease in this moment of illusion to be conscious of the means—namely, his words—which he employs for his purpose. This is the substance of what we have already said of the poetic picture. But the poet should always paint; and now let us see how far bodies with their parts set side by side are suitable for this kind of painting.

How do we arrive at the distinct representation of a thing in space? First we regard its parts singly, then the combination of these parts, and finally the whole. Our senses perform these various operations with so astonishing a swiftness that they seem to us but one, and this swiftness is imperatively necessary if we are to arrive at a conception of the whole, which is nothing more than the result of the conceptions of the parts and their combination. Provided, then, the poet leads us in the most beautiful order from one part of the object to another; provided he knows also how to make the combination of those parts equally clear—how much time does he need for that? What the eye sees at a glance, he counts out to us gradually, with a perceptible slowness, and often it happens that when we come to the last feature we have already forgotten the first. Nevertheless, we have to frame a whole from those features; to the eye the parts beheld remain constantly present, and it can run over them again and again; for the ear, on the contrary, the parts heard are lost if they do not abide in the memory. And if they so abide, what trouble, what effort it costs to renew their impressions, all of them in their due order, so vividly, to think of them together with even a moderate swiftness, and thus to arrive at an eventual conception of the whole. Let us try it by an example which may be called a masterpiece of its kind:—

Dort ragt das hohe Haupt vom edeln Enziane
Weit übern niedern Chor der Pöbelkräuter hin,
Ein ganzes Blumenvolk dient unter seiner Fahne,
Sein blauer Bruder selbst dückt sich und ehret ihn.
Der Blumen helles Gold, in Strahlen umgebogen,
Thürmt sich am Stengel auf, und krönt sein grau Gewand,
Der Blätter glattes Weiss, mit tiefem Grün durchzogen,
Strahlt von dem bunten Blitz von feuchtem Diamant.
Gerechtestes Gesetz! dass Kraft sich Zier vermähle,
In einem schönen Leib wohnt eine schöne Seele.
  Hier kriecht ein niedrig Kraut, gleich einem grauen Nebel,
Dem die Natur sein Blatt im Kreuze hingelegt;
Die holde Blume zeigt die zwei vergöldten Schnäbel,
Die ein von Amethyst gebildter Vogel trägt.
Dort wirft ein glänzend Blatt, in Finger ausgekerbet,
Auf einen hellen Bach den grünen Wiederschein;
Der Blumen zarten Schnee, den matter Purpur färbet,
Schliesst ein gestreifter Stern in weisse Strahlen ein.
Smaragd und Rosen blühn auch auf zertretner Heide,
Und Felsen decken sich mit einem Purpurkleide.

Here are weeds and flowers which the learned poet paints with much art and fidelity to Nature. Paints, but without any illusion whatever. I will not say that out of this picture he who has never seen these weeds and flowers can make no idea of them, or as good as none. It may be that all poetic pictures require some preliminary acquaintance with their subjects. Neither will I deny that for one who possesses such an acquaintance here the poet may not have awakened a more vivid idea of some parts. I only ask him, How does it stand with the conception of the whole? If this also is to be more vivid, then no single parts must stand out, but the higher light must appear divided equally amongst them all, our imagination must be able to run over them all with equal swiftness, in order to unite in one from them that which in Nature we see united in one. Is this the case here? And is not the case rather, as one has expressed it, "that the most perfect drawing of a painter must be entirely lifeless and dark compared with this poetic portrayal"? It remains infinitely below that which lines and colours on canvas can express, and the critic who bestows on it this exaggerated praise must have regarded it from an utterly false point of view: he must have looked rather at the ornaments which the poet has woven into it, at the heightening of the subject above the mere vegetative life, at the development of the inner perfection to which the outward beauty serves merely as a shell, than at the beauty itself and at the degree of life and resemblance in the picture which the painter and which the poet can assure to us from it. Nevertheless, it amounts here purely to the latter, and whoever says that the mere lines:—

> Der Blumen helles Gold, in Strahlen umgebogen,
> Thürmt sich am Stengel auf, und krönt sein grau Gewand,
> Der Blätter glattes Weiss, mit tiefem Grün durchzogen,
> Strahlt von dem bunten Blitz von feuchtem Diamant,

—that these lines in respect of their impression can compete with the imitation of a Huysum, can never have interrogated his feelings, or must be deliberately denying them. They may, indeed, if we have the flower itself in our hands, be recited concerning it with excellent effect; but in themselves alone they say little or nothing. I hear in every word the toiling poet, and I am far enough from seeing the thing itself.

Once more, then; I do not deny to speech in general the power of portraying a bodily whole by its parts: speech can do so, because its signs or characters, although they follow one another consecutively, are nevertheless arbitrary signs; but I do deny it to speech as the medium of poetry, because such verbal delineations of bodies fail of the illusion on which poetry particularly depends, and this illusion, I contend, must fail them for the reason that the *co-existence* of the physical object comes into collision with the *consecutiveness* of speech, and the former being resolved into the latter, the dismemberment of the whole into its parts is certainly made easier, but the final reunion of those parts into a whole is made uncommonly difficult and not seldom impossible.

Wherever, then, illusion does not come into the question, where one has only to do with the understanding of one's readers and appeals only to plain and as far as possible complete conceptions, those delineations of bodies (which we have excluded from poetry) may quite well find their place, and not the prose-writer alone, but the dogmatic poet (for where he dogmatises he is not a poet) can employ them with much advantage. . . .

Clive Bell

THE AESTHETIC HYPOTHESIS*

The starting-point for all systems of aesthetics must be the personal experience of a peculiar emotion. The objects that provoke this emotion we call works of art. All sensitive people agree that there is a peculiar emotion provoked by works of art. I do not mean, of course, that all works provoke the same emotion. On the contrary, every work produces a different emotion. But all these emotions are recognisably the same in kind; so far, at any rate, the best opinion is on my side. That there is a particular kind of emotion provoked by works of visual art, and that this emotion is provoked by every kind of visual art, by pictures, sculptures, buildings, pots, carvings, textiles, &c., &c., is not disputed, I think, by anyone capable of feeling it. This emotion is called the aesthetic emotion; and if we can discover some quality common and peculiar to all the objects that provoke it, we shall have solved what I take to be the central problem of aesthetics. We shall have discovered the essential quality in a work of art, the quality that distinguishes works of art from all other classes of objects.

For either all works of visual art have some common quality, or when we speak of "works of art" we gibber. Everyone speaks of

---

* From Clive Bell, *Art* (New York: G. P. Putnam's Sons, 1958). Reprinted by permission of G. P. Putnam's Sons from the Capricorn Edition of *Art* by Clive Bell and by permission of Chatto & Windus, Ltd. (London).

"art," making a mental classification by which he distinguishes the class "works of art" from all other classes. What is the justification of this classification? What is the quality common and peculiar to all members of this class? Whatever it be, no doubt it is often found in company with other qualities; but they are adventitious—it is essential. There must be some one quality without which a work of art cannot exist; possessing which, in the least degree, no work is altogether worthless. What is this quality? What quality is shared by all objects that provoke our aesthetic emotion? What quality is common to Sta. Sophia and the windows at Chartres, Mexican sculpture, a Persian bowl, Chinese carpets, Giotto's frescoes at Padua, and the masterpieces of Poussin, Piero della Francesca, and Cézanne? Only one answer seems possible—significant form. In each, lines and colours combined in a particular way, certain forms and relations of forms, stir our aesthetic emotions. These relations and combinations of lines and colours, these aesthetically moving forms, I call "Significant Form"; and "Significant Form" is the one quality common to all works of visual art.

At this point it may be objected that I am making aesthetics a purely subjective business, since my only data are personal experiences of a particular emotion. It will be said that the objects that provoke this emotion vary with each individual, and that therefore a system of aesthetics can have no objective validity. It must be replied that any system of aesthetics which pretends to be based on some objective truth is so palpably ridiculous as not to be worth discussing. We have no other means of recognising a work of art than our feeling for it. The objects that provoke aesthetic emotion vary with each individual. Aesthetic judgments are, as the saying goes, matters of taste; and about tastes, as everyone is proud to admit, there is no disputing. A good critic may be able to make me see in a picture that had left me cold things that I had overlooked, till at last, receiving the aesthetic emotion, I recognise it as a work of art. To be continually pointing out those parts, the sum, or rather the combination, of which unite to produce significant form, is the function of criticism. But it is useless for a critic to tell me that something is a work of art; he must make me feel it for myself. This he can do only by making me see; he must get at my emotions through my eyes. Unless he can make me see something that moves me, he cannot force my emotions. I have no right to consider anything a work of art to which I cannot react emotionally; and I have no right to look for the essential quality in anything that I have not *felt* to be a work of art. The critic can affect my aesthetic theories only by affecting my aesthetic experience. All systems of aesthetics must be based on personal experience—that is to say, they must be subjective.

Yet, though all aesthetic theories must be based on aesthetic judgments, and ultimately all aesthetic judgments must be matters of personal taste, it would be rash to assert that no theory of aesthetics can have general validity. For, though A, B, C, D are the works that move me, and A, D, E, F the works that move you, it may well be that x is the only quality believed by either of us to be common to all the works in his list. We may all agree about aesthetics, and yet differ about particular works of art. We may differ as to the presence or absence of the quality x. My immediate object will be to show that significant form is the only quality common and peculiar to all the works of visual art that move me; and I will ask those whose aesthetic experience does not tally with mine to see whether this quality is not also, in their judgment, common to all works that move them, and whether they can discover any other quality of which the same can be said. . . .

The hypothesis that significant form is the essential quality in a work of art has at least one merit denied to many more famous and more striking—it does help to explain things. We are all familiar with pictures that interest us and excite our admiration, but do not move us as works of art. To this class belongs what I call "Descriptive Painting"—that is, painting in which forms are used not as objects of emotion, but as means of suggesting emotion or conveying information. Portraits of psychological and historical value, topographical works, pictures that tell stories and suggest situations, illustrations of all sorts, belong to this class. That we all recognize the distinction is clear, for who has not said that such and such a drawing was excellent as illustration, but as a work of art worthless? Of course many descriptive pictures possess, amongst other qualities, formal significance, and are therefore works of art: but many more do not. They interest us; they may move us too in a hundred different ways, but they do not move us aesthetically. According to my hypothesis they are not works of art. They leave untouched our aesthetic emotions because it is not their forms but the ideas or information suggested or conveyed by their forms that affect us.

Few pictures are better known or liked than Frith's "Paddington

Station"; certainly I should be the last to grudge it its popularity. Many a weary forty minutes have I whiled away disentangling its fascinating incidents and forging for each an imaginary past and an improbable future. But certain though it is that Frith's masterpiece, or engravings of it, have provided thousands with half-hours of curious and fanciful pleasure, it is not less certain that no one has experienced before it one half-second of aesthetic rapture—and this although the picture contains several pretty passages of colour, and is by no means badly painted. "Paddington Station" is not a work of art; it is an interesting and amusing document. In it line and colour are used to recount anecdotes, suggest ideas, and indicate the manners and customs of an age: they are not used to provoke aesthetic emotion. Forms and the relations of forms were for Frith not objects of emotion, but means of suggesting emotion and conveying ideas.

The ideas and information conveyed by "Paddington Station" are so amusing and so well presented that the picture has considerable value and is well worth preserving. But, with the perfection of photographic processes and of the cinematograph, pictures of this sort are becoming otiose. Who doubts that one of those *Daily Mirror* photographers in collaboration with a *Daily Mail* reporter can tell us far more about "London day by day" than any Royal Academician? For an account of manners and fashions we shall go, in future, to photographs, supported by a little bright journalism, rather than to descriptive painting. Had the imperial academicians of Nero, instead of manufacturing incredibly loathsome imitations of the antique, recorded in fresco and mosaic the manners and fashions of their day, their stuff, though artistic rubbish, would now be an historical gold-mine. If only they had been Friths instead of being Alma Tademas! But photography has made impossible any such transmutation of modern rubbish. Therefore it must be confessed that pictures in the Frith tradition are grown superfluous; they merely waste the hours of able men who might be more profitably employed in works of a wider beneficence. Still, they are not unpleasant, which is more than can be said for that kind of descriptive painting of which "The Doctor" is the most flagrant example. Of course "The Doctor" is not a work of art. In it form is not used as an object of emotion, but as a means of suggesting emotions. This alone suffices to make it nugatory; it is worse than nugatory because the emotion it suggests is false. What it suggests is not pity and admiration but a sense of complacency in our own pitifulness and generosity. It is sentimental. Art is above morals, or, rather, all art is moral because, as I hope to show presently, works of art are immediate means to good. Once we have judged a thing a work of art, we have judged it ethically of the first importance and put it beyond the reach of the moralist. But descriptive pictures which are not works of art, and, therefore, are not necessarily means to good states of mind, are proper objects of the ethical philosopher's attention. Not being a work of art, "The Doctor" has none of the immense ethical value possessed by all objects that provoke aesthetic ecstasy; and the state of mind to which it is a means, as illustration, appears to me undesirable.

The works of those enterprising young men, the Italian Futurists, are notable examples of descriptive painting. Like the Royal Academicians, they use form, not to provoke aesthetic emotions, but to convey information and ideas. Indeed, the published theories of the Futurists prove that their pictures ought to have nothing whatever to do with art. Their social and political theories are respectable, but I would suggest to young Italian painters that it is possible to become a Futurist in thought and action and yet remain an artist, if one has the luck to be born one. To associate art with politics is always a mistake. Futurist pictures are descriptive because they aim at presenting in line and colour the chaos of the mind at a particular moment; their forms are not intended to promote aesthetic emotion but to convey information. These forms, by the way, whatever may be the nature of the ideas they suggest, are themselves anything but revolutionary. In such Futurist pictures as I have seen—perhaps I should except some by Severini—the drawing, whenever it becomes representative as it frequently does, is found to be in that soft and common convention brought into fashion by Besnard some thirty years ago, and much affected by Beaux-Art students ever since. As works of art, the Futurist pictures are negligible; but they are not to be judged as works of art. A good Futurist picture would suceed as a good piece of psychology succeeds; it would reveal, through line and colour, the complexities of an interesting state of mind. If Futurist pictures seem to fail, we must seek an explanation, not in a lack of artistic qualities that they never were intended to possess, but rather in the minds the states of which they are intended to reveal.

Most people who care much about art find that of the work that moves them most the greater part is what scholars call "Primitive." Of course there are bad primitives. For instance, I remember going, full of enthusiasm, to see one of the earliest Romanesque churches in Poitiers (Notre-Dame-la-Grande), and finding it as ill-proportioned, over-decorated, coarse, fat and heavy as any better class building by one of those highly civilised architects who flourished a thousand years earlier or eight hundred later. But such exceptions are rare. As a rule primitive art is good—and here again my hypothesis is helpful—for, as a rule, it is also free from descriptive qualities. In primitive art you will find no accurate representation; you will find only significant form. Yet no other art moves us so profoundly. Whether we consider Sumerian sculpture or pre-dynastic Egyptian art, or archaic Greek, or the Wei and T'ang masterpieces,[1] or those early Japanese works of which I had the luck to see a few superb examples (especially two wooden Bodhisattvas) at the Shepherd's Bush Exhibition in 1910, or whether, coming nearer home, we consider the primitive Byzantine art of the sixth century and its primitive developments amongst the Western barbarians, or, turning far afield, we consider that mysterious and majestic art that flourished in Central and South America before the coming of the white men, in every case we observe three common characteristics—absence of representation, absence of technical swagger, sublimely impressive form. Nor is it hard to discover the connection between these three. Formal significance loses itself in preoccupation with exact representation and ostentatious cunning.[2]

---

[1] The existence of the Ku K'ai-chih makes it clear that the art of this period (fifth to eighth centuries), was a typical primitive movement. To call the great vital art of the Liang, Chen, Wei, and T'ang dynasties a development out of the exquisitely refined and exhausted art of the Han decadence—from which Ku K'ai-chih is a delicate straggler—is to call Romanesque sculpture a development out of Praxiteles. Between the two something has happened to refill the stream of art. What had happened in China was the spiritual and emotional revolution that followed the onset of Buddhism.

[2] This is not to say that exact representation is bad in itself. It is indifferent. A perfectly represented form may be significant, only it is fatal to sacrifice significance to representation. The quarrel between significance and illusion seems to be as old as art itself, and I have little doubt that what makes most palaeolithic art so bad is a preoccupation with exact representation. Evidently palaeolithic draughtsmen had no sense of the significance of form. Their art resembles that of the more capable and sincere Royal Academicians: it is a little higher than that of Sir Edward Poynter and a little lower than that of the late Lord Leighton. That this is no paradox let the cave-drawings of Altamira, or such works as the sketches of horses found at Bruniquel and now in the British Museum, bear witness. If the ivory head of a girl from the

Naturally, it is said that if there is little representation and less saltimbancery in primitive art, that is because the primitives were unable to catch a likeness or cut intellectual capers. The contention is beside the point. There is truth in it, no doubt, though, were I a critic whose reputation depended on a power of impressing the public with a semblance of knowledge, I should be more cautious about urging it than such people generally are. For to suppose that the Byzantine masters wanted skill, or could not have created an illusion had they wished to do so, seems to imply ignorance of the amazingly dexterous realism of the notoriously bad works of that age. Very often, I fear, the misrepresentation of the primitives must be attributed to what the critics call, "wilful distortion." Be that as it may, the point is that, either from want of skill or want of will, primitives neither create illusions, nor make display of extravagant accomplishment, but concentrate their energies on the one thing needful—the creation of form. Thus have they created the finest works of art that we possess.

Let no one imagine that representation is bad in itself; a realistic form may be as significant, in its place as part of the design, as an abstract. But if a representative form has value, it is as form, not as representation. The representative element in a work of art may or may not be harmful; always it is irrelevant. For, to appreciate a work of art we need bring with us nothing from life, no knowledge of its ideas and affairs, no familiarity with its emotions. Art transports us from the world of man's activity to a world of aesthetic exaltation. For a moment we are shut off from human interests; our anticipations and memories are arrested; we are lifted above the stream of life. The pure mathematician rapt in his studies knows a state of mind which I take to be similar, if not identical. He feels an emotion for his speculations which arises from no perceived relation between them and the lives of men, but springs, inhuman or super-human, from the heart of an abstract science. I wonder, sometimes, whether the appreciators of art and of mathematical solutions are not even more closely allied. Before we feel an aesthetic emotion for a combination of forms, do we not perceive intellectually the rightness and necessity of the combination? If we do, it would ex-

Grotte du Pape, Brassempouy (_Musée St. Germain_) and the ivory torso found at the same place (_Collection St. Cric_), be, indeed, palaeolithic, then there were good palaeolithic artists who created and did not imitate form. Neolithic art is, of course, a very different matter.

plain the fact that passing rapidly through a room we recognise a picture to be good, although we cannot say that it has provoked much emotion. We seem to have recognised intellectually the rightness of its forms without staying to fix our attention, and collect, as it were, their emotional significance. If this were so, it would be permissible to inquire whether it was the forms themselves or our perception of their rightness and necessity that caused aesthetic emotion. But I do not think I need linger to discuss the matter here. I have been enquiring why certain combinations of forms move us; I should not have travelled by other roads had I enquired, instead, why certain combinations are perceived to be right and necessary, and why our perception of their rightness and necessity is moving. What I have to say is this: the rapt philosopher, and he who contemplates a work of art, inhabit a world with an intense and peculiar significance of its own; that significance is unrelated to the significance of life. In this world the emotions of life find no place. It is a world with emotions of its own.

To appreciate a work of art we need bring with us nothing but a sense of form and colour and a knowledge of three-dimensional space. That bit of knowledge, I admit, is essential to the appreciation of many great works, since many of the most moving forms ever created are in three dimensions. To see a cube or a rhomboid as a flat pattern is to lower its significance, and a sense of three-dimensional space is essential to the full appreciation of most architectural forms. Pictures which would be insignificant if we saw them as flat patterns are profoundly moving because, in fact, we see them as related planes. If the representation of three-dimensional space is to be called "representation," then I agree that there is one kind of representation which is not irrelevant. Also, I agree that along with our feeling for line and colour we must bring with us our knowledge of space if we are to make the most of every kind of form. Nevertheless, there are magnificent designs to an appreciation of which this knowledge is not necessary: so, though it is not irrelevant to the appreciation of some works of art it is not essential to the appreciation of all. What we must say is that the representation of three-dimensional space is neither irrelevant nor essential to all art, and that every other sort of representation is irrelevant.

That there is an irrelevant representative or descriptive element in many great works of art is not in the least surprising. Why it is not surprising I shall try to show elsewhere. Representation is not of necessity baneful, and highly realistic forms may be extremely significant. Very often, however, representation is a sign of weakness in an artist. A painter too feeble to create forms that provoke more than a little aesthetic emotion will try to eke that little out by suggesting the emotions of life. To evoke the emotions of life he must use representation. Thus a man will paint an execution, and, fearing to miss with his first barrel of significant form, will try to hit with his second by raising an emotion of fear or pity. But if in the artist an inclination to play upon the emotions of life is often the sign of a flickering inspiration, in the spectator a tendency to seek, behind form, the emotions of life is a sign of defective sensibility always. It means that his aesthetic emotions are weak or, at any rate, imperfect. Before a work of art people who feel little or no emotion for pure form find themselves at a loss. They are deaf men at a concert. They know that they are in the presence of something great, but they lack the power of apprehending it. They know that they ought to feel for it a tremendous emotion, but it happens that the particular kind of emotion it can raise is one that they can feel hardly or not at all. And so they read into the forms of the work those facts and ideas for which they are capable of feeling emotion, and feel for them the emotions that they can feel—the ordinary emotions of life. When confronted by a picture, instinctively they refer back its forms to the world from which they came. They treat created form as though it were imitated form, a picture as though it were a photograph. Instead of going out on the stream of art into a new world of aesthetic experience, they turn a sharp corner and come straight home to the world of human interests. For them the significance of a work of art depends on what they bring to it; no new thing is added to their lives, only the old material is stirred. A good work of visual art carries a person who is capable of appreciating it out of life into ecstasy: to use art as a means to the emotions of life is to use a telescope for reading the news. You will notice that people who cannot feel pure aesthetic emotions remember pictures by their subjects; whereas people who can, as often as not, have no idea what the subject of a picture is. They have never noticed the representative element, and so when they discuss pictures they talk about the shapes of forms and the relations and quantities of colours. Often they can tell by the quality of a single line whether or no a man is a good artist. They are concerned only with lines and colours, their relations and quantities and qualities; but from these they win an emotion more profound and far more sublime than any that can be given by the description of facts and ideas.

This last sentence has a very confident ring—overconfident, some may think. Perhaps I shall be able to justify it, and make my meaning clearer too, if I give an account of my own feelings about music. I am not really musical. I do not understand music well. I find musical form exceedingly difficult to apprehend, and I am sure that the profounder subtleties of harmony and rhythm more often than not escape me. The form of a musical composition must be simple indeed if I am to grasp it honestly. My opinion about music is not worth having. Yet, sometimes, at a concert, though my appreciation of the music is limited and humble, it is pure. Sometimes, though I have a poor understanding, I have a clean palate. Consequently, when I am feeling bright and clear and intent, at the beginning of a concert for instance, when something that I can grasp is being played, I get from music that pure aesthetic emotion that I get from visual art. It is less intense, and the rapture is evanescent; I understand music too ill for music to transport me far into the world of pure aesthetic ecstasy. But at moments I do appreciate music as pure musical form, as sounds combined according to the laws of a mysterious necessity, as pure art with a tremendous significance of its own and no relation whatever to the significance of life; and in those moments I lose myself in that infinitely sublime state of mind to which pure visual form transports me. How inferior is my normal state of mind at a concert. Tired or perplexed, I let slip my sense of form, my aesthetic emotion collapses, and I begin weaving into the harmonies, that I cannot grasp, the ideas of life. Incapable of feeling the austere emotions of art, I begin to read into the musical forms human emotions of terror and mystery, love and hate, and spend the minutes, pleasantly enough, in a world of turbid and inferior feeling. At such times, were the grossest pieces of onomatopoeic representation—the song of a bird, the galloping of horses, the cries of children, or the laughing of demons—to be introduced into the symphony, I should not be offended. Very likely I should be pleased; they would afford new points of departure for new trains of romantic feeling or heroic thought. I know very well what has happened. I have been using art as a means to the emotions of life and reading into it the ideas of life. I have been cutting blocks with a razor. I have tumbled from the superb peaks of aesthetic exaltation to the snug foothills of warm humanity. It is a jolly country.

No one need be ashamed of enjoying himself there. Only no one who has ever been on the heights can help feeling a little crestfallen in the cosy valleys. And let no one imagine, because he has made merry in the warm tilth and quaint nooks of romance, that he can even guess at the austere and thrilling raptures of those who have climbed the cold, white peaks of art. . . .

Cleanth Brooks

THE HERESY OF PARAPHRASE*

The ten poems that have been discussed were not selected because
they happened to express a common theme or to display some particular style or to share a special set of symbols. It has proved, as
a matter of fact, somewhat surprising to see how many items they
do have in common: the light symbolism as used in "L'Allegro–Il
Penseroso" and in the "Intimations" ode, for example; or, death as a
sexual metaphor in "The Canonization" and in *The Rape of the
Lock;* or the similarity of problem and theme in the "Intimations"
ode and "Among School Children."

On reflection, however, it would probably warrant more surprise
if these ten poems did not have much in common. For they are all
poems which most of us will feel are close to the central stream of
the tradition. Indeed, if there is any doubt on this point, it will have
to do with only the first and last members of the series [Donne's
"The Canonization," and Yeats' "Among School Children."]—poems
whose relation to the tradition I shall, for reasons to be given a little
later, be glad to waive. The others, it will be granted, are surely in
the main stream of the tradition.

As a matter of fact, a number of the poems discussed in this
book were not chosen by me but were chosen for me. But having
written on these, I found that by adding a few poems I could con-

* From *The Well Wrought Urn,* copyright, 1947, by Cleanth Brooks. Reprinted by permission of Harcourt, Brace & World, Inc.

struct a chronological series which (though it makes no pretension to being exhaustive of periods or types) would not leave seriously unrepresented any important period since Shakespeare. In filling the gaps I tried to select poems which had been held in favor in their own day and which most critics still admire. There were, for example, to be no "metaphysical" poems beyond the first exhibit and no "modern" ones other than the last. But the intervening poems were to be read as one has learned to read Donne and the moderns. One was to attempt to see, in terms of this approach, what the masterpieces had in common rather than to see how the poems of different historical periods differed—and in particular to see whether they had anything in common with the "metaphysicals" and with the moderns.

The reader will by this time have made up his mind as to whether the readings are adequate. (I use the word advisedly, for the readings do not pretend to be exhaustive, and certainly it is highly unlikely that they are not in error in one detail or another.) If the reader feels that they are seriously inadequate, then the case has been judged; for the generalizations that follow will be thoroughly vitiated by the inept handling of the particular cases on which they depend.

If, however, the reader does feel them to be adequate, it ought to be readily apparent that the common goodness which the poems share will have to be stated, not in terms of "content" or "subject matter" in the usual sense in which we use these terms, but rather in terms of structure. The "content" of the poems is various, and if we attempt to find one *quality* of content which is shared by all the poems—a "poetic" subject matter or diction or imagery—we shall find that we have merely confused the issues. For what is it to be poetic? Is the schoolroom of Yeats's poem poetic or unpoetic? Is Shakespeare's "new-borne babe/ Striding the blast" poetic whereas the idiot of his "Life is a tale tolde by an idiot" is unpoetic? If Herrick's "budding boy or girl" is poetic, then why is not that monstrosity of the newspaper's society page, the "society bud," poetic too?

To say this is not, of course, to say that all materials have precisely the same potentialities (as if the various pigments on the palette had the same potentialities, any one of them suiting the given picture as well as another). But what has been said, on the other hand, requires to be said: for, if we are to proceed at all, we must draw a sharp distinction between the attractiveness or beauty of any particular item taken as such and the "beauty" of the poem considered as a whole. The latter is the effect of a total pattern, and of a kind of pattern which can incorporate within itself items intrinsically beautiful or ugly, attractive or repulsive. Unless one asserts the primacy of the pattern, a poem becomes merely a bouquet of intrinsically beautiful items.

But though it is in terms of structure that we must describe poetry, the term "structure" is certainly not altogether satisfactory as a term. One means by it something far more internal than the metrical pattern, say, or than the sequence of images. The structure meant is certainly not "form" in the conventional sense in which we think of form as a kind of envelope which "contains" the "content." The structure obviously is everywhere conditioned by the nature of the material which goes into the poem. The nature of the material sets the problem to be solved, and the solution is the ordering of the material.

Pope's *Rape of the Lock* will illustrate: the structure is not the heroic couplet as such, or the canto arrangement; for, important as is Pope's use of the couplet as one means by which he secures the total effect, the heroic couplet can be used—has been used many times—as an instrument in securing very different effects. The structure of the poem, furthermore, is not that of the mock-epic convention, though here, since the term "mock-epic" has implications of attitude, we approach a little nearer to the kind of structure of which we speak.

The structure meant is a structure of meanings, evaluations, and interpretations; and the principle of unity which informs it seems to be one of balancing and harmonizing connotations, attitudes, and meanings. But even here one needs to make important qualifications: the principle is not one which involves the arrangement of the various elements into homogeneous groupings, pairing like with like. It unites the like with the unlike. It does not unite them, however, by the simple process of allowing one connotation to cancel out another nor does it reduce the contradictory attitudes to harmony by a process of subtraction. The unity is not a unity of the sort to be achieved by the reduction and simplification appropriate to an algebraic formula. It is a positive unity, not a negative; it represents not a residue but an achieved harmony.

The attempt to deal with a structure such as this may account for the frequent occurrence in the preceding chapters of such terms as "ambiguity," "paradox," "complex of attitudes," and— most frequent of all, and perhaps most annoying to the reader— "irony." I hasten to add that I hold no brief for these terms as such. Perhaps they are inadequate. Perhaps they are misleading. It is to be hoped in that case that we can eventually improve upon them. But adequate terms—whatever those terms may turn out to be—will certainly have to be terms which do justice to the special kind of structure which seems to emerge as the common structure of poems so diverse on other counts as are *The Rape of the Lock* and "Tears, Idle Tears."

The conventional terms are much worse than inadequate: they are positively misleading in their implication that the poem constitutes a "statement" of some sort, the statement being true or false, and expressed more or less clearly or eloquently or beautifully; for it is from this formula that most of the common heresies about poetry derive. The formula begins by introducing a dualism which thence-forward is rarely overcome, and which at best can be overcome only by the most elaborate and clumsy qualifications. Where it is not overcome, it leaves the critic lodged upon one or the other of the horns of a dilemma: the critic is forced to judge the poem by its political or scientific or philosophical truth; or, he is forced to judge the poem by its form as conceived externally and detached from human experience. Mr. Alfred Kazin, for example, to take an in-stance from a recent and popular book, accuses the "new formal-ists"—his choice of that epithet is revealing—of accepting the latter horn of the dilemma because he notices that they have refused the former. In other words, since they refuse to rank poems by their messages, he assumes that they are compelled to rank them by their formal embellishments.

The omnipresence of this dilemma, a false dilemma, I believe, will also account for the fact that so much has been made in the preceding chapters of the resistance which any good poem sets up against all attempts to paraphrase it. The point is surely not that we cannot describe adequately enough for many purposes what the poem in general is "about" and what the general effect of the poem is: *The Rape of the Lock* is *about* the foibles of an eighteenth-century belle. The effect of "Corinna's going a-Maying" is one of gaiety tempered by the poignance of the fleetingness of youth. We can very properly use paraphrases as pointers and as shorthand references provided that we know what we are doing. But it is highly important that we know what we are doing and that we see plainly that paraphrase is not the real core of meaning which constitutes the essence of the poem.

For the imagery and the rhythm are not merely the instruments by which this fancied core-of-meaning-which-can-be-expressed-in-a paraphrase is directly rendered. Even in the simplest poem their mediation is not positive and direct. Indeed, whatever statement we may seize upon as incorporating the "meaning" of the poem, immediately the imagery and the rhythm seem to set up tensions with it, warping and twisting it, qualifying and revising it. This is true of Wordsworth's "Ode" no less than of Donne's "Canonization." To illustrate: if we say that the "Ode" celebrates the spontaneous "naturalness" of the child, there is the poem itself to indicate that Nature has a more sinister aspect—that the process by which the poetic lamb becomes the dirty old sheep or the child racing over the meadows becomes the balding philosopher is a process that is thoroughly "natural." Or, if we say that the thesis of the "Ode" is that the child brings into the natural world a supernatural glory which acquaintance with the world eventually and inevitably quenches in the light of common day, there is the last stanza and the drastic qualifications which it asserts: it is significant that the thoughts that lie too deep for tears are mentioned in this sunset stanza of the "Ode" and that they are thoughts, not of the child, but of the man.

We have precisely the same problem if we make our example *The Rape of the Lock*. Does the poet assert that Belinda is a goddess? Or does he say that she is a brainless chit? Whichever alternative we take, there are elaborate qualifications to be made. Moreover, if the simple propositions offered seem in their forthright simplicity to make too easy the victory of the poem over any possible statement of its meaning, then let the reader try to formulate a proposition that will say what the poem "says." As his proposition approaches adequacy, he will find, not only that it has increased greatly in length, but that it has begun to fill itself up with reservations and qualifications—and most significant of all— the formulator will find that he has himself begun to fall back upon metaphors of his own in his attempt to indicate what the poem "says." In sum, his proposition, as it approaches adequacy, ceases to be a proposition.

Consider one more case, "Corinna's going a-Maying." Is the doctrine preached to Corinna throughout the first four stanzas true?
Or is it damnably false? Or is it a "harmlesse follie"? Here perhaps
we shall be tempted to take the last option as the saving mean—
what the poem really *says*—and my account of the poem at the end
of the third chapter is perhaps susceptible of this interpretation—
or misinterpretation. If so, it is high time to clear the matter up.
For we mistake matters grossly if we take the poem to be playing
with opposed extremes, only to point the golden mean in a doctrine
which, at the end, will correct the falsehood of extremes. The recon-
cilement of opposites which the poet characteristically makes is not
that of a prudent splitting of the difference between antithetical
overemphases.

It is not so in Wordsworth's poem nor in Keats's nor in Pope's.
It is not so even in this poem of Herrick's. For though the poem
reflects, if we read it carefully, the primacy of the Christian mores,
the pressure exerted throughout the poem is upon the pagan appeal; and the poem ends, significantly, with a reiteration of the
appeal to Corinna to go a-Maying, an appeal which, if qualified by
the Christian view, still, in a sense, has been deepened and made
more urgent by that very qualification. The imagery of loss and
decay, it must be remembered, comes in this last stanza after the
admission that the May-day rites are not a real religion but a "harmlesse follie."

If we are to get all these qualifications into our formulation of
what the poem says—and they are relevant—then, our formulation
of the "statement" made by Herrick's poem will turn out to be
quite as difficult as that of Pope's mock-epic. The truth of the matter
is that all such formulations lead away from the center of the poem
—not toward it; that the "prose-sense" of the poem is not a rack on
which the stuff of the poem is hung; that it does not represent the
"inner" structure or the "essential" structure or the "real" structure
of the poem. We may use—and in many connections must use—
such formulations as more or less convenient ways of referring to
parts of the poem. But such formulations are scaffoldings which
we may properly for certain purposes throw about the building.
We must not mistake them for the internal and essential structure
of the building itself.

Indeed, one may sum up by saying that most of the distempers
of criticism come about from yielding to the temptation to take

certain remarks which we make *about* the poem—statements about what it says or about what truth it gives or about what formulations it illustrates—for the essential core of the poem itself. As W. M. Urban puts it in his *Language and Reality:* "The general principle of the inseparability of intuition and expression holds with special force for the aesthetic intuition. Here it means that form and content, or content and medium, are inseparable. The artist does not first intuit his object and then find the appropriate medium. It is rather in and through his medium that he intuits the object." So much for the process of composition. As for the critical process: "To pass from the intuitible to the nonintuitible is to negate the function and meaning of the symbol." For it "is precisely because the more universal and ideal relations cannot be adequately expressed directly that they are indirectly expressed by means of the more intuitible." The most obvious examples of such error (and for that reason those which are really least dangerous) are those theories which frankly treat the poem as propaganda. The most subtle (and the most stubbornly rooted in the ambiguities of language) are those which, beginning with the "paraphrasable" elements of the poem, refer the other elements of the poem finally to some role subordinate to the paraphrasable elements. (The relation between all the elements must surely be an organic one—there can be no question about that. There is, however, a very serious question as to whether the paraphrasable elements have primacy.)

Mr. Winters' position will furnish perhaps the most respectable example of the paraphrastic heresy. He assigns primacy to the "rational meaning" of the poem. "The relationship, in the poem, between rational statement and feeling," he remarks in his latest book, "is thus seen to be that of motive to emotion." He goes on to illustrate his point by a brief and excellent analysis of the following lines from Browning:

> So wore night; the East was gray,
>   White the broad-faced hemlock flowers. . . .

"The verb *wore*," he continues, "means literally that the night passed, but it carries with it connotations of exhaustion and attrition which belong to the condition of the protagonist; and grayness is a color which we associate with such a condition. If we change the phrase to read: 'Thus night passed,' we shall have the same rational meaning, and a meter quite as respectable, but no trace of the power of the line: the connotation of *wore* will be lost, and the connotation of *gray* will remain in a state of ineffective potentiality."

But the word *wore* does not mean *literally* "that the night passed," it means literally "that the night *wore*"—whatever *wore* may mean, and as Winters' own admirable analysis indicates, *wore* "means," whether *rationally* or *irrationally*, a great deal. Furthermore, "So wore night" and "Thus night passed" can be said to have "the same rational meaning" only if we equate "rational meaning" with the meaning of a loose paraphrase. And can a loose paraphrase be said to be the "motive to emotion"? Can it be said to "generate" the feelings in question? (Or, would Mr. Winters not have us equate "rational statement" and "rational meaning"?)

Much more is at stake here than any quibble. In view of the store which Winters sets by rationality and of his penchant for poems which make their evaluations overtly, and in view of his frequent blindness to those poems which do not—in view of these considerations, it is important to see that what "So wore night" and "Thus night passed" have in common as their "rational meaning" is not the "rational meaning" of each but the lowest common denominator of both. To refer the structure of the poem to what is finally a paraphrase of the poem is to refer it to something outside the poem.

To repeat, most of our difficulties in criticism are rooted in the heresy of paraphrase. If we allow ourselves to be misled by it, we distort the relation of the poem to its "truth," we raise the problem of belief in a vicious and crippling form, we split the poem between its "form" and its "content"—we bring the statement to be conveyed into an unreal competition with science or philosophy or theology. In short, we put our questions about the poem in a form calculated to produce the battles of the last twenty-five years over the "use of poetry."[1]

If we allow ourselves to be misled by the heresy of paraphrase, we run the risk of doing even more violence to the internal order of the poem itself. By taking the paraphrase as our point of stance, we misconceive the function of metaphor and meter. We demand

---

[1] I do not, of course, intend to minimize the fact that some of these battles have been highly profitable, or to imply that the foregoing paragraphs could have been written except for the illumination shed by the discussions of the last twenty-five years.

logical coherences where they are sometimes irrelevant, and we fail frequently to see imaginative coherences on levels where they are highly relevant.

But what would be a positive theory? We tend to embrace the doctrine of a logical structure the more readily because, to many of us, the failure to do so seems to leave the meaning of the poem hopelessly up in the air. The alternative position will appear to us to lack even the relative stability of an Ivory Tower: it is rather commitment to a free balloon. For, to deny the possibility of pinning down what the poem "says" to some "statement" will seem to assert that the poem really says nothing. And to point out what has been suggested in earlier chapters and brought to a head in this one, namely, that one can never measure a poem against the scientific or philosophical yardstick for the reason that the poem, when laid along the yardstick, is never the "full poem" but an abstraction from the poem—such an argument will seem to such readers a piece of barren logic-chopping—a transparent dodge.

Considerations of strategy then, if nothing more, dictate some positive account of what a poem is and does. And some positive account can be given, though I cannot promise to do more than suggest what a poem is, nor will my terms turn out to be anything more than metaphors.[2]

The essential structure of a poem (as distinguished from the rational or logical structure of the "statement" which we abstract from it) resembles that of architecture or painting: it is a pattern of resolved stresses. Or, to move closer still to poetry by considering the temporal arts, the structure of a poem resembles that of a ballet or musical composition. It is a pattern of resolutions and balances and harmonizations developed through a temporal scheme.[3]

---

[2] For those who cannot be content with metaphors (or with the particular metaphors which I can give) I recommend Rene Wellek's excellent "The Mode of Existence of a Literary Work of Art" (*The Southern Review*, Spring, 1942). I shall not try to reproduce here as a handy, thumb-nail definition his account of a poem as "a stratified system of norms," for the definition would be relatively meaningless without the further definitions which he assigns to the individual terms which he uses. I have made no special use of his terms in this chapter, but I believe that the generalizations about poetry outlined here can be thoroughly accommodated to the position which his essay sets forth.

[3] In recent numbers of *Accent*, two critics for whose work I have high regard have emphasized the dynamic character of poetry. Kenneth Burke argues that if we are to consider a poem as a poem, we must consider it as a

Or, to move still closer to poetry, the structure of a poem resembles that of a play. This last example, of course, risks introducing once more the distracting element, since drama, like poetry, makes use of words. Yet, on the whole, most of us are less inclined to force the concept of "statement" on drama than on a lyric poem: for the very nature of drama is that of something "acted out" —something which arrives at its conclusion through conflict—something which builds conflict into its very being. The dynamic nature of drama, in short, allows us to regard it as *an action* rather than as a formula for action or as a statement about action. For this reason, therefore, perhaps the most helpful analogy by which to suggest the structure of poetry is that of the drama, and for many readers at least, the least confusing way in which to approach a poem is to think of it as a drama.

The general point, of course, is not that either poetry or drama makes no use of ideas, or that either is "merely emotional"—whatever *that* is—or that there is not the closest and most important relationship between the intellectual materials which they absorb into their structure and other elements in the structure. The relationship between the intellectual and the nonintellectual elements in a poem is actually far more intimate than the conventional accounts would represent it to be: the relationship is not that of an idea "wrapped in emotion" or a "prose-sense decorated by sensuous imagery."

The dimension in which the poem moves is not one which excludes ideas, but one which does include attitudes. The dimension includes ideas, to be sure; we can always abstract an "idea" from

---

"mode of action." R. P. Blackmur asks us to think of it as gesture, "the outward and dramatic play of inward and imagined meaning." I do not mean to commit either of these critics to my own interpretation of dramatic or symbolic action; and I have, on my own part, several rather important reservations with respect to Mr. Burke's position. But there are certainly large areas of agreement among our positions. The reader might also compare the account of poetic structure given in this chapter with the following passage from Susanne Langer's *Philosophy in a New Key:* ". . . though the *material* of poetry is verbal, its import is not the literal assertion made in the words, but *the way the assertion is made,* and this involves the sound, the tempo, the aura of associations of the words, the long or short sequences of ideas, the wealth or poverty of transient imagery that contains them, the sudden arrest of fantasy by pure fact, or of familiar fact by sudden fantasy, the suspense of literal meaning by a sustained ambiguity resolved in a long-awaited key-word, and the unifying, all-embracing artifice of rhythm."

a poem—even from the simplest poem—even from a lyric so simple and unintellectual as

> *Western wind, when wilt thou blow*
> *That the small rain down can rain?*
> *Christ, that my love were in my arms*
> *And I in my bed again!*

But the idea which we abstract—assuming that we can all agree on what that idea is—will always be *abstracted:* it will always be the projection of a plane along a line or the projection of a cone upon a plane.

If this analogy proves to be more confusing than illuminating let us return to the analogy with drama. We have argued that any proposition asserted in a poem is not to be taken in abstraction but is justified, in terms of the poem, if it is justified at all, not by virtue of its scientific or historical or philosophical truth, but is justified in terms of a principle analogous to that of dramatic propriety. Thus, the proposition that "Beauty is truth, truth beauty" is given its precise meaning and significance by its relation to the total context of the poem.

This principle is easy enough to see when the proposition is asserted overtly in the poem—that is, when it constitutes a specific detail of the poem. But the reader may well ask: is it not possible to frame a proposition, a statement, which will adequately represent the total meaning of the poem; that is, is it not possible to elaborate a summarizing proposition which will "say," briefly and in the form of a proposition, what the poem "says" as a poem, a proposition which will say it fully and will say it exactly, no more and no less? Could not the poet, if he had chosen, have framed such a proposition? Cannot we as readers and critics frame such a proposition?

The answer must be that the poet himself obviously did not—else he would not have had to write his poem. We as readers can attempt to frame such a proposition in our effort to understand the poem; it may well help toward an understanding. Certainly, the efforts to arrive at such propositions can do no harm *if we do not mistake them for the inner core of the poem*—if we do not mistake them for "what the poem *really* says." For, if we take one of them to represent the essential poem, we have to disregard the qualifications exerted by the total context as of no account, or else we have assumed that we can reproduce the effect of the total context in a condensed prose statement.[4]

But to deny that the coherence of a poem is reflected in a logical paraphrase of its "real meaning" is not, of course, to deny coherence to poetry; it is rather to assert that its coherence is to be sought elsewhere. The characteristic unity of a poem (even of those poems which may accidentally possess a logical unity as well as this poetic unity) lies in the unification of attitudes into a hierarchy subordinated to a total and governing attitude. In the unified poem, the poet has "come to terms" with his experience. The poem does not merely eventuate in a logical conclusion. The conclusion of the poem is the working out of the various tensions—set up by whatever means—by propositions, metaphors, symbols. The unity is achieved by a dramatic process, not a logical; it represents an equilibrium of forces, not a formula. It is "proved" as a dramatic conclusion is proved: by its ability to resolve the conflicts which have been accepted as the *données* of the drama.

Thus, it is easy to see why the relation of each item to the whole context is crucial, and why the effective and essential structure of the poem has to do with the complex of attitudes achieved. A scientific proposition can stand alone. If it is true, it is true. But the expression of an attitude, apart from the occasion which generates it and the situation which it encompasses, is meaningless. For example, the last two lines of the "Intimations" ode,

> *To me the meanest flower that blows can give*
> *Thoughts that do often lie too deep for tears,*

---

[4] We may, it is true, be able to adumbrate what the poem says if we allow ourselves enough words, and if we make enough reservations and qualifications, thus attempting to come nearer to the meaning of the poem by successive approximations and refinements, gradually encompassing the meaning and pointing to the area in which it lies rather than realizing it. The earlier chapters of this book, if they are successful, are obviously illustrations of this process. But such adumbrations will lack, not only the tension—the dramatic force—of the poem; they will be at best crude approximations of the poem. Moreover—and this is the crucial point—they will be compelled to resort to the methods of the poem—analogy, metaphor, symbol, etc.—in order to secure even this near an approximation.

Urban's comment upon this problem is interesting: he says that if we expand the symbol, "we lose the 'sense' or value of the symbol *as symbol*. The solution . . . seems to me to lie in an adequate theory of interpretation of the symbol. It does not consist in substituting *literal* for symbol sentences, in other words substituting 'blunt' truth for symbolic truth, but rather in deepening and enriching the meaning of the symbol."

when taken in isolation—I do not mean quoted in isolation by one who is even vaguely acquainted with the context—makes a statement which is sentimental if taken in reference to the speaker, and one which is patent nonsense if taken with a general reference. The man in the street (of whom the average college freshman is a good enough replica) knows that the meanest flower that grows does not give *him* thoughts that lie too deep for tears; if he thinks about the matter at all, he is inclined to feel that the person who can make such an assertion is a very fuzzy sentimentalist.

We have already seen the ease with which the statement "Beauty is truth, truth beauty" becomes detached from its context, even in the hands of able critics; and we have seen the misconceptions that ensue when this detachment occurs. To take one more instance: the last stanza of Herrick's "Corinna," taken in isolation, would probably not impress the average reader as sentimental nonsense. Yet it would suffer quite as much by isolation from its context as would the lines from Keats's "Ode." For, as mere statement, it would become something flat and obvious—of course our lives are short! And the conclusion from the fact would turn into an obvious truism for the convinced pagan, and, for the convinced Christian, equally obvious, though damnable, nonsense.

Perhaps this is why the poet, to people interested in hard-and-fast generalizations, must always seem to be continually engaged in blurring out distinctions, effecting compromises, or, at the best, coming to his conclusions only after provoking and unnecessary delays. But this last position is merely another variant of the para-phrastic heresy: to assume it is to misconceive the end of poetry—to take its meanderings as negative, or to excuse them (with the comfortable assurance that the curved line is the line of beauty) because we can conceive the purpose of a poem to be only the pro-duction, in the end, of a proposition—of a statement.

But the meanderings of a good poem (they are meanderings only from the standpoint of the prose paraphrase of the poem) are not negative, and they do not have to be excused; and most of all, we need to see what their positive function is; for unless we can assign them a positive function, we shall find it difficult to explain why one divergence from "the prose line of the argument" is not as good as another. The truth is that the apparent irrelevancies which metri-cal pattern and metaphor introduce do become relevant when we realize that they function in a good poem to modify, qualify, and develop the total attitude which we are to take in coming to terms with the total situation.

If the last sentence seems to take a dangerous turn toward some special "use of poetry"—some therapeutic value for the sake of which poetry is to be cultivated—I can only say that I have in mind no special ills which poetry is to cure. Uses for poetry are always to be found, and doubtless will continue to be found. But my discussion of the structure of poetry is not being conditioned at this point by some new and special role which I expect poetry to assume in the future or some new function to which I would assign it. The structure described—a structure of "gestures" or attitudes—seems to me to describe the essential structure of both the *Odyssey* and *The Waste Land*. It seems to be the kind of structure which the ten poems considered in this book possess in common.

If the structure of poetry is a structure of the order described, that fact may explain (if not justify) the frequency with which I have had to have recourse, in the foregoing chapters, to terms like "irony" and "paradox." By using the term irony, one risks, of course, making the poem seem arch and self-conscious, since irony, for most readers of poetry, is associated with satire, *vers de société*, and other "intellectual" poetries. Yet, the necessity for some such term ought to be apparent; and irony is the most general term that we have for the kind of qualification which the various elements in a context receive from the context. This kind of qualification, as we have seen, is of tremendous importance in any poem. Moreover, irony is our most general term for indicating that recognition of incongruities—which, again, pervades all poetry to a degree far beyond what our conventional criticism has been heretofore willing to allow.

Irony in this general sense, then, is to be found in Tennyson's "Tears, Idle Tears" as well as in Donne's "Canonization." We have, of course, been taught to expect to find irony in Pope's *Rape of the Lock*, but there is a profound irony in Keats's "Ode on a Grecian Urn"; and there is irony of a very powerful sort in Wordsworth's "Intimations" ode. For the thrusts and pressures exerted by the various symbols in this poem are not avoided by the poet: they are taken into account and played, one against the other. Indeed, the symbols—from a scientific point of view—are used perversely: it is the child who is the best philosopher; it is from a kind of darkness

—from something that is "shadowy"—that the light proceeds; growth into manhood is viewed, not as an extrication from, but as an incarceration within, a prison.

There should be no mystery as to why this must be so. The terms of science are abstract symbols which do not change under the pressure of the context. They are pure (or aspire to be pure) denotations; they are defined in advance. They are not to be warped into new meanings. But where is the dictionary which contains the terms of a poem? It is a truism that the poet is continually forced to remake language. As Eliot has put it, his task is to "dislocate language into meaning." And, from the standpoint of a scientific vocabulary, this is precisely what he performs: for, rationally considered, the ideal language would contain one term for each meaning, and the relation between term and meaning would be constant. But the word, as the poet uses it, has to be conceived of, not as a discrete particle of meaning, but as a potential of meaning, a nexus or cluster of meanings.

What is true of the poet's language in detail is true of the larger wholes of poetry. And therefore, if we persist in approaching the poem as primarily a rational statement, we ought not to be surprised if the statement seems to be presented to us always in the ironic mode. When we consider the statement immersed in the poem, it presents itself to us, like the stick immersed in the pool of water, warped and bent. Indeed, whatever the statement, it will always show itself as deflected away from a positive, straightforward formulation.

It may seem perverse, however, to maintain, in the face of our revived interest in Donne, that the essential structure of poetry is not logical. For Donne has been appealed to of late as the great master of metaphor who imposes a clean logic on his images beside which the ordering of the images in Shakespeare's sonnets is fumbling and loose. It is perfectly true that Donne makes a great show of logic; but two matters need to be observed. In the first place, the elaborated and "logical" figure is not Donne's only figure or even his staple one. "Telescoped" figures like "Made one anothers hermitage" are to be found much more frequently than the celebrated comparison of the souls of the lovers to the legs of a pair of compasses. In the second place, where Donne uses "logic," he regularly uses it to justify illogical positions. He employs it to overthrow a conventional position or to "prove" an essentially illogical one.

Logic, as Donne uses it, is nearly always an ironic logic to state the claims of an idea or attitude which we have agreed, with our everyday logic, is false. This is not to say, certainly, that Donne is not justified in using his logic so, or that the best of his poems are not "proved" in the only senses in which poems can be proved.

But the proof is not a logical proof. "The Canonization" will scarcely prove to the hard-boiled naturalist that the lovers, by giving up the world, actually attain a better world. Nor will the argument advanced in the poem convince the dogmatic Christian that Donne's lovers are really saints.

In using logic, Donne as a poet is fighting the devil with fire. To adopt Robert Penn Warren's metaphor (which, though I lift it somewhat scandalously out of another context, will apply to this one): "The poet, somewhat less spectacularly [than the saint], proves his vision by submitting it to the fires of irony—to the drama of the structure—in the hope that the fires will refine it. In other words, the poet wishes to indicate that his vision has been earned, that it can survive reference to the complexities and contradictions of experience."

The same principle that inspires the presence of irony in so many of our great poems also accounts for the fact that so many of them seem to be built around paradoxes. Here again the conventional associations of the term may prejudice the reader just as the mention of Donne may prejudice him. For Donne, as one type of reader knows all too well, was of that group of poets who wished to impress their audience with their cleverness. All of us are familiar with the censure passed upon Donne and his followers by Dr. Johnson, and a great many of us still retain it as our own, softening only the rigor of it and the thoroughness of its application, but not giving it up as a principle.

Yet there are better reasons than that of rhetorical vain-glory that have induced poet after poet to choose ambiguity and paradox rather than plain, discursive simplicity. It is not enough for the poet to analyze his experience as the scientist does, breaking it up into parts, distinguishing part from part, classifying the various parts. His task is finally to unify experience. He must return to us the unity of the experience itself as man knows it in his own experience. The poem, if it be a true poem is a simulacrum of reality—

in this sense, at least, it is an "imitation"—by *being* an experience rather than any mere statement about experience or any mere abstraction from experience.

Tennyson cannot be content with *saying* that in memory the poet seems both dead *and* alive; he must dramatize its life-in-death for us, and his dramatization involves, necessarily, ironic shock and wonder. The dramatization demands that the antithetical aspects of memory be coalesced into one entity which—if we take it on the level of statement—is a paradox, the assertion of the union of opposites. Keats's Urn must express a life which is above life and its vicissitudes, but it must also bear witness to the fact that its life is not life at all but is a kind of death. To put it in other terms, the Urn must, in its role as historian, assert that myth is truer than history. Donne's lovers must reject the world in order to possess the world.

Or, to take one further instance: Wordsworth's light must serve as the common symbol for aspects of man's vision which seem mutually incompatible—intuition and analytic reason. Wordsworth's poem, as a matter of act, typifies beautifully the poet's characteristic problem itself. For even this poem, which testifies so heavily to the way in which the world is split up and parceled out under the growing light of reason, cannot rest in this fact as its own mode of perception, and still be a poem. Even after the worst has been said about man's multiple vision, the poet must somehow prove that the child is father to the man, that the dawn light is still somehow the same light as the evening light.

If the poet, then, must perforce dramatize the oneness of the experience, even though paying tribute to its diversity, then his use of paradox and ambiguity is seen as necessary. He is not simply trying to spice up, with a superficially exciting or mystifying rhetoric, the old stale stockpot (though doubtless this will be what the inferior poet does generally and what the real poet does in his lapses). He is rather giving us an insight which preserves the unity of experience and which, at its higher and more serious levels, triumphs over the apparently contradictory and conflicting elements of experience by unifying them into a new pattern.

Wordsworth's "Intimations" ode, then, is not only a poem, but, among other things, a parable about poetry. Keats's "Ode on a Grecian Urn" is quite obviously such a parable. And, indeed, most of the poems which we have discussed in this study may be taken as such parables.

In one sense, Pope's treatment of Belinda raises all the characteristic problems of poetry. For Pope, in dealing with his "goddess," must face the claims of naturalism and of common sense which would deny divinity to her. Unless he faces them, he is merely a sentimentalist. He must do an even harder thing: he must transcend the conventional and polite attributions of divinity which would be made to her as an acknowledged belle. Otherwise, he is merely trivial and obvious. He must "prove" her divinity against the common-sense denial (the brutal denial) and against the conventional assertion (the polite denial). The poetry must be wrested from the context: Belinda's lock, which is what the rude young man wants and which Belinda rather prudishly defends and which the naturalist asserts is only animal and which displays in its curled care the style of a particular era of history, must be given a place of permanence among the stars.

Marvin Levich

FORM AND CONTENT
IN POETRY*

Contemporary philosophers usually admit that science and poetry are different in their techniques and objectives. The claim that poetry repeats, but in a charming way, the triumphs of science, or explores, but in a different way, the territories not yet captured by science is, I believe, either discredited or forgotten. And further, the view that science answers to uniquely aesthetic requirements such as elegance and economy has been disclaimed by serious students of scientific method who have shown that it is either a superficial caricature of the complicated obligations of science or that such conditions if applicable can be interpreted without resort to an extrascientific vocabulary.

I am not interested, therefore, in the supremely unrewarding task of establishing that science and poetry are alike. Any view which purports to establish this connection derives ultimately from a careless use of outrageous puns. It does not follow that the more rewarding business of identifying or accounting for differences obtains results which are uniformly clarifying, especially when these results are sometimes affirmed by little more than the innocent piety that science and poetry are indeed quite different. Nor does it follow that the most frequently held characterizations of these

* From *The Journal of Philosophy*, Vol. LVI, No. 13, June 1959, pp. 586–595. Reprinted by permission of *The Journal of Philosophy*.

differences are the most satisfying. In fact, the purpose of this paper is to express dissatisfaction with a well-known but nonetheless questionable view.

This view holds that the form of scientific discourse is self-effacing and not methodologically authoritative and that the form of poetical discourse is opaque and methodologically authoritative. The traditional distinction between the form and content of language is accepted where the form identifies the visual and auditory properties of language now called syntactical—the configuration, order, and relation of sign-vehicles—and where the content identifies the designata or meaning of sign-vehicles. I am using the vocabulary of Morris.

Professor Hofstadter says in one version of this popular position:

> That there are striking differences between the uses of language in science and literature is well-known. Discussions of symbolism, logic, and esthetics often refer, for instance, to the intranslatability of literary language, to the manner in which it manifests personality or exploits the characteristics of the medium or material vehicle of its meanings, in contrast with the translatability of scientific language, its impersonality, and the self-effacing transparency of its medium. . . . For the purpose of science, translatability of its propositions is necessary; a defect here would be an obstacle to the efficient conduct of the scientific enterprise. On the other hand, the purposes of literary art can be achieved only by a use of language that entails a certain resistance to complete translation into other words; so that the attempt to render the content of a piece of literature in other terms *invariably*[1] results in some degree of transformation, deformation, or destruction. . . .
>
> One of the outstanding differences between scientific and literary language has to do with the relation of the linguistic medium or vehicle to its content. In scientific language, the medium or vehicle is not itself subject-matter which is organized in the content expressed by that language. A scientific statement (except in unusual circumstances as in linguistics generally, or in particular instances such as Goedel's proof of incompleteness or the development of the semantic paradoxes) does not refer to itself or study itself in what it says. . . . In a piece of literary language, on the other hand, this distinction, even separation, between vehicle and content is difficult if at all possible to make. . . . It is *never*[2] the case that in literature

---

[1] The italics are mine.
[2] The italics are mine.

of any literary merit, some appreciable esthetic role is not played by the vehicle, both in itself and in combination with other materials of language. . . .

The character of the imaginative object achieved by the artist depends upon the character of the language he employs, whereas the language of the scientist does not operate within the involvement pattern he formulates.[3]

These remarks entail some deceptive presuppositions and consequences which I can sort out:
1. Poetical language refers reflexively while scientific language does not. 2. The form of poetical language determines to a greater or lesser extent the meaning of poetical language, while the form of scientific language does not determine uniquely the meaning of scientific language. 3. Poetical expressions are intranslatable: a modification of form invariably modifies content. Scientific expressions are translatable: modifications of form need not modify content. 4. The form and content of a poetical expression determine an effect which is different from the expression and which is called the "imaginative object."

Some difficulties in this little catalogue of presuppositions and consequences must now be considered.

Our first target will be the reflexive character of poetical language. The property of reflexivity hardly distinguishes science from poetry, if some scientific expressions are reflexive and some poetic expressions are not. If, in the first place, Goedel's proof and the semantic paradoxes are reflexive and are scientific expressions or groups of scientific expressions, then nonreflexivity is not a pervasive property of scientific expressions or Goedel's proof and the paradoxes are not scientific expressions. They could not even constitute scientific problems, since their problematic character would only occur in a vocabulary which permitted reflexive and therefore extrascientific expressions.

In the second place, most poetical expressions are not obviously self-referent. The poetical expression, "Euclid alone has looked on beauty bare," refers to itself as little or as much as the complementary scientific expression, "Euclid was the first to systematize plane geometry." Neither expression identifies or purports to identify the order or configuration of sign-vehicles.

---

[3] Albert Hofstadter, "The Scientific and Literary Uses of Language," *Symbols and Society*, ed. by Lyman Bryson and others (New York, 1955), pp. 291–295.

In the third place, self-reference is an incidental occurrence in both poetry and science. Some poetical expressions, as well as some scientific expressions, are of course self-referent. For example, Professor Hofstadter cites Mr. MacLeish, who has self-referentially declared that:

> *A poem should not mean*
> *But be.*[4]

And these lines are self-referent if we pass over the obvious quibble that they refer and mean only by the heroic sacrifice of their own poetic character.

The case of Rossetti is less troublesome when he introduces the "House of Life" with two reflexive sonnets:

> *A Sonnet is a moment's monument,—*
> *Memorial from the Soul's eternity*
> *To one dead deathless hour. . . .*

> *A Sonnet is a coin: its face reveals*
> *The soul,—its converse, to what Power 'tis due:—*
> *Whether for tribute to the august appeals*
> *Of Life, or dower in Love's high retinue,*
> *It serves; . . .*[5]

Examples could be proliferated without improving the result. Some poetry refers reflexively; some science refers reflexively. The view, therefore, which urges that "poetry studies itself" and that science does not is completely misleading.

The manifest rejoinder is that poetic content does not study poetic form, but poetic form regulates poetic content. Since the form of a scientific expression does not uniquely determine its meaning, poetic language is thereby distinguished from scientific language. The rejoinder is also the second view listed above.

This version holds that the meaning of scientific expressions is not uniquely determined by such syntactical properties as configuration and not at all determined by such syntactical properties as meter, rhyme, or alliteration. While the sign-vehicle designates a meaning and while a recognizable and repetitive physical structure permits an unambiguous designation, that designation would be unaffected by an appropriate change of sign-vehicles. A suit-

---

[4] Cited in Hofstadter, p. 302.
[5] Dante Gabriel Rossetti, "The House of Life," *The Poetical Works of Dante Gabriel Rossetti* (London, 1913), p. 176.

able announcement which described the proposed translation would license prescribed substitutions.

Furthermore, a translation which incidentally alters rhythmic or syntactical order is scientifically unobjectionable. $x^2 = 4$ is not distorted by the syntactical transformation, $4 = x^2$.

I want now to raise some doubts about these generally accepted and apparently innocuous remarks. I shall do this by constructing a tiny scientific language which contains only a few expressions, and I should like to talk about two of them.

This tiny language will contain sign-vehicles with determinate designata. It will, therefore, be a semantic language which will include among its sentences, "The snow is white." A precise scientific language would require a more exact notation, but the nonmathematical character of our language will not prejudice the result. And I shall not explicitly introduce rules of designation since their assignment raises technical rather than theoretical difficulties. I will propose and discuss, however, two semantical rules for our language as follows:

1. When any propositional set of sign-vehicles with determinate designata occurs in iambic form, that propositional set will be negated. "The snow is white" will be read, therefore, "It is not the case that the snow is white." This convention will be followed for all propositions in the language.

2. If the predicate adjective precedes the verb in any propositional set of sign-vehicles, the expression will be read as an analytic disjunction, that is, "White is the snow" will be read, "The snow is white or the snow is not white." In this case, the office of communicating the logical relations "not" and "either-or" is assumed by the form.

Now this is a rudimentary and uninteresting language. A scientist would require in addition to other qualifications a talented ear and an elementary knowledge of grammar. And this might put an insuperable obstacle in the way of its general acceptance. The language none the less places no limitations upon the precision, complexity, or translatability of expressions.

The conclusion is that a scientific language may display a form which is neither self-effacing nor transparent. The fact that the form of scientific expressions is not authoritative is an accidental property of such expressions and other languages in which the form is authoritative are equally acceptable. The distinction, therefore, between science and poetry is not established by the *unelaborated* contention that the qualities of rhythm and order are not determining properties of scientific discourse.

Such objections are sometimes overridden by a more detailed analysis of the distinctive character of poetic form. It is urged, for example, that poetic form is unique because it reinforces rather than conveys meaning. The very sound and progress of some lines illustrate and therefore reinforce their reading. "The sound," says Pope, "must seem an echo to the sense."[6]

For instance, in the following illustration, the juxtaposition of consonants creates the labored effect designated by the lines:

> *When Ajax strives some rock's vast weight to throw,*
> *The line too labours, and the words move slow.*[7]

And Coleridge has in his "Metrical Feet" echoed the simple statement with the academic meters:

> *Trochee trips from long to short;*
> *From long to long in solemn sort*
> *Slow spondee stalks; strong foot! yet ill able*
> *Ever to come up with dactyl trisyllable.*
> *Iambics march from short to long;*
> *With a leap and a bound the swift anapests throng; . . .*[8]

The above cases are too obvious and too rare to be convincing, though aestheticians dearly love them. They overlook the frequent exceptions where the echo is very hard, indeed, to hear. Consider, for example, Blake's:

> *The caterpillar on the leaf*
> *Reminds thee of thy mother's grief.*[9]

or Yeats':

> *Autumn is over the long leaves that love us,*
> *And over the mice in the barley sheaves;*
> *Yellow the leaves of the rowan above us,*
> *And yellow the wet wild-strawberry leaves.*[10]

---

[6] Cited in Hofstadter, p. 295.

[7] Cited in Hofstadter, p. 295.

[8] Samuel Taylor Coleridge, "Metrical Feet," *The Poetical Works of Samuel Taylor Coleridge* (London, 1914), p. 140.

[9] William Blake, "The Keys," *The Complete Poetry of John Donne and William Blake* (New York, 1941), p. 1020.

[10] W. B. Yeats, "The Falling of the Leaves," *The Collected Poems of W. B. Yeats* (New York, 1933), p. 17.

where this reader does not discern the proposed reinforcement. The reply which holds that the reinforcement occurs even if we cannot find it or hear it is bad logical manners, for it dismisses contrary evidence as a symptom of human infirmity and settles an empirical controversy by fiat.

The neat presumption, therefore, that poetry illustrates one and only one relation of form and content seems faulty. Many different relations of form and content may occur, so that more delicate categories than "reinforcement" and even "form" and "content" themselves should be devised to encompass them, and all these relations may or may not be quite different from the relation of form and content in scientific discourse. But the avenue of exploration opened by this alternative and by the researches of critics such as Mr. Burke and Mr. Blackmur makes even more distressing the lazy acceptance of the traditional rubrics.

I should repeat for my own safety at this juncture that I am not advocating anything so capricious as a marriage between science and poetry but am instead asking for better legal grounds of incompatibility than are supplied by the categories of form and content. It might be an illuminating exercise if aestheticians and critics foreswore the use of "form" and "content" in their working vocabulary for at least a year and exploited more promising or less tired resources. The results, at any rate, could not be worse.

The traditional commitment to "form" and "content" has generated another problem which unlike some philosophical problems has some practical consequences.

Critics who agree that poetry contains both form and content where the form in one way or another determines the content also agree that poetry cannot be translated. Everyone who is wise seems to agree that scientific expressions can be translated without loss. The form, at least in part, determines the content, goes the old refrain—and a changed form is therefore a changed content.

If we ask why, we shall usually hear at least two answers. One is impregnable but empty; the other is vulnerable and, I think, misleading.

Let us construct a specific situation in which the impregnable defense appears. Suppose that an intrepid translator translates "The light that never was on land or sea" into "The little flame that flickered" and then claims that the meaning and therefore the poem is exactly translated. The intractable defender then replies that the sense is not the whole poem, the whole poem is the sense and the words and the sounds separately and all mixed together.

Now suppose the intrepid translator retreats and maintains that he has at least translated the meaning if not the poem. The intractable defender, encouraged by the first victory, replies that the meaning of the original is conveyed by that set of words and no other. The words were changed, and therefore the meaning was changed. The poem is form and content and neither can be disturbed without altering the other. The intractable defender might even whisper to a bystander, "Doesn't this failure and the failure of everyone else who ever tried to translate poetry make it self-evident that a change in form always changes the poem?"

Now I have called this the impregnable defense, for the poem is so defined that any structural modification is automatically a distortion. A translation is disqualified not by factual specification of mistakes, but on the grounds that the words in that order in that poem are analytic of the qualities of the poem. I cannot combat this view, for the definition adamantly precludes the possibility of disconfirming evidence. It is, however, fair to expect consistent application from its advocates, who should, for instance, denounce the re-setting of a poem in a new type face for its violation of the original form.

The imaginary conversation should also illustrate the dubious tactics of the defender, since the principle that every poem is unique is invoked to discredit any translation, while the inadequacy of translation is then cited to establish the principle that every poem is unique. But what I find really bizarre about this position is that the critics who militantly defend it have thereby compromised the evidential worth of their own professional labors. I shall develop this difficulty later.

Now the other view, which is vulnerable, denies exact translations but admits approximate translations and adjudicates among better and worse translations. The traditional prefatory demurrer of translators always tells us that the proffered translation is a poor substitute for the original but is still better than any other.

Let us again consider a particular case where the vulnerable defense emerges. This time we begin with an English prose translation of Dante's *Commedia*. The sense of the original is there, we are told, but the original was a poem and this is prose, so this cannot be an exact translation. The translator then returns to his desk and produces the suggested translation in verse. This is closer, we are assured, but the original was in *terza rima* and this is not. It is only a closer approximation. But let the suggested translation in *terza rima* come forward and now the complaint is that it is English and not Italian. It is closer but not close enough. I do not know whether anyone has essayed translating Dante into other Italian but I am confident the result would be greeted with the reply that it is poetry, it is in *terza rima*, it is Italian, but it is not Dante's Italian. It is the best yet, but it is still not the original. In fact, the running rejections should make clear that only the original can reproduce itself.

We are then left in the following dilemma. If the *Commedia* or any poem is just itself and nothing else, it precludes any translation. But the translator who makes approximate translations rejects the possibility of any equivalent translation of the very grounds which preclude any translation—that is, that the poem is itself and nothing else.

The point is an elementary one which can be illustrated in another way. Assume that a painter wishes to reproduce a certain shade of green from a segment of the rainbow and mixes pigments to find a match. He rejects a yellow-green in favor of a blue-green and then finds the green which appears to be an exact match. But if he were our intractable translator he would at once refuse the match because it occurs in pigment rather than light. At the crucial juncture he invokes an *ad hoc* criterion which he previously omitted and which would have led, if it had not been omitted earlier, to the repudiation of his earlier comparisons.

The translator who is very clever can always find a condition *after* the match has been attempted which would discredit it and which he conveniently forgets when only graduated approximations are certified. But the translator who is also honest should stipulate at the beginning the self-defeating contention that only the object itself can duplicate itself.

A translator is, of course, free to claim that the *Commedia* is itself and not another thing and that every prose and poetical translation fails. But he has thereby averted the adjudication of any conflicting claims among competing translations, since the prior imputation of uniqueness prevents any warranted comparisons.

I want to suggest that another prominent set of aesthetic presuppositions would also license translations. Professor Hofstadter, you will recall, argued that "the character of the imaginative object achieved by the artist depends upon the character of the language he employs."

The adherent of this view frequently distinguishes between the poem as a spatial instance in the serial order of events, the poem as a set of meanings, and the poem as an imaginative object or effect. It is then held that the physical structure becomes poetical when it determines an imaginative event located in the reader. This imaginative event is at once a function of what has been said and the way it has been said, and it is then concluded that no other combination of words can evoke the same event. The order of words on the page is then viewed as an instrument to the poetical character which is located in the imaginative event.

The argument rests on the fundamental misconception that one and only one cause can obtain a stipulated effect, and there is no substantial evidence from any empirical domain to sustain this dubious view. A marlinespike or a baseball bat vigorously laid about the head can arouse the same sum total of pain, water or an electric grill can evoke the identical sensation of heat, and more than one identifiable order of words could conceivably evoke the same imaginative event.

Accordingly, the distinction between structure and imaginative event legitimatizes the further assumption that a multiplicity of structures could determine the same event. As a result, the replacement of an iambic or trochaic form, for example, does not in itself constitute conclusive evidence for the decision that the imaginative event has been commensurately altered. Finding alternative determining conditions which are appropriate may be very difficult, and I do not want to minimize the difficulty. But the theoretical possibility of devising equivalent structures should not be dismissed by an unyielding linguistic commitment and is consistent with at least one well-established view of poetic function.

The obvious demurrer can be entered that the imaginative effect of a poem is so vague that we cannot identify it. A translation might therefore produce an equivalent effect, but we should never know that it had. The force of this retort, however, would impose illiberal restrictions upon the conduct of literary criticism, which has frequently held that one of its objectives is the explication or identification of the imaginative effect which is evoked by a poem.

When Mr. Brooks says, for instance, that "Composed Upon

Westminster Bridge" creates the effect of surprise[11] and when Mr. Frank says that "Prufrock" creates a perception of elements spatially arranged,[12] the reader must presume that these remarks aim to identify the distinctive effect of these poems. Accordingly, if the effect of a poem eludes identification, such remarks are irresponsible and misleading. To be sure, any special claim may be either partial or distorted, but the evidential worth of special claims is not compromised by an acknowledgment of their contingent status. A translator could then say, "As far as I know, I have translated the poem exactly." He *might* be wrong, and *might* have missed something, but literary criticism is alone in discouraging an intellectual pursuit because a logical or analytic guarantee of accuracy is wanting.

Finally, the injunction that poems contain or evoke an intrinsic vagueness reduces every reading of a poem to the condition of an imperfect translation. Every reading will be to some extent arbitrary or fallible, since it will contain elements which are not completely controlled or sanctioned by the ascertainable form and content. Therefore, the integrity of *any* reading can be impugned by the same objections which are used to indict a formal translation, and the special reproaches leveled against such formal translations are arbitrary and undeserved.

The theoretical animadversions brought against translation are ill-founded, then, and convert an empirical difficulty into an analytic impossibility.

Consequently, the presently held distinction between form and content obscures the relation of science and poetry, oversimplifies the nature of poetic discourse, and excludes the possibility of exact translation through a concealed *petitio*. The distinction, then, is noxious and we will only look for better things after admitting it.

---

[11] Cleanth Brooks, "The Language of Paradox," *Criticism*, ed. by Shorer and others (New York, 1948), pp. 358–359.

[12] Joseph Frank, "Spatial Form in Modern Literature," *Criticism*, ed. by Shorer and others (New York, 1948), p. 382.

II

Style and the Form of a Work of Art

INTRODUCTION

Art historians accord a central place in their inquiries to the formulation of "period-styles" and to investigations of their conceptual structure. That the enterprise of identifying period-styles is ambitious and complex is suggested at once by the hyphenated constituents, "period" and "style." "Style" suggests one of its aims—the determination of features that are generic to works of art. "Period" suggests another and related aim—locating the generic features in the context of a determinate chronology.

Let us begin with a crude statement of the enterprise and say that it has the aim of identifying for the art-works of a given age their unities of expressive quality, form, and content. At first glance, this is quite different from defining styles *per se*. We are describing what some tragedies *are* like when we say, for example, of Greek tragedy in the fifth century B.C. that its style is such-and-such. But we are saying what tragedy *should* be like when we define tragedy *per se*, and conclude relative to that definition that *Hamlet* or *Death of a Salesman* is or is not a tragedy. The first assertion is ostensibly factual and it should be that of the possible formulations one of them is uniquely true of the fifth century B.C. The second is ostensibly evaluative and of the possible formulations, therefore, no one of them is uniquely right. We will select one of them, of course, but that will turn on our changing tastes in matters of drama.

The distinction is too easy, however. It immediately raises difficulties and seriously distorts what it seeks to clarify. In the first place, there is an obvious sense in which definitions of style *per se* are responsible to fact. There could hardly be a more crushing indictment of a definition of tragedy, for example, than the allegation that there are no dramas to which it applies. If definitions of style are formulated with some subject-matter in view, they presumably have the purpose and obligation of facilitating, and not hindering, the discussion of that subject-matter. It is not unreasonable, therefore, to require of a definition of tragedy that it include at least some dramas that, in respect of the definition, are tragedies. Definitions of style *per se* are, in this sense, subject to minimal requirements of factual worth. There is, in the second place, an obvious sense in which the use of "tragedy," when we simply say about a drama, "That is a tragedy," directly affects its use in a statement of period-style. I shall discuss at a later point why this is so.

First, however, some preliminary queries about the nature of period-styles. A high degree of energy and competence has been allocated to ascertaining period-styles, but despite this impressive investment of resources, it is not always clear what attributes of period-style belong to a designated period or what is at stake when disagreement arises about their scope or factual authority.

If we accept the crude statement, investigations into period-styles are essentially straightforward and uncomplicated. The art historian simply selects a historical epoch, examines the extant works of art from that epoch, and catalogues their common features. Of course if a period-style is to be identifying—that is, if it is to designate what is *distinctive* about that period—the art historian must in addition select the features that are characteristic *only* of that period. The result should be a period-style.

The foregoing, however, is little short of caricature. In the first place, there has never been a period in which *all* art-works are considered suitable instances of the style assigned to that period. Consequently the problem for the art historian is not to decide what is common to the art-works of a period, but of the art-works in the period which are similar enough to constitute a style. And in point of fact, the designation of a determinate chronology as a "period" presumes already that within it the requisite similarity is present.

There is, however, much more to this problem than the determination of common denominators. Paintings of the eighteenth century, for example, are said to have the period-style *rococo*. Ro-

coco is, according to one art historian, "a modification or variation of the Baroque rather than opposition to it," and in it "the irreconcilable oppositions of the Baroque were softened into sarcastic
satires, gentle ironies . . . and wistful melancholies." It is, again, "a
domesticated Baroque, better suited to fashionable townhouses than
palace halls . . ." (Art historians consider Baroque the period-style
for seventeenth-century painting and the classic statement of its
qualities is found in the selection from Wölfflin.)

The obvious point is that rococo is used to identify the qualities
in eighteenth-century painting that distinguish it from a style assumed as true of seventeenth-century painting, i.e., baroque. The
painters cited as exemplary of rococo—Watteau, Boucher, Frago-
nard, etc.—are cited because they are exemplary also of the transformations in pictorial quality that the art historian thinks important. As a result, he includes them under his period-style. The
paintings, therefore, that maintain the baroque style into the eighteenth century are excluded from a place in the period-style of that
century and relegated to the atypical. Consequently, it would be
absurd to suppose that a period-style is decided by counting all the
paintings in a century and cataloguing the traits inherent in at least
51 percent of them. A period-style is not a counting of pictorial
noses, and it is, as a result, not easy to pose the kind of question
that determines its factual authority. Clearly, it is not, "Given the
works of this period, what is it that is characteristic of them?" The
question has at least three parts: What are the characteristics of art
works in this period that are different and/or influential? Of the art
works in this period, which of them manifest these characteristics?
Given these art-works, what is the formulation that most adequately identifies their common style?

The question of what constitutes the differences that are important and influential is a troublesome one, and in one sense the
answer turns on considerations of aesthetic relevance. Suppose every
painting in the eighteenth century depicted a reclining woman surrounded by serving women and cherubs. And suppose further that
reclining women were never depicted in the paintings of the
seventeenth century. Have we discovered a suitable candidate for
inclusion in a definition of the rococo? Have we discovered something important? The answer requires still another query, "Important and influential for what?" If we reply, "To paintings as

works of art, of course," we have introduced at once the issue of aesthetic relevance.

The relation of subject-matter to artistic style is not straightforward. It depends on a framework of assumptions about which traits of an object are its traits *qua* work of art. One influential critic has maintained that "the representative element in a work of art may or may not be harmful; always it is irrelevant." Assume now that an art historian declares allegiance to this familiar maxim and to a statement of his professional purpose that proclaims, among other things, that the concern of an art historian is the examination of paintings *qua* works of art. He has committed himself, on pain of inconsistency, to the exclusion of references to subject-matter as alien to his discipline and therefore to the appropriate scope of stylistic analysis.

If the office of art history is transparent in its title, i.e., if it is concerned with objects as works of art, and if it is held that the domain of artistic traits in painting, for example, excludes subject-matter, then such traits are excluded also from statements of period-style. Any controversies, therefore, about the membership of traits in the domain of artistic traits will affect decisions about their incorporation in formulations of period-style.

There is also a more specific sense of artistic relevance that controls the formulations of period-styles. Suppose, for example, every painting in the eighteenth century contained in its upper left corner a small black line. Coloration, as distinct from subject-matter, is by common consent an aesthetic property of painting, but this fact does not warrant *any* reference to color in a period-style. There is the presumption that the reference must be *importantly* relevant to the paintings it designates, must facilitate our making critical sense of them. Therefore, the formulation of a period-style raises at once questions of critical evaluation, of what features contribute to an understanding of the objects denoted by the "period-style," and to an understanding of them as works of art. The art historian is, in other words, at once historian *and* critic.

There is, as a result, a clear relationship between what I have called definitions of style *per se* and definitions of period-style. Both introduce questions of evaluation; although both must be based on fact, their ultimate merit is not solely factual but turns on a delicate balance of fact and evaluation. When we say that tragedy has such-and-such a style, we are making claims about the properties aesthetically relevant to an understanding of drama as tragedy. When we say that Greek tragedy in the fifth century B.C. has such-and-such a period-style, we are making claims also about the properties aesthetically relevant to an understanding of those dramas as tragedies. And whatever the transformations in our critical views about the nature of drama, they will affect our views about the relevant nature and therefore the period-style of dramas. Consequently if there is no uniquely correct formulation of a style, there can be no uniquely correct formulation of a period-style.

I turn now to another and more ambitious task sometimes allotted to period-styles. Sometimes it is required that they formulate not only the characteristics in a period distinctive of a particular art, for example, painting or drama, but the characteristics in that period distinctive of all its arts, painting, drama, music, poetry, sculpture, architecture, and in case of the baroque, the apparently extraneous matters of philosophy, political organization, and military tactics. As one would expect, the problems multiply.

In the first place, the extension in scope requires a transformation of vocabulary. The styles of painting or drama are describable by a vocabulary indigenous to each in the sense that its words take their meaning from properties characteristically pictorial or dramatic. A period-style, therefore, that purports to describe what is distinctive of many arts together requires a language neutral to their differences. Obvious candidates are the languages of emotion and of intellectual history. Let us consider an example of their use and a question of meaning which the use suggests.

Professor Daniells uses both languages indifferently in his preliminary discussion of the baroque:

> A feeling of triumph, of splendour, of certainty, and of power lies behind much of this art—a belief in the attainability of truth through appeals to authority, to force, and to heavenly sanction. . . . We find the sensual in conflict with the ascetic, flesh with spirit, grace with free will. Reason fights authority, mysticism is opposed by clear intellectual perception; scholasticism and classical humanism, themselves in conflict, find a new and common foe in rationalism.

The obvious question is whether the expansion of baroque to these dimensions is damaging to or destructive of its descriptive power. There is always the danger that by inflating the subject-matter to which a word applies, we deflate the word of determinate meaning to a point of factual vacuity. In the first place, it is not clear what the words under consideration apply to, whether they still describe works of art at all, or refer instead to the attitudes of their creators, critics, or audience. It is not clear, as a result, from where the evidence comes that determines their suitability as components in a period-style. From art critics, intellectual historians, political historians, psychologists? In the second place, does the style as formulated have the use of *describing* seventeenth-century art or of *explaining* via cultural traits the fact of its occurrence? And if the role is explanatory, are the described features of seventeenth-century style simply invoked again and rebaptized as "explanation"? In the third place, what in particular does baroque style in its extended form assert, describe, or explain about the seventeenth century?

Another example might clarify the question. The view has been advanced that paradox is a characteristic of baroque art and is common to the churches of Borromini, the sculpture of Bernini, the painting of El Greco, and the poetry of Crashaw and Milton. Now there is a tolerably clear sense in which a language may express paradox and there may be also tolerably clear meanings for paradox as expressed in sculpture, architecture, and painting. What is not clear is that "paradox" in each of these uses is a species of the same genus, "paradox." What has to be established, and not assumed, is that there is a general meaning of "paradox" such that each of the uses is one of its exemplifications. Otherwise the stylistic problem is simply transferred and not resolved by exporting it from the subject-matter of works of art to that of the meaning of "paradox."

Accordingly a statement that there is a property *x*, characteristic of a class of art works, is not established by the unelaborated contention that each of them has *x*. It is necessary, in addition, to show that *x* retains a common sense on its several occasions of use. Otherwise the statement of period-style is emptied of determinate meaning or conflates otherwise determinate meanings.

Given the host of problems—methodological, factual, and evaluative—that confront the art historian, it should hardly be surprising that definitions of period-style are controversial in respect of their meaning and evidential worth. On the other hand, whatever the ultimate merit of such definitions, there is little question about the usefulness of trying to establish them. The controversies which are always raging about their adequacy, contrary to what some art-historians seem to think, are not to be deplored. They are an intellectual arena in which evidence and critical views are constantly being exchanged about the nature and aesthetic quality of works of art. They provide occasions for the accumulation of new information which contributes significantly to appreciation and understanding. One of the prime intellectual contexts in which we can find informed and responsible discussions of particular works of art is that of period-style.

The Nature of Period-Style

Heinrich Wölfflin

PERIOD-STYLE AND
THE BAROQUE*

Nothing is more natural to art history than to draw parallels between periods of culture and periods of style. The columns and arches of the High Renaissance speak as intelligibly of the spirit of the time as the figures of Raphael, and a baroque building represents the transformation of ideals no less clearly than a comparison between the sweeping gestures of Guido Reni and the noble restraint and dignity of the Sistine Madonna.

Let us this time remain on strictly architectural ground. The central idea of the Italian Renaissance is that of perfect proportion. In the human figure as in the edifice, this epoch strove to achieve the image of perfection at rest within itself. Every form developed to self-existent being, the whole freely co-ordinated: nothing but independently living parts. The column, the panel, the volume of a single element of a space as of a whole space—nothing here but forms in which the human being may find an existence satisfied in itself, extending beyond human measure, but always accessible to the imagination. With infinite content, the mind apprehends this art as the image of a higher, free existence in which it may participate.

* From Heinrich Wölfflin, *Principles of Art History*. Reprinted by permission of G. Bell & Sons, Ltd. (London).

The baroque uses the same system of forms, but in place of the perfect, the completed, gives the restless, the becoming, in place of the limited, the conceivable, gives the limitless, the colossal. The ideal of beautiful proportion vanishes, interest concentrates not on being, but on happening. The masses, heavy and thickset, come into movement. Architecture ceases to be what it was in the Renaissance, an art of articulation, and the composition of the building, which once raised the impression of freedom to its highest pitch, yields to a conglomeration of parts without true independence.

This analysis is certainly not exhaustive, but it will serve to show in what way styles express their epoch. It is obviously a new ideal of life which speaks to us from Italian baroque, and although we have placed architecture first as being the most express embodiment of that ideal, the contemporary painters and sculptors say the same thing in their own language, and whoever tries to reduce the psychic bases of style to abstract principles will probably find the decisive word here more readily than with the architects. The relationship of the individual to the world has changed, a new domain of feeling has opened, the soul aspires to dissolution in the sublimity of the huge, the infinite. "Emotion and movement at all costs." Thus does the Cicerone formulate the nature of this art.

We have, in thus sketching three examples of individual style, national style, and period style, illustrated the aims of an art history which conceives style primarily as expression, expression of the temper of an age and a nation as well as expression of the individual temperament. It is obvious that with all that, the quality of the work of art is not touched: temperament certainly makes no work of art, but it is what we might call the material element of style taken in the broad sense that the particular ideal of beauty (of the individual as of the community) is included in it too. Works of art history of this kind are still far from the perfection they might attain, but the task is inviting and grateful.

Artists are certainly not readily interested in historical questions of style. They take work exclusively from the standpoint of quality —is it good, is it self-sufficing, has nature found a vigorous and clear presentment? Everything else is more or less indifferent. We have but to read Hans van Marées when he writes that he is learning to attach less and less value to schools and personalities in order only to keep in view the solution of the artistic problem, which is ultimately the same for Michelangelo as for Bartholomew van der Helst.

Art historians who, on the other hand, take the differences between the finished products as their point of departure have always been exposed to the scorn of the artists: they have taken the detail for the essence: they cling just to the non-artistic side in man in wishing to understand art as expression only. We can very well analyse the temperament of an artist and still not explain how the work came into being, and the description of all the differences between Raphael and Rembrandt is merely an evasion of the main problem, because the important point is not to show the difference between the two but how both, in different ways, produced the same thing—namely, great art.

It is hardly necessary here to take up the cudgels for the art historian and defend his work before a dubious public. The artist quite naturally places the general canon of art in the foreground, but we must not carp at the historical observer with his interest in the variety of forms in which art appears, and it remains no mean problem to discover the conditions which, as material element—call it temperament, *Zeitgeist*, or racial character—determine the style of individuals, periods, and peoples.

Yet an analysis with quality and expression as its objects by no means exhausts the facts. There is a third factor—and here we arrive at the crux of this enquiry—the mode of representation as such. Every artist finds certain visual possibilities before him, to which he is bound. Not everything is possible at all times. Vision itself has its history, and the revelation of these visual strata must be regarded as the primary task of art history.

Let us try to make the matter clear by examples. There are hardly two artists who, although contemporaries, are more widely divergent by temperament than the baroque master Bernini and the Dutch painter Terborch. Confronted with the turbulent figures of Bernini, who will think of the peaceful, delicate little pictures of Terborch? And yet, if we were to lay drawings by the two masters side by side and compare the general features of the technique, we should have to admit that there is here a perfect kinship. In both, there is that manner of seeing in patches instead of lines, something which we can call painterly, which is the distinguishing feature of the seventeenth century in comparison with the sixteenth. We encounter here a kind of vision in which the most heterogeneous artists can participate because it obviously does not bind them to a special mode of expression. Certainly an artist like Bernini needed the painterly style to say what he had to say, and it is absurd to wonder how he would have expressed himself in the draughtsmanly style of the sixteenth century. But we are clearly dealing with other concepts here than when we speak, for instance, of the energy of the baroque handling of masses in contrast to the repose and reserve of the High Renaissance. Greater or less movement are expressional factors which can be measured by one and the same standard: painterly and draughtsmanly, on the other hand, are like two languages, in which everything can be said, although each has its strength in a different direction and may have proceeded to visibility from a different angle.

Another example. We can analyse Raphael's line from the point of view of expression, describe its great noble gait in contrast to the pettier fussiness of Quattrocento outlines: we can feel in the movement of the line in Giorgione's Venus the kinship with the Sistine Madonna and, turning to sculpture, discover in Sansovino's youthful Bacchus the new, long, continuous line, and nobody will deny that we feel in this great creation the breath of the new sixteenth century feeling: it is no mere superficial history-writing to connect in this way form and spirit. But the phenomenon has another side. By explaining great line, we have not explained line. It is by no means a matter of course that Raphael and Giorgione and Sansovino sought expressive force and formal beauty in line. But it is again a question of international connections. The same period is for the north, too, a period of line, and two artists who, as personalities, have little in common, Michelangelo and Hans Holbein the Younger, resemble each other in that they both represent the type of quite strictly linear design. In other words, there can be discovered in the history of style a substratum of concepts referring to representation as such, and one could envisage a history of the development of occidental seeing, for which the variations in individual and national characteristics would cease to have any importance. It is certainly no easy task to reveal this inward visual development, because the representational possibilities of an epoch are never shown in abstract purity but, as is natural, are always bound to a certain expressional content, and the observer is then generally inclined to seek in the expression the explanation of the whole artistic product.

When Raphael erects his pictorial edificies and, by strict observance of rules, achieves the impression of reserve and dignity to an unprecedented degree, we can find in his special problem the im-

pulse and the goal, and yet the tectonics of Raphael are not entirely
to be attributed to an intention born of a state of mind: it is rather
a question of a representational form of his epoch which he only
perfected in a certain way and used for his own ends. Similar solemn
ambitions were not lacking later, but it was impossible to revert to
his formulas. French classicism of the seventeenth century rests on
another visual basis, and hence, with a similar intention, necessarily
arrives at other results. By attributing everything to expression
alone, we make the false assumption that for every state of mind
the same expressional methods were always available.

And when we speak of the progress of imitation, of the new impressions of nature which an epoch produced, that is also a material
element which is bound to *a priori* forms of representation. The
observations of the seventeenth century were not merely woven
into the fabric of Cinquecento art. The whole groundwork changed.
It is a mistake for art history to work with the clumsy notion of the
imitation of nature, as though it were merely a homogeneous process
of increasing perfection. All the increase in the "surrender to nature" does not explain how a landscape by Ruysdael differs from
one by Patenir, and by the "progressive conquest of reality" we
have still not explained the contrast between a head by Frans Hals
and one by Dürer. The imitative content, the subject matter, may
be as different in itself as possible, the decisive point remains that
the conception in each case is based on a different visual schema—
a schema which, however, is far more deeply rooted than in mere
questions of the progress of imitation. It conditions the architectural
work as well as the work of representative art, and a Roman baroque
façade has the same visual denominator as a landscape by Van
Goyen.

THE MOST GENERAL
REPRESENTATIONAL FORMS

This volume is occupied with the discussion of these universal forms
of representation. It does not analyse the beauty of Leonardo but
the element in which that beauty became manifest. It does not
analyse the representation of nature according to its imitational
content, and how, for instance, the naturalism of the sixteenth century may be distinguished from that of the seventeenth, but the

mode of perception which lies at the root of the representative arts in the various centuries.

Let us try to sift out these basic forms in the domain of more modern art. We denote the series of periods with the names Early Renaissance, High Renaissance, and Baroque, names which mean little and must lead to misunderstanding in their application to south and north, but are hardly to be ousted now. Unfortunately, the symbolic analogy bud, bloom, decay, plays a secondary and misleading part. If there is in fact a qualitative difference between the fifteenth and sixteenth centuries, in the sense that the fifteenth had gradually to acquire by labour the insight into effects which was at the free disposal of the sixteenth, the (classic) art of the Cinquecento and the (baroque) art of the Seicento are equal in point of value. The word classic here denotes no judgment of value, for baroque has its classicism too. Baroque (or, let us say, modern art) is neither a rise nor a decline from classic, but a totally different art. The occidental development of modern times cannot simply be reduced to a curve with rise, height, and decline: it has two culminating points. We can turn our sympathy to one or to the other, but we must realise that that is an arbitrary judgment, just as it is an arbitrary judgment to say that the rose-bush lives its supreme moment in the formation of the flower, the apple-tree in that of the fruit.

For the sake of simplicity, we must speak of the sixteenth and seventeenth centuries as units of style, although these periods signify no homogeneous production, and, in particular, the features of the Seicento had begun to take shape long before the year 1600, just as, on the other hand, they long continued to affect the appearance of the eighteenth century. Our object is to compare type with type, the finished with the finished. Of course, in the strictest sense of the word, there is nothing "finished": all historical material is subject to continual transformation; but we must make up our minds to establish the distinctions at a fruitful point, and there to let them speak as contrasts, if we are not to let the whole development slip through our fingers. The preliminary stages of the High Renaissance are not to be ignored, but they represent an archaic form of art, an art of primitives, for whom established pictorial form does not yet exist. But to expose the individual differences which lead from the style of the sixteenth century to that of the seventeenth must be left to a detailed historical survey which will, to tell the truth, only do justice to its task when it has the determining concepts at his disposal.

If we are not mistaken, the development can be reduced, as a provisional formulation, to the following five pairs of concepts:

(1) The development from the linear to the painterly, *i.e.* the development of line as the path of vision and guide of the eye, and the gradual depreciation of line: in more general terms, the perception of the object by its tangible character—in outline and surfaces —on the one hand, and on the other, a perception which is by way of surrendering itself to the mere visual appearance and can abandon "tangible" design. In the former case the stress is laid on the limits of things; in the other the work tends to look limitless. Seeing by volumes and outlines isolates objects: for the painterly eye, they merge. In the one case interest lies more in the perception of individual material objects as solid, tangible bodies; in the other, in the apprehension of the world as a shifting semblance.

(2) The development from plane to recession. Classic[1] art reduces the parts of a total form to a sequence of planes, the baroque emphasises depth. Plane is the element of line, extension in one plane the form of the greatest explicitness: with the discounting of the contour comes the discounting of the plane, and the eye relates objects essentially in the direction of forwards and backwards. This is no qualitative difference: with a greater power of representing spatial depths, the innovation has nothing directly to do: it signifies rather a radically different mode of representation, just as "plane style" in our sense is not the style of primitive art, but makes its appearance only at the moment at which foreshortening and spatial illusion are completely mastered.

(3) The development from closed to open form. Every work of art must be a finite whole, and it is a defect if we do not feel that it is self-contained, but the interpretation of this demand in the sixteenth and seventeenth centuries is so different that, in comparison with the loose form of the baroque, classic design may be taken as *the* form of closed composition. The relaxation of rules, the yielding of tectonic strength, or whatever name we may give to the process, does not merely signify an enhancement of interest, but is a new mode of representation consistently carried out, and hence

---

[1] "Klassisch." The word "classic" throughout this book refers to the art of the High Renaissance. It implies, however, not only a historical phase of art, but a special mode of creation of which that art is an instance. (Tr.)

this factor is to be adopted among the basic forms of representation.

(4) The development from multiplicity to unity. In the system of a classic composition, the single parts, however firmly they may be rooted in the whole, maintain a certain independence. It is not the anarchy of primitive art: the part is conditioned by the whole, and yet does not cease to have its own life. For the spectator, that presupposes an articulation, a progress from part to part, which is a very different operation from perception as a whole, such as the seventeenth century applies and demands. In both styles unity is the chief aim (in contrast to the pre-classic period which did not yet understand the idea in its true sense), but in the one case unity is achieved by a harmony of free parts, in the other, by a union of parts in a single theme, or by the subordination, to one unconditioned dominant, of all other elements.

(5) The absolute and the relative clarity of the subject. This is a contrast which at first borders on the contrast between linear and painterly. The representation of things as they are, taken singly and accessible to plastic feeling, and the representation of things as they look, seen as a whole, and rather by their non-plastic qualities. But it is a special feature of the classic age that it developed an ideal of perfect clarity which the fifteenth century only vaguely suspected, and which the seventeenth voluntarily sacrificed. Not that artistic form had become confused, for that always produces an unpleasing effect, but the explicitness of the subject is not longer the sole purpose of the presentment. Composition, light, and colour no longer merely serve to define form, but have their own life. There are cases in which absolute clarity has been partly abandoned merely to enhance effect, but "relative" clarity, as a great all-embracing mode of representation, first entered the history of art at the moment at which reality is beheld with an eye to other effects. Even here it is not a difference of quality if the baroque departed from the ideals of the age of Dürer and Raphael, but, as we have said, a different attitude to the world.

IMITATION AND DECORATION

The representational forms here described are of such general significance that even widely divergent natures such as Terborch and Bernini—to repeat an example already used—can find room within one and the same type. The community of style in these two painters rests on what, for people of the seventeenth century, was a matter of course—certain basic conditions to which the impression of living form is bound without a more special expressional value being attached to them.

They can be treated as forms of representation or forms of beholding: in these forms nature is seen, and in these forms art manifests its contents. But it is dangerous to speak only of certain "states of the eye" by which conception is determined: every artistic conception is, of its very nature, organised according to certain notions of pleasure. Hence our five pairs of concepts have an imitative and a decorative significance. Every kind of reproduction of nature moves within a definite decorative schema. Linear vision is permanently bound up with a certain idea of beauty and so is painterly vision. If an advanced type of art dissolves the line and replaces it by the restless mass, that happens not only in the interests of a new verisimilitude, but in the interests of a new beauty too. And in the same way we must say that representation in a plane type certainly corresponds to a certain stage of observation, but even here the schema has obviously a decorative side. The schema certainly yields nothing of itself, but it contains the possibility of developing beauties in the arrangement of planes which the recessional style no longer possesses and can no longer possess. And we can continue in the same way with the whole series.

But then, if these more general concepts also envisage a special type of beauty, do we not come back to the beginning, where style was conceived as the direct expression of temperament, be it the temperament of a time, of a people, or of an individual? And in that case, would not the only new factor be that the section was cut lower down, the phenomena, to a certain extent, reduced to a greater common denominator?

In speaking thus, we should fail to realise that the second terms of our pairs of concepts belong of their very nature to a different species, in so far as these concepts, in their transformations, obey an inward necessity. They represent a rational psychological process. The transition from tangible, plastic, to purely visual, painterly perception follows a natural logic, and could not be reversed. Nor could the transition from tectonic to a-tectonic, from the rigid to the free conformity to law.

To use a parable. The stone, rolling down the mountain side, can assume quite different motions according to the gradient of the slope, the hardness or softness of the ground, etc., but all these possibilities are subject to one and the same law of gravity. So, in human psychology, there are certain developments which can be regarded as subject to natural law in the same way as physical growth. They can undergo the most manifold variations, they can be totally or partially checked, but, once the rolling has started, the operation of certain laws may be observed throughout.

Nobody is going to maintain that the "eye" passes through developments on its own account. Conditioned and conditioning, it always impinges on other spiritual spheres. There is certainly no visual schema which, arising only from its own premises, could be imposed on the world as a stereotyped pattern. But although men have at all times seen what they wanted to see, that does not exclude the possibility that a law remains operative throughout all change. To determine this law would be a central problem, the central problem of a history of art.

Roy Daniells

BAROQUE FORM IN LITERATURE*

Until recently the connotations of the word "baroque" have been almost without exception unpleasant. The *New English Dictionary* defines it as, "irregularly shaped; whimsical, grotesque, odd" and in the examples of usage we find it coupled with terms like "absurd" and "frantic." Littré, epitomizing a traditionally French hatred of the unbalanced, stigmatizes baroque as "d'une bizarrerie choquante."[1] Roget brackets the term with "gaudy," "tawdry," "bedizened," and "flamboyant." The reason for all this is not far to seek. Baroque has meant, and for many people still means, nothing more than a questionable style of architecture, that of the Seicento. Vituperation of this architecture began early: in the introduction to Campbell's *Vitruvius Britannicus* (1717) we find a sample of that unmeasured scorn which was to be poured out on the baroque for the next two centuries:

> The Italians can no more now relish the Antique Simplicity, but are entirely employed in capricious Ornaments, which must at last end in the Gothick. For Proof of this Assertion, I appeal to the Productions of the last Century. How affected and licentious are the Works of Bernini and Fontana? How wildly extravagant are the designs of Boromini, who had endeavour'd to debauch mankind with

* From the *University of Toronto Quarterly*, Vol. XIV, 1944-45, pp. 393–408. Reprinted by permission of the author and the University of Toronto Press.

[1] "Of a shocking extravagance or eccentricity." (M.L.)

his odd and chimerical Beauties, where the Parts are without Proportion, Solids without their true Bearing, Heaps of Materials without Strength, excessive Ornament without Grace, and the Whole without Symmetry? And what can be a stronger Argument, that this excellent Art is near lost in that Country, where such Absurdities meet with Applause?

The contempt of eighteenth-century connoisseurs, under the influence of a revived taste for the "classic," is at least intelligible; it is harder to see why the nineteenth century, exalting Gothic, had not a kind word for baroque. The failure of Ruskin to recognize the style should, perhaps, be taken as a tribute to its innate subtlety and sophistication. It has remained for our own generation to attempt to do critical justice to the graphic and plastic art developed by the contemporaries of Milton and the "metaphysicals."

It is to this present century, then, and particularly to the years since the first Great War, that we must look for a saner evaluation of baroque. A work such as M. S. Briggs's *Baroque Architecture* (1913) testifies to an awakening interest, and three books on baroque art by Sacheverell Sitwell between 1924 and 1931, though critically vague, are moved by a spirit of new and genuine appreciation. More significant, perhaps, because occupied with a field in which the English genius is fully at home and scarcely to be rivalled, are the new evaluations of seventeenth-century poetry: in particular, definitive editions by Grierson, Margoliouth, Martin, Miss Wade, and others, and that fresh analysis of "metaphysical" and allied verse to be found, typically, in T. S. Eliot. As an early example of the excellent periodical articles which have served both to attest and to stimulate critical interest, one should mention a series of careful and scholarly papers by M. W. Croll, culminating in 1929 in a study of the baroque style in prose. The baroque in English poetry has been admirably criticized by Mario Praz (*Secentismo e marinismo in Inghilterra*), and by Austin Warren. The greatest volume of comment is, characteristically, in German criticism, and here the disparities between points of view set forth are surprising: the reader who dips cautiously into the numerous treatises will be discouraged to find at one turn that Latimer, Whitgift, and Hooker are swept into the ranks of English baroque and at another that Crashaw stands as the sole representative of the style.

The purpose of these pages is to suggest that, whatever may be the outcome of attempts to settle the nature and scope of baroque and the validity of the kind of criticism implied by the use of the term, there remains a wide terrain where, equipped only with a tentative formulation of the qualities of baroque and urged by nothing more than his own interest in the varied shapes which the elusive breath of poetry inspires, the ordinary student may still find scope for profitable enquiry. It is to his advantage to sidestep the warfare being waged over ultimate problems of defining and applying the term, for these are of great difficulty. Should baroque be taken as meaning strictly an art-form, or may it in addition be thought of as a kind of artistic sensibility, or as a phase of general sensibility, or, indeed, as an historical period? And there are always those who exclaim that the following up of baroque is the gryphon's pursuit of the Arimaspian.

The matter of chronology is a little more urgent, for upon some limitation of baroque in this respect depends its rescue from being absorbed into the romantic movement; it is all too easy to make baroque continuous with, or even a facet of, romanticism. A good working restriction is that made by such a conservative historian as Preserved Smith, who writes, with reference to the period between 1588 and 1688: "What gives it unity and coherence is the baroque style which distinguishes all its achievements."[2] Precise limits are, of course, neither desirable nor possible. The Asam brothers were flourishing in Bavaria in the seventeen-thirties. But for practical purposes we may say that the sensibility giving rise to baroque in England took shape about the beginning of the last decade of the sixteenth century and that, about a hundred years later, baroque form in English literature had substantially fulfilled itself and the end was upon it.

The special difficulty which confronts the student of *literature* is the crucial one as to whether it is justifiable to transfer a set of values and criteria from the consideration of plastic art to that of verbal form. Efforts of this sort have not been conspicuously successful, and there is a justifiable suspicion of any effort to cross such ineradicable border lines as separate poetry from sculpture. Yet the practical conditions of critical work are favourable to such forays, as long as they are considered as such. "If we commit ourselves too absolutely to the belief that the materials and the objects and the origins and the social entanglements of the arts are too

_____

[2] *A History of Modern Culture* (London, 1930), 604.

widely distinct for them to display any essential, common, stylistic principles, when they are scrutinized strictly as pure decoration, we are likely to find our craving for an ultimate common ground among them too strong for us."[3]

There is, finally, the exceedingly interesting problem of English baroque as distinct from continental. The contrast with Italian or German baroque, with their wealth of plastic art serving as a touchstone in any discussion of form and providing innumerable points of reference to literature, is a very striking one and might seem, at first, to render futile, not to say ridiculous, the attempt to fasten upon the literature of England an apparently alien concept. Such items as the porch of St. Mary's in Oxford, the western towers of St. Paul's, Temple Bar, Castle Howard, and the gate of Plymouth Citadel do not provide a very substantial background of reference, and Blenheim Palace is a solitary, if impressive, major construction in the baroque mode. Yet the very fact that literature is the supreme artistic expression of seventeenth-century England adds zest to the effort to discover whether or no the principles of form which proved pervasive on the continent have any part in its shaping.

Besides the relative poverty of architecture, painting, and sculpture in England, there is the further complication of England's geographical remoteness and of the traditional English habit of compromise. Whereas in Italy the classical renaissance had shot its bolt by 1500, in England it had scarcely begun. There is no English Mirandola. The classical renaissance and the Protestant Reformation proceed in England *pari passu;* the court of Henry VIII is at once the centre of the cultural revival and the occasion of a break with Rome. The Elizabethan compromise in matters of the Church acts as a modifying influence; it is essentially a *via media,* and the fact of Anglicanism prevents a clean sweep by the Reformers. The English Church combats Jesuits and Calvinists with equal vigour, so that the opposition between Rome and Geneva hardly comes to a head, except momentarily during the Commonwealth. The Established Church contains within itself most of the phenomena which are, by any stretch of imagination, parallels to the Counter-Reformation, yet it remains unalterably opposed to the papacy. There are therefore lacking in England motives for reaction and proud reaffirmation which played so large a part in the formation of continental

---

[3] Merritt Hughes, "Zeitgeist and Style" (*Sewanee Review,* XLII, 1932, 485).

baroque—a triumphant curia, the court life of independent princes and bishops, an already fully exploited renaissance art technique. Everything contributes to make baroque in England more involved and concealed than elsewhere. Moreover, the overlapping of cultural influences gives rise to two special problems: in the first place, the persistence of "gothic" and medieval elements in sixteenth-century England may lead us to identify as baroque much that is really carried over from before the renaissance rather than developed in opposition to it (this is particularly true of the work of Spenser); and, in the second, the lateness of the impact of the poetic *genres* of the classical renaissance upon the practice of English writers makes it inevitable that they borrow from the continent forms which have undergone a long process of development and are already, in some of their formal aspects, baroque.

The best point of departure for the average student is undoubtedly Heinrich Wölfflin, whose five categories, the result of forty years of study of European art, differentiate the forms of baroque from those of the high renaissance.[4] The transition, Wölfflin finds, is marked by a change from the perception of an object by outline and surfaces to a perception with less tangible design; there is development from the linear and from stress upon limits toward an apprehension of the world as shifting semblance; it is Dürer as against Rembrandt. Instead of employing a plane or parallel planes in design, the new technique lays emphasis on depth, recession, and diagonal penetration of space. There is also a movement from closed to open composition, from a stable equilibrium dominated by vertical and horizonal axes to a looser form, frequently spiral in its movement and suggesting by its sweep a completion beyond its own mechanical limits. Again, the renaissance use of multiplicity in design, relying upon the union of independent parts in harmony with one another, gives way to a unity achieved by means of a single theme or by the subordination to one dominant element of all the others, i.e., to fusion instead of co-ordination. Finally, there is a change from absolute clarity, in which explicitness is the chief aim, to relative clarity, in which light and colour have their own life, and beauty is perceived in the very darkness which modifies forms.

Baroque, in the formal sense, represents a perpetuation of the art

---

[4] *Kunstgeschichtliche Grundbegriffe*, translated as *Principles of Art History* (London, 1932).

of the high renaissance accompanied by a reaction against it, the two being compatible in that the reaction amounts to intensifying or accentuating certain elements already present, dislocating or deliberately "deforming" recognized shapes in the interests of greater expressiveness, and achieving, on the same stage, a new and striking dramatic quality, informed by a sense of splendour and actuated by a fresh interest in movement, in the dynamic.

A delight in artistry for its own sake and an intellectual preoccupation with the effectiveness of techniques make themselves felt pervasively in the arts and, as a consequence, there appear certain paradoxes: a greater lifelikeness in delineation passes easily into an effect of unreal theatricality; profusion of detail is found consistent with the achievement of a single unity; and what looks like the wildest of licence may be systematically employed to make an effect: virtuosity is a keynote.

Within some such general classification we may find the churches of Borromini; such diverse productions of Bernini as the colonnaded piazza of St. Peter's and the reclining statue of Saint Teresa; and von Erlach's fusion of architecture, sculpture, and painting into a consistent whole. The vigorous movement of Rubens, Rembrandt's subtlety of design, and the intellectual and esoteric imagery of El Greco has each its filiation with the underlying movement of baroque. Baroque, then, would appear to be a comprehensive artform based upon a specific artistic sensibility, which in turn springs from a general sensibility. (One should add what is not always recognized—that similar sensibilities may occur at intervals in the history of taste but the circumstances surrounding this particular outworking in the seventeenth century, together with the much more important factor of the individuality of the artists concerned, make true baroque a unique thing.) A feeling of triumph, of splendour, of certainty, and of power lies behind much of this art—a belief in the attainability of truth through appeals to authority, to force, and to heavenly sanction. This triumph is achieved only through struggle, through an intense effort to achieve unity, for the collective mind of the age is full of diametrical oppositions, of which the wars of religion are a symbol: in England Roman Catholic wars against Protestant, Anglican against Dissenter, Presbyterian against Independent. We find the sensual in conflict with the ascetic, flesh with spirit, grace with free will. Reason fights authority, mysticism is opposed by clear intellectual perception; scholasticism and classical humanism, themselves in conflict, find a new and common foe in rationalism.

With some such tentative criteria, and without regard for the unsettled disputes into which a complete analysis of baroque must unavoidably plunge, we may make an excursion into the English literature of the baroque period.

Seventeenth-century prose may frequently be described as explorative, and, like any other kind of exploration, full of surprises, dislocations, tentative adjustments, uncertainties, and unforeseen endings. Also, paradoxically, even at its most deliberate and self-conscious moments it frequently succeeds in maintaining the air of freshness and unexpected variety, for, like certain kinds of "metaphysical" poetry, it attempts to approximate in words the actual processes of thought rather than the revised conclusion, "so that [to quote Burton] as a river runs sometimes precipitate and swift, then dull and slow; now direct, then *per ambages;* now deep, then shallow; now muddy, then clear; now broad, then narrow; doth my style flow: now serious, then light; now comical, then satirical; now more elaborate, then remiss, as the present subject required, or as at that time I was affected."

This artistic trick, the presentation of thinking itself, whether genuine or whether adopted as a device to simulate psychological realism, depends for its effect on the paradoxical but unquestionable fact that realistic observation of anything is likely to have, at first, the effect of surprise. To watch the mind in operation is to lay oneself open to surprise and shock and this was well known to the very active, if somewhat crude, psychological investigators who mark the early part of the seventeenth century. Charron follows a passage which pays nominal tribute to the dignity of the spirit of man "whereunto God hath given reason," by a plea for a closer facing of the facts:

> But I desire, that after all this we come to sound and to studie how to know this spirit; for we shall finde after all this, that it is both to itselfe and to another a dangerous instrument, a ferret that is to be feared, a little trouble-feast, a tendious and inportune parasite and which as a Jugler and plaier at fast and loose, under the shadow of some gentle motion, subtile and smiling, forgeth, inventeth, and causeth all the mischiefs of the world: and the truth is, without it there are none.[5]

---

[5] *Of Wisdome* (trans. S. Lennard, London, 1615), 57–8.

The movement in prose away from simple devices such as isocolon toward a new and often highly self-conscious simulation of the mind's actual operation takes many forms. A sentence from Milton will serve to illustrate one, at least, of these; from *Smectymnuus:*

> Some also were indued with a staid moderation and soundness of argument, to teach and convince the rational and sober-minded; yet not therefore that to be thought the only expedient course of teaching, for in times of opposition, when either against new heresies arising, or old corruptions to be reformed, this cool unpassionate mildness of positive wisdom is not enough to damp and astonish the proud resistance of carnal and false doctors, then (that I may have leave to soar awhile as the poets use) Zeal, whose substance is ethereal, arming in complete diamond, ascends his fiery chariot, drawn with two blazing meteors, figured like beasts, but of a higher breed than any the zodiac yields, resembling two of those four which Ezekiel and St. John saw; the one visaged like a lion, to express power, high authority, and indignation; the other of countenance like a man, to cast derision and scorn upon perverse and fraudulent seducers: with these the invincible warrior, Zeal, shaking loosely the slack reins, drives over the heads of scarlet prelates, and such as are insolent to maintain traditions, bruising their stiff necks under his flaming wheels.

Here the sentence breaks into unmatching parts, with an abrupt transition. The structure is loose and the thought, branching off suddenly, may produce unexpected links—"yet not therefore that to be thought." It is interesting also to note how completely the whole shape of the sentence is conditioned by the buoyant movement of the writer's immediate emotion.

In the profuse employment of emblems, epigrams, aphorisms, metaphors and "dark conceits," and perhaps also in the compressed Baconian essay and in some of the "characters," there operates a desire for significant condensation—often associated with the Tacitean style—the accompaniment of which is a deliberately sought obscurity. It is unnecessary to quote any of the numerous and well-known passages from the sermons and letters of Donne in which there is the characteristic baroque expressiveness, shrouded by varieties of simultaneous implication, by the alternate opening up of vistas and summary convergence of meanings to a single point. Donne's capacity for operating on a number of planes of thought at once and for moving irregularly from one to the other is masterly, and has obvious analogues in other baroque design.

A curious attestation of the essentially baroque manner of much of the current prose is afforded by the very careful and specific denunciation poured upon it by Sprat, Glanville, and others anxious to re-establish a simple, clear manner in writing. In his *History of the Royal-Society* (1667, pp. 111–13) there is a passage, too long to quote here, in which Sprat's denunciation turns upon two points: the tendency to expand and inflate style into "luxury," "redundance," "abundance," "volubility," "extravagance," "amplifications," "digressions," "swellings," and, second, a mysterious, unclear and figurative way of writing which leads to "mists," "uncertainties," "tropes," "figures," mysteries," "metaphors," "deceits." The style he sets up by way of contrast is not expanded, but "close" and "naked," characterized by "shortness"; it is not obscure, but "positive" and "clear," resulting in "plainness"; it does not strive for artistic expressiveness, but for "naturalness," "easiness," and "primitive purity." His condemnation, then, falls exactly and squarely on the abuse of two kinds of baroque device, that of expansion into profusion, especially the profusion of ornamentation, and that of condensation into the obscure and the shadowed. His positive demands are directed against a root principle of the baroque manner—the achievement of the maximum expressiveness by every artistic device available. Glanville has almost the same comment and criticism: he approves of a style in which:

> The Epithets are genuine, the Words proper and familiar, the Periods smooth and of middle proportion: It is not broken with ends of Latin, nor impertinent Quotations; nor made harsh by hard words, or needless terms of Art: Not rendered intricate by long Parentheses, nor gaudy by flaunting Metaphors; not tedious by wide fetches and circumferences of Speech, not dark by too much curtness of Expression: 'Tis not loose and unjointed, rugged and uneven; but as polite and as fast as Marble; and briefly, avoids all the notorious defects, and wants none of the proper ornaments of Language.[6]

In the field of drama there would appear to be evidences of baroque form, widely separated chronologically and so disparate in their nature as to make synthesis still a matter for speculation. Anxious as one might be to keep off the knotty problem of the connection, if any, between the art of Shakespeare and baroque, it is impossible not to suspect a relation between the progression from high renais-

---

[6] *Plus Ultra* (London, 1668), 84–5.

sance to baroque and the evolution of form from the symmetrical arrangements of *A Comedy of Errors* to the looser structure of, say, *Lear* in which the demands of the tragic theme are satisfied by a preoccupation with the total effect of the play—with its shape as a unified whole. At the other end of the scale are the heroic plays of Dryden. Their logical magnificence, the vigorous unreality of their action, and rhetorical insincerity of their emotion, together with the deliberate artistry of resounding rodomontade, result in a kind of massiveness which, although reminiscent of Louis Quatorze rather than of the Seicento, has, clearly enough, its place in the total pattern we are considering.

In examining the poetry of the period, it is, of course, impossible to tip Wölfflin's concepts over into another kind of art and use them immediately as criteria. But analogues cannot fail to suggest themselves. The heavy, explicit didacticism and matter-of-fact piety, exemplified in Tottel's *Miscellany*, lose their dominance over religious poetry and make way for that rich metaphor, charged with mystical implication, which we find in, say, Vaughan. The popularity of the high renaissance sonnet sequence wanes suddenly, giving place to a new interest in the semantic determination of rhythm; from Donne develops the fashion of simulating in one's stanza the motion of the thinkig mind. Chapman proclaims a cult of deliberately sought obscurity, and the minor "metaphysicals" pursue a policy of "heightening words and shadowing sense." Spenser and Milton present a contrast, to which we return presently, between metrical forms of independent stability and the enjambment of the continuous verse-paragraph. All this suggests a transition similar to that which Wölfflin discerns in his own field of the graphic and plastic arts.

The school which Johnson characterized as "on the watch for novelty" knew how to trouble the smooth course of a conventional Platonic sentiment or achieve an effect by "breaking of accent." A similar understanding of the possibilities of deformation—in the technical sense of the word—was possessed by the architects who broke the regularity of a circle of columns, indented the uniform line of a cornice with shadowy recessions or achieved movement by corkscrewing pillars. Both employed intellectually conceived devices to produce unusual and striking beauties; and Eliot's phrase defining seventeenth-century wit—"a tough reasonableness beneath the slight lyric grace"—goes as well for the logically embodied fantasies of the Brothers Asam. The "metaphysical" conceit is not infrequently itself a baroque device. In most of its varieties, and especially in its union of disparates and its concentration or dilation of ideas, it has the baroque quality of surprise, movement, and dramatic effectiveness. Frequently, too, it has a significant darkness, deliberately used for accentuation: as Bacon says of "parabolical" poetry, "it serves for obscuration; and it serveth also for illustration."

"Out of the high style developed from Marlowe through Jonson . . . the seventeenth century separated two qualities: wit and magniloquence," writes T. S. Eliot in his essay on Marvell; and on the same principle, though on a smaller scale, contraction and dilation, often immediately consecutive, are the groundwork of many a "metaphysical" conceit. The image becomes a lens to focus an idea, to effect a rapprochement between microcosm and macrocosm: Marvell's "drop of dew"

> Does, in its pure and circling thoughts, express
> The greater heaven in an heaven less.

And, as a result of this compression, of this narrow band of contact between the disparate ideas, the image easily flares off into illimitable suggestion; indeed, one may apply to it Marvell's lines on the dewdrop which follow later in the same poem:

> How loose and easy hence to go,
> How girt and ready to ascend;
> Moving but on a point below,
> It all about does upwards bend.

There is a clear analogy between the ingenious use of metaphor and the baroque employment of perspective to condense a great deal into a single line of vision, and one is tempted to see a likeness between the "O altitudo!" of "metaphysical" thinking and the topmost flourish of ornament which seems to relieve the lateral pressure in a façade or the leaping up of El Greco's tense lines into curves which fulfil themselves beyond the limits of the canvas.

The "metaphysical" image exerts its maximum effect at a single point of association; it has the air, even at its best, of an intellectual *tour de force*. The baroque architect employs similar devices: a flat ceiling, painted to simulate the interior of a dome when viewed from a single marked position, will change into ridiculously distorted proportions if seen from any other spot. And this brings us to the

common danger shared by all forms of baroque art, the danger of
allowing adroitly handled devices to become an end in themselves, of
permitting the delight in overcoming difficulties and achieving
effects by superb manipulation to run riot. Crashaw is always on
the edge of this pitfall and all the "metaphysicals" fall into it sooner
or later; even Marvell slips easily from a firmly controlled abundance of witty imagination to the mere bag of tricks:

> *Yet thus the laden House does sweat,*
> *And scarce endures the Master great:*
> *But where he comes the swelling Hall*
> *Stirs, and the Square grows Spherical.*

Donne, Crashaw, and Milton are probably the three most interesting exponents of baroque form in poetry: Donne on account of
his early and deliberate dislocation of conventional shapes, Crashaw
because of his direct connections with continental Catholic art, and
Milton for the large structure and very deliberate artistry of his
major works, which give a wide field for comparison.

As against the verse of the Elizabethan amourists, Donne's work
shows great vigour, licence, irregularity, and technical virtuosity,
and he exhibits these qualities in a way common to other baroque
artists. In his effort for complete expressiveness, he poses for himself difficult problems and strains all his resources to solve them. The
first stanza of "The Canonization," for example, seems to take its
shape from the immediate outpouring of the poet's protest—"For
Godsake hold your tongue and let me love." The succeeding stanzas
conform to the model with some difficulty and the concluding one
exemplifies in no uncertain manner Carew's lines to his brother poet:

> *Our troublesome language bends, made only fit*
> *With her tough thick-ribb'd hoops to gird about*
> *Thy giant fancy . . .*

Repeatedly in Donne we find the same sequence of outbreak, compound fracture of smooth convention and smooth line, and then a
masterly moulding of language to carry out the dramatic pattern.
Even in the sonnet form, Donne can give the effect of superimposing
continuous movement over the set frame:

> *At the round earth's imagin'd corners blow*
> *Your trumpets, angels, and arise, arise*
> *From death, you numberless infinities*
> *Of souls . . .*

His poem, "The Bait," lends itself to direct comparison with Marlowe's "Passionate Shepherd" and Raleigh's "Reply," and we find, in spite of surface similarities, that Donne had introduced the new tension and dramatic realism which might be expected. The imagery becomes more difficult and more concentrated and the whole is made to subserve a single underlying movement of the imagination in a fashion far more subtle than in the earlier pieces.

The poetry of Crashaw affords the best, or at least the most obvious, example of baroque technique, and this matter has been adequately dealt with by Praz, Warren, and Beachcroft. But a further and exceedingly important point not often recognized is that the criteria used to establish Crashaw as a baroque artist may be applied to a number of his contemporaries with a like result. Marvell's plea "To His Coy Mistress" is at one and the same time a formal argument and an emotional outburst; irresistible logic and complete extravagance combine in one, and abundant fancifulness does not interfere with the intellectual presentation of a case. Passionate, witty, formal, surprising, compressed in the extreme yet bursting with wild and even terrible imagination, the piece is, in its own way, as good baroque as anything in the century, and is almost directly reminiscent of some fantastic doorway of von Erlach's. Carew exemplifies one of the decorative aspects of baroque: "The Rapture," with its ostensible passion yet obvious theatricality, exhibits on a larger scale than usual the poet's capacity for developing a theme in the spirit of a virtuoso, and one comes, almost as definitely as when following Crashaw, into a world of words remote from things. The capacity of baroque poetry to put decoration above any other function, when this is felt to be necessary, makes it peculiarly suitable to the handling of rigid dogma, to the elaboration of a ritual, and Carew has a ritual to elaborate, a dogma to embroider, for he is concerned with the rites and doctrines of love:

> Such incense, vows, and holy rites as were
> To the involved serpent of the year
> Paid by Egyptian priests, lay I before
> Lucinda's sacred shrine . . .

As clearly as anyone, Carew exemplifies the intellectual excitement over poetry as form, over the handling of a familiar medium with the utmost technical skill and refinement; he is a master of elaboration.

There are other qualities of Crashaw's verse which distinguish it as baroque and which, far from being peculiar to Crashaw, belong also to a number of his contemporaries. The capacity for achieving unity in complication and for subordinating the validity of the single line to the internal cohesion of the total passage are well known to the student of Milton's longer works. Ingenious surprises abound in Herbert; the use of words as symbols reappears in Traherne; and the elaboration of a series of highly flexible and individual methods out of the materials supplied by the conventional formalism of the high renaissance is a feat common to an architect like Pozzo and to Donne and Milton.

Finally, one may note how often the poets present what would be a baroque subject or design if graphically portrayed: Marvell, for example, with exactly the capacity of the baroque painter for embodying an emotion in one dramatic gesture and for dealing with a subject like martyrdom with a mixture of high unreality, symbolism, and theatrical convincingness, gives us a portrait of the lover:

> *See how he nak'd and fierce does stand,*
> *Cuffing the Thunder with one hand;*
> *While with the other he does lock,*
> *And grapple, with the stubborn Rock:*
> *From which he with each Wave rebounds,*
> *Torn into Flames, and ragg'd with Wounds.*
> *And all he says, a Lover drest*
> *In his own Blood does relish best.*

It is interesting to examine the poetry of Spenser and of Milton with a view to discovering whether there are points of correspondence between the differences which separate them and those which lie between high renaissance art and baroque. The comparison is of especial value because both poets are concerned to a great extent with the same fundamental problem, the relation of the sensuousness and learning of the renaissance with the serious moral purpose and supernatural sanctions of Puritanism.

Milton tends much more strongly than Spenser to unify and universalize the situations with which he deals; he sees in his own problem the problem of all the English saints, or of the entire Church, or of mankind at large; his disappointment over Mary Powell is the occasion for a general treatise on divorce, and so on. At the same time, his emotions are more violent: Spenser's love for woman is all "pure affections" and "modest thoughts," without introversion or serious moral struggle, while Milton passes suddenly from self-conscious restraint to disillusion, and the bitterness and complication of his own experience shadow his portraits of Eve and Dalila. Spenser's eager and idealistic temperament is fundamentally gentle and his ultimate feeling for things proceeds from a belief in beauty and love; Milton sets up the standard of virtue and liberty. Spenser passes easily from epithalamia to "complaints"; he loves earthly beauty, and, because it is unstable, he turns to more lasting joys in Heaven. Milton is always aware of the interrelation of sorrow and joy and he sees the same beauties and the same moral problem in Earth as in Heaven.

The most obvious qualities of Spenser's style are, perhaps, fluency, fecundity, ease, melody, and pervasive charm; Milton may be said to embody all these in his art, but to interfuse also new seriousness, weight, and depth and deliberately to complicate his designs: extra elements of dramatic and didactic controversy are added to Milton's side of the balance.

The Spenserian stanza has an independence of its own; even in the midst of action or argument each set of nine lines contrives to maintain its own integrity. The recurrence of the second rhyme links all parts of the stanza together; the tendency to make the fifth line either a pendant to the first quatrain or the beginning of the second gives the whole scheme a pivot to turn upon and assists the internal balance of the stanza. The well-recognized use of the final alexandrine is also in keeping: it tends to close the stanza off, while, at the same time, it adds to the melodiousness and tranquillity of the total effect.

Whether we turn to the sonnets of the *Amoretti*, the books of *The Faerie Queene*—where, Spenser tells us, "many other adventures are intermedled; but rather as Accidents than intenements"— the stanzas of the *Epithalamion*, or the separate months of *The Shepheards Calender*, the effect is the same—in a word, disparate: each section is set in relation and balance with others and linked into a unity of consecutiveness, and each part possesses an independent and stable unity of its own.

Separateness and consecutiveness are marks also of Spenser's formal thought. In his *Hymne of Heavenly Beautie*, for instance, he juxtaposes the neo-Platonic world-view, which finds beauty, love, and virtue in close interaction and beholds an ascending scale of being leading to God, with the orthodox Protestant view, according to which the impassable gulf between sinful man and a holy God is only to be bridged by the sacrifice of Christ. Each view fulfills its part in the artistic structure of the piece and the violent clash goes unregarded.

Milton, on the other hand, develops verse forms remarkable for their flexible continuity—above all, in the three great poems of his maturity. The predominance of semantic rhythm over metrical structure grows greater as time goes on; the integrity of the line, consistently respected by Spenser, gives way to "deformation." Milton's renunciation of rhyme is the deliberate, conscious action of the baroque artist who prefers expressiveness and the continuity of the sense to set form: those who stick to rhyme, he writes, "express many things otherwise, and for the most part worse, than else they would have expressed them"; it is better to rely upon "apt numbers, fit quantity of syllables, and the sense variously drawn out from one verse into another." The larger units of Milton's work exhibit the same "drawing out": every episode of *Paradise Lost* has its place in the complete scheme and the various centres of interest are not so much linked in succession as united by a multitude of radiating connections.

Milton's view of the world and life is in harmony with the foregoing. We are in the midst of a complicated series of happenings, to which God alone holds the key, and His mysterious, hidden purposes are "ever best found in the close." While the allegory of *The Faerie Queene* separates out into distinct planes which require little connection with one another, in *Paradise Lost* the factual and historical form an unbroken continuity with the mythical, and no dividing line can be traced.

A necessarily vexed problem is the relation of both Spenser and Milton to the "classical." In the sense of achieving order in beauty, both are, of course, classical. But the kinds of order they bring forth are not the same. In Spenser it is chiefly a flexible adapting of style to subject, moment by moment—"dewe observing of Decorum everye where." In Milton syntheses are more complex, and incompatibilities, while less obvious, are more fundamental: the struggle to cast a Christian theme into a classical mould is unremitting. His form shows new elements of movement, weight, and surprise. As in the architectural diagrams of Pozzo, one may see the materials of the classical architecture of antiquity—its stock in trade—displayed in new alignments and perspectives, productive of saliences and recessions, of massive groupings and unexpected effects, in a similar way Milton's classicism turns out to be a baroque variety: "Classical in structure and (at bottom) in his style and rhetoric, he develops the old epical artifices to produce effects of vagueness and immateriality which they had never before been made to serve. . . . And the difference between him and Dante in general is, as should be expected, that between the Middle Ages and the Secondary Reformation, not the Middle Ages and the Renaissance."[7] In *Lycidas*, although Milton employs the method of the classical elegists and some of their materials, there is "bitter constraint" which, breaking the metrical flow and troubling the even tenor of formal lament, is only subdued by an extreme tension maintained between discordant elements. Nowhere, perhaps, does he achieve more triumphantly the peculiar unity of baroque than in this tightly strung web of opposing forces.

Examining *Paradise Lost* for evidences of baroque design and decoration we find a numerous series of resemblances, no one of which need be pushed too far, between Milton's structural methods and those of the baroque architect. And on the simply impressionistic side, such a building as the ecclesiastical foundation at Melk, by its air of proud dominance, its well-articulated design, and its striking ornamentation, conveys to one observer, at least, an impression very similar in kind to that produced by Milton's great poem. *Paradise Lost* illustrates the desire for construction on a large and comprehensive scale: it contains everything known, in space and in time, and its problem is the whole problem of God, man, the universe, good and evil. Its architectural planning is bold in the extreme and on the whole successful. And if one wishes to be fanciful, the bridge built from hell by Sin and Death may be looked upon as an example of the "solids without their true bearing" to which baroque fantasy may run. Milton assures the reader, in three sets of parentheses, that this thing is possible, yet the great incongruous arch of flotsam, bound together by the petrifying glances of the anxious architect and throwing out of balance both the physical and moral symmetry of the universe, strikes one, when viewed beside the traditional empyrean and the spheres, as a highly spectacular *tour de force*.

If we turn from structure to decoration, Milton's handling of the simile shows deliberate and unusual technical expedients. It has been

---

[7] E. E. Stoll, *Poets and Playwrights* (University of Minnesota, 1930), 289.

demonstrated elsewhere that Milton's epic similes make use, to an unprecedented degree, of prolepsis and condensed suggestion, and that their organic quality often makes it possible to extend their application, point by point, at great variety.[8] His preference for the ornate and magificent figure over the simple and homely one is an additional and congruent point. Furthermore, the distribution of figurative and decorative elements in the epic is in deliberately uneven groupings.

There is some fundamental in the baroque aesthetic which produces bold clashes of colour, difficult equilibrium in design, effects of tension and straining movement, and the unification of what individually is unbalanced into the wholeness of a designed composition. Milton makes use of similar devices in his thinking and in the formal handling of his poetry. Continually he struggles to bring comprehensive variety into unity: the great battles in Heaven epitomize all warfare and their phrases remain logically incongruous, yet their total impression satisfies the reader; the Ptolemaic system and the Copernican are made reluctantly to shake hands; on the small scale we find phrases such as "ever-burning sulphur unconsumed" and "darkness visible"; and viewing Milton's work in the largest terms we find a struggle to unify the renaissance and the Reformation. Everywhere Milton tends to reject the merely self-contained; he has little interest in a consecutive procession of ideas or events: unity through relations of dominance and subordination is his consistent desire. A motif which runs through all his writing is the conflict between passion and reason with the necessity of subjecting the former to the latter.

All this goes to explain Milton's choice of theme. Not for him the materials of Spenser and Sidney; he refuses

> ... *to dissect*
> *With long and tedious havoc, fabled knights* ...

Instead of the meandering and consecutive, Milton chooses the tangled which needs active and difficult explanation: he will justify the ways of God to man, and this effort to fuse dogmatic assertion with careful, reasoned argument shapes his whole design and not infrequently affects the very cadence of his verse. In an indignant plea for vengeance, he can superimpose the rhythm of his impreca-

---

[8] James Whaler, "The Miltonic Simile" (*P.M.L.A.*, XLVI, 1931, 1034-74).

tion over the conventional beat of the sonnet form and its division
into octave and sestet:

> Forget not: in thy book record their groans
> Who were thy sheep, and in their ancient fold
> Slain by the bloody Piemontese, that rolled
> Mother with infant down the rocks. Their *moans*
> The vales redoubled to the hills, and they
> To heaven.

As surely as the Augustan clarity of epigram is associated with the
heroic couplet, so Milton's tough and reasoned dogmatism, his
intense and splendid quality of supported asseveration are associated
with the "sense variously drawn out" into the web of a verse-paragraph and with the high, flagrant splendour of his images.

Milton's selection of images and themes will also bear examination
in the light of certain well-known preferences traditional among
baroque painters. His feeling for the ornate portal, with a decoration
of heraldic figures is, at least, interesting: the kingly palace gate of
heaven, with frontispiece of diamond and gold; the alabaster pillars
at the entrance to Eden, with celestial armoury hung high; and the
flame-wreathed gate of hell, with its writhing, shadowy figures on
either side. Sin and Death themselves, by their moral significance,
their dramatic gestures and the chiaroscuro which half conceals them
are rendered far more terrible than, say, the monsters of Spenser,
which by contrast seem merely grotesque.

Of much more importance is Milton's handling of themes of power
and triumph, of apotheosis. A magnificent piece of baroque artistry
is found in the return of Messiah when, after his victory, "He celebrated rode, Triumphant through mid Heaven"; and even better
is the ascent of the Son after the work of creation:

> The planets in their stations listening stood,
> While the bright pomp ascended jubilant.
> ...He through Heaven,
> That opened wide her blazing portals, led
> To God's eternal house direct the way—
> A broad and ample road whose dust is gold . . .

It is with some basis in critical comparison, then, as well as with
the support of impressionistic feeling, that one reads, say, the first
book of *Paradise Lost* as a baroque piece. The inherent theatricality,
accented by the most artful chiaroscuro, of the presentation of

hell; the author's delight in the most ostentatious splendour and in effectively massed images in particular; the sense of intricate, broken outline in the description of the infernal scene—the quality of these elements is characteristic of the whole treatment. Satan's rebellious verve controls by its movement of fierce defiance the whole book and carries with it much of Milton's own spirit of revolt, yet even this fiery gesture is made a part of the gigantic and organic whole of the poem, as Milton follows with relentless judgments the career of the fiend and succeeds in holding in one tense equilibrium his own strong instinct for individualistic revolt and his Christian submission to reasoned doctrine, to the revealed will of God.

The English-speaking, scholarly world has shown some distrust of baroque as a usable concept in literary classification, and in its criticism of German works on English baroque, in particular, there is a notable preponderance of light over sweetness. It is encouraging, nevertheless, to see some instances of deliberate and careful appreciation of the baroque features in the seventeenth century, as in Mr. Tillyard's "Introduction" to Milton's *Private Correspondence and Academic Exercises* (1932). Of the tone of some of the letters Tillyard remarks, "It has a kind of baroque gravity like that of a good heroic play; imperturbably and solemnly exaggerated and yet critically conscious of the exaggeration"; and of another set of correspondence, "The formality of the style which in the Cambridge letters was unpleasantly cold and stilted now seems to glow with an apt Italianate warmth. The baroque of Lecce has, as it were, supplanted the baroque of Peterhouse chapel."

There are many advantages to the use of baroque as a touchstone for the literature of the time. Now that the boundaries of seventeenth-century scholarship are clearly marked and the "metaphysicals" collectively and individually dealt with, the search for baroque, conducted with the necessary *sprezzatura* and with no desire to achieve a premature codification, is not without its pleasures. There is excellent fun to be had in the slightly disreputable pursuit of poaching across the boundaries which separate the arts.

The recognition of a baroque period means, among other things, that the century need no longer always draw apart like a pack of tapered cards. To establish unity across the chasm which is at present too often allowed to divide the age of *Samson Agonistes*, *The Pilgrim's Progress*, and the heroic play from the rest of the century, would be in itself in the nature of a baroque triumph.

Baroque stagecraft; the relation between baroque form and the Plotinian aesthetic; baroque music: these are further subjects for investigation.

Baroque, as a usable concept, will have its day and, fulfilling its purpose, pass (one hopes) into the dim limbo of worn out critical tools. At the moment, it seems opportune and useful because it readily provokes that perpetually renewed freshness in our apperception of poetry which alone justifies the labours of formal criticism. Besides providing, independent of languages, some means of comparison between English poetry and European art in general, the re-examination of familiar works on the lines here indicated—but by those whose discriminations of form are rendered more subtle by special studies—would, I believe, reveal a varied richness of artistry too often left to simply intuitive appreciation.

Bernard Heyl

MEANINGS OF BAROQUE*

Perusals of recent literature on the Baroque in either the fine arts, in literature and music, in history and philosophy, or in culture in general, will show anyone that various kinds of confusion prevail. Thus another effort to explain and clarify some of the basic issues may be welcome. A re-thinking and sorting out of some of the major problems of the Baroque should provide a helpful foundation for future investigations of a more detailed kind.

In attempting to do this, I shall concentrate upon the troublesome problems that cluster around the idea of the Baroque as the style of the period extending, roughly, from 1590–1700. Thus the concept of the Baroque as a recurrent type or phase of other styles— e.g., Hellenistic Baroque, Gothic Baroque, or nineteenth-century Baroque—is excluded from this discussion. Nor is it necessary, for my limited aim, to consider the complex and difficult problem of determining the extension of Baroque art, as specified here, into the eighteenth century. The central issue is to find a satisfactory meaning or referent for the style of seventeenth-century art. What pervading quality or what several qualities, scholars ask again and again, does one find in the Baroque period? Do these qualities pertain to everything that concerns the Baroque era or do they vary according to the field of investigation and according to time and place? Are

* From *The Journal of Aesthetics and Art Criticism*, Vol. XIX, No. 3, Spring 1961, pp. 275–287. Reprinted by permission of the author and *The Journal of Aesthetics and Art Criticism*.

the questions that arise concerning Baroque style verbal or real ones? Should the word "Baroque" be used in a narrow or wide sense? Are there degrees of Baroque?

Consideration of four approaches to the problem of the Baroque, all of which seem unsatisfactory, will clear the ground for another solution. The first and most complex of these is included in the broader problem which concerns the justification, or lack of it, for believing in a unified or pervasive period style. Does an artistic, or in broader terms, a general cultural *Zeitgeist* exist? Was Hegel right in his claim that politics, religion, art, and philosophy are all manifestations of an identical "spirit" or "essence" in a period? Many scholars appear to believe in the validity of this unifying concept. They recognize complexities within the Baroque period, yet nonetheless cling to the view that a pervasive, unifying quality, or group of closely related qualities, characterizes the age as a whole as well as each separate field of investigation within it. This widespread assumption of the intrinsic unity of the Baroque period needs to be questioned more than it has been. Although my main concern is with the fine arts, a summary of a celebrated attempt to characterize this unity in another field will illuminate the problem.

René Wellek, like many literary scholars, supports—in theory at least—the concept of a unified Baroque style. He opposes the "extreme and false nominalism" which denies that "such concepts as the baroque are organs of real historical knowledge." He asserts that the Baroque is "a general European movement whose conventions and literary style can be described fairly concretely."[1] His account of the problem is especially appealing because it frankly recognizes the many obstacles which oppose a satisfactory solution. He faithfully presents, to begin with, a summary of divergent stylistic ideas that have been held concerning Baroque literature.[2]

---

[1] "The Concept of Baroque in Literary Scholarship," *JAAC* (December 1946). The quotations of Wellek that follow all come from this article which has recently been described by Leo O. Forkey as "perhaps the best generalization of the application of the term 'baroque' to literature, and one in which Buffum and other scholars who have done considerable work in this area agree" (*JAAC* [September 1959], p. 80). Two books that attempt, without success I believe, to apply this unified concept of the Baroque to other fields are Carl J. Friedrich's *The Age of the Baroque* (New York, 1952), and Manfred F. Bukofzer's *Music in the Baroque Era* (New York, 1947).

[2] In addition to the array of contradictory views cited by Wellek about Baroque style in literature, I add the following. Whereas Grierson finds the early Milton Baroque, Wylie Sypher considers *Comus* Renaissance and *Lycidas*

Further on he avows: "Individual stylistic devices can, however, be defined fairly clearly at least for some baroque authors or schools." The weakness of this idea *as a support of the concept of stylistic unity* appears in the words "fairly" and "some." This weakness is later admitted by the author, who, after a discussion of the metaphysical and of Baroque prose style, reaches the following skeptical conclusion: "It is probably necessary to abandon attempts to define baroque in purely stylistic terms."

This conclusion leads Wellek to three other means by which he hopes to arrive at the unified concept he has assumed. First, he suggests that the presence of stylistic devices "is only important if it can be considered as symptomatic of a specific state of mind, if it expresses a 'baroque soul.' " But he abandons this suggestion because he is impressed, for example, by the contrasting attitudes or states of mind revealed in a Catholic and Protestant Baroque. Second, he avers that "much better chances of success attend the attempts at defining baroque in more general terms of a philosophy . . ." But the chances of success must indeed be slim because Wellek himself, after citing numerous attempts which have been made to define Baroque in this way, condemns them all! Third, he asserts that "the most promising way of arriving at a more closely fitting description of the baroque is to aim at analyses which would correlate stylistic and ideological criteria." The discussion of this "most promising way" seems astonishing, and comical too, because again the author opposes the many solutions he summarizes. Nor does he have any solution of his own to offer. He thus is "unconvinced that we can define baroque either in terms of stylistic devices or a peculiar world-view or even a peculiar relationship of style and belief . . ." Though Wellek, at the end of his article, reaffirms his belief in the attainment of a unified concept of Baroque literature, the cumulative effect of his analysis shows that he has refuted his basic postulate.

Mannerist. Hobbes epitomizes the Baroque for Friedrich, but Sypher urges that his "inert materialism" and his failure to believe firmly "in the efficacy of the will" prevent his achieving "the baroque resolution in exultant power." Corneille is considered Baroque by Hatzfeld and by Rousset; Borgerhoff classifies him as Mannerist. Cervantes is a Baroque ideal, according to Hatzfeld, but is expressly excluded from the Baroque by Pfandl; while Sypher considers him, "like Parmigianino or Velazquez" Mannerist! Tasso represents, according to Hatzfeld "the first great and moderate but realistic baroque," but according to Sypher, he lacks "the full baroque energy" and remains stylistically in the early Renaissance stage.

In the fine arts, Wylie Sypher has made a comparable attempt to define unified conceptions of period styles.[3] In his book *Four Stages of Renaissance Style*, Sypher defines four stylistic units in art and literature between 1400 and 1700: Renaissance, Mannerism, Baroque, and Late Baroque. Comment upon his analysis of the first of these will most clearly indicate the kind of difficulties historians of art encounter when they strive for a unified period concept. Later on, I shall refer to aspects of his discussion of the Baroque.

In the "Renaissance" stage,[4] Sypher rightly emphasizes the new conception of a universe that is "closed, intelligible," of an architecture which has, in Alberti's phrase, "a certain and regular order," of "a new coherent space and perspective," of beauty which stresses harmony and proportion, of "the sanctity of the mathematical ratio." As examples of these important Renaissance characteristics Sypher appropriately refers to the Pazzi Chapel, Santo Spirito, and Masaccio's *Trinity*. Inevitably the argument in favor of a unified style is weakened, however, when the author recognizes different characteristics. These are discussed in a section entitled "Interferences and Transformations." No one questions the existence of these other traits. But Sypher misrepresents their significance as elements of Renaissance style. Because he, too, is searching for the basic stylistic unity of a period, he considers only the first group of characteristics as the proper, correct, or right criteria of Renaissance art. The divergent traits are disposed of in summary fashion.

Thus Sypher criticizes the façade of San Francesco at Rimini as being unsatisfactory because "ambiguous." He finds "a dramatic disharmony," "a dramatic tension" in Renaissance sculpture because of conflicts in the use of both deep and shallow space and in the "opposing techniques" of carving and molding stone. Venetian painting of the sixteenth century, which is quite generally accepted

---

[3] All students of the fine arts are cognizant of such important German studies of the Baroque as those of Riegl, Wölfflin, Voss, Weisbach, and others. Although mention of Wölfflin's *Principles of Art History* occurs later in this essay, no attempt is made to discuss these German writers. My concern is primarily with more recent writing in English.

[4] *Four Stages of Renaissance Style* (New York, 1955), p. 55ff. A reader of an early draft of this essay was troubled by the attention given in it to Sypher's analyses. Undoubtedly he is a minor critic by comparison, say, with Wölfflin with whom his views are later compared. My reason for selecting aspects of his book for discussion is that they illustrate so clearly and concretely a number of issues that are pertinent to my argument.

as an important manifestation of High Renaissance art, is included in the "Interferences and Transformations." Even Raphael's *School of Athens*—a monument that is for most art historians a paradigm of High Renaissance style—is included by Sypher among the exceptional examples of Renaissance style because the great vaults in the painting "do not, in a sense, define architectural space in firm ratios but give it an acoustical quality, a momentum that seems to vibrate off into free energy." And Pollaiuolo's engraving, *The Battle of the Nudes*, we are told, "already has the tortured energy of mannerist line." These and other examples will bewilder anyone who has a broad, flexible conception of Renaissance style, who is impressed by its stylistic diversity as well as by its common stylistic traits. Sypher, I believe, misrepresents the complexity of the period in order to emphasize a unified concept of style. But the unity claimed for the style is contradicted by the evidence. Indeed, he refutes his convictions by his own words: "The renaissance humanists brought their world into a single focus, though it is hard to say whether the focus was scientific, platonic, or Christian."

Challenges to this postulate of the stylistic unity of artistic periods have of course been made by scholars who find it illusory. As Walter Friedlaender has said: "In spite of the short span of barely twenty years in which it ran its course, the particularly intensive epoch of the High Renaissance had no unified character. The very fact that Michelangelo's art cannot possibly be counted in with the 'classic' art of Leonardo, Raphael, Fra Bartolommeo, and Andrea del Sarto destroys any unity."[5] Some styles, to be sure, are more organic and homogeneous than others. In "archaic" periods, for example, when artists do not have a choice of styles, the total artistic output has more unity. But in the case of the "developed" periods that are here discussed we must reject, as an illusion, the concept of a pervasive or unified period style.

Three alternative approaches to the problem of finding a satisfactory meaning for "Baroque style" may be mentioned. Two of these show a sharp reaction against the view challenged in the foregoing pages. Recognizing the insurmountable difficulties inherent in the concept of a unified period style, some writers seem to advo-

---

[5] *Mannerism and Anti-Mannerism in Italian Painting* (New York, 1957), p. 4. Interesting and successful challenges of the postulate in regard to historical periods and to music were made in the *JAAC* by George Boas (March 1953) and by John Mueller (June 1954).

cate—or at least to yearn for—the wholesale elimination of such large stylistic concepts as Renaissance and Baroque, classic and romantic. Instead of attempting to find satisfactory referents for these terms, one should analyze only specific trends and characterize, say, decades rather than centuries. Let us settle the matter by ceasing to use words which, because they mean so many different things to different people, have, in fact, come to mean nothing. While this radical remedy to our problem is tempting in that it avoids the pitfalls of the periodizers, it is too drastic to be adopted. "Big" words—words which normally have a wide and varied significance —cannot be abolished with impunity. They retain a breadth of meaning, however vague and complex, which one is reluctant to lose. As teachers and as ordinary mortals, we need them.

The other approach which reacts against the concept of a homogeneous style restricts the meaning of "Baroque" to a single feature of to a specific time span. W. Fleming, for example, confines the meaning of "Baroque" largely to movement.[6] Others would restrict its meaning to "heroic sweep," "opulence," "magnificence," "pomp," "extravagance," and the like.[7] Walter Friedlaender believes it would be best if such terms as Gothic, Renaissance, and Baroque were used only "when they meant something very definite and circumscribed . . . a period should always be restricted to one or two generations, and not used to include completely different trends under a common denominator like 'The Art of the Baroque.' "[8] Now these and other attempts to restrict the meaning of "Baroque" have the same sorts of appeal as has the suggestion, mentioned above, to abolish the term: they avoid the inconsistencies of the unified approaches; and they seem to clarify and simplify the whole problem by eliminating much of its complexity. Yet all such solutions, I maintain, are both untenable and undesirable. They are untenable because critics and scholars will not be persuaded to agree about a preferred meaning. Proposals to restrict the sense to a relatively simple and clearly defined meaning offer an irresistible starting-point for further controversy. They are undesirable because they deliberately restrict the meaning of a big word and thus fail to

---

[6] "The Element of Motion in Baroque Art and Music," *JAAC* (December 1946), 121–128.

[7] For example, Frank Jewett Mather, Jr., *Western European Painting of the Renaissance* (New York, 1939), p. 395.

[8] *Op. cit.*, p. 81.

satisfy those who choose to conceive of the Baroque—or of Gothic or Renaissance—in a broader, more inclusive way.

To cite a specific, important example: in circumscribed meanings of Baroque style it is usually asserted that Caravaggio is not a Baroque painter—the view maintained by Berenson, Golzio, and others. Because his art, they say, does not reveal the opulence, or the sweep, or other traits which for them typify Baroque style, Caravaggio should be excluded. Most students of the Baroque, however, consider Caravaggio an important founder of that style. Breaking sharply with Mannerism, he introduced stylistic qualities that are of major significance for much seventeenth-century art: notably his new "realism" and his novel use of chiaroscuro. It seems illogical and capricious, then, to define "Baroque style" in a way that excludes Caravaggio.

The fourth and last approach to our problem that seems unsatisfactory is exemplified chiefly by Italian critics. Its novelty lies in the emphasis placed upon evaluations: either pejorative or laudatory meanings are given to the word "Baroque." Because of these meanings, stylistic traits and artists of the seventeenth century are related to the Baroque primarily on the basis of aesthetic implications. Brief illustration of this critical attitude will reveal its weakness. Having condemned the Baroque as *antiestetico* and as "il brutto relativo al secolo XVII,"[9] Giuseppe Delogu attempts to salvage from abuse most Italian painting of the seventeenth century. Not only are Caravaggio and the Carracci excluded from his concept of the Baroque; the majority of later *Seicento* painters also, he claims, are free of the stylistic vices of that style! Nearly all of the sculpture and architecture, however, are condemned as Baroque, with the notable exception of those monuments that fundamentally express classical principles. By contrast, Luigi Grassi asserts that the Baroque has a concrete and spiritual value—"un valore concreto e spirituale."[10] For this critic, then, favorable, rather than derogatory

---

[9] *La Pittura Italiana Del Seicento* (Firenze, 1931), p. 6. Of course during the past three centuries there have been changing interpretations and evaluations of Baroque art. See, for example, the historical discussion by Hans Tintelnot, "Zur Gewinning unserer Barockbegriffe" in *Die Kunstformen des Barockzeitalters* (Bern, 1956). Evaluations need not and should not, however, play a dominant part in the formulation of definitions of period styles nowadays.

[10] "Barocco E. Arti Figurative," *Emporium* (April 1945), 69–73. See also *Costruzione della Critica d'Arte* (Rome, 1955), p. 90ff.

values are the crucial criteria for Baroque style. To separate the good from the bad artists and currents of the seventeenth century, he makes the distinction between "barocco" and "barocchismo," between "Seicento" and "Seicentismo."

This disagreement between Delogu and Grassi inevitably leads to confusion. Is it not apparent that the basic cause of this confusion is the misguided application of value judgments to the concept of Baroque style? Comparable judgments unfortunately occur in critical writings of various kinds. Important terms which normally have no implications of value are given favorable or hostile connotations. As two literary critics have recently pointed out: "*Classical* means either artistically perfect or coldly artificial; *romantic* means either warmly and truly expressive or sentimental and uncontrolled."[11] Thus, "I call the classic *healthy*, the romantic *sickly*,"[12] asserted Goethe: and T. S. Eliot writes of "the classicist, or adult mind." Such evaluative uses, though often effective as polemical devices, introduce highly subjective attitudes into critical problems. By so doing, they make clear and intelligible solutions to the problems impossible.[13]

For various reasons, then, no satisfactory meaning for the term "Baroque" seems to have resulted from the four suggestions previously discussed: (1) that the word "Baroque" can properly and usefully signify a unified style pervading a cultural period; (2) that the word has been damaged beyond salvaging as a term in art history; (3) that the word can and should be given some rather narrowly defined meaning; and (4) that the word should be regarded as properly connoting an evaluation of the objects to which it is applied.

What alternative solution seems promising? The answer is suggested, I think, when flexibility and breadth of connotation are seen to be both inevitable and desirable. Style, as I conceive of it, is a function of the work of art as a whole—that is, of its medium, form, and content. And a historic style, as Thomas Munro very well puts it, "is to be described or defined not in terms of any single type or characteristic, but as a combination of several . . . it is well

---

[11] Wimsatt and Brooks, *Literary Criticism* (New York, 1957), p. 514.
[12] *Ibid.*, p. 368.
[13] An eloquent statement of this conviction occurs in Denis Mahon's *Studies in Seicento Art and Theory* (London, 1947), pp. 226–9.

to think of styles as dynamic, complex trends."[14] Big words retain their meaningfulness in spite of—or perhaps because of—multiplicity of meanings. The proposal here made, then, stresses the fact that we should understand the Baroque as a varied style, wide in scope.

Before explaining this view further, I must insist that it in no way compels one to accept an extreme "nominalism" which considers artistic periods *merely* as sections of time. They are that, undoubtedly, and one should not minimize the usefulness of time concepts in that they enable us to make rough chronological distinctions between, for example, the Baroque and the preceding Mannerism and the ensuing Rococo. But the concept of Baroque style here set forth is at once much more complex and much more valuable than a period concept. Moreover, it does not, as some writers have mistakenly argued, sanction in any way a skepticism that, in the end, abandons the problem of Baroque style. Multiple meanings for that style do not deny a certain kind of stylistic unity. The recognition by all critics of telling stylistic differences between the art of the Baroque period and of any other proves this. Thus why would one discard the idea of Baroque style? The absence of a precise and simple referent for the style, though bothersome, is inevitable. Imprecision and complexity are inherent in the only concept of Baroque style that is useful and meaningful.

This conception is meaningful in a manner similar to our conception of Gothic art: that is to say, we may recognize in Baroque art, as we do in Gothic or in Renaissance art, many different stylistic qualities. All these are implied by the general terms. The importance of each quality will vary considerably because of differences in artists, times, and places. Some qualities will be present and some may not. But together they form composite images which make up the broad stylistic concept.

At this point a critical opponent may ask: isn't the view you advocate comparable to, or perhaps even identical with, the view you have attacked of a pervasive or unified style? Isn't the word "general" applicable both to your own approach and to the first of the approaches you reject? How, if this is so, are they always and clearly distinguishable? To this objection I would reply as follows. The view I reject is that an objective referent for "Baroque" of a

---

[14] *Toward Science in Aesthetics* (New York, 1956), p. 179.

generalized sort exists—a referent that includes, at most, a group of closely related qualities. The view I champion is that whereas no such general objective referent exists, it is convenient and intelligible to employ "Baroque" with an inclusive (and in this sense "general") scope of reference, though the referents embraced within the scope of this reference may themselves be quite varied. The point in grouping them together is that they exhibit various, and sometimes intricate, sorts of inter-connectedness. Whereas "Baroque" conceived as a pervasive period style has as a referent a single characteristic, or one unified group of characteristics, the meaning of "Baroque" proposed here has as a referent all, or nearly all, of the stylistic traits found within the Baroque period. The exceptions to this inclusive concept of Baroque style are of two minor kinds: first, those artists and monuments that are notably reactionary or *retardataire* —e.g., paintings of Sassoferrato and Cerrini, or the classicistic buildings of seventeenth-century Holland; second, late Mannerist artists who continue to create in the seventeenth century—e.g., El Greco.

Further elucidation of this concept of Baroque style could be made with reference to Arnold Hauser's recent analysis of the nature of artistic style in his book, *The Philosophy of Art History.* His stimulating discussion of this basic concept includes ideas that support the conception of Baroque style recommended in this essay. But there are differences as well. Among these is the emphasis Hauser places on "ideal" and "abstract" bases of style that lead one away from the specific problems of a period style considered later in this essay. His concept, moreover, opposes the view of Baroque, here defended, that includes nearly all of the stylistic traits of the period. For Hauser, on the contrary, "when we coin a concept like the 'baroque,' we *ipso facto* leave out of account a great many traits of the works of art referred to by this concept."[15]

The referent for "Baroque style" here proposed even exceeds in its breadth and generality the connotations normally given to Renaissance art. Although the Renaissance *period* in art, that is to say, is usually considered as extending in Italy throughout the sixteenth century, Italian Renaissance *style* does not include all of the characteristics of this century. We now recognize the importance of the "stylistic crisis" of about 1520 and the three divergent styles that followed: Late Renaissance, Mannerism, and Proto-Baroque.

---

[15] *The Philosophy of Art History* (New York, 1959), p. 196.

Although the stylistic traits of Mannerism and of Proto-Baroque are not yet fully formulated, they are sufficiently differentiated from each other and from the continuation of the High Renaissance to be classified by separate broad words.[16] In the Baroque period, to be sure, marked changes also occur. We now employ the term "rococo" to characterize a great deal of eighteenth-century art that was formerly included within the Baroque style. Moreover, there seems to be a geographic split in style in the seventeenth century in that the stylistic solutions, say, of Italy and of the Netherlands in their break with Mannerist ties are quite different. However, no broad and useful terminology, that is clear and intelligible, has as yet been accepted, or even suggested, to illuminate these diverse solutions. And at the present time it seems unwise to try to coin other big words. Even so, *qualifications* in terminology, as we shall see, will connote important stylistic distinctions within the inclusive concept of Baroque that is recommended.

If one accepts the very broad concept of Baroque style proposed, it will be understood why no art historian has yet produced a satisfactory, comprehensive analysis of the style, and why such an analysis, though theoretically possible, would be an almost superhuman task. Recognizing the manifold trends within the Baroque, art historians have investigated a limited number of its component elements: for example, Wölfflin's analysis of the formal elements of Baroque style in his five famous categories;[17] and Mâle's very

---

[16] Yet this larger number of accepted categories for the style of the sixteenth century presents difficulties. As Charles de Tolnay has recently pointed out: "The fact that we are not able to determine the historical place of the *Last Judgment* with the usual stylistic categories (Renaissance, Mannerism, Baroque) does not mean that Michelangelo stands outside the historical development, but only that our categories are too narrow." *Michelangelo* (Princeton, 1960), p. 50.

[17] *Kunstgeschichtliche Grundbegriffe* (Munich, 1915; 7th ed., 1929), translated as *Principles of Art History* (New York, 1932). The various criticisms of these categories are largely invalidated, I believe, by Wölfflin's modifications of his own principles in his essay "Kunstgeschichtliche Grundbegriffe," *Eine Revision*, written in 1933 and published in his *Gedanken Zur Kunstgeschichte* (Basle, 1941). For example, he urges, p. 22, that his categories be understood in a *very* general way: "Das Ausdrucksmässige in unsern schematischen Begriffen müss in einer *sehr* allgemeinen Art bestimmt werden." For criticism of Wölfflin by German scholars see Walter Passarge, *Die Philosophie Der Kunstgeschichte* (Berlin, 1930), p. 21ff.

different study of Baroque iconography and iconology.[18] Neither writer attempts an all-embracing account of Baroque style; yet neither tries, as the periodizers do, to reduce the concept of the Baroque to a single major experience. Their material is notably rich in its variety.

Such analyses increase enormously our understanding of the Baroque. But other knotty and complex problems remain. Some of these, to be sure, are less vexing than one might at first suppose because they are essentially verbal in nature. We should ask first, then, whether disagreements among critics are, *au fond*, real or verbal. Do writers on Baroque art, that is, differ basically in their stylistic analysis of Baroque monuments, or do they find the same qualities but choose different terms to describe them? Though verbal and real questions are closely interrelated, we should know with which kind of problem we are basically dealing.

Semantic disputes occur, for example, in regard to the style of the period in Italy around 1600. Walter Friedlaender's discussion of the problem charmingly shows its complexity in that, on a single page, he suggests such different terminologies for this style as "neo-classical or neo-Renaissance" and "early, or rather, pre-Baroque."[19] Though comprehensible, the terms "neo-classical" and "neo-Renaissance" encourage confusion by separating this art from the Baroque; and "pre-Baroque" is unfortunate in that it tends to identify the style of this particular period with those characteristics of the sixteenth century that anticipate the Baroque: namely, the Proto-Baroque elements in Correggio, Michelangelo, and Tintoretto. But the epithet "Early-Baroque" seems entirely satisfactory as applied to artists of this period. It has the merits of including these artists within the broad concept of Baroque style and of differentiating them both from the late Mannerism which they reacted against and from the more developed phases of the Baroque—i.e., the Full-Baroque and the Late-Baroque. Moreover, although the styles of the artists active at this time differ in many ways—one need mention

---

[18] Émile Mâle, *L'Art Religieux après le Concile de Trente* (Paris, 1932). Other discussions of Baroque artistic content include: John Martin's essay, "The Baroque from the Viewpoint of the Art Historian," *JAAC* (December 1955); Basil Willey's book, *The Seventeenth Century Background* (London, 1942); and Erwin Panofsky's brief remarks on the "depth and width, the horror and the sublimity of the concept of time" in the Baroque in his *Studies in Iconology* (New York, 1939), p. 92.

[19] *Op. cit.*, p. 81.

only Caravaggio and Annibale Carracci—they are nonetheless related in a general tendency toward a "reform moving in the direction of the actual, the normative and reasonable, the human and the inward."[20] Thus one inclusive epithet is clearly desirable.

Verbal differences occur conspicuously when writers on the Baroque consider its relation with classicism.[21] Several writers hold that classicism is a style, contemporary with, but distinct from, the Baroque. Meyer Shapiro states, for example, that "contemporary with the Baroque of the seventeenth century is a classic style which in the late eighteenth century replaces the Baroque."[22] And T. H. Fokker, in his book, *Roman Baroque Art*, also separates classicism from Baroque style, applying the term "classicism," *tout simple*, to Poussin. Now of course one cannot compel verbal usage; but if one accepts the concept of Baroque, as here proposed, as a broad and varied style, the use of "classicism" to connote a separate and important stylistic trend is misleading. Far more satisfactory is Denis Mahon's somewhat more cumbersome expression "Baroque classicism" or, as I prefer, "Classic-Baroque." Obviously this term does not describe a style precisely, but is merely a short-hand way of suggesting a group of dominant traits. The concept of Classic-Baroque will include the Roman style of Annibale Carracci and of Poussin and will, in a very general way, designate a style that combines elements that are unquestionably Baroque—i.e., that are characteristic only of seventeenth-century art—with such "classical" elements as clarity. restraint, and emphatic orderliness. By this usage of "Classic-Baroque" one may avoid the dilemma of those critics who, like Otto Grautoff,[23] radically and arbitrarily shift their critical position, when analyzing French painting of the seventeenth century, from a style concept to a time concept.

---

[20] *Ibid.*, pp. 76–77.

[21] They occur equally in connection with academicism and the Baroque. Should one avoid the term "academic," as Mahon suggests, because of its adverse aesthetic implications? Or, as Fokker and Sypher maintain, does it well describe important stylistic features of the century? It may be useful, I think, if applied to artists and monuments that I have referred to above as reactionary or *retardataire;* but it should surely be applied with caution, as Rudolf Wittkower remarks in his usage in *Art and Architecture in Italy 1600–1750* (Baltimore, 1958), p. 241.

[22] In his article, "Style," in A. L. Kroeber's *Anthropology Today* (Chicago, 1953), p. 296.

[23] Pevsner und Grautoff, *Barokmalerei in den Romanischen Ländern* (Potsdam, 1928).

The fact that Annibale's painting is characterized as both Early-Baroque and Classic-Baroque should not create ambiguity. The application of the two qualifying terms "early" and "classic" to his art adds to the precision of the description. Indeed, as Mahon has argued, still greater precision will designate his Bolognese phase as Early-Baroque, his Roman phase as Classic-Baroque *and* Early-Baroque. In an analogous way, Caravaggio's art may be considered not only Early-Baroque but Realistic-Baroque or Naturalistic-Baroque, the referents indicating, in a very general way, a style that combines a concern for "realism" of content and of handling with characteristics that are unmistakably those of the seventeenth century. This classification is applicable as well to much Spanish and Dutch painting of the century, to the Le Nain brother, and even *faute de mieux* to Georges de la Tour. One may urge, to be sure, that, because of stylistic features exceptional in the period (the sharp edges, the sculpturesque and abstract character of his forms, for example), de la Tour should not be included within the Baroque. But to eliminate an important artist of the period from the broad meaning of Baroque at once weakens the basic idea of the preferred connotation of "Baroque." Rather than make such an exception, we should try to define the various stylistic trends of the century by coining, if necessary, new qualifying epithets, and thus refining our terminology so that it more accurately indicates the stylistic characteristics in question. By doing this, we should learn to think of different kinds of Baroque art; that is to say, we should learn to use the word "Baroque" in the plural.

Clarification of verbal differences, and agreement about the use of words cannot, however, resolve many of the contradictions found in analyses of Baroque style. We often face real, not semantic, disagreements. Consider, as examples, three opinions of Sypher which make an illuminating contrast with different views, previously expressed by other critics.

First: Sypher's contention that Baroque art is basically tactile is opposed to Wölfflin's well-known verdict. Sypher remarks: "Much baroque painting, and almost all baroque architecture and sculpture, are vigorously 'haptic,' giving us a maximum tactile value and being 'felt' in the viscera and the finger-ends as well as on the retina."[24]

---

[24] *Op. cit.,* p. 186.

Wölfflin, to the contrary, contends that in seventeenth-century painting "tactile sensations vanish" and that "the tactile picture has become the visual picture—the most decisive revolution which art history knows."[25] In his discussion of Bernini's sculpture, he stresses the absence in the forms of "immediate tangibility."

In the second place, Sypher, in the section of his Baroque chapter entitled "Baroque and Academic," is at pains to illustrate the "mighty decorum" and the "august equilibrium" of Baroque style. In so doing he cites *Paradise Lost* and Borromini's façade of Sant' Agnese as " 'tectonic' structures," and refers to the "grand simplified planes" of Italian Baroque art. This analysis plainly contradicts two of Wölfflin's categories of Baroque style: namely, the "a-tectonic" and "recession."

Thirdly, Sypher believes that "the instrument of baroque imagination is the will." "A triumphant release of the will" expresses the energy, the "dynamic fulfillment" of the Baroque. Famous previous discussions of Baroque style have insisted, on the other hand, that the will in Baroque art does not dominate but is in conflict with or actually ruled by feeling and sensation. Riegl again and again stresses the conflict. For example: "Das Neue ist, dass nun die Empfindung sich emanzipiert, in Kampf tritt mit dem Willen."[26] Wittkower, agreeing with Riegl, remarks that "à la Renaissance, c'est la volonté qui domine la sensation. La volonté est égoïste, isolante, tactile. Dans le baroque, c'est la sensation qui domine la volonté. . . ."[27]

How may we account for these and other comparable disagreements? Surely they are not primarily verbal. Sypher's meaning of "tactile," of "tectonic," and of "will" is clearly not so different from the meanings which Wölfflin, Riegl, and Wittkower give these words as to account for the differences in opinion. Although we may readily grant that different shades of meanings for these terms exist and that these are not easy to unravel, nonetheless it seems clear that the disagreements are in some sense basic.

An attempt to determine in precisely what sense they are basic suggests an important distinction. Do the differing analyses indicate that the writers actually perceive and therefore interpret dif-

---

[25] *Principles of Art History*, p. 21.
[26] *Die Entstehung der Barockkunst in Rom* (Wien, 1908), p. 36.
[27] "Le Bernin et le Baroque Romain," *Gazette des Beaux Arts* (1934), 327.

ferently? Are the opposed analyses, that is to say, the result of basically different perceptive sensibilities? Or are the differences rather the result of different emphases? That is, may they best be explained by the fact that the writers are analyzing different works of art, or different aspects of the same work, because they stress different stylistic qualities? This distinction may be illustrated by reference to the three disagreements cited above.

In the case of the contradictory opinions concerning tactility in Baroque art, I believe that they frequently reflect a difference in basic responses. From the varied experiences of hundreds of students who have worked with me at this problem, as well as from the contrasting experiences of Sypher and Wölfflin, I conclude that, in regard to tactile effects, work of Baroque art may produce reactions which are irreconcilable. The same sculptures of Bernini, for example, frequently arouse tactile sensations, yet frequently repel any feeling of tactility. At times an aesthetic experience of Bernini's *S. Teresa* includes a wish to touch and feel the intricate carving; at other times, this experience excludes any such desire. Thus the conclusions of both Sypher and Wölfflin are substantiated. We are dealing with aesthetic responses which, on empirical evidence, fundamentally differ. They are psychologically relative to differing temperaments.

This diversity of perceptions will doubtless be repudiated, or at least questioned, by many critics—notably by absolutists. Proof of *competent* diversity is, to be sure, difficult to prove. But there is substantial evidence for it in the notorious fluctuation of value judgments, in the kind of evidence given in the foregoing paragraph and later on in the discussion of the Farnese Gallery, and in the testimony, for example, of Wölfflin, Walter Abell, Arnold Hauser, and André Malraux.[28]

Consider now the other two disagreements cited above between Wölfflin and Sypher: namely, the formal problem in Baroque art of "tectonic" vs. "a-tectonic," and the psychological problem of the relative significance in Baroque art of "will" and of "feeling." In these cases, too, it is possible that disagreements result from differing responses which are basic and irreconcilable. But another

---

[28] The interested reader may find this testimony in the following: Wölfflin, *Gedanken Zur Kunstgeschichte*, p. 20; Walter Abell, *The Collective Dream in Art* (Cambridge, Mass., 1957), p. 324; Arnold Hauser, *op. cit.*, p. 3; André Malraux, *The Voices of Silence* (New York, 1953), p. 317.

solution to the difficulty—one that in all likelihood is often combined with the type just considered—seems more probable: namely, that because the writers in question stress different elements of Baroque style as basic, they analyze different monuments, or emphasize different qualities of the same monument, to support their claim.

In his discussion of Academic and Baroque art, Sypher selects the façade of Sant' Agnese to point up the existence of " 'tectonic' structures, having a mighty decorum."[29] He has deliberately chosen an example of Italian Baroque architecture which is notably "systematic," balanced, and symmetrical. The central dome and the end towers produce an effect of order and of regularity which Sypher justifiably describes as "tectonic." Wölfflin, discussing different aspects of the same monument, asserts that "the inexhaustibility of the possible pictures" and the "variation in the mode of appearance" which this façade presents, produce an effect which is "painterly."[30] By selecting, moreover, such examples of Roman Baroque architecture as S. Andrea della Valle and the Trevi Fountain for analysis, he discusses those monuments that best illustrate the characteristics which for him comprise the essence of Baroque art: namely, "painterliness," "recession," "open form," "unity," and "unclearness." Both writers consider those monuments, or aspects of monuments, which best exemplify their different stylistic criteria. The diverse conclusions result from the fact that the writers are dwelling on different aspects of a remarkably varied style.

In somewhat the same way, the predominance given either to "will" or to "feeling" (or to a conflict between them) as a psychological factor in Baroque art seems to influence the selection of works that are analyzed. Conversely, of course, one may argue that the study of the monuments determines the criteria. The interrelationship between the criteria and the works of art is indubitably complex and reciprocal. We need not argue the question of priority. One should realize, however, that an important connection exists, say, between Sypher's emphasis upon the "will" and his emphasis upon *Paradise Lost*. Milton's "baroque bodies and action are an idiom of incorrigible will."[31] Even if we do not accept Milton as a key

---

[29] *Op. cit.,* p. 219.
[30] *Principles of Art History,* p. 71.
[31] *Op. cit.,* p. 209.

Baroque figure, the presence of "will" in Baroque art can hardly be denied; a powerful will is expressed, for example, in Rubens' heroic figures. In most kinds of Baroque art, however, feeling or sensation is no doubt dominant: Van Dyck's religious pictures are obvious examples. Whether the will or sensation expressed is inherent in the attitude of the artist or in the figures he has created, or in both, seems irrelevant to the argument. In any case, both will and sensation should be recognized as elements of Baroque style. Attempts to interpret Baroque content solely in terms of one or the other are too restrictive in that they fail to recognize sufficiently the diversity of the Baroque.

The problem of the *degree* to which any seventeenth-century artist is Baroque is complex and important. Disputes concerning it largely hinge upon the three kinds of disagreement I have considered: they may be verbal; they may result from different but equally sensitive perceptions; and they may arise from the amount and kind of emphasis given to the various elements of the style. All three kinds may be involved and will, of course, vary in importance according to the type of stylistic analysis. The nature of this problem may be indicated with reference to a familiar question: to what extent is the art of Annibale Carracci Baroque? And this question may most concretely be considered with reference to the well-known debate between Rensselaer W. Lee and Denis Mahon about the style of Annibale.[32]

Lee considers Annibale an eclectic artist; Mahon does not. This disagreement is to some extent a verbal one. As Mahon himself says: the desirability of describing "certain paintings as eclectic in the sense that it provides an essential key to understanding them . . . involves semantic problems of considerable complexity." For example, Mahon rejects the significance that Lee attaches to the term "eclectic," and refers to it as "that veritable masterpiece of concise meaninglessness." Moreover, Lee's statement that the Farnese Gallery has a "patently eclectic character, essential to its classicism" means to Mahon that Lee equates classicism with eclecticism. May not, however, the phrase "essential to its classicism" refer only

---

[32] The quotations that follow come from these publications: Mahon, *Studies in Seicento Art and Theory*; Lee's review of that book in *The Art Bulletin* (September 1951); and Mahon's reply to that review in *The Art Bulletin* (September 1953).

to the particular brand of classicism that Lee finds in the Gallery?
In any case, it seems clear that verbal differences have played a
rôle in this dispute.

The question of the presence or absence of eclecticism in the style
of Annibale leads to issues more vital than semantic ones. One crucial
disagreement in the present argument concerns the artistic value of
the Farnese Gallery. According to Lee, it remains "a composite in
which individual parts tend to assert their own artistic parentage at
the expense of the kind of unity that is the mark of great genius."
Mahon, to the contrary, expresses amazement "that, at the present
time, such an approach should be made to a work of the quality of
the Galleria, which, on any balanced estimate, is one of the out-
standing monuments of European painting." This disparity in expert judgments concerning a famous monument again points to
differences in basic perceptions. Similarly, the fact that Lee finds the
art of Caravaggio and Annibale far more divergent than does
Mahon, both in respect to stylistic traits and to artistic value, reveals
a disagreement which must in large measure result from fundamentally different responses. Each writer claims that his response is
the valid or correct one. But relativist criticism is willing to accept
the judgment of each as expert. It rightly teaches that different
analyses and evaluations are frequently based, to some extent at
least, upon temperaments radically different, though equally acute
and sensitive.

The dispute in question also involves the third kind of disagreement referred to: namely, the varying *emphases* that each writer
places upon the multiple stylistic traits of the Farnese Gallery. Lee
stresses the "retrospective" and "eclectic" elements which seem to
him to link it basically and inextricably with the art of the past.
Mahon minimizes the importance of these derivative traits and
stresses the naturalism and energy, the painterly and "baroque"
character of Annibale's style. He finds Lee's conclusions a "remarkable example of allowing the sight of some of the trees to blind one
to the shape of the wood." To which Lee might respond, if the argument is continued, that the appearance of the wood is essentially
formed by the shape of many of the trees.

The problem under discussion concerning the degree to which
a seventeenth-century artist is Baroque of course depends upon the
connotation one accepts for the term "Baroque." Even the broad
and inclusive interpretation advocated in this essay implies some

norm or group of traits which receive special emphasis in this period: for example, the categories of Wölfflin, the inconography as explained by Mâle, and such prevalent stylistic features as energy and movement, pomp and splendor. General agreement about the prominence of these and other characteristics in seventeenth-century art enables one to affirm, for example, that the early works of Guercino are more Baroque than his late works, and that Rembrandt between 1630 and 1640 is more Baroque than Rembrandt after 1650. The qualifying expression "Classic-Baroque" is clearly applicable only to the late styles of these artists. But the problem of the degree of Baroqueness becomes more difficult and more intricate in the case of those artists whose style does not so clearly reveal the more prevalent traits of the period. Mere mention of Vermeer or of Vouet suggests the complexities which discussions of this kind entail. Two main ideas concerning the solution of such problems may be indicated by a consideration of some aspects of the style of Poussin.

The crucial meaning of the question: is Poussin Baroque? was clearly posed by Wolfgang Stechow. If Poussin is a Baroque artist, he wrote, "we should be able to prove that . . . a work by Poussin is basically more closely related to one by Rubens or Rembrandt that to one by Raphael or David, and this not only with regard to form but also with regard to content."[33] I suggest, first, that attempts to make this proof will depend, to a degree, upon which of Poussin's paintings are selected for analysis and upon which of his stylistic qualities are stressed—that is, the problem of emphasis, discussed above, is crucial. Second, I suggest that the complexity of the question is such that any definitive or precise answer is unobtainable; only a flexible and imprecise solution can be given to the problem of the degree to which Poussin's art is Baroque.

If one selects for analysis *The Martyrdom of S. Erasmus*, the *Neptune and Amphitrite*, and *The Dance of the Seasons*, one can point to striking differences between these works and the art of Raphael and David, both in form and content. The grander proportions and gestures, the curves and diagonals in plane and depth, the greater animation and exuberance, the sense of power, pomp, and physical strength, the heroic and ideal grandeur of these and other paintings by Poussin will be rightly interpreted as notably

---

[33] "Definitions of the Baroque in the Visual Arts," *JAAC* (December 1946), 114.

Baroque qualities. These qualities relate Poussin more directly to Rubens than to Raphael. One may also note the respective emphasis in the three paintings mentioned upon three qualities that have been characterized as Baroque by Mâle, Wölfflin, and Panofsky: namely, the emphasis upon cruelty in the *S. Erasmus,* upon "Becoming" in the *Neptune and Amphitrite,* and upon Time in the *Dance of the Seasons.* If these qualities are stressed, Poussin will be considered a distinctly Baroque painter.

But some critics may well assert that the Louvre *Et in Arcadia Ego* and *Rebecca at the Well* are more typical examples of Poussin's art. They will then reach a different conclusion. They will point to the figures parallel to the picture plane, to the clear, linear, and static character of the forms, to the metrical and regular intervals, and to a tectonic design which accepts as important the limits of the picture frame. Above all, perhaps, they will observe in these and other comparable works a style which does not reveal the painterly (or non-linear) visual level of perception that is emphasized in all of Wölfflin's Baroque categories and that one finds preeminently expressed in the art of Rubens and Rembrandt. They may even argue that none of Poussin's paintings reveal this visual level. If this quality is for them the dominant feature of Baroque style, they will hold that at no time is Poussin significantly Baroque and may thus prefer to call him "classical." For reasons already given, however, this epithet seems misleading.

The large majority of Poussin's paintings are, of course, neither so predominantly Baroque as the *S. Erasmus* nor so classical as the *Et in Arcadia Ego.* They reveal a complex, yet wholly unified, mixture of varied traits about which critics largely agree. Now how are we to weigh these traits—some emphatically Baroque, some emphatically classical—in relation to each other? I do not see how we can satisfactorily do so. If we compare Poussin's *Neptune and Amphitrite* with Raphael's *Galatea,* on the one hand, and with Rubens' *Quos Ego,* on the other, we observe in both comparisons notable similarities and differences. Most observers would probably agree that, if we analyze the three works according to Wölfflin's categories, Poussin is in this case closer to Raphael and the High Renaissance. Undeniably, however, the *Neptune and Amphitrite* reveals more "recession" and is more "a-tectonic" than the *Galatea;* it indicates an interest in space and breaks into the picture plane in a way that is more typical of seventeenth-century style. The light is more effulgent than in Raphael, less dynamic than in Rubens. In content, the Poussin expresses a mood that lies somewhere between the restrained idealism of the High Renaissance and the subjective emotionalism of the intensely Baroque.

How can one hope to determine with precision the degree to which the style of Poussin in this painting agrees with that of Raphael or of Rubens? The most objective observer imaginable would be unable, I believe, to balance the many classical qualities against the many Baroque ones. We should thus decide, reluctantly perhaps, that we are dealing with a complex problem which involves incommensurables. Stechow's demand for proof that Poussin's style is more closely related basically to that of Rubens or of Raphael will not be found. We should thus agree to discontinue a pursuit for preciseness where none exists. The suggestion, already made, to consider the style of Poussin Classic-Baroque is intended to escape the dilemma. "Classic-Baroque" connotes something broad and flexible and avoids the irksome question: is Poussin primarily classic or Baroque? "We gain much more," in the words of William James, "by a broad than by a narrow conception of our subject. At a certain stage in the development of every science a degree of vagueness is what best consists with fertility."[34]

From the several foregoing considerations about the Baroque, I should like, in conclusion, to underscore two main points. First, the many complexities of Baroque style should be accepted and explored, not oversimplified or denied. Varieties, even polarities, in points of view, hence in artistic form and content, are inevitable if one accepts the ambivalent facets of cultures. Witness the fact, for example, that the two chief emotional attitudes of the Victorian era were optimism and anxiety![35] Within the far broader scope, both chronologically and geographically, of the Baroque era, should not one naturally expect to find remarkable diversity of varying kinds?

Second: a broad, flexible view does not, it seems necessary to reaffirm, reduce the concept of Baroque style to something so vague that it is useless. Baroque should not be considered merely as a period of time. The plain fact that one can distinguish works of

---

[34] *Principles of Psychology*, Vol. II (Dover Publications), p. 6.
[35] Walter E. Houghton, *The Victorian Frame of Mind* (New Haven, 1957), Part I.

art of the seventeenth century from those of the sixteenth and
eighteenth shows that the concept of Baroque style, though highly
complex, is meaningful. Perhaps, as already suggested, by learning
to use the word "Baroque" in the plural—by consciously recognizing
the varieties of style, that is to say, within the larger concept—we
shall find the meanings of this large concept both comprehensible
and salutary.

René Wellek

LITERATURE
AND THE OTHER ARTS*

The relationships of literature with the fine arts and music are
highly various and complex. Sometimes poetry has drawn inspiration from paintings or sculpture or music. Like natural objects and
persons, other works of art may become the themes of poetry. That
poets have described pieces of sculpture, painting, or even music
presents no particular theoretical problem. Spenser, it has been
suggested, drew some of his descriptions from tapestries and
pageants; the paintings of Claude Lorrain and Salvatore Rosa influenced eighteenth-century landscape poetry; Keats derived details
of his "Ode on a Grecian Urn" from a specific picture of Claude
Lorrain. Stephen A. Larrabee has considered all the allusions and
treatments of Greek sculpture to be found in English poetry. Albert Thibaudet has shown that Mallarmé's "L'Après-midi d'un
faune" was inspired by a painting of Boucher in the London National Gallery. Poets, especially nineteenth-century poets like Hugo,
Gautier, the Parnassiens, and Tieck, have written poems on definite
pictures. Poets, or course, have had their theories about painting
and their preferences among painters, which can be studied and
more or less related to their theories about literature and their

* From *Theory of Literature* by René Wellek and Austin Warren. Copyright, 1942, 1949, 1956, by Harcourt, Brace & World, Inc. and reprinted with
their permission.

literary tastes. Here is a wide area for investigation, only partially traversed in recent decades.

In its turn, obviously, literature can become the theme of painting or of music, especially vocal and program music, just as literature, especially the lyric and the drama, has intimately collaborated with music. In an increasing number, there are studies of medieval carols or Elizabethan lyrical poetry which stress the close association of the musical setting. In art history there has appeared a whole group of scholars (Erwin Panofsky, Fritz Saxl, and others) who study the conceptual and symbolic meanings of works of art ("Iconology") and frequently also their literary relations and inspirations.

Beyond these obvious questions of sources and influences, inspiration and co-operation, there arises a more important problem: literature has sometimes definitely attempted to achieve the effects of painting—to become word painting, or has tried to achieve the effects of music—to turn into music. At times, poetry has even wanted to be sculpturesque. A critic may, as did Lessing in his *Laokoön* and Irving Babbitt in his *New Laokoön*, deplore this confusion of genres; but one cannot deny that the arts have tried to borrow effects from each other and that they have been, in considerable measure, successful in achieving these effects. One can, of course, deny the possibility of the literal metamorphosis of poetry into sculpture, painting, or music. The term "sculpturesque," applied to poetry, even to that of Landor or Gautier or Heredia, is merely a vague metaphor, meaning that the poetry conveys an impression somehow similar to the effects of Greek sculpture: coolness, induced by white marble or plaster casts, stillness, repose, sharp outlines, clarity. But we must recognize that coolness in poetry is something very different from the tactual sensation of marble, or the imaginative reconstruction of that perception from whiteness; that stillness in poetry is something very different from stillness in sculpture. When Collins' "Ode to Evening" is called a "sculptured poem" nothing is said that implies any real relationship with sculpture. The only analyzable objectivities are the slow, solemn meter and the diction, which is strange enough to compel attention to individual words and hence to enforce a slow pace in reading.

But one can hardly deny the success of the Horatian formula *ut pictura poesis*. Though the amount of visualization in the reading of poetry is likely to be overrated, there were ages and there were poets who did make the reader visualize. Lessing may have been right in criticizing the enumerative description of female beauty in Ariosto as visually ineffective (though not necessarily poetically ineffective), but the eighteenth-century addicts of the picturesque cannot be easily dismissed; and modern literature from Chateaubriand to Proust has given us many descriptions at least suggesting the effects of painting and inciting us to visualize scenes in terms frequently evocative of contemporary paintings. Though it may be doubted whether the poet can really suggest the effects of painting to hypothetical readers totally ignorant of painting, it is clear that, within our general cultural tradition, writers did suggest the emblem, the landscape painting of the eighteenth century, the impressionistic effects of a Whistler and the like.

Whether poetry can achieve the effects of music seems more doubtful, though it is a widely held view that it can. "Musicality" in verse, closely analyzed, turns out to be something entirely different from "melody" in music: it means an arrangement of phonetic patterns, an avoidance of accumulations of consonants, or simply the presence of certain rhythmical effects. With such romantic poets as Tieck and, later, Verlaine, the attempts to achieve musical effects are largely attempts to suppress the meaning structure of verse, to avoid logical constructions, to stress connotations rather than denotations. Yet blurred outlines, vagueness of meaning, and illogicality are not, in a literal sense, "musical" at all. Literary imitations of musical structures like leitmotiv, the sonata, or symphonic form seem to be more concrete; but it is hard to see why repetitive motifs or a certain contrasting and balancing of moods, though by avowed intention imitative of musical composition, are not essentially the familiar literary devices of recurrence, contrast, and the like which are common to all the arts. In the comparatively rare instances where poetry suggests definite musical sounds, Verlaine's "Les sanglots longs des violons" or Poe's "Bells," the effect of the timbre of an instrument or the very generalized clang of bells is achieved by means which are not much beyond ordinary onomatopoeia.

Poems have been, of course, written with the intention that music should be added, e.g., many Elizabethan airs and all librettos for opera. In rare instances, poets and composers have been one and the same; but it seems hard to prove that the composition of music and words was ever a simultaneous process. Even Wagner sometimes wrote his "dramas" years before they were set to music; and, no doubt, many lyrics were composed to fit ready melodies. But the relation between music and really great poetry seems rather tenuous when we think of the evidence afforded by even the most successful settings into musical terms. Poems of close-knit, highly integrated structure do not lend themselves to musical setting, while mediocre or poor poetry, like much of the early Heine or Wilhelm Müller, has provided the text for the finest songs of Schubert and Schumann. If the poetry is of high literary value, the setting frequently distorts or obscures its patterns completely, even when the music has value in its own right. One need not cite such examples as the lot of Shakespeare's *Othello* in Verdi's opera, for nearly all the settings of the Psalms or of the poems of Goethe offer adequate proof of the contention. Collaboration between poetry and music exists, to be sure; but the highest poetry does not tend towards music, and the greatest music stands in no need of words.

The parallels between the fine arts and literature usually amount to the assertion that this picture and that poem induce the same mood in me: for example, that I feel lighthearted and gay in hearing a minuet of Mozart, seeing a landscape by Watteau, and reading an Anacreontic poem. But this is the kind of parallelism which is of little worth for purposes of precise analysis: joy induced by a piece of music is not joy in general or even joy of a particular shade, but is an emotion closely following and thus tied to the pattern of the music. We experience emotions which have only a general tone in common with those of real life, and even if we define these emotions as closely as we can, we are still quite removed from the specific object which induced them. Parallels between the arts which remain inside the individual reactions of a reader or spectator and are content with describing some emotional similarity of our reactions to two arts will, therefore, never lend themselves to verification and thus to a co-operative advance in our knowledge.

Another common approach is the intentions and theories of the artists. No doubt, we can show that there are some similarities in the theories and formulas behind the different arts, in the Neo-Classical or the Romantic movements, and we can find also professions of intentions of the individual artists in the different arts which sound identical or similar. But "Classicism" in music must mean something very different from its use in literature for the simple reason that no real ancient music (with the exception of a few fragments) was known and could thus shape the evolution of music as literature was actually shaped by the precepts and practice of antiquity. Likewise painting, before the excavation of the frescoes in Pompeii and Herculaneum, can scarcely be described as influenced by classical painting in spite of the frequent reference to classical theories and Greek painters like Apelles and some remote pictorial traditions which must have descended from antiquity through the Middle Ages. Sculpture and architecture, however, were to an extent far exceeding the other arts, including literature, determined by classical models and their derivatives. Thus theories and conscious intentions mean something very different in the various arts and say little or nothing about the concrete results of an artist's activity: his work and its specific content and form.

How indecisive for specific exegesis the approach through the author's intention may be, can best be observed in the rare cases when artist and poet are identical. For example, a comparison of the poetry and the paintings of Blake, or of Rossetti, will show that the character—not merely the technical quality—of their painting and poetry is very different, even divergent. A grotesque little animal is supposed to illustrate "Tiger! Tiger! Burning bright." W. M. Thackeray illustrated *Vanity Fair*, but his smirky caricature of Becky Sharp has hardly anything to do with the complex character in the novel. In structure and quality there is little comparison between Michelangelo's *Sonnets* and his sculpture and paintings, though we can find the same Neo-Platonic ideas in all and may discover some psychological similarities. This shows that the "medium" of a work of art (an unfortunate question-begging term) is not merely a technical obstacle to be overcome by the artist in order to express his personality, but a factor performed by tradition and having a powerful determining character which shapes and modifies the approach and expression of the individual artist. The artist does not conceive in general mental terms but in terms of concrete material; and the concrete medium has its own history, frequently very different from that of any other medium.

More valuable than the approach through the artist's intentions and theories is a comparison of the arts on the basis of their common social and cultural background. Certainly it is possible to describe the common temporal, local, or social nourishing soil of the arts and literature and thus to point to common influences working on them. Many parallels between the arts are possible only because they ignore the utterly different social background to which the individual work of art appealed or from which it seems to be derived. The social classes either creating or demanding a certain type of art may be quite different at any one time or place. The Gothic cathedrals have a different social background from the French epic; and sculpture frequently appeals to and is paid for by a very different audience from the novel. Just as fallacious as the assumption of a common social background of the arts at a given time and place is the usual assumption that the intellectual background is necessarily identical and effective in all the arts. It seems hazardous to interpret painting in the light of contemporary philosophy: to mention only one example, Károly Tolnai has attempted to interpret the pictures of the elder Brueghel as evidence of a pantheistic monism paralleling Cusanus or Paracelsus and anticipating Spinoza and Goethe. Even more dangerous is an "explanation" of the arts in terms of a "time spirit," as practiced by German *Geistesgeschichte*, a movement which we have criticized in a different context.

The genuine parallelisms which follow from the identical or similar social or intellectual background scarcely ever have been analyzed in concrete terms. We have no studies which would concretely show how, for example, all the arts in a given time or setting expand or narrow their field over the objects of "nature," or how the norms of art are tied to specific social classes and thus subject to uniform changes, or how aesthetic values change with social revolutions. Here is a wide field for investigation which has been scarcely touched, yet promises concrete results for the comparison of the arts. Of course, only similar influences on the evolution of the different arts can be proved by this method, *not* any necessary parallelism.

Obviously, the most central approach to a composition of the arts is based on an analysis of the actual objects of art, and thus of their structural relationships. There will never be a proper history of an art, not to speak of a comparative history of the arts, unless we concentrate on an analysis of the works themselves and relegate to the background studies in the psychology of the reader and the spectator or the author and the artist as well as studies in the cultural and social background, however illuminating they may be from their own point of view. Unfortunately hitherto we have had scarcely any tools for such a comparison between the arts. Here a very difficult question arises: What are the common and the comparable elements of the arts? We see no light in a theory like Croce's, which concentrates all aesthetic problems on the act of intuition, mysteriously identified with expression. Croce asserts the non-existence of modes of expression and condemns "any attempt at an aesthetic classification of the arts as absurd" and thus *a fortiori* rejects all distinction between genres or types. Nor is much gained for our problem by John Dewey's insistence, in his *Art as Experience* (1934), that there is a common substance among the arts because there are "general conditions without which an experience is not possible." No doubt, there is a common denominator in the act of all artistic creation or, for that matter, in all human creation, activity, and experience. But these are solutions which do not help us in comparing the arts. More concretely, Theodore Meyer Greene defines the comparable elements of the arts as complexity, integration, and rhythm, and he argues eloquently, as John Dewey had done before him, for the applicability of the term "rhythm" to the plastic arts. It seems, however, impossible to overcome the profound distinction between the rhythm of a piece of music and the rhythm of a colonnade, where neither the order nor the tempo is imposed by the structure of the work itself. Complexity and integration are merely other terms for "variety" and "unity" and thus of only very limited use. Few concrete attempts to arrive at such common denominators among the arts on a structural basis have gone any further. G. D. Birkhoff, a Harvard mathematician, in a book on *Aesthetic Measure*, has with apparent success tried to find a common mathematical basis for simple art forms and music and he has included a study of the "musicality" of verse which is also defined in mathematical equations and coefficients. But the problem of euphony in verse cannot be solved in isolation from meaning, and Birkhoff's high grades for poems by Edgar Allen Poe seem to confirm such an assumption. His ingenious attempt, if accepted, would tend rather to widen the gulf between the essentially "literary" qualities of poetry and the other arts which share much more fully in "aesthetic measure" than literature.

The problem of the parallelism of the arts early suggested the application to literature of style-concepts arrived at in the history of the arts. In the eighteenth century, innumerable comparisons were made between the structure of Spenser's *Faerie Queene* and the glorious disorder of a Gothic cathedral. In *The Decline of the*

West, analogizing all the arts of a culture, Spengler speaks of the "visible chamber music of the bent furniture, the mirror rooms, pastorals and porcelain groups of the eighteenth century," mentions the "Titian style of the madrigal," and refers to the *allegro feroce* of Franz Hals and the *andante con moto* of Van Dyck." In Germany this mode of analogizing the arts has incited copious writing on the Gothic man and the spirit of the Baroque, has led to the literary use of the terms "Rococo" and "Biedermeier." In the periodization of literature, the clearly worked-out sequence of art styles of Gothic, Renaissance, Baroque, Rococo, Romanticism, Biedermeier, Realism, Impressionism, Expressionism has impressed literary historians and has imposed itself also on literature. The styles named are grouped into two main groups, presenting fundamentally the contrast between the Classical and the Romantic: Gothic, the Baroque, Romanticism, Expressionism appear on one line; the Renaissance, Neo-Classicism, Realism on the other. Rococo, Biedermeier, can be interpreted as late decadent, florid variations of the preceding styles—respectively Baroque and Romanticism. Frequently the parallelisms are pressed very hard; and it is easy to pick out absurdities from the writings of even the most reputable scholars who have indulged in the method.

The most concrete attempt to transfer the categories of art history to literature is Oskar Walzel's application of Wölfflin's criteria. In his *Principles of Art History*, Wölfflin distinguished, on purely structural grounds, between Renaissance and Baroque art. He constructed a scheme of contraries applicable to any kind of picture, pieces of sculpture, or specimen of architecture in the period. Renaissance art, he held, is "linear," while Baroque art is "painterly." "Linear" suggests that the outlines of figures and objects are drawn clearly, while "painterly" means that light and color, which blur the outlines of objects, are themselves the principles of comparison. Renaissance painting and sculpture use a "closed" form, a symmetrical, balanced grouping of figures or surfaces, while Baroque prefers an "open" form, an unsymmetrical composition which puts emphasis on a corner of a picture rather than its center, or even points beyond the frame of the picture. Renaissance pictures are "flat" or, at least, composed on different recessive planes, while Baroque pictures are "deep" or seem to lead the eye into a distant and indistinct background. Renaissance pictures are "multiple" in the sense of having clearly distinct parts; Baroque works are "unified," highly integrated, closely knit. Renaissance works of art are "clear," while Baroque works are relatively "unclear," blurred, indistinct.

Wölfflin demonstrated his conclusions by an admirably sensitive analysis of concrete works of art and suggested the necessity of the progression from the Renaissance to the Baroque. Certainly their sequence cannot be inverted. Wölfflin offers no causal explanation of the process, except that he suggests a change in the "manner of seeing," a process which, however, hardly can be thought of as purely physiological. This view, with its stress on changes in the "manner of seeing," on the purely structural, compositional changes, goes back to the theories of Fiedler and Hildebrand concerning pure visibility, and is ultimately derived from Zimmermann, an Herbartian aesthetician. But Wölfflin himself, especially in later pronouncements, recognized the limitations of his method and by no means thought that his history of forms had exhausted all the problems of art history. Even early he admitted "personal" and "local" styles and saw that his types could be found elsewhere than in the sixteenth and seventeenth centuries, though in a less clearly defined form.

In 1916, fresh from the reading of the *Principles of Art History*, Walzel attempted to transfer Wölfflin's categories to literature. Studying the composition of Shakespeare's plays, he came to the conclusion that Shakespeare belongs to the Baroque, since his plays are not built in the symmetrical manner found by Wölfflin in pictures of the Renaissance. The number of minor characters, their unsymmetrical grouping, the varying emphasis on different acts of the play: all these characteristics are supposed to show that Shakespeare's technique is the same as that of Baroque art, while Corneille and Racine, who composed their tragedies around one central figure and distributed the emphasis among the acts according to a traditional Aristotelian pattern, are assigned to the Renaissance type. In a little book, *Wechselseitige Erhellung der Künste*, and in many later writings, Walzel tried to elaborate and justify this transfer, at first rather modestly and then with increasingly extravagant claims.

Some of Wölfflin's categories can clearly and rather easily be reformulated in literary terms. There is an obvious opposition between an art which prefers clear outlines and distinct parts and an art with looser composition and blurred outlines. Fritz Strich's attempt to describe the opposition between German Classicism and Romanticism by applying Wölfflin's categories devised for the Renaissance and Baroque shows that these categories, liberally interpreted, can restate the old oppositions between the perfect Classical poem and the unfinished, fragmentary, or blurred Romantic poetry. But we are then left with only one set of contraries for all the history of literature. Even reformulated in strictly literary terms, Wölfflin's categories help us merely to arrange works of art into two categories which, when examined in detail, amount only to the old distinction between classic and romantic, severe and loose structure, plastic and picturesque art: a dualism which was known to the Schlegels and to Schelling and Coleridge and was arrived at by them through ideological and literary arguments. Wölfflin's one set of contraries manages to group all Classical and pseudo-Classical art together, on the one hand, and on the other to combine very divergent movements such as the Gothic, the Baroque, and Romanticism. This theory appears to obscure the undoubted and extremely important continuity between the Renaissance and Baroque, just as its application to German literature by Strich makes an artificial contrast between the pseudo-Classical stage in the development of Schiller and Goethe and the Romantic movement of the early nineteenth century, while it must leave the "Storm and Stress" unexplained and incomprehensible. Actually, German literature at the turn of the eighteenth and nineteenth centuries forms a comparative unity which it seems impossible to break up into an irreconcilable antithesis. Thus, Wölfflin's theory may help us in classifying works of art and establishing or rather confirming the old action-reaction, convention-revolt, or seesaw type of dualistic evolutionary scheme, which, however, confronted with the reality of the complex process of literature, falls far short of coping with the highly diversified pattern of the actual development.

The transfer of Wölfflin's pairs of concepts also leaves one important problem completely unsolved. We cannot explain in any way the undoubted fact that the arts did not evolve with the same speed at the same time. Literature seems sometimes to linger behind the arts: for instance, we can scarcely speak of an English literature when the great English cathedrals were being built. At other times music lags behind literature and the other arts: for instance, we cannot speak of "Romantic" music before 1800, while much Romantic poetry preceded that date. We have difficulty in accounting for the

fact that there was "picturesque" poetry at least sixty years before
the picturesque invaded architecture or for the fact, mentioned
by Burckhardt, that *Nencia*, the description of peasant life by Lo-
renzo Magnifico, preceded by some eighty years the first genre
pictures of Jacopo Bassano and his school. Even if these few examples were wrongly chosen and could be refuted, they raise a
question which cannot be answered by an over-simple theory according to which, let us say, music is always lagging by a generation after poetry. Obviously a correlation with social factors should
be attempted, and these factors will vary in every single instance.

We are finally confronted with the problem that certain times
or nations were extremely productive only in one or two arts,
while either completely barren or merely imitative and derivative
in others. The flowering of Elizabethan literature, which was not accompanied by any comparable flowering of the fine arts, is a case
in point; and little is gained by speculations to the effect that the
"national soul," in some way, concentrated on one art or that, as
Émile Legouis phrases it in his *History of English Literature*,
"Spenser would have become a Titian or Veronese had he been born
in Italy or a Rubens or Rembrandt in the Netherlands." In the case
of English literature it is easy to suggest that Puritanism was responsible for the neglect of the fine arts, but that is scarcely enough
to account for the differences between the productivity in very
secular literature and the comparative barrenness in painting. But all
this leads us far afield into concrete historical questions.

The various arts—the plastic arts, literature, and music—have
each their individual evolution, with a different tempo and a different internal structure of elements. No doubt they are in constant
relationship with each other, but these relationships are not influences which start from one point and determine the evolution of
the other arts; they have to be conceived rather as a complex scheme
of dialectical relationships which work both ways, from one art to
another and vice versa, and may be completely transformed within
the art which they have entered. It is not a simple affair of a "time
spirit" determining and permeating each and every art. We must
conceive of the sum total of man's cultural activities as of a whole
system of self-evolving series, each having its own set of norms
which are not necessarily identical with those of the neighboring
series. The task of art historians in the widest sense, including historians of literature and of music, is to evolve a set of descriptive

terms in each art, based on the specific characteristics of each art. Thus poetry today needs a new poetics, a technique of analysis which cannot be arrived at by a simple transfer or adaptation of terms from the fine arts. Only when we have evolved a successful system of terms for the analysis of literary works of art can we delimit literary periods, not as metaphysical entities dominated by a "time spirit." Having established such outlines of strictly literary evolution, we then can ask the question whether this evolution is, in some way, similar to the similarly established evolution of the other arts. The answer will be, as we can see, not a flat "yes" or "no." It will take the form of an intricate pattern of coincidences and divergences rather than parallel lines.

Georg Wilhelm Friedrich Hegel

STYLE AND THE ARTS*

THE PARTICULAR ARTS

But, now, there inhere in the idea of beauty different modifications which art translates into sensuous forms. And we find a fundamental principle by which the several particular arts may be arranged and defined—that is, the species of art contain in themselves the same essential differences which we have found in the three general types of art.[1] External objectivity, moreover, into which these types

---

* From "The Particular Arts," translated by J. Loewenberg, reprinted with the permission of Charles Scribner's Sons from *Hegel Selections*, pp. 328–337, edited by J. Loewenberg. Copyright 1929 Charles Scribner's Sons; renewal copyright 1956.

[1] The "three general types" are, according to Hegel, "symbolic art," "classical art," and "romantic art." Each general type reveals and is defined by a certain relationship of content to "sensuous medium," e.g., the colors and shapes of paintings, the words of poetry, the spatial organization of stone in sculpture. Each type occurs also in a certain historical epoch and generates problems which are solved subsequently by the introduction of another of the "general types."

"Symbolic art" attaches an "Idea" or content to a "sensuous medium" by exploiting the conventional associations between objects and concepts in its culture. Oriental art is, as a result, "symbolic." It uses animals to represent concepts—a lion stands for "strength"—but it is the culture and not the statue that establishes the connection.

"Classical art" remedies this defect by fashioning a medium that at once represents and embodies its "Idea." Hellenic sculpture is, therefore, "Classical art" because it depicts the notion of "ideal man" in a statue that iterates or expresses itself the ideality of the notion.

"Romantic art" de-emphasizes the sensuous role of the medium and aims

are molded by means of a sensuous and particular material, renders them independent and separate means of realizing different artistic functions, as far as each type finds its definite character in some one definite external material whose mode of portrayal determines its adequate realization. Furthermore, the general types of art correspond to the several particular arts, so that they (the particular arts) belong each of them *specifically* to *one* of the general types of art. It is these particular arts which give adequate and artistic external being to the general types.

ARCHITECTURE

The first of the particular arts with which, according to their fundamental principle, we have to begin, is architecture. Its task consists in so shaping external inorganic nature that it becomes homogeneous with minds, as an artistic outer world. The material of architecture is matter itself in its immediate externality as a heavy mass subject to mechanical laws, and its forms remain the forms of inorganic nature, but are merely arranged and ordered in accordance with the abstract rules of the understanding, the rules of symmetry. But in such material and in such forms the ideal as concrete spirituality cannot be realized; the reality which is represented in them remains, therefore, alien to the spiritual idea, as something external which it has not penetrated or with which it has but a remote and abstract relation. Hence the fundamental type of architecture is the *symbolical* form of art. For it is architecture that paves the way, as it were, for the adequate realization of the God, toiling and wrestling in his service with external nature, and seeking to extricate it from the chaos of finitude, and the abortiveness of chance. By this means it levels a space for the God, frames his external surroundings, and builds him his temple as the place for inner contemplation and for reflection upon the eternal objects of the spirit. It raises an inclosure around those gathered together, as a defense against the threatening of the wind, against rain, the thunderstorm, and wild beasts, and reveals the will to assemble, though externally, yet in acordance with the artistic form. A meaning

---

merely to express Ideas divorced from their material embodiments. The medium is a vehicle for transmitting the Idea but does not affect or reflect whatever is transmitted. Poetry is the romantic art *par excellence*, in this view, because the quality of a poem turns upon the character of the Ideas expressed and not upon the words which express them. (M.L.)

such as this, the art of architecture is able to mold into its material and its forms with more or less success, according as the determinate nature of the content which it seeks to embody is more significant or more trivial, more concrete or more abstract, more deeply rooted within its inner being or more dim and superficial. Indeed, it may even advance so far as to endeavor to create for such meaning an adequate artistic expression with its material and forms, but in such an attempt it has already overstepped the bounds of its own sphere, and inclines towards sculpture, the higher phase of art. For the limit of architecture lies precisely in this, that it refers to the spiritual as an internal essence in contrast with the external forms of its art, and thus whatever is endowed with mind and spirit must be indicated as something other than itself.

SCULPTURE

Architecture, however, has purified the inorganic external world, has given it symmetric order, has impressed upon it the seal of mind, and the temple of the God, the house of his community, stands ready. Into this temple now enters the God himself. The lightning-flash of individuality strikes the inert mass, permeates it, and a form no longer merely symmetrical, but infinite and spiritual, concentrates and molds its adequate bodily shape. This is the task of sculpture. Inasmuch as in it the inner spiritual element, which architecture can no more than hint at, completely abides with the sensuous form and its external matter, and as both sides are so merged into each other that neither predominates, sculpture has the *classical* form of art as its fundamental type. In fact, the sensuous realm itself can command no expression which could not be that of the spiritual sphere, just as, conversely, no spiritual content can attain perfect plasticity in sculpture which is incapable of being adequately presented to perception in bodily form. It is sculpture which arrests for our vision the spirit in its bodily frame, in immediate unity with it, and in an attitude of peace and repose; and the form in turn is animated by the content of spiritual individuality. Therefore the external sensuous matter is here not wrought, either according to its mechanical quality alone, as heavy mass, or in forms peculiar to inorganic nature, or as indifferent to color, etc., but in ideal forms of the human shape, and in the whole of the spatial dimensions. In this last respect sculpture should be credited with having first revealed the inner and spiritual essence in its eternal repose and essential self-possession. To such repose and unity with itself corresponds only that external element which itself persists in unity and repose. Such an element is the form taken in its abstract spatiality. The spirit which sculpture represents is that which is solid in itself, not variously broken up in the play of contingencies and passions; nor does its external form admit of the portrayal of such a manifold play, but it holds to this one side only, to the abstraction of space in the totality of its dimensions.

THE DEVELOPMENT
OF THE ROMANTIC ARTS

After architecture has built the temple and the hand of sculpture has placed inside it the statue of the God, then this sensuously visible God faces in the spacious halls of his house the *community*. The community is the spiritual, self-reflecting element in this sensuous realm, it is the animating subjectivity and inner life. A new principle of art begins with it. Both the content of art and the medium which embodies it in outward form now demand particularization, individualization, and the subjective mode of expressing these. The solid unity which the God possesses in sculpture breaks up into the plurality of inner individual lives, whose unity is not sensuous, but essentially ideal.

And now God comes to assume the aspect which makes him truly spiritual. As a hither-and-thither, as an alteration between the unity within himself and his realization in subjective knowledge and individual consciousness, as well as in the common and unified life of the man individuals, he is genuinely Spirit—the Spirit in his community. In his community God is released from the abstractness of a mysterious self-identity, as well as from the naïve imprisonment in a bodily shape, in which he is represented by sculpture. Here he is exalted into spirituality, subjectivity, and knowledge. For this reason the higher content of art is now this spirituality in its absolute form. But since what chiefly reveals itself in this stage is not the serene repose of God in himself, but rather his appearance, his being, and his manifestation to others, the objects of artistic representation are now the most varied subjective expressions of life and activity for their own sake, as human passions, deeds, events, and, in general, the wide range of human feeling, will, and resignation. In accordance with this content, the sensuous element must differentiate and show itself adequate to the expression of subjective feeling. Such different media are furnished by color, by the musical sound, and finally by the sound as the mere indication of inner intuitions and ideas; and thus as different forms of realizing the spiritual content of art by means of these media we obtain painting, music, and poetry. The sensuous media employed in these arts being individualized and in their essence recognized as ideal, they correspond most effectively to the spiritual content of art, and the union between spiritual meaning and sensuous expression develops, therefore, into greater intimacy than was possible in the case of architecture and sculpture. This intimate unity, however, is due wholly to the subjective side.

Leaving, then, the symbolic spirit of architecture and the classical ideal of sculpture behind, these new arts in which form and content are raised to an ideal level borrow their type from the *romantic* form of art, whose mode of expression they are most eminently fitted to voice. They form, however, a totality of arts, because the romantic type is the most concrete in itself.

PAINTING

The first art in this totality, which is akin to sculpture, is painting. The material which it uses for its content and for the sensuous expression of that content is visibility as such, in so far as it is individualized, viz. specified as color. To be sure, the media employed in architecture and sculpture are also visible and colored, but they are not, as in painting, visibility as such, not the simple light which contrasts itself with darkness and in combination with it becomes color. This visibility as a subjective and ideal attribute, requires neither, like architecture, the abstract mechanical form of mass which we find in heavy matter, nor, like sculpture, the three dimensions of sensuous space, even though in concentrated and organic plasticity, but the visibility which appertains to painting has its differences on a more ideal level, in the particular kind of color; and thus painting frees art from the sensuous completeness in space peculiar to material things only, by confining itself to a plane surface.

On the other hand, the content also gains in varied particularization. Whatever can find room in the human heart, as emotion, idea, and purpose, whatever it is able to frame into a deed, all this variety of material can constitute the many-colored content of painting. The whole range of particular existence, from the highest aspirations of the mind down to the most isolated objects of nature, can obtain a place in this art. For even finite nature, in its particular scenes and aspects, can here appear, if only some allusion to a spiritual element makes it akin to thought and feeling.

MUSIC

The second art in which the romantic form finds realization, on still a higher level than in painting, is music. Its material, though still sensuous, advances to a deeper subjectivity and greater specification. The idealization of the sensuous, music brings about by negating space. In music the indifferent extension of space whose appearance painting admits and consciously imitates is concentrated and idealized into a single point. But in the form of a motion and tremor of the material body within itself, this single point becomes a concrete and active process within the idealization of matter. Such an incipient ideality of matter which no longer appears under the spatial form, but as temporal ideality, is sound—the sensuous acknowledged as ideal, whose abstract visibility is transformed into audibility. Sound, as it were, exempts the ideal from its absorption in matter.

This earliest animation and inspiration of matter furnishes the medium for the inner and intimate life of the spirit, as yet on an indefinite level; it is through the tones of music that the heart pours out its whole scale of feelings and passions. Thus as sculpture constitutes the central point between architecture and the arts of romantic subjectivity, so music forms the centre of the romantic arts, and represents the point of transition between abstract spatial sensuousness, which belongs to painting, and the abstract spirituality of poetry. Within itself music has, like architecture, an abstract quantitative relation, as a contrast to its inward and emotional quality; it also has as its basis a permanent law to which the tones with their combinations and successions must conform.

POETRY

For the third and most spiritual expression of the romantic form of art, we must look to poetry. Its characteristic peculiarity lies in the power with which it subjugates to the mind and to its ideas the sensuous element from which music and painting began to set art free. For sound, the one external medium of which poetry avails itself, is in it no longer a feeling of the tone itself, but is a sign which is, by itself, meaningless. This sign, moreover, is a sign of an idea which has become concrete, and not merely of indefinite feeling and of its *nuances* and grades. By this means the tone becomes the *word*, an articulate voice, whose function it is to indicate thoughts and ideas. The negative point to which music had advanced now reveals itself in poetry as the completely concrete point, as the spirit or the self-consciousness of the individual, which spontaneously unites the infinite space of its ideas with the time-element of sound. But this sensuous element which, in music, was still in immediate union with inner feelings and moods, is, in poetry, divorced from the content of consciousness, for in poetry the mind determines this content on its own account and for the sake of its ideas, and while it employs sound to express them, yet sound itself is reduced to a symbol without value or meaning. From this point of view sound may just as well be considered a mere letter, for the audible, like the visible, is now relegated to a mere suggestion of mind. Thus the genuine mode of poetic representation is the inner perception and the poetic imagination itself. And since all types of art share in this mode, poetry runs through them all, and develops itself independently in each. Poetry, then, is the universal art of the spirit which has attained inner freedom, and which does not depend for its realization upon external sensuous matter, but expatiates only in the inner space and inner time of the ideas and feelings. But just in this, its highest phase, art oversteps the bounds of its own sphere by abandoning the harmoniously sensuous mode of portraying the spirit and by passing from the poetry of imagination into the prose of thought.

SUMMARY

Such, then, is the organic totality of the several arts; the external art of architecture, the objective art of sculpture, and the subjective arts of painting, music, and poetry. The higher principle from which these are derived we have found in the types of art, the symbolic, the classical, and the romantic, which form the universal phases of the idea of beauty itself. Thus symbolic art finds its most adequate reality and most perfect application in architecture, in which it is self-complete, and is not yet reduced, so to speak, to the inorganic medium for another art. The classical form of art, on the other hand, attains its most complete realization in sculpture, while it accepts architecture only as forming an inclosure round its products and is as yet not capable of developing painting and music as absolute expressions of its meaning. The romantic type of art, finally, seizes upon painting, music, and poetry as its essential and adequate modes of expression. Poetry, however, is in conformity with all types of the beautiful and extends over them all, because its characteristic element is the aesthetic imagination, and imagination is necessary for every product of art, to whatever type it may belong.

Thus what the particular arts realize in individual artistic creations are, according to the philosophic conception, simply the universal types of the self-unfolding idea of beauty. Out of the external realization of this idea arises the wide Pantheon of art, whose architect and builder is the self-developing spirit of beauty, for the completion of which, however, the history of the world will require its evolution of countless ages.

"Tragedy" as a Kind of "Style"

Aristotle

ON THE ART OF POETRY*

VI

Reserving hexameter poetry and Comedy for consideration hereafter, let us proceed now to the discussion of Tragedy; before
doing so, however, we must gather up the definition resulting from
what has been said. A tragedy, then, is the imitation of an action
that is serious and also, as having magnitude, complete in itself;
in language with pleasurable accessories, each kind brought in
separately in the parts of the work; in a dramatic, not in a narrative
form; with incidents arousing pity and fear, wherewith to accomplish its catharsis of such emotions. Here by "language
with pleasurable accessories" I mean that with rhythm and harmony
or song superadded; and by "the kinds separately" I mean that some
portions are worked out with verse only, and others in turn with
song.

I. As they act the stories, it follows that in the first place the
Spectacle (or stage-appearance of the actors) must be some part of

---

* From Aristotle, *On the Art of Poetry*, trans. by Ingram Bywater, Parts
6-15 (Oxford: The Clarendon Press, 1920). Reprinted by permission of the
publisher.

the whole; and in the second Melody and Diction, these two being the means of their imitation. Here by "Diction" I mean merely this, the composition of the verses; and by "Melody," what is too completely understood to require explanation. But further: the subject represented also is an action; and the action involves agents, who must necessarily have their distinctive qualities both of character and thought, since it is from these that we ascribe certain qualities to their actions. There are in the natural order of things, therefore, two causes, Character and Thought, of their actions, and consequently of their success or failure in their lives. Now the action (that which was done) is represented in the play by the Fable or Plot. The Fable, in our present sense of the term, is simply this, the combination of the incidents, or things done in the story; whereas Character is what makes us ascribe certain moral qualities to the agents; and Thought is shown in all they say when proving a particular point or, it may be, enunciating a general truth. There are six parts consequently of every tragedy, as a whole, that is, of such or such quality, viz. a Fable or Plot, Characters, Diction, Thought, Spectacle and Melody; two of them arising from the means, one from the manner, and three from the objects of the dramatic imitation; and there is nothing else besides these six. Of these, its formative elements, then, not a few of the dramatists have made due use, as every play, one may say, admits of Spectacle, Character, Fable, Diction, Melody, and Thought.

II. The most important of the six is the combination of the incidents of the story. Tragedy is essentially an imitation not of persons but of action and life, of happiness and misery. All human happiness or misery takes the form of action; the end for which we live is a certain kind of activity, not a quality. Character gives us qualities, but it is in our actions—what we do—that we are happy or the reverse. In a play accordingly they do not act in order to portray the Characters; they include the Characters for the sake of the action. So that it is the action in it, i.e. its Fable or Plot, that is the end and purpose of the tragedy; and the end is everywhere the chief thing. Besides this, a tragedy is impossible without action, but there may be one without Character. The tragedies of most of the moderns are characterless—a defect common among poets of all kinds, and with its counterpart in painting in Zeuxis as compared with Polygnotus; for whereas the latter is strong in character, the work of Zeuxis is devoid of it. And again: one may string together a series of characteristic speeches of the utmost finish as regards Diction and Thought, and yet fail to produce the true tragic effect; but one will have much better success with a tragedy which, however inferior in these respects, has a Plot, a combination of incidents in it. And again: the most powerful elements of attraction in Tragedy, the Peripeties and Discoveries, are parts of the Plot. A further proof is in the fact that beginners succeed earlier with the Diction and Characters than with the construction of a story; and the same may be said of nearly all the early dramatists. We maintain, therefore, that the first essential, the life and soul, so to speak, of Tragedy is the Plot; and that the Characters come second—compare the parallel in painting, where the most beautiful colours laid on without order will not give one the same pleasure as a simple black-and-white sketch of a portrait. We maintain that Tragedy is primarily an imitation of action, and that it is mainly for the sake of the action that it imitates the personal agents. Third comes the element of Thought, i.e. the power of saying whatever can be said, or what is appropriate to the occasion. This is what, in the speeches in Tragedy, falls under the arts of Politics and Rhetoric; for the older poets make their personages discourse like statesmen, and the moderns like rhetoricians. One must not confuse it with Character. Character in a play is that which reveals the moral purpose of the agents, i.e. the sort of thing they seek or avoid, where that is not obvious—hence there is no room for Character in a speech on a purely indifferent subject. Thought, on the other hand, is shown in all they say when proving or disproving some particular point, or enunciating some universal proposition. Fourth among the literary elements is the Diction of the personages, i.e. as before explained, the expression of their thoughts in words, which is practically the same thing with verse as with prose. As for the two remaining parts, the Melody is the greatest of the pleasurable accessories of Tragedy. The Spectacle, though an attraction, is the least artistic of all the parts, and has least to do with the art of poetry. The tragic effect is quite possible without a public performance and actors; and besides, the getting-up of the Spectacle is more a matter for the costumier than the poet.

VII

Having thus distinguished the parts, let us now consider the proper construction of the Fable or Plot, as that is at once the first and the most important thing in Tragedy. We have laid it down that a tragedy is an imitation of an action that is complete in itself, as a whole of some magnitude; for a whole may be of no magnitude to speak of. Now a whole is that which has beginning, middle, and end. A beginning is that which is not itself necessarily after anything else, and which has naturally something else after it; an end is that which is naturally after something itself, either as its necessary or usual consequent, and with nothing else after it; and a middle, that which is by nature after one thing and has also another after it. A well-constructed Plot, therefore, cannot either begin or end at any point one likes; beginning and end in it must be of the forms just described. Again: to be beautiful, a living creature, and every whole made up of parts, must not only present a certain order in its arrangement of parts, but also be of a certain definite magnitude. Beauty is a matter of size and order, and therefore impossible either (1) in a very minute creature, since our perception becomes indistinct as it approaches instantaneity; or (2) in a creature of vast size—one, say, 1,000 miles long—as in that case, instead of the object being seen all at once, the unity and wholeness of it is lost to the beholder. Just in the same way, then, as a beautiful whole made up of parts, or a beautiful living creature, must be of some size, a size to be taken in by the eye, so a story or Plot must be of some length, but of a length to be taken in by the memory. As for the limit of its length, so far as that is relative to public performances and spectators, it does not fall within the theory of poetry. If they had to perform a hundred tragedies, they would be timed by water-clocks, as they are said to have been at one period. The limit, however, set by the actual nature of the thing is this: the longer the story, consistently with its being comprehensible as a whole, the finer it is by reason of its magnitude. As a rough general formula, "a length which allows of the hero passing by a series of probable or necessary stages from misfortune to happiness, or from happiness to misfortune," may suffice as a limit for the magnitude of the story.

VIII

The Unity of a Plot does not consist, as some suppose, in its having one man as its subject. An infinity of things befall that one man, some of which it is impossible to reduce to unity; and in like manner there are many actions of one man which cannot be made to form one action. One sees, therefore, the mistake of all the poets who have written a *Heracleid*, a *Theseid*, or similar poems;

they suppose that, because Heracles was one man, the story also of Heracles must be one story. Homer, however, evidently understood this point quite well, whether by art or instinct, just in the same way as he excels the rest in every other respect. In writing an *Odyssey*, he did not make the poem cover all that ever befell his hero—it befell him, for instance, to get wounded on Parnassus and also to feign madness at the time of the call to arms, but the two incidents had no probable or necessary connexion with one another —instead of doing that, he took an action with a Unity of the kind we are describing as the subject of the *Odyssey*, as also of the *Iliad*. The truth is that, just as in the other imitative arts one imitation is always of one thing, so in poetry the story, as an imitation of action, must represent one action, a complete whole, with its several incidents so closely connected that the transposal or withdrawal of any one of them will disjoin and dislocate the whole. For that which makes no perceptible difference by its presence or absence is no real part of the whole.

IX

From what we have said it will be seen that the poet's function is to describe, not the thing that has happened, but a kind of thing that might happen, i.e. what is possible as being probable or necessary. The distinction between historian and poet is not in the one writing prose and the other verse—you might put the work of Herodotus into verse, and it would still be a species of history; it consists really in this, that the one describes the thing that has been, and the other a kind of think that might be. Hence poetry is something more philosophic and of graver import than history, since its statements are of the nature rather of universals, whereas those of history are singulars. By a universal statement I mean one as to what such or such a kind of man will probably or necessarily say or do—which is the aim of poetry, though it affixes proper names to the characters; by a singular statement, one as to what, say, Alcibiades did or had done to him. In Comedy this has become clear by this time; it is only when their plot is already made up of probable incidents that they give it a basis of proper names, choosing for the purpose any names that may occur to them, instead of writing like the old iambic poets about particular persons. In Tragedy, however, they still adhere to the historic names; and for this reason: what convinces is the possible; now whereas we are not yet

sure as to the possibility of that which has not happened, that which
has happened is manifestly possible, else it would not have come
to pass. Nevertheless even in Tragedy there are some plays with
but one or two known names in them, the rest being inventions;
and there are some without a single known name, e.g. Agathon's
Antheus, in which both incidents and names are of the poet's invention; and it is no less delightful on that account. So that one must
not aim at a rigid adherence to the traditional stories on which
tragedies are based. It would be absurd, in fact, to do so, as even
the known stories are only known to a few, though they are a
delight none the less to all.

It is evident from the above that the poet must be more the poet
of his stories or Plots than of his verses, inasmuch as he is a poet
by virtue of the imitative element in his work, and it is actions that
he imitates. And if he should come to take a subject from actual
history, he is none the less a poet for that; since some historic
occurrences may very well be in the probable and possible order
of things; and it is in that aspect of them that he is their poet.

Of simple Plots and actions the episodic are the worst. I call a
Plot episodic when there is neither probability nor necessity in the
sequence of its episodes. Actions of this sort bad poets construct
through their own fault, and good ones on account of the players.
His work being for public performance, a good poet often stretches
out a Plot beyond its capabilities, and is thus obliged to twist the
sequence of incident.

Tragedy, however, is an imitation not only of a complete action,
but also of incidents arousing pity and fear. Such incidents have
the very greatest effect on the mind when they occur unexpectedly
and at the same time in consequence of one another; there is more
of the marvellous in them then than if they happened of themselves
or by mere chance. Even matters of chance seem most marvellous
if there is an appearance of design as it were in them; as for instance
the statue of Mitys at Argos killed the author of Mitys' death by
falling down on him when a looker-on at a public spectacle; for
incidents like that we think to be not without a meaning. A Plot,
therefore, of this sort is necessarily finer than others.

X

Plots are either simple or complex, since the actions they represent
are naturally of this twofold description. The action, proceeding

in the way defined, as one continuous whole, I call simple, when the change in the hero's fortunes takes place without Peripety or Discovery; and complex, when it involves one or the other, or both. These should each of them arise out of the structure of the Plot itself, so as to be the consequence, necessary or probable, of the antecedents. There is a great difference between a thing happening *propter hoc* and *post hoc*.

XI

A Peripety is the change from one state of things within the play to its opposite of the kind described, and that too in the way we are saying, in the probable or necessary sequence of events; as it is for instance in *Oedipus:* here the opposite state of things is produced by the Messenger, who, coming to gladden Oedipus and to remove his fears as to his mother, reveals the secret of his birth. And in *Lynceus:* just as he is being led off for execution, with Danaus at his side to put him to death, the incidents preceding this bring it about that he is saved and Danaus put to death. A Discovery is, as the very word implies, a change from ignorance to knowledge, and thus to either love or hate, in the personages marked for good or evil fortune. The finest form of Discovery is one attended by Peripeties, like that which goes with the Discovery in *Oedipus.* There are no doubt other forms of it; what we have said may happen in a way in reference to inanimate things, even things of a very casual kind; and it is also possible to discover whether some one has done or not done something. But the form most directly connected with the Plot and the action of the piece is the first-mentioned. This, with a Peripety, will arouse either pity or fear—actions of that nature being what Tragedy is assumed to represent; and it will also serve to bring about the happy or unhappy ending. The Discovery, then, being of persons, it may be that of one party only to the other, the latter being already known; or both the parties may have to discover themselves. Iphigenia, for instance, was discovered to Orestes by sending the letter; and another Discovery was required to reveal him to Iphigenia.

Two parts of the Plot, then, Peripety and Discovery, are on matters of this sort. A third part is Suffering; which we may define as an action of a destructive or painful nature, such as murders on the stage, tortures, woundings, and the like. The other two have been already explained.

XII

The parts of Tragedy to be treated as formative elements in the whole were mentioned in a previous Chapter. From the point of view, however, of its quantity, i.e. the separate sections into which it is divided, a tragedy has the following parts: Prologue, Episode, Exode, and a choral portion, distinguished into Parode and Stasimon; these two are common to all tragedies, whereas songs from the stage and *Commoe* are only found in some. The Prologue is all that precedes the Parode of the chorus; an Episode all that comes in between two whole choral songs; the Exode all that follows after the last choral song. In the choral portion the Parode is the whole first statement of the chorus; a Stasimon, a song of the chorus without anapaests or trochees; a *Commos*, a lamentation sung by chorus and actor in concert. The parts of Tragedy to be used as formative elements in the whole we have already mentioned; the above are its parts from the point of view of its quantity, or the separate sections into which it is divided.

XIII

The next points after what we have said above will be these: (1) What is the poet to aim at, and what is he to avoid, in constructing his Plots? and (2) What are the conditions on which the tragic effect depends?

We assume that, for the finest form of Tragedy, the Plot must be not simple but complex; and further, that it must imitate actions arousing pity and fear, since that is the distinctive function of this kind of imitation. It follows, therefore, that there are three forms of Plot to be avoided. (1) A good man must not be seen passing from happiness to misery, or (2) a bad man from misery to happiness. The first situation is not fear-inspiring or piteous, but simply odious to us. The second is the most untragic that can be; it has no one of the requisites of Tragedy; it does not appeal either to the human feeling in us, or to our pity, or to our fears. Nor, on the other hand, should (3) an extremely bad man be seen falling from happiness into misery. Such a story may arouse the human feeling in us, but it will not move us to either pity or fear; pity is occasioned by undeserved misfortune, and fear by that of one like ourselves; so that there will be nothing either piteous or fear-inspiring in the situation. There remains, then, the intermediate kind of personage,

a man not pre-eminently virtuous and just, whose misfortune, however, is brought upon him not by vice and depravity but by some
error of judgment, of the number of those in the enjoyment of
great reputation and prosperity; e.g. Oedipus, Thyestes, and the
men of note of similar families. The perfect Plot, accordingly,
must have a single, and not (as some tell us) a double issue; the
change in the hero's fortunes must be not from misery to happiness,
but on the contrary from happiness to misery; and the cause of it
must lie not in any depravity, but in some great error on his
part; the man himself being either such as we have described, or
better, not worse, than that. Fact also confirms our theory. Though
the poets began by accepting any tragic story that came to hand,
in these days the finest tragedies are always on the story of some
few houses, on that of Alcmeon, Oedipus, Orestes, Meleager,
Thyestes, Telephus, or any others that may have been involved,
as either agents or sufferers, in some deed of horror. The theoretically best tragedy, then, has a Plot of this description. The
critics, therefore, are wrong who blame Euripides for taking
this line in his tragedies, and giving many of them an unhappy
ending. It is, as we have said, the right line to take. The best
proof is this: on the stage, and in the public performances, such
plays, properly worked out, are seen to be the most truly tragic;
and Euripides, even if his execution be faulty in every other point,
is seen to be nevertheless the most tragic certainly of the dramatists.
After this comes the construction of Plot which some rank first,
one with a double story (like the *Odyssey*) and an opposite issue
for the good and the bad personages. It is ranked as first only
through the weakness of the audiences; the poets merely follow
their public, writing as its wishes dictate. But the pleasure here
is not that of Tragedy. It belongs rather to Comedy, where the
bitterest enemies in the piece (e.g. Orestes and Aegisthus) walk
off good friends at the end, with no slaying of any one by any one.

XIV

The tragic fear and pity may be aroused by the Spectacle; but
they may also be aroused by the very structure and incidents of
the play—which is the better way and shows the better poet. The
Plot in fact should be so framed that, even without seeing the
things take place, he who simply hears the account of them shall
be filled with horror and pity at the incidents; which is just the

effect that the mere recital of the story in *Oedipus* would have on one. To produce this same effect by means of the Spectacle is less artistic, and requires extraneous aid. Those, however, who make use of the Spectacle to put before us that which is merely monstrous and not productive of fear, are wholly out of touch with Tragedy; not every kind of pleasure should be required of a tragedy, but only its own proper pleasure.

The tragic pleasure is that of pity and fear, and the poet has to produce it by the work of imitation; it is clear, therefore, that the causes should be included in the incidents of his story. Let us see, then, what kinds of incident strike one as horrible, or rather as piteous. In a deed of this description the parties must necessarily be either friends, or enemies, or indifferent to one another. Now when enemy does it on enemy, there is nothing to move us to pity either in his doing or in his meditating the deed, except so far as the actual pain of the sufferer is concerned; and the same is true when the parties are indifferent to one another. Whenever the tragic deed, however, is done within the family—when murder or the like is done or meditated by brother on brother, by son on father, by mother on son, or son on mother—these are the situations the poet should seek after. The traditional stories, accordingly, must be kept as they are, e.g. the murder of Clytaemnestra by Orestes and of Eriphyle by Alcmeon. At the same time even with these there is something left to the poet himself; it is for him to devise the right way of treating them. Let us explain more clearly what we mean by "the right way." The deed of horror may be done by the doer knowingly and consciously, as in the old poets, and in Medea's murder of her children in Euripides. Or he may do it, but in ignorance of his relationship, and discover that afterwards, as does the Oedipus in Sophocles. Here the deed is outside the play; but it may be within it, like the act of the Alcmeon in Astydamas, or that of the Telegonus in *Ulysses Wounded*. A third possibility is for one meditating some deadly injury to another, in ignorance of his relationship, to make the discovery in time to draw back. These exhaust the possibilities, since the deed must necessarily be either done or not done, and either knowingly or unknowingly.

The worst situation is when the personage is with full knowledge on the point of doing the deed, and leaves it undone. It is odious and also (through the absence of suffering) untragic; hence it is that no one is made to act thus except in some few instances, e.g.

Haemon and Creon in *Antigone*. Next after this comes the actual perpetration of the deed meditated. A better situation than that, however, is for the deed to be done in ignorance, and the relationship discovered afterwards, since there is nothing odious in it, and the Discovery will serve to astound us. But the best of all is the last; what we have in *Cresphontes*, for example, where Merope, on the point of slaying her son, recognizes him in time; in *Iphigenia*, where sister and brother are in a like position; and in *Helle*, where the son recognizes his mother, when on the point of giving her up to her enemy.

This will explain why our tragedies are restricted (as we said just now) to such a small number of families. It was accident rather than art that led the poets in quest of subjects to embody this kind of incident in their Plots. They are still obliged, accordingly, to have recourse to the families in which such horrors have occurred.

On the construction of the Plot, and the kind of Plot required for Tragedy, enough has now been said.

XV

In the Characters there are four points to aim at. First and foremost, that they shall be good. There will be an element of character in the play, if (as has been observed) what a personage says or does reveals a certain moral purpose; and a good element of character, if the purpose so revealed is good. Such goodness is possible in every type of personage, even in a woman or a slave, though the one is perhaps an inferior, and the other a wholly worthless being. The second point is to make them appropriate. The Character before us may be, say, manly; but it is not appropriate in a female Character to be manly, or clever. The third is to make them like the reality, which is not the same as their being good and appropriate, in our sense of the term. The fourth is to make them consistent and the same throughout; even if inconsistency be part of the man before one for imitation as presenting that form of character, he should still be consistently inconsistent. We have an instance of baseness of character, not required for the story, in the Menelaus in *Orestes;* of the incongruous and unbefitting in the lamentation of Ulysses in *Scylla*, and in the (clever) speech of Melanippe; and of inconsistency in *Iphigenia at Aulis*, where Iphigenia the suppliant is utterly unlike the later Iphigenia. The right thing, however, is in the Characters just as in the incidents of the play to endeavour always after the necessary or the probable; so that whenever such-and-such a personage says or does such-and-such a thing, it shall be the probable or necessary outcome of his character; and whenever this incident follows on that, it shall be either the necessary or the probable consequence of it. From this one sees (to digress for a moment) that the Dénouement also should arise out of the plot itself, and not depend on a stage-artifice, as in *Medea*, or in the story of the (arrested) departure of the Greeks in the *Iliad*. The artifice must be reserved for matters outside the play—for past events beyond human knowledge, or events yet to come, which require to be foretold or announced; since it is the privilege of the Gods to know everything. There should be nothing improbable among the actual incidents. If it be unavoidable, however, it should be outside the tragedy, like the improbability in the *Oedipus* of Sophocles. But to return to the Characters. As Tragedy is an imitation of personages better than the ordinary man, we in our way should follow the example of good portrait-painters, who reproduce the distinctive features of a man, and at the same time, without losing the likeness, make him handsomer than he is. The poet in like manner, in portraying men quick or slow to anger, or with similar infirmities of character, must know how to represent them as such, and at the same time as good men, as Agathon and Homer have represented Achilles.

All these rules one must keep in mind throughout, and further, those also for such points of stage-effect as directly depend on the art of the poet, since in these too one may often make mistakes. Enough, however, has been said on the subject in one of our published writings.

Joseph Wood Krutch

THE TRAGIC FALLACY*

Through the legacy of their art the great ages have transmitted to us a dim image of their glorious vitality. When we turn the pages of a Sophoclean or a Shakespearean tragedy we participate faintly in the experience which created it and we sometimes presumptuously say that we "understand" the spirit of these works. But the truth is that we see them, even at best and in the moments when our souls expand most nearly to their dimensions, through a glass darkly.

It is so much easier to appreciate than to create that an age too feeble to reach the heights achieved by the members of a preceding one can still see those heights towering above its impotence, and so it is that, when we perceive a Sophocles or a Shakespeare soaring in an air which we can never hope to breathe, we say that we can "appreciate" them. But what we mean is that we are just able to wonder, and we can never hope to participate in the glorious vision of human life out of which they were created—not even to the extent of those humbler persons for whom they were written; for while to us the triumphant voices come from far away and tell of a heroic world which no longer exists, to them they spoke of immediate realities and revealed the inner meaning of events amidst which they still lived.

When the life has entirely gone out of a work of art come down

* From *The Modern Temper* by Joseph Wood Krutch, copyright, 1929, by Harcourt, Brace & World, Inc.; renewed, 1956, by Joseph Wood Krutch. Reprinted by permission of the publishers.

to us from the past, when we read it without any emotional com-
prehension whatsoever and can no longer even imagine why the
people for whom it was intended found it absorbing and satisfying,
then, of course, it has ceased to be a work of art at all and has
dwindled into one of those deceptive "documents" from which we
get a false sense of comprehending through the intellect things
which cannot be comprehended at all except by means of a kinship
of feeling. And though all works from a past age have begun in this
way to fade there are some, like the great Greek or Elizabethan
tragedies, which are still halfway between the work of art and the
document. They no longer can have for us the immediacy which
they had for those to whom they originally belonged, but they
have not yet eluded us entirely. We no longer live in the world
which they represent, but we can half imagine it and we can
measure the distance which we have moved away. We write no
tragedies today, but we can still talk about the tragic spirit of which
we would, perhaps, have no conception were it not for the works
in question.

An age which could really "appreciate" Shakespeare or Sophocles
would have something comparable to put beside them—something
like them, not necessarily in form, or spirit, but at least in magnitude
—some vision of life which would be, however different, equally
ample and passionate. But when we move to put a modern masterpiece beside them, when we seek to compare them with, let us say,
a *Ghosts* or a *Weavers*, we shrink as from the impulse to commit
some folly and we feel as though we were about to superimpose
Bowling Green upon the Great Prairies in order to ascertain which
is the larger. The question, we see, is not primarily one of art but
of the two worlds which two minds inhabited. No increased powers
of expression, no greater gift for words, could have transformed
Ibsen into Shakespeare. The materials out of which the latter created
his works—his conception of human dignity, his sense of the importance of human passions, his vision of the amplitude of human
life—simply did not and could not exist for Ibsen, as they did not
and could not exist for his contemporaries. God and Man and
Nature had all somehow dwindled in the course of the intervening
centuries, not because the realistic creed of modern art led us to
seek out mean people, but because this meanness of human life was
somehow thrust upon us by the operation of that same process

which led to the development of realistic theories of art by which our vision could be justified.

Hence, though we still apply, sometimes, the adjective "tragic" to one or another of those modern works of literature which describe human misery and which end more sadly even than they begin, the term is a misnomer since it is obvious that the works in question have nothing in common with the classical examples of the genre and produce in the reader a sense of depression which is the exact opposite of that elation generated when the spirit of a Shakespeare rises joyously superior to the outward calamities which he recounts and celebrates the greatness of the human spirit whose travail he describes. Tragedies, in that only sense of the word which has any distinctive meaning, are no longer written in either the dramatic or any other form, and the fact is not to be accounted for in any merely literary terms. It is not the result of any fashion in literature or of any deliberation to write about human nature or character under different aspects, any more than it is of either any greater sensitiveness of feeling which would make us shrink from the contemplation of the suffering of Medea or Othello or of any greater optimism which would make us more likely to see life in more cheerful terms. It is, on the contrary, the result of one of those enfeeblements of the human spirit not unlike that described in the previous chapter of this essay, and a further illustration of that gradual weakening of man's confidence in his ability to impose upon the phenomenon of life an interpretation acceptable to his desires which is the subject of the whole of the present discussion.

To explain that fact and to make clear how the creation of classical tragedy did consist in the successful effort to impose such a satisfactory interpretation will require, perhaps, the special section which follows, although the truth of the fact that it does impose such an interpretation must be evident to any one who has ever risen from the reading of *Oedipus* or *Lear* with that feeling of exultation which comes when we have been able, by rare good fortune, to enter into its spirit as completely as it is possible for us of a remoter and emotionally enfeebled age to enter it. Meanwhile one anticipatory remark may be ventured. If the plays and the novels of today deal with littler people and less mighty emotions it is not because we have become interested in commonplace souls and their unglamorous adventures but because we have come, willy-nilly, to see the soul of man as commonplace and its emotions as mean.

II

Tragedy, said Aristotle, is the "imitation of noble actions," and though it is some twenty-five hundred years since the dictum was uttered there is only one respect in which we are inclined to modify it. To us "imitation" seems a rather naïve word to apply to that process by which observation is turned into art, and we seek one which would define or at least imply the nature of that interposition of the personality of the artist between the object and the beholder which constitutes his function and by means of which he transmits a modified version, rather than a mere imitation, of the thing which he has contemplated.

In the search for this word the aestheticians of romanticism invented the term "expression" to describe the artistic purpose to which apparent imitation was subservient. Psychologists, on the other hand, feeling that the artistic process was primarily one by which reality is modified in such a way as to render it more acceptable to the desires of the artist, employed various terms in the effort to describe that distortion which the wish may produce in vision. And though many of the newer critics reject both romanticism and psychology, even they insist upon the fundamental fact that in art we are concerned, not with mere imitation but with the imposition of some form upon the material which it would not have if it were merely copied as a camera copies.

Tragedy is not, then, as Aristotle said, the *imitation* of noble actions, for, indeed, no one knows what a *noble* action is or whether or not such a thing as nobility exists in nature apart from the mind of man. Certainly the action of Achilles in dragging the dead body of Hector around the walls of Troy and under the eyes of Andromache, who had begged to be allowed to give it decent burial, is not to us a noble action, though it was such to Homer, who made it the subject of a noble passage in a noble poem. Certainly, too, the same action might conceivably be made the subject of a tragedy and the subject of a farce, depending upon the way in which it was treated; so that to say that tragedy is the *imitation* of a *noble* action is to be guilty of assuming, first, that art and photography are the same and, second, that there may be something inherently noble in an act as distinguished from the motives which prompted it or from the point of view from which it is regarded.

And yet, nevertheless, the idea of nobility is inseparable from the idea of tragedy, which cannot exist without it. If tragedy is not the imitation or even the modified representation of noble actions it is certainly a representation of actions *considered* as noble, and herein lies its essential nature, since no man can conceive it unless he is capable of believing in the greatness and importance of man. Its action is usually, if not always, calamitous, because it is only in calamity that the human spirit has the opportunity to reveal itself triumphant over the outward universe which fails to conquer it; but this calamity in tragedy is only a means to an end and the essential thing which distinguishes real tragedy from those distressing modern works sometimes called by its name is the fact that it is in the former alone that the artist has found himself capable of considering and of making us consider that his people and his actions have that amplitude and importance which make them noble. Tragedy arises then when, as in Periclean Greece or Elizabethan England, a people fully aware of the calamities of life is nevertheless serenely confident of the greatness of man, whose mighty passions and supreme fortitude are revealed when one of these calamities overtakes him.

To those who mistakenly think of it as something gloomy or depressing, who are incapable of recognizing the elation which its celebration of human greatness inspires, and who, therefore, confuse it with things merely miserable or pathetic, it must be a paradox that the happiest, most vigorous, and most confident ages which the world has ever known—the Periclean and the Elizabethan—should be exactly those which created and which most relished the mightiest tragedies; but the paradox is, of course, resolved by the fact that tragedy is essentially an expression, not of despair, but of the triumph over despair and of confidence in the value of human life. If Shakespeare himself ever had that "dark period" which his critics and biographers have imagined for him, it was at least no darkness like that bleak and arid despair which sometimes settles over modern spirits. In the midst of it he created both the elemental grandeur of Othello and the pensive majesty of Hamlet and, holding them up to his contemporaries, he said in the words of his own Miranda, "Oh, rare new world that hath *such* creatures in it."

All works of art which deserve their name have a happy end.

This is indeed the thing which constitutes them art and through which they perform their function. Whatever the character of the events, fortunate or unfortunate, which they recount, they so mold or arrange or interpret them that we accept gladly the conclusion which they reach and would not have it otherwise. They may conduct us into the realm of pure fancy where wish and fact are identical and the world is remade exactly after the fashion of the heart's desire or they may yield some greater or less allegiance to fact; but they must always reconcile us in one way or another to the representation which they make and the distinctions between the genres are simply the distinctions between the means by which this reconciliation is effected.

Comedy laughs the minor mishaps of its characters away; drama solves all the difficulties which it allows to arise; and melodrama, separating good from evil by simple lines, distributes its rewards and punishments in accordance with the principles of a naïve justice which satisfies the simple souls of its audience, which are neither philosophical enough to question its primitive ethics nor critical enough to object to the way in which its neat events violate the laws of probability. Tragedy, the greatest and the most difficult of the arts, can adopt none of these methods; and yet it must reach its own happy end in its own way. Though its conclusion must be, by its premise, outwardly calamitous, though it must speak to those who know that the good man is cut off and that the fairest things are the first to perish, yet it must leave them, as *Othello* does, content that this is so. We must be and we are glad that Juliet dies and glad that Lear is turned out into the storm.

Milton set out, he said, to justify the ways of God to man, and his phrase, if it be interpreted broadly enough, may be taken as describing the function of all art, which must, in some way or other, make the life which it seems to represent satisfactory to those who see its reflection in the magic mirror, and it must gratify or at least reconcile the desires of the beholder, not necessarily, as the naïver exponents of Freudian psychology maintain, by gratifying individual and often eccentric wishes, but at least by satisfying the universally human desire to find in the world some justice, some meaning, or, at the very least, some recognizable order. Hence it is that every real tragedy, however tremendous it may be, is an affirmation of faith in life, a declaration that even if God is not in his Heaven, then at least Man is in his world.

We accept gladly the outward defeats which it describes for the sake of the inward victories which it reveals. Juliet died, but not before she had shown how great and resplendent a thing love could be; Othello plunged the dagger into his own breast, but not before he had revealed that greatness of soul which makes his death seem unimportant. Had he died in the instant when he struck the blow, had he perished still believing that the world was as completely black as he saw it before the innocence of Desdemona was revealed to him, then, for him at least, the world would have been merely damnable, but Shakespeare kept him alive long enough to allow him to learn his error and hence to die, not in despair, but in the full acceptance of the tragic reconciliation to life. Perhaps it would be pleasanter if men could believe what the child is taught —that the good are happy and that things turn out as they should —but it is far more important to be able to believe, as Shakespeare did, that however much things in the outward world may go awry, man has, nevertheless, splendors of his own and that, in a word, Love and Honor and Glory are not words but realities.

Thus for the great ages tragedy is not an expression of despair but the means by which they saved themselves from it. It is a profession of faith, and a sort of religion; a way of looking at life by virtue of which it is robbed of its pain. The sturdy soul of the tragic author seizes upon suffering and uses it only as a means by which joy may be wrung out of existence, but it is not to be forgotten that he is enabled to do so only because of his belief in the greatness of human nature and because, though he has lost the child's faith in life, he has not lost his far more important faith in human nature. A tragic writer does not have to believe in God, but he must believe in man.

And if, then, the Tragic Spirit is in reality the product of a religious faith in which, sometimes at least, faith in the greatness of God is replaced by faith in the greatness of man, it serves, of course, to perform the function of religion, to make life tolerable for those who participate in its beneficent illusion. It purges the souls of those who might otherwise despair and it makes endurable the realization that the events of the outward world do not correspond with the desires of the heart, and thus, in its own particular way, it does what all religions do, for it gives a rationality, a meaning, and a justification to the universe. But if it has the strength it has also the weakness of all faiths, since it may—nay, it must—be ultimately lost as reality, encroaching further and further into the realm of imagination, leaving less and less room in which that imagination can build its refuge.

III

It is indeed, only at a certain stage in the development of the realistic intelligence of a people that the tragic faith can exist. A naïver people may have, as the ancient men of the north had, a body of legends which are essentially tragic, or it may have only (and need only) its happy and childlike mythology which arrives inevitably at its happy end, where the only ones who suffer "deserve" to do so and in which, therefore, life is represented as directly and easily acceptable. A too sophisticated society on the other hand—one which, like ours, has outgrown not merely the simple optimism of the child but also that vigorous, one might almost say adolescent, faith in the nobility of man which marks a Sophocles or a Shake- speare—has neither fairy tales to assure it that all is always right in the end nor tragedies to make it believe that it rises superior in soul to the outward calamities which befall it.

Distrusting its thought, despising its passions, realizing its impotent unimportance in the universe, it can tell itself no stories except those which make it still more acutely aware of its trivial miseries. When its heroes (sad misnomer for the pitiful creatures who people con- temporary fiction) are struck down it is not, like Oedipus, by the gods that they are struck but only, like Oswald Alving, by syphilis, for they know that the gods, even if they existed, would not trouble with them, and they cannot attribute to themselves in art an im- portance in which they do not believe. Their so-called tragedies do not and cannot end with one of those splendid calamities which in Shakespeare seem to reverberate through the universe, because they cannot believe that the universe trembles when their love is, like Romeo's, cut off or when the place where they (small as they are) have gathered up their trivial treasure is, like Othello's sanctuary, defiled. Instead, mean misery piles on mean misery, petty misfortune follows petty misfortune, and despair becomes intolerable because it is no longer even significant or important.

Ibsen once made one of his characters say that he did not read much because he found reading "irrelevant," and the adjective was brilliantly chosen because it held implications even beyond those of which Ibsen was consciously aware. What is it that made the classics irrelevant to him and to us? Is it not just exactly those to him impossible premises which make tragedy what it is, those assumptions that the soul of man is great, that the universe (together with whatever gods may be) concerns itself with him and that he is, in a word, noble? Ibsen turned to village politics for exactly the same reason that his contemporaries and his successors have, each in his own way, sought out some aspect of the common man and his common life—because, that is to say, here was at least something small enough for him to be able to believe.

Bearing this fact in mind, let us compare a modern "tragedy" with one of the great works of a happy age, not in order to judge of their relative technical merits but in order to determine to what extent the former deserves its name by achieving a tragic solution capable of purging the soul or of reconciling the emotions to the life which it pictures. And in order to make the comparison as fruitful as possible let us choose *Hamlet* on the one hand and on the other a play like *Ghosts* which was not only written by perhaps the most powerful as well as the most typical of modern writers but which is, in addition, the one of his works which seems most nearly to escape that triviality which cannot be entirely escaped by anyone who feels, as all contemporary minds do, that man is relatively trivial.

In *Hamlet* a prince ("in understanding, how like a god!") has thrust upon him from the unseen world a duty to redress a wrong which concerns not merely him, his mother, and his uncle, but the moral order of the universe. Erasing all trivial fond records from his mind, abandoning at once both his studies and his romance because it has been his good fortune to be called upon to take part in an action of cosmic importance, he plunges (at first) not into action but into thought, weighing the claims which are made upon him and contemplating the grandiose complexities of the universe. And when the time comes at last for him to die he dies, not as a failure, but as a success. Not only has the universe regained the balance which had been upset by what *seemed* the monstrous crime of the guilty pair ("there is nothing either good nor ill but thinking makes it so"), but in the process by which that readjustment is made a mighty mind has been given the opportunity, first to contemplate the magnificent scheme of which it is a part and then to demonstrate the greatness of its spirit by playing a rôle in the grand style which it called for. We do not need to despair in *such* a world if it has *such* creaures in it.

Turn now to *Ghosts*—look upon this picture and upon that. A young man has inherited syphilis from his father. Struck by a to him mysterious malady he returns to his northern village, learns the hopeless truth about himself, and persuades his mother to poison him. The incidents prove, perhaps, that pastors should not endeavor to keep a husband and wife together unless they know what they are doing. But what a world is this in which a great writer can deduce nothing more than that from his greatest work and how are we to be purged or reconciled when we see it acted? Not only is the failure utter, but it is trivial and meaningless as well.

Yet the journey from Elsinore to Skien is precisely the journey which the human spirit has made, exchanging in the process princes for invalids and gods for disease. We say, as Ibsen would say, that the problems of Oswald Alving are more "relevant" to our life than the problems of Hamlet, that the play in which he appears is more "real" than the other more glamorous one, but it is exactly because we find it so that we are condemned. We can believe in Oswald but we cannot believe in Hamlet, and a light has gone out in the universe. Shakespeare justifies the ways of God to man, but in Ibsen there is no such happy end and with him tragedy, so called, has become merely an expression of our despair at finding that such justification is no longer possible.

Modern critics have sometimes been puzzled to account for the fact that the concern of ancient tragedy is almost exclusively with kings and courts. They have been tempted to accuse even Aristotle of a certain naïveté in assuming (as he seems to assume) that the "nobility" of which he speaks as necessary to a tragedy implies a nobility of rank as well as of soul, and they have sometimes regretted that Shakespeare did not devote himself more than he did to the serious consideration of those common woes of the common man which subsequent writers have exploited with increasing pertinacity. Yet the tendency to lay the scene of a tragedy at the court of a king is not the result of any arbitrary convention but of the fact that the tragic writers believed easily in greatness just as we believe easily in meanness. To Shakespeare, robes and crowns and jewels are the garments most appropriate to man because they are the fitting outward manifestation of his inward majesty, but to us they seem absurd because the man who bears them has, in our estimation, so pitifully shrunk. We do not write about kings because we do not believe that any man is worthy to be one and we do not write about courts because hovels seem to us to be dwellings more appropriate to the creatures who inhabit them. Any modern attempt to dress characters in robes ends only by making us aware of a comic incongruity and any modern attempt to furnish them with a language resplendent like Shakespeare's ends only in bombast.

True tragedy capable of performing its function and of purging the soul by reconciling man to his woes can exist only by virtue of a certain pathetic fallacy far more inclusive than that to which the name is commonly given. The romantics, feeble descendants of the tragic writers to whom they are linked by their effort to see life and nature in grandiose terms, loved to imagine that the sea or the sky had a way of according itself with their moods, of storming when they stormed and smiling when they smiled. But the tragic spirit sustains itself by an assumption much more far-reaching and no more justified. Man as it sees him lives in a world which he may not dominate but which is always aware of him. Occupying the exact center of a universe which would have no meaning except for him and being so little below the angels that, if he believes in God, he has no hesitation in imagining Him formed as he is formed and crowned with a crown like that which he or one of his fellows wears, he assumes that each of his acts reverberates through the universe. His passions are important to him because he believes them important throughout all time and all space; the very fact that he can sin (no modern can) means that this universe is watching his acts; and though he may perish, a God leans out from infinity to strike him down. And it is exactly because an Ibsen cannot think of man in any such terms as these that his persons have so shrunk and that his "tragedy" has lost that power which real tragedy always has of making that infinitely ambitious creature called man content to accept his misery if only he can be made to feel great enough and important enough. An Oswald is not a Hamlet chiefly because he has lost that tie with the natural and supernatural world which the latter had. No ghost will leave the other world to warn or encourage him, there is no virtue and no vice which he can possibly have which can be really important, and when he dies neither his death nor the manner of it will be, outside the circle of two or three people as unnecessary as himself, any more important than that of a rat behind the arras.

Perhaps we may dub the illusion upon which the tragic spirit is nourished the Tragic, as opposed to the Pathetic, Fallacy, but fallacy though it is, upon its existence depends not merely the writing of tragedy but the existence of that religious feeling of which tragedy is an expression and by means of which a people aware of the dissonances of life manages nevertheless to hear them as harmony. Without it neither man nor his passions can seem great enough or important enough to justify the sufferings which they entail, and literature, expressing the mood of a people, begins to despair where once it had exulted. Like the belief in love and like most of the other mighty illusions by means of which human life has been given a value, the Tragic Fallacy depends ultimately upon the assumption which man so readily makes that something outside his own being, some "spirit not himself"—be it God, Nature, or that still vaguer thing called a Moral Order—joins him in the emphasis which he places upon this or that and confirms him in his feeling that his passions and his opinions are important. When his instinctive faith in that correspondence between the outer and the inner world fades, his grasp upon the faith that sustained him fades also, and Love or Tragedy or what not ceases to be the reality which it was because he is never strong enough in his own insignificant self to stand alone in a universe which snubs him with its indifference.

In both the modern and the ancient worlds tragedy was dead long before writers were aware of the fact. Seneca wrote his frigid melodramas under the impression that he was following in the footsteps of Sophocles, and Dryden probably thought that his *All for Love* was an improvement upon Shakespeare, but in time we awoke to the fact that no amount of rhetorical bombast could conceal the fact that grandeur was not to be counterfeited when the belief in its possibility was dead, and turning from the hero to the common man we inaugurated the era of realism. For us no choice remains except that between mere rhetoric and the frank consideration of our fellow men, who may be the highest of the anthropoids but who are certainly too far below the angels to imagine either that these angels can concern themselves with them or that they can catch any glimpse of even the soles of angelic feet. We can no longer tell tales of the fall of noble men because we do not believe that noble men exist. The best that we can achieve is pathos and the most that we can do is to feel sorry for ourselves. Man has put off his royal robes and it is only in sceptered pomp that tragedy can come sweeping by.

IV

Nietzsche was the last of the great philosophers to attempt a tragic justification of life. His central and famous dogma—"Life is good *because* it is painful"— sums up in a few words the desperate and almost meaningless paradox to which he was driven in his effort to reduce to rational terms the far more imaginative conception which is everywhere present but everywhere unanalyzed in a Sophocles or a Shakespeare and by means of which they rise triumphant over the manifold miseries of life. But the very fact that Nietzsche could not even attempt to state in any except intellectual terms an attitude which is primarily unintellectual and to which, indeed, intellectual analysis is inevitably fatal is proof of the distance which he had been carried (by the rationalizing tendencies of the human mind) from the possibility of the tragic solution which he sought; and the confused, half-insane violence of his work will reveal, by the contrast which it affords with the serenity of the tragic writers whom he admired, how great was his failure.

Fundamentally this failure was, moreover, conditioned by exactly the same thing which has conditioned the failure of all modern attempts to achieve what he attempted—by the fact, that is to say, that tragedy must have a hero if it is not to be merely an accusation against, instead of a justification of, the world in which it occurs. Tragedy is, as Aristotle said, an imitation of noble actions, and Nietzsche, for all his enthusiasm for the Greek tragic writers, was palsied by the universally modern incapacity to conceive man as noble. Out of this dilemma, out of his need to find a hero who could give to life as he saw it the only possible justification, was born the idea of the Superman, but the Superman is, after all, only a hypothetical being, destined to become what man actually was in the eyes of the great tragic writers—a creature (as Hamlet said) "how infinite in capacities, in understanding how like a god." Thus Nietzsche lived half in the past through his literary enthusiasms and half in the future through his grandiose dreams, but for all his professed determination to justify existence he was no more able than the rest of us to find the present acceptable. Life, he said in effect, is not a Tragedy now but perhaps it will be when the Ape-man has been transformed into a hero (the *Übermensch*), and trying to find that sufficient, he went mad.

He failed, as all moderns must fail when they attempt, like him, to embrace the tragic spirit as a religious faith, because the resurgence of that faith is not an intellectual but a vital phenomenon, something not achieved by taking thought but born, on the contrary, out of an instinctive confidence in life which is nearer to the animal's unquestioning allegiance to the scheme of nature than it is to that critical intelligence characteristic of a fully developed humanism. And like other faiths it is not to be recaptured merely by reaching an intellectual conviction that it would be desirable to do so.

Modern psychology has discovered (or at least strongly emphasized) the fact that under certain conditions desire produces belief, and having discovered also that the more primitive a given mentality the more completely are its opinions determined by its wishes, modern psychology has concluded that the best mind is that which most resists the tendency to believe a thing simply because it would be pleasant or advantageous to do so. But justified as this conclusion may be from the intellectual point of view, it fails to take into account the fact that in a universe as badly adapted as this one to human as distinguished from animal needs, this ability to will a belief may bestow an enormous vital advantage as it did, for instance, in the case at present under discussion where it made possible for Shakespeare the compensations of a tragic faith completely inaccessible to Nietzsche. Pure intelligence, incapable of being influenced by desire and therefore also incapable of choosing one opinion rather than another simply because the one chosen is the more fruitful or beneficent, is doubtless a relatively perfect instrument for the pursuit of truth, but the question (likely, it would seem, to be answered in the negative) is simply whether or not the spirit of man can endure the literal and inhuman truth.

Certain ages and simple people have conceived of the action which passes upon the stage of the universe as of something in the nature of a Divine Comedy, as something, that is to say, which will reach its end with the words "and they lived happily ever after." Others, less naïve and therefore more aware of those maladjustments whose reality, at least so far as outward events are concerned, they could not escape, have imposed upon it another artistic form and called it a Divine Tragedy, accepting its catastrophe as we accept the catastrophe of an *Othello*, because of its grandeur. But a Tragedy, Divine or otherwise, must, it may again be repeated, have a hero, and from the universe as we see it both the Glory of God and the Glory of Man have departed. Our cosmos may be farcical or it may be pathetic but it has not the dignity of tragedy and we cannot accept it as such.

Yet our need for the consolations of tragedy has not passed with the passing of our ability to conceive it. Indeed, the dissonances which it was tragedy's function to resolve grow more insistent instead of diminishing. Our passions, our disappointments, and our sufferings remain important to us though important to nothing else and they thrust themselves upon us with an urgency which makes it impossible for us to dismiss them as the mere trivialities which, so our intellects tell us, they are. And yet, in the absence of tragic faith or the possibility of achieving it, we have no way in which we may succeed in giving them the dignity which would not only render them tolerable but transform them as they were transformed by the great ages into joys. The death of tragedy is, like the death of love, one of those emotional fatalities as the result of which the human as distinguished from the natural world grows more and more a desert.

Poetry, said Santayana in his famous phrase, is "religion which is no longer believed," but it depends, nevertheless, upon its power to revive in us a sort of temporary or provisional credence and the nearer it can come to producing an illusion of belief the greater is its power as poetry. Once the Tragic Spirit was a living faith and out of it tragedies were written. Today these great expressions of a great faith have declined, not merely into poetry, but into a kind of poetry whose premises are so far from any we can really accept that we can only partially and dimly grasp its meaning.

We read but we do not write tragedies. The tragic solution of the problem of existence, the reconciliation to life by means of the tragic spirit is, that is to say, now only a fiction surviving in art. When that art itself has become, as it probably will, completely meaningless, when we have ceased not only to write but to *read* tragic works, then it will be lost and in all real senses forgotten, since the devolution from Religion to Art to Document will be complete.

A. M. Quinton

TRAGEDY*

There are two points of view from which tragedy can be of interest to philosophers. First, there is the task of defining or elucidating the concept: a problem of logic in an inclusive, if familiar, sense. Secondly, there is the metaphysical problem of tragedy, an examination of the tragic view of life and the world that is held to be implied and perhaps recommended by tragic drama. I shall be concerned with both of these problems in what follows and I shall try to show how it is that the concept of tragedy implies or at least suggests a metaphysical view of the world. First of all, in part 1 of these remarks, I shall argue that there is a genuine concept of tragedy to be investigated; an indispensable preliminary in view of the assault of Croce on the reality, the more than merely labelling character, of all literary and aesthetic classification. In part 2, I shall propose a distinction between natural and institutional concepts, locating tragedy in the latter group. Institutional concepts, I shall argue, pose special problems of definition, and in part 3 I shall consider various theories of tragedy to see what kinds of definition they offer. Finally, in part 4, I shall try to give an account of the "tragic view" and to distinguish it from some metaphysical doctrines of comparable scope.

* From *Proceedings of the Aristotelian Society*, Supp. Vol. XXXIV, 1960, pp. 145–64. Reprinted by permission of the author and the Editor of the Aristotelian Society.

I. THE REALITY OF LITERARY CLASSES

In chapter 4 of his *Aesthetic* Croce asserts that "the greatest triumph of the intellectualist error lies in the theory of literary and artistic classes." He does not deny that works of art can be and have been brought together in classes in the light of resemblances between them; but he insists that these classifications are no more than labelling devices, convenient perhaps for the historian of art, but of no real significance. They are pseudo-concepts and belong, not to aesthetics, but to psychology. Creative artists should not let themselves be imposed upon by these fictions, they are concepts that anyone may define as he pleases. In general the tragic "is *everything* that is or will be so *called* by those who have employed or shall employ this *word*."

This sweeping contention has both a reason and a purpose. The reason is the essential uniqueness and individuality of works of art: the purpose is the rejection of a rigorous classicism, the aesthetically insupportable view that works of art must conform to and can be conclusively judged by a collection of fixed rules. I suggest that one might well accept both the reason and the purpose, both the principle of individuality and the view that there can be no adequate system of aesthetic canons, without committing oneself to Croce's extravagant connecting link between the two.

Let us consider first the principle of individuality. Some people might be disposed to accept it on the ground that it is a truism that applies not merely to works of art but to everything. "Every individual work of art is unique," they might argue, is a not particularly interesting special case of the tautology "every individual thing is unique." To argue in this way, however, is to insist that there is no distinction between uniqueness and individuality. If one were to reply that a thing is unique only if qualitatively distinct from everything else, but individual provided that it is numerically distinct the identity of indiscernibles might be appealed to as showing that all numerical diversity is in the end qualitative. Although I think that there is or could be merely numerical diversity, that there are or could be things whose spatio-temporal distinctness is not reducible to qualitative terms, it is fortunately not necessary to argue the point here. It will be enough to draw a provisional distinction between the unique as that whose *important* or *significant* features are, as a group, peculiar to it, and the individual as that whose features as a group, whether important or not, are peculiar to it. Here the word "feature" is being used to include quality and position with no assumption as to the reducibility or otherwise of the latter. Now on this distinction a person will ordinarily be unique (even of an identical twin it can be reasonably presumed that his memories will differ in some fairly notable respect from those of his brother) but a mass-produced article of manufacture is not. Similarly *The Tempest* is unique in a way that two particular copies, side by side on a bookseller's shelf, of a particular printed edition of it are not. As Mr. Strawson has shown (*Individuals*, p. 231) this distinction between a work of art and its "instances" is not really confined to literature and music. "The things the dealers buy and sell are particulars," he says of painting and sculpture, "but it is only because of the empirical deficiencies of reproductive techniques that we identify these with the works of art. Were it not for these deficiencies, the original of a painting would have only the interest which belongs to the original manuscript of a poem."

There is, then, a sense in which works of art are non-trivially unique, the same as that in which persons are unique, which is different from the necessary individuality of any individual whatever, even if this difference between forms of individuality should turn out to rest on nothing more definite than the importance of individuating features. This fact is not exactly an accident. That all the individuating features of a work of art are important, that they all contribute to its effect upon us and are thus relevant to our evaluation of it, is simply a more explicit rendering of the requirement that a work of art should be original or creative. A purported work of art that is not distinct from an earlier work in respect of its important, aesthetically relevant, features is an imitation or a piece of plagiarism, for such things do not seem to happen by accident, and is despised as such; it is a work not of creation but transcription.

It is this requirement of novelty in works of art that underlies reasonable hostility to the regularian obsession of an ossified classicism. The historical variety of the forms of art gives us a sense of unexploited creative possibilities and this encourages us to feel that we cannot lay down in advance the specific, formal conditions which new art must satisfy. There can be no set of aesthetic canons which is sufficient for the appraisal of new creations. Joyce with *Ulysses* is inventing a new form for fiction rather than doing badly what was done well with *David Copperfield* and *Madame Bovary*.

Again, we may admire Racine in spite of rather than because of the rigour with which he adheres to explicitly formulated rules of composition. Certainly if an artist declares his formal intentions, reference to the canons of that form will make it possible to judge his intentions' success. But the success of his intentions neither entails nor is entailed by the excellence of his work.

But the fact that the formal intentions and achievements of an artist cannot conclusively settle the critical, evaluative problem posed by his work does not mean that different works of art do not possess common features nor does it imply that these common features, whether intended or not, are critically irrelevant. The plain fact is that artists are influenced in their work by the formal characteristics that they and critics and appreciators of art generally have discerned as common to the work of other artists; that to elicit these characteristics in a new work is an essential part of the interpretative task of criticism, and that such interpretation is indispensable to any judgement or evaluation of art that is to make a rational claim to our attention. Briefly, to apply classificatory terms to a work of art, to discern features in it that it can share with other works, cannot be the whole of criticism; but *any* such classification may be relevant and *some* such classification must be made if criticism is to be more than merely demonstrative, more than quotation and excitement.

The uniqueness of persons lies behind the idea of romantic love in much the same way as the uniqueness of works of art lies behind the romantic emphasis on the essential place of originality and creativeness in art and it may be instructive to compare the two cases a little further. Although our ideas about personal relations presuppose the non-trivial uniqueness of human beings they do not entail that human beings are unclassifiable. When people protest against classifications of human beings, when they say that one should not think of men as Negroes or members of the bourgeoisie or foreigners but rather as unique individuals, they are not denying that the classification can be made; they are insisting, rather, on its inadequacy as a basis for evaluation. Nor need they hold that no classification of men can be used to support our moral or personal judgement of them. In place of a superficial and well-established classification in terms of social groups they may be recommending one based on personal character that is less obvious, harder to apply and less familiar, one that classifies men as honest or "alive" or genuine. Likewise, to protest at literary classifications may be to object to the critical superficiality of classifications in terms of content (novels of the sea, novels of hospital life, etc.) or in terms of verbally formal features (sonnets, triolets, ballads) in the interests of attention to more elusive likenesses. In each case we have to be warned against our predilection for obvious external similarities and the temptation to ignore on account of it the more important features on which a responsible and rational judgement must rest if it aims to work from the genuine sources of satisfaction.

With works of art as with people there are different levels of classification. At one extreme is the merely verbal or morphological and its equal and opposite counterpart the merely sociological. At this level are found classifications of poetry by metrical pattern and rhyme-scheme, of fiction by length and, to turn to the counterpart, all classifications in terms of subject-matter: nature poetry, detective novels, ghost stories. These have only the most modest critical utility, mainly that of suggesting a possible field of comparison. The more serious literary categories, such as tragedy, comedy, epic, romance, satire, fable, in applying to less superficial properties are harder to apply and their criteria of application are harder to formulate. This is the price of their critical importance.

There are two opposed errors that can be made about literary kinds. At one extreme is the platonism that regards the whole body of literary forms as already known and fixed. For only on the assumption that all possible forms are known and their value assessed is it possible to lay down binding rules. The opposite error is to infer from the inexhaustible character of the formal possibilities of literature that any formal resemblances there may be amongst existing works are of merely historical interest. Literature is a traditional affair, the body of existing work exercises an influence, conscious and unconscious, on the creative writer. If the tradition constituted by his immediate predecessors is exhausted he turns to a larger, more embracing tradition: either to the remoter past (as with Pound and Eliot) or to art of a "lower," less deliberate and respectable kind (as with Auden). Literary kinds exist and when not too superficial, are significant for criticism but they are not immutable. Historical things, they depend on the relation of writers to their literary tradition. The reasons for this continuity and dependence are plain if vague. Persisting literary forms reflect persisting needs for expression: there will be satire as long as society offers material for complaint. Again the use, even in a modified way, of an established form helps communication and intelligibility. Finally, and perhaps vaguest of all, there is the attraction to the writer of a finite task, a creative undertaking is too vast if every element of it has to be a new creation. The greatest literary achievements, it is worth noting, are not usually those of the most adventurous formal innovators.

2. INSTITUTIONAL CONCEPTS

We can never be sure that our conceptual apparatus is going to be adequate to our future experience. To take extreme cases first: if the human race went permanently blind the concepts of colours would soon fade away into disuse, and if we acquired new kinds of sensitivity, either by the extension of an existing range in becoming visually aware of ultra-violet colours or by the growth of a wholly new sense, new concepts would be needed and found that would be indefinable in terms of our current conceptual equipment. On a more plausible level: animal species become extinct, the summers of our youth never return, and, on the other hand, new species arise from selective breeding, new diseases and new kinds of artefact spring from civilized life. In short, concepts have histories. But in many cases the history of a concept is monotonous enough to be ignored. Such as these I shall call natural concepts and contrast with what I shall call institutional concepts. Prime examples of the natural are the adjectival concepts of colour and of sensible properties generally. Their durability derives from that of the sensory organization of our species. Among substantial concepts, those of natural objects and stuffs (trees, stones, water, smoke) fall in this class as do those of animal and plant species (always allowing for the work of the big game hunter, the dam-builder and the selective breeder) and of such things as conditions of weather. Natural concepts are the friends of the translator. They remain the same under variations of time, place and language. A good reason for this invariance is the fact that the things to which they apply are comparatively immune to the meddling Prometheanism of man.

Institutional concepts, on the other hand, are those that apply to the fruits of human contrivance. First and foremost artefacts (tools, machines, houses, furnishings); then institutions proper (marriage, property, the state); the social roles associated with them (priest, king, creditor); customs and practices (manners, games, meals). Amongst this class are to be found the concepts of literary kinds. The history of these concepts is not monotonous and because of this the more specific of them have only a chronologically local application (it is absurd to describe a Druid or the Roman *pontifex maximus* as a clergyman) while the more generic undergo substantial changes of meaning (Druid, pontifex and clergyman can all be described as priests). The elements of art, technics and society are pre-eminently subservient to the human will. They are functional in the sense that they serve human purposes more or less, and often also in the sense that they are believed to serve these purposes or others. To the extent that the purpose of art-forms, instruments and social institutions becomes recognised and explicit the way in which they serve this purpose becomes accessible to criticism and from this criticism reformed and improved means to the end in question can be derived. It is to institutional concepts, incidentally, that Mr. Hampshire's theory about the dependence of our descriptive concepts on our needs and interests (*Thought and Action*, chapter 1) most adequately applies. Our colour-classifications, for example, depend on our physiological endowment and not on our purposes, unless these are thought to stand in some evolutionary relationship to that endowment.

This account has been over-simple in assimilating social and aesthetic concepts to technical ones, for it is in the case of technical concepts that the relevance and effect of purpose are most noticeable. Kinds of artefact are commonly brought into existence for the sake of an explicitly formulated purpose; though there are accidental inventions, a man idly playing about with something suddenly finds it, or realises it, to have an unexpected use. But social institutions, it is reasonable to assume, generally antedate any conscious recognition of their functions and although their subsequent modification may be carried on with a view to formulated purposes, these will ordinarily be rather numerous in any particular case and for the most part extrinsic to the institution itself. Bentham and his followers never, at the best of times, had an entirely free hand. The social reformer, to be effective, has to compromise with the reservations of the unconvinced. On the other hand there are utopian communities and private variations on the approved pattern of marriage where the institution is separated, sometimes at a disabling cost, from its normal social surroundings. Yet again the sphere of technique can be invaded by political considerations in such large and expensive matters as the designing of a supersonic aircraft. The model of the individual technician contriving with a clearly formulated purpose fails to apply to the arts for different reasons. Here there is ordinarily only a single human will involved but in the nature of the case the purpose will be highly indeterminate. The dramatist says to himself, "I am excited by the idea of a man ready to sacrifice anything in the pursuit of power": the result, after a multitude of redirections and modifications, perhaps *Macbeth*. However, works of art are not usually, and not if they are any good, the outcome of blithe inconsequence. Even if the ostensible purpose undergoes change throughout the process of creation and even if the artist may only fully comprehend his purpose, if at all, when he contemplates his finished work, he nevertheless has some more or less statable purpose throughout. The amendments that the technical model requires before it can be applied to the work of the writer or artist are not such as to rule out the institutional account of the concepts of literary or artistic kinds. In literature, tragedies do not just happen, they are intended. To get started at all a writer must propose some form or other and unless his dislike of the prevailing tradition induces him to invent one he will take it from his tradition. But the inner, progressively revealed requirements of his particular task may lead him to modify it in a wholly original way.

Institutional concepts, then, are historically mutable and, in a wide sense, purposive. Both of these properties have a bearing on the problem of their definition. For both contribute to disputes about the proper range of their application. By contrast the definition of natural concepts is a comparatively straightforward matter. A collection of more or less universally agreed instances can be assembled and inductively inspected for common properties or resemblances. Critical scrutiny of the assemblage is required only to ensure that the applications of the concept it contains are informed, serious and careful. With institutional concepts, on the other hand, the task of assembling recognised instances presents serious difficulties. Only a proportion of the informed, serious and careful applications will be universally agreed upon. There will, therefore, be no secure starting-point for the inductive comparison. To take our particular case of tragedy: no-one is going to make a fuss about the inclusion of the *Agamemnon, Hamlet* and *Phèdre*, but there will be large and serious minorities protesting against the inclusion of *Romeo and*

Juliet and the exclusion of *The Mayor of Casterbridge*. The members of any small set of paradigm tragedies that we select will be complicated things exhibiting a mass of similarities and dissimilarities to other literary works, above all because of the inevitable historical mutation of literary forms.

It is tempting at this point to say that in fact there is no single determinate concept of tragedy and to renounce, in consequence, the attempt at definition. Different people, impressed by different resemblances, use the word in different ways as they have a perfectly good logical right to do. One might enumerate the prevailing uses and extract some such common core to them all as "plays about disasters befalling important people which end unhappily." That, it might be felt, is as far as the search for a definition can usefully go. But something more can be done with the concept, all the same: whether it be described as the proposal of a new, improved concept or as the definition of a concept already implicit in the present field or overlapping uses. The most reasonable way to proceed would be by a kind of critical induction which would extract a preliminary criterion from a central group of unquestionable paradigm cases and test it against marginal ones. To admit a marginal case would require a restatement of the criterion and consequential admissions and exclusions. Now such an activity is not to be described without qualification as the definition of an existing concept, for one thing because its result might well not coincide with any existing use. On the other hand, it is not a mere proposal, not the mere selection of an existing or brand-new concept for preferred status over all others. For the modification of the criterion is a critical process whose standards will derive from the critics' ideas of the purposes of writers of tragedy. Its aim is not mere tidiness but rather the fulfilment of existing aims. It involves, of course, the assumption that there is some unity of purpose to be found in the area loosely covered by the indeterminate, merely empirical concept of tragedy. But such an assumption is not an unreasonable one: its chief justification is the part played by tradition in the work of those who write, or seek to write, tragedies.

The same point can be made about two institutional concepts from the social field: those of democracy and marriage. The application of these to widely differing modes of political organization and of human relationships is afflicted with the same dissensions as is that of tragedy. But it is surely intellectual defeatism to main-

tain that anything is a democracy or a marriage that somebody
firmly wants to describe as one: the Athens of Pericles and the
East Germany of Ulbricht being just as much democracies as
Asquith's England; the concubines of Solomon being just as much
wives as the equal partners of modern Western monogamy.

Of the two salient properties of institutional concepts, that of
historical mutability poses a problem to which that of dependence
on human purposes suggests a solution. In describing critical induction as a solution there is no need to quarrel with those who would
prefer to call it an activity of concept-formation rather than one of
definition. The ambiguity that it aims to remove is not of a fruitful
kind; the very fact that in this area of discourse a single word is
used with an indeterminate and contention-provoking meaning is
sufficient reason to arrive, by proposal or discovery, at a single and
determinate concept. And since the concept of philosophy is an
institutional one the objectors are in no position to assert that the
undertaking is anyway no part of the business of philosophers. In
particular it does not follow from the characteristic indeterminacy
of institutional concepts that any such rectification of their outlines
must be an arbitrary business. For the dependence on comparatively
inexplicit purposes that is part of the explanation of the historical
variation of institutional concepts, can be used as a standard to guide
the critical sifting of their historical variety.

3 . DEFINITION OF TRAGEDY

"A tragedy, then, is the imitation of an action that is serious and
also, as having magnitude, complete in itself: in language with
pleasurable accessories, each kind brought in separately in the
parts of the work; in a dramatic, not in a narrative, form; with
incidents arousing pity and fear, wherewith to accomplish its
catharsis of such emotions." Aristotle's statement is the inevitable
starting-point. It is presented as, and can reasonably claim to be, a
direct induction. But Aristotle's situation was peculiar and not to
be repeated; unlike the modern investigator of the concept of
tragedy his field of instances was, as groups of literary works go,
notably determinate. His examples were all in one language, had all
sprung from a fairly unitary literary tradition and had done so
within a comparatively short space of time. All the same his
procedure had its critical elements. One departure from mere

induction is progressive refinement in the course of the *Poetics* of
his conception of the seriousness of tragedy's content. At first he
is prepared to allow the plot to run from misery to happiness as
well as from happiness to misery. But in the end he defends the unhappy endings of Euripides as "more tragic." Another example is
provided by his account of the tragic hero, who must be neither
simply good nor simply bad; yet another by his view that the
tragic sequence of events must flow, not from the depravity of the
hero, but from an error of judgement.

Most of the elements of his definition need explanation and some
need revision. A tragedy is *the imitation of an action:* this means
that it must be a literary representation of human activity, not that
it must be a strictly accurate historical record of real occurrences.
It is *serious:* it must represent things in the way that they actually
happen and not as we might more or less idly wish that they
would happen, the plot must consist of events that stand in probable
or necessary relations to one another. It must have *magnitude and
completeness:* this demand for a beginning, middle and end is not
specific to tragedy, it is an obvious requirement for any seriously
intended piece of imaginative literature. It must be expressed in
language with pleasurable accessories: this demand for "rhythm,
harmony and song" is inductively correct but critically irrelevant;
the claims of Ibsen and Eugene O'Neill cannot be ruled out by such
a comparatively trivial consideration. It must be *dramatic not
narrative:* this again is a morphological and so superficial requirement. To eliminate *Anna Karenina, Madame Bovary* and *The
Mayor of Casterbridge* we must consider what is said in these books
and not the manner of saying it. A dramatic *version* or *adaptation* of
a novel is not on that count alone a different work. It must contain
incidents arousing pity and fear: any reasonably engrossing and
believable narrative or drama may contain *incidents* of this kind, a
picaresque novel, a political thriller or an unclassifiable work like
War and Peace (consider the death of Anatole Kuragin). What is
requisite to tragedy is that the work as a whole should be calculated
to arouse these emotions. It does so by being a story of human
misfortune, suffering and disaster. It must bring about a *catharsis:*
it would seem that Aristotle understood by this, the most disputed
part of his definition, to mean that the spectator of tragedy should
derive his satisfaction from it by being purged, in a more or less
medical sense, of his emotions of pity and fear, that he should

leave the theatre emotionally evacuated. Lessing's rather pious view that *catharsis* is "purification" cannot be accepted. As a psychological account of the mechanism by which tragedy has its effect this part of the theory is both irrelevant to the matter of definition and highly dubious on its own account. To be moved by a tragedy is to be exalted rather than exhausted.

The acceptable and intelligible residue of Aristotle's formula, then, is that a tragedy should be the representation of a single and rationally connected series of events that involve misfortune and suffering and end in disaster. He later adds that the action should centre on a single person, the tragic hero, who should be impressive and admirable (or at least important, perhaps as a symbol of these qualities) and whose error of judgement, rather than depravity, should contribute causally to the disastrous sequence of events in which he is engulfed. In this revised formula the elements of form (verse and drama) and psychological effect (the *catharsis*) have been removed; what remains is a preliminary account of the purpose of tragedy. Preliminary because the question arises: why represent the misfortunes and sufferings of admirable people? A trivial answer to this question, like Hume's, takes it to ask: how is it that we enjoy the spectacle of such misfortunes? The more serious romantic theorists of tragedy of the nineteenth century—Hegel, Schopenhauer and Nietzsche— imply that the point of tragedy is that it is an image of human life, a condensed, heightened and telling representation of man's place in the universe, of his situation and of the possibilities of action open to him. The pre-eminence of tragedy, in their view, derives from its being the most metaphysical of literary forms. The differences between them are essentially metaphysical, they arise from their different opinions about the place and possibilities of man in the world. The chief virtue of Aristotle's formula is that by clearly specifying the essential character of tragedy it suggests, even if it does not explicitly raise, the question of its ultimate and underlying purpose. The answer to this question is that tragedy gives a literary, an imaginative, solution to the most humanly interesting of metaphysical problems. Where Aristotle's romantic successors differ is in the precise account they give of the nature of this solution, in their expositions of the tragic view of life. Through their dependence on the idea of purpose these theories at least approximate to the ideal of critical inductions, though they are more critical, perhaps, than inductive.

The immediate form of their disagreement concerns the causation of the tragic sequence of events. In very summary terms: Hegel requires it to develop from moral excess in the hero; Schopenhauer looks for its cause in the inexorable indifference of blind fate; Nietzsche makes no such limited demand, all he requires is that the hero's individuality should be gloriously destroyed. These three points of view imply corresponding pictures of the place of man in the world. For Hegel man is subordinate to an omnipotent and infallible principle of cosmic justice; for Schopenhauer he is the inevitable victim of a mindless, merciless cosmic will; for Nietzsche he is the creator of value in an indifferent universe. These three doctrines must be examined more closely.

For Hegel the misfortune, with its capacity of arousing pity and fear, that is characteristic of tragedy is the outcome of a conflict or collision, in particular of a collision of right with right. A conflict of right with right can only be apparent: what happens is that the "ethical institution" to which the hero is committed is given by him an improperly commanding and important place to the exclusion of other equally important ethical institutions. Thus Antigone, in Hegel's favourite and paradigmatic example, by pressing too hard the claims of the family comes into destructive conflict with the claims of the state. This situation, "the self-division of the ethical substance," a lopsidedness in the scheme of values, can only be set right by the destruction of the initiator of the conflict and a reaffirmation of eternal justice as a whole over the pretensions of its constituent parts. Hegel's view rests on a questionable interpretation of the *Antigone* (Creon is too tyrannous a monarch to be regarded as a representative of the moral claims of the state); in requiring the moral responsibility of the tragic hero for the disasters that befall him, in seeing his destruction as the reaffirmation of absolute morality, it is fundamentally a demand for poetic justice and as such inapplicable to by far the greater number of works about whose status as tragedies there would be little disagreement. A. C. Bradley amended the theory to include amongst conflicting elements not merely ethical institutions but also "universal interests," moral values that had no determinate social institution as their expression, and even "personal interests," such as Macbeth's ambition. So adjusted the theory can accommodate the tragedies of Racine, with their characteristic battle between love and duty, and to some extent the tragedies of Shakespeare, in which personal goals collide with the demands of that overriding order and harmony without which all human arrangements come to ruin. But this amendment really evacuates the Hegelian position: it allows for the reality of unrecompensed, unreconciled evil, it abandons the demand for the moral responsibility of the hero and for an essentially retributive view of his sufferings. The significance of Lear's or Othello's suffering is trivialised by seeing it as a just return for their moral offences. Certainly their follies contributed to the disasters which overtook them but only against the background of a world which allows the persistence and effectiveness of evil. Schopenhauer's protest against poetic justice is exaggerated and quaintly phrased but it makes an appropriate point: Hegel's view, he says, expresses "the dull, optimistic, Protestant-rationalistic, or peculiarly Jewish view of life." It can be said, at any rate, to have a flavour of complacent pharisaism.

Schopenhauer's position is the exact opponent of Hegel's. For him the purpose of tragedy is to represent the terrible side of life; the response it seeks to evoke is resignation, an abandonment of the will to live. The tragic hero "atones for the crime of existence," he shows us how even those most fitted to triumph in the world are really weak and powerless. Behind the world of phenomena, which, as amenable to our understandings, seems amenable to our desires, stands the thing-in-itself, the cosmic will. In the end this is the source of all tragic sequences of events, whether these are immediately initiated by chance or fate, by the will itself, or by evil men or by what Schopenhauer none too consistently preferred as a tragic initiator "the ordinary morals and relations of men." (His preference here stemmed from the belief that the third type of tragedy brought home to us the closeness of disaster to ordinary life. On the other hand misfortunes with ordinary causes are more easily thought of as preventable by human thought and effort, only the obvious workings of chance and fate can enforce an attitude of resignation.) Schopenhauer's theory derives some strength from the mild satisfaction and comfort that can be got from looking directly at the worst possibilities. This consolation, however, in so far as it does not consist in the pleasure of mere knowingness and disillusion, of having overcome the sentimental follies that afflict others, can only occur if the resignation is not total. Complete resignation that can console us and so contribute to life shows the limitation of our powers, the inexorable obstacles that we have got to recognise, and not that we have no powers at all. The resignation that tragedy does produce is not of Schopenhauer's all-engulfing kind: if, as he claims, it is the summit of art it is not because it leads to total collapse and admission of defeat. What conclusively refutes Schopenhauer's theory is the outcome of its concrete application. On his specifications *Jude the Obscure* would be far more of a tragedy than any work of Shakespeare's.

Nietzsche's *The Birth of Tragedy* is an extraordinary rhapsodic affair full of *a priori* cultural history, the mysterious combat of Apollo and Dionysus and resonant hymns to the music and metaphysics of German romanticism. In general he accepts the outlines of Schopenhauer's view, the dualism which sees the world as composed of a clear, definite, rational, harmonious order of phenomena (the world of Apollo and of plastic art) and of a dark, inchoate irrational, ecstatic order of things-in-themselves (the world of Dionysus and of music). Tragedy is the master-art that brings these two worlds together and in which the Apollonian individuality of the hero is destroyed by the wild, depersonalised forces of the Dionysian abyss. It is as if the conflicting elements in tragedy were the fixity of the intellect on the one hand and the unformed creativeness of the emotions or the unconscious on the other, as if, that is to say, the two sides to the conflict were both somehow contained in man. The tragic hero is not destroyed by impersonal forces quite external to humanity but by the more vital features of humanity. It is in these terms that Nietzsche tries to explain our delight in the tragic annihilation of individuality. We derive a metaphysical comfort, he says, from tragedy's affirmation of the power and pleasure of life that underlies the flux of phenomena. As it stands this theory seems to be of very limited application. In the tragedies of Shakespeare and Racine it is impersonal *order* and not disorder that seems to be affirmed and the individuality that is destroyed is more Dionysian and emotional than Apollonian and intellectual.

The value of Nietzsche lies in his suggestion that even if the misfortunes and sufferings of the tragic hero are real and, as unrecompensed and undeserved, not to be argued away as parts of some larger, consoling design, they can still be glorious and exalting. The words he uses of the experience of tragedy such as *joy* and *delight* seem more to the point than Aristotle's emotionally hygienic *catharsis*, Hegel's smug concept of *reconciliation* or Schopenhauer's *resignation.* The values that men create are somehow more than the men who create them and can survive the destruction of their creators. In tragedy this destruction is represented and here above all the valuable qualities of men are most strikingly revealed. The necessary impressiveness of the tragic hero is provoked to its fullest expression in the face of imminent destruction and stands out all the more noticeably against the background of disaster. Dr. Leavis, although he disowns Nietzsche ("the Nietzschean witness had better be dispensed with; at the best it introduces a disturbing vibration"), admirably states this side of Nietzsche's doctrine. "The sense of heightened life that goes with the tragic experience is conditioned by a transcending of the ego—an escape from all attitudes of self-assertion. 'Escape,' perhaps, is not altogether a good word, since it might suggest something negative and irresponsible. . . . Actually the experience is constructive or creative, and involves recognizing positive value as in some way defined and vindicated by death. It is as if we were challenged at the profoundest level with the question 'In what does the significance of life reside?' and found ourselves contemplating, for answer, a view of life, and of the things giving it value, that makes the valued appear unquestionably more important than the valuer, so that significance lies, clearly and inescapably, in the willing adhesion of the individual self to something more important than itself." (*The Common Pursuit*: pp. 131–2.) It is this Nietzschean point of view, midway between the extremes of Hegel and Schopenhauer and asserting the reality and attainability of human excellence in a world that neither guarantees the triumph of good nor the fruitlessness of human effort, that I shall consider in the final section.

4. THE TRAGIC VIEW OF LIFE

"Tragedy," says I. A. Richards, "is still the form under which the mind may most clearly and freely contemplate the human situation, its issues unclouded, its possibilities revealed. To this its value is due and the supreme position among the arts which it has occupied in historical time and still occupies. . . . [It] is too great an exercise of the spirit to be classed among amusements or even delights, or to be regarded as a vehicle for the inculcation of such crude valuations as may be codified in a moral." It is, he says elsewhere, "the most general, all-accepting, all-ordering experience known." And again, "the central experience of tragedy and its chief value is an attitude indispensable for a fully developed life." To accept this view of the metaphysical import of tragedy is not to accept the speculative psychology of aesthetic satisfaction as a balance of nervous impulses that Richards associates with it. My final object is to state more explicitly the character of this form under which the human situation may be most clearly and freely contemplated.

Its central theme, I suggest, is *the contingency of value*. Whatever is of value in the world, it asserts, is due to men. Not merely in the sense that without human purposes and satisfactions nothing would be of value at all, though this may be presupposed, but rather that the achievement and maintenance of value in the world can only be brought about by the efforts of men. There is no extra-human guarantee of the persistence and eventual triumph of value, no God or Reason, in the light of whose infallible purposes all evil, error and suffering is revealed as apparent and illusory. On the other hand, the extra-human world is not merely destructive or malevolent, men are not powerless to achieve value, their failure is no more guaranteed than their success. (I use the somewhat despised word *value* here to prevent concentration on the exclusively moral aspects of the good, whether these be taken in a conventional, negative sense related to the performance of duty, or more inclusively in relation to collective interests of humanity. One type of moral value is realised by the dutiful man, another by the saint who goes beyond the claims of duty. Distinct from both is the value achieved by the hero, a category that must be understood to cover Shakespeare and Newton as well as Cromwell and Lincoln.)

Tragedy asserts, then, that value is contingent for its realisation on the agency of men. The tragic view of life rules out both the kind of optimism represented by Hegel, which asserts the necessity of value, and the kind of pessimism represented by Schopenhauer which asserts its impossibility. Cosmic optimism holds that the good must triumph, that what seems to be bad will cease to seem so when viewed in its place in the whole scheme of things; cosmic pessimism holds that the good cannot triumph, that indeed what appears to be good is only an illusion which sharpens the suffering that must accompany its inevitable exposure. Neither of these views is easy to express too consistently, for each seems uncomfortably to combine an absolute thesis, to the effect that evil (or good) does not really exist at all but only seems to (which provokes the question

whether the seeming of evil or good is not itself evil or good),
with a temporal thesis to the effect that present evil or good will
lead in the end to the complete triumph of their opposites. Now
whether present evil or good are considered as necessary to the
realisation of the ultimate state or not, they conflict with the idea
that the final triumph of good or evil can be properly described
as total. Whether the evil there is must or merely does precede the
final triumph of good, it is real and the total situation is less good
than it might conceivably have been. For our purpose it is not the
state of the cosmic account that matters so much as the responsive-
ness of its items to the human will. Absolute optimism and pessimism
make human activity pointless: since everything that happens is
necessarily good or evil it makes no difference in point of value
what in particular it is. Similarly those versions of temporal optimism
and pessimism that hold the inevitable final state *necessarily* to require the realisation in preceding states of their opposites, rule out
justifiable or rational choice. If evil must exist so that good may find
its ultimate and necessary realisation it is something we are powerless
to prevent. The other versions of optimism and pessimism take the
world as it apparently is, as a mixture of good and evil: they add to
this the consoling or depressing assurance that good or evil will
triumph in the end but since the present state of things is logically
independent of this final state there is no good reason to suppose that
there is nothing men can do about it.

These highly schematic possibilities can now be given a more
concrete form. Redemptive religion, and its secular analogue the
theory of progress (in its liberal or Marxist form), are versions of
optimism; what might be called desperate materialism, which
emphasises human mortality, the coming death of the earth and the
universal impossibility of life that follows from entropy, is a version
of pessimism. How are these to be interpreted? Are they inconsistent
with the tragic view of life? Richards remarks, "Tragedy is only
possible to a mind which is for the moment agnostic or Manichaean.
The least touch of any theology which has a compensating Heaven
to offer the tragic hero is fatal." Is the tragic view of life consistent
with Christian belief? It is certainly not compatible with possibly
over-simple but nonetheless familiar theological interpretations of
that belief. If mystically, in the manner of absolute optimism,
Christianity contends that evil is unreal or if again the present and

temporal evils of the world are necessary to the final triumph of good, if God's best is not the best, then human action can make no difference to the value realised in the world. But if temporal evil which does not contribute to the final triumph of good is admitted to be real, evil that God could eliminate without prejudice to his final aim but in fact does not, then there is a tragic version of Christianity. I must leave others to decide whether such a theology is orthodox. A readiness to countenance such a view, at any rate, might seem to be present in the view that the reality of evil is a mystery that we cannot fathom; though in fact such reverent suspense of judgement looks like an uneasy oscillation between two equally unpalatable alternatives: on the one hand an admission of the limitation of God's power or benevolence, on the other the squalidly comfortable view that the evils of the world are nothing to worry about since they are the indispensable preliminaries to the final triumph of good. The kind of cosmic gloom represented by Mr. Joseph Wood Krutch's *The Modern Temper* can be briefly considered. If science makes it reasonable to suppose that the death of the individual is a final extinction and that the human race is also destined to pass away this does not entail that nothing of positive value can exist in the meanwhile nor that human effort is irrelevant to its achievement.

The tragic view of life, with its assertion of the contingency of value, is necessarily presupposed by the idea that human action has any point. It entails that no reasonable optimism or pessimism can be universal or cosmic in scope. I can be optimistic or pessimistic about a particular project of my own, about the possibilities of my own life, about the prospects of a particular human society and even about the long-run prospects of the human race. But there is no reason to submit passively to these expectations.

Arthur Miller

TRAGEDY AND
*DEATH OF A SALESMAN**

The play [*Death of a Salesman*] was always heroic to me, and in later years the academy's charge that Willy lacked the "stature" for the tragic hero seemed incredible to me. I had not understood that these matters are measured by Greco-Elizabethan paragraphs which hold no mention of insurance payments, front porches, refrigerator fan belts, steering knuckles, Chevrolets, and visions seen not through the portals of Delphi but in the blue flame of the hot-water heater. How could "Tragedy" make people weep, of all things?

I set out not to "write a tragedy" in this play, but to show the truth as I saw it. However, some of the attacks upon it as a pseudo-tragedy contain ideas so misleading, and in some cases so laughable, that it might be in place here to deal with a few of them.

Aristotle having spoken of a fall from the heights, it goes without saying that someone of the common mold cannot be a fit tragic hero. It is now many centuries since Aristotle lived. There is no more reason for falling down in a faint before his *Poetics* than before Euclid's geometry, which has been amended numerous times by men with new insights; nor, for that matter, would I choose to have my illness diagnosed by Hippocrates rather than the most ordinary graduate of an American medical school, despite the

* From the Introduction to *Arthur Miller's Collected Plays*, copyright © 1957 by Arthur Miller. Reprinted by permission of The Viking Press, Inc.

Greek's genius. Things do change, and even a genius is limited by his time and the nature of his society.

I would deny, on grounds of simple logic, this one of Aristotle's contentions if only because he lived in a slave society. When a vast number of people are divested of alternatives, as slaves are, it is rather inevitable that one will not be able to imagine drama, let alone tragedy, as being possible for any but the higher ranks of society. There is a legitimate question of stature here, but none of rank, which is so often confused with it. So long as the hero may be said to have had alternatives of a magnitude to have materially changed the course of his life, it seems to me that in this respect at least, he cannot be debarred from the heroic role.

The question of rank is significant to me only as it reflects the question of the social application of the hero's career. There is no doubt that if a character is shown on the stage who goes through the most ordinary actions, and is suddenly revealed to be the President of the United States, his actions immediately assume a much greater magnitude, and pose the possibilities of much greater meaning, than if he is the corner grocer. But at the same time, his stature as a hero is not so utterly dependent upon his rank that the corner grocer cannot outdistance him as a tragic figure—providing, of course, that the grocer's career engages the issues of, for instance, the survival of the race, the relationships of man to God—the questions, in short, whose answers define humanity and the right way to live so that the world is a home, instead of a battleground or a fog in which disembodied spirits pass each other in an endless twilight.

In this respect *Death of a Salesman* is a slippery play to categorize because nobody in it stops to make a speech objectively stating the great issues which I believe it embodies. If it were a worse play, less closely articulating its meanings with its actions, I think it would have more quickly satisfied a certain kind of criticism. But it was meant to be less a play than a fact; it refused admission to its author's opinions and opened itself to a revelation of process and the operations of an ethic, of social laws of action no less powerful in their effects upon individuals than any tribal law administered by gods with names. I need not claim that this play is a genuine solid gold tragedy for my opinions on tragedy to be held valid. My purpose here is simply to point out a historical fact which must be taken into account in any consideration of tragedy, and it is the sharp alteration in the meaning or rank in society between the present time and the distant past. More important to me is the fact that this particular kind of argument obscures much more relevant considerations.

One of these is the question of intensity. It matters not at all whether a modern play concerns itself with a grocer or a president if the intensity of the hero's commitment to his course is less than the maximum possible. It matters not at all whether the hero falls from a great height or a small one, whether he is highly conscious or only dimly aware of what is happening, whether his pride brings the fall or an unseen pattern written behind clouds; if the intensity, the human passion to surpass his given bounds, the fanatic insistence upon his self-conceived role—if these are not present there can only be an outline of tragedy but no living thing. I believe, for myself, that the lasting appeal of tragedy is due to our need to face the fact of death in order to strengthen ourselves for life, and that over and above this function of the tragic viewpoint there are and will be a great number of formal variations which no single definition will ever embrace.

Another issue worth considering is the so-called tragic victory, a question closely related to the consciousness of the hero. One makes nonsense of this if a "victory" means that the hero makes us feel some certain joy when, for instance, he sacrifices himself for a "cause," and unhappy and morose because he dies without one. To begin at the bottom, a man's death is and ought to be an essentially terrifying thing and ought to make nobody happy. But in a great variety of ways even death, the ultimate negative, can be, and appear to be, an assertion of bravery, and can serve to separate the death of man from the death of animals; and I think it is this distinction which underlies any conception of a victory in death. For a society of faith, the nature of the death can prove the existence of the spirit, and posit its immortality. For a secular society it is perhaps more difficult for such a victory to document itself and to make itself felt, but, conversely, the need to offer greater proofs of the humanity of man can make that victory more real. It goes without saying that in a society where there is basic disagreement as to the right way to live, there can hardly be agreement as to the right way to die, and both life and death must be heavily weighted with meaningless futility.

It was not out of any deference to a tragic definition that Willy Loman is filled with a joy, however broken-hearted, as he approaches his end, but simply that my sense of his character dictated his joy, and even what I felt was an exultation. In terms of his character, he has achieved a very powerful piece of knowledge, which is that he is loved by his son and has been embraced by him and forgiven. In this he is given his existence, so to speak—his fatherhood, for which he has always striven and which until now he could not achieve. That he is unable to take this victory thoroughly to his heart, that it closes the circle for him and propels him to his death, is the wage of his sin, which was to have committed himself so completely to the counterfeits of dignity and the false coinage embodied in his idea of success that he can prove his existence only by bestowing "power" on his posterity, a power deriving from the sale of his last asset, himself, for the price of his insurance policy.

I must confess here to a miscalculation, however. I did not realize while writing the play that so many people in the world do not see as clearly, or would not admit, as I thought they must, how futile most lives are; so there could be no hope of consoling the audience for the death of this man. I did not realize either how few would be impressed by the fact that this man is actually a very brave spirit who cannot settle for half but must pursue his dream of himself to the end. Finally, I thought it must be clear, even obvious, that this was no dumb brute heading mindlessly to his catastrophe.

I have no need to be Willy's advocate before the jury which decides who is and who is not a tragic hero. I am merely noting that the lingering ponderousness of so many ancient definitions has blinded students and critics to the facts before them, and not only in regard to this play. Had Willy been unaware of his separation from values that endure he would have died contentedly while polishing his car, probably on a Sunday afternoon with the ball game coming over the radio. But he was agonized by his awareness of being in a false position, so constantly haunted by the hollowness of all he had placed his faith in, so aware, in short, that he must somehow be filled in his spirit or fly apart, that he staked his very life on the ultimate assertion. That he had not the intellectual fluency to verbalize his situation is not the same thing as saying that he lacked awareness, even an overly intensified consciousness that the life he had made was without form and inner meaning.

To be sure, had he been able to know that he was as much the victim of his beliefs as their defeated exemplar, had he known how much of guilt he ought to bear and how much to shed from his soul, he would be more conscious. But it seems to me that there is of necessity a severe limitation of self-awareness in any character, even the most knowing, which serves to define him as a character, and more, that this very limit serves to complete the tragedy and, indeed, to make it at all possible. Complete consciousness is possible only in a play about forces, like *Prometheus*, but not in a play about people. I think that the point is whether there is a sufficient awareness in the hero's career to make the audience supply the rest. Had Oedipus, for instance, been more conscious and more aware of the forces at work upon him he must surely have said that he was not really to blame for having cohabited with his mother since neither he nor anyone else knew she was his mother. He must surely decide to divorce her, provide for their children, firmly resolve to investigate the family background of his next wife, and thus deprive us of a very fine play and the name for a famous neurosis. But he is conscious only up to a point, the point at which guilt begins. Now he is inconsolable and must tear out his eyes. What is tragic about this? Why is it not even ridiculous? How can we respect a man who goes to such extremities over something he could in no way help or prevent? The answer, I think, is not that we respect the man, but that we respect the Law he has so completely broken, wittingly or not, for it is that Law which, we believe, defines us as men. The confusion of some critics viewing *Death of a Salesman* in this regard is that they do not see that Willy Loman has broken a law without whose protection life is insupportable if not incomprehensible to him and to many others; it is the law which says that a failure in society and in business has no right to live. Unlike the law against incest, the law of success is not administered by statute or church, but it is very nearly as powerful in its grip upon men. The confusion increases because, while it is a law, it is by no means a wholly agreeable one even as it is slavishly obeyed, for to fail is no longer to belong to society, in his estimate. Therefore, the path is opened for those who wish to call Willy merely a foolish man even as they themselves are living in obedience to the same law that killed him. Equally, the fact that Willy's law—the belief, in other words, which administers guilt to him—is not a civilizing statute whose destruction menaces us all; it is rather, a deeply believed and deeply suspect "good" which, when questioned as to its value, as it is in this play, serves more to raise our anxieties than to reassure us of the existence of an unseen but humane metaphysical system in the world. My attempt in the play was to counter this anxiety with an opposing system which, so to speak, is in a race for Willy's faith, and it is the system of love which is the opposite of the law of success. It is embodied in Biff Loman, but by the time Willy can perceive his love it can serve only as an ironic comment upon the life he sacrificed for power and for success and its tokens.

III

The Work of Art and the Aesthetic Spectator

INTRODUCTION

═══════

The distinctive nature of works of art and the conditions that accompany their appreciation and appraisal are, by almost common
consent, functions of a special property, the aesthetic attitude, that is
attached to the aesthetic spectator. It is generally held, first, that the
apprehension of aesthetic qualities is always accompanied by an
occurrence in the spectator of the aesthetic attitude; second, that
an object is and becomes aesthetic only when it is observed with
this attitude; and third, that *any* object perceived under the sway
of this attitude is, for that occasion of perception, an aesthetic object.

The following example will suggest why the aesthetic attitude
is thought to play such a vital role in the determination of aesthetic
qualities. Suppose an untutored child and an art critic look at a
painting. If the child has normal vision he will see, in one sense of
"see," whatever the expert sees in the painting, but in another sense
of "see" the child sees a pointless miscellany of shapes and colors and
the critic sees something quite different, the aesthetic qualities of
design, coloration, chiaroscuro, etc. From one point of view, they
have seen the same painting; from another they have not.

An obvious solution is to say that the difference in observations
is essentially a matter of difference in spectators. The critic possesses
a trait that distinguishes him from the child and that converts his

visual sense-data into the aesthetic qualities of a painting. The trait in question is, of course, the aesthetic attitude.

And since the transforming power is in the spectator, there is no reason to suppose that it could not convert anything whatever into an object of aesthetic contemplation. Accordingly a telephone pole or a garbage can could, if apprehended through the aesthetic attitude, reveal the features more usually assigned to what are traditionally called works of art. They would, on such occasions, share the status of a string quartet or an epic poem.

The role purportedly played by the aesthetic attitude in the apprehension and interpretation of works of art makes it mandatory, therefore, that an analysis of aesthetic traits take into account the attitude which they elicit and which allegedly lends them their aesthetic character.

If we wish to define the aesthetic attitude more exactly we must distinguish between its use as an explanation of a class of uncommon occurrences and its use as a simple identification of the occurrences which it, in the first use, supposedly explains. To fail to distinguish between these two senses of the aesthetic attitude could lead to some obvious mistakes; we might think that by questioning the explanatory power of the aesthetic attitude we are questioning the existence of the phenomena which it seeks to explain. Or we might be misled into supposing that by establishing the existence of that which it identifies, we establish it for that case as adequate explanation.

First, consider another kind of situation for which the aesthetic attitude provides an explanation. Suppose that a puritan, an auctioneer, a Don Juan, and a sculptor look at and judge the merits of the *Venus di Milo*. The puritan sees it as an unclothed woman and accordingly judges it as morally repugnant: it is conducive to arousing erotic desire. The auctioneer sees it as a statue of considerable merit: it will fetch a good price. The Don Juan notices the features that concerned the puritan: he finds the *Venus*, however, an admirable instance of feminine pulchritude. The artist sees the statue in terms of balance, symmetry, three-dimensional bulk, light and shade, etc.: he concludes it merits highest commendation.

The people seem to be at once looking at the same thing and seeing different things. The discordance is the puzzle and the aesthetic attitude the explanation. It attempts to answer the question: How is it that some people apprehend in an object its qualities of, for example, balance, symmetry, design, light, and shade, and by consulting them make evaluations of aesthetic worth?

The answer runs this way: The normal or customary stance from which we consider things can be described as looking for and at "what we want." Ask ourselves what we want and the replies would be: to succeed in love, avoid war, raise children who stay out of trouble, make money, learn about mathematics, write a book, be popular, etc. The answers range over a variety of interests—moral, intellectual, emotional, economic, practical. These are what control our lookings and valuings and we select out for attention and judgment the aspects of things relevant to their satisfaction.

To summarize, our customary attitudes may be said to consist of two parts or stages. First, there is a readiness to consider things in the light of our desires, according to their utility or disutility. Then, as a result, we single out for attention and evaluation those aspects of things that are relevant to the satisfaction of such expectations.

The first two points that can be made about the aesthetic attitude are that it is everything the attitude just described is not, and that it comes about by detaching our mode of attention and judgment from personal desire. We erect a barrier, as it were, dividing our desires from our lookings and valuings. The barrier interposed, we no longer see properties in the light of what they contribute to our wants. Nothing is left but to consider them in and for themselves. Our attitude is one of disinterested contemplation and permits us to see qualities as they really are; attention and judgment is directed toward what advocates of this view call the intrinsic aspects of a thing. Of course we do not ordinarily consider objects in this light —it is a difficult exercise and therefore hard to learn. Everyone does not, in the second sense of "see," see a work of art.

There is no question but that we look for, and sometimes see, in a statue traits of balance, symmetry, three-dimensional bulk, etc., and that a suitable display and combination of such traits is sometimes used as a criterion for determining the statue's excellence. The question is whether the occurrence of these phenomena is adequately explained by the assumption that the spectator is, in such cases, possessed of the aesthetic attitude. Is it true to say first, that when we experience a work of art there is a recognizable attitude, disinterested in character, such that its presence or absence controls the suitability of that experience?

Let us consider a case where motives that are other than disinterested lead to the viewing of a work of art. Assume that a weary Mr. X comes home from his day's work and is importuned by his social-climbing wife to put away his slippers and attend an art exhibit at the local museum. And suppose that he goes only because he prefers even a museum to his wife's cackle. What if Mr. X returns home and expresses gratitude that he did not resist the entreaties of his wife? He describes each painting with the expertise of a critic and declares that he has discovered at last what contemporary painting is about. There would certainly be no temptation to denounce Mr. X as a dissembler on the ground that reasons of domestic tranquillity could not possibly initiate an adequate experience of paintings. We would admit the aesthetic authority of his experience, practical motives notwithstanding.

Nor need we say as a matter of principle that aesthetic experience is exclusive of practical consequences. Suppose that the lively interest of Mr. X in painting leads him to exchange for the pleasures of the bottle those of the easel. His pleasure in painting is not, for all that, less aesthetic nor must we regard it as simply a surrogate for membership in a temperance league.

The obvious rejoinder is that the aesthetic attitude aims to identify the experience of a spectator during, not before or after, perception of an aesthetic object. But what of the experience itself? The customary view again is that it is a disinterested contemplation of the intrinsic qualities of an object. The question is whether all this is not just a gaseous way of saying that when we pay attention to works of art, and mind our aesthetic manners, we concern ourselves with qualities such as balance, symmetry, and design rather than commercial value or sex appeal. If so, the aesthetic attitude which identifies this special sort of vision is converted without additional information into an explanation of its occurrence.

Of course, if there were distinctive *psychological* properties that always attended or facilitated aesthetic perception, that would be a different matter. But no psychologist, so far as I know, has established the fact of their occurrence, and if established, they would certainly be something more than a restatement of the phenomena which they purportedly accompany and elicit.

It is even difficult to know how we would justify the view that our experience of aesthetic objects is always accompanied by the aesthetic attitude if, as many of its advocates hold, the absence of attitude is sufficient ground for disqualifying an object as aesthetic. At any rate, we have no reliable information of a quality, disinterested or otherwise, that pervades our aesthetic experiences. We can only say that they are experiences pervaded by the recognition of aesthetic qualities.

However, we have not yet directly considered the opinion that the perception of such features as balance and symmetry in a work of art is perception of its intrinsic features. Can we say at least that this is the aesthetic attitude?

Someone might describe what he called his aesthetic experience of Botticelli's *Birth of Venus* in the following way: first he ran his hand over the canvas; next he lifted it, discovering to his pleasure that both the temperature and weight of the painting were exactly right. It was, he concluded, an aesthetic experience of the Botticelli and a highly satisfying one. I shall assume that he defends himself against the obvious retorts. If he had read some aesthetics he might offer in his defense that this pleasure in the temperature and weight of the Botticelli was not at all a practical matter. He had no ulterior aims or purposes to which either contributed. It just happened that he found the right temperature and weight an immediate delight, and since they are clearly as much internal properties of painting as color and design, and perhaps more so than subject-matter, his immediate delight was also an aesthetic delight.

We would no doubt dismiss the argument and its attendant reference to intrinsic properties. Temperature and weight are not among the aesthetic properties of painting and an experience of those properties exclusively is not an aesthetic experience of painting. But the argument, silly as it seems, poses a dilemma for those who claim that the perception of the intrinsic elements of an object is also perception qua aesthetic object. If "intrinsic" is defined independently of "aesthetic," we shall have to admit observations that are dubious or obviously aberrant into the domain of aesthetic experience. But if the internal elements of an object are the same as its aesthetic elements, it is cognitively vacuous to describe aesthetic observation as observation attending exclusively to internal elements.

All this leads to whether it is useful or informative to say of the aesthetic attitude that when it occurs in a spectator it converts nonaesthetic into aesthetic properties. It has not been successfuly construed either as psychological state, or the cognition of internal elements characterized independently of the aesthetic properties it purportedly defines and creates.

Why is it then that theories of the aesthetic attitude are so frequently urged? What is their point? It seems to me that the significance attached to such views derives from a prior assumption about the relation of aesthetic experience to aesthetic judgment. We tend to think that a good judge of a work of art is so because he is a good "experiencer" and that an education in how to judge a work of art is primarily an education in how to experience it. Consequently we tend to think of aesthetic judgment as verbal transcription of an experience and see the experience as final arbiter of the judgment's merit. It is of the utmost importance, therefore, to have the right kind of experience and to know what the having is like. Describing it becomes a supremely important task. It will tell us how to experience, therefore, how to judge a work of art.

But is it true that there is a kind of experience invariably related to aesthetic judgments and certifying their truth? The answer turns on the various meanings of "experience." Sometimes it has the sense of felt emotion, the joy, dread, excitement, exhilaration, etc., aroused by works of art. And it is also true that such emotion-words frequently appear in aesthetic appraisals. Works of art are joyous, terrifying, exhilarating, sad, pensive, calm, passionate, etc. Now the original question is more specific. Does the correct application of emotion-words require from their user a showing of the correspondiing emotion? Does "The music is sad" say and require the truth of what is expressed by "The music made me sad"? If so, the statement is autobiographical and the test of its truth remarkably simple. We need only inquire of whoever utters it what his emotional state was when he listened to the music. There is, however, little evidence from criticism that discussions of the emotional traits of art-works are primarily essays in the emotional history of the participants. If a question arises as to whether the music is sad, we talk not about ourselves but the music. We do not have to feel sad to say that John is sad. Nor do we have to feel sad to say that the music is sad. Of course we may feel sad when the music is sad, but we may feel, as some critics testify, exalted instead.

Or there is the drama critic who says that Euripides' *Medea* is terrifying. Of course he is right, but we do not, because of that, picture him in his aisle seat cowering in a cold sweat. Instead, we

rightly suspect that if he was in a state of terror he was in no condition to utter a responsible judgment.

Second, consider "experience" as total reaction of a spectator
(emotional, intellectual, moral, etc.) within the time he actually
listens to, reads, looks at a work of art. Now suppose a critic com-
plains of a novel that it shifts narrative point-of-view senselessly between first and third person. Too, he admits that he missed the flaw
while reading the novel; it came to him while he was thinking
of something else. The question is whether because judgment is not,
in this sense of "experience," borne out by experience of the novel,
it is unwarranted. Surely the critic could reply that the notion
of experience is arbitrary and unduly narrow. We do not need the
book before us to consider a novel. Thinking about it is experience
of it also.

But if experience rightly expands to these dimensions, the dictum
that there is a kind of experience that at once is expressed in aesthetic judgments and certifies their truth is reduced to truism.
Judgment of art-works, if honest, will always have as subject-
matter some experience of those art-works and experience, if the
judgments are neither tautologies nor ejaculations, will always be
that which confirms or denies them.

The point is not that there is a particular kind of experience which,
when it occurs, sanctions our judgments of works of art, or that
there is a pervasive feature of experience such that every true
judgment is accompanied by it. The dictim requires only that we
have experienced what we say we have experienced. And the question posed and not resolved by this requirement is what, in addition
to this parallelism, attends each aesthetic judgment.

The foregoing is not meant to deny the supreme value of feeling
and appreciation in the context of aesthetic activity, nor that their
character and merit depend on the character and sophistication of
our observations. The issue is whether every case of veridical feeling
and observation is accompanied, pervaded, or sanctioned by something else, whether it is in every case linked to the aesthetic
attitude. And so, the final question is whether the "aesthetic attitude" explains what goes on when we value and evaluate works
of art or whether it simply reminds us that when we do this sort of
thing, we are considering something in an object other than erotic
appeal, commercial value, utility, or some other practical value.

The following essays introduce a variety of questions about the relation of an observer to a work of art. Although I have discussed only one of them, there are others that are equally important and interesting. What I have tried to suggest is that the significance of this topic derives from the assumptions we make about the proper relationships that connect critical verdicts with the experiences in which they originate.

Kenneth Burke

PSYCHOLOGY AND FORM*

It is not until the fourth scene of the first act that Hamlet confronts the ghost of his father. As soon as the situation has been
made clear, the audience has been, consciously or unconsciously,
waiting for this ghost to appear, while in the fourth scene this
moment has been definitely promised. For earlier in the play Hamlet had arranged to come to the platform at night with Horatio
to meet the ghost, and it is now night, he is with Horatio and
Marcellus, and they are standing on the platform. Hamlet asks
Horatio the hour.

> Hor. *I think it lacks of twelve.*
> Mar. *No, it is struck.*
> Hor. *Indeed? I heard it not: then it draws near the season*
> *Wherein the spirit held his wont to walk.*

Promptly hereafter there is a sound off-stage. "A flourish of trumpets and ordnance shot off within." Hamlet's friends have established
the hour as twelve. It is time for the ghost. Sounds off-stage, and of
course it is not the ghost. It is, rather, the sound of the king's carousal, for the king "keeps wassail." A tricky, and useful, detail.
We have been waiting for a ghost, and get, startlingly, a blare
of trumpets. And, once the trumpets are silent, we feel how desolate
are these three men waiting for a ghost, on a bare "platform," feel

* From Kenneth Burke, *Counter-Statement*, 2nd ed., ch. 2 (Los Altos,
Calif.: Hermes Publications, 1953). Reprinted by permission of the author.

it by this sudden juxtaposition of an imagined scene of lights and merriment. But the trumpets announcing a carousal have suggested a subject of conversation. In the darkness Hamlet discusses the excessive drinking of his countrymen. He points out that it tends to harm their reputation abroad, since, he argues, this one showy vice makes their virtues "in the general censure take corruption." And for this reason, although he himself is a native of this place, he does not approve of the custom. Indeed, there in the gloom he is talking very intelligently on these matters, and Horatio answers, "Look, my Lord, it comes." All this time we had been waiting for a ghost, and it comes at the one moment which was not pointing towards it. This ghost, so assiduously prepared for, is yet a surprise. And now that the ghost has come, we are waiting for something further. Program: a speech from Hamlet. Hamlet must confront the ghost. Here again Shakespeare can feed well upon the use of contrast for his effects. Hamlet has just been talking in a sober, rather argumentative manner—but now the flood-gates are unloosed:

> Angels and ministers of grace defend us!
> Be thou a spirit of health or goblin damn'd,
> Bring with thee airs from heaven or blasts from hell . . .

and the transition from the matter-of-fact to the grandiose, the full-throated and full-voweled, is a second burst of trumpets, perhaps even more effective than the first, since it is the rich fulfilment of a promise. Yet this satisfaction in turn becomes an allurement, an itch for further developments. At first desiring solely to see Hamlet confront the ghost, we now want Hamlet to learn from the ghost the details of the murder—which are, however, with shrewdness and husbandry, reserved for "Scene V.—Another Part of the Platform."

I have gone into this scene at some length, since it illustrates so perfectly the relationship between psychology and form, and so aptly indicates how the one is to be defined in terms of the other. That is, the psychology here is not the psychology of the *hero*, but the psychology of the *audience*. And by that distinction, form would be the psychology of the audience. Or, seen from another angle, form is the creation of an appetite in the mind of the auditor, and the adequate satisfying of that appetite. This satisfaction—so complicated is the human mechanism—at times involves a temporary set of frustrations, but in the end these frustrations prove to be simply a more involved kind of satisfaction, and furthermore serve to make the satisfaction of fulfilment more intense. If, in a work of art, the poet says something, let us say, about a meeting, writes in such a way that we desire to observe that meeting, and then, if he places that meeting before us—that is form. While obviously, that is also the psychology of the audience, since it involves desires and their appeasements.

The seeming breach between form and subject-matter, between technique and psychology, which has taken place in the last century is the result, it seems to me, of scientific criteria being unconsciously introduced into matters of purely aesthetic judgment. The flourishing of science has been so vigorous that we have not yet had time to make a spiritual readjustment adequate to the changes in our resources of material and knowledge. There are disorders of the social system which are caused solely by our undigested wealth (the basic disorder being, perhaps, the phenomenon of overproduction: to remedy this, instead of having all workers employed on half time, we have half working full time and the other half idle, so that whereas overproduction could be the greatest reward of applied science, it has been, up to now, the most menacing condition our modern civilization has had to face). It would be absurd to suppose that such social disorders would not be paralleled by disorders of culture and taste, especially since science is so pronouncedly a spiritual factor. So that we are, owing to the sudden wealth science has thrown upon us, all *nouveaux-riches* in matters of culture, and most poignantly in that field where lack of native firmness is most readily exposed, in matters of aesthetic judgment.

One of the most striking derangements of taste which science has temporarily thrown upon us involves the understanding of psychology in art. Psychology has become a body of information (which is precisely what psychology in science should be, or must be). And similarly, in art, we tend to look for psychology as the purveying of information. Thus, a contemporary writer has objected to Joyce's *Ulysses* on the ground that there are more psychoanalytic data available in Freud. (How much more drastically he might, by the same system, have destroyed Homer's *Odyssey!*) To his objection it was answered that one might, similarly, denounce Cézanne's trees in favor of state forestry bulletins. Yet are not Cézanne's landscapes themselves tainted with the psychology of information? Has he not, by perception, *pointed out* how one object lies against another, *indicated* what takes place between two colors (which is the psychology of science, and is less successful in the medium of art than in that of science, since in art such processes are at best implicit, whereas in science they are so readily made explicit)? Is Cézanne not, to that extent, a state forestry bulletin, except that he tells what goes on in the eye instead of on the tree? And do not the true values of his work lie elsewhere—and precisely in what I distinguish as the psychology of form?

Thus, the great influx of information has led the artist also to lay his emphasis on the giving of information—with the result that art tends more and more to substitute the psychology of the hero (the subject) for the psychology of the audience. Under such an attitude, when form is preserved it is preserved as an annex, a luxury, or, as some feel, a downright affectation. It remains, though sluggish, like the human appendix, for occasional demands are still made upon it; but its true vigor is gone, since it is no longer organically required. Proposition: The hypertrophy of the psychology of information is accompanied by the corresponding atrophy of the psychology of form.

In information, the matter is intrinsically interesting. And by intrinsically interesting I do not necessarily mean intrinsically valuable, as witness the intrinsic interest of backyard gossip or the most casual newspaper items. In art, at least the art of the great ages (Aeschylus, Shakespeare, Racine) the matter is interesting by means of an extrinsic use, a function. Consider, for instance, the speech of Mark Antony, the "Brutus is an honourable man." Imagine in the same place a very competently developed thesis on human conduct, with statistics, intelligence tests, definitions; imagine it as the finest thing of the sort ever written, and as really being at the roots of an understanding of Brutus. Obviously, the play would simply stop until Antony had finished. For in the case of Antony's speech, the value lies in the fact that his words are shaping the future of the audience's desires, not the desires of the Roman populace, but the desires of the pit. This is the psychology of form as distinguished from the psychology of information.

The distinction is, of course, absolutely true only in its nonexistent extremes. Hamlet's advice to the players, for instance, has little of the quality which distinguishes Antony's speech. It is, rather, intrinsically interesting, although one could very easily prove

how the play would benefit by some such delay at this point, and
that anything which made this delay possible without violating the
consistency of the subject would have, in this, its formal justification. It would, furthermore, be absurd to rule intrinsic interest out
of literature. I wish simply to have it restored to its properly
minor position, seen as merely one out of many possible elements of
style. Goethe's prose, often poorly imagined, or neutral, in its line-
for-line texture, especially in the treatment of romantic episode—
perhaps he felt that the romantic episode in itself was enough?—is
strengthened into a style possessing affirmative virtues by his rich
use of aphorism. But this is, after all, but one of many possible
facets of appeal. In some places, notably in *Wilhelm Meisters Lehr-
jahre* when Wilhelm's friends disclose the documents they have been
collecting about his life unbeknown to him, the aphorisms are
almost rousing in their efficacy, since they involve the story. But as
a rule the appeal of aphorism is intrinsic: that is, it satisfies without
being functionally related to the context.[1] . . . Also, to return to the
matter of Hamlet, it must be observed that the style in this passage is
no mere "information-giving" style; in its alacrity, its development,
it really makes this one fragment into a kind of miniature plot.

One reason why music can stand repetition so much more sturdily
than correspondingly good prose is that music, of all the arts, is by
its nature least suited to the psychology of information, and has
remained closer to the psychology of form. Here form cannot
atrophy. Every dissonant chord cries for its solution, and whether
the musician resolves or refuses to resolve this dissonance into the
chord which the body cries for, he is dealing in human appetites.
Correspondingly good prose, however, more prone to the temptations of pure information, cannot so much bear repetition since the
aesthetic value of information is lost once that information is imparted. If one returns to such a work again it is purely because, in
the chaos of modern life, he has been able to forget it. With a
desire, on the other hand, its recovery is as agreeable as its discovery.
One can memorize the dialogue between Hamlet and Guildenstern,

---

[1] Similarly, the epigram of Racine is "pure art," because it usually serves
to formulate or clarify some situation within the play itself. In Goethe the
epigram is most often of independent validity, as in *Die Wahlverwandtschaf-
ten*, where the ideas of Ottilie's diary are obviously carried over bodily from
the author's notebook. In Shakespeare we have the union of extrinsic and
intrinsic epigram, the epigram growing out of its context and yet valuable
independent of its context.

where Hamlet gives Guildenstern the pipe to play on. For, once the speech is known, its repetition adds a new element to compensate for the loss of novelty. We cannot take a recurrent pleasure in the new (in information) but we can in the natural (in form). Already, at the moment when Hamlet is holding out the pipe to·Guildenstern and asking him to play upon it, we "gloat over" Hamlet's triumphal descent upon Guildenstern, when, after Guildenstern has, under increasing embarrassment, protested three times that he cannot play the instrument, Hamlet launches the retort for which all this was preparation:

"Why, look you now, how unworthy a thing you make of me. You would play upon me, you would seem to know my stops; you would pluck out the heart of my mystery; you would sound me from my lowest note to the top of my compass; and there is much music, excellent voice, in this little organ, yet cannot you make it speak. 'Sblood, do you think I am easier to be played on than a pipe? Call me what instrument you will, though you can fret me, you cannot play upon me."[2]

In the opening lines we hear the promise of the close, and thus feel the emotional curve even more keenly than at first reading. Whereas in most modern art this element is underemphasized. It gives us the gossip of a plot, a plot which too often has for its value the mere fact that we don't know its outcome.[3]

Music, then, fitted less than any other art for imparting information, deals minutely in frustrations and fulfilments of desire,[4] and for that reason more often gives us those curves of emotion which, because they are natural, can bear repetition without loss. It is for this reason that music, like folk tales, is most capable of lulling us to sleep. A lullaby is a melody which comes quickly to

[2] One might indicate still further appropriateness here. As Hamlet finishes his speech, Polonius enters, and Hamlet turns to him, "God bless you, sir!" Thus, the plot is continued (for Polonius is always the promise of action) and a full stop is avoided: the embarrassment laid upon Rosencrantz and Guildenstern is not laid upon the audience.

[3] Yet modern music has gone far in the attempt to renounce this aspect of itself. Its dissonances become static, demanding no particular resolution. And whereas an unfinished modulation by a classic musician occasions positive dissatisfaction, the refusal to resolve a dissonance in modern music does not dissatisfy us, but irritates or stimulates. Thus, "energy" takes the place of style.

[4] Suspense is the least complex kind of anticipation, as surprise is the least complex kind of fulfilment.

rest, where the obstacles are easily overcome—and this is precisely the parallel to those waking dreams of struggle and conquest which (especially during childhood) we permit ourselves when falling asleep or when trying to induce sleep. Folk tales are just such waking dreams. Thus it is right that art should be called a "waking dream." The only difficulty with this definition (indicated by Charles Baudouin in his *Psychoanalysis and Aesthetics,* a very valuable study of Verhaeren) is that today we understand it to mean art as a waking dream for the artist. Modern criticism, and psychoanalysis in particular, is too prone to define the essence of art in terms of the artist's weaknesses. It is, rather, the audience which dreams, while the artist oversees the conditions which determine this dream. He is the manipulator of blood, brains, heart, and bowels which, while we sleep, dictate the mould of our desires. This is, of course, the real meaning of artistic felicity—an exaltation at the correctness of the procedure, so that we enjoy the steady march of doom in a Racinian tragedy with exactly the same equipment as that which produces our delight with Benedick's "Peace! I'll stop your mouth. (*Kisses her*)" which terminates the imbroglio of *Much Ado About Nothing.*

The methods of maintaining interest which are most natural to the psychology of information (as it is applied to works of pure art) are surprise and suspense. The method most natural to the psychology of form is eloquence. For this reason the great ages of Aeschylus, Shakespeare, and Racine, dealing as they did with material which was more or less a matter of common knowledge so that the broad outlines of the plot were known in advance (while it is the broad outlines which are usually exploited to secure surprise and suspense) developed formal excellence, or eloquence, as the basis of appeal in their work.

Not that there is any difference in kind between the classic method and the method of the cheapest contemporary melodrama. The drama, more than any other form, must never lose sight of its audience: here the failure to satisfy the proper requirements is most disastrous. And since certain contemporary work is successful, it follows that rudimentary laws of composition are being complied with. The distinction is one of intensity rather than of kind. The contemporary audience hears the lines of a play or novel with the same equipment as it brings to reading the lines of its daily paper. It is content to have facts placed before it in some more or less adequate sequence. Eloquence is the minimizing of this interest in fact, *per se*, so that the "more or less adequate sequence" of their presentation must be relied on to a much greater extent. Thus, those elements of surprise and suspense are subtilized, carried down into the writing of a line or a sentence, until in all its smallest details the work bristles with disclosures, contrasts, restatements with a difference, ellipses, images, aphorism, volume, sound-values, in short all that complex wealth of minutiae which in their line-for-line aspect we call style and in their broader outlines we call form.

As a striking instance of a modern play with potentialities in which the intensity of eloquence is missing, I might cite a recent success, Capek's *R.U.R.* Here, in a melodrama which was often astonishing in the rightness of its technical procedure, when the author was finished he had written nothing but the scenario for a play by Shakespeare. It was a play in which the author produced time and again the opportunity, the demand, for eloquence, only to move on. (At other times, the most successful moments, he utilized the modern discovery of silence, with moments wherein words could not possibly serve but to detract from the effect: this we might call the "flowering" of information.) The Adam and Eve scene of the last act, a "commission" which the Shakespeare of the comedies would have loved to fill, was in the verbal barrenness of Capek's play something shameless to the point of blushing. The Robot, turned human, prompted by the dawn of love to see his first sunrise, or hear the first bird-call, and forced merely to say "Oh, see the sunrise," or "Hear the pretty birds"—here one could do nothing but wring his hands at the absence of that aesthetic mould which produced the overslung "speeches" of Romeo and Juliet.

Suspense is the concern over the possible outcome of some specific detail of plot rather than for general qualities. Thus, "Will A marry B or C?" is suspense. In *Macbeth*, the turn from the murder scene to the porter scene is a much less literal channel of development. Here the presence of one quality calls forth the demand for another, rather than one tangible incident of plot awaking an interest in some other possible tangible incident of plot. To illustrate more fully, if an author managed over a certain number of his pages to produce a feeling of sultriness, or oppression, in the reader, this would unconsciously awaken in the reader the desire for a cold, fresh northwind —and thus some aspect of a northwind would be effective if called forth by some aspect of stuffiness. A good example of this is to be found in a contemporary poem, T. S. Eliot's *The Waste Land*, where the vulgar, oppressively trivial conversation in the public house calls forth in the poet a memory of a line from Shakespeare. These slobs in a public house, after a desolately low-visioned conversation, are now forced by closing time to leave the saloon. They say good-night. And suddenly the poet, feeling his release, drops into another good-night, a good-night with *désinvolture*, a good-night out of what was, within the conditions of the poem at least, a graceful and irrecoverable past.

> *Well that Sunday Albert was home, they had a hot gammon,*
> *And they asked me in to dinner, to get the beauty of it hot*—[at this point the bartender interrupts: it is closing time]
> *Goonight Bill. Goonight Lou. Goonight May. Goonight. Ta ta. Goonight. Goonight.*
> *Good-night, ladies, good-night, sweet ladies, good-night, good-night.*

There is much more to be said on these lines, which I have shortened somewhat in quotation to make my issue clearer. But I simply wish to point out here that this transition is a bold juxtaposition of one quality created by another, an association in ideas which, if not logical, is nevertheless emotionally natural. In the case of *Macbeth*, similarly, it would be absurd to say that the audience, after the murder scene, wants a porter scene. But the audience does want the quality which this porter particularizes. The dramatist might, conceivably, have introduced some entirely different character or event in this place, provided only that the event produced the same quality of relationship and contrast (grotesque seriousness followed by grotesque buffoonery). . . . One of the most beautiful and satisfactory "forms" of this sort is to be found in Baudelaire's *Femmes Damnées*, where the poet, after describing the business of a Lesbian seduction, turns to the full oratory of his apostrophe:

> *Descendez, descendez, lamentables victimes,*
> *Descendez le chemin de l'enfer éternel . . .*

while the stylistic efficacy of this transition contains a richness which transcends all moral (or unmoral) sophistication: the efficacy of appropriateness, of exactly the natural curve in treatment. Here is morality even for the godless, since it is a morality of art, being justified, if for no other reason, by its paralleling of that staleness, that disquieting loss of purpose, which must have followed the procedure of the two characters, the *femmes damnées* themselves, a remorse which, perhaps only physical in its origin, nevertheless becomes psychic.[5]

But to return, we have made three terms synonymous: form, psychology, and eloquence. And eloquence thereby becomes the essence of art, while pity, tragedy, sweetness, humor, in short all the emotions which we experience in life proper, as non-artists, are simply the material on which eloquence may feed. The arousing of pity, for instance, is not the central purpose of art, although it may be an adjunct of artistic effectiveness. One can feel pity much more keenly at the sight of some actual misfortune—and it would be a great mistake to see art merely as a weak representation of some actual experience.[6] That artists today are content to write under such an aesthetic accounts in part for the inferior position which art holds in the community. Art, at least in the great periods when it has flowered, was the conversion, or transcendence, of emotion into eloquence, and was thus a factor added to life. I am reminded of St. Augustine's caricature of the theatre: that whereas we do not dare to wish people unhappy, we do want to feel sorry for them, and therefore turn to plays so that we can feel sorry although no real misery is involved. One might apply the parallel interpretation to the modern delight in happy endings, and say that we turn to art to indulge our humanitarianism in a well-wishing which we do not permit ourselves towards our actual neighbors. Surely the catharsis of art is more complicated than this, and more reputable.

Eloquence itself, as I hope to have established in the instance from *Hamlet* which I have analyzed, is no mere plaster added to a framework of more stable qualities. Eloquence is simply the end of art, and is thus its essence. Even the poorest art is eloquent, but in a

---

[5] As another aspect of the same subject, I could cite many examples from the fairy tale. Consider, for instance, when the hero is to spend the night in a bewitched castle. Obviously, as darkness descends, weird adventures must befall him. His bed rides him through the castle; two halves of a man challenge him to a game of nine-pins played with thigh bones and skulls. Or entirely different incidents may serve instead of these. The quality comes first, the particularization follows.

[6] Could not the Greek public's resistance to Euripides be accounted for in the fact that he, of the three great writers of Greek tragedy, betrayed his art, was guilty of aesthetic impiety, in that he paid more attention to the arousing of emotion *per se* than to the sublimation of emotion into eloquence?

poor way, with less intensity, until this aspect is obscured by others fattening upon its leanness. Eloquence is not showiness; it is, rather, the result of that desire in the artist to make a work perfect by adapting it in every minute detail to the racial appetites.

The distinction between the psychology of information and the psychology of form involves a definition of aesthetic truth. It is here precisely, to combat the deflection which the strength of science has caused to our tastes, that we must examine the essential breach between scientific and artistic truth. Truth in art is not the discovery of facts, not in addition to human knowledge in the scientific sense of the word.[7] It is, rather, the exercise of human propriety, the formulation of symbols which rigidify our sense of poise and rhythm. Artistic truth is the externalization of taste.[8] I sometimes wonder, for instance, whether the "artificial" speech of John Lyly might perhaps be "truer" than the revelations of Dostoevsky. Certainly at its best, in its feeling for a statement which returns upon itself, which attempts the systole to a diastole, it *could* be much truer than Dostoevsky.[9] And if it is not, it fails not through a mis-

---

[7] One of the most striking examples of the encroachment of scientific truth into art is the doctrine of "truth by distortion," whereby one aspect of an object is suppressed the better to emphasize some other aspect; this is, obviously, an attempt to *indicate* by art some fact of knowledge, to make some implicit aspect of an object as explicit as one can by means of the comparatively dumb method of art (dumb, that is, as compared to the perfect ease with which science can indicate its discoveries). Yet science has already made discoveries in the realm of this "factual truth," this "truth by distortion" which must put to shame any artist who relies on such matter for his effects. Consider, for instance, the motion picture of a man vaulting. By photographing this process very rapidly, and running the reel very slowly, one has upon the screen the most striking set of factual truths to aid in our understanding of an athlete vaulting. Here, at our leisure, we can observe the contortions of four legs, a head and a butt. This squirming thing we saw upon the screen showed up an infinity of factual truths anent the balances of an athlete vaulting. We can, from this, observe the marvelous system of balancing which the body provides for itself in the adjustments of movement. Yet, so far as the aesthetic truth is concerned, this on the screen was not an athlete, but a squirming thing, a horror, displaying every fact of vaulting except the exhilaration of the act itself.

[8] The procedure of science involves the elimination of taste, employing as a substitute the corrective norm of the pragmatic test, the empirical experiment, which is entirely intellectual. Those who oppose the "intellectualism" of critics like Matthew Arnold are involved in an hilarious blunder, for Arnold's entire approach to the appreciation of art is through delicacies of taste intensified to the extent almost of squeamishness.

[9] As for instance, the "conceit" of Endymion's awakening, when he forgets his own name, yet recalls that of his beloved.

take of Lyly's aesthetic, but because Lyly was a man poor in character, whereas Dostoevsky was rich and complex. When Swift, making the women of Brobdingnag enormous, deduces from this discrepancy between their size and Gulliver's that Gulliver could sit astride their nipples, he has written something which is aesthetically true, which is, if I may be pardoned, profoundly "proper," as correct in its Euclidean deduction as any corollary in geometry. Given the companions of Ulysses in the cave of Polyphemus, it is true that they would escape clinging to the bellies of the herd let out to pasture. St. Ambrose, detailing the habits of God's creatures, and drawing from them moral maxims for the good of mankind, St. Ambrose in his limping natural history rich in scientific inaccuracies that are at the very heart of emotional rightness, St. Ambrose writes "Of night-birds, especially of the nightingale which hatches her eggs by song; of the owl, the bat, and the cock at cockcrow; in what wise these may apply to the guidance of our habits," and in the sheer rightness of that program there is the truth of art.

In introducing this talk of night-birds, after many pages devoted to other of God's creatures, he says,

"What now! While we have been talking, you will notice how the birds of night have already started fluttering about you, and, in this same fact of warning us to leave off with our discussion, suggest thereby a further topic"—and this seems to me to contain the best wisdom of which the human frame is capable, an address, a discourse, which can make our material life seem blatant almost to the point of despair. And when the cock crows, and the thief abandons his traps, and the sun lights up, and we are in every way called back to God by the well-meaning admonition of this bird, here the very blindnesses of religion become the deepest truths of art.

Edward Bullough

"PSYCHICAL DISTANCE"
AS A FACTOR IN ART AND
AN AESTHETIC PRINCIPLE*

1. The conception of "Distance" suggests, in connection with Art, certain trains of thought by no means devoid of interest or of speculative importance. Perhaps the most obvious suggestion is that of *actual spatial* distance, i.e. the distance of a work of Art from the spectator, or that of *represented spatial* distance, i.e. the distance represented within the work. Less obvious, more metaphorical, is the meaning of *temporal* distance. The first was noticed already by Aristotle in his *Poetics;* the second has played a great part in the history of painting in the form of perspective; the distinction between these two kinds of distance assumes special importance theoretically in the differentiation between sculpture in the round, and relief-sculpture. Temporal distance, remoteness from us in point of time, though often a cause of misconceptions, has been declared to be a factor of considerable weight in our appreciation.

It is not, however, in any of these meanings that "Distance" is put forward here, though it will be clear in the course of this essay that the above-mentioned kinds of distance are rather special forms

* From the *British Journal of Psychology*, Vol. V, 1912. Reprinted by permission of the Editor.

of the conception of Distance as advocated here, and derive whatever aesthetic qualities they may possess from Distance in its *general* connotation. This general connotation is "Psychical Distance."

A short illustration will explain what is meant by "Psychical Distance." Imagine a fog at sea: for most people it is an experience of acute unpleasantness. Apart from the physical annoyance and remoter forms of discomfort such as delays, it is apt to produce feelings of peculiar anxiety, fears of invisible dangers, strains of watching and listening for distant and unlocalised signals. The listless movements of the ship and her warning calls soon tell upon the nerves of the passengers; and that special, expectant, tacit anxiety and nervousness, always associated with this experience, make a fog the dreaded terror of the sea (all the more terrifying because of its very silence and gentleness) for the expert seafarer no less than for the ignorant landsman.

Nevertheless, a fog at sea can be a source of intense relish and enjoyment. Abstract from the experience of the sea fog, for the moment, its danger and practical unpleasantness, just as every one in the enjoyment of a mountain-climb disregards its physical labour and its danger (though, it is not denied, that these may incidentally enter into the enjoyment and enhance it); direct the attention to the features "objectively" constituting the phenomenon—the veil surrounding you with an opaqueness as of transparent milk, blurring the outline of things and distorting their shapes into weird grotesqueness; observe the carrying-power of the air, producing the impression as if you could touch some far-off siren by merely putting out your hand and letting it lose itself behind that white wall; note the curious creamy smoothness of the water, hypocritically denying as it were any suggestion of danger; and, above all, the strange solitude and remoteness from the world, as it can be found only on the highest mountain-tops: and the experience may acquire, in its uncanny mingling of repose and terror, a flavour of such concentrated poignancy and delight as to contrast sharply with the blind and distempered anxiety of its other aspects. This contrast, often emerging with startling suddenness, is like a momentary switching on of some new current, or the passing ray of a brighter light, illuminating the outlook upon perhaps the most ordinary and familiar objects—an impression which we experience sometimes in instants of direst extremity, when our practical interest snaps like a wire from sheer over-tension, and we watch the consummation of some impending catastrophe with the marvelling unconcern of a mere spectator.

It is a difference of outlook, due—if such a metaphor is permissible—to the insertion of Distance. This Distance apepars to lie between our own self and its affections, using the latter term in its broadest sense as anything which affects our being, bodily or spiritually, e.g. as sensation, perception, emotional state or idea. Usually, though not always, it amounts to the same thing to say that the Distance lies between our own self and such objects as are the sources or vehicles of such affections.

Thus, in the fog, the transformation by Distance is produced in the first instance by putting the phenomenon, so to speak, out of gear with our practical, actual self, by allowing it to stand outside the context of our personal needs and ends—in short, by looking at it "objectively," as it has often been called, by permitting only such reactions on our part as emphasise by the "objective" features of the experience, and by interpreting even our "subjective" affections not as modes of *our* being but rather as characteristics of the phenomenon.

The working of Distance is, accordingly, not simple, but highly complex. It has a *negative*, inhibitory aspect—the cutting-out of the practical sides of things and of our practical attitude to them —and a *positive* side—the elaboration of the experience on the new basis created by the inhibitory action of Distance.

2. Consequently, this distanced view of things is not, and cannot be, our normal outlook. As a rule, experiences constantly turn the same side towards us, namely, that which has the strongest practical force of appeal. We are not ordinarily aware of those aspects of things which do not touch us immediately and practically, nor are we generally conscious of impressions apart from our own self which is impressed. The sudden view of things from their reverse, usually unnoticed, side, comes upon us a a revelation, and such revelations are precisely those of Art. In this most general sense, Distance is a factor in all Art.

3. It is, for this very reason, also an aesthetic principle. The aesthetic contemplation and the aesthetic outlook have often been described as "objective." We speak of "objective" artists as Shakespeare or Velasquez, of "objective" works or art-forms as Homer's *Iliad* or the drama. It is a term constantly occurring in discussions and criticisms, though its sense, if pressed at all, becomes very questionable. For certain forms of Art, such as lyrical poetry, are

said to be "subjective"; Shelley, for example, would usually be considered a "subjective" writer. On the other hand, no work of Art can be genuinely "objective" in the sense in which this term might be applied to a work on history or to a scientific treatise; nor can it be "subjective" in the ordinary acceptance of that term, as a personal feeling, a direct statement of a wish or belief, or a cry of passion is subjective. "Objectivity" and "subjectivity" are a pair of opposites which in their mutual exclusiveness when applied to Art soon lead to confusion.

Nor are they the only pair of opposites. Art has with equal vigour been declared alternately "idealistic" and "realistic," "sensual" and "spiritual," "individualistic" and "typical." Between the defence of either terms of such antitheses most aesthetic theories have vacillated. It is one of the contentions of this essay that such opposites find their synthesis in the more fundamental conception of Distance.

Distance further provides the much needed criterion of the beautiful as distinct from the merely agreeable.

Again, it marks one of the most important steps in the process of artistic creation and serves as a distinguishing feature of what is commonly so loosely described as the "artistic temperament."

Finally, it may claim to be considered as one of the essential characteristics of the "aesthetic consciousness," if I may describe by this term that special mental attitude towards, and outlook upon, experience, which finds its most pregnant expression in the various forms of Art.

II

Distance, as I said before, is obtained by separating the object and its appeal from one's own self by putting it out of gear with practical needs and ends. Thereby the "contemplation" of the object becomes alone possible. But it does not mean that the relation between the self and the object is broken to the extent of becoming "impersonal." Of the alternatives "personal" and "impersonal" the latter surely comes nearer to the truth; but here, as elsewhere, we meet the difficulty of having to express certain facts in terms coined for entirely different uses. To do so usually results in paradoxes, which are nowhere more inevitable than in discussions upon Art. "Personal" and "impersonal," "subjective" and "objective" are such terms, devised for purposes other than aesthetic speculation, and becoming loose and ambiguous as soon as applied outside the sphere of their special meanings. In giving preference therefore to the term "impersonal" to describe the relation between the spectator and a work of Art, it is to be noticed that it is not impersonal in the sense in which we speak of the "impersonal" character of Science, for instance. In order to obtain "objectively valid" results, the scientist excludes the "personal factor," i.e. his personal wishes as to the validity of his results, his predilection for any particular system to be proved or disproved by his research. It goes without saying that all experiments and investigations are undertaken out of a personal interest in the science, for the ultimate support of a definite assumption, and involve personal hopes of success; but this does not affect the "dispassionate" attitude of the investigator, under pain of being accused of "manufacturing his evidence."

1. Distance does not imply an impersonal, purely intellectually interested relation of such a kind. On the contrary, it describes a *personal* relation, often highly emotionally coloured, but *of a peculiar character*. Its peculiarity lies in that the personal character of the relation has been, so to speak, filtered. It has been cleared of the practical, concrete nature of its appeal, without, however, thereby losing its original constitution. One of the best-known examples is to be found in our attitude towards the events and characters of the drama: they appeal to us like persons and incidents of normal experience, except that that side of their appeal, which would usually affect us in a directly personal manner, is held in abeyance. This difference, so well known as to be almost trivial, is generally explained by reference to the knowledge that the characters and situations are "unreal," imaginary. In this sense Witasek,[1] operating with Meinong's theory of *Annahmen*, has described the emotions involved in witnessing a drama as *Scheingefühle*, a term which has so frequently been misunderstood in discussions of his theories. But, as a matter of fact, the "assumption" upon which the imaginative emotional reaction is based is not necessarily the condition, but often the consequence, of Distance; that is to say, the converse of the reason usually stated would then be true: viz. that Distance, by changing our relation to the charac-

---

[1] H. Witasek, "Zur psychologischen Analyse der aesthetischen Einfühling," *Ztsch. f. Psychol. u. Physiol. der Sinnesorg.*, 1901, xxv, 1 ff.; *Grundzüge der Aesthetik*, Leipzig, 1904.

ters, renders them seemingly fictitious, not that the fictitiousness of the characters alters our feelings towards them. It is, of course, to be granted that the actual and admitted unreality of the dramatic action reinforces the effect of Distance. But surely the proverbial unsophisticated yokel, whose chivalrous interference in the play on behalf of the hapless heroine can only be prevented by impressing upon him that "they are only pretending," is not the ideal type of theatrical audience. The proof of the seeming paradox that it is Distance which primarily gives to dramatic action the appearance of unreality and not vice versa, is the observation that the same filtration of our sentiments and the same seeming "unreality" of *actual* men and things occur, when at times, by a sudden change of inward perspective, we are overcome by the feeling that "all the world's a stage."

2. This personal, but "distanced" relation (as I will venture to call this nameless character of our view) directs attention to a strange fact which appears to be one of the fundamental paradoxes of Art: it is what I propose to call "the antinomy of Distance."

It will be readily admitted that a work of Art has the more chance of appealing to us the better it finds us prepared for its particular kind of appeal. Indeed, without some degree of pre-disposition on our part, it must necessarily remain incomprehensible, and to that extent unappreciated. The success and intensity of its appeal would seem, therefore, to stand in direct proportion to the completeness with which it corresponds with our intellectual and emotional peculiarities and the idiosyncrasies of our experience. The absence of such a concordance between the characters of a work and of the spectator is, of course, the most general explanation for differences of "tastes."

At the same time, such a principle of concordance requires a qualification, which leads at once to the antinomy of Distance.

Suppose a man, who believes that he has cause to be jealous about his wife, witnesses a performance of *Othello*. He will the more perfectly appreciate the situation, conduct and character of Othello, the more exactly the feelings and experiences of Othello coincide with his own—at least he *ought* to on the above principle of concordance. In point of fact, he will probably do anything but appreciate the play. In reality, the concordance will merely render him acutely conscious of his own jealousy; by a sudden reversal of perspective he will no longer see Othello apparently betrayed by

Desdemona, but himself in an analogous situation with his own wife. This reversal of perspective is the consequence of the loss of Distance.

If this be taken as a typical case, it follows that the qualification required is that the coincidence should be as complete as is compatible with maintaining Distance. The jealous spectator of *Othello* will indeed appreciate and enter into the play the more keenly, the greater the resemblance with his own experience—*provided* that he succeeds in keeping the Distance between the action of the play and his personal feelings: a very difficult performance in the circumstances. It is on account of the same difficulty that the expert and the professional critic make a bad audience, since their expertness and critical professionalism are *practical* activities, involving their concrete personality and constantly endangering their Distance. (It is, by the way, one of the reasons why Criticism is an art, for it requires the constant interchange from the practical to the distanced attitude and vice versa, which is characteristic of artists.)

The same qualification applies to the artist. He will prove artistically most effective in the formulation of an intensely *personal* experience, but he can formulate it artistically only on condition of a detachment from the experience *qua personal*. Hence the statement of so many artists that artistic formulation was to them a kind of catharsis, a means of ridding themselves of feelings and ideas the acuteness of which they felt almost as a kind of obsession. Hence, on the other hand, the failure of the average man to convey to others at all adequately the impression of an overwhelming joy or sorrow. His personal implication in the event renders it impossible for him to formulate and present it in such a way as to make others, like himself, feel all the meaning and fullness which it possesses for him.

What is therefore, both in appreciation and production, most desirable is the *utmost decrease of Distance without its disappearance.*

3. Closely related, in fact a presupposition to the "antinomy," is the *variability* of Distance. Herein especially lies the advantage of Distance compared with such terms as "objectivity" and "detachment." Neither of them implies a *personal* relation—indeed both actually preclude it; and the mere inflexibility and exclusiveness of their opposites render their application generally meaningless.

Distance, on the contrary, admits naturally of degrees, and differs not only according to the nature of the *object*, which may impose a greater or smaller degree of Distance, but varies also according to the *individual's capacity* for maintaining a greater or lesser degree. And here one may remark that not only do *persons differ from each other* in their habitual measure of Distance, but that the *same individual differs* in his ability to maintain it in the face of different objects and of different arts.

There exist, therefore, two different sets of conditions affecting the degree of Distance in any given case: those offered by the object and those realised by the subject. In their interplay they afford one of the most extensive explanations for varieties of aesthetic experience, since loss of Distance, whether due to the one or the other, means loss of aesthetic appreciation.

In short, Distance may be said *to be variable both according to the distancing-power of the individual, and according to the character of the object.*

There are two ways of losing Distance: either to "under-distance" or to "over-distance." "Under-distancing" is the commonest failing of the *subject,* an excess of Distance is a frequent failing of *Art,* especially in the past. Historically it looks almost as if Art had attempted to meet the deficiency of Distance on the part of the subject and had overshot the mark in this endeavour. It will be seen later that this is actually true, for it appears that over-distanced Art is specially designed for a class of appreciation which has difficulty to rise spontaneously to any degree of Distance. The consequence of a loss of Distance through one or other cause is familiar: the verdict in the case of under-distancing is that the work is "crudely naturalistic," "harrowing," "repulsive in its realism." An excess of Distance produces the impression of improbability, artificiality, emptiness or absurdity.

The individual tends, as I just stated, to under-distance rather than to lose Distance by over-distancing. *Theoretically* there is no limit to the decrease of Distance. In theory, therefore, not only the usual subjects of Art, but even the most personal affections, whether ideas, percepts or emotions, can be sufficiently distanced to be aesthetically appreciable. Especially artists are gifted in this direction to a remarkable extent. The average individual, on the contrary, very rapidly reaches his limit of decreasing Distance, his "Distance-limit," i.e. that point at which Distance is lost and appreciation either disappears or changes its character.

In the *practice,* therefore, of the average person, a limit does exist which marks the minimum at which his appreciation can maintain itself in the aesthetic field, and this average minimum lies considerably higher than the Distance-limit of the artist. It is practically impossible to fix this average limit, in the absence of data, and on account of the wide fluctuations from person to person to which this limit is subject. But it is safe to infer that, in art practice, explicit references to organic affections, to the material existence of the body, especially to sexual matters, lie normally below the Distance-limit, and can be touched upon by Art only with special precautions. Allusions to social institutions of any degree of personal importance—in particular, allusions implying any doubt as to their validity—the questioning of some generally recognised ethical sanctions, references to topical subjects occupying public attention at the moment, and such like, are all dangerously near the average limit and may at any time fall below it, arousing, instead of aesthetic appreciation, concrete hostility or mere amusement.

This difference in the Distance-limit between artists and the public has been the source of much misunderstanding and injustice. Many an artist has seen his work condemned and himself ostracised for the sake of so-called "immoralities" which to him were bona fide aesthetic objects. His power of distancing, nay, the necessity of distancing feelings, sensations, situations which for the average person are too intimately bound up with his concrete existence to be regarded in that light, have often quite unjustly earned for him accusations of cynicism, sensualism, morbidness or frivolity. The same misconception has arisen over many "problem plays" and "problem novels" in which the public have persisted in seeing nothing but a supposed "problem" of the moment, whereas the author may have been—and often has demonstrably been—able to distance the subject-matter sufficiently to rise above its practical problematic import and to regard it simply as a dramatically and humanly interesting situation.

The variability of Distance in respect to Art, disregarding for the moment the subjective complication, appears both as a general feature in Art, and in the differences between the special arts.

It has been an old problem why the "arts of the eye and of the ear" should have reached the practically exclusive predominance over arts of other senses. Attempts to raise "culinary art" to the level of a Fine Art have failed in spite of all propaganda, as completely as the creation of scent or liqueur "symphonies." There is little doubt that, apart from other excellent reasons[2] of a partly psycho-physical, partly technical nature, the actual, *spatial distance* separating objects of sight and hearing from the subject has contributed strongly to the development of this monopoly. In a similar manner *temporal remoteness* produces Distance, and objects removed from us in point of time are *ipso facto* distanced to an extent which was impossible for their contemporaries. Many pictures, plays and poems had, as a matter of fact, rather an expository or illustrative significance—as for instance much ecclesiastical Art —or the force of a direct practical appeal—as the invectives of many satires or comedies—which seem to us nowadays irreconcilable with their aesthetic claims. Such works have consequently profited greatly by lapse of time and have reached the level of Art only with the help of temporal distance, while others, on the contrary, often for the same reason have suffered a loss of Distance, through *over-distancing*.

Special mention must be made of a group of artistic conceptions which present excessive Distance in their form of appeal rather than in their actual presentation—a point illustrating the necessity of distinguishing between distancing an object and distancing the appeal of which it is the source. I mean here what is often rather loosely termed "idealistic Art," that is, Art springing from abstract conceptions, expressing allegorical meanings, or illustrating general truths. Generalisations and abstractions suffer under this disadvantage that they have too much general applicability to invite a personal interest in them, and too little individual concreteness to prevent them applying to us in all their force. They appeal to everybody and therefore to none. An axiom of Euclid belongs to nobody, just because it compels everyone's assent; general conceptions like Patriotism, Friendship, Love, Hope, Life, Death, concern as much Dick, Tom, and Harry as myself, and I, therefore, either feel unable to get into any kind of personal relation to them, or, if I do so, they become at once, emphatically and concretely, *my* Patriotism, *my* Friendship, *my* Love, *my* Hope, *my* Life and Death. By mere force of generalisation, a general truth or a universal ideal is so far distanced from myself that I fail to realise it concretely at all, or, when

---

2 J. Volkelt, "Die Bedeutung der niederen Empfindungen für die aesthetische Einfühlung," *Ztsch. f. Psychol. u. Physiol. der Sinnesorg.*, xxxii, 15, 16; *System der Aesthetik*, 1, 260 ff.

I do so, I can realise it only as part of my *practical actual being,*
i.e. it falls below the Distance-limit altogether. "Idealistic Art"
suffers consequently under the peculiar difficulty that its excess of
Distance turns generally into an *under-*distanced appeal—all the
more easily, as it is the usual failing of the subject to *under-* rather
than to *over-*distance.

The different special arts show at the present time very marked
variations in the degree of Distance which they usually impose
or require for their appreciation. Unfortunately here again the
absence of data makes itself felt and indicates the necessity of conducting observations, possibly experiments, so as to place these
suggestions upon a securer basis. In one single art, viz. the *theatre,*
a small amount of information is available, from an unexpected
source, namely the proceedings of the censorship committee,[3]
which on closer examination might be made to yield evidence of
interest to the psychologist. In fact, the whole censorship problem,
as far as it does not turn upon purely economic questions, may be
said to hinge upon Distance; if every member of the public could
be trusted to keep it, there would be no sense whatever in the
existence of a censor of plays. There is, of course, no doubt that,
speaking generally, theatrical performances *eo ipso* run a special
risk of loss of Distance owing to the material presentment[4] of its
subject-matter. The physical presence of living human beings as
vehicles of dramatic art is a difficulty which no art has to face in the
same way. A similar, in many ways even greater, risk confronts
dancing: though attracting perhaps a less widely spread human
interest, its animal spirits are frequently quite unrelieved by any
glimmer of spirituality and consequently form a proportionately
stronger lure to under-distancing. In the higher forms of dancing
technical execution of the most wearing kind makes up a great
deal for its intrinsic tendency towards a loss of Distance, and as a
popular performance, at least in southern Europe, it has retained
much of its ancient artistic glamour, producing a peculiarly subtle
balancing of Distance between the pure delight of bodily movement and high technical accomplishment. In passing, it is interesting to observe (as bearing upon the development of Distance)

---

[3] Report from the Joint Select Committee of the House of Lords and the
House of Commons on Stage Plays (Censorship), 1909.
[4] I shall use the term "presentment" to denote the manner of presenting, in
distinction to "presentation" as that which is presented.

that this art, once as much a fine art as music and considered by the Greeks as a particularly valuable educational exercise, should— except in sporadic cases—have fallen so low from the pedestal it once occupied. Next to the theatre and dancing stands *sculpture*. Though not using a *living* bodily medium, yet the human form in its full spatial materiality constitutes a similar threat to Distance. Our northern habits of dress and ignorance of the human body have enormously increased the difficulty of distancing Sculpture, in part through the gross misconceptions to which it is exposed, in part owing to a complete lack of standards of bodily perfection, and an inability to realise the distinction between sculptural form and bodily shape, which is the only but fundamental point distinguishing a statue from a cast taken from life. In *painting* it is apparently the form of its presentment and the usual reduction in scale which would explain why this art can venture to approach more closely than sculpture to the normal Distance-limit. As this matter will be discussed later in a special connection this simple reference may suffice here. *Music* and *architecture* have a curious position. These two most abstract of all arts show a remarkable fluctuation in their Distances. Certain kinds of music, especially "pure" music, or "classical" or "heavy" music, appear for many people over-distanced; light, "catchy" tunes, on the contrary, easily reach that degree of decreasing Distance below which they cease to be Art and become a pure amusement. In spite of its strange abstractness which to many philosophers has made it comparable to architecture and mathematics, music possesses a sensuous, frequently sensual, character: the undoubted physiological and muscular stimulus of its melodies and harmonies, no less than its rhythmic aspects, would seem to account for the occasional disappearance of Distance. To this might be added its strong tendency, especially in unmusical people, to stimulate trains of thought quite disconnected with itself, following channels of subjective inclinations— day-dreams of a more or less directly personal character. *Architecture* requires almost uniformly a very great Distance; that is to say, the majority of persons derive no aesthetic appreciation from architecture as such, apart from the incidental impression of its decorative features and its associations. The causes are numerous, but prominent among them are the confusion of building with architecture and the predominance of utilitarian purposes, which overshadow the architectural claims upon the attention.

4. That all art requires a Distance-limit beyond which, and a Distance within which only, aesthetic appreciation becomes possible, is the *psychological formulation of a general characteristic of Art*, viz. its *anti-realistic nature*. Though seemingly paradoxical, this applies as much to "naturalistic" as to "idealistic" Art. The difference commonly expressed by these epithets is at bottom merely the difference in the degree of Distance; and this produces, so far as "naturalism" and "idealism" in Art are not meaningless labels, the usual result that what appears obnoxiously "naturalistic" to one person, may be "idealistic" to another. To say that Art is anti-realistic simply insists upon the fact that Art is not nature, never pretends to be nature and strongly resists any confusion with nature. It emphasises the *art*-character of Art: "artistic" is synonymous with "anti-realistic"; it explains even sometimes a very marked degree of artificiality.

"Art is an imitation of nature," was the current art-conception in the eighteenth century. It is the fundamental axiom of the standard work of that time upon aesthetic theory by the Abbé Du Bos, *Réflexions critiques sur la poésie et la peinture*, 1719; the idea received strong support from the literal acceptance of Aristotle's theory of μίμησις and produced echoes everywhere, in Lessing's *Laokoon* no less than in Burke's famous statement that "all Art is great as it deceives." Though it may be assumed that since the time of Kant and of the Romanticists this notion has died out, it still lives in unsophisticated minds. Even when formally denied, it persists, for instance, in the belief that "Art idealises nature," which means after all only that Art copies nature with certain improvements and revisions. Artists themselves are unfortunately often responsible for the spreading of this conception. Whistler indeed said that to produce Art by imitating nature would be like trying to produce music by sitting upon the piano, but the selective, idealising imitation of nature finds merely another support in such a saying. Naturalism, pleinairism, impressionism, even the guileless enthusiasm of the artist for the works of nature, her wealth of suggestion, her delicacy of workmanship, for the steadfastness of her guidance, only produce upon the public the impression that Art is, after all, an imitation of nature. Then how can it be anti-realistic? The antithesis, Art *versus* nature, seems to break down. Yet if it does, what is the sense of Art?

Here the conception of Distance comes to the rescue. The solution of the dilemma lies in the "antinomy of Distance" with its demand: utmost decrease of Distance without its disappearance. The simple observation that Art is the more effective, the more it falls into line with our predispositions which are inevitably moulded on general experience and nature, has always been the original motive for "naturalism." "Naturalism," "impressionism" is no new thing; it is only a new name for an innate leaning of Art, from the time of the Chaldeans and Egyptians down to the present day. Even the Apollo of Tenea apparently struck his contemporaries as so startlingly "naturalistic" that the subsequent legend attributed a superhuman genius to his creator. A constantly closer approach to nature, a perpetual refining of the limit of Distance, yet without overstepping the dividing line of art and nature, has always been the inborn bent of art. To deny this dividing line has occasionally been the failing of naturalism. But no theory of naturalism is complete which does not at the same time allow for the intrinsic idealism of Art: for both are merely degrees in that wide range lying beyond the Distance-limit. To imitate nature so as to trick the spectator into the deception that it is nature which he beholds, is to forsake Art, its anti-realism, its distanced spirituality, and to fall below the limit into sham, sensationalism or platitude.

But what, in the theory of antinomy of Distance, requires explanation is the existence of an *idealistic, highly distanced* Art. There are numerous reasons to account for it; indeed in so complex a phenomenon as Art, *single* causes can be pronounced almost *a priori* to be false. Foremost among such causes which have contributed to the formation of an idealistic Art appears to stand the subordination of Art to some extraneous purpose of an impressive, exceptional character. Such a subordination has consisted—at various epochs of Art history—in the use to which Art was to put to subserve commemorative, hieratic, generally religious, royal or patriotic functions. The object to be commemorated had to stand out from among other still existing objects or persons; the thing or the being to be worshipped had to be distinguished as markedly as possible from profaner objects of reverence and had to be invested with an air of sanctity by a removal from its ordinary context of occurrence. Nothing could have assisted more powerfully the introduction of a high Distance than this attempt to differentiate objects of common experience in order to fit them for their exalted position. Curious, unusual things of nature met this tendency half-way and easily assumed divine rank; but others had to be distanced by an exaggeration of their size, by extraordinary attributes, by strange combinations of human and animal forms, by special insistence upon particular characteristics, or by the careful removal of all noticeably individualistic and concrete features. Nothing could be more striking than the contrast, for example, in Egyptian Art between the monumental, stereotyped effigies of the Pharaohs, and the startlingly realistic rendering of domestic scenes and of ordinary mortals, such as "the Scribe" or "the Village Sheikh." Equally noteworthy is the exceeding artificiality of Russian eikon-painting with its prescribed attributes, expressions and gestures. Even Greek dramatic practice appears to have aimed, for similar purposes and in marked contrast to our stage-habits, at an increase rather than at a decrease of Distance. Otherwise Greek Art, even of a religious type, is remarkable for its *low* Distance value; and it speaks highly for the aesthetic capacities of the Greeks that the degree of realism which they ventured to impart to the representations of their gods, while humanising them, did not, at least at first,[5] impair the reverence of their feelings towards them. But apart from such special causes, idealistic Art of great Distance has appeared at intervals, for apparently no other reason than that the great Distance was felt to be essential to its *art*-character. What is noteworthy and runs counter to many accepted ideas is that such periods were usually epochs of a low level of general culture. These were times, which, like childhood, required the marvellous, the extraordinary, to satisfy their artistic longings, and neither realised nor cared for the poetic or artistic qualities of ordinary things. They were frequently times in which the mass of the people were plunged in ignorance and buried under a load of misery, and in which even the small educated class sought rather amusement or a pastime in Art; or they were epochs of a strong practical common sense too much concerned with the rough-and-tumble of life to have any sense of its aesthetic charms. Art was to them what melodrama is to a section of the public at the present time, and its wide Distance was the safeguard of its artistic character. The flowering periods of Art have, on the contrary, always borne the evidence of a nar-

---

[5] That this practice did, in course of time, undermine their religious faith, is clear from the plays of Euripides and from Plato's condemnation of Homer's mythology.

row Distance. Greek Art, as just mentioned, was realistic to an extent which we, spoilt as we are by modern developments, can grasp with difficulty, but which the contrast with its oriental contemporaries sufficiently proves. During the Augustan period—which Art historians at last are coming to regard no longer as merely "degenerated" Greek Art—Roman Art achieved its greatest triumphs in an almost naturalistic portrait-sculpture. In the Renaissance we need only think of the realism of portraiture, sometimes amounting almost to cynicism, of the *désinvolture* with which the mistresses of popes and dukes were posed as madonnas, saints and goddesses apparently without any detriment to the aesthetic appeal of the works, and of the remarkable interpenetration of Art with the most ordinary routine of life, in order to realise the scarcely perceptible dividing line between the sphere of Art and the realm of practical existence. In a sense, the assertion that idealistic Art marks periods of a generally low and narrowly restricted culture is the converse to the oft-repeated statement that the flowering periods of Art coincide with epochs of decadence: for this so-called decadence represents indeed in certain respects a process of disintegration, politically, racially, often nationally, but a disruption necessary to the formation of larger social units and to the breakdown of outgrown national restrictions. For this very reason it has usually also been the sign of the growth of personal independence and of an expansion of individual culture.

To proceed to some more special points illustrating the distanced and therefore anti-realistic character of art: both in subject-matter and in the form of presentation Art has always safeguarded its distanced view. Fanciful, even fantastic, subjects have from time immemorial been the accredited material of Art. No doubt things, as well as our view of them, have changed in the course of time: *Polyphemus* and the *Lotus-Eaters* for the Greeks, the *Venusberg* or the *Magnetic Mountain* for the Middle Ages were less incredible, more realistic than to us. But *Peter Pan* or *L'Oiseau Bleu* still appeal at the present day in spite of the prevailing note of realism of our time. "Probability" and "improbability" in Art are not to be measured by their correspondence (or lack of it) with actual experience. To do so had involved the theories of the fifteenth to the eighteenth centuries in endless contradictions. It is rather a matter of *consistency* of Distance. The note of realism, set by a work as a whole, determines *intrinsically* the greater or smaller degree of fancy which it permits; and consequently we feel the loss of Peter Pan's shadow to be infinitely more probable than some trifling improbability which shocks our sense of proportion in a naturalistic work. No doubt also, fairy-tales, fairy-plays, stories of strange adventures were primarily invented to satisfy the craving of curiosity, the desire for the marvellous, the shudder of the unwonted and the longing for imaginary experiences. But by their mere eccentricity in regard to the normal facts of experience they cannot have failed to arouse a strong feeling of Distance.

Again, certain conventional subjects taken from mythical and legendary traditions, at first closely connected with the concrete, practical, life of a devout public, have gradually, by the mere force of convention as much as by their inherent anti-realism, acquired Distance for us today. Our view of Greek mythological sculpture, of early Christian saints and martyrs must be considerably distanced, compared with that of the Greek and medieval worshipper. It is in part the result of lapse of time, but in part also a real change of attitude. Already the outlook of the Imperial Roman had altered, and Pausanias shows a curious dualism of standpoint, declaring the Athene Lemnia to be the supreme achievement of Phidias's genius, and gazing awe-struck upon the roughly hewn tree-trunk representing some primitive Apollo. Our understanding of Greek tragedy suffers admittedly under our inability to revert to the point of view for which it was originally written. Even the tragedies of Racine demand an imaginative effort to put ourselves back into the courtly atmosphere of red-heeled, powdered ceremony. Provided the Distance is not too wide, the result of its intervention has everywhere been to enhance the *art*-character of such works and to lower their original ethical and social force of appeal. Thus in the central dome of the Church (Sta Maria dei Miracoli) at Saronno are depicted the heavenly hosts in ascending tiers, crowned by the benevolent figure of the Divine Father, bending from the window of heaven to bestow His blessing upon the assembled community. The mere realism of foreshortening and of the boldest vertical perspective may well have made the naïve Christian of the sixteenth century conscious of the Divine Presence—but for us it has become a work of Art.

The unusual, exceptional, has found its especial home in tragedy. It has always—except in highly distanced tragedy—been a popular objection to it that "there is enough sadness in life without going to the theatre for it." Already Aristotle appears to have met with this view among his contemporaries clamouring for "happy endings." Yet tragedy is not sad; if it were, there would indeed be little sense in its existence. For the tragic is just in so far different from the merely sad, as it is distanced; and it is largely the exceptional which produces the Distance of tragedy: exceptional situations, exceptional characters, exceptional destinies and conduct. Not of course characters merely cranky, eccentric, pathological. The exceptional element in tragic figures—that which makes them so utterly different from characters we meet with in ordinary experience—is a consistency of direction, a fervour of ideality, a persistence and driving-force which is far above the capacities of average men. The tragic of tragedy would, transposed into ordinary life, in nine cases out of ten, end in drama, in comedy, even in farce, for lack of steadfastness, for fear of conventions, for the dread of "scenes," for a hundred-and-one petty faithlessnesses towards a belief or an ideal: even if for none of these, it would end in a compromise simply because man forgets and time heals.[6] Again, the sympathy which aches with the sadness of tragedy is another such confusion, the under-distancing of tragedy's appeal. Tragedy trembles always on the knife-edge of a *personal* reaction, and sympathy which finds relief in tears tends almost always towards a loss of Distance. Such a loss naturally renders tragedy unpleasant to a degree: it becomes sad, dismal, harrowing, depressing. But real tragedy (melodrama has a very strong tendency to speculate upon sympathy), truly appreciated, is not sad. "The pity of it—oh, the pity of it," that essence of all genuine tragedy is not the pity of mild, regretful sympathy. It is a chaos of tearless, bitter bewilderment, of upsurging revolt and rapturous awe before the ruthless and inscrutable fate; it is the homage to the great and exceptional in the man who in a last effort of spiritual

---

[6] The famous "unity of time," so senseless as a "canon," is all the same often an indispensable condition of tragedy. For in many a tragedy the catastrophe would be even intrinsically impossible, if fatality did not overtake the hero with that rush which gives no time to forget and none to heal. It is in cases such as these that criticism has often blamed the work for "improbability"— the old confusion between Art and nature—forgetting that the death of the hero is the convention of the art-form, as much as grouping in a picture is such a convention and that probability is not the correspondence with average experience, but consistency of Distance.

tension can rise to confront blind, crowning Necessity even in his crushing defeat.

As I explained earlier, the form of presentation sometimes endangers the maintenance of Distance, but it more frequently acts as a considerable support. Thus the bodily vehicle of *drama* is the chief factor of risk to Distance. But, as if to counterbalance a confusion with nature, other features of stage-presentation exercise an opposite influence. Such are the general theatrical *milieu*, the shape and arrangement of the stage, the artificial lighting, the costumes, *mise en scène* and make-up, even the language, especially verse. Modern reforms of staging, aiming primarily at the removal of artistic incongruities between excessive decoration and the living figures of the actors and at the production of a more homogeneous stage-picture, inevitably work also towards a greater emphasis and homogeneity of Distance. The history of staging and dramaturgy is closely bound up with the evolution of Distance, and its fluctuations lie at the bottom not only of the greater part of all the talk and writing about "dramatic probability" and the Aristotelian "unities," but also of "theatrical illusion." In *sculpture*, one distancing factor of presentment is its lack of colour. The aesthetic, or rather inaesthetic, effect of realistic colouring is in no way touched by the controversial question of its use historically; its attempted resuscitation, such as by Klinger, seems only to confirm its disadvantages. The distancing use even of pedestals, although originally no doubt serving other purposes, is evident to anyone who has experienced the oppressively crowded sensation of moving in a room among life-sized statues placed directly upon the floor. The circumstance that the space of statuary is the same space as ours (in distinction to relief sculpture or painting, for instance) renders a distancing by pedestals, i.e. a removal from our spatial context, imperative.[7] Probably the framing of *pictures* might be shown to serve a similar purpose—though paintings have intrinsically a much greater Distance—because neither their space (perspective and imaginary space) nor their lighting coincides with our (actual) space or light, and the usual reduction in scale of the represented objects prevents a feeling of undue proximity. Besides, painting

---

[7] An instance which might be adduced to disprove this point only shows its correctness on closer inspection: for it was on purpose and with the intention of removing Distance, that Rodin originally intended his *citoyens de Calais* to be placed, without pedestals, upon the market-place of that town.

always retains to some extent a *two*-dimensional character, and this character supplies *eo ipso* a Distance. Nevertheless, life-size pictures, especially if they possess strong relief, and their light happens to coincide with the actual lighting, can occasionally produce the impression of actual presence which is a far from pleasant, though fortunately only a passing, illusion. For decorative purposes, in pictorial renderings of vistas, garden-perspectives and architectural extensions, the removal of Distance has often been consciously striven after, whether with aesthetically satisfactory results is much disputed.

A general help towards Distance (and therewith an anti-realistic feature) is to be found in the "unification of presentment"[8] of all art-objects. By unification of presentment are meant such qualities as symmetry, opposition, proportion, balance, rhythmical distribution of parts, light-arrangements, in fact all so-called "formal" features, "composition" in the widest sense. Unquestionably, Distance is not the only, nor even the principal function of composition; it serves to render our grasp of the presentation easier and to increase its intelligibility. It may even in itself constitute the principal aesthetic feature of the object, as in linear complexes or patterns, partly also in architectural designs. Yet, its distancing effect can hardly be underrated. For, every kind of visibly intentional arrangement or unification must, by the mere facts of its presence, enforce Distance, by distinguishing the object from the confused, disjointed and scattered forms of actual experience. This function can be gauged in a typical form in cases where composition produces an exceptionally marked impression of artificiality (not in the bad sense of that term, but in the sense in which all art is artificial); and it is a natural corollary to the differences of Distance in different arts and of different subjects, that the arts and subjects vary in the degree of artificiality which they can bear. It is this sense of artificial finish which is the source of so much of that elaborate charm of Byzantine work, of Mohammedan decoration, of the hieratic stiffness of so many primitive madonnas and saints. In general the emphasis of composition and technical finish increases with the Distance of the subject-matter: heroic conceptions lend themselves better to verse than to prose; monumental statues require a more general treatment, more elabora-

---

[8] See note 4, above.

tion of setting and artificiality of pose than impressionistic statuettes like those of Troubetzkoi; an ecclesiastic subject is painted with a degree of symmetrical arrangement which would be ridiculous in a Dutch interior, and a naturalistic drama carefully avoids the tableau impression characteristic of a mystery play. In a similar manner the variations of Distance in the arts go hand in hand with a visibly greater predominance of composition and "formal" elements, reaching a climax in architecture and music. It is again a matter of "consistency of Distance." At the same time, while from the point of view of the artist this is undoubtedly the case, from the point of view of the public the emphasis of composition and technical finish appears frequently to relieve the impression of highly distanced subjects by *diminishing the Distance of the whole*. The spectator has a tendency to see in composition and finish merely evidence of the artist's "cleverness," of his mastery over his material. Manual dexterity is an enviable thing to possess in everyone's experience, and naturally appeals to the public *practically*, thereby putting it into a directly personal relation to things which intrinsically have very little personal appeal for it. It is true that this function of composition is hardly an aesthetic one: for the admiration of mere technical cleverness is not an artistic enjoyment, but by a fortunate chance it has saved from oblivion and entire loss, among much rubbish, also much genuine Art, which otherwise would have completely lost contact with our life.

5. This discussion, necessarily sketchy and incomplete, may have helped to illustrate the sense in which, I suggested, Distance appears as a fundamental principle to which such antitheses as idealism and realism are reducible. The difference between "idealistic" and "realistic" Art is not a clear-cut dividing-line between the art-practices described by these terms, but it is a difference of degree in the Distance-limit which they presuppose on the part both of the artist and of the public. A similar reconciliation seems to me possible between the opposites "sensual" and "spiritual," "individual" and "typical." That the appeal of Art is sensuous, even sensual, must be taken as an indisputable fact. Puritanism will never be persuaded, and rightly so, that this is not the case. The sensuousness of Art is a natural implication of the "antinomy of Distance," and will appear again in another connection. The point of importance here is that the whole sensual side of Art is purified, spiritualised, "filtered" as I expressed it earlier, by Distance. The

most sensual appeal becomes the translucent veil of an underlying spirituality, once the grossly personal and practical elements have been removed from it. And—a matter of special emphasis here— *this spiritual aspect of the appeal is the more penetrating, the more personal and direct its sensual appeal would have been* BUT FOR THE PRESENCE OF DISTANCE. For the artist, to trust in this delicate transmutation is a natural act of faith which the Puritan hesitates to venture upon: which of the two, one asks, is the greater idealist?

6. The same argument applies to the contradictory epithets "individual" and "typical." A discussion in support of the fundamental individualism of Art lies outside the scope of this essay. Every artist has taken it for granted. Besides it is rather in the sense of "concrete" or "individualised," that it is usually opposed to "typical." On the other hand, "typical," in the sense of "abstract," is as diametrically opposed to the whole nature of Art, as individualism is characteristic of it. It is in the sense of "generalised" as a "general human element" that it is claimed as a necessary ingredient in Art. This antithesis is again one which naturally and without mutual sacrifice finds room within the conception of Distance. Historically the "typical" has had the effect of counteracting *under*-distancing as much as the "individual" has opposed *over*-distancing. Naturally the two ingredients have constantly varied in the history of Art; they represent, in fact, two sets of conditions to which Art has invariably been subject: the personal and the social factors. It is Distance which on one side prevents the emptying of Art of its concreteness and the development of the typical into abstractness; which, on the other, suppresses the directly personal element of its individualism; thus reducing the antitheses to the peaceful interplay of these two factors. It is just this interplay which constitutes the "antinomy of Distance."

Vincent Tomas

AESTHETIC VISION*

Just before he describes aesthetic contemplation, Schopenhauer refers to the "common way of looking at things," which a man re-
linquishes when he adopts the aesthetic attitude. When a man perceives in "the common way," Schopenhauer writes, he considers
"the where, the when, the why, and the whither of things," whereas
when he perceives aesthetically, he "looks simply and solely at
the *what*."[1]

What, precisely, is "the common way" of seeing things? Some
writers after Schopenhauer describe it in terms of a distinction between "seeing" and "really seeing" something. John Dewey writes:

> The eye and the visual apparatus may be intact; the object may be
> physically there, the Cathedral of Notre Dame, or Rembrandt's
> portrait of Hendrik Stoeffel. In some bald sense, the latter may be
> "seen." They may be looked at, possibly recognized, and have their
> correct names attached. But . . . they are not perceived, certainly
> not aesthetically.[2]

According to Henri Bergson, in ordinary vision

> we do not see the actual things themselves; in most cases we confine
> ourselves to reading the labels affixed to them.[3]

* From *The Philosophical Review*, Vol. LXVIII, No. 1, January 17, 1959.
Reprinted by permission of the author and *The Philosophical Review*.
[1] *The World as Will and Idea*, tr. by R. B. Haldane and J. Kemp (London, 1957), I, 231.
[2] *Art as Experience* (New York, 1934), p. 54.
[3] *Laughter*. In *Comedy*, ed. by Wylie Sypher (New York, 1956), p. 159.

Similarly, according to Roger Fry,

> In actual life the normal person really only reads the labels as it were on the objects around him and troubles no further. Almost all the things which are useful in any way put on more or less this cap of invisibility.[4]

Painters talk in a similar fashion. They say that with their aesthetic vision they "really see" things, whereas most of us usually do not "really see" things, however intact our visual apparatus may be, and despite the fact that we do not walk about with our eyes shut.

The distinction that painters and the writers quoted have in mind is a genuine one. But the terms they use to formulate it are less rigorous and are more suggestive of mystery and paradox than they need to be. Surely it is possible to formulate the difference between "ordinary vision" and "aesthetic vision" in a more straightforward way. I suggest that the difference may be put as follows:

(1) When we see things in "the common way," our attention is directed toward the stimulus objects that appear to us, or toward what they signify, and we do not particularly notice the ways in which these objects appear. For example, when the man on the subway train reads his newspaper, he sees the marks printed on the page. But it is a fact which any newspaper reader can verify for himself that nearly always he sees in such a way that he does not notice the ways the marks appear. Perhaps the commuter has been reading the New York *Times* for a half hour five mornings each week for five years. Yet if you asked him whether, in the *Times*, a "t" appears short and squat or long and slender, or whether an "o" has a fat and jolly look or a lean and hungry look, he would not know what to say. He never noticed how the letters looked. The ordinary perceiver is like the ordinary reader. If, when he is looking at a dark cloud, you ask him what he sees, he does not reply, "It's very like a whale." Rather, he says something like "I see a dark cloud" or "I see that it's going to rain."

(2) When we see things aesthetically, our attention is directed toward appearances and we do not particularly notice the thing that presents the appearance, nor do we care what, if anything, it is that appears. Put somewhat differently, in aesthetic vision the "what" or "aesthetic object" that we attend to when, as Schopen-

---

4 *Vision and Design* (New York, 1956), p. 25.

hauer says, we look "simply and solely at the *what*," is an appearance, and the question of reality does not arise. The preceding sentence, I believe, formulates a necessary, though not a sufficient, condition of aesthetic vision.

My first task is to make (1) and (2) clear.

How a stimulus object will appear to a perceiver depends not only on the nature of the object but on the nature of the perceiver and the conditions of observation. If a penny is viewed by a "normal" observer under "optimum" conditions, that is, when the face of the penny is perpendicular to the observer's line of vision, the penny will appear, or look, round to him. If the penny is viewed from an oblique angle, it will appear elliptical. If we look at a certain dress in direct sunlight and from close by, it will appear white. If we look at the same dress when it is worn by a girl standing fifty feet away, in the shade of a tree, it will appear blue-gray.

It is only relatively rarely that, in ordinary life, we see things under "optimum" conditions. When we see pennies, it is usually from an oblique angle, one of an infinite number of possible angles from which pennies do not look round. But how a penny does look will not be noticed, if we see it merely in "the common way."[5] Commonly, when we see a penny, we are about to pay a bill or to count our change, and it makes no difference to us how the penny looks. What is important to us is that we should not mistake a penny for, say, a subway token, and our attention is directed toward the stimulus object—as it "really is"—not toward its appearance. If, later on, an occasion should arise for us to tell about what we saw in our hand or on the counter, we probably would say, "I saw a penny." And if, for some reason, we were then asked, "How did it look?" we would probably reply, "Why —like a penny." But a penny may look dull or look shiny. Under some conditions it will look round, and under most conditions it will look elliptical. To say that a penny we saw under determinate

[5] If some epistemologist were to maintain, nonparenthetically and as a cardinal principle of his theory of perception, Gilbert Ryle's parenthetical remark that "round plates, however steeply tilted, do not usually look elliptical" (*The Concept of Mind* [London, 1949], p. 218), all I can think of to say is: either such an epistemologist usually sees tilted round plates in "the common way," i.e., he usually lacks aesthetic vision; or he is using "look" in the sense in which "The plate looks elliptical" implies "On the evidence available, the plate probably is elliptical." I am using "look" in the sense in which "The plate looks elliptical" may be part of the evidence (along with "under such-and-such conditions," etc.) for "The plate is round."

conditions looked merely "like a penny" is not to describe precisely how the penny then looked. The reply, "It looked like a penny," is an indication that the penny was seen in the common way—that the perceiver did not notice the way the penny looked.

The next time we see the girl in the white dress she may be standing indoors, under artificial light, beside a highly polished mahogany piano. Will we notice that now her dress, or this and that part of it, appears tinged with brown? Or will we only "see that she is still wearing the same white dress"?

The face, or the appearance, that the world presents to us is one of infinite, ceaselessly altering variety, but this is not noticed when we see it in "the common way." If we look at the world only in the common way, a penny is always round, and the girl's dress is always white. What Croce calls the *character*, or *individual physiognomy*,[6] of things will escape us. That is, the *appearance* of a penny or a dress or other object as seen under determinate conditions will not be noticed. As Thomas Reid says, it will "pass though the mind unobserved."[7]

When our attitude is aesthetic, however, appearances do not pass through the mind unobserved. On the contrary they are dwelt upon. And whereas for the so-called practical man (as for the epistemologist who is concerned to analyze the common way of perceiving) the distinction between "*appearing* so-and-so" and "*being* so-and-so" is of first importance, for the aesthetic perceiver it is of no importance. When he looks "simply and solely at the *what*," the question of reality does not arise.

To make clear what is meant by "the question of reality does not arise," let us perform an experiment in the imagination. It is the seventeenth century and we are somewhere in the Vatican, in a room where there are also two other men, a picture, and a mirror. One of the men is Velásquez and the other is Pope Innocent X. The picture is the one referred to in art catalogues as *Pope Innocent X* (National Gallery of Art, Washington). The visual apparatus of each man, the lighting conditions, and everything else are "normal."

Velásquez looks at Pope Innocent X. We may then justifiably

---

6 Benedetto Croce, *Aesthetic as Science of Expression and General Linguistic*, tr. by Douglas Ainslie (New York, 1956), p. 5.

7 *An Inquiry into the Human Mind*, ch. v, sec. 8. Cp. Roderick M. Chisholm, *A Philosophical Study* (Ithaca, N.Y., 1957), pp. 160–162.

assert, "He sees a man." Velásquez then looks at the picture, and we may assert, "He sees a picture"; and we may *deny*, "He sees a man." Next, when Velásquez turns his gaze toward the mirror, we may assert, "He sees a mirror"; and we may deny both "He sees a man" and "He sees a picture." After glancing at the picture, the pope looks into the mirror. Velásquez, who is standing a little behind and to one side of the pope, also looks into the mirror. We may still justifiably assert that Velásquez sees a mirror. Certainly the object by which he is being visually stimulated is not a man, nor is it a picture; it is a mirror.

Let us now start over again, at the point where Velásquez is looking at the pope. We ask him to describe what he sees. He begins, "I see a man. He has a mustache and small beard, and he is wearing a red robe and a red cap. . . ." Next Velásquez looks at the picture, and we ask him to decribe what he sees. He begins, "I see a man. He has a mustache and small beard, and he is wearing a red robe and a red cap. . . ." We notice that when he participates in our ideal experiment, Velásquez's description of what he sees when he looks at the picture is identical with his description of what he sees when he looks at the pope. The pope is now looking into the mirror, and Velásquez, from slightly behind and to one side of him is doing so, too. We ask Velásquez to describe what he sees. He begins, "I see a man. He has a mustache and small beard, and he is wearing a red robe and a red cap. . . ." So! His description of what he sees when he looks into the mirror is identical with his descriptions of what he sees when he looks at the pope and at the picture.

That is the experiment. Now, how shall we interpret its result —the fact that although, as we could observe, Velásquez looked at three different objects—a man, a picture, and a mirror—he gave one and the same reply every time he was asked, "What do you see?"

Some writers have correctly pointed out that when we aesthetically appreciate a portrait of a pope, we do not respond to it as if we took it to *be* a pope. But then they tend to say or to imply that if one describes what one sees when one looks at *Pope Innocent X* in the words we have attributed to Velásquez, then either one's attitude toward the portrait is not aesthetic or the description of what one sees is inaccurate or misleading. For Velásquez said, "I see a man," when, as we noted, it is false that he saw a man, since he saw a picture. To see a man is to see something made of flesh and blood and born of parents. Unlike Pope Innocent X, *Pope Innocent X* is not made of flesh and blood and was not born of parents. Hence, Velásquez's description of what he saw is, to say the least, misleading.

This argument is cogent only if it is assumed that the object Velásquez was attempting to describe when he said, "I see a man," while he was looking at the picture, was the stimulus object, and that he was using the word "man" to mean something made of flesh and blood and born of parents. If, however, he was not using the word "man" in this sense, and if he was describing not the picture but a way in which the picture appeared to him, his description, so far as it went, was not inaccurate and need not be misleading. The way the picture *Pope Innocent X* appeared to him was very similar, and in principle might have been exactly similar, to the way the pope himself appeared to him. In principle, the appearance of a man and the appearance of a portrait of a man could be identical, in which case the accurate descriptions of each appearance would be identical.[8] The consideration that it is two different stimulus objects that appear in the same way is, for aesthetic vision, irrelevant. The question of reality does not arise.

----

[8] I am not assuming that *Pope Innocent X* is, or was intended by Velásquez to be, a photographic likeness of Pope Innocent X—that the point in representational painting is merely to reproduce an appearance of the object depicted. One is not committed to an "imitation theory" of art just because one admits that, in principle, the appearance of a man and the appearance of a portrait of a man could be identical. Rather, one is committed to the admission that much can be learned about aesthetic vision by reflecting on what it is to see aesthetically a "work of nature," as well as by reflecting on what it is to see aesthetically a "work of art." (Consider why, otherwise, there are people so impressed by the Argument from Design.) Later on in this paper, some of my arguments might appear to have a missing premise. That premise is: for an aesthetic viewer, who describes what he sees by saying, "I see a human face," it is only an "accident" of no concern to him at the time that what he sees was made by Mother Nature (e.g., The Great Stone Face, New Hampshire) or by a man (e.g., Gutzon Borglum's mountain sculpture, South Dakota). At the same time, though this is not being argued for in this paper, an aesthetic object may be seen as "a work of art," rather than as "a work of nature." I am at present inclined to say that if one aesthetically sees the Great Stone Face as "a work of art," he is attending to a different aesthetic object from that of one who sees it as "a work of nature." Hence, if when two people are looking at the same painting, one says, "That is good" and the other says, "That is bad," this is not adequate evidence that a genuine disagreement in taste has occurred. The indexical symbol "that" may be referring to a different aesthetic object in the two cases.

Since the question of reality does not arise in *any* case of aesthetic vision, we ought not to say, when Velásquez described what he aesthetically saw when he looked at the pope himself as "a man," that he was judging the object that appeared to him to *be* a thing of flesh and blood. In this case no less than in the case of the picture he was using "man" to describe an appearance, not the object that happened to present that appearance. Hence, if it is correct to say that when we aesthetically appreciate a portrait of a pope we do not assume it to be a pope, it is equally correct to say that when we aesthetically appreciate a pope we do not assume *him* to be a pope. In every case of aesthetic vision, what is attended to is an appearance, and the question of what actual object —a picture, a mirror, or a man—presents that appearance does not arise. Perhaps this is part of what Croce meant when he wrote, "In our intuitions we do not oppose ourselves as empirical beings to external reality, but we simply objectify our impressions, whatever they be."[9] And perhaps this is the cash value of Edward Bullough's metaphor, that we achieve physical distance by "putting ourselves out of gear with our practical needs and ends."[10]

Rudolf Arnheim, in his wonderful *Film as Art,* writes (italics mine):

> From the beginning, man has excelled in making durable but immobile pictures. Up to our own day, he has hardly succeeded in presenting motion by motion in such a way as to obtain a faithful and readily available reproduction. Even film does not meet this specification: it does not render motion by motion but *gives an illusion of it* by means of immobile images shown in sequence. . . .[11]

For several pages thereafter, Arnheim discusses technical problems involved in "rendering motion by motion." Attempted solutions to these not being very successful,

> *illusory movement* attracted the attention of inventors. They found that they could create *the impression of movement* by combining still pictures with each other.[12]

---

[9] *Op. cit.,* p. 4.
[10] "Psychical Distance as a Factor in Art and an Aesthetic Principle," in *The Problems of Aesthetics,* ed. by Eliseo Vivas and Murray Krieger (New York, 1953), p. 399.
[11] Berkeley and Los Angeles, 1957, p. 162.
[12] *Ibid.,* p. 168.

What is the point of such a discussion for the understanding of aesthetic vision? To see the point of this question, one thing to bear in mind is that an aesthetic viewer is not an aesthetic producer. From the point of view of the aesthetic viewer, what he sees on the screen is not an "illusion of motion" but "motion," not an "impression of movement" but "movement." For the aesthetic viewer of a motion picture, which virtually all of us are when we slip into our seat in the theater, the question of what is real and what is illusory does not arise. Arnheim is aware of this. He points out that

> in film, the single pictures of the sequence exist only technically, not in what is experienced by the audience. As far as the eyes of the spectator go, there is no synthesis of phases but an invisible continuum . . . the displacement of the film in the camera and in the projector is not experienced directly by the audience. It is simply the mechanical means of creating the illusion of motion on the screen . . . the beat of the intermittent motion in the camera and the projector has no bearing upon the aesthetic rhythm of the picture.[13]

Among the many uses of perception words such as "see," one is appropriate to "the common way" of perceiving and one to aesthetic perception. Let us call the "ordinary" sense of "see" the sense that this word has when we say, when Velásquez looks at the picture, "He sees a picture" and "He does not see a man." When "see" is understood in this ordinary sense, the statement "He sees a picture" implies the statement "He is being visually stimulated by a picture." It implies some other statements as well, but for our purposes these may be ignored.

Let us call the "aesthetic" sense of "see" the sense that this word has when Velásquez truly says, when he is looking at the picture, "I see a man." It would be equally appropriate to call this the "phenomenological" sense. When "see" is understood in this aesthetic or phenomenological sense, the statement "I see a man" does *not* imply "I am being visually stimulated by a man (that is, by a thing of flesh and blood, born of parents, etc.)." Nor does it imply the statements "I am not being visually stimulated by a man," or "I am being visually stimulated by something," or "I am not being visually stimulated by anything." The absence of such implications reflects the fact that, in aesthetic vision, the question of reality does not arise.

---

[13] *Ibid.*, p. 169, 181.

If one sees in the movie theater "a wistful tramp shuffling down the road toward the sunset," one does not believe that one is seeing a real tramp shuffling down a real road toward a real sunset. Nor does one disbelieve it, either. This characteristic of aesthetic vision is sometimes described as "willing suspension of disbelief." The locution "The question of reality does not arise" seems preferable, because it is phenomenologically more accurate. As C. S. Peirce points out, "will" implies "resistance." Now, there seem to be people (poor souls!) for whom it involves effort, an "act of will," to adopt the aesthetic attitude toward movie tramps, real tramps, pictures of landscapes, or landscapes. Perhaps for them a willing suspension of disbelief is a precondition of being in the aesthetic attitude. Perhaps in order for them aesthetically to see anything, they must first "suspend" or "put out of gear" their so-called practical attitude. But when we are *in* the aesthetic attitude, we do not resist disbelieving or believing "a wistful tramp shuffling down the road toward the sunset." We just behold him doing so.

When Macbeth wondered, "Is this a dagger that I see before me, the handle toward my hand? . . . Art thou but a dagger of the mind, a false creation?" he was wondering whether the statement, "I see a dagger," where "see" has the ordinary sense, was true. If his attitude toward his hallucination had been aesthetic, if he had been absorbed "simply and solely" in the "what" that appeared to him, he would not have asked himself this question. When a doctor says, referring to a patient suffering from delirium tremens, "He sees pink elephants," he does not use the word "see" in the ordinary sense. He uses it in a sense that resembles the aesthetic sense in that his statement, when properly interpreted, does not imply that pink elephants are visually stimulating the patient. And he uses the phrase "pink elephants" not to describe a stimulus object but to describe the patient's phenomenological object.

Similarly, when Velásquez says, when he adopts the aesthetic attitude toward the pope, the picture, or the mirror, "I see a man," his statement does not imply that he is being visually stimulated by a thing of flesh and blood. It implies that an appearance is present to him and that it is of the kind he calls "a man." He is telling us that the phenomenological object before his mind is "a man," not "a pink elephant," "a dagger," or "a pattern of lines and colors."

Perhaps it will be said that if the aesthetic object is an appear-

ance, why not say so when we describe it? After all, if what
Velásquez aesthetically sees when he looks at the picture is not a
man but the appearance of a man, he *does* mislead us when he says
that he sees a man. He ought to say that he sees the appearance of
a man or, perhaps better, that what he sees appears or looks like
a man to him.

The reason we do not talk in this recommended way when we
describe aesthetic objects is that this recommended way of talking
presupposes a consciousness of the difference between appearance
and reality, whereas, when our attitude is aesthetic, this presupposition is lacking. If I were completely absorbed in the appearance that Velásquez's picture presents to me, I would not be aware
of it as "the appearance of a man." I would be aware of it simply
as "a man." Of course, when my first person statement, "I see
a man," is true, someone else may make the true *third* person
statement, "He sees an appearance of a man." But then the object of the verb in the third person statement, namely, "an appearance of a man," does not faithfully convey what object it is
that is object of my aesthetic vision.

The situation here is similar to the following one. Suppose that
early one morning a companion and I are walking down Park
Avenue and see a group of men going in the opposite direction.
Suppose that my companion asks me what I see and that I reply,
"I see a rather dapper elderly man walking briskly up the street
accompanied by some men carrying pencils and notebooks." My
companion might be in a position to assert truly, "You see a former
President of the United States surrounded by reporters." It does
not follow from this that, at the time that I said, "I see a dapper
elderly man," I ought to have said, "I see a former President of
the United States." In the same way in which I might see a former
President of the United States without being aware of him as
such, when my attitude is aesthetic I see an appearance that Velásquez's picture presents to me without my being aware of it as
such. And if I am not aware of what I see as an appearance, I am
not obliged to describe it as an appearance when I am asked what
I see. The object I aesthetically see when I look at the picture,
therefore, is not "the appearance of a man," but "a man."[14]

---

[14] Compare G. E. M. Anscombe, *Intention* (Oxford, 1957), sec. 20. Miss
Anscombe points out that one and the same action may be intentional "under
the description" X, and not intentional "under the description" Y. In *Philo-*

When I am looking at a picture by Breughel, I may describe what I aesthetically see by saying that the landscape recedes into the distance. If someone, motivated no doubt by the consideration that I am being visually stimulated by a picture whose surface is "really" two-dimensional, remarks that I am really experiencing or having an illusion of distance, the reply is, "That may be so, but that is not what I aesthetically see."

There are many passages in the works of Clive Bell, Roger Fry, José Ortega y Gasset, and others that suggest the following sort of objection to what is being maintained in this paper: "If your attitude were *really* aesthetic when you were looking at the portrait, you would not see anything describable as 'a man.' You would see 'a pattern of colors, lines, and shapes.' " The reply to this sort of objection is as follows. First, if looking at a picture and attending closely to how it looks is not really to be in the aesthetic attitude, then what on earth is? Second, when one does this to a Mondrian, one does indeed see "a pattern of colors, lines, and shapes." But when one does this to *Pope Innocent X*, one sees "a man." The appearance of the portrait resembles the appearance of a man much more than it resembles the appearance of the Mondrian. If one tries to see the portrait as "a pattern of colors, lines, and shapes," one gets cross-eyed, as José Ortega y Gasset suggests when he refers to works that present familiar appearances as "squinting art."[15] Ortega, by the way, attempts to define aesthetic vision in terms of an "adjustment of the optical apparatus." According to him, aesthetically to see a garden, "we must withdraw the ray of vision" until what we see is "a confused mass of color," not "shrubs and flowers."[16] But, I submit, aesthetically to see the garden is not to see "a blooming confusion," but to see appearances of a familiar sort—the sort presented by shrubs and flowers.

---

sophical Investigations (New York, 1957), when Ludwig Wittgenstein discusses how one would reply to the question "What do you see?" when one is looking at the duck-rabbit, he writes, on p. 194e, "I should have replied: 'A picture-rabbit,' " and on p. 195e, "I say 'It's a rabbit.' " If, as I think is the case, in aesthetic vision what one sees is what one says (or thinks), then when one aesthetically sees "a picture-rabbit" his aesthetic object is not the same as when one aesthetically sees "a rabbit."

[15] *The Dehumanization of Art and other Writings on Art and Culture* (New York, 1956), p. 23.
[16] *Ibid.*, p. 9.

Perhaps it will be suggested that one ought to describe what one aesthetically sees when one looks at Velásquez's portrait as a "representation of a man." To estimate the merit of this suggestion, we must first decide what is meant by "representation."

Pope Innocent X is clearly the sort of picture that most aestheticians, critics, and historians of art will refer to as a representational picture; and they will contrast it with "nonrepresentational" pictures of the sort painted by Kandinsky and Mondrian. What makes it "representational" and the latter not?

One difference between the two sorts of pictures is that when we look at *Pope Innocent X* it presents an appearance that is familiar to us from our experience of the world outside of art. In certain respects it resembles the appearances that men present to us, so that we recognize it as an appearance *of that sort*. If we wish to describe it, we borrow the term, namely "man," from the thing that, outside of art, presents that sort of appearance; but, as applied to the appearance, it is not a "thing" word, for it has lost its predictive function.[17] As applied to the appearance, "man" functions in the same way that "red" functions when it refers to a quality, as contrasted with the way "red" functions when it refers to a property of physical objects. The Kandinsky composition, on the other hand, presents an appearance that is not familiar to us from our experience of the world outside of art, and we have no convenient term to borrow for the specific Kandinsky appearance *as a whole*. We have to describe it in terms of its parts —as a combination of lines, shapes, colors, and so on.

Pope Innocent X, then, may be said to be representational because it presents an appearance which as a whole is familiar because it is similar to appearances presented by objects we experience outside of art, and the Kandinsky composition may be said to be nonrepresentational because it does not. Now if this fact were a sufficient reason for saying that the appearance presented by the portrait should be described as "a representation of a man," then, I should think, it would be a sufficient reason for saying that when Velásquez aesthetically saw the pope himself he should have said, "I see a representation of a man." For the pope himself, no less than his portrait, presented an appearance similar to appearances presented by objects outside art. For the same reason, when we are sight-

17 Compare Arnold Isenberg, "Perception, Meaning and the Subject Matter of Art," in Vivas and Krieger, *op. cit.*, p. 218.

seeing and admire the appearance of the New York City skyline,
we should describe what we are admiring not as "a skyline" but as
"a representation of a skyline."

It is sometimes said that when we aesthetically see representational
works of art, we recognize familiar objects. But we do not recognize familiar *objects* when we look aesthetically at representational
paintings (or at the subjects of such paintings). We recognize familiar *appearances*. Our recognition then is of the sort H. H. Price
has called "primary recognition." Price distinguishes between two
sorts of recognition, primary and secondary, in the following way:

> Secondary recognition [is] recognition by means of signs. Primary
> recognition, on the other hand, is not recognition by means of signs.
> It is by primary recognition that we recognize the sign-characteristics
> themselves—the dull grey colour which is a sign to us of lead, the
> blackness and the visual *gestalt*-quality which are signs to us of a
> raven. In earlier days, primary recognition would have been called
> "intuitive awareness" or "immediate apprehension," and it would have
> been said that a primarily recognized characteristic is something
> "given." It would also have been said that primary recognition is
> "logically" as well as psychologically immediate, whereas secondary
> recognition has only psychological immediacy.[18]

Thus, the recognition of physical objects—the sort that is involved in ordinary perception but which does not occur in aesthetic perception—is secondary recognition. It presupposes primary
recognition, which occurs alone in aesthetic perception. Secondary
recognition is "predictive," but primary or aesthetic recognition is
not. Price writes:

> Indeed, it would seem that most of the recognitions which interest
> us—unless we happen to be psychologists or painters or phenom-
> enologically minded philosophers—have something of this character
> which we are tempted to call indirect, or mediate, or inferential.
> Even when we recognize something as a man, or a chair, or a flower-
> pot, we go beyond the characteristics which we actually notice the
> perceived object to have. In addition, we attribute other character-
> istics to it which we are not at the moment noticing at all; though
> we believe, or rather take for granted without question, that further

---

[18] *Thinking and Experience* (Cambridge, Mass., 1953), p. 47. Cp. Isenberg,
op. cit., pp. 215–216. On this and some other points, see also Arnold Isenberg,
"The Esthetic Function of Language," *Journal of Philosophy*, XLVI (1949),
5–20.

examination of the object would enable us to notice them if we wished. For instance, when I recognize the thing over there to be a chair, I am assuming without question that it is a moderately rigid body capable of supporting a man or a pile of books, and unlikely to change its shape or its chemical constitution within the next five minutes; but the only characteristics I actually notice it to have at the moment are a certain set of colours . . . and a certain visible shape.[19]

Using Price's distinction, we may now say that when an aesthetic perceiver describes what he sees when he looks at Van Gogh's painting of his room and says, "and beside the bed is a chair," he is describing a visual gestalt which he apprehends as "a chair beside a bed" by primary recognition; but he does not assume without question that what he so recognizes as "a chair" is a moderately rigid body capable of supporting a man or a pile of books.

When, as in the case of secondary recognition, a presented appearance functions as a sign of something not present, it is sometimes said to *represent* what it signifies. It seems clear that if the analysis of aesthetic vision here proposed is correct, for an aesthetic perceiver a presented appearance does not function as a sign. Therefore it is not, and it should not be described as, a representation in this sense of the word. If this is what he meant by "representation," Clive Bell was right when he said that representation is irrelevant to the aesthetic appreciation of a work of art. All that needs to be added is that it is irrelevant to the aesthetic appreciation of works of nature as well.

Here we have a suggestion that may explain, at least in part, why some writers such as S. K. Langer speak of aesthetic objects as "presentational symbols." Some years ago, in a review, Professor Ernest Nagel objected to the concept of a "presentational symbol" on the ground that if by the term "symbol" we mean something that represents something to someone, a merely presentational symbol is a contradiction in terms.[20] Perhaps bringing forward the notion of a "presentational symbol," which does seem to be a contradiction in terms, was nevertheless an attempt to point out a genuine phenomenon, namely, that in our aesthetic perception of nature, and in much of our aesthetic perception

---

[19] *Op. cit.*, p. 45.
[20] *Journal of Philosophy*, XL (1943), 323–329.

of works of art, there are appearances which we recognize in the primary sense and which in ordinary perception would function as signs, yet which do not function as signs. Our attention is arrested and dwells upon what in ordinary perception would be a mere "sign vehicle" and scarcely noticed. It is then no longer a vehicle "representing" an object, but a "presented" object, about which the question of reality does not arise.

Clive Bell also wrote that to appreciate a work of art, we need bring nothing from life, nothing but a sense of form and color and three-dimensional space. By this he may have meant to eliminate as irrelevant to the appreciation of works of art not only appearances that were representations in the sense that they were functioning as signs, but also familiar appearances of forms—what we grasp by primary recognition. Only then, according to Bell, would a work of art evoke in us a unique aesthetic emotion. If Bell had realized that by primary recognition we are made aware of familiar *appearances*, not of familiar *objects* or *events*, and that when we attend to these appearances we are attending to something "in the picture" in precisely the same sense that lines, colors, shapes, and volumes are, would he have allowed the familiar appearances back in?

If the analysis of aesthetic vision presented above is on the whole correct, there seems to be no reason why they should not be allowed back in. If it is on the whole correct, then, contrary to what Ortega wrote in *The Dehumanization of Art*, it is false that "preoccupation with the human content of the work is in principle incompatible with aesthetic enjoyment proper."[21]

---

21 P. 9.

Frank Sibley

AESTHETICS AND THE
LOOKS OF THINGS*

Many questions of aesthetics are concerned with the looks of things or with appearances. "In at least the simpler cases," says J. O. Urmson,[1] we are interested in "the way the object . . . looks, the way it sounds, smells, tastes or feels." Sometimes it is claimed that an aesthetic approach to things is *always* concerned with looks or appearances; more strongly still, that *only* appearances are relevant. Vincent Tomas, discussing the special case of aesthetic *vision*,[2] says that when we see things with "ordinary vision" we notice the things, but do not notice how they appear or look; but "When we see things aesthetically, our attention is directed toward appearances and we do not particularly notice the thing that presents the appearance, nor do we care what, if anything, it is that appears . . . the question of reality does not arise." This he be-

* From *The Journal of Philosophy*, Vol. LVI, No. 10, Nov. 5, 1959, pp. 905–915. Reprinted by permission of the author and of *The Journal of Philosophy*.

Presented in the symposium on "Aesthetics" at the 56th annual meeting of the American Philosophical Association, Eastern Division, at Columbia University, December 30, 1959. (Small revisions have been made in the present version of this paper. The aim of these revisions has been greater clarity; the views expressed remain the same. Author's note.)

[1] "What Makes a Situation Aesthetic?" *Proc. Arist. Soc.*, Supp. Vol. XXXI.
[2] "Aesthetic Vision," *The Philosophical Review*, January 1959.

lieves "formulates a necessary, though not a sufficient, condition of aesthetic vision." He adds that "the distinction between '*appearing* so-and-so' and '*being* so-and-so,' " which for the practical man and "the common way" of perceiving "is of first importance," is "of no importance" for the aesthetic perceiver. These are interesting claims; but Appearance and Reality are a shifty couple, liable to multiply senses on the sly. I want first, therefore, to elucidate some senses in which a claim like Tomas' about appearances and aesthetic *vision* may and may not be taken. Later, broadening the discussion to include not only how an object looks but how it feels, etc., I shall suggest that only *certain* looks, feels, etc. can be ultimate grounds of aesthetic admiration.

Even at the outset, one way of taking Tomas' words which would render his claim false springs to mind. We try hard, rightly, to see what paintings and statues are *really* like, what their characteristics really are, not what they might appear to a casual or careless observer to be. Of course Tomas tries to make clear how his remarks quoted are to be taken, and, if they are interpreted in a certain way, I believe the broad bearing of his thesis must be correct. But some of his examples and formulations tend to suggest much less plausible interpretations of the thesis; I think, therefore, that if we are to assess the claim that attention to appearances is a necessary condition of aesthetic vision, we must examine the senses that "appearances" can and cannot bear. In any case, since the subject is liable to confusion and is of interest in its own right, I want to make independently and in greater detail a number of distinctions.

I begin with some of the examples Tomas uses to illustrate looks or appearances; in each case he suggests that by "the common way" of seeing we fail to notice these appearances. The implication is therefore that, for the aesthetic way of seeing, we are required to notice them. In reading a newspaper, he says, one commonly does not notice "how the letters look." He then gives two examples which seem to me to need distinguishing. I shall number them. We do not notice (1) "whether, in the *Times*, a 't' appears short . . . or long," or (2a) "whether an 'o' has a fat and jolly look or a lean and hungry look." He also gives other examples which seem to me to be different again. (3) The ordinary perceiver does not notice that a dark cloud may be "very like a whale." (4) A penny from one angle "will appear, or look, round," from another, elliptical; a white dress in sunlight looks white, at another time, blue-grey. We

ordinarily do not notice these apparent variations of sensible qualities. (5) "The appearance of a man and the appearance of a portrait of a man could be identical"; one might look just like the
other, the same description of features and coloring might apply to
each. One might even be mistaken for the other. (6) I shall add a
further distinction, not discussed by Tomas, but suggested by and
perhaps the most normal understanding of the pair of phrases he
mentions, "appearing so-and-so" and "being so-and-so." This is the
distinction between the penny which *merely looks* elliptical but is
round, or the dress which *merely looks* bluish but is white. Other
uses of "looks" and "appearances" are relevant to aesthetics; but this
is enough to begin.³

The foregoing examples vary greatly. If aesthetic vision requires
attention to appearances in one sense, it may not require it in another. For instance, we can dispose of the sense illustrated by (3),
the "very like a whale" example, at once. To notice that a cloud
has the appearance of a whale is to note a (fanciful) resemblance.
But noticing resemblances is *certainly* not necessary for aesthetic
vision. We may comment appreciatively on a building or statue by
mentioning its mass, solidity, or grandeur; these are primary aesthetic observations. We might perhaps (though we rarely do) say
"It's like a whale (or a mountain)"; but such remarks are of a
secondary kind, neither necessary nor self-explanatory. If someone uses them we ask "Why?" or "How do you mean?" and the
reply is, "Well, it has an extraordinary solidity and grandeur."
These are the important features, and we note them independently
of seeing resemblances to whales, etc.

Consider next example (1). Truly we often do not notice how
the letters in a newspaper look. But if asked to describe how they
look, we are being asked whether they *are* long or short, round
or oval, straight or slanting. Failing to notice their appearance is
failing to notice what their features, colors, shapes *are*. "Appearance"
in example (1) simply means the visible features (features that
appear or *show*) which a thing actually has. Features of this sort
are amongst those which we praise when we praise a person's

---

³ In this paper, for the sake of brevity, I followed Tomas in using "appears"
and "looks" interchangeably. I should certainly agree with Professor Cohen
(p. 917) that this is to ignore many niceties of their usage. But I do not believe that the argument of this paper is prejudiced thereby. (Note added
by author.)

appearance; and they may be included, for instance, in a police
description of someone's appearance. We exclude from such a description the features (e.g., "a greyish face") that someone or something merely appears to have, say, under unusual lighting or from
odd angles. Similarly, it would be foolish if, asked suddenly to
describe how the letter "t" in the newspaper looked, we held it at an
angle and replied, "Very short and dumpy." "Appearance" here
then concerns the *reality*, and falls, for a familiar use of those expressions, on the side of "*being* so-and-so," not of "*appearing* so-
and-so." This is surely the most obvious sense suggested by the
newspaper letters example. It contrasts sharply with the "mere appearance" sense which I introduced in (6): the penny is round
and merely *looks* elliptical, the grass is green and merely *looks*
blue-grey under the trees. "Appearance" in (6), or "the look it has,"
includes only visual characteristics the object does *not* really possess.

I have isolated these possible meanings of "appearance" in order to
make clear that there are many ways in which the dictum "Aesthetic vision requires attention to appearances" might be taken. Unfortunately, Tomas' examples suggest a variety of interpretations.
One normal interpretation of the newspaper example might suggest
that the dictum is concerned with the sense illustrated in (1); yet
his emphasis on "appearing so-and-so" as against "being so-and-so"
might suggest on the contrary that it concerns the sense illustrated in
(6). In fact, however, I think his claim is not really concerned with
just one or another of these senses. For others of his examples, which
I quote under (4), include *both* circular *and* elliptical appearances
of the penny, etc., and so obviously involve a broader sense which
embraces *both* the real visual qualities of (1) *and* the apparent
qualities of (6). The examples in (4), I suspect, despite other possible interpretations of some of his examples, illustrate more nearly
the sense of "appearance" Tomas intended.

There are several other kinds of "looks" worth mentioning. One
is illustrated by Tomas' example in (2a) above, "The 'o' looks fat
and jolly"; others, somewhat similar, which I will introduce, by
(2b) "The building has a top-heavy (solid) look," "The car looks
fast," and by (2c) "The picture has a warm look." In these new
examples, the contrast between "looks" and "is" is not a contrast
between the thing's appearance in unusual conditions and its appearance in normal conditions. If a thing *is* red, that is still part
of its appearance; but when something *is* fast or top-heavy, this is not

a part of its appearance at all (cf. "intelligent" and "intelligent-looking"). *Being* white and *merely looking* white are both appearances in the broad sense (4), but it is only *looking* top-heavy that is an appearance. However, these new examples also differ among themselves in various ways. A building might really *be* top-heavy or a car fast. Similarly a picture or a color might even really *be* warm (e.g., if standing in the sun) as well as having a warm look. But a "t" could not literally be hungry or an "o" jolly. Nevertheless "fast-looking" and "warm" also *differ* from each other; "fast looking" connects closely with appearances or expectations of speed whereas warm colors are not usually, or expected to be, literally warm. Notice also that all these looks grouped under (2) can themselves be veridical or non-veridical, real or apparent; the contrast of (1) and (6) applies to them. A building that does not *really* look top-heavy might look this way in a mist or from an unusual angle; the colors of a picture might look warm under unusual lighting, but in ordinary light not really look warm at all.

When the looks just discussed are veridical, they may be classified along with (1) as part of the appearance of a thing in the "police description" sense, and when non-veridical, they may be classified with (6). Thus, whether veridical or not, they may be grouped along with (4) as part of the totality of real and non-veridical visual qualities of things. So also with the example mentioned in (5); having "a mustache and small beard" may be part of the description of the appearance of both men and portraits. Thus we may consider the sense illustrated by (4) as the broadest sense we have encountered, consisting of real and non-veridical looks of all kinds.

We can now ask whether the thesis that aesthetic vision *requires* attention to appearances is acceptable, and with these distinctions behind us we can understand it more clearly by seeing in which senses it is not true. Will anything narrower than the sense illustrated by (4) suffice? Clearly sense (6) will not do; aesthetic vision does not require attention simply to *mere* appearances. With works of art we must attend to *real* looks or appearance. We look at pictures and statues in good light and judge them on their "intrinsic" qualities, not for qualities lent them accidentally by tricks of lighting. This might lead us to conclude that aesthetic vision requires attention to appearances only in sense (1). But our everyday aesthetic experiences prove this conclusion false; the appearances we find beautiful are usually heavily dependent on sun and shadow, etc. It is not the uniform green of the field but the apparent variation of color that matters. If one wanted to give sense to sayings like "Beauty is in the object" and "Beauty lies in mere appearances, in the eye of the observer," the case of art tends to favor the former, that of nature often favors the latter. But even with art there are exceptions; eye-shadows in the uniformly white marble of a statue are important, so are shadows and fore-shortening of figures high on a building or column, the colors of an altar piece may be adapted to the dim light of the church, and the pigment a painter uses may be dictated by how it looks when surrounded by the other colors on the canvas.

Of the multiple senses of "looks" and "appearances" mentioned, then, only the broadest is suitable for the dictum under discussion. Anything less renders it false; we need not always pay attention to veridical appearances nor always to non-veridical ones. But if we interpret the dictum thus, is it true? For it then claims that *all* cases of aesthetic vision require attention to appearances in this very broad sense. If we hold tightly to *vision*, I think it certainly is true, indeed analytic. To take a *visual* aesthetic interest in anything, we must certainly be concerned with what appears, can be seen. (Parallel arguments hold for aesthetic listening, touch, or smell.) The main interest of the claim lies in making clear, as I have tried to do, what exactly "appearances" must mean if it is to be true. Otherwise it might be taken to imply that we are never interested in what really is; but I have shown that this is false. Taken in one obvious way, "We do not particularly notice the thing that presents the appearance" is untenable. Notice too, in passing, that if we replace "*aesthetic vision*" by "*aesthetic interest*," the dictum does not hold. In literature we are not mainly concerned with appearances in the sense outlined; elsewhere too. The comment that two people are perfectly suited, each setting off the other, might be an aesthetic one; but it concerns their characters, temperaments, or interests, not their appearances only.[4]

---

4 My conclusion here is that if the dictum is applied only to *vision* and if "appearances" is taken in the broad way suggested, the dictum is not only true but analytic. Without saying, as Professor Cohen does, that it is trifling (p. 924), I certainly meant to suggest that by this time it has ceased to be very interesting. I also conclude explicitly that if the dictum is not restricted to *vision*, or if any narrower interpretation of "appearances" is given, the dictum seems to be false. Perhaps it was some infelicity of expression in my original version that led Cohen to think I was agreeing with Tomas and that I subscribed to the doctrine that "appearance is the object of the aesthetic attitude" (p. 915). (Note added by author.)

I want also to comment briefly on the further claim that for aesthetic vision "the question of reality does not arise" and that we are not concerned with something "*being* so-and-so." I have given one sense in which this is false. In another sense it is doubtless true: with looks of the restricted types falling under (2), the question whether something *is* warm, fast, or top-heavy never arises. But the view Tomas intends seems different again. The question of reality which he holds never arises for aesthetic vision is, I think, the question "What is it?" or "Is it really a . . . ?" a question of classification or identification. But such questions do seem to arise often. We might distinguish three cases. (i) Tomas' example, "Is it a penny or a subway token?"; we might add "Is it a tie or a girl's sash?" "Is it a man or a bearded lady?" (ii) Speaking of a painting, "Is it a bunch of flowers, a rocky landscape, or purely non-representational?" (iii) "Is it a man or a portrait?" "Is it a painting or a view through a window?" The third is Tomas' main concern. I shall comment on this only. Some features we may remark on aesthetically, independently of the question whether the object is a painting or the real thing; e.g., "The colors are rich and varied," "The face is serene (ecstatic, sad)." But there are also appreciative comments we can make on the one but not on the other. Comments (in tones of admiration) like "It really lives," "It has the very air of life about it," "So powerful as to be more than real" (and these do *not* mean merely "lifelike") are not infrequently made about statues and portraits. "You can almost see the clouds and spray flying, almost taste the salt air" and "It has such depth" can be said about seascapes and landscapes but not about seaside and country. If some aesthetic comments on the looks of things can be made only when we know we are dealing with works of art, the question of reality in the sense indicated does arise. Perhaps Tomas did not mean to deny this. Perhaps he meant that *after* such questions are answered, no further concern with whether it is a real man or a portrait arises. From then on we care only about how it looks. But this, I have said, is analytic for aesthetic *vision;* it seems misleading to express it by saying that the question of reality never arises.

I have given a partial elucidation of the claim that attention to appearances is a necessary condition of aesthetic vision. I want now to take up the further question, which of the many appearances and qualities of things (not necessarily visual only) *can* one admire (or disapprove) aesthetically?

Tomas says that attention to appearances is not a sufficient condition of aesthetic vision, and this is, broadly speaking, true. Noticing the appearance of a white dress in shadow or a penny at an angle does not entail that one has looked with an aesthetic eye. But it is not always true. There are some qualities, typically aesthetic ones, the very noticing of which does betoken an aesthetic eye. If one notices how graceful, delicate, or elegant something is or appears, this is sufficient to prove *ipso facto* that one's vision has been in some degree aesthetic. And there are many other typically aesthetic qualities and appearances. Many (but not all) are noted by using certain expressions in a metaphorical or quasi-metaphorical way. If someone describes a letter as "jolly" or a painting as "warm," "placid," or "violent," speaks of the "dull glow" of a velvet, or of "rich" or "vehement" colors (as opposed to saying simply "It's red," "It's angular," "It has a mat surface"), his way of talking and the features he has noticed again indicate some degree of aesthetic sensitivity. If we are to discern and comment on certain qualities at all, some degree of aesthetic sensitivity is required. With perfect eyesight and intelligence but without this sensitivity, people do not see these qualities or make these comments. I cannot discuss these aesthetic qualities further here.[5] It is to the qualities and appearances that remain, aside from these "typically aesthetic" ones, that I wish to confine my attention from now on. For there are many appearances that we do not need an aesthetic eye to notice. Anyone might be brought to see that things are smooth, white, square, transparent, or regular, that white looks bluish-grey in shadow, or that things look elliptical or trapezoid from certain angles. Yet though the noticing of these qualities or appearances does not itself require aesthetic sensitivity, many of them nevertheless can be admired aesthetically. Here we are noticing not "typically aesthetic" features, but ordinary features which we are responding to in a certain way, with admiration, delight or distaste. It seems not so much *what* we attend to as *how* we attend to it that makes our attention aesthetic. This often shows in the way we remark on these qualities. "It is very smooth," said in a scientific or matter-of-fact tone, does not indicate aesthetic interest. "It's *so* smooth (so wonderfully smooth, etc.)," said with admiration, usually has an aesthetic ring.

---

[5] I have said something on this topic elsewhere; see *The Philosophical Review*, October 1959.

Now the point I want to make is that, of the great variety of qualities the noticing of which does *not* require aesthetic sensitivity, only certain ones *can* be admired aesthetically for themselves. Urmson says, rightly, that the "really basic" grounds for aesthetic admiration or evaluation often consist in the looks, feel, etc., of things; "Things may have sensible qualities which affect us favorably or unfavourably with no ulterior grounds." But there are limits to the qualities which can sensibly serve as ultimate grounds for aesthetic judgments, in much the same way as a man's height cannot in itself be of moral interest. Aestheticians sometimes speak as though, by simply changing to an aesthetic approach or "attitude" or "contemplation," we can value or admire for itself *any* quality or appearance; but this is not so. There are, first, those looks and qualities we can admire in things for themselves, smoothness, high gloss, simplicity, translucence, and so on; no further explanation or justification is needed. We can express admiration by "It's so smooth (highly polished, bright, pale, soft, pure, regular, transparent, clear, simple, intricate, vivid)." We can qualify these remarks by suitable adverbs: "beautifully," "wonderfully." (We can do this too with some colors: "It's so blue [green, white]"; but see below.) Secondly, there are qualities that cannot stand alone as basic grounds; "It's so (wonderfully) angular" seems to call for explanation in a way "so smooth" and "so brilliant" do not. But an explanation can often be supplied by a linkage with qualities that *can* stand alone aesthetically: "Well, its angularity makes it so forbidding, violent, grotesque." We can admire smoothness just for itself, but we cannot admire angularity *tout court*. And there may, thirdly, be some qualities where no linkage can be provided and which we cannot admire aesthetically at all. There is something logically very odd about saying "It's so (wonderfully, beautifully) elliptical, equilateral, serrated, etc."

As an aside here it is interesting to ask where colors stand in this regard. They seem frequently to be the object of aesthetic admiration. Yet I believe we do not admire colors for themselves as we do brilliance, smoothness, or softness. In admiring colors we make use of two forms of words: "It is *so* (beautifully) blue," and "It is *such* a beautiful blue." These expressions have different uses. I believe that when we use the former there has to be some special context; we can say "The sky (lake, sea) is so wonderfully blue" but not "Her dress is so wonderfully blue." "So blue" (said admiringly) seems to be used of objects that are supposed at their best or most typical to be blue. "So wonderfully brown (red, pink)" as expressions of admiration sound somewhat strange; they call up a context less readily. But if we supply one, all is well: "Those apples, so wonderfully red," "The flesh, so pink." I wonder, therefore, whether the possibility of admiring colors by using expressions like "so blue" always depends on some connection and fittingness to subject-matter. It does not otherwise seem comprehensible to praise something just for its blueness or greenness. We admire fields for being so very green, but we do not admire or praise vases or pictures for being very green, or blue, or red. But we *can* praise things for being pure, soft, smooth, colorful, and bright, independently of special subject matter. The second expression, however, "*such* a beautiful color," "*a* beautiful blue," is not necessarily related to the typical or expected colors of things. We don't say "Her dress is so beautifully blue," but we may say "It is such a beautiful blue." Here, then, we might seem to admire a color, *simpliciter*, after all. But I believe this is still not so. "It's such a wonderful blue" calls for "In what way?" or "How?" (just as "a wonderful texture" calls for "so smooth" or "so soft"). We reply, "Well, it's such a delicate (cool, pure, bright) blue" or "such a rich (brilliant, vivid, flaming, cheerful) red." We admire a color for its character, the qualities it has, qualities which *are* capable of admiration *tout court;* it is not blueness we admire. But praise for smoothness, softness, purity, brilliance, or variety is not like this; such words do not raise, but answer, questions like "In what way is it beautiful?" Colors then, despite appearances, seem not to be praised for themselves in the way some qualities are; we do not admire things simply for being blue or green. Rather we praise colors either for "suitability" to subject, or for their qualities of warmth, purity, brilliance, glow, etc.

   I have suggested a threefold division of the qualities and appearances I am discussing: we can take a favorable (or unfavorable) aesthetic interest in some for themselves, in others only with a suitable explanation, in others, again, perhaps not at all. Is it possible to say why this is so, or find principles that mark off the first class from the other two? Urmson suggests some such principle for the restricted class of looks I called (2b) above, e.g., "It looks fast"; he says, "It is looking to possess some quality which is non-aesthetically desirable that matters." Whether this principle is too broad or too narrow I shall not stop to inquire. Certainly it seems that things might look to possess *some* non-aesthetically desirable qualities and yet not thereby be capable of being aesthetically admired, e.g., "It looks hygienic (sanitary, arable, fertile)." But it is not this class (2b) I am mainly considering, but rather appearances like red, square, elliptical, smooth, soft, translucent, and brilliant.

About them I shall merely make a suggestion of a quite vague and tentative kind. Is it, perhaps, that the qualities and appearances that can be admired aesthetically for themselves must be ones which somehow, putting aesthetic questions aside, are vitally involved in human experience? Awareness of and concern with warmth, light, brilliance, clarity, purity, regularity, cleanness, richness, softness, smoothness, and simplicity go deep into human life and interests. There is nothing artificial or accidental or superficial about them. They are as basic as the passions, fear, anger, hope, pity, longing, ecstasy, and despair, with which other aspects of art are concerned. By contrast, many of the qualities which, it seems, could not in themselves be ultimate grounds of aesthetic favor are abstract or specialized or artificial. "Equilateral," "elliptical," and "square" are of this sort; if we come across such qualities in nature they are of no special concern to us for themselves, any more than mere curiosities like a hexagonal stone or a rock that looks like a face. But we cannot survive without warmth, peace, energy; we cannot avoid anger, violence, fear; and we concern ourselves deeply over purity, clarity, and simplicity. These are qualities we may value for themselves. Again, qualities like serrated, or hygienic, or sanitary are more specialized or peripheral, of interest less for themselves than for their instrumental value (contrast with them "sharp" and "biting," "pure" and "clean"). When we do praise something for being, e.g., fast-looking, we notice that "fast" is not confined, like "hygienic," to its instrumental value; it suggests dash, bravado, a way of life valued for itself. As for colors, while qualities like brilliance, light, and variety startle and attract us, and while warmth and purity mean much to us, redness as such means nothing to us. If it impresses us, it is by its vividness or brilliance or warmth, or else by what it indicates, suggests, or stands for, ripeness, richness, violence.

This is, I know, vague and speculative. It is not an explanation of why we can value some qualities aesthetically and not others, but rather a comment on those qualities. It suggests that qualities that can be objects of aesthetic interest reflect our vital concerns and the sort of creatures we are. As we saw, to make a quality like angularity aesthetically acceptable, we link it with some of these deeper concerns, with what touches home; we say it is violent or energetic or menacing. More artificial, specialized, or abstract notions, or purely instrumental ones, can be linked up in this way only with greater difficulty, if at all.

I do not know if these last vague comments throw any light upon the division between qualities that can and qualities that cannot be ultimate aesthetic grounds. In any case, the suggestion might be worth exploring further and my hints replaced by something more precise and adequate. But that there is such a division I am sure. Some qualities may be admired aesthetically without further explanation, but not others. It is sometimes said that what is aesthetically admired is wholly relative to a particular culture, and that other cultures might admire quite other things than we do. In its broadest sense I believe this is not so. If someone professed aesthetic admiration for equiangular or elliptical appearances as such, this would not mark an unusual, seldom met with sensitivity on his part; we should not understand him. Similarly, we should be puzzled if we were told of a people who admired ellipses or redness as such; we should ask what significance these qualities had for them. We do not ask this of people who admire smoothness, fine finish, brilliance, simplicity, or softness. If we were asked to imagine creatures who really do admire ellipticality or redness purely for themselves, it is not at all obvious that we could call their admiration aesthetic. For it to be so, these qualities, if my hints are correct, would have to be involved in their vital interests in a way they are not in human life; that being so, it is not clear what kind of creatures we are being asked to imagine.

I began by trying to elucidate the senses in which aesthetic vision does and does not require attention to *appearances*. I then noted that there are appearances and qualities that require, as well as those that do not require, aesthetic sensitivity on our part if we are to notice them at all. Of the latter I said that only some can be admired for themselves or serve as ultimate grounds for aesthetic admiration. And I offered a very tentative suggestion on why this is so.

Marshall Cohen

APPEARANCE AND THE
AESTHETIC ATTITUDE*

The concept of appearance has had a long career in the history of aesthetics, going back, if not to Plato, at least to Kant. It achieved real celebrity, however, in Schiller's *Letters*.[1] In that illusive essay

* Slightly revised from "Appearance and the Aesthetic Attitude," *The Journal of Philosophy*, Vol. LVI, No. 10, pp. 915–926. Reprinted by permission of the author and of *The Journal of Philosophy*.

Presented in the symposium on "Aesthetics" at the 56th annual meeting of the American Philosophical Association, Eastern Division, at Columbia University, December 30, 1959. I would like to acknowledge here my indebtedness to Professor J. L. Austin for certain of the ideas which are exploited in this essay. I do not know, however, because his formulations are not in print, whether he would endorse any of the formulations which are made in this essay.

[1] Kant anticipates Schiller's view in sec. 53 of the *Critique of Judgment*, tr. J. H. Bernard (New York: Hafner, 1951), p. 171. He says there that "(Poetry) plays with the illusion (*spielt mit dem Schein*), without deceiving by it. . . ." In his division of the arts in sec. 51, p. 165, however, poetry is defined as "the art of conducting a free play of the imagination (*ein unterhaltendes Spiel mit Ideen an*) as if it were a serious business of the understanding." It is painting which, p. 166, he identifies as the art of *Sinnenschein*. Schiller speaks in the 26th Letter of his *Upon the Aesthetic Culture of Man, In a Series of Letters*, in *The Aesthetic Letters, Essays, and the Philosophical Letters of Schiller*, tr. J. Weiss (Boston: Little, Brown, 1845), p. 131, of "all the fine arts, generally, whose existence depends on show (*alle schöne Kunst . . . deren Wesen der Schein ist*)." The notion can be found in Hegel, but there and in Schopenhauer the notion of *Erscheinung* is basic. It is surprising, then, to find in sec. 16 of Nietzsche, *The Birth of Tragedy*, tr. F. Golfing

Schein becomes the material of *Spiel,* and the doctrine that appearance is the object of the aesthetic attitude is complete in outline. Something like that doctrine is to be found in innumerable writers since, in the essays of Messrs. Tomas[2] and Sibley,[3] and most elaborately in Mrs. Langer's *Feeling and Form,*[4] where she explicitly acknowledges an indebtedness to Schiller. Yet the doctrine has nowhere been given a satisfactory statement, and most of the formulations have only a tenuous and verbal connection with one another. Tomas, for instance, and Mrs. Langer too, hold to a number of versions of the view (some actually incompatible with one another), and it will be necessary to distinguish at least five distinct theses for discussion. Sibley has already made a large contribution to the effort, and I shall not hesitate to reiterate and expand some of his points. I find myself less attracted by the doctrine than he does, and dissatisfied with the way he formulates a number of points which are in essence acceptable.

II

Tomas cites a crucial passage from Schopenhauer[5] in which the aesthetic way of seeing things is distinguished from the "common" way, and seems to think that it is in the spirit of his own essay. But Schopenhauer, if he ranks with Kant and Schiller in conjuring the notion of an aesthetic attitude, differs from them and their tradition in thinking that the aesthetic attitude, far from being incompatible with the cognitive attitude, is in the fact the highest form of it. As a consequence, the object of that attitude, "the what of things," is not the sensory idea manifested but the Platonic Idea embodied. It is not the inspection of metaphysical Ideas but attention of the

---

(Garden City: Doubleday and Co., 1956), p. 97, "Apollo embodies the transcendent genius of the *principium individuationis;* through him alone is it possible to achieve redemption in illusion (*Erlösung im Scheine*); the mystical jubilation of Dionysus, on the other hand, breaks the spell of individuation and opens a path to the maternal womb of being (*den Müttern des Seins*)."

2 V. Tomas "Aesthetic Vision," *The Philosophical Review,* January, 1959.

3 F. Sibley, "Aesthetics and the Looks of Things," *The Journal of Philosophy,* November 5, 1959.

4 S. K. Langer, *Feeling and Form* (New York: Charles Scribner's Sons, 1953).

5 A. Schopenhauer, *The World as Will and Idea,* tr. R. B. Haldane and J. Kemp (London: Routledge and Kegan Paul Ltd., 1957), I, p. 231.

appearance of things that is the basis of the doctrine which we are to examine.

Tomas calls our attention to the generous variety of appearances which each object of our quotidian world freely presents for our delectation, only to be ignored, labeled, used. As if this kind of philistinism weren't enough, Tomas has to face the Ryles of the world, who insist that the penny, to stick to the consecrated example, looks round even from beside and above.[6] But surely Tomas would have to admit that if he announced without further ado that some penny looked elliptical, a most natural response would be for him to be told to look again, or to be asked how he supposes that it got that way. The statement that the penny *appears* elliptical from *here* at least does not imply that we take the penny to *be* elliptical (although it does not imply that we don't either). With some instructions designed to counteract the suggestion that it is the *penny* that appears elliptical, and after establishing that we may transform the verbal into the substantive form at will (which is not ordinarily sanctioned), we might grant Tomas that in certain circumstances the penny has an elliptical appearance in the sense that he wants. Having gone so far, I am not inclined to go any further and admit to Tomas that I think there is anything of aesthetic interest about pennies, still less about their appearances. In this got-up sense of appearances it seems to me that they are of no special interest to the aesthetics of nature. An attempt to cultivate an aesthetic attitude along these lines would not promote more looking and liking, but more squinting and staring. And, as Santayana says, staring at brute experience is the lot of madmen and idiots, not of the *fine fleur* of aesthetically sensitive mankind. When we consider the case of art proper this suggestion is even less appealing. Are we being asked to encourage readers to make more remarks like, "I don't care what the word meant to Shakespeare, that's what it means to us," or to join those sophisticated members of the international set who go through the museums with their sun glasses on? It could not be in this sense of looks or appearances that Tomas expects us to treat his "If looking at a picture and attending closely to how it looks is not really to be in the aesthetic attitude, then what on earth is?"[7] as a rhetorical question.

---

[6] G. Ryle, *The Concept of Mind* (New York: Barnes and Noble, Inc., 1949), p. 218.

[7] *Loc. cit.*, p. 63.

I think Sibley is wrong in trying to sustain Tomas here. First of all I think he is wrong in supposing that there is in fact a sense of "appearance" which implies *mere* appearance. That office, as I have suggested, falls to auxiliary expressions, as in "just appears," "appears from here," "appears to me." And these differ among themselves. "Appears from here" suggests that from here it will appear this way to you too, and it does not imply that the thing really isn't the way it appears. Is this what is meant by a "mere" appearance? If so, this is quite a different matter from "appears to me" (and apparently *only* to me). The latter is what I should have supposed a "mere" appearance to be. If it is, I cannot think that "mere" appearances are of any importance whatever to aesthetics. I do not mean, however, to deny that "our" song may mean something very special to us, or even that a man might get to like the sight of his pink rats. It is clearly the "from here" type of (mere) appearance that Sibley has in mind when he undertakes a defense of Tomas. He calls attention to the fact that the angel on the chancel screen is properly foreshortened (to follow his loose usage) only from below, and that only in certain light will the sculpture have the proper eye shadowing. These are not "subjective" appearances, certainly, and if they are public appearances obtained from the right spot and under the proper conditions they are, far from being mere appearances, the way the things actually look. Any art critic who assessed the angel on aesthetic grounds from a ladder in the nave or the sculpture when it was badly lit would be comparable to the man (brought to fame by Meier, Kant, and Croce) who examined the complexion of a rose-cheeked maiden under a microscope. I do not wish, incidentally, to take the view, which many have taken, that between Meier's microscopist and Malraux's photographer there is no distinction to be drawn. Support may, I believe, be extended to the *musée sans murs* without surrendering the judgment that (mere) appearances have no real place in aesthetic theory.

III

Sibley's concession on this point is meant to apply only to a few special cases. The reason for not making it is, however, that if Sibley's principle is admitted we shall immediately be precipitated into the widespread view that *all* art is an illusion or appearance. Sibley remarks, for instance, that "the pigment the painter uses may be dictated by how it looks when surrounded by other colors on the canvas." The shade the green looks in the tube is the shade the green in the painting really is; the green as it appears in the picture is a "mere" appearance or illusion. This leads directly to the view that "really" the painting is the pigments arranged on the flat canvas; the green of the trees, the three-dimensional space they occupy, all that we should describe if we were asked to describe the picture, is but an appearance, even a "mere" appearance of the painting. Tomas is almost certainly thinking about things this way when he distinguishes between the "stimulus" object and its "appearance" and contends that "when we see things aesthetically, our attention is directed toward appearances and we do not particularly notice the thing that presents the appearance, nor do we care what, if anything, it is that appears."[8] Of course, if the *thing* is the pigments, the physical words, the vibrations in the air, while the three-dimensional picture, the fugue, the tale is the appearance, mere appearance, or illusion, then when we are attending to the work of art we are paying primary, sometimes exclusive, attention to the appearance rather than to the thing. (Notice, incidentally, that we are now talking about *one* particular appearance. *The* mere appearance?) Mrs. Langer, who is also given to this notion, gives an extreme but revealing expression of the kind of mistake which is behind it. "All forces," she says, "that cannot be scientifically established and measured must be regarded, from a philosophical standpoint, as illusory."[9] The argument for the two works of art relies on the very same principle as did the once prestigious argument for the two tables. The table isn't really solid because it is penetrable by "scientific" gamma rays; the green in the painting isn't real because it doesn't match the green in what is now the "test" tube. If you pick a sufficiently irrelevant criterion of reality anything can be shown to be an illusion (as almost everything has been). This type of argument has no special interest for aesthetics, as can be seen by the fact that if we allow the equally valid two tables argument we could conclude that the *common* way of seeing pays "no attention to the thing but to the appearance." If art is appearance in this sense, Tomas' discovery that the aesthetic attitude is directed to appearance can be seen in its full

---

8 *Ibid.*, p. 53.
9 *Op. cit.*, p. 188.

triviality. It has not been discovered by studying aesthetic responses but by reading tired manuals of epistemology.

Because Tomas wants to say that the aesthetic attitude is directed to appearances (as opposed to things) he must argue that when (in his example) Velasquez looks (aesthetically) at the pope he is looking at his appearance in a sense which excludes his looking at the pope himself. As a consequence, when Velasquez uses the phrase, "a man," to describe what he sees he is using the word "man" in a special sense which applies only to appearances. Tomas seems to suppose that when we describe an appearance we cannot be describing the thing that appears that way. But, surely, when we describe a person's appearance we describe the person. Even when we speak of the way things appear from unusual angles we are describing the way *they* appear. And these "appearances" are public and must not be compared (as Tomas compares them) with Macbeth's seeing the dagger which, some producers of the play notwithstanding, is not. We do, of course, describe the appearance of the image on the screen and of the mirage on the horizon without describing the *film* image or the *occasion* of the image, but there is no analogy to these in the case of looking at the pope. So far there is no reason to suppose either that we are describing the pope's appearance but not the pope, or that the word "man" is being used in a peculiar sense. Next we must approach the question from the side of the portrait of the pope. We have already seen how Tomas has convinced himself that the portrait of the pope is only an appearance. (Of which we now get an appearance? Tomas speaks ambiguously of the appearance of the portrait.) He will now want to establish that when we describe the portrait as the portrait of a man we are using the word "man" in the sense, already mentioned, which is peculiar to appearances. And so he observes that when you do *say* (being asked in the presence of the portrait when you see), "a man," you are being misleading. Indeed, "to say the *least* (italics mine) misleading" if you are describing the "stimulus object." But this is alarming. Nobody to whom you might actually make this remark in the presence of the portrait would conceivably be misled into thinking that you were saying that pigments and a piece of canvas are a real live man. (And if he were, how would the other sense of "man" avoid the difficulty, since he would still hear the very same physical word? It might mitigate it.) Tomas now clinches his argument by asserting that "in principle the appearance of the picture and the appearance of the pope could be identical,"[10] and this is why we can use the word in its narrow sense of them both. But surely, the reason we can, and do, use the word in its only (relevant) sense of them both is not that in principle they could be identical, but that in practice it is impossible that they should ever be confused with one another.

Tomas' motive for trying to convince us that in principle the appearance of the pope and the appearance of the portrait might be identical is that he thinks it a matter of indifference whether the appearance is an appearance of the one or the other. For aesthetic vision the question of reality does not arise, he avers, giving his own formulation of Kant's notion that the aesthetic judgment is indifferent to existence and of Schiller's that the claim to reality is actually repudiated. Even granting the propriety of the notion that the aesthetic situation can be analyzed into the presence or absence of some single property, it would seem fairly clear that the "property" of existence could not be it. Responding aesthetically to a woman *may* involve not raising questions about her morals; it does not require "bracketing" her existence. Responding aesthetically to a pope might require the "remission" of papal politics; it would not entail meeting with equanimity the news that one had been gushing over a particularly startling creation from Madame Tussaud's.

Objections arise even more pressingly from the side of art. How *could* the question arise in the case of the non-representational arts? (I omit the consideration that a group of touring epistemologists—sightseers—could raise the question of the existence of Chartres Cathedral at any moment.) And in those cases where we can make *sense* of the claim that the question of existence might arise, the point is not that the matter is one of indifference, but that it must normally be decided in the negative from the very start. (A better way of putting this point might be to say that the question of reality does not *arise*, if that form of expression had not been appropriated for Tomas' purposes.) If the question of existence were *not* decided in the negative from the start, how, as Sibley demands, could one say, for instance, "it has the very air of life about it"? (The logical point remains even if we do have to imagine an offensive piece of *trompe l'oeil* art, or a philistine observer, to occasion it.) It would be absurd to admire the brilliant craftsmanship, the stylistic originality, the relationship to the tradition of an image which might turn out to be a

---

[10] *Loc. cit.*, p. 57.

real live man. In addition to being absurd it would be immoral. Hobbes would *obviously* be right in ascribing our pleasure in tragedy to sadism if it were not perfectly clear that the tragic events did not transpire. Nietzsche would have more right than he does to imply what he implies in saying that it is "at tragedies, bull-fights, and crucifixions (that man) has so far felt best on earth."[11] *Aficionados* to the contrary, the moment of truth is not an aesthetic moment. And the worst possible argument they might use in claiming that it is would be to suggest that the question of reality does not arise. If it did not this could not be a moment of *truth*.

I V

Mrs. Langer's view proceeds not from the notion that in the aesthetic experience we treat things as appearances, but rather from the notion that there is no other way to treat appearances than by adopting an aesthetic attitude toward them. For the Kantian tradition (if not for Kant) the aesthetic problem might be understood as that of *adopting* the aesthetic attitude toward objects which by their own nature might elicit an existential concern. For Mrs. Langer the problem is solved by adopting the theory that the artist creates an appearance which by its very nature could not sustain an existential interest. Kant's formula *ohne Interesse* is displaced by Schiller's *Interesse am Schein*. We guarantee an impractical attitude by taking it to impractical things. There are, of course, a number of senses in which Mrs. Langer might hold that the artist creates an appearance, senses which, unfortunately, Mrs. Langer fails to distinguish. The one which is specially relevant here is the sense in which she wants to say that a work of art is an appearance because of the features it has in common with such appearances as rainbows or shadows. Any object which does not meet the criteria of "scientific" reality is an appearance or illusion. Thus the impalpable rainbow, the weightless shadow, the inaccessible space of the picture make them all appearances. It is important, in passing, to distinguish this reason for calling the picture an appearance from the reason we examined in the last section (and which Mrs. Langer often seems to hold). Here we are saying that the picture is an appearance because its space lacks some dimension

---

11 F. Nietzsche, *Thus Spake Zarathustra*, tr. W. Kaufmann, in *The Portable Nietzsche* (New York: The Viking Press, 1954), p. 300.

of *physical* space. There we were saying that it is an appearance because, really, there is no space at all, only pigments on canvas.

One's immediate reaction to this thesis is to object that after all it is based on the patent error of supposing that rainbows and shadows are appearances or illusions. They may be special types of objects, not material objects, but it does not follow from this that they are appearances or illusions. And it may appear that Mrs. Langer is prepared to deal with this objection since she herself points out that rainbows and shadows, and in consequence works of art may, alternatively, be considered "virtual" objects in the scientific sense—"objects" which are real but are not real *objects*. It is at this point, however, that Mrs. Langer is guilty of perilous confusion. She does not distinguish the thesis that each work of art is an appearance or illusion, in the sense that it presents the appearance or gives the illusion of something, from the thesis that each work of art is a virtual object. That is to say, she confuses being virtually *something* with being virtually an *object*. I think she does this because her main example is painting, and in the case of painting the arguments which go to show that the space of the painting is only virtual *space* (can't measure it) also go to show that the space of the picture is only a virtual *object* (can't measure it). But, of course, it is not true, in general, that when something is virtually this or that it is a virtual object. It does not follow, for instance, that if Mrs. Langer is right in saying that dance is virtual *gesture* that the gesture of dance is thereby shown to be a virtual *object*. Perfectly "real" objects may give the appearance of, or virtually be, other objects. Either Mrs. Langer will have to argue that virtual gestures *are* virtual objects or she will have to admit that works of art are not all appearances in the sense of being virtual objects. I do not think that she should even want to argue the more modest thesis which on occasion she suggests: that works of art *function* as virtual objects. What sense is a real gesture of despair perceived by, which is functionally irrelevant to the perception of a dance gesture? The repudiation of the thesis that art is an appearance in the sense of being a virtual object will be no great loss, however, for, after all, even if there is less to the existence of rainbows and shadows, even if all one can do is to *look* at them, is it inevitable that one will? It is easy to be negligent and unappreciative of shadows and rainbows, and guaranteeing that works of art are like them will not guarantee an aesthetic response. Because one can only look it does not follow that one will look, or that one will look appreciatively.

V

It remains to consider Mrs. Langer's view that a work of art is an appearance because it creates the appearance or gives the illusion of something. One might well object that it does not follow from the fact that something gives the appearance of (being) something that it is an appearance itself. Let us waive this objection, however, and examine the view that every art does in fact create such an illusion or give such an appearance. Every work of painting or sculpture or architecture gives the illusion of space; every piece of music the illusion of time; every dance the illusion of gesture; every literary work the illusion of life. The task requires heroism but the path is clear. When an art does not exploit illusion in all cases, either ignore the remaining cases, or deny that they exist; when the art never exploits illusion, discover some property which is present in every work of that art, and then declare it to be there only apparently. Thus we simply ignore those painters who have eschewed the illusion of space and frankly identified the pigments on the canvas with the painting. To them Mrs. Langer would doubtless reply: "To keep the virtual and the actual materials separate is not easy for anyone without philosophical training."[12] Sculpture is said to give the appearance of life. This might seem plausible enough if only living beings were represented, but what are we to say of the many distinguished modern sculptors in the constructivist tradition who have in some measure occasioned Ortega to observe "that it is not an exaggeration to say that modern paintings and sculptures betray a real loathing of living forms and forms of living beings."[13] Mrs. Langer's approach here is to take the bull by the horns. The appearance of life does not require the representation of it, the *expression* of biological feeling will suffice, and presumably we shall find it in the Gabos and the David Smiths if we look hard enough. In the case of the dance, where it *might* appear that gesture is always present, Mrs. Langer takes it into her head that gesture in the sense relevant

---

[12] *Op. cit.*, p. 181.
[13] J. Ortega y Gasset, *The Dehumanization of Art* (Garden City: Doubleday and Co., 1956), p. 37.

to the dance requires self-expression, embraces Diderot's paradox, and concludes that it is only the *appearance* of gesture which
is actually present. While Isadora Duncan thought she was expressing herself she was only deceiving herself. In sum, it seems
to me that Mrs. Langer's taking of the high priori is both an im-
pediment to genuine critical insight and, as usual with such constructions, unnecessarily ambitious. Indeed, one wonders at Mrs.
Langer's elaborate attempt to show that each work of art is an
image *of* something when she herself has said early in her book
"that the difference between images and actualities is functional.
That is why the character of an illusion may cling to works that
do not represent anything."[14] If so, why this valiant attempt to
establish that every work is indeed an image or appearance? Far
better to avoid such sweeping assumptions, and investigate the
techniques which do in fact make the arts function.

V I

Certainly some looks are aspects of realities; some even exhaust
them. A man with a mean look has it even if he is a saint. And it
is downright absurd to suggest that a pretty-looking girl isn't
pretty. It is in this sense that the "o" of Tomas' *Times* has a fat
look, and if attending to the looks of things is aesthetic it cannot
be because there is any conflict or distinction between appearance
and reality here. It is only in this sense of "look" that his "if
looking at a picture and attending to how it looks is not really to be
in the aesthetic attitude, then what on earth is?" is even plausible. Sibley, who joins Tomas in drawing no distinction between
looks and appearances, goes so far as to say that, taken appropriately, the thesis is analytic. Of course, if the statement only means
that it is necessary to look at a picture in order to have an aesthetic
experience (of it), the thesis is not only analytic but trifling. I
shall assume that this is not what is meant. Perhaps not "looking
at it" but "attending to how it looks" is the operative phrase.
And "attending to how it looks" (no easy phrase) would seem to
mean attending to its looks (Tomas) or to its appearances (Sibley).
But I am not sure that attending to looks or appearances can be
a necessary condition of aesthetic response.

Tomas and Sibley are indifferent to any distinctions between

---

[14] *Op. cit.*, p. 47

"looks" and "appears" and their cognates, and I should agree if they objected that there are exceptions and, indeed, that usage is extremely fuzzy in this area. Yet I think it would be wrong to conclude that nothing can be said. The natural way to rebut "he *looks* angry" is to deny that he does *look* angry, while the natural way to rebut "he *appears* angry" is to deny that he *is* angry. "Looks" has primarily to do with the visual properties of things, "appears" with how they are taken to be in certain circumstances or on certain occasions. (Of course, they may be taken to be the way they are.) Perhaps this is reflected in the distinction between a person's looks and his appearance. His appearance is relative to (now probably to his) circumstances and is different on different occasions. This is not true of his looks (or was not before plastic surgery). Tomas is right, I think, in speaking of the putative pudginess of the "o" as a look. He and Sibley are both wrong, however, if they think that the verbal and substantive forms of these words may be shuffled with impunity. It does not follow from the fact that one appears angry that he has an angry appearance or look. Nor does it follow from the fact that one looks at something that what one looks at is a look. Figures appear in paintings and one may look at them, but it does not follow that they are looks or appearances (of the painting). And whether or not it follows, they are *not* looks or appearances. Is it clear that *any* pictures have looks or appearances? Some of them have a look, to be sure—an unfinished, a glazed, an elegant look. (To forestall objections: a glazed and elegant *look*.) But does *every* painting have a look? I am not sure that it does. And if it doesn't, attending to looks (or appearances) could not be a necessary condition of having an aesthetic response. It is not even a necessary condition for having such a response in cases where there is a look. It is not necessary to attend to, but rather to ignore, the faded look of the Milan *Last Supper* in order to have an, or certainly, *the* aesthetic response to it. Interpreted one way Tomas' thesis is trivially obvious, another, very probably false. Incidentally, if Tomas' criterion is meant to apply, *mutatis mutandis*, to aesthetic experience in general, it might be well to point out that listening to music is not the same as listening to the way it sounds. It might sound far-off (key), or as if the hall were an echo chamber, but does all music sound some way, have a sound? And does the music have a far-off appearance? The mind boggles as we approach the literary arts.

Although Tomas says that attending to appearances or looks is only a *necessary* condition of aesthetic experience his remarks imply that he considers it a *sufficient* condition ("If looking is not really . . . then what . . . is?"), and Sibley alludes anonymously to people who hold this view. The first version of Tomas' thesis becomes interesting if it is put forward as a sufficient condition of the aesthetic experience. *Is* looking (closely) at the picture sufficient? Are, then, the restorer, the curator, the dealer in the aesthetic attitude whenever they happen to be looking at a painting? (They are probably still further from it when they are looking closely.) And even if one were looking from where one should, and with honorable intentions, is this enough? Does looking (no matter how closely) suffice even for the notation of all the "visual" features—color relationships and significant repetitions? It is even less plausible that it could account for the response to structure, tone, theme. Seeing the point requires more than looking at it. The aesthetic attitude is an illusion and art a reality.

IV

Types of Evidence
and Their Relevance
to Critical Judgment

The "Meaning" of
a Work of Art

INTRODUCTION

Philosophers, sometimes critics turned philosopher, have disagreed about whether "meaning" can be ascribed to works of art and, if so, whether it is a kind of meaning that can or does refer to matters of fact. The task of adjudicating these disputes is not facilitated if, as is frequently the case, the question of what the issues are that divide them is left open by the disputants. The following material aims to identify one objective of philosophical claims about the nature of artistic meaning, and so to provide a basis for understanding and evaluating the intellectual merit of these claims.

Suppose a critic denied that Dante's *Divine Comedy* is good poetry for the following reasons: (1) Typical among the beliefs expressed in the *Divine Comedy* are that God exists and that He is our creator and judge. It holds to a theistic view of ultimate reality. (2) The articles of theism, including the Christian version, are, at best, museum relics. They are inheritances from a pre-scientific past. We have come to recognize that whatever is knowable about the universe is authenticated not by visions or fables but by the methods of the empirical sciences. And the result has been the exposure of Christianity as a tissue of deceptions disguised by the solemnity of its piety and high moral conviction. (3) The *Divine Comedy* affirms as certain truth the doctrinal absurdities of medieval Christianity. It is, therefore, bad poetry.

Now suppose there is another critic who also agrees that in no sense is Christianity a privileged oracle of revealed truth. But he still believes that the *Divine Comedy* is superb poetry. He continues to hold, therefore, that his estimate is the right one. How can he show that the high regard in which he continues to hold the poem turns on something more substantial than intransigence or an idle whim? How can he justify, on the one hand, his rejection of the Christian verities as manifestly preposterous and, on the other, his commendation of a poem that is pre-eminently a vehicle of their expression?

First, he might return to the poem to discover whether he had read it correctly, whether it had, in fact, a distinctively Christian character. And suppose he concludes that the problem is not one of a mistaken reading. The Christian references throughout the poem are too clear; its basic structure—Inferno, Purgatory, Paradise—is dictated by the Christian theory of punishment and redemption. There is no question either of forcing an interpretation upon a language which will not bear it because it is obscure, or misinterpreting a language that is clear in the direction of another viewpoint than Christianity.

Second, he might consider whether there are not other merits of the poem that outweigh the defects of its intellectual content. Suppose he cannot agree this is so, that Christianity infects everything in the *Divine Comedy*—imagery, structure, diction, theme. Remove it and nothing is left.

Our critic has now rejected two of the defensive strategies which are, in principle at least, available to him. There is a third: His problem began with the fact that he thought certain beliefs false and reprehensible and the poem that contained them praiseworthy. And does not that suggest that to hold both judgments simultaneously is possible because beliefs are not part of a poem and, therefore, not one of the things that count in a judgment of its quality? If he then tried to understand how this could be so, there is a theory of language which makes it so and provides a general warrant for asserting otherwise incompatible judgments of artistic merit and intellectual content.

That is the "emotive theory" of language and it can be adapted to poetry as follows: We know that there are words and combinations of words that have meaning and that, in their ordinary use, have the purpose of stating facts. The grammatical unit for stating a fact is the sentence and, in such a case, we call that which the sentence expresses a "proposition." The meaning of a sentence is what it states and if it states nothing it is not a proposition and it does not have meaning.

Now we think that, because the words and grammatical units of poetry are like the words and grammatical units of fact-stating discourse, there is between then an identity of meaning. This is a mistake. Poetry has the function not of stating facts but of expressing or communicating emotion. For that function, the grammatically intelligible units of poetry are not propositions—are not, therefore, units of meaning. They are units expressive of feeling. They have no more meaning than a smile or groan which are in their rudimentary way also expressions of feeling. It is easy to see that a smile expresses happiness but does not mean what it expresses and that we would not evaluate it according to whether it is true or false. It is harder to see, because poetry is composed of words, that it is uniquely expressive of feeling also and like a smile lacks the features of cognitive meaning.

Accordingly grammatically well-formed sentences may not say anything for either of two reasons: There may be an abuse of language, a collection of words whose combined meaning lack a sense, e.g., *Time is larger than space.* Or there may be a use of language for a purpose other than asserting some condition of the world. The language of poetry falls under the second category. It does not follow, however, that because a sentence does not *say* anything, it does not *do* anything. Poetry is a case in point; it does something by expressing and communicating our emotional states.

To be sure, there is much more that could be said about and for the emotive theory. What I have presented is greatly oversimplified but it points up a crucial implication of the theory for questions of aesthetic judgment. Once accepted, it prevents us from saying about poems such as the *Divine Comedy* that if bad theology (or bad science) then bad poetry. The *Divine Comedy*, if it is meaningless, cannot assert that which is true or false, cannot be fact-stating. Consequently, we cannot condemn it on the now-irrelevant ground that what it says is false.

Of course, the theory is not propounded in order to show that poetry, since meaningless, is inconsequential gibberish and thereby to provide for those who do not understand it the consolation that there is nothing to understand. The purpose, if not the result, of the theory is to salvage the prestige of poetry by taking it out of a losing race with science. If the value of poetry is measured by the extent to which it expresses true propositions, it is a primitive and unsatisfactory alternative to the special sciences. And if the merit of particular poems were to be measured by the same criterion, the standard rankings of works of literature would be up for wholesale revision. On this ground, probably the only poetry exempt from censure would be that exhibiting the novel virtue of simple-mindedness.

Unfortunately, the surgery involved in excising meaning has the effect of creating complications as damaging to a view of poetry as the complaints it hopes to eliminate. In the first place, it is plausible to take the position that when it comes to expression or communication of emotion, there are a host of devices simpler and less devious than those of poetry. In this regard, as in the case of poetry being a vehicle of fact-stating, it is quite possible to conclude that it comes off second-best. A tritely sentimental letter may express a certain condition of love as well as, if not better than, for example, Andrew Marvell's "To His Coy Mistress." The letter has the advantage of not being burdened with sophisticated and—to the uninitiated—opaque diction and imagery. And for the expression of religious awe and wonder, the Church is probably right in preferring a celebration of the Mass to the long and tortuous development of the *Divine Comedy*.

In the second place, to say that poetry is literally meaningless seems to separate it completely from matters of the mind. It places poetry closer to gibberish than to reasoned discourse and demeans its character by suggesting that the writing or reading of it is not an intellectual exercise.

It should be obvious why this doctrine (a more subtle version can be found in the early writings of I. A. Richards) could ruffle the sensibilities of literary critics and arouse them to a defense of poetry as something at once intellectual and possessed of its own qualities of merit. The part of their defense that was positive took the form of restating the notion of poetic meaning. And it was at this point that they invoked a position discussed earlier in this book—that in the nature of a work of art it is always true that form and content are inseparable.

It will be recalled that according to this view the meaning of a work of art could not be construed apart from the manner of its expression. A change of form, it follows, is always a change of meaning. For poetry, therefore, among the elements of form, among the determinants of meaning, are the words and their order of deployment, meter, rhyme, imagery, structure, etc. No two poems are exactly alike in all these matters (if they were they would not be different poems); consequently, they can never have the same meaning. No words or groups of words in poetry and in prose discourse, however identical in every other respect, can have the same meaning. The meaning of a work of art is particular to and exhausted by the vehicle of its expression.

The result is twofold: First, poetry is restored to the life of the mind; it has meaning. It is, therefore, deserving of the attention and concern that we devote to an intellectual enterprise. Second, poetry is not susceptible of analysis or evaluation relative to the truth or falsity of what it says. The meaning of poetry is different in kind from that of prose discourse. The standard techniques of evaluating factual worth were developed with reference to the latter. They have no bearing on the qualitatively distinct problems of identifying the meaning and estimating the truth of poetic utterance.

We can now return to the dilemma with which we began: the critic's apparently incompatible views of the intellectual content of Christianity and the aesthetic merit of the *Divine Comedy*. Under this view of meaning, the dilemma disappears. If, for example, he regards the sentence "God exists" as false, it is because he thinks its meaning is lacking of an objective counterpart. But as the meaning of a prose sentence, neither the *Divine Comedy* nor any of its parts can iterate it and, therefore, the ascription of falsity is logically independent of his literary judgment. What the critic regards as false is the meaning of a prose sentence and that is not, and cannot be, the meaning of the *Divine Comedy*.

There is a sense in which this doctrine, taken straight, is a palpable absurdity. If, for example, we ask about the meaning of a poem there is no form of words other than the poem itself capable of stating the answer. For poetry, in other words, meaning is no longer a property distinguishable among others: it is another name for poetry, whatever its properties.

However, it should be clear that I have been suggesting that, in another light, the notion of poetic meaning has a point and performs an intellectual service. In the cases considered, theses about meaning were advanced to sustain what seemed to be imperiled judgments of poems or the discipline of poetry. To that extent, they are instruments of strategy and have to be evaluated in relation to the problems that gave them birth.

It is from this point of view that the last notion, that of poetic meaning, takes on a point. The meaning of a sentence is, in prose discourse, that which we consider in evaluating its acceptability. That is to say, we do not consider, in the course of evaluating the truth of an indicative sentence, its qualities of meter, rhyme, assonance, etc. If it is true, it is true regardless of the ugliness or felicity of its rhetoric. Consequently, the redefinition of meaning attempts to preserve its sense of being that which we consider in a language in making an evaluation. All the different features that we weigh in a judgment of poetry (discursive meaning, imagery, diction, theme, structure, etc.) become part of what a critic will call "poetic meaning." And it is by this use of meaning that he avoids the presumption that any one of these factors is sufficient to a total judgment of artistic merit.

Of course, this leaves aside the question of whether a critic is right in thinking that the view of Christianity in a poem such as the *Divine Comedy* is such an important element that rejecting it is tantamount to condemning the poem.

Suppose a teacher of elocution says and his class repeats, "Our room is cold." The class understand what is said in a sense in which it would not understand the collection of nonsense syllables, "tiz bif gil." Let us call that which they understand "the meaning of a sentence."

Now the class might hear and repeat "Our room is cold," on a hot day. But we could not criticize them for having misstated the weather. If the sentence has, in this case, the use of teaching elocution, it is not a statement and it is irrelevant to consider its merits according to the predicates of evaluation that apply to statements. It is irrelevant to evaluate it as true or false. Let us call a sentence which has the use of stating a fact an "assertion," and say that a sentence is "uttered" if its use is other than assertive.

By preserving the distinction between uttering and asserting, we could say that the *Divine Comedy* expresses the beliefs of Christianity but does not state that what it expresses is true. It utters but does not assert them. Then we could admit meaning, in a standard sense, into the *Divine Comedy* without committing ourselves to the relevance of factual evaluation.

This seems a neat way of dispatching our problem, but it is, unfortunately, much too neat. The attribution of utterance rather than assertion to poetry would itself be without foundation. In most cases there are contextual clues which tell us whether or not a sentence is asserted. If a meteorologist says in a forecast that the weather will be hot, we have no doubt he is asserting. If an elocution master says, "Repeat after me. The room is hot," we have no doubt that he is uttering. Should we be mistaken, the speaker is able to correct us.

There are no such settled conventions or clues that enable us to decide whether or not a poem is asserting. Dead poets cannot correct our errors and we frequently disbelieve the living ones who try. It seems to me, therefore, that in judging poetry we use the distinction of uttering and asserting in quite a different way. For the most part, we tend to assume that a poem is asserting and to count what it asserts as part of its aesthetic quality. But for a troublesome case, we may reverse standard procedure and allow a prior estimate of aesthetic merit to decide that the meaning is uttered and not asserted. If, in our consideration of a poem, we decide that the grandeur of its theme or the brilliance of its language deserve the title of greatness but cannot accept what we think of as its meaning, we will not allow this to count against our judgment. That is another way of saying we will regard it as utterance.

There is, however, one thing we cannot do. We cannot both say that a poem asserts and refuse to take into account, when we judge it, the truth or falsity of what it asserts. To assert is to take responsibility for what is asserted and to assert falsely is to fail. That is why claims about whether literary works can express assertions are prompted by, have an effect upon, and must be understood in the light of our evaluations of their quality as works of art.

Roy Harvey Pearce

THE POET AS PERSON[*]

In 1920 William Carlos Williams, publishing a collection of self-consciously experimental poems under the title "Kora in Hell: Improvisations," began his volume with a long rambling preface on the state of the world and American letters. He came to the conclusion that the proper credo for the true poet was this: "There is nothing in literature but change and change is mockery. I'll write whatever I damn please, whenever I damn please and as I damn please and it'll be good if the authentic spirit of change is on it." His desire was that the poet discover and rediscover his world exclusively in terms of himself. As he wrote, "It is in the continual and violent refreshing of the idea [of discovery of self] that love and good writing have their security." And poets who looked elsewhere than into the violence of the self for a means of discovering the spirit of change in the world, were to be anathemized: "Our prize poems are especially to be damned not because of superficial bad workmanship, but because they are rehash, repetition—just as Eliot's more exquisite work is rehash, repetition in another way of Verlaine, Baudelaire, Maeterlinck—conscious or unconscious—just as were Pound's early paraphrases from Yeats and his constant later cribbing from the renaissance, Provence and the modern French: Men content with the connotations of their masters."

[*] From *The Yale Review*, Vol. XLI, No. 3, March, 1952. Copyright Yale University Press. Reprinted by permission of *The Yale Review* and of the author.

It was, in fact, the "connotations of their masters" that Williams feared would somehow destroy the connotations of the self. And it was such connotations that he felt his friend Pound was teaching as the only means by which American poets might discipline themselves out of their moribund Victorianism. All this Pound cheerfully admitted in a series of letters he sent Williams on receiving a copy of "Kora in Hell." Justifying himself, he said that he had "sweated like a nigger to break up the clutch of the old . . . Harper's etc. That [he had] tried to enlighten . . . Chicago, so as to make a place for the real thing. That [he had] sent over French models, which [had] given six hundred people a means of telling something nearer the truth than they would have done senza."

We may reduce the question that Pound and Williams debated to this: How could the twentieth-century American tell the truth in poetry? For Williams it was by letting nothing interfere with the poet's need to know himself primarily as an individuated, violently individuated, self. For Pound it was by going to school to other poets and learning thereby to delimit and to give precise form to that need—as it were, to put an end to the violence of the self.

But the problem is only an aspect of a far larger one: the eternal problem of community, of finding a moral and social order which men can accept, while yet remaining sufficiently differentiated and egocentric to be aware that the acceptance is an individual matter. It is the problem of constructing a society in which men can remain individuals and at the same time share values, ideas, and beliefs, in which they can realize themselves as somehow at once different and alike, separate and together, democratic and en masse.

We are told by our social scientists that we participate in society doubly, so to speak, as individuated and as socialized selves, and that the struggle to survive as whole men is the struggle to make one kind of participation coördinate with the other. Calling the elements in this double participation culture and personality, the anthropologist Edward Sapir wrote:

> The interests connected by the terms culture and personality are necessary for intelligent and helpful growth because each is based on a distinctive kind of imaginative participation by the observer in the life around him. The observer may dramatize such behavior as he takes note of it in terms of a set of values, a conscience which is beyond self and to which he must conform, actually or

imaginatively, if he is to preserve his place in the world of authority or impersonal social necessity. Or, on the other hand, he may feel the behavior as self-expressive, as defining the reality of individual consciousness against the mass of environing social determinants. Observations coming within the framework of the former of these two kinds of participation constitute our knowledge of culture. Those which come within the framework of the latter constitute our knowledge of personality. One is as subjective or objective as the other, for both are essentially modes of projection of personal experience into the analysis of social phenomena.

This puts the matter at its most general, as is fitting for the social scientist, but it also, I think, achieves, through its very generalization, a perspective which will let us see that our poetry, being the intensest kind of "imaginative participation" in the life around us, must also tend to express, on the one hand, our sense of personality, and, on the other, our sense of culture. If our social scientists have become aware of the culture-personality split primarily because our society is so constituted as to make them aware of it, then our poets, by virtue of being poets operating according to the canons of *their* mode of knowledge, will be even more intensely aware of it, and even more intensely committed to it. But if our social scientists posit an ideal society wherein the demands of culture and personality are exactly reciprocal, our poets cannot; for they live not by positing generalities but by realizing particulars. Being artists, not scientists, they cannot speak in terms of that which is abstractly and generally desirable. They must speak of what is and of what they desire, whether psychologically or metaphysically, in terms of what they have empirically. If what they see in the world around them manifests a split between personality and culture, if all forms of culture seem alien to the modern personality as it discovers and reveals itself, and if the choice of one cancels out the choice of the other, then they must try to discover the kind of a community (or, strictly speaking, substitute for a community) that is possible when they have chosen one or the other. Which is to say, they must discover what it is to need a sense of community and not to have it. Thus they must write their poems and let us know fully what one or the other choice comes to.

What I want to get at from this perspective of sociological generalization is this: that Pound and Williams, in making their separate choices, were willy-nilly—as men in some sense limited by

the language and values-in-language which their world gave them
—touching at the heart of our cultural crisis; that, as poets, they
asked the right and necessary questions. For them a sense of community—and the ability to write poetry in and to a community—
had to be searched for, had to be discovered. For Pound the possibility of community (again, strictly speaking, of a substitute kind)
lay in a source ultimately outside the individual poet's sensibility, in
authoritative models, and he proceeded to shape his sensibility in accordance with those models. In short, he gave primary devotion to
culture. Williams, on the other hand, found the possibility of community in his own radically individuated sensibility and made it
his business either to deny the usefulness of models or to make
them into something genuinely his own; he insisted that they have
no meaning except as the poet gives them meaning. He gave primary devotion to personality.

It is this latter devotion, especially as it appears in the work of
Wallace Stevens, William Carlos Williams, and E. E. Cummings,
that is my main interest in this essay. Not that these are the only
poets who have chosen this course; there are many more—from
Imagists to Activists, from a Marianne Moore through a Theodore
Roethke; and I write with all of them in mind. Taken all in all,
their work makes up, if not a school, at least a strain in our poetry,
a strain so clear and vibrant that it lets us know surely and certainly one way that the poet works in our world—and, beyond
that, one way that our world makes the poet work.

But we must remember that the greater number of our poets have
chosen the other course; they have chosen to celebrate culture—as
in our society and its search for a sense of community, more of us
have followed the way to authority which guarantees order and
runs the risk of denying the self, than the way to free and full
selfhood which runs the risk of denying order and achieving only
chaos or isolation—the violence of change, as Williams put it. Thus
before we look more closely at that minor strain in our poetry
which centers on personality, we must glance hastily, by way of
recall, at that major strain which centers on culture.

The most obvious instance besides Pound himself is, of course,
T. S. Eliot. The history of Eliot's enterprise, it is now obvious, has
been that of seeking an adequate culture—artistic and moral and
political. He began by writing small poems of objective description,
which were yet more than descriptive because they were cast in an

ironic evaluative form; "Sweeney among the Nightingales" is a characteristic example. Here the situation of one of our bourgeoisie is found negatively meaningful by being contrasted with a larger, alien kind of order. The very texture of the poem depends not upon our perception of the situation as it is objectively, in and of itself—but rather historically, in relation to something larger, more stable than itself; the situation is worth looking at only in relation to this larger order which it reflects in a bitter and dumb irony.

So it is, on a much larger scale, with "The Waste Land." The obscurity of this poem derives from Eliot's dependence upon authorities nominally extraneous to the situation of the poem; yet we must feel the order immanent in these authorities if we are to know the disorder, twentieth-century disorder, which is the subject of the poem. The poet continually makes us aware of what he is not, not of what he is, by means of such fragments of folklore, myth, and his literary heritage as he can shore against his ruins. "Shore against his ruins" is precise, I think; for insofar as Eliot's poet-protagonist is to have a self, it is literally a self shored up—held together by forces derived from something outside, not from something within.

"Ash Wednesday" moves towards the positive, certainly. But it is positive denial and discipline: "Teach us to care and not to care" —which I take it means to know, even to love, the world for what it is, so as to be able to renounce it fully. The structure of "Ash Wednesday" depends upon a continual, if only implicit, reference to received Christian doctrine. The ruins of the self begin to be reconstituted into a whole; yet the principle of reconstitution is the will of God and not of the individual. The perceptions that the poet registers for us are his only secondarily. First they are those of what he takes to be universal Christendom; his secondary perceptions make uniform sense only as they are those of this universal Christendom.

The poems which make up "Four Quartets" record this seeking of order most fully and most brilliantly; likewise they push this seeking to its logical end. The task is, within the structure of time, to achieve the timeless. There is still, but much more subtly than in "The Waste Land," the dependence upon history and tradition and myth for points of reference around which the poems may be organized. The perceiving self still values most what he is not, not what he is. He comes to know what he is not, in terms of the material qualities which mark his earthly nature: air, earth, water, fire. These qualities are held together, as I have noted, by something which is outside of man; he can know what that something is only by denying, insofar as he can, his material nature. Thus in "The Dry Salvages":

> *. . . to apprehend*
> *The point of intersection of the timeless*
> *With time, is an occupation for the saint—*
> *No occupation either, but something given*
> *And taken, in a lifetime's death in love,*
> *Ardour and selflessness and self-surrender.*
> *For most of us, there is only the unattended*
> *Moment, the moment in and out of time . . .*

"hints and guesses. . . . Hints followed by guesses": this is the lot of the modern self. One presumes that the guesses are possible because they are based on a certainty that there are saints. And saints are part of a larger order to which one must appeal to find his place in the world—if one is so disposed, to write poetry; "Four Quartets," we remember, is also a series of poems about language, the mystery of the Word. It is not out of context, I think, to recall Eliot's pronouncement in "Tradition and the Individual Talent": "What happens [to the poet] is a continual surrender of himself as he is at the moment to something which is more valuable. The progress of the artist is a continual self-sacrifice, a continual extinction of personality."

Eliot, of course, has been the great example for our poets, though there are others. One thinks of Ransom and Tate and of all the young men who have gone to school to them. The kind of order differs, certainly; but the conviction that there is order somewhere —in the past, or in tradition, or in formal religion—is there. And for our purposes it is important to note that the older Southerners were by no means influenced by their reading of Eliot into writing the kind of poetry that they wrote and continue to write. Their own cultural situation, as the history of the Agrarian-Fugitive movement shows, directed them to a search for models or order; their discovery that Eliot's search was like theirs only served to authenticate and to verify their own need and their own procedure and to make it possible for them to go to school to Eliot.

But the tendency to search for an order and an authority alien to the modern world is not confined to poets such as these. It is the product of too deep a need in our society to be so. Thus it seems to me that Robert Frost is, in his own way, a poet whose work is equally characterized by devotion to culture. Frost achieves his celebrated individualism, what on first glance may seem to be a devotion to personality, simply by refusing to have anything to do with a modern world which, so his poems report, lacks a principle capable of supporting any kind of individualism. His is an individualism out of a nineteenth-century agrarian America, a Transcendentalism which has barked its shins on evil and has come to be skilled at avoiding or facing it where it is most easily identifiable, in the New England mountains. Frost strikes us as an individualist because he will have none of our more usual kinds of authority. Yet we must be sure to note that he will have none of the modern self either. Seeking to find a personality, yet turning away from whatever there is of personality in his own time, he has found—for us as his readers—only culture.

Recently, putting Job in the twentieth century, Frost has made him complain to God:

> *We don't know where we are, or who we are,*
> *Don't know one another; don't know You;*
> *Don't know what time it is....*

Starting from a position something like this, Eliot finally located himself in the world of Christian orthodoxy. Frost will have none of that. Yet he has found a place and a condition in which he can know himself well enough to be a whole poet and write whole poems. With the farm, country, and mountain settings of his longer poems, with the simple and direct relationship set up between man and the natural world in his lyrics, he is able to record a sense of community and self-awareness as satisfying, in its way, as Eliot's. But that sense is achieved only by virtue of such a setting and such a relationship. The principle of order is immanent in a sensibility most fully aware of life in the country, life apart from centralization, industrialization, and urbanization. Because in our world culture and personality are not consonant, Frost has withdrawn (not retreated) to a place where they can be consonant, where he can write as an individual living in a community; and our memory, however acquired, of that sense of community is such that we can follow him, or his poems.

The community which is in Frost's poems does not rise directly out of the world we find about us; for us it is a community limited, restricted, apart from our workday concerns. Thus the poems must embody for us something superimposed, a culture sought for so as to give order to, even to create, a modern personality which has no proper culture of its own. Frost's poems, above all because they are such beautifully adequate poems, make a figure somewhat too neat and ordered for those of us who go to them to see what we might be, under conditions alien to our own, if we were not what we are. If Frost can write (in "New Hampshire") "Me for the hills I don't have to choose," we must feel that he has nonetheless chosen, chosen to work out his poems in terms of a set of relationships which derive from the past and from an agrarian, individualistic tradition which can function in the present only as a superimposed culture. If, like Eliot, he satisfies us most because his verses seem completely to control and judge a portion of our world, so too, like Eliot, he achieves that control and is enabled to make that judgment only by virtue of withdrawing from our world. In effect, his verses, like Eliot's, manifest a denial of the irreducibly private and idiosyncratic and a holding-fast to a principle of order which, as it must enforce that denial, makes withdrawal inevitable.

At once the complement to and the polar opposite of such a denial is, of course, an affirmation of the irreducibly private and idiosyncratic in man, and thus of personality. The choice for the poet, so far as I can understand it, has tended towards the either/or. This very extremity of choice, indeed, has set its mark on, perhaps made possible, the writing of poetry in our generation; for ours is, if nothing else, an extreme poetry. The situation is worth remarking here, because we haven't been sufficiently aware that the choice existed in all its extremity, that poets have chosen compulsively, and, most important, that some have chosen personality, with *its* affirmations and denials. We can see then, in the work of three of our poets of "established" reputation, the evidence of this choice and all that it implies for practice and achievement in our poetry. These three are William Carlos Williams, who celebrates perception; E. E. Cummings, who celebrates emotion; and Wallace Stevens, who celebrates creative imagination—all celebrations stemming from a sense of the personality as simple, separate, and immediately doomed when lost in the mass.

Celebration of the perceiving self has been for some thirty years William Carlos Williams' stock-in-trade. There is, for example, this celebrated piece:

> so much depends
> upon
>
> a red wheel
> barrow
>
> glazed with rain
> water
>
> beside the white
> chickens

This says, if I may run the risk of making indirect that which depends for its quality upon directness: So much depends upon our continuing clear and coherent perception of such a little scene; so much depends, because we depend upon seeing objects thus; what is important is the perceptive act; it is a way we have of taking possession of our world without destroying it. The bare claim of the first line literally "depends" upon the effectiveness of what follows; the generalization comes alive only if the instance is fresh and strong, forever new. Always in Williams' work the procedure is to discover other things, other selves—and to discover them sharply and precisely and separately; then to discover that the paradox of relatedness is in non-relatedness.

The bulk of Williams' poems over the past thirty years has been such small poems as the one I have quoted, poems in which the personality has realized itself by appropriating esthetically part of its world—a world of things and events, big and little, in a doctor's life. There has been no search for a highest authority, but rather for a community of perceiving selves. When Williams has occasionally written about authority from above—for example, in the much-anthologized "The Yachts"—he has imaged it as something fearful and monstrous and destructive, yet beautiful, and so all the more dangerous.

The form and movement of his poems reflect the sentiments. Or can one say that they make the sentiments? Williams characteristically begins with a natural situation and sticks to it as hard as he can, searching out its every immediate quality. If the situation bodies forth a "meaning" larger than itself, that meaning is made literally to force itself on the poet's sensibility, so that he can register it in his poems as being, in all its uniqueness, integral to his own full and clear knowledge of the world. The meaning is immanent in the perceptive act, in the separateness and uniqueness of the subject-object relationship.

This is the structural principle of the poems, realized most fully in the long work which Williams has just completed: "Paterson." He attached this note to the section of the poem published in 1946: "This is the first part of a long poem in four parts—that a man in himself is a city, beginning, seeking, achieving and concluding his life in ways which the various aspects of a city may embody— if imaginatively conceived—any city, all the details of which may be made to voice his most intimate convictions." The poem is a portrait of the poet-protagonist wandering over his city, meditating upon it, recalling its history and his life in it, and fusing what he sees, meditates upon, and recalls into one continuing image. What unifies the poem is the poet who is at its center; structurally it moves by a kind of associationism; the poet is gifted with an eloquent and lyrical recall. He discovers not so much that he is a city, but that by virtue of being a poet he has made the city himself. It is the self, his and others', which he discovers in all its possible fullness, and discovering, celebrates. If there is to be a community, it is a community of infinitely different, infinitely varied selves. In the form of his poem, as well as in its sentiments, Williams manifests a fear of any kind of order which would make those selves deny any part of their being. Order itself is denied—unless it be the order of living, discovering, and dying. Order becomes process; so that whatever form there is in Williams' poem is one deriving from a sense of the process which constitutes the life-principle for each man and object in his world.

For Williams the poet's job is to work with language; and language is of separate and unique things which must be perceived for what they are and so saluted. Language must be saved from itself, from the death-drive which is in the necessity to communicate by abstracting and destroying the particular. The poet's job is a large one, not to be subordinated to any authority; for only he can discover the uniqueness of the self and through that discovery give life to language. In the words of the fairly recent "Convivio":

We forget sometimes that no matter what
our quarrels we are the same brotherhood:
the rain falling or the rain withheld,
—berated by women, barroom smells
or breath of Persian roses! our wealth
is words. And when we go down to defeat,
before the words, it is still within and
the concern of, first, the brotherhood.
Which should quiet us, warm and arm us
besides to attack, always attack—but to
reserve our worst blows for the enemy, those
who despise the word, flout it, stem
leaves and root; the liars who decree laws
with no purpose other than to make a screen
of them for larceny, murder—for our
murder, we who salute the word and would
have it clean, full of sharp movement.

Devotion to the word—"clean, full of sharp movement"—and all that such devotion implies has been the way of another poet who in yet another way is marked by obsession with personality. This is E. E. Cummings. Saluting him in 1946, Williams wrote, "I think of cummings as Robinson Crusoe at the moment when he first saw the print of a naked human foot in the sand. That . . . implied a new language—and a readjustment of conscience," And further, "cummings is the living presence of the drive to make all our convictions evident by penetrating through their costumes to the living flesh of the matter." Williams and Cummings are by no means poets teaching in the same school. But they are devoted to what is, in the last analysis, the same cause.

In an essay called, appropriately enough, "Technique as Joy," Theodore Spencer thus described Cummings' cause: "There is no doubt about what Mr. Cummings stands for. He has said it again and again. He is for the individual human being against mechanical regimentation, for the living Now—in flower, bird, mountain and man; he is for 'the remembrance of miracle . . . by somebody who can love and be continually reborn.' He hates standardization, communism, all planning and ordering that kills the sensuous and emotional awareness by which people are kept alive.

my specialty is living said
a man(who could not earn his bread
because he would not sell his head)."

Cummings' mode is the lyric; for his concern is to make us
aware of awareness, of the act of living and feeling all the riches
of our world; and not the least of these riches is ourselves. His
characteristic strategy is to wrench the common and the ordinary
from the context which would abstract it into negativeness and
to make it positive. For him, what is most common and most ordinary is, of course, man and his experience of living.

His earlier poems, say those published before 1938, shock us
into awareness primarily by their typographical misbehavior; poems
are set up on a page so as to force us to attend to the quality of an
individual experience as it is occurring. Another way of forcing
awareness in these poems is by going to nominally "unpoetic" subject matters and exhibiting the poetry immanent in them. So there
are poems on violent love, self-consciously tough-tender—many of
these; and in straining for effect, Cummings is too often like a
Bret Harte come to the Village. What saves the poems, when they
are saved, is Cummings' good humor, his knowledge that only the
most sacred things of the self can be kidded and still remain sacred.
The end of the poems is to register joy, any kind of joy; and the
source of joy is always in the uniqueness of the self. So, in general,
the earlier poems are attempts to define maximally individuated experience in such a way as to show that its only end is realization of
self. The poems range from this:

                                                    i will be
        M o ving in the Street of her
        bodyfee l inga ro undMe the traffic of
        lovely;muscles-sinke x p i r i n   g S
                    uddenl
        Y   *totouch*
                            the curvedship of
                                        Her-
    . . . . *kIss* . . .

to this:

            since feeling is first
            who pays any attention
            to the syntax of things
            will never wholly kiss you

and this:

        I'd rather learn from one bird how to sing
        than teach ten thousand stars how not to dance.

In his more recent poetry Cummings has worked to refine this technique by trying literally to rescue abstract language from the abstractness that deadens it. He has wrenched words out of the regular grammatical and syntactical functions, more closely to associate them with the men and women whose experience they are to represent:

> my father moved through dooms of love
> through sames of am through haves of give,
> singing each morning out of each night
> my father moved through depths of height

for example, or this:

> all ignorance toboggans into know
> and trudges up to ignorance again:
> but winter's not forever,even snow
> melts;and if spring should spoil the game,what then?

or this:

> when faces called flowers float out of the ground
> and breathing is wishing and wishing is having—
> but keeping is downward and doubting and never
> —it's april(yes, april; my darling)it's spring!
> yes the pretty birds frolic as spry as can fly
> yes the little fish gambol as glad as can be
> (yes the mountains are dancing together)

Here language has somehow been restored to the feeling self from which it has been too long absent. This is Cummings' achievement, this is how he has chosen personality in preference to culture.

His choice continues to make him speak loudly and to follow out its fullest implications. He is now, I suppose, a self-admitted philosophical anarchist, an unreconstructed Bohemian. "The Enormous Room" and "Eimi" only point to something which the poems realize. Recently Cummings has written a preface to a collection of Krazy Kat comic strips. Krazy, he finds, represents the highest of our realities; for she is all love, loving most of all Ignatz Mouse, even though he continually heaves bricks at her. The villain of the piece, for Cummings, is Offisa Pup—who in trying to protect Krazy from Ignatz only succeeds in setting up abstract authority. But, then, Offisa Pup is always defeated; and Krazy's love, if it does not conquer Ignatz, at least conquers Krazy herself, and in a

dim way even conquers Offisa Pup. So love conquers all, because the
self, conquering nothing, gives all. Cummings' lyricism is absolute,
because it is a lyricism which celebrates personality as purely and
directly as possible.

The most commanding of modern American poets who celebrate personality is Wallace Stevens. He is, in his own way, a
philosophical poet; and striving to be as inclusive and exact as a
philosophical poet must be, he demands most of his poetry and his
audience. For, from the beginning, he has poetized about what he
has called reality and the imagination—which is to say, the world
we live in and our selves, considered as interacting forces. His
problem has been: What is the relation of one to the other? And he
has treated it literally as a problem. As a result, his recent poems,
instead of celebrating the self, have been concerned with studying
it. And he has by now evolved a kind of informal, rhetorically-
stated philosophic position on the problem. The development is long
and complex; his production has been voluminous; I shall be able
only to note its high points.

What is central in Stevens' earliest poems (those published before
1935) is an awareness of the texture of reality (in Stevens' sense
of the thing-in-itself) as a factor at once for the enriching and for
the limiting of the experience of the self. Here he is akin to Williams. The driving concern of these early poems is with the sensuously flowing aspect of reality as we come to know, to partake
of, and thus to inform it and be informed by it. These are specifically
poems of the creative imagination, of the creative self. On the one
hand, Stevens writes lyrics, in which the self is, as it were, caught
in the act of experiencing and organizing the world, thus giving it
meaning; on the other hand, he writes dramatic poems, in which
men and women puzzle over the limitations that their selfhood imposes on them and try to comprehend their relations to the world
outside. Thus there is a poem like "Peter Quince at the Clavier,"
which ends:

> *Beauty is momentary in the mind—*
> *The fitful tracing of a portal;*
> *But in the flesh it is immortal.*

And there is a poem like "Sunday Morning" the argument of which
turns on the predicament of a sensitive woman who is disturbed
by her awareness of a "holy hush of ancient sacrifice" in which

she cannot participate. She tries to break through the limits of her bright warm world and to achieve realization of the world of received religion and of the authority which might be outside herself. But she cannot; she can only know what her sensitive self will let her know. Stevens does not let her, and many another like her in his earlier poetry, deny reality or authority outside herself. He makes her accept its possibility; yet he will not let her know it unless she somehow makes it by and through herself.

Since the middle 'thirties Stevens' subject has been this problem of finding a sense of authority which is generated in signficant part by the personality (for him, the creative imagination) and of facing frankly the inadequacy of such culture or cultures as are available to modern man. His poems through the 'forties continually speak of the need for such a sense and of the part which poetry should play in achieving it. One poem from "The Man with the Blue Guitar" ends with what might be taken as the text of this essay:

> *Poetry*
>
> *Exceeding music must take the place*
> *Of empty heaven and its hymns,*
>
> *Ourselves in poetry must take their place*
> *Even in the chattering of your guitar.*

He sees clearly that the question of the role of the self is not simply one of realization but of belief, not simply of awareness but of understanding the fundamental role of awareness in making knowledge possible. In another poem of this period, he writes:

> *The prologues are over. It is a question, now,*
> *Of final belief. So, say that final belief*
> *Must be in a fiction. It is time to choose.*

Further, this belief must somehow be in the self, in that

> *... impossible possible philosopher's man,*
> *The man who has had the time to think enough,*
> *The central man, the human globe, responsive*
> *As a mirror with a voice, the man of glass,*
> *Who in a million diamonds sums us up.*

Personality must dominate.

And Stevens' latest poems, those in his last two volumes, have been devoted to defining the fiction in which we must believe and the role of the self in generating that fiction. If the fiction is to be authoritative for us, it is to be so because it results from a man's meditating his private relation to reality, because it is a product of the imaginative self giving shape to reality, because only it will allow for the primacy of existence of an infinite number of selves. Poetry, Stevens concluded in a lecture a few years ago, is the product of a violence within which protects us from the violence without. One recalls Williams and his talk about the quality of "continual and violent refreshing" which characterizes worth-while poetry.

The two poems in which Stevens has most fully treated this problem are "Notes toward a Supreme Fiction" and "Esthétique du Mal." These are explicitly philosophical poems, poems of ideas. But they are also poems of the imaginative, artistic self. For imaginative experience is shown to be the only means we have of initiating the inquiry by which we arrive at philosophical ideas and to be, moreover, the only means we have of realizing and believing in those ideas. Thus the poetry is at once an expression and an exposition of a philosophical attitude. Since the authenticity of that attitude depends on an origin in imaginative experience, it depends on the sensibility of the poet, on the self—a self divorced, ideally, from any kind of external authority. The place of dialectic is taken by rhetoric; for rhetoric is of the self and dialectic of authority. Stevens has said that when he writes "poet," he means "any man of imagination." Presumably, all good men must be men of imagination, knowing the world in acts of imagination—in poems.

The Supreme Fiction which is generated and realized thus will compel belief because it will be a product of the act of the believer. This Supreme Fiction has the following attributes: abstractness, change, good, and evil. For these qualities which we discover in all our imaginative experience of reality; these are qualities which we can know imaginatively and so must believe in. The poems in which the qualities are elucidated are long and difficult. They are elegantly worded, discursive, modulating from perceived idea to perceived idea, cast in a language which registers as precisely as possible the imaginative qualities of the perceptions out of which they are made. Beginning with the notion of a radically free self and an utterly alien reality, Stevens has created an object for a kind of religious belief, a God of four attributes, a God literally made (so far as He is known) by the self, a God who is literally a fiction. To return to the central generalization of this essay, he has celebrated the creative imagination in such a way as to define culture in terms of personality and to deny culture any existence except as a fiction— however compelling, however supreme.

The very end of "Esthétique du Mal" reads thus:

> ... out of what one sees and hears and out
> Of what one feels, who could have thought to make
> So many selves, so many sensuous worlds,
> As if the air, the mid-day air, was swarming
> With the metaphysical changes that occur
> Merely in living as and where we live.

This, with its insistence on sees, hears, feels, changes, living, is at the opposite pole from and complementary to Eliot's

> ... to apprehend
> The point of intersection of the timeless
> With time, is an occupation for the saint—
> No occupation either, but something given
> And taken, in a lifetime's death in love,
> Ardour and selflessness and self-surrender.
> For most of us, there is only the unattended
> Moment, the moment in and out of time. . .

The two passages read together tell us a great deal about our world, our society, and ourselves—in all, about our present discontents. I suggest that we must "use" the two passages—and all that leads up to and follows from them—in a way analogous to that in which we use concepts like culture and personality; for the poetry fills out and realizes the concepts, as the concepts generalize and make operative the poetry. And I suggest further that, as with the concepts, we cannot really understand the one passage of poetry and the place it has in our lives unless we understand the other. A poetry whose strength is manifest in a denial of the radically free self makes final sense to men living in this world only in relation to a poetry whose strength is manifest in an affirmation of that self. In the end we must come from Eliot and Stevens, as from culture and personality, to ourselves in our world. Then, if we look about carefully, we shall discover that with Eliot and Stevens, as with culture and personality, we have already been there.

I. A. Richards

BELIEFS AND THE FUTURE

OF POETRY*

I

The business of the poet, as we have seen, is to give order and coherence, and so freedom, to a body of experience. To do so through words which act as its skeleton, as a structure by which the impulses which make up the experience are adjusted to one another and act together. The means by which words do this are many and varied. To work them out is a problem for linguistic psychology, that embarrassed young heir to philosophy. What little can be done shows already that most critical dogmas of the past are either false or nonsense. A little knowledge is not here a danger, but clears the air in a remarkable way.

Roughly and inadequately, even in the dim light of present knowledge, we can say that words work in the poem in two main fashions. As sensory stimuli and as (in the *widest* sense) symbols. We must refrain from considering the sensory side of the poem, remarking only that it is *not* in the least independent of the other side, and that it has for definite reasons prior importance in most poetry. We must confine ourselves to the other function of words in the poem, or rather, omitting much that is of secondary rele-

* Part I is from I. A. Richards, *Science and Poetry*, pp. 61–67 (London: Kegan Paul, Trench, Trubner & Co., Ltd., 1935). Slightly revised by and reprinted with the permission of the author. Part II is from *The Screens and Other Poems*, © 1959, 1960, by I. A. Richards. Reprinted by permission of Harcourt, Brace & World, Inc.

vance, to one form of that function, let me call it *pseudo-statement*.

It will be admitted—by those who distinguish between scientific statement, where truth is ultimately a matter of verification as this is understood in the laboratory, and emotive utterance, where "truth" is primarily acceptability *by* some attitude, and more remotely is the acceptability *of* this attitude itself—that it is *not* the poet's business to make scientific statements. Yet poetry has constantly the air of making statements, and important ones; which is one reason why some mathematicians cannot read it. They find the alleged statements to be *false*. It will be agreed that their approach to poetry and their expectations from it are mistaken. But what exactly is the other, the right, the poetic, approach and how does it differ from the mathematical?

The poetic approach evidently limits the framework of possible consequences into which the pseudo-statement is taken. For the scientific approach this framework is unlimited. Any and every consequence is relevant. If any of the consequences of a statement conflicts with acknowledged fact then so much the worse for the statement. Not so with the pseudo-statement when poetically approached. The problem is—just how does the limitation work? One tempting account is in terms of a supposed universe of discourse, a world of make-believe, of imagination, of recognized fictions common to the poet and his readers. A pseudo-statement which fits into this system of assumptions would be regarded as "poetically true"; one which does not, as "poetically false." This attempt to treat "poetic truth" on the model of general "coherence theories" is very natural for certain schools of logicians but is inadequate, on the wrong lines from the outset. To mention two objections, out of many; there is no means of discovering what the "universe of discourse" is on any occasion, and the kind of coherence which must hold within it, supposing it to be discoverable, is not an affair of logical relations. Attempt to define the system of propositions into which

O Rose, thou art sick!

must fit, and the logical relations which must hold between them if it is to be "poetically true"; the absurdity of the theory becomes evident.

We must look further. In the poetic approach the relevant consequences are not logical or to be arrived at by a partial relaxation of logic. Except occasionally and by accident logic does not enter at all. They are the consequences which arise through our emotional organization. The acceptance which a pseudo-statement receives is primarily governed by its effects upon our feelings and attitudes. Logic only comes in, if at all, in subordination, as a servant to our emotional response. It is an unruly servant, however, as poets and readers are constantly discovering. A pseudo-statement is "true" if it suits and serves some attitude or links together attitudes which on other grounds are desirable. This kind of "truth" is so different from scientific "truth" that it is a pity to use so similar a word, but at present it is difficult to avoid the malpractice.[1]

This brief analysis may be sufficient to indicate the fundamental disparity between pseudo-statements as they occur in poetry and statements as they occur in science. A pseudo-statement is a form of words which is justified entirely by its effect in organizing or releasing our impulses and attitudes (due regard being had for the better or worse organizations of these *inter se*); a statement, on the other hand, is justified by its truth, *i.e.*, its correspondence, in a highly technical sense, with the fact to which it points.

Statements true and false alike do, of course, constantly touch off attitudes and action. Our daily practical existence is largely guided by them. On the whole true statements are of more service to us than false ones. None the less we do not and, at present, cannot order our emotions and attitudes by true statements alone. Nor is there any probability that we ever shall contrive to do so. This is one of the great new dangers to which civilization is exposed. Countless pseudo-statements—about God, about the universe, about human nature, the relations of mind to mind, about the soul, its ranks and destiny—pseudo-statements which are pivotal points in the organization of the mind, vital to its well-being, have suddenly become, for sincere, honest and informed minds, impossible to believe as for centuries they have been believed. The accustomed incidences of the modes of believing are changed irrecoverably; and the knowledge which has displaced them is not of a kind upon which an equally fine organization of the mind can be based.

For the mind I am considering here the question "Do I believe

---

[1] A pseudo-statement, as I use the term, is not necessarily false in any sense. It is merely a form of words whose scientific truth or falsity is irrelevant to the purpose in hand.

x?" is no longer the same. Not only the "What" that is to be believed but the "How" of the believing has changed—through the segregation of science and its clarification of the techniques of proof. This is the danger; and the remedy suggested is a further differentiation of the "Hows." To these differences correspond differences in the senses of "is so" and "being" where, as is commonly the case, "is so" and "being" assert believings. As we admit this, the world that "is" divides into worlds incommensurable in respect of so called "degrees of reality." Yet, and this is all-important, these worlds have an order, with regard to one another, which is the order of the mind; and interference between them imperils sanity. . . .

I I

. . . Take this question "What sort of a thing is a poem?" just as you might take: "What sort of a thing is a pin, a table, a TV receiver, a moon-observation satellite, a cell, an eye, a brain?"—or, going down below the pin, "What sort of a thing is a molecule, an atom, an electron and so on?" Put this way, the question "What sort of a thing is a poem?" yields to reflection an interesting outcome, an outcome not found with any of the things in the list I have just run over.

I have put "What is a poem?" in this sharp contrast with "What is a pin, a table . . . a moon-observation satellite, a cell, an eye, a brain . . . and so on?" for two reasons. (1) To remind us that poems are among the most complex products (if that is a wise word to use here) of the most complex organisms known; and (2) to remark that the phrase "this poem" has a duality not shown by any of the things in my list of artificial and natural objects.

This duality it shares with all the words which denote parts of a poem, *e.g., verse, sentence, line, phrase, word.* Also with the *person* in whom the poem originated and all the persons in whom it may, as it were, be reincarnated as they read it.

Contrast the two components of this duality which is the poem. On the one hand, evidently, we have one of the most identifiable, problem-free entities imaginable: the black marks on white paper that are printed and may be bought, the physical, visual poem—a configuration of letters on a page. As this, it is almost, if not quite, as clear and reliable as a fingerprint; it is a public object of the highest status.

But, alas, this public object, with such high public credentials, is not what any reader, any critic even, any historian of cultures, any philosopher of civilizations is interested in. Only bibliopoles and compositors care for the page. What the rest are interested in is something else, a something else most intimately connected with the visual printed page, but quite other: something that isn't a physical object with at all the same status as the printed page—something which is an outcome, an agitation, an activity, an endeavor . . . a phantasm, a fiction, a vision . . . a *what-not* arising in readers who read, as we say, the poem. And these readers care for the page only insofar as it supports this something else.

The trouble about this something else is that—in contrast to the black marks on the white page—it is among the least identifiable, the least honest-to-goodness-this-is-it entities that can be sought. Its credentials—however it appears, and its appearances are endlessly variable—are, whenever they are critically examined, most shaky.

I realize what a subversive thing this almost comical contrast between the perfectly identifiable *page* and the dimly-if-at-all identifiable *something else* can become. If the poem, as opposed to its vehicle, is really as elusive as I am suggesting, then this contrast would seem to cut at the very roots of much current educational endeavor; it should pull the chairs from under innumerable professors and leave reviewers little or nothing to stand on. There are tremendous investments of energy, routine, and prestige threatened here, and massive resistances are to be expected. Whatever the outcome, let us not be too much uplifted or downcast. Sir Douglas Haig —who in Flanders in World War I had surely plenty of opportunity for judging—used to remark, "No news is ever so good or so bad as it seems!" And, in this instance, we may add, this news is by no means so new. . . .

At a time when linguistics is paying more and more heed to the development of speech in the infant (and to its inverse: loss of speech in the aphasic; see Jakobson and Halle, *Fundamentals of Language*, Mouton, 1956), we will do very well to hark back again to *The Prelude* . . . to note how "the infant Babe" becomes—

> *An inmate of this active universe . . .*
> *And powerful in all sentiments of grief,*
> *Of exultation, fear, and joy, his mind,*
> *Even as an agent of the one great mind,*

Creates, creator and receiver both,
Working but in alliance with the works
Which it beholds.

The linguistic structuralist is so often in danger of confining his attention to the relations of words with other words only, that it is salutary to be reminded that the initial charges of the poet's earliest worlds come to them, normally (I stress the normative meaning of *normal*), from his mother's face: in her tones of voice, in her frowns and smiles,

> *there exists*
> *A virtue which irradiates and exalts*
> *All objects through all intercourse of sense.*
> *No outcast he, bewilder'd and depress'd;*
> *Along his infant veins are interfus'd*
> *The gravitation and the filial bond*
> *Of nature, that conect him with the world.*
>
> *—Such, verily, is the first*
> *Poetic spirit of our human life.*

Poetic plaiting is threefold: there is the duality we have discussed of the meaningful words and there is "the filial bond" that connects us with "this *active* universe," which, if we will take *interfusion* seriously and considerately enough, weaves that duality. The strength of a passage comes from all three: from the phonologic and morphologic network linking words with words (their rhyme fields, root-branching, and so on); from the semantic network of substitutions, oppositions, implications (and how much more) which by countless routes links every word with every other; and from the mutual control of the contexts[2] (recurrences of utterances in situations) which give all reference and concern to whatever may be uttered. Through these threefold ways language has built up its strange power. If I may quote some sentences I wrote some time ago:

> So far from verbal language being a "compromise for a language of intuition" (T. E. Hulme's misleading phrase)—a thin, but better-than-nothing, substitute for real experience,—language, well used, is a *completion* and does what the intuitions of sensation by them-

---

[2] See *The Meaning of Meaning*, Appendix B; *Interpretation in Teaching*, Preface, VIII, IX; *Philosophy of Rhetoric*, pp. 28–42.

selves cannot do. Words are the meeting points at which regions of experience which can never combine in sensation or intuition, come together. They are the occasion and the means of that growth which is the mind's endless endeavour to order itself. That is why we have language. It is no mere signalling system. It is the instrument of all our distinctively human development, of everything in which we go beyond the other animals.[3]

Structuralists stress for their purposes, for the sake of an operable technique, opposition (mutual preclusiveness) among linguistic elements. For poetics, we need also to note the multiplicity, the limitless variety, of the linkages among phrases, the threefold web of potential interinanimations. They are of course dispositional: no one is actually aware of more than a very few of them at any one time. None the less, these verbal potentials—potentials in a sense which looks for help to the mathematicians' and the physicists' senses—are what the poet works with.

No one will deny that there are meanings (to call them that: virtualities, dispositional conspiracies) which are active before they embody themselves. The process of writing a poem—in many instances—consists of cajoling an unembodied something into its incarnation. The formal aspects of poetry—rhyme, meter, et cetera—are largely dodges which have been found to be propitious, in slowing down selection and widening the scan. Before it has found itself in its words by finding the words for itself, that *something else* has as little character, is as indescribable, as a name that we are failing to recall.

One thing, I suggest, is clear and certain as well as highly familiar: it is tested and verified billions of times a minute in human experience, entirely trustworthy and reliable. And what is this reassuring and comfortable truth? It is that *what is said* depends on *how it is said,* and *how it is said* on *what is said. What we say* and *How we say it* are inseparable—in utterances which are entire.

There are exceptions—in various measure. Briefly: what can be translated in any utterance without change—put into other words, into another language without changes—is a sort of precipitate, a derivative from the entire living fluid utterance. There are sci-

---

[3] *Philosophy of Rhetoric,* pp. 130–31. See on this Allen Tate, *Reason in Madness,* "Literature as Knowledge," p. 55. I am indebted to Mr. Tate for drawing my attention to the passage. See also, as to mutual control of recurrences of sentences in situation: *First Steps in Reading English, English Through Pictures,* I and II, Pocket Books Inc.

ences, there are technologies which operate almost exclusively with and in such precipitates; they can be translated without trouble: you can make up new terms, if need be, to fill gaps and so on. That is one end of a continuous series—spectrum, shall I call it? At the other end is the sort of poetry for which there is either no precipitate—no factual or propositional or directive derivative— or what there is that could be separated as such is trivial, negligible. In between there are all sorts of poetry. Near the center there is the sort exemplified in the lines from *The Prelude* I have quoted, where there is a very important propositional precipitate but where the interpretations—the further signs and further signs and so on —for the parts of the utterance and for their connections with one another are not what they are in the precipitate. The words moderate one another, give and take among themselves in ways mostly beyond the means, as yet, of linguistic analysis.

I am not talking, however, of the future of linguistic analysis— which I imagine as illimitable—but of the future of poetry. The great danger there which a crude use of *encode* and *decode*, *message* and *signal* would bring in would be a recrudescence of the separation between *what is said* and the *how of saying it*.

Back to the engineer for a moment. His *message* is typically a script, a telegram, or a photographic image (for TV, for example). This he transforms to suit his channel into a *signal* he can send. Ideally, he can reverse the transformation process at the Receiver end, *decode* and regain the message. Well and good!

Contrast that, now, with what happens when an utterance is forming here in me and I am trying to speak so that a sufficiently similar utterance may arise in you.

We are dealing with whole utterances, mind you, not with precipitates.

In whole utterances rhythm, stress, intonation, pausing, the expression of a face, gestures are as important as choice of words, all these things moderating one another, qualifying one another, adjusting one another to the over-all aim. And the over-all aim, we can add, only finds itself through all this. What sort of separation can you make here between message and signal?

You can't make any: the coming into being of the signal is too closely interinanimated with the coming into being of the message.

The more minutely and imaginatively we examine the process by which an utterance forms—and, correspondingly, is understood—

the more fully we realize how interdependent WHAT and HOW here are. This unity of content and form, of spirit and letter, of intuition and expression, is, of course, a perennial theme of criticism and of poetry itself.

> *O body swayed to music, o brightening glance,*
> *How can we know the dancer from the dance!*

The most important thing about poetry, the thing which most makes its future a matter of concern, is that it exemplifies this interdependence, this unity. It strives to be exemplary in this; it is our exemplar—for that kind of mutual and just control of part by part which is health.

So now: if we suddenly leap into the middle of this delicate subtle mutuality (bull-in-the-china-shop fashion) with a bad metaphor and old error mistaken for a bit of scientific discovery and teach that what we do in using language is to make up messages which we then encode in words and transmit with our vocal organs . . . and so for the other side . . . look what happens: we are flung back into what I want to label now (damagingly, destroyingly, I hope) as the VULGAR PACKAGING VIEW.

According to this, here's the poet having a !poetic experience! poor fellow. (I should put shrieks of derision round every phrase of this account.) Then he wraps it up well in a neat and elegant verbal package—air, damp and rust, mold, moth and fungus proof, guaranteed to keep forever . . . and sells us it so! We unwrap it, if we can, and enjoy the contents. We have the !poetic experience,! believe it or not!

You may suppose I am pulling your leg. But no. This sort of thing, with garnishings, is being served up as the latest word in scientific theory of communication under cover of talk about *message* and *signal, information, coding* and *encoding.* How is it, I wonder, in Toronto? In my classes at Harvard I have for some time been meeting graduate students—in good standing and pretty certain to climb to important positions in educational administration, designing and directing programs of instruction in reading and so forth—whose handling of Theory of Communication jargon amounts to just that.

Of course, it is an old error—this Vulgar Packaging View—but that does not mean that, under new labels and new management,

it won't be successful. Indeed, no; in general, it is the oldest errors
—newly dressed up—that most often get the market. And—I am
sorry as I say it—you can catch both Wordsworth and Shelley,
though not Coleridge, I think, preaching the Vulgar Packaging
View like anything.

We have, of course, to bear in mind how constantly language
leads us to talk in ways which do not correspond with our thought.
I will borrow a convenient label from Roman Jakobson and call
it the Sunrise-Sunset, or pre-Copernican, or pre-Einsteinian Style.
It may be that many people who use Vulgar Packaging expressions
really know better—just as people talking of sunsets have not forgotten, and are not denying, that the Earth rotates. I am suggesting,
though, that very often people not only use Vulgar Packaging
Language but *think with* and are attached to Vulgar Packaging
THOUGHT. And that these people are finding this scientific lingo:
of *message*, *signal*, and so on an intellectual Godsend.

What's chiefly wrong with it? This. It stands squarely in the
way of our practical understanding and command of language.
It hides from us both how we may learn to speak (and write)
better, and how we may learn to comprehend more comprehen-
sively. Managing the variable connections between words and what
they mean: what they might mean, can't mean, and should mean—
that—not as a theoretical study only or chiefly, but as a matter
of actual control—that is the technique of poetry. If anyone is led
into a way of thinking—a way of proceeding, rather—as though
composing were a sort of catching a nonverbal butterfly in a
verbal butterfly net, as though comprehending were a releasing of
the said butterfly from the net, then he is deprived of the very thing
that could help him: exercise in comparing the various equivalences
of different words and phrases, their interdependencies, in varying
situations.

Every word of phrase in a language known to any one person
(one utterer-comprehender) is—I have been insisting—potentially
linked with all his other words and phrases in an unimaginably
multifarious manner. Some words *substitute* for others (in a given
situation), some *modify*, some *oppose*, some *exclude* others; some
invite others, some *repel* . . . it is endless. Roman Jakobson, who
has done so much to enlighten us on all this, is fond of recurring
to the suggestive example of the NAME that you have temporarily
forgotten. You don't know it—except perhaps that it begins with

C. But of any name that comes up you know undoubtingly that it is NOT THAT. And equally, if the name were said, you would know it. Here is this vacuum that is so exactly choosy as to what could fill it. There are similar exactly choosy relationships of partial synonymy, modification, implication, opposition, et cetera uniting a language in any mind.

Consider what we know in knowing some part of a language. We know to some extent which words will *work how* with which, in the varying vicissitudes in which we meet them and in which we may try to use them. Every word, through this potential work, this network of possible co-operations, is connected *via* other words with all the rest in a *living*—growing, changing, decaying—lexical-structural would-be system. That system has its claims—as we know —to be *you*, in your case, or *me*, in mine. I don't myself support these claims, but this much seems certain: the quality of our living —not only of our thinking, but for our feeling, desiring, willing and the rest—is most intimately mixed up with the state of order-disorder within our lexical-structural would-be system. And Poetry, as I have been saying, is our exemplar of that would-be system at its most entire—being most itself.

Perhaps *system* is too daunting a word; suggesting something doctrinaire. The cure is to remember Shakespeare. He is, it seems to me, the ink well, the crystal ball in which we may best see our visions of poetry's future.

Shakespeare has been—has he not?—the most variously interpreted and interpretable of poets; and, moreover, the most widely influential. I connect these three: influence, range of interpretations, and the prophetic. This brings me back to my opening point— the connection of poetry with prophecy. Poetry offers, with the widest scope, exercise in choices. Prophecy demands, with equally wide scope, the exercise of choice. They are both concerned— acknowledged or unacknowledged—with legislation: what to feel, to do, to be, or to try to be.

So, now, after these preliminaries: three short remarks on what may and should happen to poetry.

(1) I have dwelt on the dangers of badly applied and misunderstood linguistics. Let me proclaim the hopes that well-applied, well-understood linguistics might warrant.

There really have been astounding advances in linguistics in the last few decades—not only in detailed description, but in principle, too. Some of this offers new promise, new power, new hope, and new sanction to poetry. Chiefly, the view that behind a line of verse may stand, not the mere experience of the poet, but the immense reserves, the accumulated potentials, of language, due to the equivalences, the oppositions, reinforcements, resistances and so on of phrase to phrase within it. Though all this language can really represent, can really speak for human experience as the poet's !experiences! (the things his biographer shakes his head over, sobs, giggles, or goggles at) can't. It is this same vast interconnexity among phrases, of course, which is responsible for our understanding one another at all. The meanings we share are the possibilities, the potentials, we can rely on in explaining our words to ourselves in parallel fashion.

(2) My second remark is that *for a good future* poetry *needs a good audience.* Its present audience is, I fear, very small and very poor; indeed, highly incompetent. I doubt if it is improving. The root of this, I believe, is bad techniques in the teaching of Reading and in the early stages of language teaching. I believe these can be remedied, and that an audience much more capable of reading well enough to explore and enjoy and appraise poetry could be produced pretty quickly if we really tried. The trouble is—as I see it—the prevalence of methods which appeal to those who think that the ideal pupil, the dream-student, is one with the right surface for the stencil of the mimeograph—one who takes in, to give back unchanged, just what he is told. Mind you, every teacher will indignantly disown *this* as his educational philosophy. I am thinking, though, of what teachers do.

Somehow I have for the last few decades been deep in this field, and out of Poetics and Literary Criticism. But, you know, it is the same everywhere. When, at different hours of the same day, you may be busy on, say, *Troilus and Cressida* with graduate students and on early pages of a pre-primer for complete beginners to Reading, it is enheartening to perceive that *learning itself*—when it is the outcome of successful exploration—is renewing and refreshing, a self-reinforcement at all levels; and that rote instruction, tamped down by drill, is everywhere the same: a dehumanizing replacement of spontaneity by psittacism, which, being interpreted, is parroting. But it is in the earliest years that obstacles to poetry —to *poiesis*—are most firmly set up.

(3) My third and last remark can be brief. Poetry needs to

wake up. It is being neglectful of, irresponsive to what is happening. In a spring dawn such as never broke, dazzling with promise and power never offered before, there is poetry—as though it were old and frail—all huddled up and with, I fear, its head under the bedclothes.

wake life, it is being perfected of. It repudiates to what is [...]
ing, in a spring down [...] with profane and
power never burst outside the world of poetry—as though it were
cold and mulfled muffled up, and visible keep its head under the
coddlefies.

Susanne Langer

THE SYMBOL OF FEELING*

In the book to which the present one is a sequel there is a chapter
entitled "On Significance in Music." The theory of significance
there developed is a special theory, which does not pretend to any
further application than the one made of it in that original realm,
namely music. Yet, the more one reflects on the significance of art
generally, the more the music theory appears as a lead. And the
hypothesis certainly suggests itself that the oft-asserted fundamental
unity of the arts lies not so much in parallels between their respective
elements or analogies among their techniques, as in the singleness of
their characteristic import, the meaning of "significance" with
respect to any and each of them. "Significant Form" (which really
has significance) is the essence of every art; it is what we mean by
calling anything "artistic."

If the proposed lead will not betray us, we have here a principle
of analysis that may be applied within each separate art gender in
explaining its peculiar choice and use of materials; a criterion of
what is or is not relevant in judging works of art in any realm; a
direct exhibition of the unity of all the arts (without necessitating
a resort to "origins" in fragmentary, doubtful history, and still more
questionable prehistory); and the making of a truly general theory

* The material from *Feeling and Form*, pp. 24–34, 39–41, 45–50, by Susanne
Langer is reprinted with the permission of Charles Scribner's Sons. Copyright
1953 Charles Scribner's Sons. Some extracts from the above selections are
requoted from Mrs. Langer's *Philosophy in a New Key* and reprinted by
permission of Harvard University Press.

of art as such, wherein the several arts may be distinguished as well as connected, and almost any philosophical problems they present— problems of their relative values, their special powers or limitations, their social function, their connection with dream and fantasy or with actuality, etc., etc.—may be tackled with some hope of decision. The proper way to construct a general theory is by generalization of a special one; and I believe the analysis of musical significance in *Philosophy in a New Key* is capable of such generalization, and of furnishing a valid theory of significance for the whole Parnassus.

The study of musical significance grew out of a prior philosophical reflection on the meaning of the very popular term "expression." In the literature of aesthetics this word holds a prominent place; or rather, it holds prominent places, for it is employed in more than one sense and consequently changes its meaning from one book to another, and sometimes even from passage to passage in a single work. Sometimes writers who are actually in close agreement use it in incompatible ways, and literally contradict each other's state- ments, yet actually do not become aware of this fact, because each will read the word as the other intended it, not as he really used it where it happens to occur. Thus Roger Fry tried to elucidate Clive Bell's famous but cryptic phrase, "Significant Form," by identifying it with Flaubert's "expression of the Idea"; and Bell probably subscribes fully to Fry's exegesis, as far as it goes (which, as Fry remarks, is unfortunately not very far, since the "Idea" is the next hurdle). Yet Bell himself, trying to explain his meaning, says: "It is useless to go to a picture gallery in search of expression; you must go in search of Significant Form." Of course Bell is thinking here of "expression" in an entirely different sense. Perhaps he means that you should not look for the artist's *self*-expression, i.e. for a record of his emotions. Yet this reading is doubtful, for elsewhere in the same book he says: "It seems to me possible, though by no means certain, that created form moves us so profoundly because it expresses the emotion of its creator." Now, is the emotion of the creator the "Idea" in Flaubert's sense, or is it not? Or does the same work have, perhaps, two different expressive functions? And what about the kind we must *not* look for in a picture gallery?

We may, of course, look for any kind of expression we like, and there is even a fair chance that, whatever it be, we shall find it. A work of art is often a spontaneous expression of feeling, i.e., a symptom of the artist's state of mind. If it represents human beings it is probably also a rendering of some sort of facial expression which suggests the feelings those beings are supposed to have. Moreover, it may be said to "express," in another sense, the life of the society from which it stems, namely to *indicate* customs, dress, behavior, and to reflect confusion or decorum, violence or peace. And besides all these things it is sure to express the unconscious wishes and nightmares of its author. All these things may be found in museums and galleries if we choose to note them.

But they may also be found in wastebaskets and in the margins of schoolbooks. This does not mean that someone has discarded a work of art, or produced one when he was bored with long division. It merely means that all drawings, utterances, gestures, or personal records of any sort express feelings, beliefs, social conditions, and interesting neuroses; "expression" in any of these senses is not peculiar to art, and consequently is not what makes for artistic value.

Artistic significance, or "expression of the Idea," is "expression" in still a different sense and, indeed, a radically different one. In all the contexts mentioned above, the art work or other object functioned as a *sign* that pointed to some matter of fact—how someone felt, what he believed, when and where he lived, or what bedeviled his dreams. But *expression of an idea*, even in ordinary usage, where the "idea" has no capital *I*, does not refer to the signific function, i.e. the indication of a fact by some natural symptom or invented signal. It usually refers to the prime purpose of language, which is discourse, the presentation of mere ideas. When we say that something is well expressed, we do not necessarily believe the expressed idea to refer to our present situation, or even to be true, but only to be given clearly and objectively for contemplation. Such "expression" is the function of symbols: articulation and presentation of *concepts*. Herein symbols differ radically from signals.[1] A signal is comprehended if it serves to make us notice the object or situation it bespeaks. A symbol is understood when we conceive the idea it presents.

---

[1] In *Philosophy in a New Key* (cited hereafter as *New Key*) the major distinction was drawn between "signs" and "symbols"; Charles W. Morris, in *Signs, Language and Behavior*, distinguishes between "signals" and "symbols." This seems to me a better use of words, since it leaves "sign" to cover both "signal" and "symbol," whereas my former usage left me without any generic term. I have, therefore, adopted his practice, despite the fact that it makes for a discrepancy in the terminology of two books that really belong together.

The logical difference between signals and symbols is sufficiently explained, I think, in *Philosophy in a New Key* to require no repetition here, although much more could be said about it than that rather general little treatise undertook to say. Here, as there, I shall go on to a consequent of the logical studies, a theory of significance that points the contrast between the functions of art and of discourse, respectively; but this time with reference to all the arts, not only the non-verbal and essentially non-representative art of music.

The theory of music, however, is our point of departure, wherefore it may be briefly recapitulated here as it finally stood in the earlier book:

The tonal structures we call "music" bear a close logical similarity to the forms of human feeling—forms of growth and of attenuation, flowing and stowing, conflict and resolution, speed, arrest, terrific excitement, calm, or subtle activation and dreamy lapses—not joy and sorrow perhaps, but the poignancy of either and both—the greatness and brevity and eternal passing of everything vitally felt. Such is the pattern, or logical form, of sentience; and the pattern of music is that same form worked out in pure, measured sound and silence. Music is a tonal analogue of emotive life.

Such formal analogy, or congruence of logical structures, is the prime requisite for the relation between a symbol and whatever it is to mean. The symbol and the object symbolized must have some common logical form.

But purely on the basis of formal analogy, there would be no telling which of two congruent structures was the symbol and which the meaning, since the relation of congruence, or formal likeness, is symmetrical, i.e. it works both ways. (If John looks so much like James that you can't tell him from James, then you can't tell James from John, either.) There must be a motive for choosing, as between two entities or two systems, one to be the symbol of the other. Usually the decisive reason is that one is easier to perceive and handle than the other. Now sounds are much easier to produce, combine, perceive, and identify, than feelings. Forms of sentience occur only in the course of nature, but musical forms may be invented and intoned at will. Their general pattern may be reincarnated again and again by repeated performance. The effect is actually never quite the same even though the physical repetition may be exact, as in recorded music, because the exact degree of one's familiarity with a passage affects the experience of it, and this factor can never be made permanent. Yet within a fairly wide range such variations are, happily, unimportant. To some musical forms even much less subtle changes are not really disturbing, for instance certain differences of instrumentation and even, within limits, of pitch or tempo. To others, they are fatal. But in the main, sound is a negotiable medium, capable of voluntary composition and repetition, whereas feeling is not; this trait recommends tonal structures for symbolic purposes.

Furthermore, a symbol is used to articulate ideas of something we wish to think about, and until we have a fairly adequate symbolism we cannot think about it. So *interest* always plays a major part in making one thing, or realm of things, the meaning of something else, the symbol or system of symbols.

Sound, as a sheer sensory factor in experience, may be soothing or exciting, pleasing or torturing; but so are the factors of taste, smell, and touch. Selecting and exploiting such somatic influences is self-indulgence, a very different thing from art. An enlightened society usually has some means, public or private, to support its artists, because their work is regarded as a spiritual triumph and a claim to greatness for the whole tribe. But mere epicures would hardly achieve such fame. Even chefs, perfumers, and upholsterers, who produce the means of sensory pleasure for others, are not rated as the torchbearers of culture and inspired creators. Only their own advertisements bestow such titles on them. If music, patterned sound, had no other office than to stimulate and soothe our nerves, pleasing our ears as well-combined foods our palates, it might be highly popular, but never culturally important. Its historic development would be too trivial a subject to engage many people in its lifelong study, though a few desperate Ph.D. theses might be wrung from its anecdotal past under the rubric of "social history." And music conservatories would be properly rated exactly like cooking schools.

Our interest in music arises from its intimate relation to the all-important life of feeling, whatever that relation may be. After much debate on current theories, the conclusion reached in *Philosophy in a New Key* is that the function of music is not stimulation of feeling, but expression of it; and furthermore, not the symptomatic expression of feelings that beset the composer but a symbolic expression of the forms of sentience as he understands them. It bespeaks his imagination of feelings rather than his own emotional state, and expresses what he *knows about* the so-called "inner life"; and this may exceed his personal case, because music is a symbolic form to him through which he may learn as well as utter ideas of human sensibility.

There are many difficulties involved in the assumption that music is a symbol, because we are so deeply impressed with the paragon of symbolic form, namely language, that we naturally carry its characteristics over into our conceptions and expectations of any other mode. Yet music is not a kind of language. Its significance is really something different from what is traditionally and properly called "meaning." Perhaps the logicians and positivistic philosophers who have objected to the term "implicit meaning," on the ground that "meaning" properly so-called is always explicable, definable, and translatable, are prompted by a perfectly rational desire to keep so difficult a term free from any further entanglements and sources of confusion; and if this can be done without barring the concept itself which I have designated as "implicit meaning," it certainly seems the part of wisdom to accept their strictures.

Probably the readiest way to understand the precise nature of musical symbolization is to consider the characteristics of language and then, by comparison and contrast, note the different structure of music, and the consequent differences and similarities between the respective functions of those two logical forms. Because the prime purpose of language is discourse, the conceptual framework that has developed under its influence is known as "discursive reason." Usually, when one speaks of "reason" at all, one tacitly assumes its discursive pattern. But in a broader sense any appreciation of form, any awareness of patterns in experience, is "reason"; and discourse with all its refinements (e.g. mathematical symbolism, which is an extension of language) is only one possible pattern. For practical communication, scientific knowledge, and philosophical thought it is the only instrument we have. But on just that account there are whole domains of experience that philosophers deem "ineffable." If those domains appear to anyone the most important, that person is naturally inclined to condemn philosophy and science as barren and false. To such an evaluation one is entitled; not, however, to the claim of a better way to philosophical truth through instinct, intuition, feeling, or what have you. Intuition is the basic process of all understanding, just as operative in discursive thought as in clear sense perception and immediate judgment; there will be more to say about that presently. But it is no substitute for discursive logic in the making of any theory, contingent or transcendental.

The difference between discursive and non-discursive logical forms, their respective advantages and limitations, and their consequent symbolic uses have already been discussed in the previous book, but because the theory, there developed, of music as a symbolic form is our starting point here for a whole philosophy of art, the underlying semantic principles should perhaps be explicitly recalled first.

In language, which is the most amazing symbolic system humanity has invented, separate words are assigned to separately conceived items in experience on a basis of simple, one-to-one correlation. A word that is not composite (made of two or more independently meaningful vocables, such as "omni-potent," "com-posite") may be assigned to mean any object *taken as one*. We may even, by fiat, take a word like "omnipotent," and regarding it as one, assign it a connotation that is not composite, for instance by naming a race horse "Omnipotent." Thus Praisegod Barbon ("Barebones") was an indivisible being although his name is a composite word. He had a brother called "If-Christ-had-not-come-into-the-world-thou-wouldst-have-been-damned." The simple correlation between a name and its bearer held here between a whole sentence taken as one word and an object to which it was arbitrarily assigned. Any symbol that names something is "taken as one"; so is the object. A "crowd" is a lot of people, but *taken as a lot*, i.e. as one crowd.

So long as we correlate symbols and concepts in this simple fashion we are free to pair them as we like. A word or mark used arbitrarily to denote or connote something may be called an associative symbol, for its meaning depends entirely on association. As soon, however, as words taken to denote different things are used in combination, something is expressed by the way they are combined. The whole complex is a symbol, because the combination of words brings their connotations irresistibly together in a complex, too, and this complex of ideas is analogous to the word-complex. To anyone who knows the meanings of all the constituent words in the name of Praisegod's brother, the name is likely to sound absurd, because it is a sentence. The concepts associated with the words form a complex concept, the parts of which are related in a pattern analogous to the word-pattern. Word-meanings and grammatical forms, or rules for word-using, may be freely assigned; but once they are accepted, propositions emerge automatically as the meanings of sentences. One may say that the elements of propositions are *named* by words, but propositions themselves are *articulated* by sentences.

A complex symbol such as a sentence, or a map (whose outlines correspond formally to the vastly greater outlines of a country), or a graph (analogous, perhaps, to invisible conditions, the rise and fall of prices, the progress of an epidemic) is an *articulate form*. Its characteristic symbolic function is what I call *logical expression*. It expresses relations; and it may "mean"—connote or denote—any complex of elements that is of the same articulate form as the symbol, the form which the symbol "expresses."

Music, like language, is an articulate form. Its parts not only fuse together to yield a greater entity, but in so doing they maintain some degree of separate existence, and the sensuous character of each element is affected by its function in the complex whole. This means that the greater entity we call a composition is not merely produced by mixture, like a new color made by mixing paints, but is *articulated*, i.e. its internal structure is given to our perception.

Why, then, is it not a *language* of feeling, as it has often been called? Because its elements are not words—independent associative symbols with a reference fixed by convention. Only as an articulate form is it found to fit anything; and since there is no meaning assigned to any of its parts, it lacks one of the basic characteristics of language—fixed association, and therewith a single, unequivocal reference. We are always free to fill its subtle articulate forms with any meaning that fits them; that is, it may convey an idea of anything conceivable in its logical image. So, although we do receive it as a significant form, and comprehend the processes of life and sentience through its audible, dynamic pattern, it is not a language, because it has no vocabulary.

Perhaps, in the same spirit of strict nomenclature, one really should not refer to its content as "meaning," either. Just as music is only loosely and inexactly called a language, so its symbolic function is only loosely called meaning, because the factor of conventional reference is missing from it. In *Philosophy in a New Key* music was called an "unconsummated" symbol.[2] But meaning, in the usual sense recognized in semantics, includes the condition of conventional

_____
[2] Harvard University Press edition, p. 240; New American Library (Mentor) edition, p. 195.

reference, or consummation of the symbolic relationship. Music has *import*, and this import is the pattern of sentience—the pattern of life itself, as it is felt and directly known. Let us therefore call the significance of music its "vital import" instead of "meaning," using "vital" not as a vague laudatory term, but as a qualifying adjective restricting the relevance of "import" to the dynamism of subjective experience.

So much, then, for the theory of music; music is "significant form," and its significance is that of a symbol, a highly articulated sensuous object, which by virtue of its dynamic structure can express the forms of vital experience which language is peculiarly unfit to convey. Feeling, life, motion and emotion constitute its import.

Here, in rough outline, is the special theory of music which may, I believe, be generalized to yield a theory of art as such. The basic concept is the articulate but non-discursive form having import without conventional reference, and therefore presenting itself not as a symbol in the ordinary sense, but as a "significant form," in which the factor of significance is not logically discriminated, but is felt as a quality rather than recognized as a function. If this basic concept be applicable to all products of what we call "the arts," i.e. if all works of art may be regarded as significant forms in exactly the same sense as musical works, then all the essential propositions in the theory of music may be extended to the other arts, for they all define or elucidate the nature of the symbol and its import.

That crucial generalization is already given by sheer circumstance: for the very term "significant form" was originally introduced in connection with other arts than music, in the development of another special theory; all that has so far been written about it was supposed to apply primarily, if not solely, to visual arts. Clive Bell, who coined the phrase, is an art critic, and (by his own testimony) not a musician. His own introduction of the term is given in the following words:

> Every one speaks of "art," making a mental classification by which he distinguishes the class "works of art" from all other classes. What is the justification of this classification? . . . There must be some one quality without which a work of art cannot exist; possessing which, in the least degree, no work is altogether worthless. What is this quality? What quality is shared by all objects that provoke our aesthetic emo-

tions? What quality is common to Santa Sophia and the Windows at Chartres, Mexican sculpture, a Persian bowl, Chinese carpets, Giotto's frescoes at Padua, and the masterpieces of Poussin, Piero della Francesca, and Cézanne? Only one answer seems possible—significant form. In each, lines and colours combined in a particular way, certain forms and relations of forms, stir our aesthetic emotions. These relations and combinations of lines and colours, these aesthetically moving forms, I call "Significant Form"; and "Significant Form" is the one quality common to all works of visual art.[3]

Bell is convinced that the business of aesthetics is to contemplate the aesthetic emotion and its object, the work of art, and that the reason why certain objects move us as they do lies beyond the confines of aesthetics.[4] If that were so, there would be little of interest to contemplate. It seems to me that the *reason* for our immediate recognition of "significant form" is the heart of the aesthetical problem; and Bell himself has given several hints of a solution, although his perfectly justified dread of heuristic theories of art kept him from following out his own observations. But, in the light of the music theory that culminates in the concept of "significant form," perhaps the hints in his art theory are enough.

"Before we feel an aesthetic emotion for a combination of forms," he says (only to withdraw hastily, even before the end of the paragraph, from any philosophical commitment) "do we not perceive intellectually the rightness and necessity of the combination? If we do, it would explain the fact that passing rapidly through a room we recognize a picture to be good, although we cannot say that it has provoked much emotion. We seem to have recognized intellectually the rightness of its forms without staying to fix our attention, and collect, as it were, their emotional significance. If this were so, it would be permissible to inquire whether it was the forms themselves or our perception of their rightness and necessity that caused aesthetic emotion."[5]

Certainly "rightness and necessity" are properties with philosophical implications, and the perception of them a more telling incident than an inexplicable emotion. To recognize that something is right and necessary is a rational act, no matter how spontaneous

---

[3] *Ibid.*, p. 8.
[4] *Ibid.*, p. 10.
[5] *Ibid.*, p. 26.

and immediate the recognition may be; it points to an intellectual principle in artistic judgment, and a rational basis for the feeling Bell calls "the aesthetic emotion." This emotion is, I think, a result of artistic perception, as he suggested in the passage quoted above; it is a personal reaction to the discovery of "rightness and necessity" in the sensuous forms that evoke it. Whenever we experience it we are in the presence of Art, i.e. of "significant form." He himself has identified it as the same experience in art appreciation and in pure musical hearing, although he says he has rarely achieved it musically. But if it is common to visual and tonal arts, and if indeed it bespeaks the artistic value of its object, it offers another point of support for the theory that significant form is the essence of all art.

That, however, is about all that it offers. Bell's assertion that every theory of art must begin with the contemplation of "the aesthetic emotion," and that, indeed, nothing else is really the business of aesthetics,[6] seems to me entirely wrong. To dwell on one's state of mind in the presence of a work does not further one's understanding of the work and its value. The question of what gives one the emotion is exactly the question of what makes the object artistic; and that, to my mind, is where philosophical art theory begins. . . .

The concept of significant form as an articulate expression of feeling, reflecting the verbally ineffable and therefore unknown forms of sentience, offers at least a starting point for such inquiries. All articulation is difficult, exacting, and ingenious; the making of a symbol requires craftsmanship as truly as the making of a convenient bowl or an efficient paddle, and the techniques of expression are even more important social traditions than the skills of self-preservation, which an intelligent being can evolve by himself, at least in rudimentary ways, to meet a given situation. The fundamental technique of expression—language—is something we all have to learn by example and practice, i.e. by conscious or unconscious training.[7] People whose speech training has been very casual are less sensitive to what is exact and fitting for the expression of an idea than those of cultivated habit; not only with regard to arbitrary rules of usage, but in respect of logical *rightness and necessity* of expression, i.e.

---

6 See note 4 above.
7 Cf. *New Key*, Chap. v, "Language."

saying what they mean and not something else. Similarly, I believe, all making of expressive form is a craft. Therefore the normal evolution of art is in close association with practical skills—building, ceramics, weaving, carving, and magical practices of which the average civilized person no longer knows the importance;[8] and therefore, also, sensitivity to the rightness and necessity of visual or musical forms is apt to be more pronounced and sure in persons of some artistic training than in those who have only a bowing acquaintance with the arts. Technique is the means to the creation of expressive form, the symbol of sentience; the art process is the application of some human skill to this essential purpose.

At this point I will make bold to offer a definition of art, which serves to distinguish a "work of art" from anything else in the world, and at the same time to show why, and how, a utilitarian object may be *also* a work of art; and how a work of so-called "pure" art may fail of its purpose and be simply bad, just as a shoe that cannot be worn is simply bad by failing of its purpose. It serves, moreover, to establish the relation of art to physical skill, or making, on the one hand, and to feeling and expression on the other. Here is the tentative definition, on which the following chapters are built: Art is the creation of forms symbolic of human feeling.

The word "creation" is introduced here with full awareness of its problematical character. There is a definite reason to say a craftsman *produces* goods, but *creates* a thing of beauty; a builder *erects* a house, but *creates* an edifice if the house is a real work of architecture, however modest. An artifact as such is merely a combination of material parts, or a modification of a natural object to suit human purposes. It is not a creation, but an arrangement of given factors. A work of art, on the other hand, is more than an "arrangement" of given things—even qualitative things. Something emerges from the arrangement of tones or colors, which was not there before, and this, rather than the arranged material, is the symbol of sentience.

The making of this expressive form is the creative process that enlists a man's utmost technical skill in the service of his utmost conceptual power, imagination. Not the invention of new original turns, nor the adoption of novel themes, merits the word "creative," but

---

[8] Yet a pervasive magical interest has probably been the natural tie between practical fitness and expressiveness in primitive artifacts. See *New Key*, chap. ix, "The Genesis of Artistic Import."

the making of any work symbolic of feeling, even in the most canonical context and manner. A thousand people may have used every device and convention of it before. A Greek vase was almost always a creation, although its form was traditional and its decoration deviated but little from that of its numberless forerunners. The creative principle, nonetheless, was probably active in it from the first throw of the clay.

To expound that principle, and develop it in each autonomous realm of art, is the only way to justify the definition, which really is a philosophical theory of art in miniature. . . .

It is a curious fact that people who spend their lives in closest contact with the arts—artists, to whom the appreciation of beauty is certainly a continual and "immediate" experience—do not assume and cultivate the "aesthetic attitude." To them, the artistic value of a work is its most obvious property. They see it naturally and constantly; they do not have to make themselves, first, unaware of the the world. Practical awareness may be there, in a secondary position, as it is for anyone who is engrossed in interesting talk or happenings; if it becomes too insistent to be ignored, they may become quite furious. But normally, the lure of the object is greater than the distractions that compete with it. It is not the percipient who discounts the surroundings, but the work of art which, if it is successful, detaches itself from the rest of the world; he merely sees it as it is presented to him.

Every real work of art has a tendency to appear thus dissociated from its mundane environment. The most immediate impression it creates is one of "otherness" from reality—the impression of an illusion enfolding the thing, action, statement, or flow of sound that constitutes the work. Even where the element of representation is absent, where nothing is imitated or feigned—in a lovely textile, a pot, a building, a sonata—this air of illusion, of being a sheer image, exists as forcibly as in the most deceptive picture or the most plausible narrative. Where an expert in the particular art in question perceives immediately a "rightness and necessity" of forms, the unversed but sensitive spectator perceives only a peculiar air of "otherness," which has been variously described as "strangeness," "semblance," "illusion," "transparency," "autonomy," or "self-sufficiency."

This detachment from actuality, the "otherness" that gives even a bona fide product like a building or a vase some aura of illusion, is a crucial factor, indicative of the very nature of art. It is neither chance nor caprice that has led aestheticians again and again to take account of it (and in a period dominated by a psychologistic outlook, to seek the explanation in a state of mind). In the element of "unreality," which has alternately troubled and delighted them, lies the clue to a very deep and essential problem: the problem of creativity.

What is "created" in a work of art? More than people generally realize when they speak of "being creative," or refer to the characters in a novel as the author's "creations." More than a delightful combination of sensory elements; far more than any reflection or "interpretation" of objects, people, events—the figments that artists *use* in their demiurgic work, and that have made some aestheticians refer to such work as "re-creation" rather than genuine creation. But an object that already exists—a vase of flowers, a living person —cannot be re-created. It would have to be destroyed to be re-created. Besides, a picture is neither a person nor a vase of flowers. It is an image, created for the first time out of things that are not imaginal, but quite realistic—canvas or paper, and paints or carbon or ink.

It is natural enough, perhaps, for naive reflection to center first of all round the relationship between an image and its object; and equally natural to treat a picture, statue, or a graphic description as an imitation of reality. The surprising thing is that long after art theory had passed the naive stage, and every serious thinker realized that imitation was neither the aim nor the measure of artistic creation, the traffic of the image with its model kept its central place among philosophical problems of art. It has figured as the question of form and content, of interpretation, of idealization, of belief and make-believe, and of impression and expression. Yet the idea of copying nature is not even applicable to all the arts. What does a building copy? On what given object does one model a melody?

A problem that will not die after philosophers have condemned it as irrelevant has still a gadfly mission in the intellectual world. Its significance merely is bigger, in fact, than any of its formulations. So here: the philosophical issue that is usually conceived in terms of image and object is really concerned with the nature of images as such and their essential difference from actualities. The difference is functional; consequently real objects, functioning in a way that is normal for images, may assume a purely imaginal status. That is why the character of an illusion may cling to works of art that do not represent anything. Imitation of other things is not the essential power of images, though it is a very important one by virtue of which the whole problem of fact and fiction originally came into the compass of our philosophical thought. But the true power of the image lies in the fact that it is an abstraction, a symbol, the bearer of an idea.

How can a work of art that does not represent anything—a building, a pot, a patterned textile—be called an image? It becomes an image when it presents itself purely to our vision, i.e. as a sheer visual form instead of a locally and practically related object. If we receive it as a completely visual thing, we abstract its appearance from its material existence. What we see in this way becomes simply a thing of vision—a form, an image. It detaches itself from its actual setting and acquires a different context.

An image in this sense, something that exists only for perception, abstracted from the physical and causal order, is the artist's creation. The image presented on a canvas is not a new "thing" among the things in the studio. The canvas was there, the paints were there; the painter has not added to them. Some excellent critics, and painters too, speak of his "arranging" forms and colors, and regard the resultant work primarily as an "arrangement." Whistler seems to have thought in these terms about his paintings. But even the forms are not phenomena in the order of actual things, as spots on a table-cloth are; the forms in a design—no matter how abstract—have a *life* that does not belong to mere spots. Something arises from the process of arranging colors on a surface, something that is created, not just gathered and set in a new order: that is the image. It emerges suddenly from the disposition of the pigments, and with its advent the very existence of the canvas and of the paint "arranged" on it seems to be abrogated; those actual objects become difficult to perceive in their own right. A new appearance has superseded their natural aspect.

An image is, indeed, a purely virtual "object." Its importance lies in the fact that we do not use it to guide us to something tangible and practical, but treat it as a complete entity with only visual attributes and relations. It has no others; its visible character is its entire being.

The most striking virtual objects in the natural world are optical —perfectly definite visible "things" that prove to be intangible, such as rainbows and mirages. Many people, therefore, regard an image or illusion as necessarily something visual. This conceptual limitation has even led some literary critics, who recognize the essentially imaginal character of poetry, to suppose that poets must be visual-minded people, and to judge that figures of speech which do not conjure up visual imagery are not truly poetic.[9] F. C. Prescott, with consistency that borders on the heroic, regards "The quality of mercy is not strained" as unpoetic because it suggests nothing visible.[10] But the poetic image, is, in fact, not a painter's image at all. The exact difference, which is great and far-reaching, will be discussed in the following chapters; what concerns us right here is the broader meaning of "image" that accounts for the genuinely artistic character of non-visual arts without any reference to word painting, or other substitute for spreading pigments on a surface to make people see pictures.

The word "image" is almost inseparably wedded to the sense of sight because our stock example of it is the looking-glass world that gives us a visible copy of the things opposite the mirror without a tactual or other sensory replica of them. But some of the alternative words that have been used to denote the virtual character of so-called "aesthetic objects" escape this association. Carl Gustav Jung, for instance, speaks of it as "semblance." His exemplary case of illusion is not the reflected image, but the dream; and in a dream there are sounds, smells, feelings, happenings, intentions, dangers —all sorts of invisible elements—as well as sights, and all are equally unreal by the measures of public fact. Dreams do not consist entirely of images, but everything in them is imaginary. The music heard in a dream comes from a virtual piano under the hands of an apparent musician; the whole experience is a semblance of events. It may be as vivid as any reality, yet it is what Schiller called "Schein."

Schiller was the first thinker who saw what really makes "Schein," or semblance, important for art: the fact that it liberates perception —and with it, the power of conception—from all practical pur-

---

[9] See, for example, Remy de Gourmont, *Le problème du style*, especially p. 47, where the author declares that the only people who can "write" are visual-minded people.

[10] *The Poetic Mind*, p. 49.

poses, and lets the mind dwell on the sheer appearance of things. The function of artistic illusion is not "make-believe," as many philosophers and psychologists assume, but the very opposite, disengagement from belief—the contemplation of sensory qualities without their usual meanings of "Here's that chair," "That's my telephone," "These figures ought to add up to the bank's statement," etc. The knowledge that what is before us has no practical significance in the world is what enables us to give attention to its appearance as such.

Everything has an aspect of appearance as well as of causal importance. Even so non-sensuous a thing as a fact or a possibility *appears* this way to one person and that way to another. That is its "semblance," whereby it may "resemble" other things, and—where the semblance is used to mislead judgment about its causal properties —is said to "dissemble" its nature. Where we know that an "object" consists entirely in its semblance, that apart from its appearance it has no cohesion and unity—like a rainbow, or a shadow—we call it a merely virtual object, or an illusion. In this literal sense a picture is an illusion; we see a face, a flower, a vista of sea or land, etc., and know that if we stretched out our hand to it we would touch a surface smeared with paint.

The object seen is given only to the sense of sight. That is the chief purpose of "imitation," or "objective" painting. To present things to sight which are known to be illusion is a ready (though by no means necessary) way to *abstract* visible forms from their usual context.

Normally, of course, semblance is not misleading; a thing is what it seems. But even where there is no deception, it may happen that an object—a vase, for instance, or a building—arrests one sense so exclusively that it seems to be given to that sense alone, and all its other properties become irrelevant. It is quite honestly there, but is *important* only for (say) its visual character. Then we are prone to accept it as a vision; there is such a concentration on appearance that one has a sense of seeing sheer appearances—that is, a sense of illusion. . . .

Herein lies the "unreality" of art that tinges even perfectly real objects like pots, textiles, and temples. Whether we deal with actual illusions or with such quasi-illusions made by artistic emphasis, what is presented is, in either case, just what Schiller called "Schein"; and a pure semblance, or "Schein," among the husky substantial realities of the natural world, is a strange guest. Strangeness, separateness, otherness—call it what you will—is its obvious lot.

The semblance of a thing, thus thrown into relief, is its direct aesthetic quality. According to several eminent critics, this is what the artist tries to reveal for its own sake. But the emphasis on quality, or essence, is really only a stage in artistic conception. It is the making of a rarified element that serves, in its turn, for the making of something else—the imaginal art work itself. And this form is the non-discursive but articulate symbol of feeling. . . .

John Hospers

IMPLIED TRUTHS
IN LITERATURE*

Many things have been identified as "the function of art": to express emotions, to edify or ennoble mankind, to promote communism, to bring about a moral society. But among the functions it has often been supposed to have is to give us *truth*. This claim for art was made by Aristotle when he said that art (poetry) gives us universal truth; and a long line of critics and philosophers since Aristotle has defended this view.

When one examines this claim, however, it seems highly peculiar. One would have thought that the task of the natural sciences was to give us truth in the form of general laws and theories about the physical universe; of history, to give us truth about what has happened in the past; and of philosophy, to give us truth about—well, opinions differ on this point. Perhaps even aesthetics gives us truth about the arts; but what is it that the arts give us truth about?

II

One of the arts at any rate, literature, uses words as its medium, and thus it can make statements; therefore, it would seem, it is in

* From *The Journal of Aesthetics and Art Criticism*, Vol. XIX, No. 1, Fall 1960, pp. 37–64. Reprinted by permission of the author and *The Journal of Aesthetics and Art Criticism*.

an excellent position to make true statements, that is, to state truths.
Whether true or false, statements do indeed occur in literature,

> *Life is real! Life is earnest!*
> *And the grave is not its goal.*
> *"Dust thou art, to dust returneth"*
> *Was not spoken of the soul.*

If a poem is defined as whatever doesn't extend all the way across
the page, the above passage may be called poetry. But whether or
not one decides to call it poetry, one could not ask for a more outright statement anywhere. Many statements occurring in poetry
are undoubtedly true; so it can hardly be denied that poetry gives
us truth in this sense.

Of course, it is not always clear what the sentences in poems mean:

> *Life, like a dome of many-colored glass,*
> *Stains the white radiance of eternity.*

True or false? We must first know what is being stated. Some would
say that nobody can tell for sure what is being stated; others would
say that this is not a statement at all, that we are merely being
regaled with exotic images. No doubt this sometimes occurs;
whether the above couplet is a case of it is for critics to determine.
When it does occur, no question of truth, of course arises. Nor does
it arise in the case of sentences which contain only exclamations, suggestions, commands, or questions.

Such sentences, however, constitute only a small minority of the
sentences in literature, as in daily discourse. For the vast remainder,
questions of truth do arise. Some of these questions, as we shall
see, are extremely puzzling. But it is important at the outset that
we should not dismiss literature as "non-cognitive." (1) First, we
cannot easily relegate poetry to the category of "emotive language."

> *Stars, I have seen them fall.*
> *And when they drop and die,*
> *No star is lost at all*
> *From all the star-sown sky.*
>
> *The tears of all that be*
> *Help not the primal fault.*
> *It rains into the sea,*
> *And still the sea is salt.*

These lines of Housman are, to be sure, deeply moving. But to understand their meaning we do not suddenly have to "shift gears" from ordinary discourse into an entirely different domain (or "function") of language. We understand what these sentences mean as we understand any other sentences in the language. They have meaning—or, if one wants the usual qualifying adjective, "descriptive meaning"—just as non-poetic sentences do. Perhaps the author of them is expressing a feeling, but this does not prevent him from making statements which he believes to be true. In daily life also we often express feelings by making true-or-false statements: "I wish the war would end," "She's changed so much in the last few years," and so on. Whether the author uses the sentence to express a feeling (or to arouse feeling in others) is something we would have to ask the author to discover. Whether the sentence contains a true or false statement, however, is something for which we examine not the author but the sentence itself. The words, especially in the combinations and juxtapositions we find them in the poem, may, then, move us emotionally, as do many expressions of deep feeling, but this does not prevent them from being true or false. (2) Nor do they fall into the category that has sometimes been called "pictorial meaning." It is true that a poem may present us with an interesting array of mental pictures, but this is something that may or may not occur, depending on the pictorial capacities of the reader; and many readers who have no mental pictures at all while reading poems still claim that they get the full impact of the poems. Even the use of metaphor, which is so important in poetry that poetry has often been defined in terms of it, does not imply that language is being used pictorially. Some metaphors evoke no pictures whatever, and even if one claims that they should, the fact is that metaphor is not to be defined in terms of mental pictures but in terms of linguistic devices. The whole attempt to relegate poetry to the realms of "emotive meaning" or "pictorial meaning" is, I believe, a mistake.

To be sure, the sentences in poetry are richer in suggestion than most of the sentences we utter, but this does not make them "mean" in a different way; it only shows that we respond to them somewhat differently. We are moved, but not (usually) to action. When we read that "Poor Tom's a-cold," we do not go out to fetch a blanket, nor do we gather flowers to put on Cordelia's casket. But the problem of how we do or should *respond* to various linguistic utterances (to religious language, to political speeches, to statements in textbooks, etc.)—and our responses are varied indeed—is not to be confused with understanding the *meaning* of these utterances. The meaning of a sentence does not vary with the use to which it happens to be put on a particular occasion. In particular, the meaning does not vary with either (a) the feelings of the speaker, which it may express, or (b) the response which it evokes in the listener. If two readers respond differently to the same sentence, this does not show that the sentence has two different meanings. Talk about "emotive meaning" would be far less misleading if the term "meaning" were scrapped in favor of the term "effects." A sentence in a poem may powerfully affect the emotions, but it does not follow that its *meaning* is "emotive." (The term "emotive" is misleading even in describing the effects. As the term "emotive" is ordinarily used, at any rate, I would suggest that the language of poetry is considerably more emotive in its effects than the telephone directory, somewhat more emotive than scientific treatises, not quite as emotive as day-to-day conversations—consisting as they usually do of an inelegant mixture of assertion, persuasion, suggestion, and loaded language—and not nearly as emotive as propaganda or the language of political and moral persuasion.)

Let us say no more about the explicit statements that occur in literature. Some of them may well be true, and may thus give us knowledge we did not previously possess, whether or not the imparting of such knowledge was the intent of the author when he wrote.[1] The main problem that confronts us now has to do not with explicit statements, but with statements which the author nowhere makes.

We are probably convinced that the novels of Balzac give us a reasonably accurate picture of certain aspects of life in Paris in the early nineteenth century, that in fact they were intended to do this; but whether or not they were so intended, they do. Yet we do not encounter, on reading any of these novels, any sentence such as "This is a true picture of life in Paris in my time; I do hereby assert it." Nor do the novels of Thomas Hardy contain sentences

---

[1] The language of fiction seems to raise special problems: Is it true that Hamlet was the prince of Denmark? Of course; just read the play. But how can it be true, since there never was a Hamlet at all? But then it's false. Still, Shakespeare's Hamlet *was* prince of Denmark, wasn't he? These have been dealt with abundantly in the recent literature. (See Monroe C. Beardsley, *Aesthetics,* pp. 411–414, and the numerous references on the topic listed on pp. 441–443, 446–447.) Once the peculiar logic of fictional sentences has been cleared up, no *special* problem of truth, I think, arises.

telling us what Hardy's view of life and human destiny was; yet, from the way the novels are plotted, and the chance character of the events upon which the major developments turn, even the least perceptive reader, before he finishes even one of the novels, has a pretty good idea of what that view was. Psychological novels customarily contain many remarks describing the psychological traits of the characters; these are stated, but what seems actually to be the concern of such novels is not singular propositions about the characters but general, even universal, propositions about human nature; yet none of these general propositions is stated outright.[2] These statements often seem to contain the most important things in the novel, and are often the novel's chief excuse for existing; yet they seem to operate entirely behind the scenes. The most important statements, views, theories in a work of literature are seldom stated in so many words. What is more natural, then, than to say that they are *implied?*

We can say it, and doubtless it is true. The difficulty, however, is to track down the relevant meaning of the term "imply." The logic-book senses of implication will not suffice here. There are, of course, statements in works of literature which imply other statements, just as they do anywhere else. If the sentence "Jones is a father" occurred in a novel, it would surely imply "Jones is a male." And if we read "If Smith was surprised, he gave no sign of it" and were later told that Smith was surprised (on this same occasion) but gave no sign of it, we could accuse the author of inconsistency in his narrative. But this is hardly the kind of case we are interested in here. What those who talk about implied truths in literature are referring to is seldom individual propositions at all; they talk about large segments of a work of literature, sometimes an entire novel or drama, as all together implying certain propositions. But what is the meaning of such a claim? What sense of "imply" is being used?

III

Let us try a few obvious candidates. Perhaps what you imply is what you *meant* to say, or intended to say, even though you did not actually say it. If someone says to a student in a somewhat sar-

---

[2] For example, the psychological observations of Marcel Proust are excellently described by Morris Weitz in his paper "Truth in Literature," *Revue Internationale de Philosophie,* IX (1955), 116–129.

castic tone of voice after an examination, "Some people don't do their own work," the student may retort, "Are you implying that I cheat?" The proposition "You cheat" is the one he *meant* to convey to the student, though without having said it. Similarly, when I say during a miserable rain, "Lovely weather, isn't it?" I may be said to imply (intend) the opposite of what I said—what I meant to communicate to my hearer is that the weather is foul. So, it may be said, it can be the same in a work of literature. When we say that the author implied this proposition even though he did not state it, perhaps we mean simply that this is the proposition he wanted or intended to get across to his hearers through his work.

Why should people say one thing and mean (intend) another, either in daily conversation or in works of literature? Why should the proposition they most want to impress upon their hearers or readers be never stated? Because, surely, they can often impress it on their readers with greater force and effectiveness by this means. When Jonathan Swift wrote *A Modest Proposal*, his words would not have been so devastatingly effective had he said outright what he meant; he said, with multiplied examples, just the opposite. Sometimes, indeed, when an author has meant to communicate something throughout an entire work, and then goes on to say it explicitly, we are pained and disappointed. "The President of the Immortals had had his sport with Tess," wrote Thomas Hardy, thus spoiling at the end (as Collingwood quite rightly, I think, points out in a different connection) the effect of what was otherwise a fine novel. The reader who has not surmised for himself by page 300 that this is what Hardy wants to communicate to us, hardly deserves to be told it at the end.

But this sense of "imply" is subject to an interesting objection. The test of whether a given proposition is implied in a work of art, as thus far explained, is simply whether the artist meant to communicate it to his audience by means of the work. If p is the proposition he meant to convey, then p is the proposition implied in the work. But can't the artist be wrong? Suppose he meant to convey one proposition, p, but didn't succeed, or succeeded in conveying to his readers another one, q, which he never intended or even thought of. And if all readers agree that q is the proposition implied, are we still to say that it is p that is implied because the author said so?

The main trouble here is that what is implied (in this sense) seems to require no connection with the words and sentences that are actually to be found in the work of literature. If Hardy (in a document just discovered) were to tell us that what he meant to convey in his novels is that humanity is nearing perfection, then this is implied in the novels, even though the novels seem to contradict such an assertion utterly at every point. If the poet says sincerely that what he meant to say in the poem is that reality is circular (and artists have said stranger things than this about their work), then this proposition is what is implied in the poem; and if the poet changes his mind and says that what he meant to convey is that blue is seven, then this (if it can be called a proposition at all) is implied. He said that he meant p or q; but does it follow that p or q is implied? Is he the final test? We might read the poem till doomsday without any such notion entering our heads as that reality is circular; but, one might say, this only shows that the poet did not *succeed* in communicating this proposition to us, not that he did not mean to communicate it; and thus far what he meant to communicate has been the test of what proposition or propositions are implied.

IV

Let us, then, try to find a criterion of implication other than what the artist meant or wanted to convey; following the hint just given, why not say that the criterion is what proposition he *succeeded in conveying?* What he meant to convey and what he did actually convey to his readers may, after all, be two very different things.

But now another objection occurs at once: here the criterion of what is implied does not depend on the author, but it does depend on his readers. If the poem does not succeed in communicating to the readers proposition p, then the poem does not imply p. Moreover, it would follow that the poem may imply one proposition to one reader and a very different one (or none at all) to another reader, or even to the same reader at a different time. If the audience is dull, stupid, or sleepy, no proposition is implied no matter how much the poet meant to convey one and how much care he took to convey it, while if the audience is sensitive, alert, and imaginative, that same poem may imply a whole host of propositions, including many that never occurred to the poet at all or to any reader but one. This is, to say the least, an extremely relativistic kind of implying. Surely, one is tempted to say, a proposition is implied or it is not, and whether it is or is not doesn't vary with the intelligence or imaginative capacity of the audience or whether they have just been fed tranquillizing pills and taken the road to Miltown. I do not deny that we *can*, if we please, use the word "imply" in this sense, but I doubt very much whether it is a sense which anyone ever gives the word in practice, and it is certainly not a sense which (once we realize what it involves) would be at all acceptable to those who speak of propositions as being implied in works of literature.

V

The trouble with the attempts at pinpointing the notion of implication we have considered thus far is that whether or not something is implied is determined by the artist's intention or by the audience's response, but not by the work of art itself. We want to be able to say that something is implied even though the author may not intend it and be quite unaware of it, and even though the audience may be so unperceptive as not to grasp it. In that way we shall at least be released from having to know the author's intentions to know what is implied.

Let us begin again with our previous example. "Some people don't do their own work," the person says to the student in an accusing tone of voice. Doubtless he intended to accuse him of cheating. But one might well allege that quite apart from this, he implied it: by what he said, by his tone of voice, by the whole context of the utterance (in connection with having finished an examination, and so on). A speaker uttering these words in this tone and in this context *does*, we would say, imply this, and if he later says that he didn't imply it because he didn't intend to, this does not exonerate him from the charge of implying it just the same.

It is surely this sense that G. E. Moore had in mind when he gave his classic example of implication: when I say that I went to the pictures last Tuesday, I thereby imply that I believe that I went. Of course I did not *say* that I believed it; this is no part of the statement I made, and one cannot formally deduce the proposition that I believed I went (q) from the proposition that I went (p). It is not the proposition *per se* that implies this, but my *utterance* of the proposition, in a normal tone of voice, without evidence of joking or playing tricks on my listener. I do imply q when I utter *p* in this way, in that anyone who knows the language and can interpret facial expression and manner is *entitled*, by virtue of all these, to infer *q*. If I later disavow this and claim that I was only exercising my vocal cords, I would not be excused (say, in a court of law) from having implied *q* in my utterance. "But you implied that you believed it by what you said and the way you said it. So you did imply it, whether you intended to or not."

Can we apply this kind of implication to works of literature? There is one difficulty at the outset: there is an enormous difference between literature and the examples we have just considered from everyday conversation, in that when Jones speaks to us, we have not only his spoken utterance to go by but all the other cues such as his facial expression and gestures and tone of voice and the environmental circumstances accompanying the utterance. When Jones writes a letter, however, we have only his written word as a guide. There are many inferences we might make if we *saw* him speaking that we are unable to make when we have before us only the sentences he has recorded. There are not as many clues in the written word alone. This makes things more difficult; but still, it is not as if there were *no* clues. What a person writes *may* give us good evidence of what he thinks or believes, even though he nowhere tells us that he thinks or believes these things.

Works of literature, of course, are a special case of the written word, and we can sometimes make inferences from them. We can infer many things about Theodore Dreiser's beliefs, without knowing anything about him as a man, by reading his novels: that his view of life was (roughly) materialistic; that he saw man as a pawn of destiny, caught in a tangled web of circumstances not of his own making which nevertheless lead him to his doom; that he was a champion of the underdog and the downtrodden, a humanitarian, even a sentimentalist. How can we infer these things? By observing carefully which passages contain the greatest passion and intensity, which themes are most often reiterated, how the plot is made to evolve, which characters are treated with the greatest sympathy, and so on. There are countless clues in the novels themselves that we could cite as evidence for the author's beliefs. (Not for the truth of the beliefs, but for the truth of the proposition that the author entertained them.) And there are no contrary clues. From observing all this, we can say with considerable confidence that the work implies that the author had these beliefs. We are entitled to make this inference, even if by some chance it should turn out that he actually did not have these beliefs. The belief-clues are still there, even if (though this would be surprising, for normally they would not get there if he had not purposely put them there) the beliefs in this case did not exist. (A somewhat analogous kind of case is well known in discussion of scientific method: our judgment that the next raven will be black is one we are entitled to make on the basis of the thousands of ravens already observed to be black and the absence of any contrary cases; and we are justified in making this inference, even if the next raven should turn out to be an albino.)

"Perhaps, however," an objector may say, "the point is not so much that the author believed this as that he wants *us* to believe it. As long as he can make us believe it, his own beliefs are irrelevant." This introduces the topic of the aesthetic relevance of belief, which is not my subject now. But I would venture this suggestion: Perhaps it doesn't matter whether the author believed *p*. But neither is it necessary, for understanding a work of literature, that *we* believe what the author may have wanted us to believe. Some would say that if we are in a state of belief or conviction, we are already far removed from a state of aesthetic receptivity. Do we know what beliefs Shakespeare had, or what beliefs (if any) he was trying to instill in us? And as far as the appreciation of his plays is concerned, who cares? There are many beliefs stated by the *characters* in Shakespeare's plays; but these cannot all be Shakespeare's beliefs, unless Shakespeare was pathologically addicted to changing his mind, for they constantly conflict with one another; nor can they all be our beliefs, unless we are so irrational as to believe whatever we hear regardless of whether it contradicts what we heard just before. Rather, it is necessary that we *understand* the beliefs to which the characters give voice, that we appreciate why they believe it, and what difference it makes to their motivation and behavior in the drama.

Whatever we may conclude, then, about the relevance of the author's beliefs, we can sometimes make highly probable inferences as to what they were; and when we do so, we can correctly say that the author was, in his written work, implying that he had these beliefs. But if we can infer what his beliefs were, why not his feelings, his attitudes, his intentions? Such inferences again are vulnerable, but they can often be made—perhaps not with Shakespeare, but with Dreiser. The written word often contains intent-clues as well as belief-clues.

Much of the writing of literary critics is given over to discovering from these clues, what the author's intentions were (sometimes exclusively from these, and not from independent sources outside the work). The critic becomes a kind of sleuth, and from a careful reading of the work he tells us what the author probably felt or intended. Is this going back to intentions again? Not in the same way as before. Here we are not concerned with what he intended —i.e. in his intentions apart from the work—but with what he implied *in* the work *about* his intentions. (Not that there is anything sinful about discovering his intentions through outside sources, such as his autobiography. If we want to know what his intentions were, the work itself may offer no clues to this, and we have to discover it in other ways. There is no "fallacy" involved in this. We are in no position to cut ourselves off *a priori* from sources of information which may turn out to be useful, and if the author— outside his work—can enlighten us, we are cheating only ourselves if we refuse to accept this source of enlightenment. And if one objects, "But if you have to go outside the work to the artist to find such clues, the work is not self-sufficient, autonomous, etc., for the intentions should be embodied in the work and be wholly inferrable from it," we can reply that this is a counsel of perfection. Works of art may not be entirely self-sufficient—whatever exactly that is —and moreover there appears to be no compelling reason why they should be. Can we deny that some works, at any rate, mean more to us than they would if we had no such outside knowledge?)

A work of literature may also provide clues about the author's *unconscious* intentions, and a critic well versed in psychiatry may discover them. Just as we say in daily life that a man does not intend, consciously, to be unpleasantly aggressive, he nevertheless has many such unconscious intentions (he says things in a hostile manner without meaning to, and unconsciously chooses situations for saying them that would strike any observer as calculated to arouse resentment), so we may make similar discoveries from the written word, though it takes someone who is both a sensitive critic and an astute psychiatrist to do this. (When Ernest Jones attempts it with *Hamlet*, I find his conclusions convincing, but when Ella Freeman-Sharpe attempts it with *King Lear*, I do not.) When this is well done, we have not merely a series of inferences about the author's personality—which would be of interest principally to clinicians—but clues to the interpretation of a work, or at least *an* interpretation of a work, which might otherwise have puzzled us forever.

One final point: although we sometimes draw inferences from works of literature to their authors, it may happen that we *think* we are doing this when we are actually doing something else.[3] Suppose that on walking through an empty building I see written on the blackboard a great many incendiary remarks and obscene epithets. I do not know who the author is, and presumably the words were not intended specifically for me. I may suspect that the author had vitriolic feelings when he wrote it, but this is not the inference that I normally make. He may have written it as a joke, or at random as a kind of verbal doodling, or seriously for someone's attention; I do not know. Accordingly I do not infer anything at all about the author. I conclude only that inflammatory language is being used—no matter by whom or for what purpose. Nor do I *infer* this; this language *is* inflammatory, and I do not so much infer this as *recognize* it as such; I make no inferences from it whatever.

We are sometimes in this situation with regard to works of literature. When we see the line "I fall upon the thorns of life! I bleed!" whether or not we know that Shelley wrote it, we can say that the lines are despairing in character. This is what they are, and they remain so even if neither Shelley nor the reader was despairing. We simply recognize them as lines of a certain character; the word "despairing" refers to a property of the poem, not of its author. Often what may first pass as inductive inference to propositions about the author is not only not inductive but is not inference at all.

V I

But let us have an end of intentions. We have considered how an author's work, or parts thereof, can be said to imply that the author had certain beliefs, attitudes, or intentions. But this is not the end of the matter. Does not a work of literature often imply propositions, not about its author, but about the world, about human life, human traits, the human situation, the cosmos? Through reading the work we somehow arrive at these propositions—*not* the rather

---

[3] This point was suggested to me by Professor Isabel Hungerland.

incidental proposition that the author believed them, although we may infer this also. (We might say in such cases, not that the *author* implied this or that of his work, but that *the very words* imply it. But this distinction is not a sharp one, and I am not sure how far we would have to stretch our ordinary use of such expressions in order to make such a distinction sharp.) [4]

Before trying to be more precise about this, I shall give a few examples of sentences implying propositions which are never stated and which have nothing to do with the speaker's beliefs. A reporter asks an anthropologist, "Would you say that the Bongoese are a clean people?" and the anthropologist replies, "I would not say that the Bongoese are clean." Note that he did not say that they were *not* clean; he said only what he would *not* say—he would not say that they were clean, but he would not say that they were not clean either; perhaps he knew nothing one way or the other about the Bongoese. But though he did not say they were not clean, it does seem plausible to hold that the sentence *implies* this to anyone who is at all aware of the English idiom (whether or not the speaker intended any such thing). Or, the physician says, "Yes, of course the patient died. I wasn't his physician." He does not *say* that the patient would have lived if he had been the patient's physician, but this certainly seems to be what is implied. (Note that what the sentence implies is that the patient died because this man was not his physician, *not* that the physician *believed* that the patient died because he was not the physician.)

There is surely a relation here which in daily life we do not hesitate to call implication. Nor is it bizarre or mysterious; it is a garden variety sort of thing which we constantly recognize. What exactly does it consist in? There does not seem to be any term (other than "implication" itself) that describes it precisely; it seems to be closest to what, in one sense, we call *suggestion*.[5] Statements often suggest other statements, which need not at all be about the person who utters them. "They had children and got married" suggests that they had illegitimate children, even though the utterance was a slip of the tongue and the order of the two clauses should have been reversed. "He saw the dragon and fell down dead" sug-

---

4 See Max Black, "Presupposition and Implication," in S. Uyeda (ed.), *A Way to the Philosophy of Science* (Tokyo, 1958), pp. 443–448.
5 See Monroe C. Beardsley, *Aesthetics*, p. 123.

gests, though it does not state, that he fell down dead because he saw the dragon. What is actually *said* is usually very limited, and when pressure is applied it tends to narrow still further: "Did he actually *say* he was going to kill you? True, he said he was going to make mincemeat out of you, but . . ." And as our conception of what was actually said narrows, our conception of what was implied (suggested) tends to expand.

Why not conclude, then, that literature implies many propositions in the sense of suggesting them? The word "suggest," however, as it is presently employed, is not quite tailor-made for this job:

(1) The word "suggest" ordinarily has a far wider range than that of "imply" as we are now considering it. "To me this poem suggests the sounding surf, tropical islands, wine-red sunsets . . ." This is a perfectly legitimate sense of "suggest," one in which what is suggested is not a proposition at all, and it is not at all synonymous with "imply." Is this because what the poem suggests here is not a proposition? No, for most of the cases in which what is suggested *is* a proposition will not do either: "To me this play suggests that the hero was struggling, afraid to face the truth about himself, trying to repress it without knowing it himself . . ." This may indeed be what the play suggests to a particular reader, and it may do so even if the reader is just "imagining things" and there is not the slightest textual basis for such a claim. What a line suggests to you, it may not suggest to me; in our ordinary use of "suggest" there is virtually unlimited subjectivity, whether what is suggested is or is not a proposition. But this is not true of the cases we are now concerned with. I want to say that a line suggests this or that, not to you or to me, but suggests, period; or at least that it suggests it to anyone who understands the words and is acquainted with the idiom of the language. "They had children and got married," though it does not *say* that they had illegitimate children, *does* suggest this, and if a person does not catch the suggestion (whether it is an intentional one on the part of the speaker or not), he is stupid or blind to any subtlety of linguistic expression. If we continue to use "suggest," then, we shall have to limit its application rather arbitrarily to these "objective" cases, excluding the to-you-but-not-to-me cases. And in view of our common use of this term, it is difficult to make this stricture stick.

(2) Even when the stricture is accepted, the term "suggest" seems unsatisfactory for another reason: it is far too pallid, too va-

nilla-flavored. The term "suggestion" suggests (!) something not quite there, lurking in the background, or visible through the trees if one squints. But works of literature, as well as sentences in daily discourse, may suggest in a far stronger way than this. The implied proposition, or thesis, or moral, of the work (when there is one), far from being "suggested" in this way, may be the most prominent thing in it; it may leap out at you, scream at you, bowl you over. Shall we say that Ibsen's *A Doll's House* only *suggests* that a woman should develop her personality and have a life of her own as much as her husband, or that Swift's *A Modest Proposal* only *suggests* that perhaps England was not treating Ireland in a humane manner? Perhaps we should say, not that these propositions are suggested by the work, but that they are *intimated* by it.[6] Or perhaps simply, "He said it all right, but not in so many words!"

Still, subject to these severe limitations, and because "imply" seems to have no ready synonym for this context, let us proceed with "suggest." Swift's *A Modest Proposal* is an instance of irony. Must irony be defined intentionalistically, as saying the opposite of what one intends? The disadvantage of this is, of course, that to know whether a given work was ironical, one would have to know whether it was so intended. It seems preferable to define "irony" as implying (suggesting) the opposite of what one says. One can even apply this to parody, which is often used as an incontrovertible example of a genre in which reference to the author's intention is indispensable. "To know that something is a parody, you have to know whether the author *meant* to parody this or that. If he didn't, you can hardly criticize him for failing to do something he didn't intend to do." In the intentionalistic sense, this is true; but we *can* criticize the work for not suggesting an interpretation other than the one it bears on its face. A good parody always contains countless such marks, whether or not the author so intended.

A frustrating and at the same time fascinating aspect of complex works of literature is their resistance to a single interpretation, in that many propositions seems to be implied, some of them contradicting others. The work would be far less rich in texture without this feature. Nor need any of the conflicting interpretations be wrong; both of two contradictory propositions may really be suggested by a work of literature, and though of course they cannot both be true, they may both really be implied, and both may live

6 This term was suggested to me by Professor Max Black.

in aesthetic harmony in the same work, giving it a kind of piquancy by the very tension which is thus set up. How is *Paradise Lost* to be interpreted? There is some evidence in the text that man's fall is a dire catastrophe, a work of Satan in defiance of God; there is other evidence that the entire series of events was fore-ordained by omnipotence, and thus, in view of divine benevolence, not a catastrophe at all; and there is some evidence that man's state after the Fall is much better, in that he has free-will in a sense which he lacked before ("a paradise within thee, happier farr"). It is, I think, only of marginal interest to ask, what did Milton believe? or what did Milton intend? The question is: Regardless of what he believed or intended, what beliefs got embodied in the poem? Which propositions are stated, and what further ones are implied?

One fruitful field of suggested propositions is the following: Works of literature are able, through the delineation of character and the setting forth of situations which are followed through in the details of the plot, to suggest *hypotheses* about human behavior, human motivation, human actions, and sometimes about the social structure. In doing so it doubtless enters upon the domain of the the social sciences; but in the present undeveloped state of these sciences, I do not think that a bit of supplementation from the literary artists (who are, at the least, excellent observers of the human scene) will be thought to crowd the scientists unduly. In any event, many writers have believed themselves, and with good reason, to be commentators on and interpreters of human behavior and the social situation in their time. Zola certainly considered himself to be one, and John Dos Passos another. Works of literature may suggest hypotheses of various kinds. Some are empirical in character—for example, Tolstoy's *War and Peace*, even apart from the explicitly stated philosophy of history at the end, suggests a hypothesis about the genesis of great events in history in relation to their leaders; and Dreiser's novels suggest semi-empirical and semi-metaphysical hypotheses about the help-lessness of human beings caught in a web of circumstances beyond their control and carried on willy-nilly to their destruction. Many works of literature suggest what one might call *moral* hypotheses —Dostoyevsky, George Eliot, Victor Hugo. Works of literature do not, of course, *verify* these hypotheses; that is the task of the empirical sciences. But they can suggest hypotheses which may be empirically fruitful; and this is, of course, a far more difficult task than verification.

Now, what has all this to do with the topic of truth in literature, with which we began? Simply this: we were looking for propositions, and especially true propositions, in works of literature, other than explicitly stated ones. And we have found, first, that works of literature may provide us with evidence for propositions about the author's beliefs, attitudes, and intentions, thus entitling us to infer these propositions; and, second, that quite apart from any reference to their authors, these works may suggest or intimate (say without saying) numerous propositions which are not about the author but about the world, about the subject-matter of the work itself. And since some of these suggested propositions are doubtless true, we have here, surely, an important sense of truth in literature, and one which it seems to me that many critics who have made claims for truth in literature have had in mind without being fully aware of it.

Two final precautions: (1) I am not saying that truth in literature is an important feature of these works *aesthetically*. On this point, as far as the present paper is concerned, I am quite content to agree with Professor Arnold Isenberg when he says, "What is so glorious about truth? Why should a quality which all except the demented commonly attain in the greater number of their ideas be considered so precious as to increase the stature of a Milton or a Beethoven if it can be ascribed to him?"[7] Though in fact I would not go so far as this, the matter would have to be separately argued. (Roughly, I would hold that the thesis implied in a work of literature may be the most important single feature of that work, and that it may be an important thesis, never before thought of by anyone; but not that we must accept the thesis as *true*.) (2) Nor am I saying that the author of the work of literature means to *assert* the propositions he implies. He may, and in most cases he certainly does, wish to assert them, or he would not have taken such pains to suggest them; but this has to be discovered by checking the relevant data (including the work itself) that will enlighten us about the author's beliefs. I am saying only that a work of literature may imply certain propositions and that these implied propositions may be true; it is not even necessary that the author mean to *assert* that they are true. This too is a separate consideration.

---

[7] *JAAC*, XIII (March 1955), 3, 400.

The Intention of the Artist

INTRODUCTION

The judgments that we make about works of art are neither formal truths nor simple expressions of sentiment. They are always open to objection, but an objection, if it is to be taken seriously, must be more than unelaborated opinion. A critic cannot refuse to adduce reasons or justification. To do so would be a breach of the conventions that govern the discipline of criticism. But there is no breach if he does not reply to an objection that offers nothing more in its defense than the sincerity of the objector; the appropriate response on such an occasion is instruction rather than argument.

Although there is no disagreement about whether artistic judgments require some kind of justification, there is disagreement about what kinds of properties can be assigned to works of art and so figure in a relevant justification. That disagreement we shall now consider.

First, some broad categories. Let us say that an artistic judgment takes the form: This work of art is such-and-such ("such-and-such" may include terms of description or evaluation). And let us say that a "backing" is whatever is offered in favor of an artistic judgment. These categories suggest different ways in which we can counter an artistic judgment. We can say that the backing is factually false. We say it is true but not sufficient to support the judgment. Or we can say that the backing is simply irrelevant.

If someone said that Donne's "The Canonization" is marvelous poetry because it is an exquisite delineation of a country scene, we would respond by telling him, in effect, that his backing was false. We would remind him that "The Canonization" has nothing to do with a country scene; it is about lovers and the features of their love that elevate them to a kind of sainthood. That would be an example of the first case.

Suppose, next, someone argues for the greatness of the same poem because of the technically interesting rhyme-scheme a-b-b-a-c-c-c-a-a. That is definitely a property of the poem, and can certainly occur in a backing. But rhyme-schemes are not of primary importance and no one would regard any verdict about poetry as adequately supported by their citation alone.

In both of these cases the backing was accepted as relevant and then refused; in one case because it was false, in the other because it was insufficient. In both cases it was thought appropriate to enter a rejoinder. And it is thus that we admit the relevance of a backing. Otherwise, we would not bother to answer; we would simply throw it out.

But what if someone praised "The Canonization" as great poetry because its first edition is now worth five hundred thousand dollars. This is a case in which we would throw the backing out. We might reply that a backing must refer to the *aesthetic* properties of a poem and we need not show that this backing is false or insufficient. We need simply disregard it. The monetary value of a book in which a poem appears is neither a good nor bad reason for judging it. It is not a reason at all.

There is another way in which a dispute could arise about the suitability of an artistic judgment. Suppose that someone praises the poem, citing as a backing the unusually subtle and complex imagery of the poem and referring to the fact that the author intended "die" in the poem to designate not only physical death but the culmination of the sexual act. The backing might be rejected on the grounds that the author's intentions are not part of the poem, and that if the double sense of "die" is not clear in the poem, it cannot be made clear by evidence derived from the biography of its author. But what if the person then answers that the intention of the author *is* a feature of the poem and therefore provides acceptable evidence for a critical analysis of "die"? Who is right? Is the intention inside or outside the poem? The problems suggested by these questions cannot be settled by any of the means used in the previous examples. In the first two cases, the reasons provided were clearly relevant—albeit less than adequate as backing. And in the third case, there was also no problem: the reason given was clearly irrelevant.

The last example is more troublesome because the dispute turns on different views about what is properly a part of a poem and whether a property neither clearly relevant nor clearly irrelevant to a poem can serve as a backing. There is no dispute over whether the author's intentions suggest to the reader the presence of properties in the poem that he has otherwise overlooked but which, once suggested, can be identified by scrutiny of its structure and subject-matter. Neither is there dispute over whether evidence of intention suggests what *might* be found in a poem. The point of controversy is whether evidence from intention *establishes* of a property that it is a part of a poem.

An advocate of the view that critics should construe poetry through the intentions of the poet might argue that every poem is an expression of the self and that therefore the best information for construing a poem is biographical. It is easy to think of examples which convert such a view into an exercise in intellectual futility. Austin Warren, in his important and revealing book on Crashaw,* has pointed out that it is difficult to reconcile the known tempera-ment of the man with the religious complexities of his verse. He suggests that Crashaw's poetry expresses his "creative" and not his "private" self.

If it is the poetry rather than the biography of an author that establishes the nature of his creative self, the principle that every poem is an instance of self-expression is immune to factual ap-praisal. Any evidence that differentiates the known temperament of an author from the character of his poetry would simply be relegated to his private self. Accordingly the method for deriving the features inherent to the creative self of a poet precludes its use as an explanation of the motivational or causal conditions of crea-tivity. The factual vacuity of the claim makes it irrelevant also to the conduct of criticism, since the method of interpretation that it endorses presumes, but cannot affect, the adequacy of a literary analysis.

However, the foregoing arguments are not decisive against the use of evidence from intention in support of an artistic judgment. Let us restate the points against: 1. There is a class of properties such that for every poem some of them are inside and some of them outside the poem. 2. Among the properties that are inside a poem is its language; among the properties that are outside is the intention of the poet. 3. Whatever property counts in favor of a judgment about a poem is inside the poem. 4. Therefore evidence from in-tention cannot count in favor of such a judgment.

The argument has the defect, however, of presuming that a work of art, like a spatial body, has clearly defined boundaries such that

---

* Austin Warren, *Richard Crashaw* (*Ann Arbor*, 1957), pp. 194–206.

any property can be determined either foreign or indigenous. Someone might write a letter, for example, saying there was buried treasure in my back yard. Were I to excavate, I could resolve any suspicions about the veracity of the letter writer. That would conclusively settle the question of whether the treasure, as described, was in my back yard. We can for this case delimit an area such that we can determine for any physical body whether it is or is not a part of that area. There could be no reasonable doubt that if the treasure were in my neighbor's cellar, it would be outside and not inside the legal boundaries of my property. And if it were said that the letter was not self-confirming, that it suggested and did not establish the existence of what it described, there could be no reasonable doubt about that.

But a work of art is not my back yard or anything like it. I can consult a surveyor, find the boundaries of my property, and catalogue whatever objects fall within the lines. But it is a quite different and puzzling kind of act to draw a line around a poem, catalogue whatever class of elements are encircled, and then conclude of any other element that it is not a member of that class.

Yet a standard criticism of the use of evidence from intention seems to presume that the perimeter of a poem can be drawn and that after drawing it we shall see "intention" on the outside looking in. Words such as "inside" and "outside" are, however, especially misleading in determinations of this kind. They impart a specious clarity to the otherwise difficult question of whether intention is admissible into poetry as one of its aesthetic properties.

Though the foregoing remarks may be obvious, they are not irrelevant to the question before us. Arguments about the propriety of admitting evidence from intention are frequently couched in a vocabulary that pictures works of art as quasi-physical objects with the attendant property of determinate boundaries. Since critics, in the contexts of these discussions, apparently view the discovery of such boundaries as the object of their investigations, and since they never find them, the controversies about intention continue in the vain hope that somehow and someday the fog will lift.

More light is thrown on the debate about intention if we look for another source. It is now a commonplace of aesthetics that the rules which govern the use of "poem" and similar aesthetic words are sufficiently flexible and loose so that the words whose applications they control do not refer on every occasion to an identical sector of subject-matter: that is, "poem" has a variety of different, albeit related, uses and, as a result, refers differently on different occasions. And we cannot say of the different uses, simply because they are different, that they are *prima facie* mistaken and that they violate the meaning of "poem." For example, someone might use "poem" so that its meaning includes the intention of the poet; someone else, for good reason, might not. And if in such a situation a dispute emerges, it would be futile to attempt a reconciliation by reciting rules.

This does not mean that disputes about intention are simply semantic, nor that participating in them is, in principle, futile. A comparable case from another field illuminates the issue. Suppose that a political tract written in seventeenth-century England contains a word whose meaning has puzzled scholars for generations; "blesh," a word which the writer of the tract uses to describe politicians. A student of political science finally unearths a secret diary hidden by the author which discloses that the author used "blesh" to designate corruption. In a sense, we have discovered something: that the tract said that politicians are corrupt. But in another sense it has not said so. Because of the coined word, no one to whom the tract was addressed understood it as saying that politicians were corrupt, and in that sense the secret meaning is not part of the tract. As a result, the scholar, by incorporating the discovered meaning into the tract, is placed in the peculiar position of tacitly admitting that the tract said or communicated that which it did not say or communicate.

This might lead the scholar to say that what had been discovered pertained to the document *qua* autobiography and not *qua* political tract. If a tract is that which communicates the political views of its author, then understanding and evaluating it in this light requires attention to what it actually communicated and not what it might have communicated had a secret meaning been accessible. It would be difficult to say at once, for example, that the tract was a failure because the views it expressed were concealed by a coined word with an inaccessible meaning and that the meaning in question was part of the tract. In other words, a dispute about whether the intended meaning should be incorporated into the text would turn not upon the reliability of the author's diary, but upon whether it in this way clouded an understanding of the text as political document.

In much the same way, a poet may use a word or phrase whose meaning baffles his critics, and evidence may eventually be uncovered that unravels its sense. If the ascertained meaning is then allocated to the poem, the understanding and evaluation of it should take account of the added increment of meaning. But a critic may hold the view that a poem is a social act; it communicates and must communicate a sense to an audience; and if that is his view of poetry, he will be unwilling to agree that an essentially esoteric meaning deserves a place in the poem. He would otherwise have to describe and evaluate the poem in terms that he considers incompatible with the nature and objectives of poetry.

On the other hand, there is the view that poetry is expression of self, that it provides clues instrumental to the understanding of creative personalities. According to this version, any evidence is germane to a poem if it is explicative of an otherwise unclear meaning; and that meaning, in turn, is part of a poem because it is explicative of its creator.

The arguments about intention thus illustrate different views about the nature of poetry and are part of the battleground on which the authority of such views is alternately attacked and defended. They are not silly arguments, although they are unlikely to be resolved. They will continue as long as we disagree about the nature of poetry. And that will be a long time.

John Wain, F. W. Bateson,
W. W. Robson

"INTENTION"

AND BLAKE'S *JERUSALEM**

I

The question of "intention" is one of the most obstinate difficulties in literary criticism; that it has received so little formal discussion in this country is merely one more indication of the policy of *laissez-faire* which governs academic thinking. Most people are familiar with the clumsy but valuable article by Wimsatt and Beardsley, "The Intentional Fallacy" (*Sewanee Review*, LIV, 3), but, although some influential critics have signified assent, nothing like general agreement has been reached. Yet the subject is of such pervasive significance that even critics who normally show an unusual degree of indifference to the theoretic bases of their craft have had to come to some kind of terms with it (e.g. M. R. Ridley, *Shakespeare's Plays*, 1937, pp. 5–6).

It is probable, in fact, that no piece of critical reasoning which ignores, or begs the question of, "intention" can really stand up. A good recent example occurs on p. 7 of Mr. Bateson's *English Poetry: A Critical Introduction.* Under the heading "The Primacy of Meaning," the author is belabouring the modern lack of concern

---

* From *Essays in Criticism*, Vol. II, No. 1, January 1952, pp. 105–114. Reprinted by permission of the publisher, Basil Blackwell, Ltd.

with what a poem is actually *saying*. As an example we are told that Blake's "And did those feet in ancient time" (note the "intentionalism" implicit in steering clear of the name *Jerusalem*, a title given to the poem not by its author but by subsequent editors) has a meaning very remote from anything imagined by the "millions" who "chant these lines every year." Someone should explain to them (i) that the phrase "ancient time" refers to the legend that Pythagoras derived his system of philosophy from the British druids—the point being that British artists need feel no undue reverence for Greek and Latin models, (ii) that "Jerusalem" means, not an ideally happy England, but "something much more abstract," and in particular, sexual liberty, (iii) that by "dark Satanic Mills" Blake refers to the altars of the Churches. In order to establish this, a good deal of proof is needed, and it is accordingly fetched from elsewhere in *Milton*, and from the Prophetic Books in general (for "Clouds are a recurrent symbol in the Prophetic Books of the Church's repression of the instinctive energies, and gold is generally a specifically sexual symbol"). The point about Pythagoras, though for all I know it is an agreed fact among Blake scholars, is supported by no evidence beyond the information that Milton himself alludes to the legend in *Areopagitica*.

I am far from wishing to dispute that this is the real meaning of Blake's verses—if we reserve the term "real" for the meaning which the author himself attaches to the work. But are we to do so? The lines themselves would never, in a thousand years, yield this meaning; it has to be supplied from outside. But few would oppose Coleridge's "Every work of art must contain within itself the reason why it is thus and not otherwise." Strictly speaking, the point may not arise, since the lyric is not in itself a work of art but a part of one. But does the "intentionalist" assert that no lyric can ever be abstracted from a longer work? If it is self-sufficient (that is, if it yields a paraphrasable meaning answering the normal demands of logic and syntax) and if—as here—it is manifestly superior to the rest of the work, what hinders?

The usual objection to a reading of a poem which obfuscates, or ignores, the author's meaning, is that it is an injustice to the merit of the poem. But in this case it seems to be rather an improvement. By what principle of literary criticism will the "intentionalist" demonstrate that the simple surface meaning of these lines is inferior to the hotch-potch of altars, legends and repression-symbols that Blake "really meant"?

I wish only to open the question, and am sure that many readers would be grateful if it could be thrashed out, by authoritative critics, in these pages.

JOHN WAIN

II

I am not an authoritative critic, but I share Mr. Wain's concern at the muddled thinking that prevails on this issue; I particularly welcome his note, since it enables me to define my own position in rather different terms from those I used in my book.

To simplify the discussion, may I confine myself to "dark Satanic mills"? And for my own non-expert interpretation of the phrase's meaning, may I now substitute that provided by Northrop Frye (*Fearful Symmetry: a Study of William Blake*, Princeton, 1947, p. 290):

> The mill also represents the dissolving of "living form," and the "dark Satanic mills" in Blake mean any unimaginative mechanism: the mechanical logical method of Aristotle, the industrial machinery that requires slave-labour, the mathematical co-ordination of the Newtonian universe, the mechanical ability to turn out uninspired art—anything that compels Albion, of whom Samson is a reminiscence, to remain "Eyeless in Gaza at the mill with slaves."

This, or something not unlike it, is what the phrase meant to Blake—and presumably to such early readers of *Milton* as Thomas Butts. To Mr. Wain, on the other hand, Blake's mills are, I suppose, a nineteenth-century textile-factory: "dark" with the soot from its steam-engines, "Satanic" because of capitalism's indifference to human suffering. Aesthetically this interpretation may perhaps be preferable to Blake's, but if so it derives its beauty from the historical accident that Mr. Wain was born *after* the Industrial Revolution, whereas Blake was born *before* it. There can be no question of Blake or his original readers giving "dark Satanic mills"—in however muzzy or subconscious a way—the sense that Mr. Wain prefers. There *were* no grim steam-driven textile factories when Blake wrote Milton (1800–4), nor apparently did capitalism, as a coherent economic theory, ever penetrate his consciousness. To substitute for the Old Testament hand-mills (a civic institution) the steam-driven mills of the nineteenth century (the children of the capitalist *entrepreneur*) is, in fact, to re-write Blake's poem. And, in the last analysis, this is what Mr. Wain is really encouraging the modern reader to do.

It is not, of course, a crime to re-write Blake. But the procedure should surely be distinguished from *reading*. To attribute to a poet's words what neither he nor his original readers can possibly have meant by them, even subconsciously, is to exceed the province of a mere *reader*. The parallel is rather with such things as Laforgue's *Hamlet* or Browning's "Caliban upon Setebos," in which a literary classic is made the pretext for what is essentially an original creation. No doubt most of Eliot's quotations and allusions also come into this category. It is, I agree, a not unamusing *genre*, but its successful practice calls for a high degree of sophistication and mental agility. It cannot possibly be recommended, even in the smallest doses, to the Common Reader.

Mr. Wain's criterion will not, in fact, bear inspection. His advice to the modern reader, faced with two possible interpretations of a phrase or a poem, is to choose the more attractive one. That is, I think, what it boils down to. The modern interpretation of "dark Satanic mills" is, he assures us, an "improvement" on what the works meant to Blake. It is, therefore, the "right" meaning today presumably. But Blake can hardly have been "wrong" in thinking his phrase meant something like Northrop Frye's paraphrase. It follows, then, that the phrase has at least two meanings, both equally—though perhaps not simultaneously—correct. And if somebody should come along with an improvement on the "improvement"—based, for example, on some twentieth-century underground factory for the manufacture of armaments—there would then be three meanings. Nor need the process stop there. If the test of a poem's meaning is simply the degree of its attractiveness to the reader, the number of meanings need only be limited by the number of readers. In the last resort, *any* word can mean *any* thing. What hinders, Mr. Wain asks? Why, only that if the meaning of the poet's words is to be entirely at this or that reader's beck and call, there ceases to be any point at this stage in reading the poem at all!

If the criterion is not the individual reader's preference, what is it? Are the intentionalists right after all in referring us, when we run into difficulties, to what was going on in the poet's mind? The compromise that I tried to elaborate in my second chapter was to identify the meaning of a poem with the interaction of four constant factors: (i) the poet, (ii) the poet's original audience, (iii) their common language, (iv) their inherited literary conventions. In terms of this formula the poet's intentions are relevant only to the extent to which the audience, the language and the literary tradition permit their expression. Anything that is not directly or indirectly implicit in the actual words of the poem must therefore be eliminated. But this does not mean that a phrase or a poem is restricted to what Mr. Wain calls its "simple surface meaning." If Coleridge meant that by the *obiter dictum* quoted by Mr. Wain, Coleridge was talking nonsense. Even a Coleridge cannot understand a poem unless he knows or can guess a good deal about the conventions of style and form which it presupposes. And for a precise understanding the poet's exact position, chronological and qualitative, within the particular tradition must also be known—a process that inevitably entails the accumulation of as much relevant information as possible about the poem's author and its original audience. I conclude, indeed, that these two participants in the poetic act are not really separable. The proper question to put is not "What did Blake mean?", but "What meaning did Blake succeed in conveying to the best of his early readers?"

Language, after all, is a social device, and its function is to reduce, not to extend, the area of our mutual misunderstanding. A good speaker is the man who minimizes the distortions inherent in the use of words. A good poem is a linguistic complex that is specially resistant to misinterpretation. But even good poems are not immune from the action of time, and in their case the modern reader, who is worthy of his cultural heritage, must be prepared *to reverse the time-process*—even if this does result in a "hotch-potch of altars, legends and repression-symbols." May I without offence remind Mr. Wain of Coleridge's rebuke of Hayley (who had echoed Johnson's disgust at Milton's "controversial merriment"):

> The man who reads a work meant for immediate effect on one age with the notions and feelings of another, may be a refined gentleman, but must be a sorry critic. (*Essays and Lectures*, Everyman ed., p. 289.)

The changes of connotation that sometimes seem to give a phrase a meaning it did not originally have must be regarded, I suggest, as historic accidents. To applaud such accidental accretions is as perverse as to prefer the ruins of a medieval cathedral to the original fabric. It is also uncritical, since the critic's basic assumption must be that the essential meaning of the particular work under discussion, "the object as in itself it really is," remains continuously the *same*. The final formulation of that one ultimate meaning may be infinitely remote, but a provisional approximation to it, one commanding a wide measure of intelligent assent, is surely a constant possibility. To deny that, Mr. Wain, is to deny our craft.

F. W. BATESON

III

In slapping me down Mr. Bateson has stated his own position in what seems a rather simplified form. Let me select two points. (1) Apparently intention is to be admitted, but only to the extent that it *succeeded* with the *best* of the poet's contemporary readers. (If it failed with them, its last chance was gone.) Is it really true that any interpretation of, say, the *Ode on a Grecian Urn* must pass the test, not of "Does this reveal the kind, and degree, of poetic achievement embodied in the poem?" but of "Is this what the poem meant to the 'best' of Keats's contemporaries?" If so, who are these "best"? Since they are obviously not precisely identifiable, the answer must be, "The best contemporary readers are those who would probably, or did actually, agree with the view I hold myself in the mid-twentieth century." The spectre of the "most attractive" interpretation is thus not so easily laid. (ii) "Meaning" is an ambiguous word, and when Mr. Bateson takes it as axiomatic that "the essential meaning" of a work of literature "remains continuously the same," he is trying on the adjective "essential" to protect himself from the other sense of the word, namely, the kind and intensity of importance and appositeness which a work has for a given society or individual. In this second sense it is obviously *not* "continuously the same," but alive and developing. "Jerusalem" may be a comically crude example in which a poem is furnished by time with an entirely new meaning, but what of *Hamlet* or the *Odyssey?* Is the critic's task to be restricted to prim warnings against extending the original area of a poem's usefulness and truth, or is it, as I think, to create and maintain a balance between the "original" and the "developed" significances, and by this difficult act to recognize that subtle tension which is the mode of existence of a work of literature?

JOHN WAIN

IV

"The object," says Mr. Bateson, replying to Mr. Wain, "remains the same." This interesting controversy does not, to my mind, clear up some general difficulties about the status of the "object"; and I think an indication of these difficulties is relevant to the problems of "meaning" and "intention" raised above.

In discussing a poem with (say) a class of students it should be established first of all just what is being discussed—to create the common basis for discussion. This establishment, assuming it to be successful, is the result of a series of agreed decisions by teacher and class about the words and phrases of the given poem: which references, associations, implications, etc., are in this case present, and, if present, relevant. (All this serves to rule out, *inter alia*, the kind of elementary irrelevances found in many of the Richards protocols.) Such a procedure requires in part historical information (whether certain "meanings," or certain references, etc., were possible "then"—cf. Mr. Bateson's four cultural factors): in part it requires simply ordinary sensitiveness and good sense. But this procedure is certainly not "criticizing" the poem, hardly even "interpreting" it, at any rate not at a very deep level. It is merely an extension to a group of the kind of individual activity demonstrated in one's making an acceptable prose paraphrase of the poem; it assumes, as a working hypothesis, the possibility of a sort of conceptual equivalent of the poem being placed beside the poem for comparison, contrast, illumination; hence it is a process of *reduction*. Now I contend (*a*) that the further stages of "interpretation" and of "criticism" are not processes of reduction; (*b*) that the poem, the "object," is in some sense not fully "there" until the final stage, that of criticism; (*c*) that an evaluative attitude is necessarily co-present and continuous with the process of criticism, manifesting itself, not only explicitly in incidental or local valuations, but implicitly in the control of the whole process by the critic's concern for a total judgment of value; and so (*d*) that the question of the "intention" of the poem, or of the poet, cannot be adequately discussed, let alone settled, until the poem is fully "there" as an object of value.

Mr. Bateson's account of the "meaning" of a poem ignores the evaluative (hence, in my view, quasi-creative) function of interpretation and criticism, and pictures the critic only as a "reducer" or "translator." I answer that the poem cannot be fully exploited even for the purposes of historical scholarship until it exists as a poem, and that it can only exist as a poem when the approach described in (c) above has operated on the raw material of the text. "What is it like?" or, more fundamentally still, "What *is* it?" is a question both the scholar and the critic must try to answer; but the poem can never, as Mr. Bateson wants, be engaged with as a noumenon, only as a phenomenon, and the question can only be answered in the form: "What is it like *now*? What is it *now*?" (Let me observe here that analogies with painting, or other arts where the "object" is said to be constant, are misleading, since words are not a specific non-utilitarian medium, and poems, among other means of verbal communication, enjoy no specially privileged status.)

This is not, however, to accept Mr. Wain's position (or Mr. Bateson's account of Mr. Wain's position) that, faced with a number of alternative "meanings," one should choose the "meaning" which is most attractive to modern ears. Historical considerations *are* relevant, and they are taken into account at the "establishment" or "reduction" stage. Thus, if there were no unpleasant factories in 1800 (weren't there?), this will have a bearing on our reading of "dark Satanic mills." But even the most historically minded scholar, in discussing that phrase of the poem, and its relation to the total complex of the poem, is discussing that phrase, and that poem, as they are now. For, if a poem can be said to have an eternal, or, as I should prefer to call it, a "public" meaning, this meaning is not this or that "interpretation," but the resultant *now* of all plausible interpretations; and, if the scholar's duty is to decide which interpretations are plausible, perhaps the critic's duty is to find their resultant. But the scholar, too, is a reader *now*, and the poem can only fully exist for him, even *qua* scholar, in so far as he is a reader *now*. And he is not, in my sense, a "reader" until he is, in his reading, interpreting, evaluating, choosing; and, in so far as he is doing so, he is entitled to *his* say about the poem's "intention."

W. W. ROBSON

V

It is an Editor's privilege to have the last word. I agree, of course, with Mr. Wain that I have oversimplified this issue. My object was simply to show, in a rough and ready way, that a poem's meaning to its original audience provides the only workable criterion of relevance in the case of a disputed interpretation. I cannot, I am afraid, accept the ingenious compromise he offers me in the last sentence of his reply. In the last resort, Blake's readers must choose between Samson's mills and the steam-driven textile factories. Mr. Wain seems to expect them to do a balancing act—precariously perched on his "subtle tension"—between Gaza and Lancashire! I am grateful to Mr. Robson for his elucidation of some of the implications of our problem. I suspect, however, that his emphasis on evaluation is a red herring. The object remains the same only in so far as its value continues to be *implicit*. My concern is with the poem as artifact. There must be some poetic equivalent to the artist's painting and the musician's score, and my suggestion is that it is to be found in the experience that the original audience ideally underwent when reading the poem. This experience was occasioned by certain words and a certain literary tradition, or combination of traditions, that the original audience shared with the poet. It follows that the poem's proper use today—the analogy would be with learning to play a piece of music—demands the recreation of the occasions by the modern reader. Here we have the justification of the academic study of literature. We struggle through the commentators on Blake to ensure the authenticity of our reaction to his poems. And as our reactions (by which I mean the pre-critical phenomenal "experience" that accompanies the actual reading of a poem) approach authenticity, we are in fact responding to "the object as in itself it really is" (the unchanging artifact).

F. W. BATESON

T. M. Gang

─────

INTENTION*

─────

In the years that have passed since Professors Wimsatt and Beardsley
first enriched our vocabulary by the phrase "The Intentional Fallacy" (in an article so entitled, *Sewanee Review*, liv, 1946), the
problem they treated has been discussed a number of times, notably
in the controversy between Messrs. Bateson and Wain (" 'Intention'
and Blake's Jerusalem," *Essays in Criticism*, ii, 1952) and in Mr. F.
W. Leakey's article, "Intention in Metaphor" (ib., iv, 1954); but
these discussions have not gone to the roots of the question.

The problem is how far the author's intention in writing a work
is relevant to the critic's judgment on it. "The Intentional Fallacy"
consists in judging a work by measuring the author's achievement
against "what he was trying to do." It is not difficult to show that
this is a completely circular process; on the other hand, Mr. Leakey
(op. cit.) shows that the circularity arises from our formulation.
It remains to show whether other ways of talking about the author's
intention are meaningful, and useful to the critic. Professors Wimsatt
and Beardsley's basic position, with which most modern critics will
sympathise, is that criticism should concern itself with the poem
as something existing "objectively," rather than with the mental
processes which engendered it, or those it produces. This position
I accept; the philosophical puzzle *how* a poem (or for that matter,
a word) can "objectively exist" is no concern of the literary critic's.
In practice we know that it does, and not merely as marks on paper

─────

* From *Essays in Criticism*, Vol. VII, No. 2, April 1957, pp. 175–186. Reprinted by permission of the publisher, Basil Blackwell, Ltd.

or sounds in the air. If we allow ourselves to believe that the poem
only exists in the minds of the poet and the individual reader, we
soon discover that in that case no two readers will have read "the
same poem"; so that there can never be any discussion, and hence
criticism, of any work.

But granted the objective existence of poems and words, there
is a difference between the status of words in isolation (as, for
example, when we put them between inverted commas) and words
in a context: an isolated word probably has a number of meanings,
and that number does not remain constant. But the meanings
of a word in a context are strictly limited: most obviously, by its
syntactical position; but also by the occasion on which it was
uttered, and by various things we know about the speaker. We are
often in doubt as to the meaning of a sentence, or even a whole
book, until we know the identity of the author. If we believe *The
Young Visiters* to be written by Daisy Ashford, aged nine, we
shall understand it in one way; but in quite another, if we credit
J. M. Barrie, aged fifty odd, with the authorship. The same is true
in ordinary life: we are constantly limiting the possible meanings
a phrase might possess, with the help of our knowledge of the
speaker. We know that double negatives, in some people's usage,
do not cancel out; and that when an army order says "Sandwiches
will be provided" this is a command, not a promise, to provide them.
There is no ambiguity here, *if* we know that this is an army order.
Yet although special knowledge is required to interpret it, we can
say that the order "exists objectively."

It does not, then, follow from our premise (the objective existence
of poems, or other works of literature) that we can ignore all information about the author. We must know *something* about him,
and about the historical context of the poem, in order to eliminate
the inappropriate meanings. So much we can grant without necessarily saying anything about the poet's *intention*. But the question
we are going to discuss is the narrower one, whether a critic can
discover anything about that intention, and, if he can, whether
he should try to do so.

II

The verb "to mean" conveys two senses, often simultaneously: that
of intending, and that of signifying. When we talk about the meaning of a poem, we usually mean its significance alone; but when we

ask what the poet meant by it, we are asking what he intended it to signify. And here let us enter a caveat against those who would ask "Signify: for whom?" There *is* a sense in which we can talk about the significance of words for particular persons; but normally "significance" means the significance which is open for all to discover and therefore to discuss. For the present, at any rate, it is with this that we are concerned.

In ordinary life we do not hesitate to consider the intentions of people who say things: of friends who upbraid us or enemies who wish us well, of those who promise or of those who threaten. As a rule we presume that there *is* an intention, even though we know from experience how often we speak without having any clear antecedent intention—without, in other words, meaning thereby to produce a particular effect. Nevertheless, we do not usually try to reconstruct the complex and perhaps even confused mental processes of other persons when we look for the "intention" with which they uttered their words: where it is possible to suppose a simple purpose on the speaker's part, which would account both for his words and his subsequent conduct, we call this his "intention." We envisage intentions as the sort of thing people might write in their secret diaries, which God's spies, and the lucky historian, may read. It is this simple kind of intention that the historian and politician must suppose and reconstruct. They know, as we all do, that in fact we don't "*have* intentions," as we might "*have* a brainwave"; but in order to avoid the multiplication of hypotheses (which merely leads to uncontrolled speculation), they, and we, are obliged to construct simple "intentions" in order to make sense of other people's behaviour.

The intentions of which we have spoken up to now have all been what one might call "practical" intentions—that is, intentions to achieve a certain result. But of everything that is spoken or written, we could suppose another kind of intention, namely, that of conveying a certain significance. This, which we shall call the "literary" intention, will include intentions as to the tone of voice in which words are to be read, the sense in which they are to be taken, and even the emotions with which they are to be accompanied; but with this last we have reached the frontiers of "practical" intention. If we go one step farther, and speak of the intention to produce a certain emotional effect (as, for example, when we go from saying "This is a sad poem" to saying "This poem is to make you sad"), we are speaking of an effect to be produced, a result to be achieved. Practical intentions can be directed to the most diverse ends: such as arousing an emotion, justifying the ways of God to man, wooing the fair sex, obtaining a pension for the author, or purging the audience of pity and terror. And although the critic will judge the poem as a poem, not as a means of achieving any of these objects, his understanding of it may be greatly influenced by what he knows of the poet's practical intentions. He will not judge a love-lyric by its efficacy in wooing the lady to whom it was addressed; but his reading of it will depend to some degree on the knowledge that it was, or was not, written in order to woo someone. Where we find it difficult to construct a practical intention, as for example with Shakespeare's sonnets, we may find it exceedingly difficult to know in what tone, with what degree of seriousness, or irony, we are to read the poem: criticism which evades these questions, while it may be the only kind possible here, is thin and unsatisfactory. Or, to take another example, how very differently the *Lyrical Ballads* will strike the reader who knows, and the reader who does not know, that these poems are intended to demonstrate a theory of the imagination.

I have said that we could suppose a literary intention, as well as a practical one, for whatever is written or spoken. But can we, in fact, construct such an intention? Whenever something is quite plainly and unambiguously said, it hardly makes sense to ask the speaker what he intended his words to signify: and if he produces a paraphrase of his words, it will be very odd to call this his "intention": his original words have as good a claim to that title. Only where there is some difficulty—where the language is being used in an unfamiliar way, or there is some ambiguity, or something has apparently been omitted, for example—only there does it make sense to talk about the speaker's or writer's literary intention.

But there is a further difficulty. Practical intentions are intentions to produce effects: and the effect produced, whatever it may be, is one of the data from which we construct the intention. That the novelist shot his mistress, or that the poet moved us, are the fixed points in our enquiries into what they meant to do. But for literary intentions there is no corresponding certain datum. The object of a literary intention is a significance: yet it is only where significance is in doubt that it makes sense to ask what the intention is. Moreover, our inevitable uncertainty about mental processes, which compelled us to regard practical intentions as constructs, now threatens to prevent us from constructing any literary intentions whatever. With no external data to take into account, on what grounds are we to distinguish between all the possible hypotheses about the meaning intended by the poet? Nor can we evade this dilemma by thinking of the poet's intention otherwise than as a construct. We know from experience how often we have no clear idea of what we want to say until we have said it; how rhymes will determine sense; how something we say suddenly appears to have meanings we had not thought of, but which we appropriate in our next remark. And when something we say spontaneously is not quite clear, and we are asked to explain it, how often do we find ourselves saying "I suppose I must have meant . . ."

We find, then, that far from being able to construct literary intentions for whatever is said and spoken, we are often unable to do so at all. But there are cases when we can, and usually do. The speaker who has prepared his subject may say something his audience cannot follow; they ask him what he meant, and he can tell them. A poet who has planned and written an epic; a novelist; a dramatist: all writers who formulate what they are going to say before they say it—all these could tell us, and often they do, what meaning they intended to convey. The problem for the critic is to know whether any given work belongs to this category; usually it is not hard to tell. Sometimes it is even possible to say of a work that the author changed his intention in the course of writing; *Piers Plowman* springs to mind as an example.

To complete our analysis of "meaning," we must look at its other component, "significance." "Significance" (like "meaning," whenever they are synonymous), has a range of meanings extending from what we may call its "weak" to its "strong" sense. The weak significance of a word is given by its synonyms, and that of a passage, by paraphrase, translation or précis: and it is this we intend when we say "Give the meaning of five of the following phrases." The strong meaning of a word or of a whole work of art is its implication or even its message: we talk of "The meaning of Easter" or say that Elmer Rice's plays possess Social Significance. Very roughly, the weak sense corresponds to "what it says," the strong to "what it is telling us": notices in the imperative (such as "Go home, Yankees") provide borderline cases, where what is being said is identical with what someone is being told. A whole poem can hardly be said to have a weak significance; it would be odd to call a paraphrase of *Hamlet* its "meaning." We take "the meaning of Hamlet" to be what it tells us about the world, or about ourselves. But even single words and sentences are sometimes said to be "charged with significance"—as, for example, when they carry tragic or ironic implications. Again, slogans, mottoes, notices, and the kind of symbols used in art and literature (but not those of mathematics and logic) all have strong meanings. "Walls have ears" exhorted us to guard our talk: "Private" tells us to keep out: "Dominus Illuminatio Mea" tells members of an ancient university in what spirit they are to pursue their studies. Again, a symbol will tell us about the thing it represents: the bandage on Cupid's eyes indicates something about the nature of love.

The distinction between strong and weak meanings introduces a new complication. For we are more inclined to believe that an author knows the weak significance of his words, than that he knows the strong. We sometimes talk as if a work could possess a strong meaning without the author's wish, or even against his wishes. (This does, of course, imply that there is also a strong significance which he intended.) Thus we know that faint praise is not always uttered with the intention of damning; circumstances may lend ironic significance to remarks innocently made; a poet may employ a charming lyric, written at another period of his life—or written by someone else—in a play of sordid content, so that it assumes a new and sinister significance. On the other hand, we tend to hold authors responsible for weak meanings. Mr. Eliot may claim not to know what *The Confidential Clerk* means; but if a translator was in doubt whether he had correctly rendered a sentence or a word in it, he would no doubt expect Mr. Eliot to be able to tell him. Only a poet who composes in a vatic trance would deny that he knew what his individual words and sentences signified. At all events, when we ask what the author meant by such a word or such a line, it is not really about his intention that we are asking, but about the weak significance he would have said it possessed: which is neither a biographical, nor a psychological question. It is therefore a matter of complete indifference whether we ask what Shakespeare meant by a "handsaw," or what "handsaw" means in a particular context in *Hamlet*.

But with some poets it is not a matter of indifference whether we ask what they meant, or what their words mean. A poet may

use a private language. If this is merely a kind of code, which with
the help of a key can be translated into an ordinary public language,
then we can continue to talk about what the poem means without
invoking the author; but if the language expresses concepts which
the ordinary language does not embody, we may not be able to do
so. Blake writes in such a language. When he says "Heaven" or
"Hell," "Angel" or "Devil," "Good" or "Evil," the words do not refer
to things which an orthodox Christian would call by these names;
yet by using the same words, Blake implies that they are the same
things, and that the orthodox Christian is ignorant of their true
nature. Blake's language will not permit us to talk about the orthodox Christian hell and Blake's hell as two distinct concepts: in fact,
it will not permit us to talk about the orthodox concept at all.

When we are talking about the meaning of a poem written in a
private language of this kind, we cannot avoid invoking the author's meaning, except by elaborate evasions. For such a poem
cannot simply be translated into ordinary language with the help
of a key; to understand even its weak meanings, knowledge of
the author's whole view of the world is required. To understand
Blake, it is useless to try to imagine what his poetry must have
meant to his contemporaries: we should have to ask ourselves what
it would have signified to a man in every way like Blake. And
we might just as well ask what Blake thought it meant. But this,
let us remember, is not a question about his intentions.

III

We can now return to our original question, whether the author's
intention is relevant to criticism. It has been argued that we can
know something about his practical intention, and under certain
circumstances about his literary intention. We said at the beginning that the possible meanings of a word were limited by its
syntactical position, and those of a piece of discourse by its context
—which may include all we know about the circumstances of its
composition. Only a full-time hedonist can claim for himself the
right to read any meaning he chooses into any work; he, of course,
will be able to enjoy *Macbeth*, as we enjoy *Maria Marten*, by treating it as a huge joke; but he will not be able to set up as a critic:
for we cannot compare notes on a work which we allow to mean
anything anyone likes. But if we admit that many meanings are

ruled out, for example by context, then we shall be rather perverse if we refuse to admit limitations on the meaning which may be derived from the author's intentions. Of course, where this intention is reconstructed entirely from data which would in themselves serve equally well to limit the meaning, there will be no point in constructing it, and some danger that we may give the construct more authority than it deserves. It is probably better to talk about the meaning of *King Lear* than about Shakespeare's intention in writing this play. But where external data, such as note-books, prefaces or letters, have contributed to our construction, the author's literary intention will be worth invoking. We can and should talk about Milton's intention when we discuss the meaning of *Paradise Lost*.

But should we take it into account when we evaluate the poem? The question will hardly arise where the intention, as we have constructed it, is fulfilled, since a judgment on the poem will automatically also be a judgment on the intention. It is only where there is a discrepancy between the intention and the work that a problem presents itself.

In ordinary life, discrepancies between intentions and, for example, the tone in which they are announced, or the behaviour that follows the announcement, can be regarded in two ways. When, for example, a visitor repeatedly refuses a drink, but in an uncertain voice, and when he is clearly unhappy that his refusal is accepted, we may either pass a moral judgment ("Slightly disingenuous in his refusal") or we may make a psychological statement ("Obviously he was inhibited, afraid of seeming greedy, etc."): and both interpretations of his behaviour are given as *explanations*. The moral judgment is explanatory in a very restricted sense; perhaps it implies that he is simply the sort of person who will behave in that kind of way; at all events, however, it is incapable of further analysis or explanation in moral terms. On the other hand, psychological explanations are never final: there always remains the probability that further and further causes may be discovered if new evidence comes to light. A psychological explanation is sufficient when it has used up all the available data, and (clinically) when it has produced the result we want; it is never more than a working hypothesis.

Faced with a work in which there is a radical inconsistency, we may, on the one hand, merely point out that there is one; but to base a literary judgment on this alone is not so easy. On what principle do we distinguish between different degrees and kinds of discrepancy? Why should we be harder (or why should we not be harder) on *David Copperfield* than on *Measure for Measure?* But we can go beyond merely pointing out discrepancies: we can try to account for them, either in moral or in psychological terms. Pope's *Essay on Man* provides a good example of a poem ruined by an inner contradiction. The poet is committed to telling us about an orderly universe, inhabited by men whose motives can be reduced to a simple scheme, who are middling creatures in a middle state, and whose golden rule should be to follow the mean; yet at the least excuse the poet produces images of chaos, cataclysm, lawless multiplicity, and extremes of every kind: and these are infinitely better done and more memorable than his descriptions of the universe as it is, or of man as he ought to be. The moralising commentator can say that Pope in some deep sense did not believe in Bolingbroke's theory, and was deceiving himself; the psychologiser might argue that Pope needed to attach himself to a system to which he was emotionally averse—a contention which could be supported or refuted with the help of Pope's correspondence, his alterations to the *Essay*, and any other information we may have about his life and opinions. Both approaches involve the assumption that we *can* talk about his intention, though not always the necessity of constructing it.

The moral appraisals I have mentioned have all been in terms of honesty: for the simple reason that this is the appropriate moral concept for explaining consistency. But other, related, terms can be used: such as sincerity—a word which modern critics do not much like. It has probably fallen into disrepute because it is too easy to use with reference to the author's practical, rather than his literary, intention; if the poet's biographer could show that he did not love the mistress to whom he addressed his verses, it was sometimes thought that these were necessarily insincere. As messages to his mistress, doubtless they were; as poems, they may not have been. When we say that a poem, as a poem, is sincere, we are commenting on a peculiar congruity of its tone and its matter, for which I know no other name. But because this usually implies a particular kind of tone, that tone, too, is called "sincere"; and sincerity can be faked, simply by the adoption of a sincere tone. As well as describing a tone, and being a moral term, "sincere" has stronger psychological implications than "honest." It is therefore a dangerous, but also a very useful word. Just such a word seems to me to be required in criticising, for instance, *Jane Eyre,* where something so clearly goes wrong in the last twelve chapters. The tone changes; the moral judgments become less clear; events happen arbitrarily; issues are blurred; the style slackens. We can say that there has been a falling off in sincerity, by which we mean, both that Charlotte Brontë shirked the implications of what she had been saying, and that we blame her for this evasion.

Whether we prefer to make psychological or moral statements will largely depend on our general preconceptions, and on the kind of criticism we are trying to produce. To pass judgments, the psychologiser must of course go beyond purely psychological statements; but his value-judgments will surely differ from the moraliser's: for example, he may applaud health and deplore unhealthiness (it is often unclear whether he deplores it *per se* or as a cause of unhealthiness in others), or he may use the sociologist's value-judgments of "life-affirming" and "life-denying."

One device by which psychologisers have attempted to account for difficulties in works of art, such as discrepancies between the avowed intention and the achievement, is the concept of "subconscious intention." Whatever the philosophical respectability of this concept may be, it does make some sense, in ordinary life, to suppose the existence of such a thing. We know that people do things "accidentally on purpose"; odd behaviour, which we cannot satisfactorily explain by reference to conscious motivation, is conveniently explained in terms of subconscious motives, or even subconscious intentions. But even if we believe that our behaviour is largely governed by such, we are not at liberty to start looking for them in isolated pieces of *normal* conduct in persons about whom we know nothing; or, for that matter, in works of literature which can be quite adequately explained without recourse to such a hypothesis, which is, after all, incapable of any degree of verification without far more information than we possess about most authors. Where nothing has gone wrong, we cannot know what was consciously, what subconsciously intended: we cannot give an explanation designed to explain inconsistencies where there are none. And even where something has clearly gone wrong, as for example, in *Paradise Lost,* a hypothesis which does not involve the subconscious will be more economical, and more easily verifiable. That Milton should write about Satan as if he sympathised with him, and that he should make God tedious and severe, can surely be explained in terms of Milton's consciously held beliefs and attitudes; and even if we hazard a shrewd guess as to the subconscious roots of these attitudes, we shall not thereby be saying anything about his "subconscious intention" in writing *Paradise Lost*.

On another view, however, the subconscious, or unconscious is not merely invoked to explain neurotic behaviour, but is thought of as the *discoverable* source of all behaviour and of all art. A practical consequence of the assumption that it is always discoverable (even in the work of artists about whose lives nothing is known) is that there must be a universally valid set of rules by which the products of conscious action (e.g. works of art) can be related to their origins in the unconscious. A particular pattern, or a particular image, will always be said to have the same meaning in the unconscious, however little the artist may be aware of it. Now if this meaning is *inevitably* present, whether or not the artist was aware of it, and irrespective of anything he may have actively wished to say, then clearly this meaning is in no sense "intended." At the same time, such unconscious meanings are public, in the sense that they are accessible to everybody, even though our conscious minds may fail to see them. We are left with the curious conclusion that the "unconscious meaning" of a symbol is rather like the dictionary meaning of a word: we can look up our book of archetypal patterns to know what it is.

The real objection to such a hypothesis is not that it is incapable of proof, but that it always carries with it the implication that these unintended public meanings, of which we are not consciously aware, are in some sense the true, the most important, meanings of a work. We have already seen that there is a sense in which we can admit the existence of unintended strong meanings, as when a work is given a new significance by changed historical circumstances. That is how Shakespeare's plays can be given different "interpretations" by different ages. But we are always aware that these strong meanings *are* independent of the author's intentions; we would never say that such a meaning is the "true" or the primary one.

IV

We have argued that the concept of intention need not involve us in circular reasoning, provided we always remember how we arrived at our hypothesis about any particular intention. By differentiating practical and literary intention, we have distinguished between a sense which cannot be directly relevant to critical judgments, and a sense which can: both kinds can be indirectly useful, by allowing us to limit the meaning of a work. It is possible to construct a literary intention with certain kinds of work, particularly those which are evidently the result of planning; and this intention becomes of interest to the critic when something has gone wrong with such a work.

In short, we need not be afraid of the word "intention." We can use it, and yet treat the poem as something objectively existing. When we find ourselves writing "The poet intended . . ." we need not automatically blush and reach for the eraser.

H. S. Eveling

COMPOSITION AND CRITICISM*

Literary scholars spend a great deal of time trying to establish who wrote what, to whom (if anyone), when, in what circumstances, and so on. They try to arrive at an accurate presentation of the author's final text and attach lengthy footnotes glossing some of the more difficult terms and giving earlier versions of the same text. Clearly the main point of such activity is to make the text available to the common reader and critic for interpretation and evaluation. Equally clearly no critic would want to deny the importance of much of what the scholar provides. Presumably he would like to know what Shakespeare really did write in the disputed description of Falstaff's death in *Henry V* and presumably the discovery of a letter by the author himself on this subject would settle the issue. According to many modern critics and philosophers, however, there are certain limits to what the scholar may produce as determining, in an authoritative way, the meaning and interpretation of a particular text. Beyond a certain point the poem must speak for itself, and this point is reached, so they say, when we come to information about the author himself or comments by the author on the way in which his work is to be read. For purposes of literary criticism a work may be treated as anonymous and in cases of doubt or disagreement what would normally be considered a decisive step, that of consulting the author himself or, if this is

* From *Proceedings of the Aristotelian Society*, Vol. LIX, 1958–59, pp. 213–232. Reprinted by permission of the author and of the Editor of the Aristotelian Society.

not possible, letters or other sources of information as to what he may have had in mind or may have meant, is not considered decisive in this case. Neither the author nor his ghost shadows the work, nor does he stand in any privileged position with respect to what he writes, apart, presumably, from the fact that he managed to write it. If this view is correct it ought to throw some light on the logical character of the kind of writing of which it is true and, with this in mind, I want to examine some of the reasons that may be or have been suggested in its favour.

Of course, this putative anonymity of certain forms of literature may only be an instance of a feature shared by anything with a claim to be considered a work of art and it is more than likely that other uses of language prohibit an appeal to the person or persons originating what is said or written. It is surely true of the interpretation of law, and a less austere example would be the case of bidding in a Bridge contract. However, I shall resist the temptation to look for a single explanation to cover these diverse examples, although I do want to begin by considering whether the mere fact of a poem or play having a title to be considered a work of art confers upon it a certain independence of its author.

Mr. Henry Moore is reported to have said recently, in reply to a question about one of his sculptures, that it means whatever anyone thinks it means. This appears to solve the problem of interpretation by denying that there is anything to interpret, for if something "means" whatever we think it means then it means nothing at all, except, perhaps, in the sense in which something may have a personal significance for someone. Of course, part of the force and effectiveness of a particular work of art for a particular person may lie in certain incidental associations which it has for him but it seems odd to suppose that the sole point and significance of a work of art lies in its power to evoke responses of this kind. In any case, the work of art has to be recognised *as* something before it can achieve anything at all, and since this is so, we are still left with a question of recognition, which implies, or may imply, that problems of interpretation can arise. However, Moore may be saying that works of art lack the kind of intention-shadowed content which makes questions of interpretation appropriate. This view could be expressed by saying that there is no logical discontinuity between works of art, *objets trouvés* or, indeed, anything to which we apply aesthetic criteria. A work of art differs only in that it is *devised* for an aesthetic end. It is easy to see how such a theory might be used to justify or explain the practice of abstract art, at least of that form of it that is not to be taken as the distorted representation of an object or person, but is to be viewed as having as much or as little meaning as the pattern on a carpet or a coloured stone. It might be argued that this kind of work is, in a sense, *pure* art, that is, art which is *solely* devised for an aesthetic end. More traditional forms derive their status as aesthetic objects from precisely those features which they share with abstract presentations and they differ from these only in that they have been burdened with many other functions as well, some of which can now be performed as well or better in other ways. This is not to denigrate Munnings' horses, but any aesthetic merit such paintings may have, their claim to being works of art, is founded upon their claim to possess features which are possessed by works which Sir Alfred Munnings would not recognise as art at all.

One difficulty about this view is that it seems to suppose that to say of something that it has a pleasing, charming or beautiful shape or colour is to suppose that the shape or colour is beautiful *per se,* and not because it is a feature of this or that particular thing. Of course, shapes and colours may be pleasing when placed upon a canvas and having no obvious or arcane representational function, but then again, seen in this way, they may be tedious or positively unpleasant. This point may be obscured by the fact that the abstract artist may acquire the capacity to see objects as coloured masses in space and may come to regard those objects as pleasing which seem pleasing when seen in this way. But it does not follow that the same shape, when seen as the shape of this or that particular thing, is either pleasing because as an abstract shape it would be pleasing, or unpleasing because as an abstract composition, or considered in this light, it would be unpleasing. A woman with a certain shape may be pleasing to look at and a pot with a certain shape may also be pleasing to look at, but a pot with the shape of a woman, or worse, a woman with the shape of a pot, may not be pleasing to look at, and neither or either may be pleasing when viewed merely as shapes. Naturally none of this implies a condemnation of abstract art but it does show the possibility of criticising it in the way in which Salvador Dali or Wyndham Lewis have criticised it, for it is possible to go on to say that it is *merely* pleasing, charming or (more doubtfully) beautiful. It is not enough, that is, simply to say that aesthetic appreciation is concerned with the sensuous appearance of things, since it is intricately and intimately connected with a thousand other factors concerning our responses to and relationships with the objects and persons we appraise. Of course it is true that a knife is beautiful because of its shape and so on, but our response to its shape is conditioned by, or may be conditioned by, our sense of the way in which the shape reflects the object's function. Similarly, our appreciation of faces or portraits reflects, or may reflect, our awareness of the way in which the face or portrait expresses, visibly, a mood, a predicament, a character or a history.

Further than this, it seems reasonable to object to the argument's main premiss, namely that there is no logical discontinuity between works of art and anything else to which we apply aesthetic criteria. The force of this assumption is to restrict the range of epithets that may be legitimately applied to a work of art, as a work of art, to those epithets which are properly applied to non-interpretable objects. Yet it is clear that a whole complex of terms may be legitimately applied which would be out of place when referring to such objects. We do not think it correct to find stones, flowers or stars profound or moving, unless, that is, we see in them a hint of design, or take them to have the sort of significance that Wordsworth sometimes seemed to find in them. The point here is not that art has different functions which might be performed as well or better by something not claiming to be a work of art—although art does have these functions—but that the concept of a work of art is richer than a concept determined by a range of epithets appropriate to the aesthetic appraisal of natural phenomena.

If this is true of the visual arts it is even more obviously true of literature. Here it seems inevitable that questions of interpretation and meaning should arise. Still, words do have a physical dimension, and in poetry in particular, more than in any other use of language, the physical dimension of words is important, sufficiently important for it to be difficult to conceive of a poem where this aspect does not need to be considered. Nevertheless a similar point to the one made when considering the visual arts seems in order here. Clearly poems may differ in the degree to which they tolerate questions of meaning and significance, one end of the scale consisting of poems where the physical aspect of the verse is more important than any sense we may try to make of it. In this kind of

verse it may be that we have a piece of nonsense, or, higher on the
scale, it may be of the kind—Swinburne's or Dame Edith Sitwell's—
where a too close attention to the sense destroys the effectiveness of
the poem. In such verse it is rather as if there is an appearance of
sense which lulls our intellectual expectations while the flow of
the words achieves its effect. And if Empson[1] is right, this is the
best that can be said for the celebrated lines in *Tintern Abbey*, whose
emotional afflatus derives more from the mere occurrence of certain
intellectually weighted words, the gravity and insistence of the
verse, than from anything seriously and coherently said.

Here again, however, it would be a mistake to suppose that what
is true, or at best true, of certain poems indicates how we are to approach any poem at all. On the other hand this last point must not
be taken as asserting that in poems where a deliberately casual attitude to meaning would be out of place it is anything other than the
sensuous qualities of the verse that is, or may be, the major factor in
determining our appreciation of the work, any more, that is, than
denying that a painting or sculpture has to be regarded as an abstract
shape implies that our praise or condemnation is not directed towards its sensuous characteristics, although these are now to be
evaluated in the light of what it is understood to portray.

So far, then, there is no reason to suppose that to classify something as a work of art necessarily excludes the possibility of interpretation, although it has been recognised that certain works may be
treated in this way. Equally, nothing has been said to show any
significant connexion between the artist and what he produces. This
could only be shown if one regards interpretation itself in a certain
way, as, so to speak, a discovery of the true character of the entity
with which one has to deal. It may be, however, that interpretation
is itself creative, limited only by the sense which the words bear as
part of a common language. A critic of genius may impose his interpretation upon us but there is no necessity even about this. Interpretations may vary from person to person, age to age, they may
differ in subtle, slight or gross ways, and our only justification for
speaking of the same work is the fact that there is a common text
from which each interpretation is derived.

There is, I believe, a sense of "interpretation" in which the foregoing view does correspond to something we do when we approach

---

[1] *Seven Types of Ambiguity*, Ch. IV, pp. 151–153.

a work of art. Margaret Macdonald,[2] as evidence for the sort of view
outlined above, cites the fact that actors present characters in widely
different ways, that the language of Shakespeare differs widely from
the language as we now speak it, and that the background and circumstances of his Elizabethan audience were very different from
ours. Facts of this sort are supposed to support the conclusion that
different interpretations of a work are of equal validity, and indeed,
that a work of art, as she puts it, only exists in so far as an interpretation
has been given to it. But other facts, or alleged facts, are claimed
to be really clinching. It is argued that the only feasible alternative
to this is to suppose that a poem or play really expresses the state
of mind of the author, and that this is an absurd view to take since,
whatever one wants to say about works like *King Lear* or *Paradise
Lost*, it is at least certain that these are not to be taken as concerning
or in any way about the minds of Shakespeare or Milton. It is
claimed, and not merely by Margaret Macdonald in her article, that
to suppose that in establishing a definitive interpretation one is attempting to discover what went on in the author's mind, or what
the author meant, is to suppose that a work of art simply mirrors, or
is in some sense about, the author's state of mind.

But surely this is itself absurd. To ask someone what he meant
or what he had in mind when he said or wrote something is certainly,
in a way, to find out something about him, and perhaps what we find
out may be described as information about his state of mind, but
the point of asking is clearly not to discover *this* but how we are to
take what he has written or said; just as to find out what someone
meant to do we may ask him what he had in mind, but this does not
transform what he does into the physical reflection of a mental state;
whatever that may mean. Professor Passmore[3] does not argue in this
way but he does want to maintain that we need to know nothing of
what the author had in mind when writing his work. He is delighted
to concur with F. W. Leakey who argues, according to Passmore,
that when we have the poem, this is all we need, and to speak
of what is "intended" is simply to speak of how all the details of a
poem may be seen to fit together in the light of some theme. Pass-

---

[2] "Some Distinctive Features of Arguments Used in Criticism of the Arts."
Aesthetics and Language, edited by W. Elton.

[3] "Intentions," *Aristotelian Society, Supplementary Volume*, Vol. XXIX
(1955), pp. 141–143.

more's reason for adopting this view is that he thinks that this "model" of intention is the appropriate one to apply in the case of literature. The alternative, which he finds implausible, is to suppose that to read the intention one must have access to some kind of mental preamble to the act of writing, some kind of preliminary planning which has gone on before the work is completed. But one can agree with this, and go on to assert that in many cases no such planning ever takes place, without inferring that what has been written means anything other than what the author means by it. In speaking one's mind no kind of elaborate or brief rehearsal or en-visaging need take place and yet it would be absurd to suppose that what I say I mean, if I am asked, does not settle the issue once and for all; always assuming, of course, that I *can* mean, by what I said, what I say I mean.

It is an important fact about language and our understanding of its employment that words and sentences mean only in so far as *we* mean something by them, express what we mean in terms of them, and in the light of agreed conventions for their use. To understand the way in which language functions, therefore, is to understand, among other things, that words and sentences have a meaning only within a community of people and in relationship to their ways of dealing with and entering into association with other members of the same community. More than this, however, more than the fact that to understand what is meant on any given occasion we need to take into account not merely the speaker but the relationship in which he stands to his audience, we have to take into account the way in which what is meant, what we are to understand by what is said, is determined by the particular social setting within which the sentences are employed. It is not merely that in order to understand something we may need to know who said it, in reply to what, or against what background of events and attitudes to these events it is said (note, for example, the obscurity of the lines beginning "The mortal moon hath her eclipse endur'd," in Shakespeare's sonnet)[4] but also that what, in some circumstances, may be a simple and straightforward recital of facts may, in others, be a studied insult or a piece of immodest praise. And what, on one occasion, may be clear and unequivocal may, on another, seem confused, or may be delicately ambiguous, poised impolitely or ironically be-

---

[4] Sonnet No. 97. *The New Temple Shakespeare,* edited by M. R. Ridley.

tween one sense and another. The significance of a sentence, the way in which it carries its sense and the point with which it is used, understood in this way, is something that cannot be expressed simply but depends upon our ability to envisage the sentence in action in some circumstance or other. A sentence in action is a possibility realised within a milieu of tacit understandings, attitudes, actions and events, and to understand a given sentence is either to understand that sentence in its possibilities for employment or to grasp which, within a field of possibilities, is realised in a particular case. It is sometimes supposed that to give the meaning of a sentence it is enough to provide another sentence or set of words which are (in the circumstances) equivalent to it. Of course, we sometimes do this, but at least as often we explain what is meant by putting someone in the picture, by giving him certain information, by establishing, for the questioner, the setting within which the sentences take on life. No doubt as a statement of the *modus operandi* of language this is grossly oversimplified and it won't indeed cover certain of the ways in which language operates. There is a kind of scale of dependence against which language may, in some of its uses, be shown as deeply implicated in the circumstances of its use or, as in the extreme case of mathematics, standing aloof from the fortuitous and mundane settings within which less formal modes of expression exist.

However, if anything is certain about literature, and particularly poetry, it is that there we have language at its most fluent, concrete and localised. What the view outlined earlier seems to suggest is that we take language of this kind and in seeking to interpret it we consider it apart from the living situation within which one would expect it to be understood. It is not surprising, therefore, that competing interpretations should now be of equal validity, for we are left with the mere sentences on the page whose significance awaits and is only determined by whatever interpretation the critic finds he can put upon them. The poem is to be regarded as an autonomous entity, whose criterion of identity is determined solely by the words themselves, and not connected in any logically significant way with the person who wrote it nor the setting within which it is written. Indeed, once we detach the work in this way, it ceases to be of any significance whether the work has been incidentally composed by different authors at different times.

Perhaps the main difficulty of this view is that, although it appears to make sense of some of the things critics do, it is extremely difficult to make sense of what the author does. The effect of regarding literature, or even only some works of literature, in this light, is to present the poet as the mere cause or occasion of what is written, of a piece with Eddington's monkeys battering out Shakespeare's plays on a typewriter. But surely this is to see the situation from entirely the wrong way round, making the author the initiator of the critic's creative activity. And yet, when the critic finds a work ironic, witty, moving, solemn, intense, disturbing, passionate or obscure, he is surely not constructing the work in the act of examining it nor, as in the latter case, expressing his failure to achieve such a construction. The critic's vocabulary of elucidation and comment only makes sense in the light of sentences taken as having already an active function. To say that the critic determines the interpretation implies that the author writes as a man might write sentences on a blackboard, merely as sentences, writing, that is, which is neither ironic, grave, pointed nor anything else. Nor is the case that it is of no importance to the critic who wrote the work he is considering. A recent discussion illustrates this. Dr. Donald Davie,[5] reviewing Professor Frank Kermode's book *The Romantic Image*, argued that Kermode had placed too high a value on a poem by Yeats. He went on to say that the poem is a bad pastiche of early Blake and commented, among other things, upon the forced archaism of the inverted word orders. It was pointed out by Kermode that the poem is in fact by Blake, and *one* of the morals to be drawn from this is that it *is* important to locate the author, since this determines what kind of comment may be apt, felicitous, and so on. Miss Ruby Meager[6] has argued that if two persons wrote down a poem consisting of the same words we should have to say that they had written the same poem. I do not see that we *have* to say this at all. If such a situation did arise then I am more inclined to say that it would not be at all clear how we should want to describe the situation. The difficulty here is that there is not one criterion of identity and difference involved in the individuation of poems but that one individuating feature is that they are written by particular persons. The difficulty about

---

[5] *The Twentieth Century*, Vol. CLXII, Nos. 969, 970 (Nov. & Dec. 1957).
[6] *Aristotelian Society, Proceedings*, Vol. LIX (1958–59), pp. 57–58 *supra*.

the situation Miss Meager envisages is that there is a clash of criteria, one feature inclining us to say that it is one poem, the other, in virtue of the fact that it only becomes possible to make sense of poetry on the presumption of a particular author, inclining us to suppose that we ought to speak of two poems. When Empson[7] says of the lines "Bare ruined choirs where late the sweet birds sang" that they suggest ruined monastery choirs of the period, and so on, one may doubt whether he is correct in supposing that the lines are there to suggest this (and much else besides) but the fact that they may require to be taken in this way implies that the sentence is to be read as having an active function, a particular use. Empson, quite properly, attempts to justify his remarks by referring to the contemporary background and to the fact that many of the sonnets were addressed to a particular person. To suggest that the "same" poem might have been written by someone else can only mean that someone, similarly placed, *might* have used this sentence in this way. On the other hand, given a different author, the exegesis might have to be quite different.

Once we grant the obvious, therefore, namely that it is relevant to the interpretation of poetry and other forms of literature that it is written by particular people, sometimes for a particular occasion, sometimes concerning a particular person, and for a particular public, it is possible to make sense of a great deal of the actual practice of literary critics when they examine and evaluate a particular work. Much of their talk is talk *around* the poem or play, talk about the author, about the immediate circumstances associated with the writing of the work, and in the case of works of different and more or less remote periods, about the attitudes and general state of the society to which the author belongs. No doubt some critics have felt that what might be called "life and times" criticism is too remote and not obviously concerned with the actual elucidation of the text. No doubt it is often difficult to see what relevance certain information may have and no doubt, also, certain scholarly critics tend to become more interested in the background to interpretation than in the actual work. From the critic's point of view it is the work itself that counts, but then its elucidation is not merely a matter of staring at the actual words on the page, for how they are to be taken is disclosed in part by coming to see them as

---

[7] *Loc. cit.*, Ch. I, p. 2.

located in their appropriate setting. Talking around the poem, therefore, is itself a form of elucidation, although this is not to say that it does not require a great deal of insight into the complex allusiveness of language in order to make this kind of examination pay.

It would be equally improper, in rejecting an exaggerated picture of the isolation of a literary work, to go to the other extreme and assert that we understand nothing unless we see it in its full setting, or that all works are, to an equal degree, embedded in the circumstances of their writing. Some works do approximate to an ideal of isolation, and sometimes this is a function of the theme or subject matter. A poem may be concerned with this or that particular event—Dryden's *Annus Mirabilis*—with some particular person, or simply with the weather, or love, or failure, etc. Again, works may operate upon different levels and when, through ignorance or indifference, we ignore or do not take note of one level, we may assess the work at another level. This is not to say that we lose nothing by this, but sometimes what we lose cannot be saved anyway, and sometimes what is lost is what is least important. Thus, for instance, Swift's *Gulliver's Travels* operates upon at least two levels. It is, by means of its mock narrative, a satire upon certain contemporary absurdities, or what Swift regarded as absurdities, the differences between high and low Churchmen, for example, and the behaviour of certain mathematicians and scientists of the Royal Society. We lose something of its satirical force by not knowing this, for the appositeness of some of the situations depicted depends, at some points, upon taking their targets into account. But since it achieves its effect by means of a mock narrative, it has to succeed at that level too. Also it is a feature of the work, as of many others that survive the loss of contemporary relevance, that what is said concerning this or that event or situation it is appropriate to say about this *kind* of event or situation. What it is momentous or amusing to say about, for instance, a pompous concern over certain trivial issues it may be momentous or amusing to say about human pomposity in general. Hence it may be possible to consider a work in a way which ignores, in some measure, how it was originally meant to be taken, always providing the form that the work really has facilities this kind of treatment. Some works, of course, do not survive this kind of treatment. Sometimes their significance fades with the situation that initiated them or with the passing of the society within which they were created.

An audience or public, as I have been trying to indicate, is not a passive entity, and the brilliance of a work may be in the skill with which the author plays upon the public for whom he writes. Thus it is difficult to establish again the precise effect of Donne's use of sexual imagery in his religious verse. The extravagance of the gesture is lost. One can, perhaps, note that it is there but not respond to it. Similarly a work may exist within an agreed context of belief. Thus, in *Paradise Lost* it is not that Milton argues for or against a particular view of the world, but that his imagery presupposes such a view. It is pointless to argue with the poem but obviously not pointless to take into account the fact that it is a Puritan poem. We are not invited to suspend disbelief, nor to say that poetry is essentially disconnected from questions of truth or falsity, but rather that it presupposes a milieu as the condition for its assessment. In the absence of this milieu the status of the poem is impossible to define and it becomes an insoluble problem for criticism. Of course it is possible to take what else the poem has to offer, which is not to reinterpret the poem as an elaborate myth but to respond to the quality of the writing, the scenes and situations depicted in it, and so forth.

It may even be the case that conditions in society so change that a work which has appeared dead suddenly takes on life. This is not simply or solely a question of a change in taste, although it can be that. It is not merely that what was thought dull and bad is now seen to be miraculously good but that the language is now understood in a way in which it was difficult or impossible to understand against the background within which it has, up to this point, been interpreted. It is for this reason that with a kind of historical imagination or scholarly understanding we can at times reconstitute a work as a living expression. This kind of understanding is, naturally enough, very difficult to pass on. The blank wall of difference between two persons concerning the merits or otherwise of a certain poem need not be the ultimate difference, which is so popular among philosophers, between two sets of irreconcilable aesthetic attitudes; it may simply be that one understands what the other does not, that to one the sentences are seen as active and meaningful while to the other they remain merely sentences on the page. Here no amount of talk about the words themselves will achieve the required effect.

They are, one might say, agreed about the facts. What is required is something more elusive and difficult to describe, as elusive and difficult as it may be to describe what is required in order to grasp the meaning and significance of a religious ceremony to someone not himself used to participate.

It has still not been shown, however, that what an author says he meant *is* what he meant, determining how we are to take what he says, nor that in order to discover what a work is about we need to know that the author intended us to take it in the way in which we do take it. It might appear from what I have been saying that we do need to know this and that we have to accept what the author says as mandatory. But this is not so since all that follows from the preceding remarks is simply that in the case of some works, those written in past times, for a public other than ourselves, it may be necessary to acquire the sort of information which is presupposed by the act of communication which constitutes the poem. In some cases the best way, or the only way, in which one can place oneself in this position is to find out about the author and what he himself intended to say. It does not follow that a contemporary of the author needs to do this or to accept what the author meant to say as a definitive criterion of what he did say. This follows from the way in which a sentence or set of sentences carries its meaning in the conditions within which it is to be understood. The position is analogous to that in painting where, say, a painter may use live models in depicting a religious theme and where, nevertheless, this fact does not figure as a significant part of the completed work, although if the painting is meant to be viewed by those who can be expected to know this fact, it may figure in the significance of what is painted.

What a work means, therefore, is a function of the conditions within which it is to be read or viewed and nothing more is required of its public, by way of investigation, other than an examination of the work itself. There is thus a kind of asymmetry in criticism which creates the impression, either that nothing more is required for interpretation other than the work itself, or that the work cannot be understood unless a great deal of background information is obtained. In fact what is required depends upon the position from which the work is considered, either from a privileged, contemporary standpoint or from a position similar to that of the outsider overhearing a private conversation. It is not up to the author to say that what he has written expresses what he meant, and hence, whether what he writes *does* mean what he intended it to mean is not for him to decide. Thus Dr. Ian Gregor,[8] discussing D. H. Lawrence's short story *The Fox,* argues that critics have been misled into taking the achievement for the intention and have, therefore, read into the story a significance that it cannot properly sustain. In some cases, of course, it may be very difficult to decide whether a set of words do or do not carry the sense they are meant to have. For instance, it may be that after we have been unable to make anything of a particular philosophical text we are guided to an understanding of it by what the author or a sympathetic commentator says about it. And then we may be able to read the text with understanding and yet be dubious as to whether the author has managed to say what he exactly and minutely meant to say. It would, perhaps, be nearer to the truth to maintain that the author's remarks create a new set of conditions within which the work has to be read, but to say *this* is to admit that the work has failed within the circumstances within which it was meant to be read. However, even if it is agreed that there may be border-line cases, this should not be allowed to obscure the fact that in the vast majority of cases it must be possible to say that someone has or has not succeeded in saying what he meant to say, and that in the last resort it is not up to the author to decide the degree to which he has accomplished his aim.

However, Dr. Gregor seems to imply more than this, since he goes on to quote, with approval, some remarks of Dr. F. R. Leavis in which Leavis says: "Intentions in art are nothing except when realised . . . the tests of realisation are a matter of the critic's sense, derived from his literary experience, of what the living thing feels like—of the difference between that which has been willed and put there . . . and that which grows from a deep centre of life. These tests may well reveal that the deep animating intention is something very different from the intention the author would declare."

I have no very strong objection to the first part of these remarks; indeed, if I understand them correctly they summarise some of the things I have been trying to say earlier in the paper. The difficulty arises when we come to the phrase "that which has been willed and put there . . . and that which comes from a deep centre of life." It looks as if this antithesis corresponds to the antithesis which may

---

8 "The Fox—A Caveat," *Essays in Criticism,* Vol. IX (Jan. 1959).

exist between the author's declared intentions and what Leavis describes as "the deep animating intention." This invites us to read the expression "willed" as meaning "that which the author intended to say, or meant to say" and if this is "put there" it seems to follow that what the author meant to say he said. But then, how is this adversely contrasted with what "grows from a deep centre of life"? The difficulties multiply when we come to the last part of the quotation for here we learn that the "intention" which is deep and animating may conflict with what the author claims his intentions to be. The phrase "the intention the author would declare" suggests either that someone may know what I intend better than I know myself, which is inadmissible, or that Leavis does not mean by "intention" in the second part of the phrase what he means by it in the first part. But if he means something other than what is normally meant, what *does* he mean by it?

In ordinary circumstances we sometimes speak of someone as not really meaning what he says, or as speaking from no great conviction or in a manner which reveals or evinces no great concern. It is sometimes possible to detect those cases in which a person's sympathies or interests are engaged, from those in which he is merely lukewarm or feigning an interest, or even expressing what he believes to be a genuine concern though, from what he says and his manner of saying it, it is possible to see that his feelings are not actively engaged. What Leavis may be contrasting, therefore, when he speaks of that which comes from a deep centre of life and that which is merely willed and put there, is the poem or story which has this ring of authenticity about it as opposed to the work which conveys the impression of mechanical and unfelt contrivance. Now it may be the case, and possibly Leavis would want to say that it is the case, that a poem or work of art having this ring of conviction about it, cannot be fabricated; it may be that such works, as a matter of fact, do spring from a genuine concern. It does not follow, however, that they *have* to do so. It may be that those works which strike one as contrived and those which have the hall-mark of spontaneity and conviction upon them, are psychologically inexplicable except we equate the appearance with the reality, but the point is that nothing of importance as to the interpretation and evaluation of the work hangs upon whether this is so or not. In any case, whatever view one takes about this, it is clear that the artist occupies no special privileges concerning the question of how well he has succeeded in conveying his concern or an impression of concern. One must distinguish this case, however, one of really meaning or conveying the impression of really meaning what one says, from the case in which one succeeds (or fails) in saying what one means, where it is relevant to ask not "does he (really, in all sincerity) mean what he says?" but "does he mean this or that? how is what he says to be taken? has he managed to say what he means?" If someone, in this latter sense, fails to say what he means, then there is no sense in asking what he means by what is *actually* said; there is no further intention to which an appeal can be made. The speaker or author cannot fail in one sense to say what he means only to succeed triumphantly and unwittingly in another. In so far as he fails, what is said or written can only be interpreted as a guide or pointer to what he failed to say, or only to show what might have been meant by saying this. Poems, and kindred works, are in a more extreme position, in respect of this sort of failure, than other forms of expression. In the case of a certain sort of remark it may be extremely important to grasp what the speaker was trying to say: it may be, for example, that he is trying to warn us or convey an important piece of information. In poems, however, the interest lies, not in the attempt but, as Leavis remarks, in the accomplishment. There is a sense in which we are not interested in what the poet intended to say, and also a sense in which we are not interested in anything else.

A literary work is impersonal, not because it is open to us to take it in any way we please or because it is unimportant to decide who wrote it, but because it is, I have argued, a social act whose meaning is determined by the conditions within which it is to be read. This implies that whether or not the author has succeeded in expressing what he means to express is not something concerning which *his* judgment is final. This in turn implies that we must distinguish between, say, the expression of a mood or feeling in a lyric poem, and what is a merely personal expression of feeling. The former is difficult and the latter is not. The former is an act of communication and the latter merely gives vent to one's feelings, relieves one's feelings or manifests them. With the former it is possible to succeed or fail, but with the latter the question does not arise. In one way, there is nothing more expressive than a sigh, or a start, in another there is nothing less expressive. A lyric poem is not the extension of a sigh in print, but a totally different means of expression, as different as expressing one's enthusiasm and conveying it. Because this is so, it is important to consider a work of art against its appropriate setting, since without this there are no grounds for estimating its success or failure. To be moved by a poem is one thing, to be moved by an expression of feeling outside of poetry is another. In the latter one feels *for* the person, but with the former one is moved *by* the poem within which the feeling is expressed. Anything at all may be personally expressive and may be moving to others, providing they can establish the occasion and circumstances surrounding the expression of feeling. A word or a single sentence may be moving taken together with knowledge of the situation of the person who has uttered it, but such words or sentences do not compete in effectiveness with poetry, since nothing has been attempted and hence, there are no criteria for determining success or failure. It is for this reason, perhaps, that some critics have been chary of admitting certain sorts of information, particularly information concerning the author, since practically any work, and particularly poetry, can be made to seem interesting and expressive if viewed against such a background. It is important, therefore, to distinguish between the way in which background knowledge may enter into the interpretation and evaluation of literature and the way in which it may enter into our response to the non-literary expression of feeling, etc.

Hence, it is somewhat paradoxical to find critics both claiming that works of art are autonomous and yet trying to account for this by construing works of literature on the model of personal expressions of feeling. Certainly, when expressing feelings in either a verbal or non-verbal way, one may be unaware of what feelings are thereby expressed. It is possible, for example, to detect in what someone says, or in what he does, an unconscious vein of hostility.[9] In the Leavis remarks there is, I think, this hesitation between two ways of regarding works of art. The talk about what comes from a

----

[9] This raises a large number of questions which unfortunately can't be adequately discussed here. I take expressions of feeling to be something we do neither intentionally nor unintentionally—although we can deliberately conceal our feelings or pretend to feelings we don't have. I also think that there is a difference between telling or conveying to someone *that* one is angry, and expressing this anger *in* what one does and says. But the expression of feelings, emotions, etc., in poetry, is different from either of these, as the expression of feeling and emotion by an actor differs from the expression of feeling in normal cases. The former is an art, it merits or fails to merit applause, the latter is not, and does not.

deep centre of life, coupled with the suggestion that there may be
a difference between what the artist says is in the work and what is
really there, suggests that he may be thinking of literature as being
the expression, *i.e.*, the personal expression, of attitudes and feelings,
concerning which the artist may be right or wrong. But the suggestion that there may or must be a deeper intention—corresponding,
one would suppose, to what he really feels, and which really gets
into the work—suggests that he wants to treat literature as expressive in its proper sense. However, as I suggested, this notion of intention is inadmissible; but if one's practice seems to require that
one treat poetry in the appropriate way, and one's account of its
autonomy requires that one consider or describe it in another, one
would expect the outcome to be the introduction of a bogus notion
of a possibly unconscious intention.

It follows from what I have been saying that there could not be
an essentially *private* poem or literary work. Of course one can
write a poem without intending it to be published but one could
not write a poem which is not, necessarily, an act of communication,
one, that is, which does not require to be assessed in this way. It may
be argued, therefore, that some modern poetry is obscure in a new
way, not, that is, obscure in the way in which Donne and Hopkins
are obscure, but rather that it has an obscurity of status, in part the
result of an ill-defined relation between the author and those for
whom he writes. The reasons for this state of affairs need not be
discussed but the consequences are peculiar. It has resulted in a kind
of verse, for example, which seems to have the form and order of
words one gets in conducting a silent conversation with oneself,
with all the gaps, changes or apparent changes of theme which this
may have. But in so far as a work approximates to the status of a private act one is unable to determine whether what is said carries or
does not carry a certain sense. One must ask how one's private ru-
minations carry a sense, how questions of success or failure could
arise, whether it makes sense to say that one "inly ruminates" well or
badly. One might be inclined to think that talking to oneself is a
limiting case of talking to others, where, however, there is never
any question of one's failing to understand, where there is the odd
privilege of being certain of what one means. It is as if one were
conversing under ideal conditions, with no failure of communication
possible, since the listener is oneself. And yet we know quite well
that our thoughts may be confused, but to know this is to envisage

how we might try to communicate them to someone else, so that our internal musings take on the character of a mock performance or rehearsal for saying what we want to say. The final test of this, however, lies in the actual performance, not in the rehearsal, and then the conditions governing success or failure are determined in the usual public way. The idea, therefore, that words carry a sense is bound up with the idea of communication with others. Hence, the notion of a language from which this condition is excluded, a logically private language, is one in which saying what we mean, and therefore of words *having* a meaning, has no place, which entails that such a "language" would be no language at all. Whether this is so or not, there does seem to be something anomalous in the idea of a work of art which has the status of, or appears to have the status of, a meditative or otherwise private form, and this is so because we cannot say whether anything has been achieved or not.

The Moral and/or Social Properties of a Work of Art

INTRODUCTION

Many disputes about moral and/or social features of the arts turn on considerations discussed already as questions of meaning and intention. They are not simply disagreements about the presence or absence of the properties designated by these terms, and so a determination of their factual status will not resolve them. They are disagreements about whether it is true to say, even if the properties in question are assignable to any object, that they are therefore among the *aesthetic* properties of that object.

The fact that the El Greco *Cardinal de Guevera* is hung in the Metropolitan Museum is an undoubted property of that painting, but not a property of it *qua* work of art. That is to say, if asked to describe the artistic features of the *Cardinal de Guevera*, we would not include in our answer that it is hung in the Metropolitan Museum. We would refer instead to its use of color, design, perspective, etc. But what if we all agreed that the painting depicts a face so austere and self-righteous that it undoubtedly reflects El Greco's disapproval of the Cardinal? Should we then add this information to our description of the artistic features of the painting? To answer that question is to raise the issue of whether a moral trait is like the property of location or the property of design. We are being asked to decide whether a moral trait is also an aesthetic trait.

We could, further, read a book, detect in it a recognizable group of moral preferences, and connect them with the cultural features of the era in which the book was written. An obvious case is Sinclair Lewis' treatment of the bourgeois businessman in *Babbitt*. And though the evidence is at present indecisive, there is, in principle, no obstacle to ascertaining the moral effects of a work of art upon its audience. Of course, we must first identify the effect which *Babbitt*, for example, has upon its readers, and then evaluate it according to some generally agreed-upon notions of what it is that constitutes morally acceptable behavior. This leaves aside the question of how we arrive at or defend such canons of value. But assuming that a successful resolution of these inquiries gives us a knowledge of the moral effect of *Babbitt* upon its readers and the cultural traits of the twenties which it exhibits, the issue remains of whether they are legitimately included, along with such matters as characterization and narrative structure, among the aesthetic traits of the novel.

There are, of course, a host of technical questions that must be settled before any such decision. What is it that we do to determine the appropriate moral features of a work of art? Are we concerned, as in the case of Shakespeare's *Othello*, with the views expressed by any one or all of the characters about the proprieties of human conduct? Which one of the characters shall it be, Othello, Iago, or Desdemona? Or is the morality of the play something over and above what is said by any one of its speakers? Is it, for example, that Othello is brought to a bad end, and that it is wrong, therefore, to suspect one's wife of infidelity?

The last question is particularly difficult since it is not the same to provide a subject-matter for moral judgment as it is to make a moral judgment appropriate to that subject-matter. We may read in a newspaper of someone guilty of philandering and condemn him for it, but it is silly to think that the act of philandering itself expresses the judgment that subsequently condemns it. We may judge that Othello is brought to a bad end because he behaved as he did, but there is still the problem of whether it is the play or the reader that has judged him so. We may say of course that Shakespeare constructed the play in order to exhibit the moral weakness of Othello, but this simply reintroduces the question of whether it is relevant to invoke the intention of the playwright as a way of identifying the moral verdicts expressed in his plays.

Or we may investigate the morality of *Othello* in the light of its effect on its viewers or readers. This will be quite different from its morality in light of the view that it advocates or expresses about the nature of human behavior. Suppose that a minister urges us at every opportunity to attend the church of our choice on Sunday. We would have no difficulty in answering what it is that he thinks we should do on Sunday. But he may express himself so sanctimoniously, or on such inappropriate occasions, that his effect is to arouse in us a distinct disinclination to attend the church of our choice on Sunday. The *effect* of what he says, in this case, is quite different from what he *urges* or *advocates*. Consequently, the fact that a play appears to take a position on the verities of human conduct does not necessarily mean that its effect upon an audience is identical with the moral recommendations that it presumably endorses.

However these difficulties are resolved, what must be determined is whether the moral and/or social features of a painting or book or drama are a legitimate basis for construing their nature or evaluating their worth as works of art. In so doing, there are two questions that need to be distinguished. First, is it possible, and relevant, to take the moral message of a work of art into account in evaluating its aesthetic quality? Second, can the judgment of quality, in such a case, be itself a moral judgment? The latter question raises a problem to be discussed in the section, "The Nature and Uses of Critical Judgment"—that of the differences and/or similarities in the logical structure of moral and aesthetic judgments.

Jerome Frank

OBSCENITY AND THE LAW*

For a time, American courts adopted the test of obscenity contrived in 1868 by Cockburn, L.J., in Queen v. Hicklin: "I think the test of obscenity is this, whether the tendency of the matter charged as obscenity is to deprave and corrupt those whose minds are open to such immoral influences, and into whose hands a publication of this sort might fall." He added that the book there in question "would suggest . . . thoughts of a most impure and libidinous character."

The test in most federal courts has changed: They do not now speak of the thoughts of "those whose minds are open to . . . immoral influences" but, instead, of the thoughts of average adult normal men and women, determining what these thoughts are, not by proof at the trial, but by the standard of "the average conscience of the time," the current "social sense of what is right." Yet the courts still define obscenity in terms of the assumed average normal adult reader's sexual thoughts or desires or impulses, without reference to any relation between those "subjective" reactions and his subsequent conduct. The judicial opinions use such key phrases as this: "suggesting lewd thoughts and exciting sensual desires"; "arouse the salacity of the reader"; " 'allowing or implanting . . . obscene, lewd, or lascivious thoughts or desires' "; "arouse sexual desires." The judge's charge in the instant case reads accordingly: "It must

---

* Title supplied by editor. From 2 Cir., 237 F. 2d 796, *United States v. Roth.* By permission of West Publishing Co. Some footnotes and case citations are omitted.

tend to stir sexual impulses and lead to sexually impure thoughts." Thus the statute, as the courts construe it, appears to provide criminal punishment for inducing no more than thoughts, feelings, desires.

No Adequate Knowledge Is Available Concerning the Effects on the Conduct of Normal Adults of Reading or Seeing the "Obscene"

Suppose we assume, *arguendo*, that sexual thoughts or feelings, stirred by the "obscene," probably will often issue into overt conduct. Still it does not at all follow that that conduct will be anti-social. For no sane person can believe it socially harmful if sexual desires lead to normal, and not anti-social, sexual behavior since, without such behavior, the human race would soon disappear.

Doubtless, Congress could validly provide punishment for mailing any publications if there were some moderately substantial reliable data showing that reading or seeing those publications probably conduces to seriously harmful sexual conduct on the part of normal adult human beings. But we have no such data.

Suppose it argued that whatever excites sexual longings might *possibly* produce sexual misconduct. That cannot suffice: Notoriously, perfumes sometimes act as aphrodisiacs, yet no one will suggest that therefore Congress may constitutionally legislate punishment for mailing perfumes. It may be that among the stimuli to irregular sexual conduct, by normal men and women, may be almost anything—the odor of carnations or cheese, the sight of a cane or a candle or a shoe, the touch of silk or a gunny-sack. For all anyone now knows, stimuli of that sort may be far more provocative of such misconduct than reading obscene books or seeing obscene pictures. Said John Milton, "Evil manners are as perfectly learnt, without books, a thousand other ways that cannot be stopped."

Effect of "Obscenity" on Adult Conduct

To date there exist, I think, no thorough-going studies by competent persons which justify the conclusion that normal adults' reading or seeing of the "obscene" probably induces anti-social conduct. Such competent studies as have been made do conclude that so complex and numerous are the causes of sexual vice that it is impossible to assert with any assurance that "obscenity" represents a ponderable causal factor in sexually deviant adult behavior. "Although the whole subject of obscenity censorship hinges upon the unproved assumption that 'obscene' literature is a significant factor in causing sexual deviation from the community standard, no report can be found of a single effort at genuine research to test this assumption by singling out as a factor for study the effect of sex literature upon sexual behavior."[1] What little competent research has been done, points definitely in a direction precisely opposite to that assumption.

Alpert reports[2] that, when, in the 1920s, 409 women college graduates were asked to state in writing what things stimulated them sexually, they answered thus: 218 said "Man"; 95 said books; 40 said drama; 29 said dancing; 18 said pictures; 9 said music. Of those who replied "that the source of their sex information came from books, not one specified a 'dirty' book as the source. Instead, the books listed were: The Bible, the dictionary, the encyclopedia, novels from Dickens to Henry James, circulars about venereal diseases, medical books, and Motley's Rise of the Dutch Republic." Macaulay, replying to advocates of the suppression of obscene books, said: "We find it difficult to believe that in a world so full of temptations as this, any gentleman whose life would have been virtuous if he had not read Aristophanes or Juvenal, will be vicious by reading them." Echoing Macaulay, "Jimmy" Walker remarked that he had never heard of a woman seduced by a book. New Mexico has never had an obscenity statute; there is no evidence that, in that state, sexual misconduct is proportionately greater than elsewhere.

Effect on Conduct of Young People

Most federal courts (as above noted) now hold that the test of obscenity is the effect on the "mind" of the average normal adult, that effect being determined by the "average conscience of the time," the current "sense of what is right"; and that the statute does

---

[1] Lockhart and McClure, "Obscenity and the Courts," 20 L. & Contemp.P. (1955) 587, 595.

[2] See Alpert, "Judicial Censorship and the Press," 52 Harv.L.Rev. (1938) 40, 72.

not intend "to reduce our treatment of sex to the standard of a child's library in the supposed interest of a salacious few."

However, there is much pressure for legislation, designed to prevent juvenile delinquency, which will single out children, i. e., will prohibit the sale to young persons of "obscenity" or other designated matter. That problem does not present itself here, since the federal statute is not thus limited. The trial judge in his charge in the instant case told the jury that the "test" under that statute is not the effect of the mailed matter on "those comprising a particular segment of the community," the "young" or "the immature."

Therefore a discussion of such a children's protective statute is irrelevant here. But, since Judge Clark does discuss the alleged linkage of obscenity to juvenile delinquency, and since it may perhaps be thought that it has some bearing on the question of the effect of obscenity on adult conduct, I too shall discuss it.

The following is a recent summary of studies of that subject: [3] "(1) Scientific studies of juvenile delinquency demonstrate that those who get into trouble, and are the greatest concern of the advocates of censorship, are far less inclined to read than those who do not become delinquent. The delinquents are generally the adventurous type, who have little use for reading and other nonactive entertainment. Thus, even assuming that reading sometimes has an adverse effect upon moral behavior, the effect is not likely to be substantial, for those who are susceptible seldom read. (2) Sheldon and Eleanor Glueck, who are among the country's leading authorities on the treatment and causes of juvenile delinquency, have recently published the results of a ten-year study of its causes. They exhaustively studied approximately 90 factors and influences that might lead to or explain juvenile delinquency; but the Gluecks gave no consideration to the type of reading material, if any were read by the delinquents. This is, of course, consistent with their finding that delinquents read very little. When those who know so much about the problem of delinquency among youth—the very group about whom the advocates of censorship are most concerned —conclude that what delinquents read has so little effect upon their conduct that it is not worth investigating in an exhaustive study of

---

[3] Lockhart and McClure, "Literature, the Law of Obscenity and the Constitution," 38 Minn.L.Rev. (1954) 295, 385–386.

Perhaps some of the reasoning of this summary is a bit too sweeping. For a more cautious summary, see the Jahoda report, discussed infra.

causes, there is good reason for serious doubts concerning the basic hypothesis on which obscenity censorship is dependent. (3) The many other influences in society that stimulate sexual desire are so much more frequent in their influence and so much more potent in their effect that the influence of reading is likely, at most, to be relatively insignificant in the composite of forces that lead an individual into conduct deviating from the community sex standards. . . . And the studies demonstrating that sex knowledge seldom results from reading indicates the relative unimportance of literature in sexual thoughts and behavior as compared with other factors in society."[4]

---

[4] Novick, Superintendent of the New York Training School for Girls, writes: "In the public eye today juvenile delinquency is alternately the direct result of progressive education, horror comics, T.V. programs, and other pet peeves of our present society . . . This is not a new phenomenon. Each generation of adults has been concerned about the behavior of its children and has looked for a scapegoat on which to place the blame for its delinquency. At the same time, adults have always sought a panacea which would cure the problem. It is sufficient to note that delinquency has always risen during periods of stress and strain, and the era in which we are living is no exception . . . Neither do restrictive measures such as . . . censorship of reading matter . . . prevent delinquency. They merely have an effect upon the manner in which the delinquency will be expressed." Novick, "Integrating the Delinquent and His Community," 20 Fed.Probation (1956) 38, 40.

Charles Lamb (whose concern with children he manifested in his *Tales from Shakespeare*) had no belief that uncensored reading harmed children: In his *Essays of Elia* he wrote of the education of his cousin Bridget, "She was tumbled early into a spacious closet of good old English reading" (which included Elizabethan and Restoration dramas and 18th century novels) "without much selection or prohibition and browsed at will upon that fair and wholesome pasturage. Had I twenty girls, they should be brought up exactly in this fashion."

Judge Curtis Bok, perhaps remembering Lamb's remarks, said of the publications before him in Commonwealth v. Gordon, 1949, 66 Pa.Dist. & Co.R. 101: "It will be asked whether one would care to have one's young daughter read these books. I suppose that by the time she is old enough to wish to read them she will have learned the biologic facts of life and the words that go with them. There is something seriously wrong at home if those facts have not been met and faced and sorted by them; it is not children so much as parents that should receive our concern about this. I should prefer that my own three daughters meet the facts of life and the literature of the world in my library than behind a neighbor's barn, for I can face the adversary there directly. If the young ladies are appalled by what they read, they can close the book at the bottom of page one; if they read further, they will learn what is in the world and in its people, and no parents who have been discerning with their children need fear the outcome. Nor can they hold it back, for life is a series of little battles and minor issues, and the burden of choice is on us all, every day, young and old. Our daughters must live in the world and decide what sort of women they are to be, and we should be willing to

Judge Clark, however, speaks of "the strongly held views of those
with competence in the premises as to the very direct connection"
of obscenity "with the development of juvenile delinquency." He
cites and quotes from a recent opinion of the New York Court of
Appeals and an article by Judge Vanderbilt, which in turn, cite the
writings of persons thus described by Judge Clark as "those with
competence in the premises." One of the cited writings is a report,
by Dr. Jahoda and associates, entitled *The Impact of Literature: A
Psychological Discussion of Some Assumptions in the Censorship
Debate* (1954).[5] I have read this report (which is a careful survey
of all available studies and psychological theories). I think it expresses an attitude quite contrary to that indicated by Judge Clark.
In order to avoid any possible bias in my interpretation of that
report, I thought it well to ask Dr. Jahoda to write her own summary of it, which, with her permission, I shall quote. (In doing so,
I am following the example of Mr. Justice Jackson who, in Federal
Trade Commission v. Ruberoid Co., acknowledged that he relied
on "an unpublished treatise," i. e., one not available to the parties. If
that practice is proper, I think it similarly proper to quote an
author's unpublished interpretation of a published treatise.) Dr.
Jahoda's summary reads as follows:

> Persons who argue for increased censorship of printed matter
> often operate on the assumption that reading about sexual matters or
> about violence and brutality leads to anti-social actions, particularly
> to juvenile delinquency. An examination of the pertinent psycho-
> logical literature has led to the following conclusions:
>   1. There exists no research evidence either to prove or to dis-
> prove this assumption definitively.
>   2. In the absence of scientific proof two lines of psychological ap-
> proach to the examination of the assumption are possible: (a) a re-

prefer their deliberate and informed choice of decency rather than an innocence that continues to spring from ignorance. If that choice be made in the
open sunlight, it is more apt than when made in shadow to fall on the side
of honorable behavior."
   [5] Cited in a passage in Brown v. Kingsley Books, Inc., 1 N.Y.2d 177, 151,
N.Y.S.2d 639, 134 N.E.2d 461, quoted by Judge Clark. Judge Clark cites and
quotes from this opinion only in connection with his statement of our
judicial "lack of knowledge of the social bearing of this problem." However,
his quotation from that New York opinion cites the Jahoda report, and I
therefore assume that Judge Clark intended to include Dr. Jahoda among
"those with competence in the premises."

view of what is known on the causes of juvenile delinquency; and (b) review of what is known about the effect of literature on the mind of the reader.

3. In the vast research literature on the causes of juvenile delinquency there is no evidence to justify the assumption that reading about sexual matters or about violence leads to delinquent acts. Experts on juvenile delinquency agree that it has no single cause. Most of them regard early childhood events, which precede the reading age, as a necessary condition for later delinquency. At a later age, the nature of personal relations is assumed to have much greater power in determining a delinquent career than the vicarious experiences provided by reading matter. Juvenile delinquents as a group read less, and less easily, than non-delinquents. Individual instances are reported in which so-called "good" books allegedly influenced a delinquent in the manner in which "bad" books are assumed to influence him.

Where childhood experiences and subsequent events have combined to make delinquency psychologically likely, reading could have one of two effects: it could serve a trigger function releasing the criminal act or it could provide for a substitute outlet of aggression in fantasy, dispensing with the need for criminal action. There is no empirical evidence in either direction.

4. With regard to the impact of literature on the mind of the reader, it must be pointed out that there is a vast overlap in content between all media of mass communication. The daily press, television, radio, movies, books and comics all present their share of so-called "bad" material, some with great realism as reports of actual events, some in clearly fictionalized form. It is virtually impossible to isolate the impact of one of these media on a population exposed to all of them. Some evidence suggests that the particular communications which arrest the attention of an individual are in good part a matter of choice. As a rule, people do not expose themselves to everything that is offered, but only to what agrees with their inclinations.

Children, who have often not yet crystallized their preferences and have more unspecific curiosity than many adults, are therefore perhaps more open to accidental influences from literature. This may present a danger to youngsters who are insecure or maladjusted who find in reading (of "bad" books as well as of "good" books) an escape from reality which they do not dare face. Needs which are not met in the real world are gratified in a fantasy world. It is likely, though not fully demonstrated, that excessive reading of comic books will intensify in children those qualities which drove them to the comic book world to begin with: an inability to face the world, apathy, a belief that the individual is hopelessly impotent and driven by uncontrollable forces and, hence, an acceptance of violence and brutality in the real world.

It should be noted that insofar as causal sequence is implied, insecurity and maladjustment in a child must precede this exposure to the written word in order to lead to these potential effects. Unfortunately, perhaps, the reading of Shakespeare's tragedies or of Andersen's and Grimm's fairy tales might do much the same.

Most of the current discussion of the relation between children's reading and juvenile delinquency has to do with so-called "comic books" which center on violence (sometimes coupled with sex) rather than mere obscenity. Judge Vanderbilt, in an article from which Judge Clark quotes, cites Feder, *Comic Book Regulation* (University of California, Bureau of Public Administration, 1955 Legislative Problems No. 2).[6] Feder writes: "It has never been determined definitely whether or not comics portraying violence, crime and horror are a cause of juvenile delinquency."

Judge Vanderbilt, in the article from which Judge Clark quotes, also cites Wertham, *Seduction of the Innocent* (1954).[7] Dr. Wertham is the foremost proponent of the view that "comic books" do contribute to juvenile delinquency. The Jahoda report takes issues with Dr. Wertham, who relies much on a variety of the *post-hoc-ergo-propter-hoc* variety of argument, i. e., youths who had read "comic books" became delinquents. The argument, at best, proves too much: Dr. Wertham points to the millions of young readers of such books; but only a fraction of these readers become delinquents. Many of the latter also chew gum, drink Coca-Cola, and wear soft-soled shoes. Moreover, Dr. Wertham specifically says (p. 298) that he is little concerned with allegedly obscene publications designed for reading by adults, and (pp. 303, 316, 348) that the legislation which he advocates would do no more than forbid the sale or display of "comic books" to minors. As previously noted, the federal obscenity statute is not so restricted.

Maybe some day we will have enough reliable data to show that obscene books and pictures do tend to influence children's sexual conduct adversely. Then a federal statute could be enacted which

---

[6] Vanderbilt, "Impasse in Justice," Wash.U.L.Q. (1956), 267, 302.
[7] *Ibid.*

would avoid constitutional defects by authorizing punishment for using the mails or interstate shipments in the sale of such books and pictures to children.

It is, however, not at all clear that children would be ignorant, in any considerable measure, of obscenity, if no obscene publications ever came into their hands. Youngsters get a vast deal of education in sexual smut from companions of their own age.[8] A verbatim report of conversations among young teen-age boys (from average respectable homes) will disclose their amazing proficiency in obscene language, learned from other boys.[9] Replying to the argument of the need for censorship to protect the young Milton said: "Who shall regulate all the . . . conversation of our youth . . . appoint what shall be discussed . . . ?" Most judges who reject that view are long past their youth and have probably forgotten the conversational ways of that period of life: "I remember when I was a little boy," said Mr. Dooley, "but I don't remember how I was a little boy."

---

[8] Alpert (*loc. cit.* at 74) writes of the American Youth Commission study of the conditions and attitudes of young people in Maryland between the ages of sixteen and twenty-four, as reported in 1938: "For this study Maryland was deliberately picked as a 'typical' state, and, according to the Commission, the 13,528 young people personally interviewed in Maryland can speak for the two hundred and fifty thousand young people in Maryland and the twenty millions in the United States. 'The chief source of sex "education" for the youth of all ages and all religious groups was found to be the youth's contemporaries.' Sixty-six percent of the boys and forty percent of the girls reported that what they knew about sex was more or less limited to what their friends of their own age had told them. After 'contemporaries' and the youth's home, the source that is next in importance is the school, from which about 8 percent of the young people reported they had received most of their sex information. A few, about 4 percent, reported they owed most to books, while less than 1 percent asserted that they had acquired most of their information from movies. Exactly the same proportion specified the church as the chief source of their sex information. These statistical results are not offered as conclusive; but that they do more than cast doubt upon the assertion that 'immoral' books corrupt and deprave must be admitted. These statistical results placed in the scale against the weight of the dogma upon which the law is founded lift the counterpane high. Add this: that 'evil manners' are as easily acquired without books as with books; that crowded slums, machine labor, barren lives, starved emotions, and unreasoning minds are far more dangerous to morals than any so-called obscene literature. True, this attack is tangential, but a social problem is here involved, and the weight of this approach should be felt."

[9] For such a report, slightly expurgated for adult readers, see Cleckley, *The Mask of Sanity* (1950) 135-137.

The Obscenity Statute and the Reputable Press

Let it be assumed, for the sake of the argument, that contemplation of published matter dealing with sex has a significant impact on children's conduct. On that assumption, we cannot overlook the fact that our most reputable newspapers and periodicals carry advertisements and photographs displaying women in what decidedly are sexually alluring postures,[10] and at times emphasizing the importance of "sex appeal." That women are there shown scantily clad, increases "the mystery and allure of the bodies that are hidden," writes an eminent psychiatrist. "A leg covered by a silk stocking is much more attractive than a naked one; a bosom pushed into shape by a brassiere is more alluring than the pendant realities."[11] Either, then, the statute must be sternly applied to prevent the mailing of many reputable newspapers and periodicals containing such ads and photographs, or else we must acknowledge that they have created a cultural atmosphere for children in which, at a maximum, only the most trifling additional effect can be imputed to children's perusal of the kind of matter mailed by the defendant.

The Obscenity Statute and the Newspapers

Because of the contrary views of many competent persons, one may well be sceptical about Dr. Wertham's thesis. However, let us see what, logically, his crusade would do to the daily press: After referring repeatedly to the descriptions, in "comic books" and other "mass media," of violence combined with sadistic sexual behavior, descriptions which he says contribute to juvenile delinquency, he writes, "Juvenile delinquency reflects the social values current in a society. Both adults and children absorb these social values in their daily lives . . . and also in *all the communications through the mass*

---

[10] Cf. Larrabee, "The Cultural Context of Sex Censorship," 20 L. & Contemp.Prob. (1955) 672, 684.

[11] Myerson, *Speaking of Man* (1950) 92. See also the well known chapter on clothes in Anatole France's *Penguin Island*.

Dr. Wertham discussing "comic books," makes much of the advertisements they carry. He speaks of their "breast ads," and also of their playing up of "glamour girls," their stress on the "sexy," their emphasis on women's "secondary sexual characteristics." Is not this also descriptive of the advertisements in our "best periodicals"?

media . . . Juvenile delinquency holds up a mirror to society . . . It is self-understood that such a pattern in a mass medium does not come from nothing . . . Comic books are not the disease, they are only a symptom . . . The same social forces that made comic books make other social evils, and the same social forces that keep comic crime books keep the other social evils the way they are." (Emphasis added.)

Now the daily newspapers, especially those with immense circulations, constitute an important part of the "mass media"; and each copy of a newspaper sells for much less than a "comic book." Virtually all the sorts of descriptions, of sex mingled with violence, which Dr. Wertham finds in the "comic books," can be found, often accompanied by gruesome photographs, in those daily journals. Even a newspaper which is considered unusually respectable, published prominently on its first page, on August 26, 1956, a true story of a "badly decomposed body" of a 24 year old woman school teacher, found in a clump of trees. The story reported that police had quoted a 29 year old salesman as saying that "he drove to the area" with the school teacher, that "the two had relations on the ground, and later got into an argument," after which he "struck her three times on the back of the head with a rock, and, leaving her there, drove away." Although today no one can so prove, one may suspect that such stories of sex and violence in the daily press have more impact on young readers than do those in the "comic books," since the daily press reports reality while the "comic books" largely confine themselves to avowed fiction or fantasy.[12] Yet Dr. Wertham, and most others who propose legislation to curb the sale of "comic books" to children, propose that it should not extend to newspapers.[13] Why not?

The question is relevant in reference to the application of the obscenity statute: Are our prosecutors ready to prosecute reputable newspaper publishers under that Act? I think not. I do not at all urge such prosecutions. I do suggest that the validity of that statute

---

[12] It is arguable that the fact that a publication is regarded by the reader as "pornography" influences its impact on him. No relevant reliable data, however, is available.

[13] "No one would dare ask of a newspaper that it observe the same restraints that are constantly being demanded of . . . the comic book." Larrabee, "The Cultural Context of Sex Censorship, 20 Law & Contemp.Problems (1955) 673, 679.

has not been vigorously challenged because it has not been applied
to important persons like those publishers but, instead, has been enforced principally against relatively inconspicuous men like the
defendant here.

Da Capo: Available Data Seem Wholly Insufficient to Show That the Obscenity Statutes Come Within Any Exception to the First Amendment

I repeat that, because that statute is not restricted to obscene
publications mailed for sale to minors, its validity should be tested
in terms of the evil effects of adult reading of obscenity on adult
conduct.[14] With the present lack of evidence that publications probably have such effects, how can the government discharge its burden
of demonstrating sufficiently that the statute is within the narrow
exceptions to the scope of the First Amendment? One would think
that the mere possibility of a causal relation to misconduct ought
surely not be enough.

Even if Congress had made an express legislative finding of the
probable evil influence, on adult conduct, of adult reading or seeing
obscene publications, the courts would not be bound by that finding,
if it were not justified in fact. See, e. g., Chastleton Corp. v. Sinclair,
where the Court (per Holmes, J.) said of a statute (declaring the
existence of an emergency) that "a Court is not at liberty to shut its
eyes to an obvious mistake, when the validity of the law depends
upon the truth of what is declared." And the Court there and
elsewhere has held that the judiciary may use judicial notice in
ascertaining the truth of such a legislative declaration.

If the Obscenity Statute Is Valid, Why May Congress Not Validly Provide Punishment for Mailing Books Which Will Provoke Thoughts It Considers Undesirable About Religion or Politics?

If the statute is valid, then, considering the foregoing, it would
seem that its validity must rest on this ground: Congress, by statute,
may constitutionally provide punishment for the mailing of books
evoking mere thoughts or feelings about sex, if Congress considers

---

14 See United States v. Levine, 2 Cir., 83 F.2d 156, 157 to the effect that
"what counts is its effect, not upon any particular class, but upon all those
whom it is likely to reach."

them socially dangerous, even in the absence of any satisfactory evidence that those thoughts or feelings will tend to bring about socially harmful deeds. If that be correct, it is hard to understand why, similarly, Congress may not constitutionally provide punishment for such distribution of books evoking mere thoughts or feelings, about religion or politics, which Congress considers socially dangerous, even in the absence of any satisfactory evidence that those thoughts or feelings will tend to bring about socially dangerous deeds.

II. THE JUDICIAL EXCEPTION
OF THE ''CLASSICS''

As I have said, I have no doubt the jury could reasonably find, beyond a reasonable doubt, that many of the publications mailed by defendant were obscene within the current judicial definition of the term as explained by the trial judge in his charge to the jury. But so, too, are a multitude of recognized works of art found in public libraries. Compare, for instance, the books which are exhibits in this case with Montaigne's "Essay on Some Lines of Virgil" or with Chaucer. Or consider the many nude pictures which the defendant transmitted through the mails, and then turn to the reproductions in the articles on painting and sculpture in the *Encyclopædia Britannica* (14th edition): some of the latter are no less "obscene" than those which led to the defendant's conviction. Yet these *Encyclopædia* volumes are readily accessible to everyone, young or old, and, without let or hindrance, are frequently mailed to all parts of the country. Catalogues, of famous art museums, almost equally accessible and also often mailed, contain reproductions of paintings and sculpture, by great masters, no less "obscene."

To the argument that such books (and such reproductions of famous paintings and works of sculpture) fall within the statutory ban, the courts have answered that they are "classics"—books of "literary distinction" or works which have "an accepted place in the arts," including, so this court has held, Ovid's *Art of Love* and Boccaccio's *Decameron*.[15] There is a "curious dilemma" involved in

---

[15] No one can argue with a straight face (1) that reading an obscene "classic" in a library has less harmful effects or (2) that, as the "classics" often are published in expensive volumes, they usually affect only persons who have large incomes, and that such persons' right to read is peculiarly privileged.

this answer that the statute condemns "only books which are dull and without merit," that in no event will the statute be applied to the "classics," i.e., books "of literary distinction." The courts have not explained how they escape that dilemma, but instead seem to have gone to sleep (although rather uncomfortably) on its horns.

This dilemma would seem to show up the basic constitutional flaw in the statute: No one can reconcile the currently accepted test of obscenity with the immunity of such "classics" as e. g., Aristophanes' *Lysistrata*, Chaucer's *Canterbury Tales*, Rabelais' *Gargantua and Pantagruel*, Shakespeare's "Venus and Adonis," Fielding's *Tom Jones*, or Balzac's *Droll Stories*. For such "obscene" writings, just because of their greater artistry and charm, will presumably have far greater influence on readers than dull inartistic writings.

It will not do to differentiate a "classic," published in the past, on the ground that it comported with the average moral attitudes at the time and place of its original publication. Often this was not true. It was not true, for instance, of Balzac's *Droll Stories,* a "classic" now freely circulated by many public libraries, and which therefore must have been transported by mail (or in interstate commerce). More to the point, if the issue is whether a book meets the American common conscience of the present time, the question is how "average" Americans now regard the book, not how it was regarded when first published, here or abroad. Why should the age of an "obscene" book be relevant? After how many years—25 or 50 or 100—does such a writing qualify as a "classic"?

The truth is that the courts have excepted the "classics" from the federal obscenity statute, since otherwise most Americans would be deprived of access to many masterpieces of literature and the pictorial arts, and a statute yielding such deprivation would not only be laughably absurd but would squarely oppose the intention of the cultivated men who framed and adopted the First Amendment.

This exception—nowhere to be found in the statute[16]—is a judge-made device invented to avoid that absurdity. The fact that the judges have felt the necessity of seeking that avoidance, serves to suggest forcibly that the statute, in its attempt to control what our

---

[16] The importation statute relating to obscenity, 19 U.S.C.A. § 1305, does make an explicit exception of the "so-called classics or books of recognized and established literary . . . merit," but only if they are "imported for non-commercial purposes"; if so, the Secretary of the Treasury has discretion to admit them.

citizens may read and see, violates the First Amendment. For no one can rationally justify the judge-made exception. The contention would scarcely pass as rational that the "classics" will be read or seen solely by an intellectual or artistic elite; for, even ignoring the snobbish, undemocratic nature of this contention, there is no evidence that that elite has a moral fortitude (an immunity from moral corruption) superior to that of the "masses." And if the exception, to make it rational, were taken as meaning that a contemporary book is exempt if it equates in "literary distinction" with the "classics," the result would be amazing: Judges would have to serve as literary critics; jurisprudence would merge with aesthetics; authors and publishers would consult the legal digests for legal-artistic precedents; we would some day have a Legal Restatement of the Canons of Literary Taste.

The exception of the "classics" is therefore irrational. Consequently, it would seem that we should interpret the statute rationally—i. e., without that exception. If, however, the exception, as an exception, is irrational, then it would appear that, to render the statute valid, the standard applied to the "classics" should be applied to all books and pictures. The result would be that, in order to be constitutional, the statute must be wholly inefficacious.

III. HOW CENSORSHIP UNDER THE STATUTE ACTUALLY OPERATES

(a) Prosecutors, as Censors, Actually Exercise Prior Restraint

Fear of punishment serves as a powerful restraint on publication, and fear of punishment often means, practically, fear of prosecution. For most men dread indictment and prosecution; the publicity alone terrifies, and to defend a criminal action is expensive. If the definition of obscenity had a limited and fairly well known scope, that fear might deter restricted sorts of publications only. But on account of the extremely vague judicial definition of the obscene,[17] a person threatened with prosecution if he mails (or otherwise sends in interstate commerce) almost any book which deals in an unconventional, unorthodox manner with sex,[18] may well apprehend that, should the

---

[17] See infra, point IX, for further discusion of that vagueness.

[18] See Kaplan, "Obscenity as an Esthetic Category," 20 Law & Contemp. Problems (1955) 544, 551–552 as to "conventional obscenity," which he defines as "the quality of any work which attacks sexual patterns and practices. In

threat be carried out, he will be punished. As a result, each prosecutor becomes a literary censor (i. e., dictator) with immense unbridled power, a virtually uncontrolled discretion. A statute would be invalid which gave the Potsmaster General the power, without reference to any standard, to close the mails to any publication he happened to dislike. Yet, a federal prosecutor, under the federal obscenity statute, approximates that position: Within wide limits, he can (on the advice of the Postmaster General or on no one's advice) exercise such a censorship by threat, without a trial, without any judicial supervision, capriciously and arbitrarily. Having no special qualifications for that task, nevertheless, he can, in large measure, determine at his will what those within his distinct may not read on sexual subjects. In that way, the statute brings about an actual prior restraint of free speech and free press which strikingly flouts the First Amendment.

(*b*) Judges as Censors

When a prosecution is instituted and a trial begins, much censorship power passes to the trial judge: If he sits without a jury, he must decide whether a book is obscene. If the trial is by jury, then, if he thinks the book plainly not obscene, he directs a verdict for the accused or, after a verdict of guilt, enters a judgment of acquittal. How does the judge determine whether a book is obscene? Not by way of evidence introduced at the trial, but by way of some sort of judicial notice. Whence come the judicial notice data to inform him?

Those whose views most judges know best are other lawyers. Judges can and should take judicial notice that, at many gatherings of lawyers at Bar Association or of alumni of our leading law schools,[19]

---

essence, it is the presentation of a sexual heterodoxy, a rejection of accepted standards of sexual behavior. Zola, Ibsen and Shaw provide familiar examples. It surprises no one that the author of *Nana* also wrote *J'Accuse;* of *Ghosts, An Enemy of the People;* of *Mrs. Warren's Profession, Saint Joan.*"

[19] See Roth v. Goldman, 2 Cir., 172 F.2d 788, at page 796 (concurring opinion): "One thinks of the lyrics sung at many such gatherings by a certain respected and conservative member of the faculty of a great law-school which considers itself the most distinguished and which is the Alma Mater of many judges sitting on upper courts."

Aubrey's *Lives,* containing many "salacious" tales, delights some of our greatest judges.

Mr. Justice Holmes was a constant reader of "naughty French novels." See Bent, *Justice O. W. Holmes* (1932) 16, 134.

tales are told fully as "obscene" as many of those distributed by men, like defendant, convicted for violation of the obscenity statute. Should not judges, then set aside such convictions? If they do not, are they not somewhat arrogantly concluding that lawyers are an exempt elite, unharmed by what will harm the multitude of other Americans? If lawyers are not such an elite then, since, in spite of the "obscene" tales lawyers frequently tell one another, data are lacking that lawyers as a group become singularly addicted to depraved sexual conduct, should not judges conclude that "obscenity" does not importantly contribute to such misconduct, and that therefore the statute is unconstitutional?

(c) Jurors as Censors

If in a jury case, the trial judge does not direct a verdict or enter a judgment of acquittal, the jury exercises the censorship power. Courts have said that a jury has a peculiar aptitude as a censor of obscenity, since, representing a cross-section of the community, it knows peculiarly well the "common conscience" of the time. Yet no statistician would conceivably accept the views of a jury—twelve persons chosen at random—as a fair sample of community attitudes on such a subject as obscenity. A particular jury may voice the "moral sentiments" of a generation ago, not of the present time.

Each jury verdict in an obscenity case has been sagely called "really a small bit of legislation ad hoc." So each jury constitutes a tiny autonomous legislature. Any one such tiny legislature, as experience teaches, may well differ from any other, in thus legislating as to obscenity. And, one may ask, was it the purpose of the First Amendment, to authorize hundreds of divers jury-legislatures, with discrepant beliefs, to decide whether or not to enact hundreds of divers statutes interfering with freedom of expression? (I shall note, infra, the vast difference between the applications by juries of the "reasonable man" standard and the "obscenity" standard.)

IV. THE DANGEROUSLY INFECTIOUS NATURE OF GOVERNMENTAL CENSORSHIP OF BOOKS

Governmental control of ideas or personal preferences is alien to a democracy. And the yearning to use governmental censorship of any kind is infectious. It may spread insidiously. Commencing with suppression of books as obscene, it is not unlikely to develop into official lust for the power of thought-control in the areas of religion, politics, and elsewhere. Milton observed that "licensing of books . . . necessarily pulls along with it so many other kinds of licensing." J. S. Mill noted that the "bounds of what may be called moral police" may easily extend "until it encroaches on the most unquestionably legitimate liberty of the individual." We should beware of a recrudescence of the undemocratic doctrine uttered in the 17th century by Berkeley, Governor of Virginia: "Thank God there are no free schools or preaching, for learning has brought disobedience into the world, and printing has divulged them. God keep us from both."

The People as Self-Guardians: Censorship by Public Opinion, Not by Government

Plato, who detested democracy, proposed to banish all poets; and his rulers were to serve as "guardians" of the people, telling lies for the people's good, vigorously suppressing writings these guardians thought dangerous. Governmental guardianship is repugnant to the basic tenet of our democracy: According to our ideals, our adult citizens are self-guardians, to act as their own fathers, and thus become self-dependent. When our governmental officials act towards our citizens on the thesis that "Papa knows best what's good for you," they enervate the spirit of the citizens: To treat grown men like infants is to make them infantile, dependent, immature.

So have sagacious men often insisted. Milton, in his *Areopagitica,* denounced such paternalism: "We censure them for a giddy, vicious and unguided people, in such sick and weak [a] state of faith and discretion as to be able to take down nothing but through the pipe of a licensor." "We both consider the people as our children," wrote Jefferson to Dupont de Nemours, "but you love them as infants whom you are afraid to trust without nurses, and I as adults whom I freely leave to self-government." Tocqueville sagely remarked: "No form or combination of social policy has yet been devised to make an energetic people of a community of pusillanimous and enfeebled citizens." "Man," warned Goethe, "is easily accustomed to slavery and learns quickly to be obedient when his freedom is taken from him." Said Carl Becker, "Self-government, and the spirit of freedom that sustains it, can be maintained only if the people have sufficient intelligence and honesty to maintain them with a minimum of legal compulsion. This heavy responsibility is the price of freedom."[20] The "great art," according to Milton, "lies to discern in what the law is to bid restraint and punishment, and in what things persuasion only is to work." So we come back, once more, to Jefferson's advice: The only completely democratic way to control publications which arouse mere thoughts or feelings is through non-governmental censorship by public opinion.

V. THE SEEMING PARADOX OF THE FIRST AMENDMENT

Here we encounter an apparent paradox: The First Amendment, judicially enforced, curbs public opinion when translated into a statute which restricts freedom of expression (except that which will probably induce undesirable conduct). The paradox is unreal: *The Amendment ensures that public opinion—the "common conscience of the time"—shall not commit suicide through legislation which chokes off today the free expression of minority views which may become the majority public opinion of tomorrow.*

Private Persons or Groups, May Validly Try to Influence Public Opinion

The First Amendment obviously has nothing to do with the way persons or groups, not a part of government, influence public opinion as to what constitutes "decency" or "obscenity." The Catholic Church, for example, has a constitutional right to persuade or instruct its adherents not to read designated books or kinds of books.

VI. THE FINE ARTS ARE WITHIN THE FIRST AMENDMENT'S PROTECTION

"The framers of the First Amendment," writes Chafee, "must have had literature and art in mind, because our first national statement on the subject of 'freedom of the press,' the 1774 address of the Continental Congress to the inhabitants of Quebec, declared, 'The importance of this (freedom of the press) consists, beside the advancement of truth, science, morality and *arts* in general, in its diffusion of liberal sentiments on the administration of govern-

---

[20] Becker, *Freedom and Responsibility in the American Way of Life* (1945) 42.

ment.' "[21] 165 years later, President Franklin Roosevelt said, "The arts cannot thrive except where men are free to be themselves and to be in charge of the discipline of their own energies and ardors. The conditions for democracy and for art are one and the same. What we call liberty in politics results in freedom of the arts." The converse is also true.

In our industrial era when, perforce, economic pursuits must be, increasingly, governmentally regulated, it is especially important that the realm of art—the non-economic realm—should remain free, unregimented, the domain of free enterprise, of unhampered competition at its maximum. An individual's taste is his own, private, concern. *De gustibus non disputandum* represents a valued democratic maxim.

Milton wrote: "For though a licenser should happen to be judicious more than the ordinary, yet his very office . . . enjoins him to let pass nothing but what is vulgarly received already." He asked, "What a fine conformity would it starch us all into? . . . We may fall . . . into a gross conformity stupidly . . . ." In 1859, J. S. Mill, in his essay on "Liberty," maintained that conformity in taste is not a virtue but a vice. "The danger," he wrote, "is not the excess but the deficiency of personal impulses and preferences. By dint of not following their own nature [men] have no nature to follow . . . Individual spontaneity is entitled to free exercise . . . That so few men dare to be eccentric marks the chief danger of the time." Pressed by the demand for conformity, a people degenerate into "the deep slumber of a decided opinion," yield a "dull and torpid consent" to the accustomed. "Mental despotism" ensues. For "whatever crushes individuality is despotism by whatever name it be called . . . It is not by wearing down into uniformity all that is individual in themselves, but by cultivating it, and calling it forth, within the limits imposed by the rights and interests of others, that human beings become a noble and beautiful object of contemplation; and as the works partake the character of those who do them, by the same process human life also becomes rich, diversified, and animating . . . In proportion to the development of his individuality, each person becomes more valuable to himself, and is therefore capable of being more valuable to others. There is a greater fullness of life about his own existence, and when there is more life in the units there is more in the mass which is composed of them."

---

[21] Chafee, *Government and Mass Communication* (1947) 53.

To vest a few fallible men—prosecutors, judges, jurors—with vast powers of literary or artistic censorship, to convert them into what J. S. Mill called a "moral police," is to make them despotic arbiters of literary products. If one day they ban mediocre books as obscene, another day they may do likewise to a work of genius. Originality, not too plentiful, should be cherished, not stifled. An author's imagination may be cramped if he must write with one eye on prosecutors or juries; authors must cope with publishers who, fearful about the judgments of governmental censors, may refuse to accept the manuscripts of contemporary Shelleys or Mark Twains or Whitmans.[22]

Some few men stubbornly fight for the right to write or publish or distribute books which the great majority at the time consider loathsome. If we jail those few, the community may appear to have suffered nothing. The appearance is deceptive. For the conviction and punishment of these few will terrify writers who are more sensitive, less eager for a fight. What, as a result, they do not write might have been major literary contributions. "Suppression," Spinoza said, "is paring down the state till it is too small to harbor men of talent."

VII. THE MOTIVE OR INTENTION OF THE AUTHOR, PUBLISHER OR DISTRIBUTOR CANNOT BE THE TEST

Some courts once held that the motive or intention of the author, painter, publisher or distributor constituted the test of obscenity. That test, the courts have abandoned: That a man who mails a book or picture believes it entirely "pure" is no defense if the court finds it obscene. United States v. One Book Entitled Ulysses. Nor, conversely, will he be criminally liable for mailing a "pure" publication—Stevenson's *Child's Garden of Verses* or a simple photograph of the Washington Monument—he mistakenly believes obscene. Most courts now look to the "objective" intention, which can only mean the effect on those who read the book or see the picture; the motive of the mailer is irrelevant because it cannot affect that effect.

---

[22] Milton remarked that "not to count him fit to print his mind without a tutor or examiner, lest he should drop . . . something of corruption, is the greatest . . . indignity to a free and knowing spirit that can be put upon him."

VIII. JUDGE BOK'S DECISION AS TO THE CAUSAL RELATION TO ANTI-SOCIAL CONDUCT

In Commonwealth v. Gordon, Judge Bok said: "A book, however sexually impure and pornographic . . . cannot be a present danger unless its reader closes it, lays it aside, and transmutes its erotic allurement into overt action. That such action must inevitably follow as a direct consequence of reading the book does not bear analysis, nor is it borne out by general human experience; too much can intervene and too many diversions take place . . . The only clear and present danger . . . that will satisfy . . . the Constitution . . . is the commission or the imminence of the commission of criminal behavior resulting from the reading of a book. Publication alone can have no such automatic effect." The constitutional operation of "the statute," Judge Bok continued, thus "rests on narrow ground . . . I hold that [the statute] may constitutionally be applied . . . only where there is a reasonable and demonstrable cause to believe that a crime or misdemeanor has been committed or is about to be committed as the perceptible result of the publication and distribution of the writing in question: the opinion of anyone that a tendency thereto exists or that such a result is self-evident is insufficient and irrelevant. The causal connection between the book and the criminal behavior must appear beyond a reasonable doubt."

I confess that I incline to agree with Judge Bok's opinion. But I think it should be modified in a few respects: (a) Because of the Supreme Court's opinion in the Dennis case, 1951, decided since Judge Bok wrote, I would stress the element of probability in speaking of a "clear danger." (b) I think the danger need not be that of probably inducing behavior which has already been made criminal at common law or by statute, but rather of probably inducing any seriously anti-social conduct (i. e., conduct which, by statute, could validly be made a state or federal crime). (c) I think that the causal relation need not be between such anti-social conduct and a particular book involved in the case on trial, but rather between such conduct and a book of the kind or type involved in the case.[23]

---

[23] According to Judge Bok, an obscenity statute may be validly enforced when there is proof of a causal relation between a particular book and undesirable conduct. Almost surely, such proof cannot ever be adduced. In the instant case, the government did not offer such proof.

IX. THE VOID-FOR-VAGUENESS ARGUMENT

There is another reason for doubting the constitutionality of the obscenity statute. The exquisite vagueness of the word "obscenity" is apparent from the way the judicial definition of that word has kept shifting: Once (as we saw) the courts held a work obscene if it would probably stimulate improper thoughts or desires in abnormal persons; now most courts consider only the assumed impact on the thoughts or desires of the adult "normal" or average human being. A standard so difficult for our ablest judges to interpret is hardly one which has a "well-settled" meaning, a meaning sufficient adequately to advise a man whether he is or is not committing a crime if he mails a book or picture.

If we accept as correct the generally current judicial standard of obscenity—the "average conscience of the time"—that standard still remains markedly uncertain as a guide to judges or jurors—and therefore to a citizen who contemplates mailing a book or picture. To be sure, we trust juries to use their common sense in applying the "reasonable man" standard in prosecutions for criminal negligence (or the like); a man has to take his chances on a jury verdict in such a case, with no certainty that a jury will not convict him although another jury may acquit another man on the same evidence. But that standard has nothing remotely resembling the looseness of the "obscenity" standard.

F. R. Leavis

POETRY AND
THE MODERN WORLD*

Poetry matters little to the modern world. That is, very little of
contemporary intelligence concerns itself with poetry. It is true
that a very great deal of verse has come from the press in the last
twenty years, and the uninterested might take this as proving the
existence both of a great deal of interest in poetry and of a great
deal of talent. Indeed, anthologists do. They make, modestly, the
most extravagant claims on behalf of the age. "It is of no use asking
a poetical renascence to conform to type," writes Mr J. C. Squire
in his *Prefatory Note* to *Selections from Modern Poets*. "There are
marked differences in the features of all those English poetical
movements which have chiefly contributed to the body of our "im-
mortal" poetry. . . . Should our literary age be remembered by
posterity solely as an age during which fifty men had written lyrics
of some durability for their truth and beauty, it would not be remembered with contempt. It is in that conviction that I have com-
piled this authology." Mr Harold Monro, introducing *Twentieth
Century Poetry*, is more modest and more extravagant: "Is it a
great big period, or a minutely small? Reply who can! Somebody
with whom I was talking said: 'They are all of them only poetical

* From F. R. Leavis, *New Bearings in English Poetry*, ch. 1 (London:
Chatto & Windus Ltd., 1932). Reprinted by permission of Chatto & Windus
Ltd.

persons—*not* poets. Who will be reading them a century hence?'
To which I answered: 'There are so many of them that, a century
hence, they may appear a kind of Composite Poet; there may be
500 excellent poems proceeding from 100 poets mostly not so very
great, but well worth remembering a century hence.' "

Such claims are symptoms of the very weakness that they deny:
they could have been made only in an age in which there were no
serious standards current, no live tradition of poetry, and no public
capable of informed and serious interest. No one *could* be seriously
interested in the great bulk of the verse that is culled and offered to
us as the fine flower of modern poetry. For the most part it is not
so much bad as dead—it was never alive. The words that lie there
arranged on the page have no roots: the writer himself can never
have been more than superficially interested in them. Even such
genuine poetry as the anthologies of modern verse do contain is
apt, by its kind and quality, to suggest that the present age does not
favour the growth of poets. A study of the latter end of *The Oxford
Book of Victorian Verse* leads to the conclusion that something has
been wrong for forty or fifty years at the least.

For it seems unlikely that the number of potential poets born
varies as much from age to age as literary history might lead one to
suppose. What varies is the use made of talent. And the use each age
makes of its crop of talent is determined largely by the preconceptions of "the poetical" that are current, and the corresponding
habits, conventions and techniques. There are, of course, other very
important conditions, social, economic, philosophical and so on; but
my province is that of literary criticism, and I am confining myself
as far as possible to those conditions which it rests with the poet
and the critic to modify—those which are their immediate concern.

Every age, then, has its preconceptions and assumptions regarding
poetry: these are the essentially poetical subjects, these the poetical
materials, these the poetical modes. The most influential are apt to
be those of which we are least aware. The preconceptions coming
down to us from the last century were established in the period of
the great Romantics, Wordsworth, Coleridge, Byron, Shelley and
Keats. To attempt to define them is to risk misrepresenting them,
for it is largely in their being vague and undefined that their power
has lain. Their earliest formulation is to be found, perhaps, in the
Dedication (dated 1756) of Joseph Warton's *Essay on the Genius
and Writings of Pope*. What Warton, consciously challenging the

prevailing ideas, puts explicitly, afterwards came to be implicitly assumed.

> We do not, it should seem, sufficiently attend to the difference there is between a MAN OF WIT, a MAN OF SENSE, and a TRUE POET. Donne and Swift were undoubtedly men of wit, and men of sense: but what traces have they left of PURE POETRY?

The question would seem to determine the spirit of the affirmation: any doubt that may remain, both affirmation and question in the following combine to settle:

> The sublime and the pathetic are the two chief nerves of all genuine poesy. What is there transcendently sublime or pathetic in Pope?

Warton goes on to classify the English Poets:

> In the first class I would place our only three sublime and pathetic poets; SPENSER, SHAKESPEARE, MILTON.

The collocation is decisive: it defines with sufficient precision the nineteenth-century idea of the poetical. Donne, we may note, Warton places in the third class. The reign of the idea is challenged when Donne comes to be associated with Shakespeare in contrast to Spenser and Milton. How universal and unquestioned it had become in the Victorian Age Matthew Arnold may be cited to prove. His evidence is the more significant in that it was unwitting, for he regarded himself as a critic of the ideas about poetry current in his day.

> Though they may write in verse, though they may in a certain sense be masters of the art of versification, Dryden and Pope are not classics of our poetry, they are classics of our prose.[1]
> The difference between genuine poetry and the poetry of Dryden, Pope, and all their school, is briefly this: their poetry is conceived and composed in their wits, genuine poetry is conceived and composed in the soul.[2]

—Arnold, that is, shares with his age a prejudice against recognizing as poetry anything that is not, in the obvious sense of Milton's formula, "simple, sensuous, and passionate." Poetry, it was assumed,

---

[1] *Essays in Criticism.* Second Series: *The Study of Poetry.*
[2] *Ibid., Thomas Gray.*

must be the direct expression of simple emotions, and these of a limited class: the tender, the exalted, the poignant, and, in general, the sympathetic. (It is still quite common to come to the University from school doubting whether satire can be poetry.) Wit, play of intellect, stress of cerebral muscle had no place: they could only hinder the reader's being "moved"—the correct poetical response.[3]

There is something further to be noted of "the poetical" in the nineteenth century. It comes out if one considers these half-a-dozen well-known and representative poems: *La Belle Dame Sans Merci*, *Mariana*, *The Lady of Shalott*, *The Blessed Damozel*, Morris's *The Nymph's Song to Hylas*, *A Forsaken Garden*, O'Shaughnessy's *Ode*. Nineteenth-century poetry, we realize, was characteristically preoccupied with the creation of a dream-world.[4] Not all of the poetry, or all of the poets: but the preoccupation was characteristic. So that when a poetaster like O'Shaughnessy, with nothing personal to communicate, was moved by the desire to write poetry he produced this:

> *We are the music-makers,*
> *And we are the dreamers of dreams,*
> *Wandering by lone sea-breakers,*
> *And sitting by desolate streams;*
> *World-losers and world forsakers,*
> *On whom the pale moon gleams....*

The preoccupation, the habit, then, became a dominant element in the set of ideas, attitudes and sentiments constituting "the poetical" for the nineteenth century, and may often be seen to be present and potent when it is not avowed or even wittingly entertained. Consider, for instance, Andrew Lang's sonnet, *The Odyssey*. Lang (born in 1844) was a scholar and a man of taste, with a feeling for language and a desire to write poetry—with, in short, all the qualifications of a poet except the essential one, the need to communicate

---

[3] "Poetry tells you about things that have happened long ago, and it tells you about them in language that is rich with an antique idiom. . . . The poet must, I think, be regarded as striving after the simplicity of a childish utterance. His goal is to think as a child, to understand as a child. He must deliver himself—and the poetic task is the same in every age—from the burden of the intellect of his day and the complexity of the forms of speech which it involves."—J. M. Thorburn, *Art and the Unconscious*, p. 70.

[4] Mr Eliot has pointed this out in *Homage to John Dryden*.

something of his own. His sonnet is one of the most interesting of
the many documents of like value that are to be found in *The Oxford Book of English Verse*. It illustrates very neatly the kind of
thing that cultured people in the latter part of the nineteenth
century took poetry to be.

> *As one that for a weary space has lain*
>   *Lull'd by the song of Circe and her wine*
>   *In gardens near the pale of Proserpine,*
> *Where that Aeaean isle forgets the main,*
> *And only the low lutes of love complain,*
>   *And only shadows of wan lovers pine—*
>   *As such an one were glad to know the brine*
> *Salt on his lips, and the large air again—*
> *So gladly from the songs of modern speech*
>   *Men turn, and see the stars, and feel the free*
>   *Shrill wind beyond the close of heavy flowers,*
>   *And through the music of the languid hours*
>   *They hear like Ocean on a western beach*
>   *The surge and thunder of the Odyssey.*

This is a very representative document. To begin with, there is
about the whole thing an atmosphere such as we have learnt to
associate with the 'nineties. It is quite in keeping, then, that Swinburne should be very much in evidence: "gardens near the pale of
Proserpine," "the low lutes of love," "the close of heavy flowers,"
etc. Morris, too, is there, suggesting a general Pre-Raphaelite collaboration. Then, as we should expect in late Victorian poetastry, we
are aware of the pervasive presence of Tennyson. And when Lang
wishes to escape from "the music of the languid hours" into the
"larger air" of "a western beach" he naturally has recourse to
Matthew Arnold. But in spite of the explicit intention to end in the
larger air, and the success with which Lang achieves "the traditional
trumpet blast of the close" (as the reviewers say), it is the music of
the languid hours that predominates in his sonnet.

> *We are the music-makers*
>   *And we are the dreamers of dreams,*

and if we dream of Homer and of waking up, it is still dreaming.
And there is in the sonnet yet another presence, that of Keats—the
Keats of *La Belle Dame Sans Merci* ("And only shadows of wan

lovers pine") which counts for so much in "the poetical" of the nineteenth century.

It is not only in the practice of poetasters that such preconceptions, habits and conventions assert themselves: they exercise a decisive influence over the use of genuine talent. Poetry tends in every age to confine itself by ideas of the essentially poetical which, when the conditions which gave rise to them have changed, bar the poet from his most valuable material, the material that is most significant to sensitive and adequate minds of his own day; or else sensitive and adequate minds are barred out of poetry. Poetry matters because of the kind of poet who is more alive than other people, more alive in his own age. He is, as it were, at the most conscious point of the race in his time. ("He is the point at which the growth of the mind shows itself," says Mr I. A. Richards.[5]) The potentialities of human experience in any age are realized only by a tiny minority, and the important poet is important because he belongs to this (and has also, of course, the power of communication). Indeed, his capacity for experiencing and his power of communicating are indistinguishable; not merely because we should not know of the one without the other, but because his power of making words express what he feels is indistinguishable from his awareness of what he feels. He is unusually sensitive, unusually aware, more sincere and more himself than the ordinary man can be. He knows what he feels and knows what he is interested in. He is a poet because his interest in his experience is not separable from his interest in words; because, that is, of his habit of seeking by the evocative use of words to sharpen his awareness of his ways of feeling, so making these communicable. And poetry can communicate the actual quality of experience with a subtlety and precision unapproachable by any other means. But if the poetry and the intelligence of the age lose touch with each other, poetry will cease to matter much, and the age will be lacking in finer awareness. What this last prognostication means it is perhaps impossible to bring home to any one who is not already convinced of the importance of poetry. So that it is indeed deplorable that poetry should so widely have ceased to interest the intelligent.

The mischievousness of the nineteenth-century conventions of "the poetical" should by now be plain. They had behind them the prestige of the Romantic achievement and found their sanction in

[5] *The Principles of Literary Criticism*, p. 61.

undoubted poetic successes. But as the situation changed and the incidence of stress for the adult sensitive mind shifted, more and more did they tend to get between such a mind and its main concerns. It clearly could not take the day-dream habit seriously, though to cut free from the accompanying conventions and techniques would not be so easy as one might think. The other habits and conventions that have been indicated would be still harder to escape. But they would be equally disabling. For a sensitive adult in the nineteenth century could not fail to be preoccupied with the changed intellectual background, and to find his main interests inseparable from the modern world. Tennyson did his best. But, in spite of a great deal of allusion to scientific ideas ("If that hypothesis of theirs be sound"), and in spite of the approval of contemporary savants, his intellectual interests (of which, therefore, we need not discuss the quality) have little to do with his successful poetry, which answers to the account of "the poetical" given above. Indeed, there could be no better illustration. To justify his ambition would have taken a much finer intelligence and a much more robust original genius than Tennyson's—much greater strength and courage. He might wrestle solemnly with the "problems of the age," but the habits, conventions and techniques that he found congenial are not those of a poet who could have exposed himself freely to the rigours of the contemporary climate. And in this he is representative. It was possible for the poets of the Romantic period to believe that the interests animating their poetry were the forces moving the world, or that might move it. But Victorian poetry admits implicitly that the actual world is alien, recalcitrant and unpoetical, and that no protest is worth making except the protest of withdrawal.

A comparison between any comparable passages of Tennyson and Keats will suggest readily how even Keats,[6] who might at first seem to resist this generalized distinction, may be reconciled with it: Tennyson, in the comparison, will show as literary and Alexandrian, a senior contemporary of the Pre-Raphaelites. His case is well put by *The Palace of Art:* the explicit moral of this poem is that withdrawal will not do; but when he comes to the moral Tennyson's art breaks down: the poetry belongs to the palace. Pre-Raphaelite art is frankly withdrawn—the appropriate metaphor would suggest some-

---

[6] There is no need to insist on the significance of the revised *Hyperion* and Keats's reasons for the revision.

thing not only beglamoured, but also ritualistic and religiose. Swinburne sings Liberty and Revolution, but it would be difficult to illustrate more forcibly the distinction I have pointed to than by comparing him with Shelley.

The causes of this peculiar other-worldliness of Victorian poetry are sufficiently indicated by Matthew Arnold's recurrent note—his references to

> . . . *this strange disease of modern life,*
> *With its sick hurry, its divided aims,*
> *Its heads o'ertaxed, its palsied hearts . . .*

and to this age that

> *had bound*
> *Our souls in its benumbing round*

and

> . . . *this iron time*
> *Of doubts, disputes, distractions, fears.*

The frankness of this explicit recognition distinguishes Arnold from among his fellow poets, but it is not enough to constitute the poetic "criticism of life" that he desiderated. Alas! the past was out of date, the future not yet born, and Arnold's response to these conditions does not differ fundamentally from that of his fellows. Whatever reasons of discipline he may give for valuing Wordsworth and the Greeks, it is plain that he frequents them largely as means of escape to "the freshness of the early world." His debt to Wordsworth,[7] in fact, is hardly separable from a debt to Coleridge, and he bears much the same kind of relation to these two as Tennyson bears to Coleridge and Keats. If we note further the relation of *Sohrab and Rustum*, for instance, to the "ineffectual angel" we shall have a fair idea of Arnold's general relation to the Romantic period. He derives from it in the same kind of way as Tennyson and the Pre-Raphaelites do. This obvious point seems worth dwelling on because he certainly aimed to be a very different kind of poet from these, and his unwitting testimony to the strength of the

---

[7] And of Wordsworth he says: "The gravest of them, Wordsworth, retired (in Middle-Age phrase) into a monastery. I mean, he plunged himself in the inward life, he voluntarily cut himself off from the modern spirit." —*Essays in Criticism.* First Series: *Heinrich Heine.*

prevailing atmosphere and conventions is even more striking in his poetry than in his criticism.

I am not thinking of his frankly romantic poems so much as of his work in the manner of *A Summer Night,* in which he is explicitly concerned with "this strange disease of modern life." Except as the explicit occasion of his thin, sweet, meditative melancholy, "modern life," "its sick hurry," "its divided aims," "its heads o'ertaxed" are not there. They could have been put there only by genius of the order of Gerard Manley Hopkins—genius, that is, in which technical originality is inseparable from the rare adequacy of mind, sensibility and spirit that it vouches for. Arnold—and we have no reason to say that will and intelligence more than technical abilities were lacking—slips away from "this uncongenial place, this human life" to moonlight transformations, and the iron time dissolves in wistful, melodious sentiment.

To explain why moonlight appears so often in Arnold's poetry is to explain why, in *Empedocles on Etna,* it should be in two songs of Callicles that the sap suddenly flows. One of these songs is so obviously significant that a phrase or two from it will be enough to clinch the argument:

> *Far, far from here*
> *The Adriatic breaks in a warm bay . . .*
> *There those two live, far in the Illyrian brakes.*
> *. . . but were rapt, far away . . .*

Arnold's manner of evasion distinguishes him from his fellows mainly in the cool, meditative lucidity of his waking dream. In his poems of the English countryside his quest is the Scholar-Gypsy's— sanctuary from the modern world, "its sick hurry, its divided aims." And even in poems that do not fall naturally under the head of "evasion" the sentiment has the same well-bred innocence as always, the same sweet, limpid solemnity: one could hardly have divined in the poet the scourge of the Philistines.

No, Matthew Arnold was not qualified either as critic or poet to give English poetry a new direction. When he predicted that poetry would—advocated that it should—more and more take the place of religion, he intended something very different from an indulging of religious sentiment in a hushed cult of Beauty, a religiose sensuality, a retreat out of the profane world into an exquisite cloistral art; but this describes fairly enough the development from the Pre-Raphaelites and Swinburne through Pater and Oscar Wilde to the 'nineties.

Where, it might be asked, does Browning come in these generalizations? His can hardly be described as a poetry of withdrawal. It belongs to the world he lives in, and he lives happily in the Victorian world with no sense of disharmony. But is this altogether by reason of qualities that should recommend a poet? There are kinds of strength a poet is best without. And it is too plain that Browning would have been less robust if he had been more sensitive and intelligent. He did indeed bring his living interests into his poetry, but it is too plain that they are not the interests of an adult sensitive mind. He did not need to withdraw into a dream-world, because he was able to be a naïve romantic of love and action on the waking plane. If he lived in the Victorian world, it was only as *l'homme moyen sensuel* might live there; unaware of disharmonies because for him there were none, or, rather, only such as were enough to exhilarate, to give him a joyous sense of physical vitality. It is possible to consider him as a philosophical or psychological poet only by confusing intelligence with delight in the exercise of certain grosser cerebral muscles. When he is a poet he is concerned merely with simple emotions and sentiments: the characteristic corrugation of his surface is merely superficial, and not the expression of a complex sensibility. And yet it was a truly remarkable force that broke as Browning did with the current poetical habits. His use, if only it had been finer, of spoken idiom in verse might have been worth a great deal to later poets: at the end of the century Mr Pound found it worth study. But so inferior a mind and spirit as Browning's could not provide the impulse needed to bring back into poetry the adult intelligence.

As for Meredith, if any one should comment that I have taken no account of him, I can only say that *Modern Love* seems to me the flashy product of unusual but vulgar cleverness working upon cheap emotion: it could serve later poets, if at all, only as a warning.

The further on we go in *The Oxford Book* the more apparent does it become that the age did not make full use of its talent. Who, for instance, would guess from his poetry that William Morris was one of the most versatile, energetic and original men of his time, a force that impinged decisively in the world of practice? He reserved poetry for his day-dreams.

And if we look through any anthologies covering the last fifty years, it becomes impossible to doubt that distinguished minds that should have gone into poetry have gone elsewhere. It is hard to explain otherwise the dearth of original talent in any form or degree. When original talent of a minor order does manifest itself, as, for instance, in Mr. A. E. Housman, or, though the collocation is unfair to Mr Housman, Rupert Brooke, it is apt to exert a disproportionate influence. The books of "Georgian" verse abound with tributes, more or less unconscious, to these two poets (not to insist on R. L. Stevenson's part): indeed it was largely in terms of them that the Victorian bequest of habits and conventions was brought up to date. But these remained essentially the same, as a perusal of the representative anthology, Mr J. C. Squire's *Selections from Modern Poets*, will show. The modernity manifests itself, for the most part, in a complacent debility; the robust, full-blooded emotional confidence of the Victorians is lacking, a modest quietness being the Georgian study; and technical liberation, accordingly, takes the form of loose, careless, unconvinced craftsmanship.

To make a fresh start in poetry under such conditions is a desperate matter. It is easy enough to say that poetry must be adequate to modern life, and it has often been said. But nothing has been done until such generalities have been realized in particulars, that is, in the invention of new techniques, and this, in an age when the current conventions will not serve even to provide a start, is something beyond any but a very unusually powerful and original talent. The established habits form a kind of atmosphere from which it is supremely difficult to escape. Mr J. C. Squire, for instance, reviewing in *The Observer* the late Poet Laureate's *The Testament of Beauty*, wrote:

> . . . the old poet has done triumphantly what none of his juniors have managed to do—he has, assisted by courage, a natural sincerity, a belief in the function of poetry, contrived to bring within the borders of a poem, and avoiding flatness, all his feelings, knowledge, speculations, interests, hopes and fears. For generations, owing to the reaction of the aesthetic against the new scientific, industrial and largely materialistic world, we have become accustomed to the idea that certain things are "not poetical," that a poet can mention a rose, but not a Rolls-Royce, that poetry is a refuge and not an attack, that a poet is a sensitive refugee and not a man facing life, the whole of it, and sounding a clarion call to his more speechless and encumbered fellows.

The first sentence might seem to be in the spirit of this essay, though the phrase "bring within the borders of a poem" should put us on our guard. On the next sentence—"we have become accustomed to the idea that certain things are not poetical"—our commentary runs: worse, we have become accustomed to the idea that certain things *are* poetical, e.g. flowers, dawn, dew, birds, love, archaisms and country place-names;[8] "that a poet can mention a rose, but not a Rolls-Royce"—suspicious; "that poetry is a refuge and not an attack, that a poet is a sensitive refugee and not a man facing life, the whole of it, and sounding a clarion call"—this will not do: it is plain by now that the critic is trying to put a misconception right by turning it upside-down. For we are no more justified in demanding that poetry shall be an attack than in demanding that it shall be a refuge. Indeed, it is very unlikely that a significant modern poem will be anything in the nature of a clarion call. The passage betrays a total misconception of the way in which such a poem will exhibit modernity. It will not be by mentioning modern things, the apparatus of modern civilization, or by being about modern subjects or topics. If the Rolls-Royce enters significantly into poetry it will be, perhaps, in some such way as Mr T. S. Eliot suggests[9] when he says that probably the modern's perception of rhythm has been affected by the internal combustion engine. All that we can fairly ask of the poet is that he shall show himself to have been fully alive in our time. The evidence will be in the very texture of his poetry.

Mr Alfred Noyes wrote (is still writing?) a long work in verse, *The Torch-Bearers*, about the succession of great astronomers. A few glances were enough to establish its complete insignificance as poetry. For such an undertaking would have to justify itself in the texture of the verse, by an unmistakable newness of tone, rhythm and imagery, by an utterly unfamiliar "feel." Mr Noyes's verse is such as any one with a feeling for language, and a close acquaintance with the poets of the past, could learn to write. On like grounds a subtler performance, Mr Laurence Binyon's *The Sirens*, an ode on the questing spirit of man, must be dismissed. The ode has been praised for its technical accomplishment, and in a sense it does exhibit skilled craftsmanship. But the only technique that matters is that which compels words to express an intensely personal way of feeling, so that the reader responds, not in a general way that he

---

8 If it be remarked that the cultivated no longer hold this idea, then the cultivated are reduced to a very small minority indeed.

9 *Savonarola*, Charlotte Eliot. *Introduction*, xi.

knows beforehand to be "poetical," but in a precise, particular way that no frequenting of *The Oxford Book* could have made familiar to him. To invent techniques that shall be adequate to the ways of feeling, or modes of experience, of adult, sensitive moderns is difficult in the extreme. Until it has been once done it is so difficult as to seem impossible. One success makes others more probable because less difficult.

That is the peculiar importance of Mr T. S. Eliot. For, though there is, inevitably, a great deal of snobbism in the cult he suffers from, mere snobbism will not account for his prestige among the young. Having a mind unquestionably of rare distinction he has solved his own problem as a poet, and so done more than solve the problem for himself. His influence has been the more effective in that he is a critic as well as a poet, and his criticism and his poetry reinforce each other. It is mainly due to him that no serious poet or critic to-day can fail to realize that English poetry in the future must develop (if at all) along some other line than that running from the Romantics through Tennyson, Swinburne, *A Shropshire Lad*, and Rupert Brooke. He has made a new start, and established new bearings. . . .

Leo Tolstoy

WHAT IS ART?*

What is art if we put aside the conception of beauty, which confuses the whole matter? The latest and most comprehensible definitions of art, apart from the conception of beauty, are the following:
—(1) *a*, Art is an activity arising even in the animal kingdom, and
springing from sexual desire and the propensity to play (Schiller,
Darwin, Spencer), and *b*, accompanied by a pleasurable excitement
of the nervous system (Grant Allen). This is the physiological-
evolutionary definition. (2) Art is the external manifestation, by
means of lines, colours, movements, sounds, or words, of emotions
felt by man (Véron). This is the experimental definition. According
to the very latest definition (Sully), (3) Art is "the production of
some permanent object or passing action which is fitted not only to
supply an active enjoyment to the producer, but to convey a pleasurable impression to a number of spectators or listeners, quite apart
from any personal advantage to be derived from it."

Notwithstanding the superiority of these definitions to the metaphysical definitions which depended on the conception of beauty,
they are yet far from exact. The first, the physiological-evolutionary
definition (1) *a*, is inexact, because instead of speaking about the
artistic activity itself, which is the real matter in hand, it treats of
the derivation of art. The modification of it, *b*, based on the physiological effects on the human organism, is inexact because within the

---

* From Leo Tolstoy, *What Is Art?* trans. by Aylmer Maude (London:
Oxford University Press, 1930). Reprinted by permission of the publisher.

limits of such definition many other human activities can be included, as has occurred in the neo-aesthetic theories which reckon as art the preparation of handsome clothes, pleasant scents, and even of victuals.

The experimental definition, (2), which makes art consist in the expression of emotions, is inexact because a man may express his emotions by means of lines, colours, sounds, or words and yet may not act on others by such expression—and then the manifestation of his emotions is not art.

The third definition (that of Sully) is inexact because in the production of objects or actions affording pleasure to the producer and a pleasant emotion to the spectators or hearers apart from personal advantage, may be included the showing of conjuring tricks or gymnastic exercises, and other activities which are not art. And further, many things the production of which does not afford pleasure to the producer and the sensation received from which is unpleasant, such as gloomy, heart-rending scenes in a poetic description or a play, may nevertheless be undoubted works of art.

The inaccuracy of all these definitions arises from the fact that in them all (as also in the metaphysical definitions) the object considered is the pleasure art may give, and not the purpose it may serve in the life of man and of humanity.

In order to define art correctly it is necessary first of all to cease to consider it as a means to pleasure and to consider it as one of the conditions of human life. Viewing it in this way we cannot fail to observe that art is one of the means of intercourse between man and man.

Every work of art causes the receiver to enter into a certain kind of relationship both with him who produced or is producing the art, and with all those who, simultaneously, previously, or subsequently, receive the same artistic impression.

Speech transmitting the thoughts and experiences of men serves as a means of union among them, and art serves a similar purpose. The peculiarity of this latter means of intercourse, distinguishing it from intercourse by means of words, consists in this, that whereas by words a man transmits his thoughts to another, by art he transmits his feelings.

The activity of art is based on the fact that a man receiving through his sense of hearing or sight another man's expression of feeling, is capable of experiencing the emotion which moved the man who expressed it. To take the simplest example: one man laughs, and another who hears becomes merry, or a man weeps, and another who hears feels sorrow. A man is excited or irritated, and another man seeing him is brought to a similar state of mind. By his movements or by the sounds of his voice a man expresses courage and determination or sadness and calmness, and this state of mind passes on to others. A man suffers, manifesting his sufferings by groans and spasms, and this suffering transmits itself to other people; a man expresses his feelings of admiration, devotion, fear, respect, or love, to certain objects, persons, or phenomena, and others are infected by the same feelings of admiration, devotion, fear, respect, or love, to the same objects, persons, or phenomena.

And it is on this capacity of man to receive another man's expression of feeling and to experience those feelings himself, that the activity of art is based.

If a man infects another or others directly, immediately, by his appearance or by the sounds he gives vent to at the very time he experiences the feeling; if he causes another man to yawn when he himself cannot help yawning, or to laugh or cry when he himself is obliged to laugh or cry, or to suffer when he himself is suffering— that does not amount to art.

Art begins when one person with the object of joining another or others to himself in one and the same feeling, expresses that feeling by certain external indications. To take the simplest example: a boy having experienced, let us say, fear on encountering a wolf, relates that encounter, and in order to evoke in others the feeling he has experienced, describes himself, his condition before the encounter, the surroundings, the wood, his own lightheartedness, and then the wolf's appearance, its movements, the distance between himself and the wolf, and so forth. All this, if only the boy when telling the story again experiences the feelings he had lived through, and infects the hearers and compels them to feel what he had experienced—is art. Even if the boy had not seen a wolf but had frequently been afraid of one, and if wishing to evoke in others the fear he had felt, he invented an encounter with a wolf and recounted it so as to make his hearers share the feelings he experienced when he feared the wolf, that also would be art. And just in the same way it is art if a man, having experienced either the fear of suffering or the attraction of enjoyment (whether in reality or in imagination), expresses these feelings on canvas or in marble so that others are infected by them.

And it is also art if a man feels, or imagines to himself, feelings of delight, gladness, sorrow, despair, courage, or despondency, and the transition from one to another of these feelings, and expresses them by sounds so that the hearers are infected by them and experience them as they were experienced by the composer.

The feelings with which the artist infects others may be most various—very strong or very weak, very important or very insignificant, very bad or very good: feelings of love of one's country, self-devotion and submission to fate or to God expressed in a drama, raptures of lovers described in a novel, feelings of voluptuousness expressed in a picture, courage expressed in a triumphal march, merriment evoked by a dance, humour evoked by a funny story, the feeling of quietness transmitted by an evening landscape or by a lullaby, or the feeling of admiration evoked by a beautiful arabesque —it is all art.

If only the spectators or auditors are infected by the feelings which the author has felt, it is art.

To evoke in oneself a feeling one has once experienced and having evoked it in oneself then by means of movements, lines, colours, sounds, or forms expressed in words, so to transmit that feeling that others experience the same feeling—this is the activity of art.

Art is a human activity consisting in this, that one man consciously by means of certain external signs, hands on to others feelings he has lived through, and that others are infected by these feelings and also experience them.

Art is not, as the metaphysicians say, the manifestation of some mysterious Idea of beauty or God; it is not, as the aesthetic physiologists say, a game in which man lets off his excess of stored-up energy; it is not the expression of man's emotions by external signs; it is not the production of pleasing objects; and, above all, it is not pleasure but it is a means of union among men joining them together in the same feelings, and indispensable for the life and progress towards well-being of individuals and of humanity.

As every man, thanks to man's capacity to express thoughts by words, may know all that has been done for him in the realms of thought by all humanity before his day, and can in the present, thanks to this capacity to understand the thoughts of others, become a sharer in their activity and also himself hand on to his contemporaries and descendants the thoughts he has assimilated from others as well as those that have arisen in himself; so, thanks to man's capacity to be infected with the feelings of others by means of art, all that is being lived through by his contemporaries is accessible to him, as well as the feelings experienced by men thousands of years ago, and he has also the possibility of transmitting his own feelings to others.

If people lacked the capacity to receive the thoughts conceived by men who preceded them and to pass on to others their own thoughts, men would be like wild beasts, or like Kasper Hauser.[1]

And if men lacked this other capacity of being infected by art, people might be almost more savage still, and above all more separated from, and more hostile to, one another.

And therefore the activity of art is a most important one, as important as the activity of speech itself and as generally diffused.

As speech does not act on us only in sermons, orations, or books, but in all those remarks by which we interchange thoughts and experiences with one another, so also art in the wide sense of the word permeates our whole life, but it is only to some of its manifestations that we apply the term in the limited sense of the word.

We are accustomed to understand art to be only what we hear and see in theatres, concerts, and exhibitions; together with buildings, statues, poems, and novels. . . . But all this is but the smallest part of the art by which we communicate with one another in life. All human life is filled with works of art of every kind—from cradle-song, jest, mimicry, the ornamentation of houses, dress, and utensils, to church services, buildings, monuments, and triumphal processions. It is all artistic activity. So that by art, in the limited sense of the word, we do not mean all human activity transmitting feelings but only that part which we for some reason select from it and to which we attach special importance.

This special importance has always been given by men to that part of this activity which transmits feelings flowing from their religious perception, and this small part they have specifically called art, attaching to it the full meaning of the word.

That was how men of old—Socrates, Plato, and Aristotle—looked on art. Thus did the Hebrew prophets and the ancient Christians

---

[1] "The foundling of Nuremberg," found in the market place of that town on 23rd May 1828, apparently some sixteen years old. He spoke little and was almost totally ignorant even of common objects. He subsequently explained that he had been brought up in confinement underground and visited by only one man, whom he saw but seldom.

regard art. Thus it was, and still is, understood by the Mohammedans, and thus it still is understood by religious folk among our
own peasantry.

Some teachers of mankind—such as Plato in his *Republic,* and
people like the primitive Christians, the strict Mohammedans, and
the Buddhists—have gone so far as to repudiate all art.

People viewing art in this way (in contradiction to the prevalent
view of to-day which regards any art as good if only it affords
pleasure) held and hold that art (as contrasted with speech, which
need not be listened to) is so highly dangerous in its power to infect
people against their wills, that mankind will lose far less by banish-
ing all art than by tolerating each and every art.

Evidently such people were wrong in repudiating all art, for they
denied what cannot be denied—one of the indispensable means of
communication without which mankind could not exist. But not less
wrong are the people of civilized European society of our class and
day in favouring any art if it but serves beauty, that is, gives people
pleasure.

Formerly people feared lest among works of art there might
chance to be some causing corruption, and they prohibited art altogether. Now they only fear lest they should be deprived of any enjoyment art can afford, and they patronize any art. And I think the
last error is much grosser than the first and that its consequences are
far more harmful. . . .

Art in our society has become so perverted that not only has bad
art come to be considered good, but even the very perception of
what art really is has been lost. In order to be able to speak about
the art of our society it is, therefore, first of all necessary to distinguish art from counterfeit art.

There is one indubitable sign distinguishing real art from its
counterfeit—namely, the infectiousness of art. If a man without
exercising effort and without altering his standpoint, on reading,
hearing, or seeing another man's work experiences a mental condition which unites him with that man and with others who are also
affected by that work, then the object evoking that condition is a
work of art. And however poetic, realistic, striking, or interesting,
a work may be, it is not a work of art if it does not evoke that feeling (quite distinct from all other feelings) of joy and of spiritual

union with another (the author) and with others (those who are also infected by it).

It is true that this indication is an *internal* one and that there are people who, having forgotten what the action of real art is, expect something else from art (in our society the great majority are in this state), and that therefore such people may mistake for this aesthetic feeling the feeling of diversion and a certain excitement which they receive from counterfeits of art. But though it is impossible to undeceive these people, just as it may be impossible to convince a man suffering from colour-blindness that green is not red, yet for all that, this indication remains perfectly definite to those whose feeling for art is neither perverted nor atrophied, and it clearly distinguishes the feeling produced by art from all other feelings.

The chief peculiarity of this feeling is that the recipient of a truly artistic impression is so united to the artist that he feels as if the work were his own and not some one else's—as if what it expresses were just what he had long been wishing to express. A real work of art destroys in the consciousness of the recipient the separation between himself and the artist, and not that alone, but also between himself and all whose minds receive this work of art. In this freeing of our personality from its separation and isolation, in this uniting of it with others, lies the chief characteristic and the great attractive force of art.

If a man is infected by the author's condition of soul, if he feels this emotion and this union with others, then the object which has effected this is art; but if there be no such infection, if there be not this union with the author and with others who are moved by the same work—then it is not art. And not only is infection a sure sign of art, but the degree of infectiousness is also the sole measure of excellence in art.

The stronger the infection the better is the art, as art, speaking of it now apart from its subject-matter—that is, not considering the value of the feelings it transmits.

And the degree of the infectiousness of art depends on three conditions:—

(1) On the greater or lesser individuality of the feeling transmitted; (2) on the greater or lesser clearness with which the feeling is transmitted; (3) on the sincerity of the artist, that is, on the greater or lesser force with which the artist himself feels the emotion he transmits.

The more individual the feeling transmitted the more strongly does it act on the recipient; the more individual the state of soul into which he is transferred the more pleasure does the recipient obtain and therefore the more readily and strongly does he join in it.

Clearness of expression assists infection because the recipient who mingles in consciousness with the author is the better satisfied the more clearly that feeling is transmitted which, as it seems to him, he has long known and felt and for which he has only now found expression.

But most of all is the degree of infectiousness of art increased by the degree of sincerity in the artist. As soon as the spectator, hearer, or reader, feels that the artist is infected by his own production and writes, sings, or plays, for himself, and not merely to act on others, this mental condition of the artist infects the recipient; and, on the contrary, as soon as the spectator, reader, or hearer, feels that the author is not writing, singing, or playing, for his own satisfaction— does not himself feel what he wishes to express, but is doing it for him, the recipient—resistance immediately springs up, and the most individual and the newest feelings and the cleverest technique not only fail to produce any infection but actually repel.

I have mentioned three conditions of contagion in art, but they may all be summed up into one, the last, sincerity; that is, that the artist should be impelled by an inner need to express his feeling. That condition includes the first; for if the artist is sincere he will express the feeling as he experienced it. And as each man is different from every one else, his feeling will be individual for every one else; and the more individual it is—the more the artist has drawn it from the depths of his nature—the more sympathetic and sincere will it be. And this same sincerity will impel the artist to find clear expression for the feeling which he wishes to transmit.

Therefore this third condition—sincerity—is the most important of the three. It is always complied with in peasant art, and this explains why such art always acts so powerfully; but it is a condition almost entirely absent from our upper-class art, which is continually produced by artists actuated by personal aims of covetousness or vanity.

Such are the three conditions which divide art from its counterfeits, and which also decide the quality of every work of art considered apart from its subject-matter.

The absence of any one of these conditions excludes a work from the category of art and relegates it to that of art's counterfeits. If the work does not transmit the artist's peculiarity of feeling and is therefore not individual, if it is unintelligibly expressed, or if it has not proceeded from the author's inner need for expression—it is not a work of art. If all these conditions are present even in the smallest degree, then the work even if a weak one is yet a work of art.

The presence in various degrees of these three conditions: individuality, clearness, and sincerity, decides the merit of a work of art as art, apart from subject-matter. All works of art take order of merit according to the degree in which they fulfil the first, the second, and the third, of these conditions. In one the individuality of the feeling transmitted may predominate; in another, clearness of expression; in a third, sincerity; while a fourth may have sincerity and individuality but be deficient in clearness; a fifth, individuality and clearness, but less sincerity; and so forth, in all possible degrees and combinations.

Thus is art divided from what is not art, and thus is the quality of art, as art, decided, independently of its subject-matter, that is to say, apart from whether the feelings it transmits are good or bad.

But how are we to define good and bad art with reference to its content or subject-matter?

How in the subject-matter of art are we to decide what is good and what is bad?

Art like speech is a means of communication and therefore of progress, that is, of the movement of humanity forward towards perfection. Speech renders accessible to men of the latest generations all the knowledge discovered by the experience and reflection both of preceding generations and of the best and foremost men of their own times; art renders accessible to men of the latest generations all the feelings experienced by their predecessors and also those felt by their best and foremost contemporaries. And as the evolution of knowledge proceeds by truer and more necessary knowledge dislodging and replacing what was mistaken and unnecessary, so the evolution of feeling proceeds by means of art—feelings less kind and less necessary for the well-being of mankind being replaced by others kinder and more needful for that end. That is the purpose of art. And speaking now of the feelings which are its subject-matter, the more art fulfils that purpose the better the art, and the less it fulfils it the worse the art.

The appraisement of feelings (that is, the recognition of one or other set of feelings as more or less good, more or less necessary for the well-being of mankind) is effected by the religious perception of the age.

In every period of history and in every human society there exists an understanding of the meaning of life, which represents the highest level to which men of that society have attained—an understanding indicating the highest good at which that society aims. This understanding is the religious perception of the given time and society. And this religious perception is always clearly expressed by a few advanced men and more or less vividly perceived by members of the society generally. Such a religious perception and its corresponding expression always exists in every society. If it appears to us that there is no religious perception in our society, this is not because there really is none, but only because we do not wish to see it. And we often wish not to see it because it exposes the fact that our life is inconsistent with that religious perception.

Religious perception in a society is like the direction of a flowing river. If the river flows at all it must have a direction. If a society lives, there must be a religious perception indicating the direction in which, more or less consciously, all its members tend.

And so there always has been, and is, a religious perception in every society. And it is by the standard of this religious perception that the feelings transmitted by art have always been appraised. It has always been only on the basis of this religious perception of their age, that men have chosen from amid the endlessly varied spheres of art that art which transmitted feelings making religious perception operative in actual life. And such art has always been highly valued and encouraged, while art transmitting feelings already outlived, flowing from the antiquated religious perceptions of a former age, has always been condemned and despised. All the rest of art transmitting those most diverse feelings by means of which people commune with one another was not condemned and was tolerated if only it did not transmit feelings contrary to religious perception. Thus for instance among the Greeks, art transmitting feelings of beauty, strength, and courage (Hesiod, Homer, Phidias) was chosen, approved, and encouraged, while art transmitting feelings of rude sensuality, despondency, and effeminacy, was condemned and despised. Among the Jews, art transmitting feelings of devotion and submission to the God of the Hebrews and to His will (the epic of

Genesis, the prophets, the Psalms) was chosen and encouraged, while art transmitting feelings of idolatry (the Golden Calf) was condemned and despised. All the rest of art—stories, songs, dances, ornamentation of houses, of utensils, and of clothes—which was not contrary to religious perception, was neither distinguished nor discussed. Thus as regards its subject-matter has art always and everywhere been appraised and thus it should be appraised, for this attitude towards art proceeds from the fundamental characteristics of human nature, and those characteristics do not change.

I know that according to an opinion current in our times religion is a superstition humanity has outgrown, and it is therefore assumed that no such thing exists as a religious perception common to us all by which art in our time can be appraised. I know that this is the opinion current in the pseudo-cultured circles of to-day. People who do not acknowledge Christianity in its true meaning because it undermines their social privileges, and who therefore invent all kinds of philosophic and aesthetic theories to hide from themselves the meaninglessness and wrongfulness of their lives, cannot think otherwise. These people intentionally, or sometimes unintentionally, confuse the notion of a religious cult with the notion of religious perception, and think that by denying the cult they get rid of the perception. But even the very attacks on religion and the attempts to establish an idea of life contrary to the religious perception of our times, most clearly demonstrate the existence of a religious perception condemning the lives that are not in harmony with it.

If humanity progresses, that is, moves forward, there must inevitably be a guide to the direction of that movement. And religions have always furnished that guide. All history shows that the progress of humanity is accomplished no otherwise than under the guidance of religion. But if the race cannot progress without the guidance of religion—and progress is always going on, and consequently goes on also in our own times—then there must be a religion of our times. So that whether it pleases or displeases the so-called cultured people of to-day, they must admit the existence of religion—not of a religious cult, Catholic, Protestant, or another, but of religious perception—which even in our times is the guide always present where there is any progress. And if a religious perception exists amongst us, then the feelings dealt with by our art should be appraised on the basis of that religious perception; and as has been the case always and everywhere, art transmitting feelings flowing from the religious perception of our time should be chosen from amid all the indifferent art, should be acknowledged, highly valued, and encouraged, while art running counter to that perception should be condemned and despised, and all the remaining, indifferent, art should neither be distinguished nor encouraged.

The religious perception of our time in its widest and most practical application is the consciousness that our well-being, both material and spiritual, individual and collective, temporal and eternal, lies in the growth of brotherhood among men—in their loving harmony with one another. This perception is not only expressed by Christ and all the best men of past ages, it is not only repeated in most varied forms and from most diverse sides by the best men of our times, but it already serves as a clue to all the complex labour of humanity, consisting as this labour does on the one hand in the destruction of physical and moral obstacles to the union of men, and on the other hand in establishing the principles common to all men which can and should unite them in one universal brotherhood. And it is on the basis of this perception that we should appraise all the phenomena of our life and among the rest our art also: choosing from all its realms and highly prizing and encouraging whatever transmits feelings flowing from this religious perception, rejecting whatever is contrary to it, and not attributing to the rest of art an importance that does not properly belong to it.

The chief mistake made by people of the upper classes at the time of the so-called Renaissance—a mistake we still perpetuate—was not that they ceased to value and attach importance to religious art (people of that period could not attach importance to it because, like our own upper classes, they could not believe in what the majority considered to be religion), but their mistake was that they set up in place of the religious art that was lacking, an insignificant art which aimed merely at giving pleasure, that is, they began to choose, to value, and to encourage, in place of religious art, something which in any case did not deserve such esteem and encouragement.

One of the Fathers of the Church said that the great evil is not that men do not know God, but that they have set up instead of God, that which is not God. So also with art. The great misfortune of the people of the upper classes of our time is not so much that they are without a religious art as that, instead of a supreme religious art chosen from all the rest as being specially important and valuable, they have chosen a most insignificant and, usually, harmful art, which aims at pleasing certain people and which therefore, if only by its exclusive nature, stands in contradiction to that Christian principle of universal union which forms the religious perception of our time. Instead of religious art, an empty and often vicious art is set up, and this hides from men's notice the need of that true religious art which should be present in life to improve it.

It is true that art which satisfies the demands of the religious perception of our time is quite unlike former art, but notwithstanding this dissimilarity, to a man who does not intentionally hide the truth from himself, what forms the religious art of our age is very clear and definite. In former times when the highest religious perception united only some people (who even if they formed a large society were yet but one society among others—Jews, or Athenian or Roman citizens), the feelings transmitted by the art of that time flowed from a desire for the might, greatness, glory, and prosperity, of that society, and the heroes of art might be people who contributed to that prosperity by strength, by craft, by fraud, or by cruelty (Ulysses, Jacob, David, Samson, Hercules, and all the heroes). But the religious perception of our times does not select any one society of men; on the contrary it demands the union of all—absolutely of all people without exception—and above every other virtue it sets brotherly love of all men. And therefore the feelings transmitted by the art of our time not only cannot coincide with the feelings transmitted by former art, but must run counter to them.

Christian, truly Christian, art has been so long in establishing itself, and has not yet established itself, just because the Christian religious perception was not one of those small steps by which humanity advances regularly, but was an enormous revolution which, if it has not already altered, must inevitably alter the entire conception of life of mankind, and consequently the whole internal organization of that life. It is true that the life of humanity, like that of an individual, moves regularly; but in that regular movement come, as it were, turning-points which sharply divide the preceding from the subsequent life. Christianity was such a turning-point; such at least it must appear to us who live by the Christian perception of life. Christian perception gave another, a new direction to all human feelings, and therefore completely altered both the content and the significance of art. The Greeks could make use of Persian art and the Romans could use Greek art, or, similarly, the

Jews could use Egyptian art—the fundamental ideals were one and the same. Now the ideal was the greatness and prosperity of the Persians, now the greatness and prosperity of the Greeks, now that of the Romans. The same art was transferred to other conditions and served new nations. But the Christian ideal changed and reversed everything, so that, as the Gospel puts it, "That which was exalted among men has become an abomination in the sight of God." The ideal is no longer the greatness of Pharaoh or of a Roman emperor, not the beauty of a Greek nor the wealth of Phoenicia, but humility, purity, compassion, love. The hero is no longer Dives, but Lazarus the beggar; not Mary Magdalene in the day of her beauty but in the day of her repentance; not those who acquire wealth but those who have abandoned it; not those who dwell in palaces but those who dwell in catacombs and huts; not those who rule over others, but those who acknowledge no authority but God's. And the greatest work of art is no longer a cathedral of victory[2] with statues of conquerors, but the representation of a human soul so transformed by love that a man who is tormented and murdered, yet pities and loves his persecutors.

And the change is so great that men of the Christian world find it difficult to resist the inertia of the heathen art to which they have been accustomed all their lives. The subject-matter of Christian religious art is so new to them, so unlike the subject-matter of former art, that it seems to them as though Christian art were a denial of art, and they cling desperately to the old art. But this old art, having no longer in our day any source in religious perception, has lost its meaning, and we shall have to abandon it whether we wish to or not.

The essence of the Christian perception consists in the recognition by every man of his sonship to God and of the consequent union of men with God and with one another, as is said in the Gospel (John xvii. 21[3]). Therefore the subject-matter of Christian art is of a kind that feeling can unite men with God and with one another.

The expression *unite men with God and with one another* may seem obscure to people accustomed to the misuse of these words that

---

[2] There is in Moscow a magnificent "Cathedral of our Saviour," erected to commemorate the defeat of the French in the war of 1812.—A. M.

[3] "That they may all be one; even as thou, Father, art in me, and I in Thee, that they also may be in us."

is so customary, but the words have a perfectly clear meaning nevertheless. They indicate that the Christian union of man (in contradiction to the partial, exclusive, union of only certain men) is that which unites all without exception.

Art, all art, has this characteristic, that it unites people. Every art causes those to whom the artist's feeling is transmitted to unite in soul with the artist and also with all who receive the same impression. But non-Christian art while uniting some people, makes that very union a cause of separation between these united people and others; so that union of this kind is often a source not merely of division but even of enmity towards others. Such is all patriotic art, with its anthems, poems, and monuments; such is all Church art, that is, the art of certain cults, with their images, statues, processions, and other local ceremonies. Such art is belated and non-Christian, uniting the people of one cult only to separate them yet more sharply from the members of other cults, and even to place them in relations of hostility to one another. Christian art is such only as tends to unite all without exception, either by evoking in them the perception that each man and all men stand in a like relation towards God and towards their neighbour, or by evoking in them identical feelings, which may even be the very simplest, provided that they are not repugnant to Christianity and are natural to every one without exception.

Good Christian art of our time may be unintelligible to people because of imperfections in its form or because men are inattentive to it, but it must be such that all men can experience the feelings it transmits. It must be the art not of some one group of people, or of one class, or of one nationality, or of one religious cult; that is, it must not transmit feelings accessible only to a man educated in a certain way, or only to an aristocrat, or a merchant, or only to a Russian, or a native of Japan, or a Roman Catholic, or a Buddhist, and so on, but it must transmit feelings accessible to every one. Only art of this kind can in our time be acknowledged to be good art, worthy of being chosen out from all the rest of art and encouraged.

Christian art, that is, the art of our time, should be catholic in the original meaning of the word, that is, universal, and therefore it should unite all men. And only two kinds of feeling unite all men: first, feelings flowing from a perception of our sonship to God and of the brotherhood of man; and next, the simple feelings of common

life accessible to every one without exception—such as feelings of
merriment, of pity, of cheerfulness, of tranquillity, and so forth.
Only these two kinds of feelings can now supply material for art
good in its subject-matter.

And the action of these two kinds of art apparently so dissimilar,
is one and the same. The feelings flowing from the perception of
our sonship to God and the brotherhood of man—such as a feeling of
sureness in truth, devotion to the will of God, self-sacrifice, respect
for and love of man—evoked by Christian religious perception;
and the simplest feelings, such as a softened or a merry mood caused
by a song or an amusing jest intelligible to every one, or by a
touching story, or a drawing, or a little doll: both alike produce
one and the same effect—the loving union of man with man. Sometimes people who are together, if not hostile to one another, are at
least estranged in mood and feeling, till perhaps a story, a performance, a picture, or even a building, but oftenest of all music, unites
them all as by an electric flash, and in place of their former isolation or even enmity they are conscious of union and mutual love.
Each is glad that another feels what he feels; glad of the communion
established not only between him and all present, but also with all
now living who will yet share the same impression; and, more than
that, he feels the mysterious gladness of a communion which, reaching beyond the grave, unites us with all men of the past who have
been moved by the same feelings and with all men of the future who
will yet be touched by them. And this effect is produced both by
religious art which transmits feelings of love of God and one's
neighbour, and by universal art transmitting the very simplest feelings common to all men.

The art of our time should be appraised differently from former
art chiefly in this, that the art of our time, that is, Christian art
(basing itself on a religious perception which demands the union
of man), excludes from the domain of art good in its subject-matter,
everything transmitting exclusive feelings which do not unite men
but divide them. It relegates such work to the category of art that
is bad in its subject-matter; while on the other hand it includes in
the category of art that is good in subject-matter a section not
formerly admitted as deserving of selection and respect, namely,
universal art transmitting even the most trifling and simple feelings
if only they are accessible to all men without exception, and therefore unite them. Such art cannot but be esteemed good in our

time, for it attains the end which Christianity, the religious perception of our time, sets before humanity.

Christian art either evokes in men feelings which through love of God and of one's neighbour draw them to closer and ever closer union and make them ready for, and capable of, such union; or evokes in them feelings which show them that they are already united in the joys and sorrows of life. And therefore the Christian art of our time can be and is of two kinds: first, art transmitting feelings flowing from a religious perception of man's position in the world in relation to God and to his neighbour—religious art in the limited meaning of the term; and secondly, art transmitting the simplest feelings of common life, but such always as are accessible to all men in the whole world—the art of common life—the art of the people—universal art. Only these two kinds of art can be considered good art in our time.

The first, religious art—transmitting both positive feelings of love of God and one's neighbour, and negative feelings of indignation and horror at the violation of love—manifests itself chiefly in the form of words, and to some extent also in painting and sculpture: the second kind, universal art, transmitting feelings accessible to all, manifests itself in words, in painting, in sculpture, in dances, in architecture, and most of all in music.

If I were asked to give modern examples of each of these kinds of art, then as examples of the highest art flowing from love of God and man (both of the higher, positive, and of the lower, negative kind), in literature I should name *The Robbers* by Schiller; Victor Hugo's *Les Pauvres Gens* and *Les Misérables;* the novels and stories of Dickens—*The Tale of Two Cities, The Christmas Carol, The Chimes,* and others—*Uncle Tom's Cabin;* Dostoevski's works —especially his *Memoirs from the House of Death*—and *Adam Bede* by George Eliot.

Plato

ART AND MORALITY*

In the next place our youth must be temperate?[1]

Certainly.

Are not the chief elements of temperance, speaking generally, obedience to commanders and command of oneself in the pleasures of eating and drinking, and of sexual relations?

True.

Then we shall approve such language as that of Diomede in Homer,

> *Friend, sit still and obey my word,*[2]

and the verses which follow,

> *The Greeks marched breathing prowess,*[3]
> *. . . in silent awe of their leaders,*[4]

and other sentiments of the same kind.

We shall.

What of this line,

---

* Reproduced from *The Dialogues of Plato* edited by Benjamin Jowett (4th edition 1953) by permission of the Clarendon Press, Oxford, Bk. III, 389d–398b, pp. 234–245.

[1] Socrates is speaking to Adeimantus and is in the course of establishing the characteristics of a state that is organized around the principle of "justice." (M.L.)

[2] *ll.* iv. 412.

[3] *ll.* iii. 3.

[4] *ll.* iv. 431.

> *O heavy with wine, who hast the eyes of a dog*
> *and the heart of a stag,*[5]

and of the words which follow? Would you say that these, or any similar impertinences which private individuals are supposed to address to their rulers, whether in verse or prose, are well or ill spoken?

They are ill spoken.

They may very possibly afford some amusement, but they do not conduce to temperance. And therefore they are likely to do harm to our young men—you would agree with me there?

Yes.

And then, again, to make the wisest of men say that nothing in his opinion is more glorious than

> *When the tables are full of bread and meat, and the cup-bearer carries*
> *round wine which he draws from the bowl and pours into the cups;*[6]

is it fit or conducive to self-control for a young man to hear such words? Or the verse

> *The saddest of fates is to die and meet destiny from hunger?*[7]

What would you say again to the tale of Zeus, who, while other gods and men were asleep and he the only person awake, lay devising plans, but forgot them all in a moment through his lust, and was so completely overcome at the sight of Hera that he would not even go into the hut, but wanted to lie with her on the ground, declaring that he had never been in such a state of rapture before, even when they first used to meet one another

> *Without the knowledge of their parents;*[8]

or that other tale of how Hephaestus, because of similar goings-on, cast a chain around Ares and Aphrodite?[9]

Indeed, he said, I am strongly of opinion that they ought not to hear that sort of thing.

But any instances of endurance of various ills by famous men

---

[5] *Il.* i. 225.
[6] *Od.* ix. 8.
[7] *Od.* xii. 342.
[8] *Il.* xiv. 294 foll.
[9] *Od.* viii. 266.

which are recounted or represented in drama, these they ought to
see and hear; as, for example, what is said in the verses,

> *He smote his breast, and thus reproached his heart,*
> *Endure, my heart; far worse hast thou endured!*[10]

Certainly, he said.

In the next place, we must not let them be receivers of bribes or
lovers of money.

Certainly not.

Neither must we sing to them of

> *Gifts persuading gods, and persuading reverend kings.*[11]

Neither is Phoenix, the tutor of Achilles, to be approved or deemed
to have given his pupil good counsel when he told him that if the
Greeks offered him gifts he should assist them;[12] but that without
a gift he should not lay aside his anger. Neither will we believe or
acknowledge Achilles himself to have been such a lover of money
that he took Agamemnon's gifts, or that when he had received pay-
ment he restored the dead body of Hector, but that without pay-
ment he was unwilling to do so.[13]

Undoubtedly, he said, these are not sentiments which can be
approved.

Loving Homer as I do,[14] I hardly like to say that to attribute these
feelings to Achilles, or to accept such a narrative from others, is
downright impiety. As little can I believe the narrative of his inso-
lence to Apollo, where he says,

> *Thou hast wronged me, O far-darter, most abominable of deities.*
> *Verily I would be even with thee, if I had only the power;*[15]

or his insubordination to the river-god,[16] on whose divinity he is
ready to lay hands; or his offering to the dead Patroclus of his own
hair,[17] which had been previously dedicated to the other river-god

---

[10] *Od.* xx. 17.
[11] Quoted by Suidas as attributed to Hesiod.
[12] *Il.* ix. 515.
[13] *Il.* xxiv. 175.
[14] Cf. *infra*, x. 595.
[15] *Il.* xxii. 15 foll.
[16] *Il.* xxi. 130, 223 foll.
[17] *Il.* xxiii. 151.

Spercheius, and that he actually performed this vow; or that he dragged Hector round the tomb of Patroclus,[18] and slaughtered the captives at the pyre;[19] all this we shall declare to be untrue, and shall not allow our citizens to be persuaded that he, the wise Cheiron's pupil, the son of a goddess and of Peleus who was the most modest of men and third in descent from Zeus, was so confused within as to be afflicted with two seemingly inconsistent diseases, meanness, not untainted by avarice, and overweening contempt of gods and men.

You are quite right, he replied.

And let us equally refuse to believe, or allow to be repeated, the tale of Theseus son of Poseidon, and Peirithous son of Zeus, going forth as they did to perpetrate a horrid rape; or of any other hero or son of a god daring to do such impious and dreadful things as they falsely ascribe to them in our day: and let us further compel the poets to declare either that these acts were not done by them, or that they were not the sons of gods—both in the same breath they shall not be permitted to affirm. We will not have them trying to persuade our youth that the gods are the authors of evil, and that heroes are no better than men—sentiments which, as we were saying, are neither pious nor true, for we have already proved that evil cannot come from the gods.

Assuredly not.

And further they are likely to have a bad effect on those who hear them; for everybody will begin to excuse his own vices when he is convinced that similar wickednesses are always being perpetrated by—

The kindred of the gods, near descendants of Zeus, who worship him their ancestor at his altar, aloft in air on the peak of Ida,

and who have

The blood of deities yet flowing in their veins.[20]

And therefore let us put an end to such tales, lest they engender laxity of morals among the young.

By all means, he replied.

But now that we are determining what classes of tales are or are

---

[18] *Il.* xxii. 395.
[19] *Il.* xxiii. 175.
[20] From the *Niobe* of Aeschylus.

not to be told, let us see whether any have been omitted by us. The manner in which gods and demigods and heroes and the world below should be treated has been already laid down.

Very true.

And it remains for us to decide what to say about men?

Clearly so.

But we are not in a condition to answer this question at present, my friend.

Why not?

Because, if I am not mistaken, we shall have to say that, about men, poets and story-tellers are guilty of making the gravest mis-statements when they tell us that wicked men are often happy and the good miserable; and that injustice is profitable when undetected, but that justice is a man's own loss and another's gain—these things we shall forbid them to utter, and command them to sing and de-scribe the opposite.

To be sure we shall, he replied.

But if you admit that I am right in this, then I shall maintain that you have implied the principle for which we have been all along contending.

I grant the truth of your inference.

That such things are or are not to be said about men is a question which we cannot determine until we have discovered what justice is, and how naturally advantageous to the possessor, whether he seem to be just or not.

Most true, he said.

Enough of the subjects of poetry: let us now speak of the style; and when this has been considered, both matter and manner will have been completely treated.

I do not understand what you mean, said Adeimantus.

Then I must make you understand; and perhaps I may be more intelligible if I put the matter in this way. You are aware, I sup-pose, that all mythology and poetry is a narration of events, either past, present, or to come?

Certainly, he replied.

And narration may be either simple narration, or imitation, or a union of the two?

That again, he said, I do not quite understand.

I fear that I must be an absurdly vague teacher. Like a bad speaker, therefore, I will not take the whole of the subject, but will break a

piece off in illustration of my meaning. You know the first lines of
the Iliad, in which the poet says that Chryses prayed Agamemnon
to release his daughter, and that Agamemnon flew into a passion
with him; whereupon Chryses, failing of his object, invoked the
anger of the god against the Achaeans. Now as far as these lines,

> *And he prayed all the Greeks, but especially the two sons of Atreus,*
> *the chiefs of the people,*

the poet is speaking in his own person; he never even tries to distract
us by assuming another character. But in what follows he takes the
person of Chryses, and then he does all that he can to make us believe that the speaker is not Homer, but the aged priest himself. And
in this double form he has cast the entire narrative of the events
which occurred at Troy and in Ithaca and throughout the Odyssey.

Yes.

And a narrative it remains both in the speeches which the poet
recites from time to time and in the intermediate passages?

Quite true.

But when the poet speaks in the person of another, may we not
say that he assimilates his style to that of the person who, as he informs you, is going to speak?

Certainly we may.

And this assimilation of himself to another, either by the use
of voice or gesture, is the imitation of the person whose character
he assumes?

Of course.

Then in this case the narrative of the poet, whether Homer or
another, may be said to proceed by way of imitation?

Very true.

Or, if the poet were at no time to disguise himself, then again the
imitation would be dropped, and his poetry become simple narration. However, in order that you may not have to repeat that you do
not understand, I will show how the change might be effected. If
Homer had said, "The priest came, having his daughter's ransom in
his hands, supplicating the Achaeans, and above all the kings"; and
then if, instead of speaking in the person of Chryses, he had continued in his own person, the words would have been, not imitation,
but simple narration. The passage would have run as follows (I am
no poet, and therefore I drop the metre), "The priest came and

prayed the gods on behalf of the Greeks that they might capture Troy and return safely home, but begged that they would give him back his daughter, and take the ransom which he brought, and respect the god. Thus he spoke, and the other Greeks revered the priest and assented. But Agamemnon was wroth, and bade him depart and not come again, lest the staff and chaplets of the god should be of no avail to him, and told him that before his daughter should be released, she should grow old with him in Argos. And then he told him to go away and not to provoke him, if he intended to get home unscathed. And the old man went away in fear and silence, and, when he had left the camp, he called upon Apollo by his many names, reminding him of everything which he had done pleasing to him, whether in building his temples or in offering sacrifice, and praying that his good deeds might be returned to him and that the Achaeans might expiate his tears by the arrows of the god"—and so on. In this way the whole becomes simple narrative.

I understand, he said.

And you must realize that an opposite case occurs, when the poet's comments are omitted and the passages of dialogue only are left.

That also, he said, I understand; you mean, for example, as in tragedy.

You have conceived my meaning perfectly; and I think I can now make clear what you failed to apprehend before, that some poetry and mythology are wholy imitative (and, as you say, I mean tragedy and comedy); there is likewise the opposite style, in which the poet is the only speaker—of this the dithyramb affords the best example; and the combination of both is found in epic, and in several other styles of poetry. Do I take you with me?

Yes, he said; I see now what you meant.

I will ask you to remember also what I began by saying, that we had done with the subject and might proceed to the style.

Yes, I remember.

In saying this, I intended to imply that we must come to an understanding about the mimetic art—whether the poets, in narrating their stories, are to be allowed by us to imitate, and if so, whether in whole or in part, and if the latter, in what parts; or should all imitation be prohibited?

You mean, I suspect, to ask whether tragedy and comedy shall be admitted into our State?

Perhaps, I said; but there may be more than this in question:

I really do not know as yet, but whither the argument may blow, thither we go.

And go we will, he said.

Then, Adeimantus, let me ask you to consider whether our guardians should or should not be fond of imitation; or rather, has not this question been decided by the rule already laid down that one man can only do one thing well, and not many; and that one who grasps at many will altogether fail of gaining much reputation in any?

Certainly.

And this is equally true of imitation; no one man can imitate many things as well as he would imitate a single one?

He cannot.

Then the same person will hardly be able to play a serious part in life, and at the same time to be an imitator and imitate many other parts as well; for even when two species of imitation are nearly allied, the same persons cannot succeed in both, as, for example, the writers of tragedy and comedy—did you not just now call them imitations?

Yes, I did; and you are right in thinking that the same persons cannot succeed in both.

Any more than they can be rhapsodists and actors at once?

True.

Neither do comic and tragic writers employ the same actors; yet all these things are imitations.

They are so.

And human nature, Adeimantus, appears to have been coined into yet smaller pieces, and to be as incapable of imitating many things well, as of performing well the actions of which the imitations are copies.

Quite true, he replied.

If then we adhere to our original notion and bear in mind that our guardians, released from every other business, are to dedicate themselves wholly to the maintenance of the freedom of the State, making this their craft and engaging in no work which does not bear on this end, then they ought not to practise or even imitate anything else; if they imitate at all, they should imitate from youth upward only those characters which are suitable to their profession—the courageous, temperate, holy, free, and the like; but they should not depict or be skilful at imitating any kind of illiberality or baseness, lest the fruit of imitation should be reality. Did you never observe how imitations, beginning in early youth and continuing far into life, at length grow into habits and become a second nature, affecting body, voice, and mind?

Yes, certainly, he said.

Then, I said, we will not allow those for whom we profess a care and of whom we say that they ought to be good men, to imitate a woman, whether young or old, quarrelling with her husband, or striving and vaunting against the gods in conceit of her happiness, or when she is in affliction, or sorrow, or weeping; and certainly not one who is in sickness, love, or labour.

Very right, he said.

Neither must they represent slaves, male or female, performing the offices of slaves?

They must not.

And surely not bad men, whether cowards or any others, who do the reverse of what we have just been prescribing, who scold or mock or revile one another in drink or out of drink, or who in any other manner sin against themselves and their neighbours in word or deed, as the manner of such is. Neither should they be trained to imitate the action or speech of madmen; they must be able to recognize madness and vice in man or woman, but none of these things is to be practised or imitated.

Very true, he replied.

Neither may they imitate smiths or other artificers, or oarsmen, or boatswains, or the like?

How can they, he said, when they are not allowed to apply their minds to the callings of any of these?

Nor may they imitate the neighing of horses, the bellowing of bulls, the murmur of rivers and the roll of the ocean, thunder, and all that sort of thing?

Nay, he said, if madness be forbidden, neither may they copy the behaviour of madmen.

You mean, I said, if I understand you aright, that there is one sort of narrative style which is likely to be employed by an upright and good man when he has anything to say, and another sort, very un-like it, which will be preferred by a man of an opposite character and education.

And which are these two sorts? he asked.

As for the man of orderly life, I answered, when the time comes to describe some saying or action of another good man—I think he will be willing to personate him, and will not be ashamed of this sort of imitation: he will be most ready to play the part of the man when he is acting firmly and wisely; less often and in a less degree when he is overtaken by illness or love or drink, or has met with any other disaster. But when he comes to a character which is unworthy of him, he will not seriously assume the likeness of his inferior, and will do so, if at all, for a moment only when he is performing some good action; at other times he will be ashamed, both because he is not trained in imitation of such characters, and because he disdains to fashion and frame himself after the baser models; he feels the employment of such an art, unless in jest, to be beneath him.

So I should expect, he replied.

Then he will adopt a mode of narration such as we have illustrated out of Homer, that is to say, his style will be both imitative and narrative; but there will be, in a long story, only a small proportion of the former. Do you agree?

Certainly, he said; that is the model which such a speaker must necessarily take.

But there is another sort of character who will narrate anything, and, the worse he is, the more unscrupulous he will be; nothing will be too bad for him: and he will be ready to imitate anything, in right good earnest, and before a large company. As I was just now saying, he will attempt to represent the roll of thunder, the noise of wind and hail, or the creaking of wheels, and pulleys, and the various sounds of flutes, pipes, trumpets, and all sorts of instruments: he will bark like a dog, bleat like a sheep, or crow like a cock; his entire art will consist in imitation of voice and gesture, or will be but slightly blended with narration.

That, he said, will be his mode of speaking.

These, then, are the two kinds of style I had in mind.

Yes.

And you would agree with me in saying that one of them is simple and has but slight changes; and that if an author expresses this style in fitting harmony and rhythm, he will find himself, if he does his work well, keeping pretty much within the limits of a single harmony (for the changes are not great), and in like manner he will make a similar choice of rhythm?

That is quite true, he said.

Whereas the other requires all sorts of harmonies and all sorts of rhythms if the music and the style are to correspond, because the style has all sorts of changes.

That is also perfectly true, he replied.

And do not the two styles, or the mixture of the two, comprehend all poetry and every form of expression in words? No one can say anything except in one or other of them or in both together.

They include all, he said.

And shall we receive into our State all the three styles, or one only of the two unmixed styles? or would you include the mixed?

I should prefer only to admit the pure imitator of virtue.

Yes, I said, Adeimantus; and yet the mixed style is also charming: and indeed the opposite style to that chosen by you is by far the most popular with children and their attendants, and with the masses.

I do not deny it.

But I suppose you would argue that such a style is unsuitable to our State, in which human nature is not twofold or manifold, for one man plays one part only?

Yes; quite unsuitable.

And this is the reason why in our State, and in our State only, we shall find a shoemaker to be a shoemaker and not a pilot also, and a husbandman to be a husbandman and not a dicast also, and a soldier a soldier and not a trader also, and the same throughout?

True, he said.

And therefore when any one of these pantomimic gentlemen, who are so clever that they can imitate anything, comes to us and makes a proposal to exhibit himself and his poetry, we will fall down and worship him as a sacred, marvellous and delightful being; but we must also inform him that in our State such as he are not permitted to exist; the law will not allow them. And so when we have anointed him with myrrh, and set a garland of wool upon his head, we shall send him away to another city. For we mean to employ for our souls' health the rougher and severer poet or story-teller, who will imitate the style of the virtuous only, and will follow those models which we prescribed at first when we began the education of our soldiers.

We certainly will, he said, if we have the power.

Then now, my friend, I said, that part of music or literary education which relates to the story or myth may be considered to be finished; for the matter and manner have both been discussed.

V

The Nature and Uses
of Critical Judgment

W. K. Wimsatt, Jr.

EXPLICATION AS CRITICISM*

My aim in this essay is to talk about the question whether explication of a poem is itself an act of criticism and hence of evaluation. Not whether it is necessary to understand a poem *in order* to evaluate it (The question in that form is little better than rhetorical), but whether to understand a poem is the same as to evaluate it. This indeed I conceive to be the only critical question that can be asked about explication. And this is far from a rhetorical question. The correct answer to it lies, I believe, not in a simple affirmation or denial, but in an adjustment. My effort to give an answer will move toward a "monism" of evaluation through explication, but it will insist at the same time on certain other principles.

As both the method and the philosophy of explicative criticism are strongly established in our day, it has seemed to me easiest to make my own approach to the philosophy from the direction of its difficulties. I find my own account of explication caught constantly in a pull between certain opposed pairs of ideas, and these will be my main topics of discussion—namely, (1) part and whole, or the rival claims of these entities to critical consideration; (2) value and disvalue, or the difficulty of describing *dis*value in a philosophy of value which rises above the principles of pleasure and pain; (3) value and neutrality, or the difficulty of merging value with what we com-

* From W. K. Wimsatt, Jr., *The Verbal Icon*, pp. 235–251 (Lexington: University of Kentucky Press, 1954). Reprinted by permission of the author and the University of Kentucky Press.

monly speak of as the neutral facts. Running parallel to these three pairs and tending to involve and unite them and hence to appear in one way or another at all points of the discussion is a fourth pair, the ideas of the explicit and the implicit—or the difference between these, yet their interdependence in the meaning of the poem. In the course of an attempt to show that these four pairs of ideas are to be considered as coming inside the theory of explication, I shall have occasion to inquire if another pair, the affective and the cognitive, are to be considered in the same way.

The thesis that explication *is* criticism, or is at least immediately and intimately related to criticism, proceeds quite reasonably from any theory of poetry which sees the poem as a wholeness of meaning established through internally differentiated form, the reconciliation of diverse parts. And this will be more or less true no matter whether the kind of holism invoked be the realistic and Aristotelian, the idealistic (either neo-Platonic or romantic), or the affective, the synaesthesis of Richards—although, as I have hinted a moment ago, the course of our argument may develop certain relevant differences among these theories. The success of explication in persuading us of literary value is a kind of practical test of how well aesthetic theories of order and wholeness do apply to literary works. More precisely, a practical affinity between holism and *ex*plication arises because organization and wholeness are matters of structure and hence also of *im*plication. Organization and wholeness are at stake, for instance, if we undertake to ask what kind of coherence actually obtains between two main parts of some poem—let us say Donne's *Extasie*, where one part is mystical, the other apparently seductive. It is not clear to me, indeed, that Dryden, in providing a motto for the organ of the contemporary explicators' guild—"The last verse is not yet sufficiently explicated"—had in mind more than the explication of the explicit. But the thoroughgoing explicator will surely not conceive that he has employed his talent to the full unless he performs not only that service (as in glosses and other linguistic and historical observations) but beyond that the *explicit*ation of the implicit. For poetry is never altogether, or even mainly, "poetry of statement." The very difference between those two sides of the explicable, the explicit and the implicit, and the ways in which one may relate to the other are matters with which the explicator is bound to be deeply engaged.

II

One of the main difficulties for explicative holism is that which arises in one form or another from what we may roughly describe as the competition of parts with whole. At the metaphysical level, holistic theories of beauty have had difficulty in coping with the fact that such simple things as bright colors and sweet sounds are usually called beautiful. Our idea of beauty usually does begin with such experiences and persists naively in including them, except in the face of the most studious self-denial. As the sophist Hippias was made to remark, "Gold is a beautiful thing." One escape from the equivocation thus apparently arising for the term "beauty" is the assignment of the name *pleasant* or *agreeable* (the Kantian *Angenehm*) to such simpler experiences, the name *beauty* being reserved for the higher and more complex. A bright color or a note on a French horn will be pleasant; painting or music, beautiful. Another kind of escape, however, and one I believe to be of more interest to us as literary theorists, was that provided by the neo-Platonic and medieval aesthetic of the luminous, and to some extent by its parallel the aesthetic of numerical harmony. The latter of these, proceeding on Pythagorean and Platonic conceptions concerning relations between mathematics, music, and astronomy (the affinities of the quadrivium), arrived at a synthesis of beauty in order and unity with far less of an analogical leap. The aesthetic of the luminous was more daring and solved a bigger difficulty, saying in effect that the reason why we apply the term *beautiful* to simple bright things and to complex harmonies alike is the Platonic reason that light is an analogue of intelligible reality—light is to the eye as truth is to the mind. The radiant color of a Byzantine mosaic or of a painting of saints by Fra Angelico is an analogue of the ordered brilliance of the whole composition. The doctrine has a close relation to the equally ancient doctrine that sight, along with hearing, is a chief aesthetic sense—a sense that can understand things—not just be stimulated by them or amorphously rubbed against them. It is a doctrine which is echoed in our own inevitable habits of aesthetic praise, our metaphoric vocabulary of positive evaluation—not *dirty, drab, muddy*, or *dark* but *clean, bright, radiant, fiery, brilliant, gorgeous*. And we are likely to feel that with these terms of approval we are doing more justice to the worth of the poem than if we were to say it is smooth or sweet.

When Plotinus devised his own expression of the theory which I have just sketched, in the sixth essay of his first *Ennead*, he did so in order to refute a notion which seemed to him implied in the Stoic theory of symmetry, that the parts of a pattern can have beauty only in virtue of their relation to the whole. And in this perhaps the relevance of the ancient problem to our own thinking can be most readily seen. For one of the most persistent implications of holism and explicationism is that the parts do have value only as interacting and making the whole. And this is an article of the philosophy which is bound to impose some hard work here and there on the explicator —even when he is working on the most highly finished poems. Perhaps the difficulty of eliciting the significance of every detail will be the greater in proportion to the largeness and greatness of the poem. Extreme holism is obviously contrary to our experience of literature. (We do not wait until the end of the play or novel to know whether the first scene or chapter is brilliant or dull—no long work in fact would ever be witnessed or read if this were so.) A poem, said Coleridge, the father of holism in English criticism, is a composition which proposes "to itself such delight from the *whole*, as is compatible with a distinct gratification from each component part." The value of a whole poem, while undoubtedly reflecting something back to the parts, has to grow out of parts which are themselves valuable. *The Rape of the Lock* would not come off were not the couplets witty. We may add that good poems may have dull parts; bad poems, bright parts. How minutely this principle could be urged without arriving at a theory of Longinian "sudden flashes," of "cathartically charged images," or Arnoldian touchstones, of poetic diction, or of irrelevant local texture, I do not know. Nor what the minimal dimension of wit or local brilliance of structure may be; nor to what extent a loosely constructed whole may be redeemed by the energy of individual chapters or scenes. Yet the validity of partial value as a general principle in tension with holism seems obvious. The whole with which explication is concerned is something elastic and approximate.

III

And yet again what I have just been saying is not true in the sense that the poetic part could ever be literally like the bright color or the sweet sound of our direct experience. Poetic theory, of all the branches of aesthetics, most easily resolves the competition between part and whole which we have been describing. For poetry entertains no beautiful ideas or words as such. Its materials, unlike those of sculpture, do not have to be high-class. They include everything, "the weariness, the fever, and the fret," dung, poison, pain, deformity, and death. All, we are convinced, may be assimilated by the peculiar process of the given poem. Poetry is the art which most readily transcends the simple pleasure principle and illustrates the principle of structure and harmonious tension.

For somewhat the same reason, however, poetic theory appears to me to be that branch of aesthetic theory which has the greatest difficulty with a certain other thing. I mean *disvalue*—not the absence only of value, a vacuum, and not just an inferior value, a minor pattern of order, but actual disvalue—sources of displeasure in our reading of bad poetry or pseudo-poetry, and not only locally, in blemishes or partial defects, but in total structures, poems which are wholly bad. The aesthetic of harmonious order is closely related to an ontology which sees evil in general, and hence ugliness, as a special kind of negative, an absence, or privation, where something is needed to fill out a harmony. The meaning of this doctrine is most easily realized in such examples as a man without an eye or a leg or a kidney. But even here our realization of disvalue comes about most readily through our positive sense of the inconvenient and the painful. Sheer disvalue in an ontological sense, complete, substantive chaos or disorder, is not conceivable. Anything that is anything at all has a minimal kind of order and being. Our experience of the painful, the evil, and the ugly is not actually negative:—the knife in the dark, the cunning plot, the riotous passion, the distorted countenance. If their evil lies in a deviation from the fullness and rightness of human nature, this evil is none the less powered by a violent positive activity of the human substance. Yet poetry, as we have noted, transcends and subsumes all this evil and by perspective makes it part of aesthetic value. So, we might think of poetry, the reflection of the universe and its intensification through our spirit's activity, as the art in which the ontological principle would be most easily realized—where indeed, as Keats yearned to experience, the ideal would be the real, and there would be no disvalue—only greater and lesser values, only expression and lack of expression. (A good poem, we have often heard, is simply a real poem, a genuine poem.) And how, on this theory of value, could we explicate disvalue? Would not a bad poem be simply one about which we could say little or nothing at all?

Perhaps we ought to begin by confessing that many poems which we are accustomed to call bad, or at least about which we are accustomed to profess discomfort, are not actually bad, but only less good. The element of discomfort attached to them may be a part of our snobbery—or it may come through a reflexive light cast upon the author's vanity or obtuseness. If he had not professed to write a poem, if he had not called it a poem and printed it on fine paper, the offense might be far less.

This kind of escape, however, will hardly be complete. We shall have yet to examine a matter of more critical importance; that is, the peculiar way in which two kinds of truth, that of correspondence (the accent of explicitness) and that of coherence (the accent of implication) are united in verbal discourse and depend on each other. The simplest kind of verbal assertion (let us say, hawthorn is white) if it is true has a truth both of correspondence and of coherence. The whole expression corresponds to reality; but looked at internally and verbally, this correspondence consists of a coherence between subject and predicate. They go together. Poetry is a complex kind of verbal construction in which the dimension of coherence is by various techniques of implication greatly enhanced and thus generates an extra dimension of correspondence to reality, the symbolic or analogical. But all this structure of meaning rises upon a certain element of unavoidably direct reference to outside reality and a minimal truth of such reference.

If it were otherwise, then indeed would poetry achieve the status of a pure idealism. Elements of falsity could scarcely creep into the poet's discourse. Poetry could not go wrong. Everything the poet said would simply have more or less being or character and be more or less valuable. Some such idealistic assumption or desire surely prompted Leibniz to the remark quoted with approval by Herder: "I like almost everything I read." A kind of inversion of that assumption, but equally simplistic, could produce in Tolstoy the view that clarity of meaning is so much a characteristic of sincerity and of moral value that the unintelligibility of Baudelaire was almost the same thing as his immorality. A more cautious neo-Platonic statement had been that of Joubert, that clarity "is so eminently one of the characteristics of truth, that often it even passes for truth itself."

The response of reality to verbal expression while to some extent elastic and plastic (we can in some sense see best what we can best

express) is at the same time in important ways obdurate and recalcitrant. The elasticity comes in the nexus which obtains *between*
words and things, one by which words can be twisted and stretched
a long way and yet maintain a coherence and validity of their own—
so long as the referential relation to reality is not entirely broken.
A theory of poetic wholeness and coherence need not proceed to the
extreme—either idealistic or positivistic—of making the only kind
of *un*truth the unmeaningful. The kind of truth found in poetry (if
either our poetry or our criticism is to survive) will have to be
more than the satisfaction aroused by the contemplation of a system of symbols. Most of us are in fact practically equipped to resist
this kind of total submersion of knowledge into the dimension of
coherence. The routine technique of our historical studies may
sometimes betray us into writing a defence of some mean work of
literature just because we have come to understand the conventions
according to which it was written. But we don't really think that
way. We know all along that some historically understandable
things are wicked or silly.

Actual disvalue in poetry arises when some abstractly true assertion or correct attitude is blurred or garbled in symbolic or stylistic
incoherencies, or (more flagrantly) when some false assertion or
attitude is invested with specious forms of coherence. A sentimental,
that is an excessive or oversimplified, feeling about an object can
be endowed, for instance, with such a pattern of coherence and
suggestion of deep resonance as the metrical and rhyming scheme of
a sonnet. The very fact that a poem is a sonnet may create a greater
opportunity for badness than if it were a ramble in free verse. Or
again, a poem can be given an illusion of depth through the introduction of apparently real but actually phantasmal or irrelevant
symbols. In such cases explication reveals disvalue by explicating the
absence of the truly explicable. In such cases, there is more (and
less) than mere lack or meagerness of meaning. There is the positive and active carelessness and self-deception of the human will
and imagination. This is disvalue and from it comes our experience
of displeasure.

IV

It is a curious testimony to the inseparability of the topics which I
have proposed to discuss in this essay that the difficulty concerning
disvalue which we have just seen, along with such solution as I

may have suggested, greatly facilitates the discussion of what I conceive to be the advantage of a fully explicative criticism—though I have to ask your patience in waiting a short space before I can show how these ideas go together. The great advantage in keeping our explicative activity as close as possible to our evaluative is that we thereby keep a clear distance from affective ways of talking about poems—ways which emphasize our minds exactly so far as they are individual agents reacting to impulses and tending to move in separate directions. The issue is not always clearly recognized; it is often disguised by a terminology of ends and means. Thus David Daiches in his *Study of Literature for Readers and Critics:*

> Pattern by itself does not make literature; it must be the kind of pattern which communicates insight. A mistake made by many contemporary critics, particularly in the discussion of poetry, is to regard subtlety or complexity of arrangement as itself a criterion of literary worth. But pattern in literature is a means to an end, not an end in itself. (p. 80)

But in literature a part is never a means to another part which is the end, or to a whole which is the end—unless in the organistic sense that all parts and the whole are reciprocally ends and means, the heart, the head, and the hand. The end-means relation in literature (so far as the end is outside the means) is a relation between us the readers and the poem, by means of which the poet indeed may be aiming at us. Inside the poem there are no ends and means, only whole and parts.

The affective theory of Richards, or the affective side of his theory, was implicitly an end-means theory, about poetry as a means of working on us—except that here and there this theory got mixed up with a cognitive part-whole terminology, as in the following single sentence of his chapter on "The Language of Criticism."

> This trick of judging the whole by the detail, instead of the other way about, of mistaking the means for the end, the technique for the value, is in fact much the most successful of the snares which waylay the critic.

I suggest that the separation of technique from value which results from confusing means and end with part and whole was in the case of Richards a far more successful snare. It was the resolute unification of technique and value, of knowledge and value, in the system of Croce which provoked the sneering remarks about him in the early books of Richards. And Croce's idealism is indeed one plausible though extreme terminus of the cognitive tendency in criticism—a joining of reality and mind so thorough that all is united in one, the absolute reality of spirit.

The rift between technique and value accomplished by Richards' *Principles* appeared most clearly and curiously in the chapter on "Badness in Poetry." And it is here that I meant we may see disvalue (with its inherently divisive tendency) as a severe test of just how cognitive and hence how coherent a theory of poems may be. Richards distinguished two kinds of bad poems. In one the "original experience" was somehow recognized to have "had some value," but there was a serious failure to communicate the value. This was illustrated by a tiny scrap of H.D.'s imagism. In the other the reproduction of "the state of mind of the writer" was thought to be exact, but the values thus reproduced or communicated were sadly inferior. This was illustrated by a heavy-footed sonnet of Ella Wheeler Wilcox's on Love and Friendship. It is to be noted in passing that this kind of division in badness produced an especially mysterious instance of "intentionalistic" interpretation. (How could he tell that H.D.'s poem proceeded from a valuable experience?) But the more important thing to note is that once the merit of perfect communication (that is, expression and hence structure and meaning) was conceded to the sonnet by Ella Wheeler Wilcox, there was no way left of explaining how it was bad. Richards spoke of the "pleasure and admiration" which ensue for many readers from "the soothing effect of aligning the very active Love-Friendship groups of impulses with so settled yet rich a group as the Summer-Autumn simile brings in." "The value" of the reconciliation, he said, "depends upon the level of organization at which it takes place, upon whether the reconciled impulses are adequate or inadequate. In this case those who have adequate impulses . . . are not appeased. Only for those who make certain conventional, stereotyped maladjustments instead, does the magic work." My objection to this as a critique of the poem is that instead of talking about the poem to you or to me, Richards backed off and started talking equally about the poem and about you and me—what it was going to do to our impulses if they were set in a certain way, what if not. Those remarks about our adequate or inadequate impulses were an opaque substitute for a discourse that could easily have focused an embarrassing light on the poem itself. What kind of Love was it (not Cupid, one assumed, not Venus) who had managed to *lead* us by an action composed entirely of "his own throes and torments, and desires"? Did this allegorical figure, appearing so strangely in a landscape of midsummer burned to ashes, stand for something inside us, or for something outside? What kind of love had we experienced anyway? Why *indeed* were we haunted with a sense of loss? Not only the "triteness" of the close, as Richards put it, but its fatuity was to be noted. In short, what was wrong with the poem was that neither in its main explicit statement nor in the implications of its imagistic parts (and of its overemphatic metrical pattern) did it make sense. The criticism of this poem might have been much more closely unified with that of the first, even though one wished to insist that while neither poem actually conveyed anything coherent, the second was more offensive because it made an elaborate pretense of doing so.

v

We have now arrived at a point in our argument where it is convenient to introduce a final, and as it appears to me the most troublesome, difficulty that confronts a philosophy of explicative criticism—that is, a difficulty in the relation between value and neutrality. It is one which arises with peculiar force from a proposition clearly enunciated in our day—if not often perfectly illustrated—namely, that the critic's job is never to judge a poem (never, that is, to use either valuative or hortatory terms), but only to place the poem in its historical context and to elucidate, to compare and analyze. Thus Richards in one of his later statements, the "Introductory" to his *Practical Criticism* (altering his earlier view):

> There is, it is true, a valuation side to criticism. When we have solved, completely, the communication problem, when we have got, perfectly, the experience, *the mental condition* relevant to the poem, we have still to judge it, still to decide upon its worth. But the later question nearly always settles itself; or rather, our own inmost nature and the nature of the world in which we live decide it for us.

And Eliot in several of his essays:

> Comparison and analysis . . . are the chief tools of the critic. . . .
> Any book, any essay, any note in *Notes and Queries*, which produces
> a fact even of the lowest order about a work of art is a better piece
> of work than nine-tenths of the most pretentious critical journalism.
> . . . *Fact* cannot corrupt taste.

> In the dogmatic or lazy mind comparison is supplied by judgment,
> analysis replaced by appreciation. Judgment and appreciation are
> merely tolerable avocations, no part of the critic's serious business.

> The critic must not coerce, and he must not make judgments of
> worse or better. He must simply elucidate: the reader will form the
> correct judgment for himself.

Eliot was presumably not thinking about the cosmic aspects of
such statements, but the other terminus of the scale of thought
intimated in his simple defence of *Notes and Queries* might be
illustrated in this passage from Plotinus:

> In the single system of Intelligence are embraced as in an envelope
> other envelopes within, other systems and powers and intuitions: it
> may be analysed not by a straight severance, but by progressive ex-
> plication of the implicit.

That is to say, values are continuous with and embodied in experience, in the facts and the structure of the facts. You don't
stick them in or add them on, as in a mere psychology of values.
Furthermore, since value is an indefinitely flexible and analogical
concept, coextensive with form and being, a something which
is always different yet always the same—there is no excuse for
intruding special terms of appreciation and evaluation into our
elucidative criticism. Value is always implicit and indefinable. It
looks after itself. "Beauty Looks after Herself." Criticism is the
"progressive explication of the implicit."

Those seem to me to be the full entailments of the holistic and
elucidative position. And how often have we not all been tempted
to pursue just that policy—prune away the terms of warmth, of
pleasure, of admiration (our subjective impertinences), cut close
to the contour of fact in a neutral and only implicitly critical
style? How often has Eliot himself perhaps not tried to do that?
How often, however, have any of us succeeded?

If you look at *Catiline*—that dreary Pyrrhic victory of tragedy—you find two passages to be successful: Act II, sc. i, the dialogue of the political ladies, and the Prologue of Sylla's ghost. These two passages are genial. The soliloquy of the ghost is a characteristic Jonson success in content and versification. This is the learned, but also the creative Jonson. Without concerning himself with the character of Sulla, and in lines of invective, Jonson makes Sylla's ghost, while the words are spoken, a living and terrible force. The words fall with as determined beat as if they were the will of the morose Dictator himself. . . . What Jonson has done here is not merely a fine speech. It is the careful, precise filling in of a strong and simple outline.

This passage, so bristly with several kinds of evaluative terms, was not unfairly chosen. So far have the more influential critics of our time been from practicing a style of neutral explication (and I think here not only of Eliot but especially of Leavis and Pound) that it would be nearer the truth to say that they have mainly depended on two nonexplicative powers: a confident good taste in pointing out passages and quoting them and an energetic, authoritarian bent for exhortation—that is, telling us we ought to admire these passages. I for one am prepared to defend this use of critical instruments, or at any rate to argue that the greatest influence of the critic is often exercised that way. But at the moment I am more concerned to describe and justify the kind of middle style of evaluative explication which is illustrated to some extent in the passage from Eliot just quoted.

Our critical vocabulary, I venture, may be divided roughly into three classes of terms: at one extreme the terms of most general positive and negative valuing (of which "good poem" or "excellent poem" may be taken as the center and type), at the other extreme the numerous neutral or nearly neutral terms of more or less technical description (*verse, rhyme, spondee, drama, narrative*) and along with these the whole vocabulary of referential content (*love, war, life,* and *death*), and then in between those extremes the numerous and varied terms of special valuation—*dreary, determined, careful, precise, strong, simple*—terms which of course assume their character of positive or negative valuing partly from the complex of more neutral terms among which they are set and partly from the flow of valuing started by more general and explicit value terms—*success, successful, genial, creative.*

It is true that the history of literary criticism shows a more or

less constant regression of key value terms toward the level of neutrality—that is, a movement of value predicates into neutral subject
positions—as the growth of poetic styles and the appearance of inferior repetitions, or the maneuvers of critical dialectic itself, the
assaults and counterassaults of theory, compel ever new discrimination. Croce has commented amusingly on the utility of such terms
as *realistic* and *symbolic, classic* and *romantic* for either positive or
negative valuing. We have heard of *true wit* and *false wit* (even
mixed wit), of *fruitful* and *unfruitful ambiguities*. This Protean
character of our valuative terminology is a function of the analogical
and indefinable character of the poetic, the individual concreteness
which in each different poem is strictly relevant to the requirements
of the poetic formula. The *je-ne-sais-quoi* or magic of the poem, we
understand, is not a mere finishing touch, a stroke or note, added
here and there. It is the form itself, in which the material and neutral
elements of the work of art transcend neutrality and are beautiful.
The reasons for approval and disapproval given in our criticism are
never quite literally universal reasons but must always be taken
in the light of the example we are talking about. When Pope in his
Peri Bathous (ch. X) gives the mock rule, "Whenever you start a
Metaphor, you must be sure to *run it down*, and pursue it as far as
it can go," there can be no doubt that he puts his finger on the absurdity of the passages which he quotes from Blackmore's *Job* and
Isaiah. Yet the same standard, that of consistency in the working
out of metaphor, is that according to which critics of our generation
have praised metaphysical poetry and one of them has even found
the measure for patronizing the sonnets of Shakespeare.

Another way of stating what this means for critical terminology
is to say that the terms at the bottom of the critical scale, the
merely neutral, can never add up to a demonstration of the top term,
"excellent poem." That is, no definition of "excellent poem" has
even been achieved in a merely neutral, scientifically measurable
predicate. Value is not translatable into neutrality. If value resides in
the whole, then analysis must tend toward neutrality.

Nevertheless, our intuition of any complex whole will be improved by analysis. The effort of critical analysis and of explication
is inevitably an effort to bring the two extremes of the critical scale
together, the means or boosters toward this end being the intermediate terms of value—of luster or dullness, warmth or chill,

speed or slowness—as such terms happen to be appropriate to our criticism, and in all the variety of ways in which they can fit the contours of the poem and interpret these in the direction of value. Such value terms may be quite subdued; they may rely little if at all on pointing by explicit and general value terms. It is perhaps under these conditions that they are most serviceable—that is, when they add to a strongly concrete and determinate coloration merely the accent of value.

It is easy to imagine instances, and to produce them from our scholarly literature, of simply neutral, philological, or otherwise historical explanation—where "explication" means glossing, that is, going outside the poem to understand its references, or where this shades into telling the content of the poem. ("This poem alludes to a society prank and tiff in the time of Queen Anne; it deals with the vanity of beaux and belles, with courtship and maidenly resistance.") It is also possible to conceive adding to such description certain simply technical notes—concerning, for instance, burlesque narrative or heroic couplets. It is further possible to conceive and produce instances where these types of neutral explication are enhanced by the addition of some general value term, like *successful, aesthetically satisfying,* or *brilliant,* but where in fact nothing has been done to bridge the gap between the neutral explicative materials and the value terms or to establish the right of the former to the wedding with the latter. But then, finally, it is possible to conceive and to produce instances where explication in the neutral senses is so integrated with special and local value intimations that it rises from neutrality gradually and convincingly to the point of total judgment. It is important to observe that in such instances the process of explication tends strongly to be not merely the explication of the explicit but the e*xplicit*ation of the implicit or the interpretation of the structural and formal, the truth of the poem under its aspect of coherence.

The problem of explication which we have been examining is one which puts before us in a compelling way both the desirability and the difficulty of finding an escape between the two extremes of sheer affectivism and of sheer scientific neutralism. I can make that point clearer by continuing the quotation which I made above from Eliot's passage about the laziness of the critic who judges. Eliot went on to say:

If the critic has performed his laboratory work well, his understanding will be evidence of appreciation; but his work is by the intelligence, not the emotions. . . . Where he judges or appreciates he simply . . . is missing out a link in the exposition.

But on these terms it scarcely makes much difference to rational criticism which side we take—whether we say the critic should judge or say he should not. One of the latest warnings against the use of judgment in criticism has been sounded by Professor George Boas in his *Wingless Pegasus, a Handbook for Critics.* And a reviewer in the *T.L.S.* takes issue with him as follows:

This attempt would lead to the dehumanization of the whole relationship between the beholder and the work of art. Criticism has, inevitably, as much concern with the emotions as with logic.

That is, both Eliot and the *T.L.S.* reviewer (though on opposite sides of the argument) put judgment and appreciation in the area of emotion, separated from the area of intelligence. And that is just what Richards did in his chapter on "Badness in Poetry," except that instead of "logic" or "intelligence" he spoke of "communication." And later he said, in the passage I have quoted, that "communication" is the only thing the critic can deal with. The extreme theory of explicative criticism cuts apart understanding and value just as much as the avowed theory of affects—and that is another way of saying that our main critical problem is always how to push both understanding and value as far as possible in union, or how to make our understanding evaluative.

At higher levels of abstraction, certain terms by which poetry has been defined have tended to lose all specific coloration and to become value predicates nearly if not quite synonymous with the subject "good poetry." Yet it may be that the best of these terms, those which define poetry as a kind of order and wholeness, are able to preserve on one side their character of the analyzable while on the other taking on the indefinable and unanalyzable meaning of poetry or beauty. For these are terms which point toward the intelligible and perspicuous (toward the implicit which may be explicated), rather than toward the opaqueness of the merely individual, concrete, or vivid. Terms of form and order keep to the public object and enable a critic to make more and more relevant observations about any specific work. And translated into a statement about theory, this is to say that formal and intellectual theory is theory par excellence. It is what is implied in the very concept of a theory—if, that is, there is to be any correspondence between the form of our thoughts and their content—more simply if we are to *know* what we are talking about.

Immanuel Kant

THE BASIS OF
AESTHETIC JUDGMENT*

FIRST DIVISION
ANALYTIC OF THE
AESTHETICAL JUDGEMENT

FIRST BOOK
ANALYTIC OF THE BEAUTIFUL

FIRST MOMENT
OF THE JUDGEMENT OF TASTE[1]
ACCORDING TO QUALITY

§ 1. *The Judgement of Taste Is Aesthetical*

In order to decide whether anything is beautiful or not, we refer
the representation, not by the Understanding to the Object for cognition but, by the Imagination (perhaps in conjunction with the Understanding) to the subject, and its feeling of pleasure or pain. The
judgement of taste is therefore not a judgement of cognition, and

---

* From Immanuel Kant, *The Critique of Judgement*, 2nd ed., rev., trans.
by J. H. Bernard (London: Macmillan & Co., Ltd., 1931). Reprinted by permission of the publisher.

1 The definition of taste which is laid down here is that it is the faculty
of judging of the beautiful. But the analysis of judgements of taste must
show what is required in order to call an object beautiful. The moments, to
which this Judgement has regard in its reflection, I have sought in accordance
with the guidance of the logical functions of judgement (for in a judgement
of taste a reference to the Understanding is always involved). I have considered the moment of quality first, because the aesthetical judgement upon
the beautiful first pays attention to it.

is consequently not logical but aesthetical, by which we understand that whose determining ground can be *no other than subjective*. Every reference of representations, even that of sensations, may be objective (and then it signifies the real in an empirical representation); save only the reference to the feeling of pleasure and pain, by which nothing in the Object is signified, but through which there is a feeling in the subject, as it is affected by the representation.

To apprehend a regular, purposive building by means of one's cognitive faculty (whether in a clear or a confused way of representation) is something quite different from being conscious of this representation as connected with the sensation of satisfaction. Here the representation is altogether referred to the subject and to its feeling of life, under the name of the feeling of pleasure or pain. This establishes a quite separate faculty of distinction and of judgement, adding nothing to cognition, but only comparing the given representation in the subject with the whole faculty of representations, of which the mind is conscious in the feeling of its state. . . .

§ 2. *The Satisfaction Which Determines the Judgement of Taste Is Disinterested*

The satisfaction which we combine with the representation of the existence of an object is called interest. Such satisfaction always has reference to the faculty of desire, either as its determining ground or as necessarily connected with its determining ground. Now when the question is if a thing is beautiful, we do not want to know whether anything depends or can depend on the existence of the thing either for myself or any one else, but how we judge it by mere observation (intuition or reflection). If any one asks me if I find that palace beautiful which I see before me, I may answer: I do not like things of that kind which are made merely to be stared at. Or I can answer like that Iroquois *sachem* who was pleased in Paris by nothing more than by the cook-shops. Or again after the manner of *Rousseau* I may rebuke the vanity of the great who waste the sweat of the people on such superfluous things. In fine I could easily convince myself that if I found myself on an uninhabited island without the hope of ever again coming among men, and could conjure up just such a splendid building by my mere wish, I should not even give myself the trouble if I had a sufficiently comfortable hut. This may all be admitted and approved; but we are not now talking of this. We wish only to know if this mere representation of the object is accompanied in me with satisfaction, however indifferent I may be as regards the existence of the object of this representation. We easily see that in saying it is *beautiful* and in showing that I have taste, I am concerned, not with that in which I depend on the existence of the object, but with that which I make out of this representation in myself. Every one must admit that a judgement about beauty, in which the least interest mingles, is very partial and is not a pure judgement of taste. We must not be in the least prejudiced in favour of the existence of the things, but be quite indifferent in this respect, in order to play the judge in things of taste. . . .

§ 5. *Comparison of the Three Specifically Different Kinds of Satisfaction*

The pleasant and the good have both a reference to the faculty of desire; and they bring with them—the former a satisfaction pathologically conditioned (by impulses, *stimuli*)—the latter a pure practical satisfaction, which is determined not merely by the representation of the object, but also by the represented connexion of the subject with the existence of the object. [It is not merely the object that pleases, but also its existence.[2]] On the other hand, the judgement of taste is merely *contemplative; i.e.* it is a judgement which, indifferent as regards the being of an object, compares its character with the feeling of pleasure and pain. But this contemplation itself is not directed to concepts; for the judgement of taste is not a cognitive judgement (either theoretical or practical), and thus is not *based* on concepts, nor has it concepts as its *purpose*.

The Pleasant, the Beautiful, and the Good, designate then, three different relations of representations to the feeling of pleasure and pain, in reference to which we distinguish from each other objects or methods of representing them. And the expressions corresponding to each, by which we mark our complacency in them, are not the same. That which GRATIFIES a man is called *pleasant;* that which merely PLEASES him is *beautiful;* that which is ESTEEMED [or *approved*[3]] by him, *i.e.* that to which he accords an objective worth, is *good*. Pleasantness concerns irrational animals also; but Beauty only

---

[2] [Second Edition.]
[3] [Second Edition.]

concerns men, *i.e.* animal, but still rational, beings—not merely *quâ* rational (e.g. spirits), but *quâ* animal also; and the Good concerns every rational being in general. This is a proposition which can only be completely established and explained in the sequel. We may say that of all these three kinds of satisfaction, that of taste in the Beautiful is alone a disinterested and *free* satisfaction; for no interest, either of Sense or of Reason, here forces our assent. Hence we may say of satisfaction that it is related in the three aforesaid cases to *inclination*, to *favour*, or to *respect*. Now *favour* is the only free satisfaction. An object of inclination, and one that is proposed to our desire by a law of Reason, leave us no freedom in forming for ourselves anywhere an object of pleasure. All interest presupposes or generates a want; and, as the determining ground of assent, it leaves the judgement about the object no longer free.

As regards the interest of inclination in the case of the Pleasant, every one says that hunger is the best sauce, and everything that is eatable is relished by people with a healthy appetite; and thus a satisfaction of this sort does not indicate choice directed by taste. It is only when the want is appeased that we can distinguish which of many men has or has not taste. In the same way there may be manners (conduct) without virtue, politeness without good-will, decorum without modesty, etc. For where the moral law speaks there is no longer, objectively, a free choice as regards what is to be done; and to display taste in its fulfilment (or in judging of another's fulfilment of it) is something quite different from manifesting the moral attitude of thought. For this involves a command and generates a want, whilst moral taste only plays with the objects of satisfaction, without attaching itself to one of them.

EXPLANATION OF THE BEAUTIFUL
RESULTING FROM THE FIRST MOMENT

Taste is the faculty of judging of an object or a method of representing it by an *entirely disinterested* satisfaction or dissatisfaction. The object of such satisfaction is called *beautiful*.

§ 41. *Of the Empirical Interest in the Beautiful*

That the judgement of taste by which something is declared beautiful must have no interest *as its determining ground* has been sufficiently established above. But it does not follow that after it has been given as a pure aesthetical judgement, no interest can be combined with it. This combination, however, can only be indirect, *i.e.* taste must first of all be represented as combined with something else, in order that we may unite with the satisfaction of mere reflection upon an object a *pleasure in its existence* (as that wherein all interest consists). For here also in aesthetical judgements what we say in cognitive judgements (of things in general) is valid; *a posse ad esse non valet consequentia.* This something else may be empirical, viz. an inclination proper to human nature, or intellectual, as the property of the Will of being capable of *a priori* determination by Reason. Both these involve a satisfaction in the presence of an Object, and so can lay the foundation for an interest in what has by itself pleased without reference to any interest whatever.

Empirically the Beautiful interests only in *society*. If we admit the impulse to society as natural to man, and his fitness for it, and his propension towards it, *i.e. sociability*, as a requisite for man as a being destined for society, and so as a property belonging to *humanity*, we cannot escape from regarding taste as a faculty for judging everything in respect of which we can communicate our *feeling* to all other men, and so as a means of furthering that which every one's natural inclination desires.

A man abandoned by himself on a desert island would adorn neither his hut nor his person; nor would he seek for flowers, still less would he plant them, in order to adorn himself therewith. It is only in society that it occurs to him to be not merely a man, but a refined man after his kind (the beginning of civilisation). For such do we judge him to be who is both inclined and apt to communicate his pleasure to others, and who is not contented with an Object if he cannot feel satisfaction in it in common with others. Again, every one expects and requires from every one else this reference to universal communication [of pleasure], as it were from an original compact dictated by humanity itself. Thus, doubtless, in the beginning only those things which attracted the senses, *e.g.* colours for painting oneself (roucou among the Carabs and cinnabar among the Iroquois), flowers, mussel shells, beautiful feathers, etc.—but in time beautiful forms also (*e.g.* in their canoes, and clothes, etc.), which bring with them no gratification, or satisfaction of enjoyment—were important in society, and were combined with great interest. Until at last civilisation, having reached its highest point, makes out of this almost the main business of refined inclination; and sensations are only regarded as of worth in so far as they can be universally communicated. Here, although the pleasure which every one has in such an object is inconsiderable and in itself without any marked interest, yet the Idea of its universal communicability increases its worth in an almost infinite degree.

But this interest that indirectly attaches to the Beautiful through our inclination to society, and consequently is empirical, is of no importance for us here; because we have only to look to what may have a reference, although only indirectly, to the judgement of taste *a priori*. For if even in this form an interest bound up therewith should discover itself, taste would discover a transition of our judging faculty from sense-enjoyment to moral feeling; and so not only would we be the better guided in employing taste purposively, but there would be thus presented a link in the chain of the human faculties *a priori*, on which all legislation must depend. We can only say thus much about the empirical interest in objects of taste and in taste itself. Since it is subservient to inclination, however refined the latter may be, it may easily be confounded with all the inclinations and passions, which attain their greatest variety and highest degree in society; and the interest in the Beautiful, if it is grounded thereon, can only furnish a very ambiguous transition from the Pleasant to the Good. But whether this can or cannot be furthered by taste, taken in its purity, is what we now have to investigate.

SECOND MOMENT
OF THE JUDGEMENT OF TASTE, VIZ.
ACCORDING TO QUANTITY

§ 6. *The Beautiful Is That Which Apart from Concepts Is Represented as the Object of a Universal Satisfaction*

This explanation of the beautiful can be derived from the preceding explanation of it as the object of an entirely disinterested satisfaction. For the fact of which every one is conscious, that the satisfaction is for him quite disinterested, implies in his judgement a ground of satisfaction for every one. For since it does not rest on any inclination of the subject (nor upon any other premeditated interest), but since he who judges feels himself quite *free* as regards the satisfaction which he attaches to the object, he cannot find the ground of this satisfaction in any private conditions connected with his own subject; and hence it must be regarded as grounded on what he can presuppose in every other man. Consequently he must believe that he has reason for attributing a similar satisfaction to every one. He will therefore speak of the beautiful, as if beauty were a characteristic of the object and the judgement logical (constituting a cognition of the Object by means of concepts of it); although it is only aesthetical and involves merely a reference of the representation of the object to the subject. For it has this similarity to a logical judgement that we can presuppose its validity for every one. But this universality cannot arise from concepts; for from concepts there is no transition to the feeling of pleasure or pain (except in pure practical laws, which bring an interest with them such as is not bound up with the pure judgement of taste). Consequently the judgement of taste, accompanied with the consciousness of separation from all interest, must claim validity for every one, without this universality depending on Objects. That is, there must be bound up with it a title to subjective universality.

§ 7. *Comparison of the Beautiful with the Pleasant and the Good by Means of the Above Characteristic*

As regards the Pleasant every one is content that his judgement, which he bases upon private feeling, and by which he says of an object that it pleases him, should be limited merely to his own person. Thus he is quite contented that if he says "Canary wine is pleasant," another man may correct his expression and remind him that he ought to say "It is pleasant *to me*." And this is the case not only as regards the taste of the tongue, the palate, and the throat, but for whatever is pleasant to any one's eyes and ears. To one violet colour is soft and lovely, to another it is faded and dead. One man likes the tone of wind instruments, another that of strings. To strive here with the design of reproving as incorrect another man's judgement which is different from our own, as if the judgements were logically opposed, would be folly. As regards the pleasant therefore the fundamental proposition is valid, *every one has his own taste* (the taste of Sense).

The case is quite different with the Beautiful. It would (on the contrary) be laughable if a man who imagined anything to his own taste, thought to justify himself by saying: "This object (the house we see, the coat that person wears, the concert we hear, the poem submitted to our judgement) is beautiful *for me*." For he must not call it *beautiful* if it merely pleases himself. Many things may have for him charm and pleasantness; no one troubles himself at that; but if he gives out anything as beautiful, he supposes in others the same satisfaction—he judges not merely for himself, but for every one, and speaks of beauty as if it were a property of things. Hence he says "the *thing* is beautiful"; and he does not count on the agreement of others with this his judgement of satisfaction, because he has found this agreement several times before, but he *demands* it of them. He blames them if they judge otherwise and he denies them taste, which he nevertheless requires from them. Here then we cannot say that each man has his own particular taste. For this would be as much as to say that there is no taste whatever; *i.e.* no aesthetical judgement, which can make a rightful claim upon every one's assent.

At the same time we find as regards the Pleasant that there is an agreement among men in their judgements upon it, in regard to which we deny Taste to some and attribute it to others; by this not meaning one of our organic senses, but a faculty of judging in respect of the pleasant generally. Thus we say of a man who knows how to entertain his guests with pleasures (of enjoyment for all the senses), so that they are all pleased, "he has taste." But here the universality is only taken comparatively; and there emerge rules which are only *general* (like all empirical ones), and not *universal;* which latter the judgement of Taste upon the beautiful undertakes or lays claim to. It is a judgement in reference to sociability, so far as this rests on empirical rules. In respect of the Good it is true that judgements make rightful claim to validity for every one; but the Good is represented only *by means of a concept* as the Object of a universal satisfaction, which is the case neither with the Pleasant nor with the Beautiful.

§ 8.   *The Universality of the Satisfaction Is Represented in a Judgement of Taste Only as Subjective*

This particular determination of the universality of an aesthetical judgement, which is to be met with in a judgement of taste, is noteworthy, not indeed for the logician, but for the transcendental philosopher. It requires no small trouble to discover its origin, but we thus detect a property of our cognitive faculty which without this analysis would remain unknown.

First, we must be fully convinced of the fact that in a judgement of taste (about the Beautiful) the satisfaction in the object is imputed to *every one*, without being based on a concept (for then it would be the Good). Further, this claim to universal validity so essentially belongs to a judgement by which we describe anything as *beautiful*, that if this were not thought in it, it would never come into our thoughts to use the expression at all, but everything which pleases without a concept would be counted as pleasant. In respect of the latter every one has his own opinion; and no one assumes, in another, agreement with his judgement of taste, which is always the case in a judgement of taste about beauty. I may call the first the taste of Sense, the second the taste of Reflection; so far as the first lays down mere private judgements, and the second judgements supposed to be generally valid (public), but in both cases aesthetical (not practical) judgements about an object merely in respect of the relation of its representation to the feeling of pleasure and pain. Now here is something strange. As regards the taste of Sense not only does experience show that its judgement (of pleasure or pain connected with anything) is not valid universally, but every one is content not to impute agreement with it to others (although actually there is often found a very extended concurrence in these judgements). On the other hand, the taste of Reflection has its claim to the universal validity of its judgements (about the beautiful) rejected often enough, as experience teaches; although it may find it possible (as it actually does) to represent judgements which can demand this universal agreement. In fact for each of its judgements of taste it imputes this to every one, without the persons that judge disputing as to the possibility of such a claim; although in particular cases they cannot agree as to the correct application of this faculty.

Here we must, in the first place, remark that a universality which does not rest on concepts of Objects (not even on empirical ones) is not logical but aesthetical, *i.e.* it involves no objective quantity of the judgement but only that which is subjective. For this I use the expression *general validity* which signifies the validity of the reference of a representation, not to the cognitive faculty but, to the feeling of pleasure and pain for every subject. (We can avail ourselves also of the same expression for the logical quantity of the judgement, if only we prefix *objective* to "universal validity," to distinguish it from that which is merely subjective and aesthetical.)

A judgement with *objective universal validity* is also always valid subjectively; *i.e.* if the judgement holds for everything contained under a given concept, it holds also for every one who represents an object by means of this concept. But from a *subjective universal validity*, *i.e.* aesthetical and resting on no concept, we cannot infer that which is logical; because that kind of judgement does not extend to the Object. Hence the aesthetical universality which is ascribed to a judgement must be of a particular kind, because it does not unite the predicate of beauty with the concept of the *Object*, considered in its whole logical sphere, and yet extends it to the whole sphere of judging persons.

In respect of logical quantity all judgements of taste are *singular* judgements. For because I must refer the object immediately to my feeling of pleasure and pain, and that not by means of concepts, they cannot have the quantity of objective generally valid judgements. Nevertheless if the singular representation of the Object of the judgement of taste in accordance with the conditions determining the latter, were transformed by comparison into a concept, a logically universal judgement could result therefrom. *E.g.* I describe by a judgement of taste the rose, that I see, as beautiful. But the judgement which results from the comparison of several singular judgements, "Roses in general are beautiful" is no longer described simply as aesthetical, but as a logical judgement based on an aesthetical one. Again the judgement "The rose is pleasant" (to smell) is, although aesthetical and singular, not a judgement of Taste but of Sense. It is distinguished from the former by the fact that the judgement of Taste carries with it an *aesthetical quantity* of universality, *i.e.* of validity for every one; which cannot be found in a judgement about the Pleasant. It is only judgements about the Good which—although they also determine satisfaction in an object—have logical and not merely aesthetical universality; for they are valid of the Object, as cognitive of it, and thus are valid for every one.

If we judge Objects merely according to concepts, then all representation of beauty is lost. Thus there can be no rule according to which any one is to be forced to recognise anything as beautiful. We cannot press [upon others] by the aid of any reasons or fundamental propositions our judgement that a coat, a house, or a flower is beautiful. We wish to submit the Object to our own eyes, as if the satisfaction in it depended on sensation; and yet if we then call the object beautiful, we believe that we speak with a universal voice, and we claim the assent of every one, although on the contrary all private sensation can only decide for the observer himself and his satisfaction.

We may see now that in the judgement of taste nothing is postulated but such a *universal voice*, in respect of the satisfaction without the intervention of concepts; and thus the *possibility* of an aesthetical judgement that can, at the same time, be regarded as valid for every one. The judgement of taste itself does not *postulate* the agreement of every one (for that can only be done by a logically universal judgement because it can adduce reasons); it only *imputes* this agreement to every one, as a case of the rule in respect of which it expects, not confirmation by concepts, but assent from others. The universal voice is, therefore, only an Idea (we do not yet inquire upon what it rests). It may be uncertain whether or not the man, who believes that he is laying down a judgement of taste, is, as a matter of fact, judging in conformity with that Idea; but that he refers his judgement thereto, and, consequently, that it is intended to be a judgement of taste, he announces by the expression "beauty." He can be quite certain of this for himself by the mere consciousness of the separation of everything belonging to the Pleasant and the Good from the satisfaction which is left; and this is all for which he promises himself the agreement of every one —a claim which would be justifiable under these conditions, provided only he did not often make mistakes, and thus lay down an erroneous judgement of taste.

§ 9. *Investigation of the Question Whether in the Judgement of Taste the Feeling of Pleasure Precedes or Follows the Judging of the Object*

The solution of this question is the key to the Critique of Taste, and so is worthy of all attention.

If the pleasure in the given object precedes, and it is only its universal communicability that is to be acknowledged in the judgement of taste about the representation of the object, there would be a contradiction. For such pleasure would be nothing different from the mere pleasantness in the sensation, and so in accordance with its nature could have only private validity, because it is immediately dependent on the representation through which the object *is given*.

Hence, it is the universal capability of communication of the mental state in the given representation which, as the subjective condition of the judgement of taste, must be fundamental, and must have the pleasure in the object as its consequent. But nothing can be universally communicated except cognition and representation, so far as it belongs to cognition. For it is only thus that this latter can be objective; and only through this has it a universal point of reference, with which the representative power of every one is compelled to harmonise. If the determining ground of our judgement as to this universal communicability of the representation is to be merely subjective, *i.e.* is conceived independently of any concept of the object, it can be nothing else than the state of mind, which is to be met with in the relation of our representative powers to each other, so far as they refer a given representation to *cognition in general.*

The cognitive powers, which are involved by this representation, are here in free play, because no definite concept limits them to a particular[4] rule of cognition. Hence, the state of mind in this representation must be a feeling of the free play of the representative powers in a given representation with reference to a cognition in general. Now a representation by which an object is given, that is to become a cognition in general, requires *Imagination*, for the gathering together the manifold of intuition, and *Understanding*, for the unity of the concept uniting the representations. This state of *free play* of the cognitive faculties in a representation by which an object is given, must be universally communicable; because cognition, as the determination of the Object with which given representations (in whatever subject) are to agree, is the only kind of representation which is valid for every one.

The subjective universal communicability of the mode of representation in a judgement of taste, since it is to be possible without presupposing a definite concept, can refer to nothing else than the state of mind in the free play of the Imagination and the Understanding (so far as they agree with each other, as is requisite for *cognition in general*). We are conscious that this subjective relation, suitable for cognition in general, must be valid for every one, and thus must be universally communicable, just as if it were a definite cognition, resting always on that relation as its subjective condition.

This merely subjective (aesthetical) judging of the object, or of

---

4 [Reading *besondere* with Windelband; Hartenstein reads *bestimmte*.]

the representation by which it is given, precedes the pleasure in it, and is the ground of this pleasure in the harmony of the cognitive faculties; but on the universality of the subjective conditions for judging of objects is alone based the universal subjective validity of the satisfaction bound up by us with the representation of the object that we call beautiful.

The power of communicating one's state of mind, even though only in respect of the cognitive faculties, carries a pleasure with it, as we can easily show from the natural propension of man towards sociability (empirical and psychological). But this is not enough for our design. The pleasure that we feel is, in a judgement of taste, necessarily imputed by us to every one else; as if, when we call a thing beautiful, it is to be regarded as a characteristic of the object which is determined in it according to concepts; though beauty, without a reference to the feeling of the subject, is nothing by itself. But we must reserve the examination of this question until we have answered another, viz. "If and how aesthetical judgements are possible *a priori?*"

We now occupy ourselves with the easier question, in what way we are conscious of a mutual subjective harmony of the cognitive powers with one another in the judgement of taste; is it aesthetically by mere internal sense and sensation? or is it intellectually by the consciousness of our designed activity, by which we bring them into play?

If the given representation, which occasions the judgement of taste, were a concept uniting Understanding and Imagination in the judging of the object, into a cognition of the Object, the consciousness of this relation would be intellectual (as in the objective schematism of the Judgement of which the Critique[5] treats). But then the judgement would not be laid down in reference to pleasure and pain, and consequently would not be a judgement of taste. But the judgement of taste, independently of concepts, determines the Object in respect of satisfaction and of the predicate of beauty. Therefore that subjective unity of relation can only make itself known by means of sensation. The excitement of both faculties (Imagination and Understanding) to indeterminate, but yet, through the stimulus of the given sensation, harmonious activity, viz. that which belongs to cognition in general, is the sensation whose universal communicability is postulated by the judgement of taste. An objective relation can only be thought, but yet, so far as it is sub-

_____
5 [*I.e. The Critique of Pure Reason*, Analytic, bk. ii. c. i.]

jective according to its conditions, can be felt in its effect on the mind; and, of a relation based on no concept (like the relation of the representative powers to a cognitive faculty in general), no other consciousness is possible than that through the sensation of the effect, which consists in the more lively play of both mental powers (the Imagination and the Understanding) when animated by mutual agreement. A representation which, as singular and apart from comparison with others, yet has an agreement with the conditions of universality which it is the business of the Understanding to supply, brings the cognitive faculties into that proportionate accord which we require for all cognition, and so regard as holding for every one who is determined to judge by means of Understanding and Sense in combination (*i.e.* for every man).

EXPLANATION OF THE BEAUTIFUL RESULTING FROM THE SECOND MOMENT

The *beautiful* is that which pleases universally, without a concept.

THIRD MOMENT
OF JUDGEMENTS OF TASTE, ACCORDING TO THE PURPOSES WHICH ARE BROUGHT INTO CONSIDERATION THEREIN

§ 10. *Of Purposiveness in General*

. . . The faculty of desire, so far as it is determinable only through concepts, *i.e.* to act in conformity with the representation of a purpose, would be the Will. But an Object, or a state of mind, or even an action, is called purposive, although its possibility does not necessarily presuppose the representation of a purpose, merely because its possibility can be explained and conceived by us only so far as we assume for its ground a causality according to purposes, *i.e.* a will which would have so disposed it according to the representation of a certain rule. There can be, then, purposiveness without[6] purpose, so far as we do not place the causes of this form in a will, but yet can only make the explanation of its possibility intelligible to ourselves by deriving it from a will. Again, we are not always forced to regard what we observe (in respect of its possi-

---

6 [The editions of Hartenstein and Kirchmann omit *ohne* before *zweck*, which makes havoc of the sentence. It is correctly printed by Rosenkranz and Windelband.]

bility) from the point of view of Reason. Thus we can at least observe a purposiveness according to form, without basing it on a purpose (as the material of the *nexus finalis*), and we can notice it in objects, although only by reflection.

§ 11. *The Judgement of Taste Has Nothing at Its Basis But the Form* of the Purposiveness *of an Object* (*or of Its Mode of Representation*)

Every purpose, if it be regarded as a ground of satisfaction, always carries with it an interest—as the determining ground of the judgement—about the object of pleasure. Therefore no subjective purpose can lie at the basis of the judgement of taste. But neither can the judgement of taste be determined by any representation of an objective purpose, *i.e.* of the possibility of the object itself in accordance with principles of purposive combination, and consequently it can be determined by no concept of the good; because it is an aesthetical and not a cognitive judgement. It therefore has to do with no *concept* of the character and internal or external possibility of the object by means of this or that cause, but merely with the relation of the representative powers to one another, so far as they are determined by a representation.

Now this relation in the determination of an object as beautiful is bound up with the feeling of pleasure, which is declared by the judgement of taste to be valid for every one; hence a pleasantness, accompanying the representation, can as little contain the determining ground [of the judgement] as the representation of the perfection of the object and the concept of the good can. Therefore it can be nothing else than the subjective purposiveness in the representation of an object without any purpose (either objective or subjective); and thus it is the mere form of purposiveness in the representation by which an object is *given* to us, so far as we are conscious of it, which constitutes the satisfaction that we without a concept judge to be universally communicable; and, consequently, this is the determining ground of the judgement of taste.

§ 56. *Representation of the Antinomy of Taste*

The first commonplace of taste is contained in the proposition, with which every tasteless person proposes to avoid blame: *every one has his own taste.* That is as much as to say that the determining ground of this judgement is merely subjective (gratification or grief), and that the judgement has no right to the necessary assent of others.

The second commonplace invoked even by those who admit for judgements of taste the right to speak with validity for every one is: *there is no disputing about taste*. That is as much as to say that the determining ground of a judgement of taste may indeed be objective, but that it cannot be reduced to definite concepts, and that consequently about the judgement itself nothing can be *decided* by proofs, although much may rightly be *contested*. For *contesting* [quarrelling] and *disputing* [controversy] are doubtless the same in this, that by means of the mutual opposition of judgements they seek to produce their accordance; but different in that the latter hopes to bring this about according to definite concepts as determining grounds, and consequently assumes *objective concepts* as grounds of the judgement. But where this is regarded as impracticable, controversy is regarded as alike impracticable.

We easily see that between these two commonplaces there is a proposition wanting, which, though it has not passed into a proverb, is yet familiar to every one, viz. *there may be a quarrel about taste* (although there can be no controversy). But this proposition involves the contradictory of the former one. For wherever quarrelling is permissible, there must be a hope of mutual reconciliation; and consequently we can count on grounds of our judgement that have not merely private validity, and therefore are not merely subjective. And to this the proposition, *every one has his own taste*, is directly opposed.

There emerges therefore in respect of the principle of taste the following Antinomy:—

(1) *Thesis*. The judgement of taste is not based upon concepts; for otherwise it would admit of controversy (would be determinable by proofs).

(2) *Antithesis*. The judgement of taste is based on concepts; for otherwise, despite its diversity, we could not quarrel about it (we could not claim for our judgement the necessary assent of others).

§ 57. *Solution of the Antinomy of Taste*

There is no possibility of removing the conflict between these principles that underlie every judgement of taste (which are nothing

else than the two peculiarities of the judgement of taste exhibited
above in the Analytic), except by showing that the concept to
which we refer the Object in this kind of judgement is not taken
in the same sense in both maxims of the aesthetical judgement. This
twofold sense or twofold point of view is necessary to our transcendental Judgement; but also the illusion which arises from the
confusion of one with the other is natural and unavoidable.

The judgement of taste must refer to some concept; otherwise
it could make absolutely no claim to be necessarily valid for every
one. But it is not therefore capable of being proved *from* a concept;
because a concept may be either determinable or in itself unde-
termined and undeterminable. The concepts of the Understanding
are of the former kind; they are determinable through predicates of
sensible intuition which can correspond to them. But the transcendental rational concept of the supersensible, which lies at the
basis of all sensible intuition, is of the latter kind, and therefore
cannot be theoretically determined further.

Now the judgement of taste is applied to objects of Sense, but
not with a view of determining a *concept* of them for the Understanding; for it is not a cognitive judgement. It is thus only a private
judgement, in which a singular representation intuitively perceived is
referred to the feeling of pleasure; and so far would be limited as
regards its validity to the individual judging. The object is *for me*
an object of satisfaction; by others it may be regarded quite differently—every one has his own taste.

Nevertheless there is undoubtedly contained in the judgement
of taste a wider reference of the representation of the Object (as
well as of the subject), whereon we base an extension of judgements of this kind as necessary for every one. At the basis of
this there must necessarily be a concept somewhere; though a concept which cannot be determined through intuition. But through a
concept of this sort we know nothing, and consequently it can
supply no proof for the judgement of taste. Such a concept is the
mere pure rational concept of the supersensible which underlies
the object (and also the subject judging it), regarded as an Object
of sense and thus as phenomenon.[7] For if we do not admit such a
reference, the claim of the judgement of taste to universal validity
would not hold good. If the concept on which it is based were only

---

[7] [Cf. p. 241 *infra.*]

a mere confused concept of the Understanding, like that of perfection, with which we could bring the sensible intuition of the
Beautiful into correspondence, it would be at least possible in itself
to base the judgement of taste on proofs; which contradicts the
thesis.

But all contradiction disappears if I say: the judgement of taste
is based on a concept (viz. the concept of the general ground of the
subjective purposiveness of nature for the Judgement); from which,
however, nothing can be known and proved in respect of the Object, because it is in itself undeterminable and useless for knowledge.
Yet at the same time and on that very account the judgement has
validity for every one (though of course for each only as a singular
judgement immediately accompanying his intuition); because its
determining ground lies perhaps in the concept of that which may
be regarded as the supersensible substrate of humanity.

The solution of an antinomy only depends on the possibility of
showing that two apparently contradictory propositions do not
contradict one another in fact, but that they may be consistent;
although the explanation of the possibility of their concept may
transcend our cognitive faculties. That this illusion is natural and
unavoidable by human Reason, and also why it is so, and remains
so, although it ceases to deceive after the analysis of the apparent
contradiction, may be thus explained.

In the two contradictory judgements we take the concept, on
which the universal validity of a judgement must be based, in the
same sense; and yet we apply to it two opposite predicates. In the
Thesis we mean that the judgement of taste is not based upon
determinate concepts; and in the Antithesis that the judgement of
taste is based upon a concept, but an *indeterminate* one (viz. of the
supersensible substrate of phenomena). Between these two there
is no contradiction.

We can do nothing more than remove this conflict between the
claims and counter-claims of taste. It is absolutely impossible to give
a definite objective principle of taste, in accordance with which its
judgements could be derived, examined, and established; for then
the judgement would not be one of taste at all. The subjective
principle, viz. the indefinite Idea of the supersensible in us, can
only be put forward as the sole key to the puzzle of this faculty
whose sources are hidden from us: it can be made no further intelligible.

The proper concept of taste, that is of a merely reflective aesthetical Judgement, lies at the basis of the antinomy here exhibited and adjusted. Thus the two apparently contradictory principles are reconciled—*both can be true;* which is sufficient. If, on the other hand, we assume, as some do, *pleasantness* as the determining ground of taste (on account of the singularity of the representation which lies at the basis of the judgement of taste), or, as others will have it, the principle of perfection (on account of the universality of the same), and settle the definition of taste accordingly; then there arises an antinomy which it is absolutely impossible to adjust except by showing that *both* the contrary (though not contradictory) *propositions are false.* And this would prove that the concept on which they are based is self-contradictory. Hence we see that the removal of the antinomy of the aesthetical Judgement takes a course similar to that pursued by the Critique in the solution of the antinomies of pure theoretical Reason. And thus here, as also in the Critique of practical Reason, the antinomies force us against our will to look beyond the sensible and to seek in the supersensible the point of union for all our *a priori* faculties; because no other expedient is left to make our Reason harmonious with itself.

Ruby Meager

THE UNIQUENESS OF A
WORK OF ART*

We can hardly today be suspected of dogmatic slumbers in philosophy, but in aesthetics we are haunted by the dream of a rather
new ghost: that of the essential Individual which, if not now to be
comprehended only by Intuition, is still at least to be evaluated
only by standards uniquely applicable to itself. I speak, of course,
of the Work of Art. Everything is an individual thing, but some
are more individual than others, and a true Work of Art is now
said to be so importantly individual that the application of general
standards of evaluation to it is simply inappropriate. Yet the only
familiar rational procedure of evaluation is that of applying general
standards to particular objects. Hence in aesthetics we find the admission that we do offer reasons for our evaluations qualified by an
often visible aura of inverted commas. I call this a new ghost, for
clearly individuality has not always been the hall-mark of aesthetic
merit. A visit to the Assyrian and Egyptian Rooms of the British
Museum would suggest that conformity rather than originality was
de rigueur in art in those days. Yet the requirement of individuality
seems to be generally accepted in current philosophy, and is indeed
offered in explanation of the poverty of philosophical aesthetic
theory. I want to consider what sort of individual thing a work of

* From *Proceedings of the Aristotelian Society*, Vol. LIX, 1958–59, pp.
49–70. Reprinted by permission of the author and of the Editor of the
Aristotelian Society. The author has revised the text slightly.

art must be; whether this means that general standards of evaluation cannot be applied to it; and if not, what sort of rational evaluation is possible in art.

I shall first quote three authors representing what I have called the "current view." The quotations are all from articles appearing in the collection *Aesthetics and Language.*

Professor Gallie writes: "Every work of art is what it is and not another thing . . . the job of criticism is to show what is unique, and therefore important, in a given work."[1] (The force of the argument "important because unique" is a little weakened when we remember Butler's original dictum in this form.) Miss Macdonald similarly writes: "For every work of art is unique and in the last resort, perhaps, can be judged by no standards but its own."[2] And later: "To affirm that a work of art is good or bad is to commend or condemn, but not describe. To justify such a verdict is not to give general criteria as 'reasons' but to 'convey' the work as a pianist might 'show' the value of a sonata by playing it."[3] (But the puzzle is how there can be a "standard" set by, and applicable only to, one and the same object; and performing a work, however sympathetically, seems essentially a different undertaking from, or at least not the whole of, offering a critical evaluation of it.) Stuart Hampshire treats the question at greater length in a long but obscure contrast between works of art and actions as objects of evaluation, in the course of which he says that, since an artist sets himself to produce, not Beauty, but some particular thing essentially of his own devising, "the canons of success and failure, of perfection and imperfection, are in this sense internal to the work itself, if it is regarded as an original work of art."[4] (But we may wonder whether a perfectly executed artist's project is always a perfect work of art.) And further: "An aesthetic judgment has to point to the arrangement of elements, and to show what constitutes the originality of the arrangement in this particular case."[5] (But not any sort of originality is held to be "important," and we may

---

[1] W. B. Gallie: "The Function of Philosophical Aesthetics," *Aesthetics and Language,* ed. W. Elton, Blackwell, p. 26.
[2] Margaret Macdonald: "Some Distinctive Features of Arguments Used in Criticism of the Arts," *ibid.,* p. 118.
[3] *Ibid.,* p. 129.
[4] Stuart Hampshire: "Logic and Appreciation," *ibid.,* p. 162.
[5] *Ibid.,* p. 168.

ask whether even the right sort of originality is always the criterion of aesthetic merit. In the whole history of aesthetic appreciation this might appear as a local and temporary, rather than universal and essential, demand.)

These short quotations do not of course do justice to the careful explanations given by the authors of the positions stated, but
they exemplify the current tendency to regard works of art as
being essentially and in a special sense individuals, unique, and to
regard this as an obstacle to reasoning in any familiar form in support of aesthetic evaluations. It is interesting also to find R. M.
Hare, in his paper on "Universalisability" (P.A.S., 1954-55, N.S.,
Vol. LV), holding what seems to be a contradictory view. At least
some works of art (notably poems and the Union Jack), he takes
to be *not* individuals in any "down-to-earth" sense,[6] and, further,
he takes this to show that at least some aesthetic judgments, namely
those about such works, *are* supportable by reasons of the familiar
sort, or are "U-type" or "universalisable" valuations, in his terms.
I shall proceed to consider in what ways we individuate works
of art (what types of individual are presented by works of art), and
how far these rival conclusions as to the possibility of general aesthetic evaluations are justified.

It is of course true that works of art comprise many different
sorts of individual things, and perhaps none is a down-to-earth
individual thing like a pebble on Brighton beach. No one principle
of individuation can account for all that we say of works of art,
even of works of one art. There is an obvious sense in which paintings and statues, e.g., just are individual things like pebbles. Leonardo's "Last Supper," like the Parthenon and the trees of Birnam
Wood, is in the course of being destroyed by time and wars, despite
the stained-glass copy of it, good for all time, so reverently preserved
at Forest Lawn. But the sense in which Michelangelo's "David" is
an individual thing like these (uniquely located, at present in the
Galleria dell'Accademia in Florence), is clearly different from the
sense in which "Paradise Lost" is an individual thing. "Paradise
Lost" is not to be identified with any *one* spatio-temporal thing.
It exists as a poem by being related to many different spatio-

---

[6] Cf. "When we say that a poem is a good one, we are not appraising an
individual in the ordinary sense. The *Iliad* is like the Union Jack . . . Writing
a poem for recitation on many occasions is like designing a flag for printing
on many pieces of bunting." *Op. cit.*, p. 296.

temporal phenomena: persons reading, persons reciting, the books
they are reading or reciting from, etc. No one of these phenomena
is the poem (rather than *a* recitation, *a* reading, *a* copy of it; even
Milton's dictation was the dictation *of* a poem equally to be heard
to-day in the schoolroom), as the block of marble chiselled by
Michelangelo *is* his "David." Let us call the spatio-temporal phenomena so related to a work of art that when a person sees or hears
them he is seeing or hearing the work, *manifestations* of the work.
Then an original painting or statue both is the work of art itself
and is one of its manifestations, where a poem is like a universal
in being capable of multiple manifestations of which no single one
can count as *the* poem itself. Signatures can be forged, but not
names. Hence though we can (and usually do) use the familiar
material-object principle of individuation to individuate paintings
and statues, this cannot be used to individuate poems.

We do not, of course, always use it to individuate even those
phenomena to which it would sensibly apply, when we refer to
them as works of art. It was not a professional philosopher who said
that Beauty was in the eye of the beholder, and non-philosophers
know what he meant; and for him, presumably, the successful work
of art (say a Braque of the Cubist period) is also in the eye of
(some of) its beholders. But we do not need reminding by now
that seeing, in any sense of "seeing," involves understanding, and
the aesthetic sense is not alone in admitting of degrees of compre-
hension. It seems unnecessary then to go to the poetic extreme of
subjectivism on this account.

More importantly, much of our talk about paintings and statues,
etc., is such that we treat copies, when not mechanically produced,
as also works of art, but not additional works of art. A copy of
"David," provided it is a good one and produced by hand, is also
a work of art, but is the same work of art as its original, namely,
Michelangelo's "David" (in replica). And the Board of Regents of
Forest Lawn Funeral Park, California, U.S.A., who claim that theirs
is not only the only cemetery in the world where *all* mortuary
facilities are gathered together on the one site, including the
beautician's parlour, but also the only place in the world where
all Michelangelo's sculptural masterpieces are gathered together on
the one site (in replica), would no doubt suspect of un-American
sympathies anyone who questioned this complex supposition. We
can support them, moreover, by considering how we should treat

the work of Smith who, desiring to produce a new work of art, and considering Leonardo's "Madonna of the Rocks" beautiful, sits down and copies it, painstakingly and successfully, on to yet another stretch of canvas. We should feel that he has missed the point of art (unless his is the copyist's art, criterion: indistinguishability; class: not fine). What we have gained is not a new work of art, but once more Leonardo's "Madonna of the Rocks," reproduced by Smith as it might be by Ganymede Prints.

But this subtle principle, on which we allow for both the material-object principle, of individuation (two works of art) and a pure work-of-art principle (one work reproduced) would run us into difficulties if we tried to apply it consistently and explicitly at all widely in practice. What would we make of an artist's own repeated attempts at the same subject, e.g.: Do the three representations of "The Healing of the Blind," all (it seems) the work of El Greco between c. 1569 and 1577, showing roughly the same composition but appropriate development in style from a Venetian period to his early Spanish style, count as one work or three? And if three, as seems most appropriate, what becomes of the demand of uniqueness in conception, so far acquiesced in as an essential characteristic of the work of art? A similar problem of deciding when a copy is a copy would arise in connexion with one artist's (*not* a copyist's) deliberate but characteristic copies of another's work, e.g. Van Gogh's copies of paintings by Delacroix. We can decide by definition that such characteristic works embody different conceptions from those contained in their originals; but at least such conceptions will have a great deal in common, and the indeterminacy of the border-line between inspired copy and derivative original work also blurs the import of the demand for uniqueness. And if this is compromised, what becomes of the consequent claim that there is no room for general rules for good art, or for general principles of evaluation for works of art? We in fact do make reasoned comparative evaluations among works sharing what is so obviously a similar aim, or a similar conception. But perhaps this would represent only a minor qualification to the demand; perhaps it would affect only those art-forms where representation is clearly the general aim, and within these, only those works (a very restricted group in any one case) which may be seen as attempts at representing a similar conception of the same theme.

With this qualification, then, we can, in view of our treatment of Smith, recognise as dominant in our use of the title "work of art" a principle by which any deliberate, pure copy of a work is a manifestation of the same work. But it is only the same work in virtue of being, and in so far as it is, qualitatively indistinguishable from the original work. The Forest Lawn statue is Michelangelo's "David" (in replica) only in so far as it reproduces the block chiselled by Michelangelo, now in Florence. Here we find an object functioning very much like a Platonic Form. For in a sense Michelangelo's work of art is identical with the block he worked on; but in the sense which justifies the claim of the block in Forest Lawn to be his "David" in replica, his block is a model-universal; at one and the same time an individual thing, and the defining model of a class of things, more or less imperfect copies of it, which take their identity as works of art (though not as blocks of marble) from it.

In being able to perform this function, a work of art does not differ from any more ordinary spatio-temporal phenomenon. Any individual spatio-temporal object, or temporal phenomenon, *can* be regarded both as a particular thing and as a model or sample of a class of things (or events) qualitatively indistinguishable from itself. So a pin is itself a particular pin but can be regarded as a sample of *the* pin produced by the million in Messrs. Ackrill & Ponsonby's factory. But for instrumental objects like pins, we are not normally interested in one particular specimen to the extent that the importance we give to the others derives from their resemblance to it, and we identify them as more or less imperfect copies of it; we are interested in pins generally for their instrumental efficiency, and identify them in their own right as roughly equally good pins, whether or not they exactly reproduce all the characteristics of the sample pin. So we find, in the model-universal function we accord to a work of art, and the uniqueness it thus acquires, the positive aspect of a traditional negative view of it as an object valued, if at all, not for any instrumental use it may have, but in itself.

In its function as a model-universal, a painting or statue approaches the condition of a poem as being capable of multiple instantiation, though with the difference that one particular instance of the painting is the painting itself, of which the other instances are mere copies, whereas there is no such distinction among the instances in which the poem is manifested. For what the poet produces is usually a specification for his work (in writing), and not itself a manifestation of it. And even if he happens to dictate his poem, and not merely dictate it but declaim it for the record, in suitable tones to produce a master-manifestation of it in the way that the original statue is a master-manifestation of "David," we should probably not accept this degree of dictation. A poem consists of words; and sounds or marks of such a kind as to count as words will specify a literary work independently of what their other characteristics are, even if these help to indicate the *author's* intentions in an ambiguity. Harold Hobson did not feel it inconsistent to give Ralph Richardson a laudatory notice for revealing a Timon of Athens undreamt of by Shakespeare. Poems and plays, as works of art, must bear their identity on their own face, not in the stage-directions or elucidatory comments appended by their authors; and the face of a literary work of art is the words it comprises. Even if poets take generally to the habit of specifying their work on the tape-recorder rather than the typewriter, we shall probably use such records as mere specifications of the words, and not as master-manifestation of the status of Michelangelo's "David."

Even more obviously a composer's work is produced by specification and not by manifestation, except perhaps in in the special case of instrumentalist-composers composing extempore solo works for their own instrument. In general, a composer may well hum or strum as he works, but most would be dismayed if these performances were take as models specifying their completed work. The normal score is plainly a specification for a musical work; it would make no sense to take it for the work itself. In the way that Michelangelo's block is a complete specification of his "David," the specification offered by the score for a musical work is in some ways more, in some ways less, nearly complete than that offered by the words of a poem. The composer can specify in more detail the dynamic development of his work, the accentuation, tempi, and character of playing he requires; these are all more clearly accepted as part of his proper job than is a particular interpretation of his words accepted as mandatory from a poet. But the need for performance in the case of the composer's works opens the way to the performer's art of interpretation, an art which in the case of literature the reader must generally practise for himself; and hence to difficulties in practice in identifying a composer's work which do not arise in the case of the poet's. For compared with the familiar material-object identity underlying our individuation of paintings and statues (even when refined by our treatment of the original objects as model-universals), and our identification of literary works by reference to the spatio-temporal objects or performances first specifying them, we may find the identity of a musical work difficult to establish. How do we, in fact, distinguish for critical comment Mozart's Symphony No. 40 from Klemperer's or Bruno Walter's interpretation of it? In so far as we can do this, it would seem that we do so by considering the other works of both composer and conductors, yielding general (but probably unformulated) conclusions enabling us to recognize the characteristic traits of each in their combined work. (That we can do this at all brings out how remote from the realities of art is the ghostly, absolutely isolated, unique and incomparable work of art which seems to be postulated by the current view.)

However, granting that there are these practical difficulties in identification, and that these are such differences in the types of individuals presented by works of different arts as those which we have briefly considered, it may be that these do not affect the demand for uniqueness in a work of art with which we are concerned. We could well agree that a poem is a type-thing rather than a token-thing, whereas a statue is more obviously to be taken as a token-thing with a type-function, without regarding this as showing in any way that a poem is less of an individual, less unique, as an object of critical evaluation than a statue, or that an aesthetic judgment of the poem might be, whereas one of the statue could not be, such as we could support by reasons of the familiar, generally applicable kind.

What then is the principle of individuation by which a work of art-form is equally an individual for the purposes of critical evaluation? It is tempting to take a clue from our account of Michelangelo's and Milton's role in setting up either the model or the specification for a given work of art and its replicas for the first time, and to find it in our habit of referring identifyingly to such works by reference to the artist and his original activity in producing them. We may take "original activity" here to mean an activity not wholly determined in detail by its being mere obedience to specifications already laid down; and by "mere obedience to specifications" we can mean the execution of specifications without reflective choice between the possible ways of carrying them out resulting in different possible manifestations. An episode of such

activity may result in an object or the specification for a performance intended for appreciation as a work of art, or so appreciated
in fact. Then a work of art may be identifyingly referred to by
reference to the artist and this episode in his history. If this were
also the principle of individuation of works of art, it would account for the sense in which "work of art" is used as entailing
"work not produced solely in obedience to specifications already
laid down"; and thus for our treatment of Smith's pure, deliberate
copy of Leonardo's work as on the one hand the same work, but on
the other hand only a copy and not the work itself. It is undoubtedly
the usual way in which we refer identifyingly to works of art,
and it is a way which is important in understanding the connexion
claimed to hold between the uniqueness required of a work of art
and the impossibility of general rules for its production or criteria
for its evaluation. If a work of art is *individuated* as what results,
either in the form of an object, or in the form of specifications for a
performance, from an episode of original activity in the life of an
artist, then it would seem to be essentially a personal feat, un-
repeatable and individual like any datable phenomenon. But is this
the way in which we individuate works as objects of critical
evaluation?

Let us consider a situation which I cannot see to be wholly impossible though no doubt incredible. Imagine Joyce Cary's Mister
Johnson when young, pupil at a native school in Darkest Africa,
whose Eng. Lit. syllabus had consisted entirely of the Bible and
Basic English, and who had had no other contact with the tongue
of Shakespeare; whose girl-friend's name was Pippa, and who one
year for his school magazine threw off "Pippa Passes," word for word
the replica of Browning's poem. (No doubt such a supposition
would utterly subvert the art-historian's science, but we may not
yet regard its basic presuppositions as not only synthetic and *a priori*
but also constitutive of experience and necessary.) The question is
whether, *if* two men independently produced qualitatively indistinguishable works, their products would be two poems or one?
Surely Mister Johnson has somehow come to write the *same* poem
as Browning? I can see no reason why this situation is impossible
as distinct from suspicious, and it does seem to me that in the case
as stated we should wish to treat the poem as a single poem despite
its two authors. If we take words to constitute a poem, then this is
clearly so. If we take it to be an intuition, or a set of responses,

the answer is no clearer than the supposition. But if we do take it to be the same poem in both cases, we cannot treat our usual identifying reference to works of art by way of their artists as constituting the only principle of individuation we use of them.

The principle implied in this example, by which we call the results of Browning's and of Mister Johnson's original activities the same poem, is that of their consisting of the same elements (English words) in the same arrangement (order), just as a good copy of Leonardo's "Last Supper" would consist of the same elements (colour-patches of what appears to be the same sort of material— stained-glass is so alien a material and the original is now so far ruined as a material object that the Forest Lawn artist's work runs the risk of being a new work and not Leonardo's) in the same arrangement. But though pattern-of-elements is according to this example the individuating principle used of works of art, not just any pattern of elements, even one appreciated aesthetically, counts as a work of art. To count as a work of art the pattern must be produced, as we have noticed, by a person or persons under special conditions. If we knew for a fact that an object was the result of erosion and not of Barbara Hepworth, or of a chimpanzee and not Joan Miro, this would disqualify it altogether from the work-of-art stakes, though not, *pace* Alexander, from the beauty stakes nor from the aesthetic object stakes. And this essential characteristic is so absorbed into the individuating principle of works of art that the patterns of elements they present do not function as ordinary universals, of which all manifestations would be democratically equal instances, but as model-universals where the original object or specification for manifesting the pattern has master-status, defining the work in question. But the model-universals presented by works of art differ from their Platonic forbears in that there is a possibility of their being reduplicated themselves, owing to the spatio-temporal character of their models and the activity producing them. Any activity of an artist of the kind indicated will serve as a model-universal, but in the unlikely case of one artist's independently producing a qualitatively indistinguishable replica of the work of another, there may be two (or more, of course) models defining the same work of art.

To summarise the features elicited of our concept of a work of art, in respect of which the object of aesthetic evaluation is individuated: a work of art is (i) a spatio-temporal object or a spatio-temporal, or, if mental events are not spatial, temporal performance manifesting a pattern of elements which is (ii) the product of a person's or group of persons' activity, where (iii) the activity was not mere obedience to specifications previously laid down, in the sense explained, and where (iv) the object or performance is evaluated as more or less worth having in itself and apart from any purposes it may serve instrumentally. These conditions we have seen to result in a concept which operates in a rather special way as a universal defined by a spatio-temporal particular, which may itself therefore be regarded as a type-universal. Must we now agree that the individual works so picked out have a kind of individuality which prohibits the use of general standards of evaluation in their case? Are the innumerable reasoned comparative evaluations made of works of art misleadingly expressed avowals of mere personal preference, fallaciously supported by invalid general considerations? And, more importantly, if the reason why these are not applicable to works of art is that works of art must be evaluated not for their instrumental worth but for their own, does this not apply equally in the case of the moral evaluation of actions?

At the beginning of the paper we noticed that Mr. Hare seemed aware of a connexion between the type of individual presented by an object and the possibility of its evaluation by general standards, to the extent that he took his denial of a poem's being an ordinary individual to prove that some aesthetic judgments were "universalisable" or "U-type" valuations. We can therefore perhaps throw light on the connexion by considering his argument.

Universalisable, or U-type, valuations are, very roughly, those which can be expressed without using proper names or singular terms. In effect they are what I have been calling the 'quite familiar rational type' of evaluation, done in terms of a general description used as a criterion of value generally applicable to such objects as it makes sense to speak of as having the characteristic in question. An example of such a universalisable valuation would be "Rosie is admirable (because she is utterly reliable)." The "because" here can naturally be taken to invoke the related universal valuation that utterly reliable persons are admirable. The valuation could have been formulated without change of meaning as "Rosie, being an utterly reliable person, is admirable." By contrast, a typically non-universalisable valuation would be "Rosie is admirable (because I love her)." Whatever the "because" is doing here (and it is of course hard to see what it *is* doing), it cannot be invoking the related universal valuation "Persons someone loves are admirable." The speaker would not accept as the *same* valuation "Rosie, being a person someone loves, is admirable." A more persuasive and common example, but of the same kind of valuation (non-U?) would be the patriotic man's "English soldiers are the best (because they are my conutrymen." . . . "My countrymen are the best soldiers" is not a universal valuation, and the related universal form "Any speaker's countrymen are the best soldiers" is logically incoherent.

Hare's argument for the universalisable character (or, we may say, the quite familiar rational character) of at least some aesthetic judgments remains obscure. What he has to show is that at least such valuation as, e.g., " 'Paradise Lost,' being a ø poem, is magnificent," invoking the related universal valuation "ø poems are magnificent." This would represent precisely that application of general standards ("being ø" to evaluate a particular poem that the current view holds to be inadmissible. Hare's argument is extremely elliptical. He says truly that a poem, e.g., can be uniquely specified without the use of proper names or singular terms to refer to it, by listing its words in order. (Instead of mentioning "Paradise Lost" by name I could recite it.) He calls such a listing a "description" of the poem. He then says: "Thus at least some aesthetic judgments are U-type valuations, for if the object of a valuation can be specified without using proper names or singular terms it is hard to see how these can be required for evaluating it."[7] It is, surely, much harder to see the connexion here appealed to. Perhaps he is misled through having called the quotation of the poem a description of it; but even if it were an ordinary description his argument would be unsound. For his argument to be sound, he must take the quotation of the poem to be *both* an ordinary description, generally applicable though in face only applying to "Paradise Lost," *and* a manifestation of the poem itelf, which is nonsensical to treat as generally applicable like a description.

For let us consider Rosie as *in fact* the only utterly reliable person in the universe. Then we can specify her uniquely either as "Rosie" or as "The utterly reliable person", and evaluate her indifferently either in the statement "Rosie is admirable" or in the statement "The utterly reliable person is admirable." But this latter

---

[7] R. M. Hare: "Universalisability," *loc. cit.,* p. 296.

formulation does not entail the universal valuation "Utterly reliable persons are admirable," any more than does the former. It might be that other qualities *in fact* possessed by the person *in fact* picked out by this description are what make her admirable. On the other hand, in the case of the poem, we can take the quotation of the poem to be the specification of the poem itself and not a (generally applicable) description of it. An evaluation of the poem as so specified cannot be made in view of other characteristics of the poem than those so specified, for it has no others; but now there is no sense in the notion of the universal form of this evaluation. " 'Paradise Lost' is magnificent" can be rephrased " 'Of Man's first disobedience, etc.' is magnificent," but what would be the universal form of this evaluation? The quotation can function as *part* of an apparently descriptive phrase: "The poem that goes as follows: . . ." (though this is rather a definition than a description); but the universal form of an evaluation in this form would be: "Any poem that goes as follows: 'Of Man's first disobedience, etc.' is magnificent." The oddity of this universal formulation may throw doubt on Hare's doubt about the individual character of poems in the operative respect as objects of evaluation; it cannot throw light on the character of reasoning in support of such evaluations.

However, the conditions bringing about the failure of Hare's connexion (between an object's being uniquely specifiable by description and an evaluation of it being necessarily universalisable) again point to a necessary condition of universalisable evaluation in terms of particular characteristics, the absence of which in the case of works of art we have already found to be the ground of their uniqueness. Hare seemed to hold that when an object X is the only ϕ thing in the universe (is uniquely specifiable by description), any evaluation of it must be universalisable, presumably in the form "ϕ things are valuable." We saw that the evaluation "The ϕ thing is valuable" is only universalisable when ϕ is a genuine characteristic of a genuine *object* X, such that X must have other characteristics, for it must logically be able to share ϕ with other objects without losing its identity. Then X must be an object with characteristics other than ϕ which are irrelevant to this evaluation of it, since this evaluation is made in terms of its possession of the characteristic ϕ; it might have run "X, *being a ϕ thing*, is valuable." That is, a genuinely universalisable evaluation is an evaluation of things having characteristics irrelevant to this evaluation. Hence this must be an evaluation by which many different things *might* qualify as equally valuable; hence the evaluation must be done in view of some aim, function or desired effect which *might* be achieved by any of many different things, since on this evaluation anything can qualify, in so far as it possesses the characteristic ø, as *pro tanto* valuable.

In denying that works of art can be the objects of universalisable evaluations of this kind, then, philosophers of the current view are drawing the logical conclusion from the traditional view of a work of art already noticed, that if it is valuable as a work of art, it must be so in itself, and not for anything we can do with it but might equally do with something else, or for anything it does for us which other things might equally have done. If we accept this view of a work of art, that it is unique in precisely the respect of being evaluated for itself and not for its instrumental possibilities, it is plain that no universal evaluation of particular characteristics can apply to it, or rather, that any such evaluation could not be aesthetic, but must be, e.g., moral, where art is treated functionally as say, a character-developing force. It is also plain that any evaluation of the particular characteristics of a work of art must be made by reference to their contribution to the total effect of the work to which they belong (and indeed from this condition flow many of the general aesthetic criteria we do in fact recognise and apply).

This leaves open a question, however, which these philosophers seem to regard as thereby closed: is there no general evaluation of objects possible except in terms of characteristics they may share? and except in terms of aims, functions or effects which it makes sense to think may be achieved indifferently by any one of many objects so evaluated? These are questions of some importance, since in so far as we accept the account of the work of art on which they rest, the rationality of critical aesthetic evaluation seems to stand or fall by the answer to them. Moreover it is often held that the moral evaluation of actions, as distinct from a prudential or hedonistic one, must be made in view of the characteristics (and surely *all* the characteristics so far as *prima facie* relevance goes) of the action evaluated, and not in view of its further consequences. If this is a possible view of moral evaluation, it would seem to fall under the same ban as the evaluation of works of art in so far as we have succeeded in accounting for it. Stuart Hampshire, in the article referred to above, attempts to point out the difference between these two types of evaluation which in his view permits the former to be carried on by reference to general principles, but not the latter. We may consider his argument.

Hampshire's argument seems to be as follows: a procedure is recognisably rational if it consists of subsuming a particular case under a general rule or principle. Grading X's is a recognisably rational procedure if it is supportable by generally applicable reasons. Ethics is largely the rational grading of actions. Aesthetics purports to be largely the rational grading of works of art. There is ground for the possibility of such grading in ethics in the exigencies of the human situation, in which we must all act and be acted upon, often to common ends and often relying upon co-operation, and therefore requiring general compliance with common standards and ways of behaving. There is no ground for the possibility of such grading in aesthetics, for nobody *need* produce a work of art or take an interest in one; and such production and such interest are essentially individual performances. "Virtue and good conduct are essentially repeatable and imitable, in a sense in which a work of art is not. To copy a right action is to act rightly; but the copy of a work of art is not necessarily or generally a work of art."[8]

Now it may be that the exigencies of the human predicament force common ethical standards upon us, whereas, since we may spend our lives untroubled with the desire to produce a work of art for the contemplation of others, or with the attempt to understand or appreciate one produced by another, there is no *need* to formulate or apply common aesthetic standards. But this seems so far to be a pragmatic reflection on the usefulness of such common standards rather than a philosophical reflection on their possibility. The philosophical question would seem to be, not, are we *forced* to appreciate and to justify appreciation of works of art, but *if* we want to justify this appreciation, is there any logical possibility of doing this—is there any *contradiction* in the appeal to general standards? We have seen that, given our concept of a work of art, and given that the appeal to general standards must take the form of universalisable evaluations of particular characteristics of works, there is. But how is it that actions, which are after all unique events taking place in unique situations, any of whose characteristics *might* be relevant to their moral evaluation, are nevertheless sus-

---

[8] *Op. cit.*, p. 164.

ceptible of evaluation by general standards, however useful the human predicament would make these?

What Hampshire's contrast between actions and works of art brings out is that the very terms of moral evaluation are set by the general standards or rules which we require people to comply with in their behaviour, whereas there need be no general terms of aesthetic appreciation in order to constitute this response.

Aesthetic appreciation must be a direct response to a particular work, to which "justification" may be irrelevant or impossible, whereas moral appraisal can only take place in a context in which *general* requirements ("authenticity," if nothing less formal) are made of our own and each other's behaviour. In a sense, justification is constitutive of moral appraisal, which must take place in terms of these general requirements. Hence we can only evaluate an action morally as *an instance of* the fulfilment or violation of one of these general requirements. But we must evaluate a work of art, if our account of the concept is accepted, as a whole individual valuable in itself, and therefore not adequately to be treated simply as an instance of some general characteristic. Aesthetic appraisal may take the form of noticing in a particular work those features which render it effective or ineffective most strikingly, but their value will be attributed to them only in the context of the particular work considered; only, therefore, in a context where all the other features present are relevantly present, making the work the work that it is. Clearly there need be no general rule or principle implied in such an appraisal.

There may *be* general rules *in fact* about what gives us aesthetic satisfaction *in most cases*. It is a safe bet that ending a composition on the chord of the diminished 13th is liable to have an untranquillising effect inimical to the appeal of most compositions, but this is merely an *a posteriori* observation, and may well be flouted deliberately in the interests of some special desired effect. It is obvious that there are general rules which artists and composers use and critics appeal to; to bundle all of these into the "technique" pigeon-hole, except by defining any operation guided by general rules as techniques, would seem impossible. "The aged Haydn lamented, as he lay dying," according to Gordon Jacob,[9] that he

---

[9] Gordon Jacob: *The Composer and His Art*, Oxford University Press, p. 30.

had to leave the world just as he was beginning to learn what to do with the wind instruments"—what to do with them in general, that is; a rule concerned with their potentialities; a rule he had no doubt picked up from comparing his own use of them with that of his predecessors and contemporaries, especially Mozart, a rule possibly impossible to formulate in words and certainly very subtle; a purely technical rule? How is one to decide, except by definition? Nevertheless, that there are such rules is a matter of fact logically independent of the fact that we do appreciate works aesthetically.

By contrast, moral appraisal, we have agreed, is defined in terms of the general requirements made of people's behaviour. A moral evaluation of an action must evaluate it as an instance of a generally valued or deplored type of action. Yet this cannot mean that actions, as objects of moral evaluation, are any less unique or individual than are works of art as objects of aesthetic evaluation. Though the evaluation is ultimately done in terms of the general types of action instantiated in this particular event, both the agent and his critic have first to classify the situation and projected actions in it in these terms in an appropriate way; and there is ultimately no rule showing how to classify, any more than there is a rule for acquiring original conceptions. Spontaneity marks the agent as well as the artist. But whereas the artist's evaluations may never get so far as to be subsumed under very general rules for aesthetic merit (there may so far be none covering a new type of satisfactory effect), the agent and his critic must work in universal terms; but all their work is already done when classification in these terms is suitably made. This becomes apparent if we compare Jones the imitative agent with Smith the imitative artist. If Jones does X because Napoleon did Y and Jones admired Y and thinks X copies Y in its admirable characteristics, X will be Jones' action and not Napoleon's; the responsibility not only for doing X but for classifying it as a copy of Y, is Jones'.

It is because he minimises this responsibility and task that Hampshire is led to make the surely extraordinary statement that "to copy a right action is to act rightly." Actions, no less than works of art, have each a unique frame of reference within which they must be evaluated—though in the case of actions it is their spatio-temporal situation which provides this frame, whereas in the case of the work of art it is the artist's conception, or more accurately but less definitely, whatever principles or organisation can be perceived as informing the work as a whole in its completed form. It is plainly false to say, in any ordinary sense of the words, that to copy a right action will be to act rightly. It is right to dance at your rival's wedding but not on her grave. Even if we take a more promising type of action, say, being helpful: it may be right to help young Tom with his homework one night but not the next. Given that we should act consistently and virtuously, we cannot do so by simply copying actions which at one point manifested a virtuous disposition. The up-turning of the usurers' tables was in one context a manifestation of virtue, but it would be unsafe to copy it lavishly in the hope of acting rightly at the Personal Loan counters of the Midland Bank. Imitating Christ is no doubt cultivating certain dispositional characteristics, and no doubt such dispositions to act in certain general ways—to do kind, honest, brave, temperate, forbearing, etc., actions. But this so far gives us no unmistakable general prescriptions for action in any particular situation. We must also act with a sense of proportion; with judgment as to what is relevant in evaluating different possibilities. How can we have general prescriptions for achieving this? Is any such general prescription possible? Only, it seems, if it were possible to present one in a form allowing for each situation to which it is to be applied to be viewed as a whole, rather as we have seen that we must look on a work of art, in which the elements are properly evaluated only as they appear in this particular whole, and not in universal evaluations valid of such elements whenever they occur, in combination with whatever other elements. If we could perform general evaluations of objects as wholes without the mediation of universal evaluations of characteristics, we might here also find that we could *a posteriori* build up general rules as to those features which we generally find to have a satisfactory effect. But in any case we seem here to be under the same threat of irrationalism as we face in aesthetics. For how can any rational evaluation of objects be done except in terms of universal evaluations of their particular characteristics?

For hope in this situation we may turn to the therapeutist; in particular to an interesting discussion of reasoning in aesthetics by Wittgenstein, reported by Moore in the third of his articles on Wittgenstein's lectures to appear in *Mind*, 1955.

Reasons in aesthetics, Wittgenstein is reported as saying, are of the nature of descriptions designed to show what the point of a work is. If this is clear, and the work still doesn't appeal, the question must be dropped. But he also considers possible reasons for not liking a work, e.g., "The bass moves too much." He suggests that this judgment could perhaps be supported by indicating another work in which the relevant feature was "perfectly right." He suggests that aesthetic criticism in general usually takes this problem-solving terminology, as if there were an Ideal of which a work falls short, although of course there is no such Ideal and artists do not work by trying to reproduce one.

It seems to me that Wittgenstein has here indicated a very common form for aesthetic reasoning to take, involving the presumption, but not the specification, of a general point to a work, in terms of which its features can be assessed as contributing or not contributing to it. For the purposes of rational discussion the trouble is, of course, that this "point" cannot be clearly or exhaustively stated; hence no simple functional evaluation of the features of the work can be made, and the work as a whole is not adequately summarisable and evaluatable as an instance of something with such-and-such a point. How then can evaluation proceed? The interesting suggestion is that evaluations of features of works (and if so, also of works as wholes) can be supported, if at all, by reference to what may be taken as a model of the successful use of a criticised feature (or of a successful work with a similar point), indicated *in situ* in its own successful work.

This seems an unexpected place for a paradigm-case method to be evoked, in a context where the "problems" more or less correctly "solved" (where the feature is "right" or "not quite right") *must* differ so completely that any such device would seem to be put out of court. But the paradigm-case method of support has precisely this advantage over the more usual general-formula method, that it allows us to present a model problem-plus-solution instead of reducing a given problem to general terms where a single generally applicable formula can give an answer. The paradigm-case method allows us to use a kind of ostensive general principle of evaluation, in a situation where the resemblance assumed and that to be required is too subtle and complex, rather than too simple, to be verbally formulated in a precise descriptive standard. The suggestion is that we *can* apply general criteria of evaluation (although only of a very restricted scope), but that they will take the form of models together with the demand for some very free kind of imitation (guided essentially by judgment in the use of the model), rather than of written-out requirements. Kant, of course, made a similar point in his pioneer work on the aesthetic judgment. If Haydn had attempted to formulate what he had learnt about the use of the wind instruments for the benefit of his pupils, his only hope of doing so would surely have been by means of examples from his and Mozart's works (together no doubt for contrast with examples from their own). If such general principles can be found and used, they will allow for the individual framework of reference presented by each work, and the policy of despair emerging from the current view of aesthetics may seem premature.

If this is a typical form of support available in aesthetic evaluation, can it be called rational? Let us consider the question of rational support for a judgment of very much this kind, namely, her young man's judgment that Rosie is lovable; a judgment which he would wish to treat as fully rational but precisely of the kind which Miss Macdonald prescribed for aesthetic judgments: Rosie, he feels, can be judged by no standards but her own. We can now provide the young man with an ostensive general principle of the type we have outlined. It would have to be *formulated* in an uninformative way: "Rosie is lovable just because she is Rosie"; but this verbal formulation would invoke a display of Rosie herself in action, in support of the judgment. It is thus quite different from the universalisable judgment: "Rosie is lovable because she has all and only the characteristics she does have," for this would be equivalent to a principle in which her characteristics were merely listed, and any occurrence of the combination of the characteristics in the list would count as of equal lovableness. The ostensive principle is quite different from this in allowing for the fact that it is the particular form in which Rosie manifests them, and the particular way in which they are combined in her, that make just this occurrence of them together lovable. It is not *insouciance* in general, but Rosie's particular actions and attitudes which for want of a better name we call *insouciance*, and which are combined in her with an unexpected gravity on certain significant occasions, etc., etc., which are so supremely lovable in Rosie. However precisely we discriminate Rosie's peculiar virtues in *general* terms, and without the help of pointing to her, we cannot pin Rosie down in this way, and it is just her individual manifestation of her characteristics which makes them lovable *in her*.

Given a highly complex object like Rosie or a symphony, to be evaluated for its own sake and not functionally with some general end in mind, it seems perfectly rational to refuse to commit oneself to generalisable evaluations of particular characteristics, however precisely defined. On the other hand it seems an adequate acknowledgment of the demand of reason for consistency and general evaluations rather than avowals of atomic particular preferences, to provide a general principle of the ostensive form: "Anything sufficiently closely reproducing the features of Rosie, in the excellent way and excellent combination in which they are manifested by her, is lovable." These features may then even be isolated for special mention, like the characteristic movement of the bass in Wittgenstein's example. "Anyone *insouciante* in a way sufficiently like Rosie has a good chance of being lovable." "Any passage in a work resembling this one sufficiently closely where the bass moves as much as this bass moves has a good chance of being spoilt." But the force of these comments as general principles of evaluation clearly resides in the model, and not in the general value of the characteristics mentioned.

What the ostensive general principle allows for, then, is the comparative evaluation of objects in virtue of certain of their common characteristics, together with the recognition that these characteristics can only be evaluated in terms of their contribution to the effect of each object separately, where this provides a separate framework of reference in each case. Such comparative and general evaluations will be possible to the extent that the resemblances between the total effects of the objects concerned are close enough to allow for it; but this is ultimately a question for the judgment of those making the evaluations; if they cannot agree on it, then indeed the attempt must fail.

In this paper I have come a very long and pedantic way round to the venerable old conclusion that the uniqueness demanded of a work of art is that consequent on its essentially being evaluated for itself and not for its instrumental potentialities; and have given an old problem of the possibility of rational aesthetic evaluation an answer at least as old as Kant's. But I hope that by taking the long way round I have raised a few of the complexities buried in our familiar talk of works of art and have thereby succeeded in laying a promising metaphysical ghost.

Arnold Isenberg

CRITICAL COMMUNICATION*

That questions about meaning are provisionally separable, even if finally inseparable, from questions about validity and truth, is shown by the fact that meanings can be exchanged without the corresponding convictions or decisions. What is imparted by one person to another in an act of communication is (typically) a certain idea, thought, content, meaning, or claim—not a belief, expectation, surmise, or doubt; for the last are dependent on factors, such as the checking process, which go beyond the mere understanding of the message conveyed. And there is a host of questions which have to do with this message: its simplicity or complexity, its clarity or obscurity, its tense, its mood, its modality, and so on. Now, the theory of art criticism has, I think, been seriously hampered by its headlong assault on the question of validity. We have many doctrines about the objectivity of the critical judgment but few concerning its import, or claim to objectivity, though the settlement of the first question probably depends on the clarification of the second. The following remarks are for the most part restricted to meeting such questions as: What is the content of the critic's argument? What claim does he transmit to us? How does he expect us to deal with this claim?

* From The Philosophical Review, Vol. LVIII, 1949, pp. 330–344. Reprinted by permission of the author and The Philosophical Review.

Read at the annual meeting of the American Society for Aesthetics, Cambridge, Mass., September 1–3, 1948. The author is indebted to Mr. Herbert Bohnert for assistance with this paper.

A good starting point is a theory of criticism, widely held in spite of its deficiencies, which divides the critical process into three parts. There is the value judgment or *verdict* (V): "This picture or poem is good—." There is a particular statement or *reason* (R): "—because it has such-and-such a quality—." And there is a general statement or *norm* (N): "—and any work which has that quality is *pro tanto* good."[1]

V has been construed, and will be construed here, as an expression of feeling—an utterance manifesting praise or blame. But among utterances of that class it is distinguished by being in some sense conditional upon R. This is only another phrasing of the commonly noted peculiarity of aesthetic feeling: that it is "embodied" in or "attached" to an aesthetic content.

R is a statement describing the content of an art work; but not every such descriptive statement is a case of R. The statement, "There are just twelve flowers in that picture" (and with it nine out of ten descriptions in Crowe and Cavalcaselle), is without critical relevance, that is, without any bearing upon V. The description of a work of art is seldom attempted for its own sake. It is controlled by some purpose, some interest; and there are many interests by which it might be controlled other than that of reaching or defending a critical judgment. The qualities which are significant in relation to one purpose—dating, attribution, archaeological reconstruction, clinical diagnosis, proving or illustrating some thesis in sociology—might be quite immaterial in relation to another. At the same time, we cannot be sure that there is any *kind* of statement about art, dictated by no matter what interest, which cannot also act as R; or, in other words, that there is any *kind* of knowledge about art which cannot influence aesthetic appreciation.

V and R, it should be said, are often combined in sentences which are at once normative and descriptive. If we have been told that the colors of a certain painting are garish, it would be astonishing to find that they were all very pale and unsaturated; and to this extent the critical comment conveys information. On the other hand,

---

[1] Cf., for instance, C. J. Ducasse, *Art, the Critics, and You* (p. 116): "The statement that a given work possesses a certain objective characteristic expresses at the same time a judgment of value if the characteristic is one that the judging person approves, or as the case may be, disapproves; and is thus one that he regards as conferring, respectively, positive or negative value on any object of the given kind that happens to possess it." See, further, pp. 117–120.

we might find the colors bright and intense, as expected, without being thereby forced to admit that they are garish; and this reveals the component of valuation (i.e., distaste) in the critical remark. This feature of critical usage has attracted much notice and some study; but we do not discuss it here at all. We shall be concerned exclusively with the descriptive function of R.

Now if we ask what makes a description critically useful and relevant, the first suggestion which occurs is that it is *backed up by* N. N is based upon an inductive generalization which describes a relationship between some aesthetic quality and someone's or everyone's system of aesthetic response. Notice: I do not say that N *is* an inductive generalization; for in critical evaluation N is being used not to predict or to explain anybody's reaction to a work of art but to vindicate that reaction, perhaps to someone who does not yet share it; and in this capacity N is a precept, a rule, a *generalized value statement.* But the *choice* of one norm, rather than another, when that choice is challenged, will usually be given some sort of inductive justification. We return to this question in a moment. I think we shall find that a careful analysis of N is unnecessary, because there are considerations which permit us to dismiss it altogether.

At this point it is well to remind ourselves that there is a difference between *explaining* and *justifying* a critical response. A psychologist who should be asked "why X likes the object y" would take X's enjoyment as a datum, a fact to be explained. And if he offers as explanation the presence in y of the quality Q, there is, explicit or latent in this causal argument, an appeal to some generalization which he has reason to think is true, such as "X likes any work which has that quality." But when we ask X as a critic "why he likes the object y," we want him to give us some reason to like it too and are not concerned with the causes of what we may so far regard as his bad taste. This distinction between the genetic and the normative dimension of inquiry, though it is familiar to all and acceptable to most of us, is commonly ignored in the practice of aesthetic speculation; and the chief reason for this—other than the ambiguity of the question "Why do you like this work?"—is the fact that some statements about the object will necessarily figure both in the explanation and in the critical defense of any reaction to it. Thus, if I tried to explain my feeling for the line

But musical as is Apollo's lute

I should certainly mention "the pattern of u's and l's which reinforces the meaning with its own musical quality," because this
quality of my sensations is doubtless among the conditions of my
feeling response. And the same point would be made in any effort
to convince another person of the beauty of the line. The remark
which gives a reason also, in this case, states a cause. But notice
that, though as criticism this comment might be very effective, it
is practically worthless as explanation, because we have no phonetic
or psychological laws (nor any plausible "common-sense" generalizations) from which we might derive the prediction that such a
pattern of u's and l's should be pleasing to me. In fact, the formulation ("pattern of u's and l's," etc.) is so vague that one could not
tell just what general hypothesis it is that is being invoked or assumed; yet it is quite sharp enough for critical purposes. On the
other hand, suppose that someone should fail to be "convinced" by
my argument in favor of Milton's line. He might still readily admit that the quality which I mentioned might have something to
do with *my* pleasurable reaction, given my peculiar psychology.
Thus the statement which is serving both to explain and to justify
is not equally effective in the two capacities; and this brings out
the difference between the two paths of discussion. Coincident
at the start, they diverge in the later stages. A *complete* explanation of any of my responses would have to include certain propositions about my nervous system, which would be irrelevant in any
critical argument. And a critically relevant observation about some
configuration in the art object might be useless for explaining a
given experience, if only because the experience did not yet contain that configuration.[2]

Now it would not be strange if, among the dangers of ambiguity

---

[2] I should like to add that when we speak of "justifying" or "giving reasons"
for our critical judgments, we refer to something which patently does go on
in the world and which is patently different from the causal explanation of
tastes and preferences. We are not begging any question as to whether the
critical judgment can "really" be justified, i.e., established on an objective basis.
Even if there were no truth or falsity in criticism, there would still be
agreement and disagreement; and there would be argument which arises out
of disagreement and attempts to resolve it. Hence, at the least there exists the
purely "phenomenological" task of elucidating the import and intention of
words like "insight," "acumen," "obtuseness," "bad taste," all of which have a
real currency in criticism.

to which the description of art, like the rest of human speech, is exposed, there should be some which derive from the double purpose—critical and psychological—to which such description is often being put. And this is, as we shall see, the case.

The necessity for sound inductive generalizations in any attempt at aesthetic explanation is granted. We may now consider, very briefly, the parallel role in normative criticism which has been assigned to N. Let us limit our attention to those metacritical theories which *deny* a function in criticism to N. I divide these into two kinds, those which attack existing standards and those which attack the very notion of a critical standard.

(1) It is said that we know of no law which governs human tastes and preferences, no quality shared by any two works of art that makes those works attractive or repellent. The point might be debated; but it is more important to notice what it assumes. It assumes that if N *were* based on a sound induction, it would be (together with R) a real ground for the acceptance of V. In other words, it would be reasonable to accept V on the strength of the quality Q if it could be shown that works which possess Q tend to be pleasing. It follows that criticism is being held back by the miserable state of aesthetic science. This raises an issue too large to be canvassed here. Most of us believe that the idea of progress applies to science, does not apply to art, applies, in some unusual and not very clear sense, to philosophy. What about criticism? Are there "discoveries" and "contributions" in this field? Is it reasonable to expect better evaluations of art after a thousand years of investigation than before? The question is not a simple one: it admits of different answers on different interpretations. But I do think that some critical judgments have been and are every day being "proved" as well as in the nature of the case they ever can be proved. I think we have already numerous passages which are not to be corrected or improved upon. And if this opinion is right, then it could not be the case that the validation of critical judgments waits upon the discovery of aesthetic laws. Let us suppose even that we *had* some law which stated that a certain color combination, a certain melodic sequence, a certain type of dramatic hero has everywhere and always a positive emotional effect. To the extent to which this law holds, there is of course that much less disagreement in criticism; but there is no better method for resolving disagreement. We are not more fully convinced in our own judgment because we know its

explanation; and we cannot hope to convince an imaginary opponent by appealing to this explanation, which by hypothesis does not hold for him.

(2) The more radical arguments against critical standards are spread out in the pages of Croce, Dewey, Richards, Prall, and the great romantic critics before them. They need not be repeated here. In one way or another they all attempt to expose the absurdity of presuming to judge a work of art, the very excuse for whose existence lies in its *difference* from everything that has gone before, by its degree of *resemblance* to something that has gone before; and on close inspection they create at least a very strong doubt as to whether a standard of success or failure in art is either necessary or possible. But it seems to me that they fail to provide a positive interpretation of criticism. Consider the following remarks by William James on the criticism of Herbert Spencer: "In all his dealings with the art products of mankind he manifests the same curious dryness and mechanical literality of judgment. . . . Turner's painting he finds untrue in that the earth-region is habitually as bright in tone as the air-region. Moreover, Turner scatters his detail too evenly. In Greek statues the hair is falsely treated. Renaissance painting is spoiled by unreal illumination. Venetian Gothic sins by meaningless ornamentation." And so on. We should most of us agree with James that this is bad criticism. But *all* criticism is similar to this in that it cites, as reasons for praising or condemning a work, one or more of its qualities. If Spencer's reasons are descriptively true, how can we frame our objection to them except in some such terms as that "unreal illumination does not make a picture bad," that is, by attacking his standards? What constitutes the relevance of a reason but its correlation with a norm? It is astonishing to notice how many writers, formally committed to an opposition to legal procedure in criticism, *seem* to relapse into a reliance upon standards whenever they give reasons for their critical judgments. The appearance is inevitable; for as long as we have no alternative interpretation of the import and function of R, we must assume *either* that R is perfectly arbitrary *or* that it presupposes and depends on some general claim.

With these preliminaries, we can examine a passage of criticism. This is Ludwig Goldscheider on *The Burial of Count Orgaz:*

Like the contour of a violently rising and falling wave is the outline of the four illuminated figures in the foreground: steeply upwards

and downwards about the grey monk on the left, in mutually inclined curves about the yellow of the two saints, and again steeply
upwards and downwards about . . . the priest on the right. The depth
of the wave indicates the optical center; the double curve of the
saints' yellow garments is carried by the greyish white of the shroud
down still farther; in this lowest depth rests the bluish-grey armor of
the knight.

This passage—which, we may suppose, was written to justify
a favorable judgment on the painting—conveys to us the idea of a
certain quality which, if we believe the critic, we should expect to
find in a certain painting by El Greco. And we do find it: we can
verify its presence by perception. In other words, there is a quality
in the picture which agrees with the quality which we "have in
mind"—which we have been led to think of by the critic's language.
But the same quality ("a steeply rising and falling curve," etc.)
would be found in any of a hundred lines one could draw on the
board in three minutes. It could not be the critic's purpose to inform us of the presence of a quality as banal and obvious as this.
It seems reasonable to suppose that the critic is thinking of another
quality, no idea of which is transmitted to us by his language, which
he *sees* and which by his use of language he *gets us to see*. This
quality is, of course, a wavelike contour; but it is not the quality designated by the expression "wavelike contour." Any object which
has this quality will have a wavelike contour; but it is not true that
any object which has a wavelike contour will have this quality. At
the same time, the expression "wavelike contour" *excludes* a great
many things: if anything is a wavelike contour, it is not a color,
it is not a mass, it is not a straight line. Now the critic, besides imparting to us the idea of a wavelike contour, gives us directions
for perceiving, and does this *by means* of the idea he imparts to us,
which narrows down the field of possible visual orientations and
guides us in the discrimination of details, the organization of parts,
the grouping of discrete objects into patterns. It is as if we found
both an oyster and a pearl when we had been looking for a seashell
because we had been told it was valuable. It *is* valuable, but not
because it is a seashell.

I may be stretching usage by the senses I am about to assign to
certain words, but it seems that the critic's *meaning* is "filled in,"
"rounded out," or "completed" by the act of perception, which
is performed not to judge the truth of his description but in a certain

sense to *understand* it. And if *communication* is a process by which a mental content is transmitted by symbols from one person to another, then we can say that it is a function of criticism to bring about communication at the level of the senses, that is, to induce a sameness of vision, of experienced content. If this is accomplished, it may or may not be followed by agreement, or what is called "communion"—a community of feeling which expresses itself in identical value judgments.

There is a contrast, therefore, between critical communication and what I may call normal or ordinary communication. In ordinary communication, symbols tend to acquire a footing relatively independent of sense-perception. It is, of course, doubtful whether the interpretation of symbols is at any time completely unaffected by the environmental context. But there is a difference of degree between, say, an exchange of glances which, though it means "Shall we go home?" at one time and place, would mean something very different at another—between this and formal science, whose vocabulary and syntax have relatively fixed connotations. With a passage of scientific prose before us, we may be dependent on experience for the definition of certain simple terms, as also for the confirmation of assertions; but we are not dependent on experience for the interpretation of compound expressions. If we are, this exposes semantic defects in the passage—obscurity, vagueness, ambiguity, or incompleteness. (Thus: "Paranoia is marked by a profound egocentricity and deep-seated feelings of insecurity"—the kind of statement which makes every student think he has the disease—is suitable for easy comparison of notes among clinicians and all who know how to recognize the difference between paranoia and other conditions; but it does not explicitly set forth the criteria which they employ.) Statements about immediate experience, made in ordinary communication, are no exception. If a theory requires that a certain flame should be blue, then we have to report whether it is or is not blue—regardless of shades or variations which may be of enormous importance aesthetically. We are bound to the letters of our words. Compare with this something like the following:

"The expression on her face was delightful."

"What was delightful about it?"

"Didn't you see that smile?"

The speaker does not mean that there is something delightful about smiles as such; but he cannot be accused of not stating his meaning clearly, because the clarity of his language must be judged in relation to his purpose, which in this case is the *evaluation* of the immediate experience; and for that purpose the reference to the smile will be sufficient if it gets people to feel that they are "talking about the same thing." There is understanding and misunderstanding on this level; there are marks by which the existence of one or the other can be known; and these are means by which misunderstanding can be eliminated. But these phenomena are not identical with those that take the same names in the study of ordinary communication.

Reading criticism, otherwise than in the presence, or with direct recollection, of the objects discussed is a blank and senseless employment—a fact which is concealed from us by the co-operation, in our reading, of many noncritical purposes for which the information offered by the critic is material and useful. There is not in all the world's criticism a single purely descriptive statement concerning which one is prepared to say beforehand, "If it is true, I shall like that work so much the better"—and *this* fact is concealed by the play of memory, which gives the critic's language a quite different, more specific, meaning than it has as ordinary communication. The point is not at all similar to that made by writers who maintain that value judgments have no objective basis because the reasons given to support them are not logically derivable from the value judgments themselves. I do not ask that R be related *logically* to V. In ethical argument you have someone say, "Yes, I would condemn that policy if it really did cause a wave of suicides, as you maintain." Suppose that the two clauses are here only psychologically related—still, this is what you never have in criticism. *The truth of R never adds the slightest weight to V*, because R does not designate any quality the perception of which might induce us to assent to V. But if it is not R, or what it designates, that makes V acceptable, then R cannot possibly require the support of N. The critic is not committed to the general claim that the quality named Q is valuable because he never makes the particular claim that a work is good in virtue of the presence of Q.

But he, or his readers, can easily be misled into *thinking* that he has made such a claim. You have, perhaps, a conflict of opinion about the merits of a poem; and one writer defends his judgment by mentioning vowel sounds, metrical variations, consistent or inconsistent imagery. Another critic, taking this language at its face value in ordinary communication, points out that "by those standards" one would have to condemn famous passages in *Hamlet* or *Lear* and raise some admittedly bad poems to a high place. He may even attempt what he calls an "experiment" and, to show that his opponent's grounds are irrelevant, construct a travesty of the original poem in which its plot or its meter or its vowels and consonants, or whatever other qualities have been cited with approval, are held constant while the rest of the work is changed. This procedure, which takes up hundreds of the pages of our best modern critics, is a waste of time and space; for it is the critic abandoning his own function to pose as a scientist—to assume, in other words, that criticism explains experiences instead of clarifying and altering them. If he saw that the *meaning* of a word like "assonance"—the quality which it leads our perception to discriminate in one poem or another—is in critical usage never twice the same, he would see no point in "testing" any generalization about the relationship between assonance and poetic value.

Some of the foregoing remarks will have reminded you of certain doctrines with which they were not intended to agree. The fact that criticism does not actually designate the qualities to which it somehow directs our attention has been a ground of complaint by some writers, who tell us that our present critical vocabulary is woefully inadequate.[3] This proposition clearly looks to an eventual improvement in the language of criticism. The same point, in a stronger form and with a different moral, is familiar to readers of Bergson and Croce, who say that it is impossible by means of concepts to "grasp the essence" of the artistic fact; and this position has seemed to many people to display the ultimate futility of critical analysis. I think that by returning to the passage I quoted from Goldscheider about the painting by El Greco we can differentiate the present point of view from both of these. Imagine, then, that the painting should be projected onto a graph with intersecting co-ordinates. It would then be possible to write complicated mathematical expressions which would enable another person who knew the system to construct for himself as close an approximation to the exact outlines of the El Greco as we might desire. Would this be an advance toward precision in criticism? Could we say that we had devised a more specific terminology for drawing and painting? I think not, for the most refined

3 See D. W. Prall, *Aesthetic Analysis*, p. 201.

concept remains a concept; there is no vanishing point at which it becomes a percept. It is the idea *of* a quality, it is not the quality itself. To render a critical verdict we should still have to perceive the quality; but Goldscheider's passage already shows it to us as clearly as language can. The idea of a new and better means of communication presupposes the absence of the sensory contents we are talking about; but criticism always assumes the presence of these contents to both parties; and it is upon this assumption that the vagueness or precision of a critical statement must be judged. Any further illustration of this point will have to be rough and hasty. For the last twenty or thirty years the "correct" thing to say about the metaphysical poets has been this: They think with their senses and feel with their brains. One hardly knows how to verify such a dictum: as a psychological observation it is exceedingly obscure. But it does not follow that it is not acute criticism; for it increases our awareness of the difference between the experience of Tennyson and the experience of Donne. Many words—like "subtlety," "variety," "complexity," "intensity"—which in ordinary communication are among the vaguest in the language have been used to convey sharp critical perceptions. And many expressions which have a clear independent meaning are vague and fuzzy when taken in relation to the content of a work of art. An examination of the ways in which the language of concepts mediates between perception and perception is clearly called for, though it is far too difficult to be attempted here.

We have also just seen reason to doubt that any aesthetic quality is ultimately ineffable. "What can be said" and "what cannot be said" are phrases which take their meaning from the purpose for which we are speaking. The aesthetics of obscurantism, in its insistence upon the incommunicability of the art object, has never made it clear what purpose or demand is to be served by communication. If we devised a system of concepts by which a work of art could be virtually reproduced at a distance by the use of language alone, what human intention would be furthered? We saw that *criticism* would not be improved: in the way in which criticism strives to "grasp" the work of art, we could grasp it no better then than now. The scientific *explanation* of aesthetic experiences would not be accomplished by a mere change of descriptive terminology. There remains only the *aesthetic* motive in talking about art. Now if we set it up as a condition of communicability that our language should *afford* the experience which it purports to describe, we shall of course reach the conclusion that art is incommunicable. But by that criterion all reality is unintelligible and ineffable, just as Bergson maintains. Such a demand upon thought and language is not only preposterous in that its fulfillment is logically impossible; it is also baneful, because it obscures the actual and very large influence of concepts upon the process of perception (by which, I must repeat, I mean something more than the ordinary *reference* of language to qualities of experience). Every part of the psychology of perception and attention provides us with examples of how unverbalized apperceptive reactions are engrained in the content and structure of the perceptual field. We can also learn from psychology how perception is affected by verbal cues and instructions. What remains unstudied is the play of critical comment in society at large; but we have, each of us in his own experience, instances of differential emphasis and selective grouping which have been brought about through the concepts imparted to us by the writings of critics.

I have perhaps overstressed the role of the critic as teacher, that is, as one who affords *new* perceptions and with them new values. There is such a thing as discovering a community of perception and feeling which already exists; and this can be a very pleasant experience. But it often happens that there are qualities in a work of art which are, so to speak, neither perceived nor ignored but felt or endured in a manner of which Leibniz has given the classic description. Suppose it is only a feeling of monotony, a slight oppressiveness, which comes to us from the style of some writer. A critic then refers to his "piled-up clauses, endless sentences, repetitious diction." This remark shifts the focus of our attention and brings certain qualities which had been blurred and marginal into distinct consciousness. When, with a sense of illumination we say "Yes, that's it exactly," we are really giving expression to the *change* which has taken place in our aesthetic apprehension. The postcritical experience is the true commentary on the precritical one. The same thing happens when, after listening to Debussy, we study the chords that can be formed on the basis of the whole-tone scale and then return to Debussy. New feelings are given which bear some resemblance to the old. There is no objection in these cases to our saying that we have been made to "understand" why we liked (or disliked) the work. But such understanding, which is the legitimate fruit of criticism, is nothing but a second moment of aesthetic experience, a retrial of experienced values. It should not be confused with the psychological study which seeks to know the causes of our feelings.

Note

In this article I have tried only to mark out the direction in which, as I believe, the exact nature of criticism should be sought. The task has been largely negative: it is necessary to correct preconceptions, obliterate false trails. There remain questions of two main kinds. Just to establish the adequacy of my analysis, there would have to be a detailed examination of critical phenomena, which present in the gross a fearful complexity. For example, I have paid almost no attention to large-scale or summary judgments—evaluations of artists, schools, or periods. One could quote brief statements about Shakespeare's qualities as a poet or Wagner's as a composer which seem to be full of insight; yet it would be hard to explain what these statements do to our "perception"—if that word can be used as a synonym for our appreciation of an artist's work as a whole.

But if the analysis is so far correct, it raises a hundred new questions. Two of these—rather, two sides of one large question—are especially important. What is the semantical relationship between the language of criticism and the qualities of the critic's or the reader's experience? I have argued that this relationship is not designation (though I do not deny that there *is* a relationship of designation between the critic's language and *some* qualities of a work of art). But neither is it denotation: the critic does not *point* to the qualities he has in mind. The ostensive function of language will explain the exhibition of *parts* or *details* of an art object but not the exhibition of abstract *qualities;* and it is the latter which is predominant in criticism. The only positive suggestion made in this paper can be restated as follows. To say that the critic "picks out" a quality in the work of art is to say that if there did exist a designation for that quality, then the designation which the critic employs would be what Morris calls an analytic implicate of that designation. (Thus, "blue" is an analytic implicate of an expression "$H_3B_5S_2$" which designates a certain point on the color solid.) This definition is clearly not sufficient to characterize the critic's method; but, more, the antecedent of the *definiens* is doubtful in meaning. A study of terms like "Rembrandt's chiaroscuro," "the blank verse of *The Tempest*," etc., etc., would probably result in the introduction of an idea analogous to that of the proper name (or of Russell's "definite description") but with this difference, that the entity uniquely named or labeled by this type of expression is not an object but a quality.

If we put the question on the psychological plane, it reads as follows: How is it that (a) we can "know what we like" in a work of art without (b) knowing what "causes" our enjoyment? I presume that criticism enlightens us as to (a) and that (b) would be provided by a psychological explanation; also that (a) is often true when (b) is not.

Contrary to Ducasse[4] and some other writers I cannot see that the critic has any competence as a self-psychologist, a specialist in the explanation of his own responses. There is no other field in which we admit the existence of such scientific insight, unbridled by experimental controls and unsupported by valid general theory; and I do not think we can admit it here. (For that reason I held that critical insight, which does exist, cannot be identified with scientific understanding.) The truth is that, in the present stone age of aesthetic inquiry, we have not even the vaguest idea of the form that a "law of art appreciation" would take. Consider, "It is as a *colorist* that Titian excels"; interpret this as a causal hypothesis, e.g., "Titian's colors give pleasure"; and overlook incidental difficulties, such as whether "color" means tone or the hue (as opposed to the brightness and the saturation) of a tone. Superficially, this is similar to many low-grade hypotheses in psychology: "We owe the *color* of the object to the retinal rods and cones," "It is the *brightness* and not the color that infuriates a bull," "Highly *saturated* colors give pleasure to American schoolboys." But the difference is that we do not know what test conditions are marked out by the first proposition. Would it be relevant, as a test of its truth, to display the colors of a painting by Titian, in a series of small rectangular areas, to a group of subjects in the laboratory? I cannot believe this to be part of what is meant by a person who affirms this hypothesis. He is committed to no such test.

Anyone with a smattering of Gestalt psychology now interposes that the colors are, of course, pleasing *in* their context, not out of it. One has some trouble in understanding how in that case one could know that it is the *colors* that are pleasing. We may believe in study-

---

[4] *Op. cit.*, p. 117.

ing the properties of wholes; but it is hard to see what scientific formulation can be given to the idea that a quality should have a certain function (that is, a causal relationship to the responses of an observer) in one and only one whole. Yet that appears to be the case with the color scheme in any painting by Titian.

We can be relieved of these difficulties simply by admitting our ignorance and confusion; but there is no such escape when we turn to criticism. For it *is* as a colorist that Titian excels—this is a fairly unanimous value judgment, and we should be able to analyze its meaning. (I should not, however, want the issue to turn on this particular example. Simpler and clearer judgments could be cited.) Now when our attention is called, by a critic, to a certain quality, we respond to that quality *in its context*. The context is never specified, as it would have to be in any scientific theory, but always assumed. Every descriptive statement affects our perception of— and our feeling for—the work as a whole. One might say, then, that we agree with the critic if and when he gets us to like the work about as well or as badly as he does. But this is clearly not enough. For he exerts his influence always through a specific discrimination. Art criticism is analytic, discriminating. It concerns itself less with over-all values than with merits and faults in specified respects. It is the quality and not the work that is good or bad; or, if you like, the work is good or bad "on account of" its qualities. Thus, we may agree with his judgment but reject the critic's grounds (I have shown that the "grounds" to which he is really appealing are not the same as those which he explicitly states or designates); and when we do this, we are saying that the qualities which he admires are not those which we admire. But then we must know what we admire: we are somehow aware of the special attachment of our feelings to certain abstract qualities rather than to others. Without this, we could never reject a reason given for a value judgment with which we agree—we could never be dissatisfied with descriptive evalua- tion. There must therefore exist an analyzing, sifting, shredding process within perception which corresponds to the conceptual dis- tinctness of our references to "strong form but weak color," "pow- erful images but slovenly meter," and so on.

This process is mysterious; but we can get useful hints from two quarters. Artists and art teachers are constantly "experimenting" in their own way. "Such a bright green at this point is jarring." "Shouldn't you add more detail to the large space on the right?" We can compare two wholes in a single respect and mark the difference in the registration upon our feelings. Implicit comparisons of this kind, with shifting tone of feeling, are what are involved in the isolation of qualities from the work, at least in *some* critical judgments. I am afraid that as psychology, as an attempt to discover the causes of our feelings, this is primitive procedure; but as a mere analysis of what is meant by the praise and blame accorded to special qualities, it is not without value.

If, in the second place, we could discover what we mean by the difference between the "object" and the "cause" of an emotion, *outside* the field of aesthetics; if we could see both the distinction and the connection between two such judgments as "I hate his cheek" and "It is his cheek that inspires hatred in me"; if we knew what happens when a man says, "Now I know why I have always disliked him—it is his pretense of humility," there would be a valuable application to the analysis of critical judgments.

VI

The Nature and Uses
of Definition

Benedetto Croce

INTUITION,
EXPRESSION, AND ART*

INTUITION AND EXPRESSION

Knowledge has two forms: it is either *intuitive* knowledge or *logical* knowledge; knowledge obtained through the *imagination* or knowledge obtained through the *intellect;* knowledge of the *individual* or knowledge of the *universal;* of *individual things* or of the *relations* between them; it is, in fact, productive either of *images* or of *concepts.*

In ordinary life, constant appeal is made to intuitive knowledge. It is said that we cannot give definitions of certain truths; that they are not demonstrable by syllogisms; that they must be learnt intuitively. The politician finds fault with the abstract reasoner, who possesses no lively intuition of actual conditions; the educational theorist insists upon the necessity of developing the intuitive faculty in the pupil before everything else; the critic in judging a work of art makes it a point of honour to set aside theory and abstractions, and to judge it by direct intuition; the practical man professes to live rather by intuition than by reason.

But this ample acknowledgment granted to intuitive knowledge in ordinary life, does not correspond to an equal and adequate

* From Benedetto Croce, *Aesthetic,* trans. by Douglas Ainslie, chs. 1–2 (London: Macmillan & Co., 1922). Reprinted by permission of Vision Press, Ltd.

acknowledgment in the field of theory and of philosophy. There exists a very ancient science of intellectual knowledge, admitted by all without discussion, namely, Logic; but a science of intuitive knowledge is timidly and with difficulty asserted by but a few. Logical knowledge has appropriated the lion's share; and if she does not slay and devour her companion outright, yet yields to her but grudgingly the humble place of maid-servant or doorkeeper. —What can intuitive knowledge be without the light of intellectual knowledge? It is a servant without a master; and though a master find a servant useful, the master is a necessity to the servant, since he enables him to gain his livelihood. Intuition is blind; intellect lends her eyes.

Now, the first point to be firmly fixed in the mind is that intuitive knowledge has no need of a master, nor to lean upon any one; she does not need to borrow the eyes of others, for she has excellent eyes of her own. Doubtless it is possible to find concepts mingled with intuitions. But in many other intuitions there is no trace of such a mixture, which proves that it is not necessary. The impression of a moonlight scene by a painter; the outline of a country drawn by a cartographer; a musical motive, tender or energetic; the words of a sighing lyric, or those with which we ask, command and lament in ordinary life, may well all be intuitive facts without a shadow of intellectual relation. But, think what one may of these instances, and admitting further the contention that the greater part of the intuitions of civilized man are impregnated with concepts, there yet remains to be observed something more important and more conclusive. Those concepts which are found mingled and fused with the intuitions are no longer concepts, in so far as they are really mingled and fused, for they have lost all independence and autonomy. They have been concepts, but have now become simple elements of intuition. The philosophical maxims placed in the mouth of a personage of tragedy or of comedy, perform there the function, not of concepts, but of characteristics of such personage; in the same way as the red in a painted face does not there represent the red colour of the physicists, but is a characteristic element of the portrait. The whole is that which determines the quality of the parts. A work of art may be full of philosophical concepts; it may contain them in greater abundance and they may there be even more profound than in a philosophical dissertation, which in its turn may be rich to overflowing with descriptions and intuition. But notwithstanding all these concepts the total effect of the work of art is an intuition; and not withstanding all those intuitions, the total effect of the philosophical dissertation is a concept. The *Promessi Sposi* contains copious ethical observations and distinctions, but does not for that reason lose as a whole its character of simple story or intuition. In like manner the anecdotes and satirical effusions to be found in the works of a philosopher like Schopenhauer do not deprive those works of their character of intellectual treatises. The difference between a scientific work and a work of art, that is, between an intellectual fact and an intuitive fact, lies in the difference of the total effect aimed at by their respective authors. This it is that determines and rules over the several parts of each, not these parts separated and considered abstractly in themselves.

But to admit the independence of intuition as regards concept does not suffice to give a true and precise idea of intuition. Another error arises among those who recognize this, or who at any rate do not explicitly make intuition dependent upon the intellect, to obscure and confuse the real nature of intuition. By intuition is frequently understood *perception*, or the knowledge of actual reality, the apprehension of something as *real*.

Certainly perception is intuition: the perceptions of the room in which I am writing, of the ink-bottle and paper that are before me, of the pen I am using, of the objects that I touch and make use of as instruments of my person, which, if it write, therefore exists—these are all intuitions. But the image that is now passing through my brain of a me writing in another room, in another town, with different paper, pen and ink, is also an intuition. This means that the distinction between reality and non-reality is extraneous, secondary, to the true nature of intuition. If we imagine a human mind having intuitions for the first time, it would seem that it could have intuition of actual reality only, that is to say, that it could have perceptions of nothing but the real. But since knowledge of reality is based upon the distinction between real images and unreal images, and since this distinction does not at the first moment exist, these intuitions would in truth not be intuitions either of the real or of the unreal, not perceptions, but pure intuitions. Where all is real, nothing is real. The child, with its difficulty of distinguishing true from false, history from fable, which are all one to childhood, can furnish us with a sort of very vague and only remotely approximate idea of this ingenuous state. Intuition is the undifferentiated unity of the perception of the real and of the simple image of the possible. In our intuitions we do not oppose ourselves as empirical beings to external reality, but we simply objectify our impressions, whatever they be.

Those, therefore, who look upon intuition as sensation formed and arranged simply according to the categories of space and time, would seem to approximate more nearly to the truth. Space and time (they say) are the forms of intuition; to have an intuition is to place it in space and in temporal sequence. Intuitive activity would then consist in this double and concurrent function of spatiality and temporality. But for these two categories must be repeated what was said of intellectual distinctions, when found mingled with intuitions. We have intuitions without space and without time: the colour of a sky, the colour of a feeling, a cry of pain and an effort of will, objectified in consciousness: these are intuitions which we possess, and with their making space and time have nothing to do. In some intuitions, spatiality may be found without temporality, in others, *vice versa*; and even where both are found, they are perceived by later reflexion: they can be fused with the intuition in like manner with all its other elements: that is, they are in it *materialiter* and not *formaliter*, as ingredients and not as arrangement. Who, without an act of reflexion which for a moment breaks in upon his contemplation, can think of space while looking at a drawing or a view? Who is conscious of temporal sequence while listening to a story or a piece of music without breaking into it with a similar act of reflexion? What intuition reveals in a work of art is not space and time, but *character, individual physiognomy*. The view here maintained is confirmed in several quarters of modern philosophy. Space and time, far from being simple and primitive functions, are nowadays conceived as intellectual constructions of great complexity. And further, even in some of those who do not altogether deny to space and time the quality of formative principles, categories and functions, one observes an effort to unite them and to regard them in a different manner from that in which these categories are generally conceived. Some limit intuition to the sole category of spatiality, maintaining that even time can only be intuited in terms of space. Others abandon the three dimensions of space as not philosophically necessary, and conceive the function of spatiality as void of all particular spatial determination. But what could such a spatial function be, a simple arrangement that should arrange even time? It represents, surely, all that criticism and refutation have left standing—the bare demand for the affirmation of some intuitive activity in general. And is not this activity truly determined, when one single function is attributed to it, not spatializing nor temporalizing, but characterizing? Or rather, when it is conceived as itself a category or function which gives us knowledge of things in their concreteness and individuality?

Having thus freed intuitive knowledge from any suggestion of intellectualism and from every later and external addition, we must now explain it and determine its limits from another side and defend it from a different kind of invasion and confusion. On the hither side of the lower limit is sensation, formless matter, which the spirit can never apprehend in itself as simple matter. This it can only possess with form and in form, but postulates the notion of it as a mere limit. Matter, in its abstraction, is mechanism, passivity; it is what the spirit of man suffers, but does not produce. Without it no human knowledge or activity is possible; but mere matter produces animality, whatever is brutal and impulsive in man, not the spiritual dominion, which is humanity. How often we strive to understand clearly what is passing within us! We do catch a glimpse of something, but this does not appear to the mind as objectified and formed. It is in such moments as these that we best perceive the profound difference between matter and form. These are not two acts of ours, opposed to one another; but the one is outside us and assaults and sweeps us off our feet, while the other inside us tends to absorb and identify itself with that which is outside. Matter, clothed and conquered by form, produces concrete form. It is the matter, the content, which differentiates one of our intuitions from another: the form is constant: it is spiritual activity, while matter is changeable. Without matter spiritual activity would not forsake its abstractness to become concrete and real activity, this or that spiritual content, this or that definite intuition.

It is a curious fact, characteristic of our times, that this very form, this very activity of the spirit, which is essentially ourselves, is so often ignored or denied. Some confound the spiritual activity of man with the metaphorical and mythological activity of what is called nature, which is mechanism and has no resemblance to human activity, save when we imagine, with Aesop, that *"arbores loquuntur non tantum ferae."* Some affirm that they have never observed in themselves this "miraculous" activity, as though there were no difference, or only one of quantity, between sweating and thinking, feeling cold and the energy of the will. Others, certainly with greater reason, would unify activity and mechanism in a more general concept, though they are specifically distinct. Let us, however, refrain for the moment from examining if such a final unification be possible, and in what sense, but admitting that the attempt may be made, it is clear that to unify two concepts in a third implies to begin with the admission of a difference between the two first. Here it is the difference that concerns us and we set it in relief.

Intuition has sometimes been confused with simple sensation. But since this confusion ends by being offensive to common sense, it has more frequently been attenuated or concealed with a phraseology apparently designed at once to confuse and to distinguish them. Thus, it has been asserted that intuition is sensation, but not so much simple sensation as *association* of sensations. Here a double meaning is concealed in the word "association." Association is understood, either as memory, mnemonic association, conscious recollection, and in that case the claim to unite in memory elements which are not intuited, distinguished, possessed in some way by the spirit and produced by consciousness, seems inconceivable: or it is understood as association of unconscious elements, in which case we remain in the world of sensation and of nature. But if with certain associationists we speak of an association which is neither memory nor flux of sensations, but a *productive* association (formative, constructive, distinguishing); then our contention is admitted and only its name is denied to it. For productive association is no longer association in the sense of the sensationalists, but *synthesis*, that is to say, spiritual activity. Synthesis may be called association; but with the concept of productivity is already posited the distinction between passivity and activity, between sensation and intuition.

Other psychologists are disposed to distinguish from sensation something which is sensation no longer, but is not yet intellectual concept: the *representation* or *image*. What is the difference between their representation or image and our intuitive knowledge? Everything and nothing: for "representation" is a very equivocal word. If by representation be understood something cut off and standing out from the psychic basis of the sensations, then representation is intuition. If, on the other hand, it be conceived as complex sensation we are back once more in crude sensation, which does not vary in quality according to its richness or poverty, or according to whether the organism in which it appears is rudimentary or highly developed and full of traces of past sensations. Nor is the ambiguity remedied by defining representation as a psychic product of secondary degree in relation to sensation, defined as occupying the first place. What does secondary degree mean here? Does it mean a qualitative, formal difference? If so, representation is an elaboration of sensation and therefore intuition. Or does it mean greater complexity and complication, a quantitative, material difference? In that case intuition is once more confused with simple sensation.

And yet there is a sure method of distinguishing true intuition, true representation, from that which is inferior to it: the spiritual fact from the mechanical, passive, natural fact. Every true intuition or representation is also *expression*. That which does not objectify itself in expression is not intuition or representation, but sensation and mere natural fact. The spirit only intuits in making, forming, expressing. He who separates intuition from expression never succeeds in reuniting them.

Intuitive activity *possesses intuitions to the extent that it expresses them.* Should this proposition sound paradoxical, that is partly because, as a general rule, a too restricted meaning is given to the word "expression." It is generally restricted to what are called verbal expressions alone. But there exist also non-verbal expressions, such as those of line, colour and sound, and to all of these must be extended our affirmation, which embraces therefore every sort of manifestation of man, as orator, musician, painter, or anything else. But be it pictorial, or verbal, or musical, or in whatever other form it appear, to no intuition can expression in one of its forms be wanting; it is, in fact, an inseparable part of intuition. How can we really possess an intuition of a geometrical figure, unless we possess so accurate an image of it as to be able to trace it immediately upon paper or on the blackboard? How can we really have an intuition of the contour of a region, for example of the island of Sicily, if we are not able to draw it as it is in all its meanderings? Every one can experience the internal illumination which follows upon his success in formulating to himself his impressions and feelings, but only so far as he is able to formulate them. Feelings or impressions, then, pass by means of words from the obscure region of the soul into the clarity of the contemplative spirit. It is impossible to distinguish intuition from expression in this cognitive process. The one appears with the other at the same instant, because they are not two, but one.

The principal reason which makes our view appear paradoxical as we maintain it, is the illusion or prejudice that we possess a more complete intuition of reality than we really do. One often hears people say that they have many great thoughts in their minds, but that they are not able to express them. But if they really had them, they would have coined them into just so many beautiful, sounding words, and thus have expressed them. If these thoughts seem to vanish or to become few and meagre in the act of expressing them, the reason is that they did not exist or really were few and meagre. People think that all of us ordinary men imagine and intuit countries, figures and scenes like painters, and bodies like sculptors; save that painters and sculptors know how to paint and carve such images, while we bear them unexpressed in our souls. They believe that any one could have imagined a Madonna of Raphael; but that Raphael was Raphael owing to his technical ability in putting the Madonna upon canvas. Nothing can be more false than this view. The world which as a rule we intuit is a small thing. It consists of little expressions, which gradually become greater and wider with the increasing spiritual concentration of certain moments. They are the words we say to ourselves, our silent judgments: "Here is a man, here is a horse, this is heavy, this is sharp, this pleases me," etc. It is a medley of light and colour, with no greater pictorial value than would be expressed by a haphazard splash of colours, from among which one could barely make out a few special, distinctive traits. This and nothing else is what we possess in our ordinary life; this is the basis of our ordinary action. It is the index of a book. The labels tied to things (it has been said) take the place of the things themselves. This index and these labels (themselves expressions) suffice for small needs and small actions. From time to time we pass from the index to the book, from the label to the thing, or from the slight to the greater intuitions, and from these to the greatest and most lofty. This passage is sometimes far from easy. It has been observed by those who have best studied the psychology of artists that when, after having given a rapid glance at any one, they attempt to obtain a real intuition of him, in order, for example, to paint his portrait, then this ordinary vision, that seemed so precise, so lively, reveals itself as little better than nothing. What remains is found to be at the most some superficial trait, which would not

even suffice for a caricature. The person to be painted stands before
the artist like a world to discover. Michael Angelo said, "One paints,
not with his hands, but with the brain." Leonardo shocked the
prior of the Convent of the Graces by standing for days together
gazing at the "Last Supper," without touching it with the brush. He
remarked of this attitude: "The minds of men of lofty genius are
most active in invention when they are doing the least external
work." The painter is a painter, because he sees what others only
feel or catch a glimpse of, but do not see. We think we see a smile,
but in reality we have only a vague impression of it, we do not
perceive all the characteristic traits of which it is the sum, as the
painter discovers them after he has worked upon them and is thus
able to fix them on the canvas. We do not intuitively possess more
even of our intimate friend, who is with us every day and at all
hours, than at most certain traits of physiognomy which enable
us to distinguish him from others. The illusion is less easy as regards
musical expression; because it would seem strange to every one to
say that the composer had added or attached notes to a motive
which was already in the mind of him who is not the composer; as
if Beethoven's Ninth Symphony were not his own intuition and
his intuition the Ninth Symphony. Now, just as one who is deluded
as to the amount of his material wealth is confuted by arithmetic,
which states its exact amount, so he who nourishes delusions as to the
wealth of his own thoughts and images is brought back to reality,
when he is obliged to cross the *Pons Asinorum* of expression. Let
us say to the former, count; to the latter, speak; or, here is a pencil,
express yourself.

Each of us, as a matter of fact, has in him a little of the poet, of
the sculptor, of the musician, of the painter, of the prose writer: but
how little, as compared with those who bear those names, just because they possess the most universal dispositions and energies of
human nature in so lofty a degree! How little too does a painter
possess of the intuitions of a poet! And how little does one painter
possess those of another painter! Nevertheless, that little is all our
actual patrimony of intuitions or representations. Beyond these are
only impressions, sensations, feelings, impulses, emotions, or whatever else one may term what still falls short of the spirit and is not
assimilated by man; something postulated for the convenience of
exposition, while actually non-existent, since to exist also is a fact
of the spirit.

We may thus add this to the various verbal descriptions of intuition, noted at the beginning: intuitive knowledge is expressive
knowledge. Independent and autonomous in respect to intellectual
function: indifferent to later empirical discriminations, to reality
and to unreality, to formations and apperceptions of space and time,
which are also later: intuition or representation is distinguished as
form from what is felt and suffered, from the flux or wave of sensation, or from psychic matter; and this form, this taking possession,
is expression. To intuit is to express; and nothing else (nothing
more, but nothing less) than *to express*.

INTUITION AND ART

Before proceeding further, it may be well to draw certain consequences from what has been established and to add some explanations.

We have frankly identified intuitive or expressive knowledge with
the aesthetic or artistic fact, taking works of art as examples of intuitive knowledge and attributing to them the characteristics of intuition, and *vice versa*. But our identification is combated by a view
held even by many philosophers, who consider art to be an intuition
of an altogether special sort. "Let us admit" (they say) "that art is
intuition; but intuition is not always art: artistic intuition is a distinct
species differing from intuition in general by something *more*."

But no one has ever been able to indicate of what this something
more consists. It has sometimes been thought that art is not a simple
intuition, but an intuition of an intuition, in the same way as the
concept of science has been defined, not as the ordinary concept,
but as the concept of a concept. Thus man would attain to art by
objectifying, not his sensations, as happens with ordinary intuition,
but intuition itself. But this process of raising to a second power
does not exist; and the comparison of it with the ordinary and scientific concept does not prove what is intended, for the good reason
that it is not true that the scientific concept is the concept of a
concept. If this comparison proves anything, it proves just the opposite. The ordinary concept, if it be really a concept and not a simple
representation, is a perfect concept, however poor and limited.
Science substitutes concepts for representations; for those concepts
that are poor and limited it substitutes others, larger and more
comprehensive; it is ever discovering new relations. But its method

does not differ from that by which is formed the smallest universal in the brain of the humblest of men. What is generally called *par excellence* art, collects intuitions that are wider and more complex than those which we generally experience, but these intuitions are always of sensations and impressions.

Art is expression of impressions, not expression of expression.

For the same reason, it cannot be asserted that the intuition, which is generally called artistic, differs from ordinary intuition as intensive intuition. This would be the case if it were to operate differently on the same matter. But since the artistic function is extended to wider fields, yet does not differ in method from ordinary intuition, the difference between them is not intensive but extensive. The intuition of the simplest popular love-song, which says the same thing, or very nearly, as any declaration of love that issues at every moment from the lips of thousands of ordinary men, may be intensively perfect in its poor simplicity, although it be extensively so much more limited than the complex intuition of a love-song by Leopardi.

The whole difference, then, is quantitative, and as such is indifferent to philosophy, *scientia qualitatum*. Certain men have a greater aptitude, a more frequent inclination fully to express certain complex states of the soul. These men are known in ordinary language as artists. Some very complicated and difficult expressions are not often achieved, and these are called works of art. The limits of the expression-intuitions that are called art, as opposed to those that are vulgarly called non-art, are empirical and impossible to define. If an epigram be art, why not a simple word? If a story, why not the news-jottings of the journalist? If a landscape, why not a topographical sketch? The teacher of philosophy in Molière's comedy was right: "Whenever we speak, we create prose." But there will always be scholars like Monsieur Jourdain, astonished at having spoken prose for forty years without knowing it, who will have difficulty in persuading themselves that when they call their servant John to bring their slippers, they have spoken nothing less than— prose.

We must hold firmly to our identification, because among the principal reasons which have prevented Aesthetic, the science of art, from revealing the true nature of art, its real roots in human nature, has been its separation from the general spiritual life, the having made of it a sort of special function or aristocratic club. No one is astonished when he learns from physiology that every cell is an organism and every organism a cell or synthesis of cells. No one is astonished at finding in a lofty mountain the same chemical elements that compose a small stone fragment. There is not one physiology of small animals and one of large animals; nor is there a special chemical theory of stones as distinct from mountains. In the same way, there is not a science of lesser intuition as distinct from a science of greater intuition, nor one of ordinary intuition as distinct from artistic intuition. There is but one Aesthetic, the science of intuitive or expressive knowledge, which is the aesthetic or artistic fact. And this Aesthetic is the true analogue of Logic, which includes, as facts of the same nature, the formation of the smallest and most ordinary concept and the most complicated scientific and philosophical system.

Nor can we admit that the word *genius* or artistic genius, as distinct from the non-genius of the ordinary man, possesses more than a quantitative signification. Great artists are said to reveal us to ourselves. But how could this be possible, unless there were identity of nature between their imagination and ours, and unless the difference were only one of quantity? It were better to change *poeta nascitur* into *homo nascitur poeta:* some men are born great poets, some small. The cult of the genius with all its attendant superstitions has arisen from this quantitative difference having been taken as a difference of quality. It has been forgotten that genius is not something that has fallen from heaven, but humanity itself. The man of genius who poses or is represented as remote from humanity finds his punishment in becoming or appearing somewhat ridiculous. Examples of this are the *genius* of the romantic period and the *superman* of our time.

But it is well to note here, that those who claim unconsciousness as the chief quality of an artistic genius, hurl him from an eminence far above humanity to a position far below it. Intuitive or artistic genius, like every form of human activity, is always conscious; otherwise it would be blind mechanism. The only thing that can be wanting to artistic genius is the *reflective* consciousness, the super-added consciousness of the historian or critic, which is not essential to it.

The relation between matter and form, or between *content* and *form*, as is generally said, is one of the most disputed questions in Aesthetic. Does the aesthetic fact consist of content alone, or of form alone, or of both together? This question has taken on various meanings, which we shall mention, each in its place. But when these words are taken as signifying what we have above defined, and matter is understood as emotionality not aesthetically elaborated, or impressions, and form as intellectual activity and expression, then our view cannot be in doubt. We must, that is to say, reject both the thesis that makes the aesthetic fact to consist of the content alone (that is, the simple impressions), and the thesis which makes it to consist of a junction between form and content, that is, of impressions plus expressions. In the aesthetic fact, expressive activity is not added to the fact of the impressions, but these latter are formed and elaborated by it. The impressions reappear as it were in expression, like water put into a filter, which reappears the same and yet different on the other side. The aesthetic fact, therefore, is form, and nothing but form.

From this was inferred not that the content is something superfluous (it is, on the contrary, the necessary point of departure for the expressive fact); but that *there is no passage* from the qualities of the content to those of the form. It has sometimes been thought that the content, in order to be aesthetic, that is to say, transformable into form, should possess some determined or determinable qualities. But were that so, then form and content, expression and impression, would be the same thing. It is true that the content is that which is convertible into form, but it has no determinable qualities until this transformation takes place. We know nothing about it. It does not become aesthetic content before, but only after it has been actually transformed. The aesthetic content has also been defined as the *interesting*. That is not an untrue statement; it is merely void of meaning. Interesting to what? To the expressive activity? Certainly the expressive activity would not have raised the content to the dignity of form, had it not been interested in it. Being interested is precisely the raising of the content to the dignity of form. But the word "interesting" has also been employed in another and an illegitimate sense, which we shall explain further on.

The proposition that art is *imitation of nature* has also several meanings. Sometimes truths have been expressed or at least shadowed forth in these words, sometimes errors have been promulgated. More frequently, no definite thought has been expressed at all. One of the scientifically legitimate meanings occurs when "imitation" is understood as representation or intuition of nature, a form of knowledge. And when the phrase is used with this intention, and in order to emphasize the spiritual character of the process, another proposition becomes legitimate also: namely, that art is the *idealization* or *idealizing* imitation of nature. But if by imitation of nature be understood that art gives mechanical reproductions, more or less perfect duplicates of natural objects, in the presence of which is renewed the same tumult of impressions as that caused by natural objects, then the proposition is evidently false. The coloured waxen effigies that imitate the life, before which we stand astonished in the museums where such things are shown, do not give aesthetic intuitions. Illusion and hallucination have nothing to do with the calm domain of artistic intuition. But on the other hand if an artist paint the interior of a wax-work museum, or if an actor give a burlesque portrait of a man-statue on the stage, we have work of the spirit and artistic intuition. Finally, if photography have in it anything artistic, it will be to the extent that it transmits the intuition of the photographer, his point of view, the pose and grouping which he has striven to attain. And if photography be not quite an art, that is precisely because the element of nature in it remains more or less unconquered and ineradicable. Do we ever, indeed, feel complete satisfaction before even the best of photographs? Would not an artist vary and touch up much or little, remove or add something to all of them?

The statements repeated so often, that art is not knowledge, that it does not tell the truth, that it does not belong to the world of theory, but to the world of feeling, and so forth, arise from the failure to realize exactly the theoretic character of simple intuition. This simple intuition is quite distinct from intellectual knowledge, as it is distinct from perception of the real; and the statements quoted above arise from the belief that only intellectual cognition is knowledge. We have seen that intuition is knowledge, free from concepts and more simple than the so-called perception of the real. Therefore art is knowledge, form; it does not belong to the world of feeling or to psychic matter. The reason why so many aestheticians have so often insisted that art is *appearance* (*Schein*), is precisely that they have felt the necessity of distinguishing it from the more complex fact of perception, by maintaining its pure intuitiveness. And if for the same reason it has been claimed that art is *feeling* the reason is the same. For if the concept as content of art, and historical reality as such, be excluded from the sphere of art, there remains no other content than reality apprehended in all its ingenuousness and immediacy in the vital impulse, in its *feeling*, that is to say again, pure intuition.

The theory of the *aesthetic senses* has also arisen from the failure to establish, or from having lost to view, the character of expression as distinct from impression, of form as distinct from matter.

This theory can be reduced to the error just indicated of wishing to find a passage from the qualities of the content to those of the form. To ask, in fact, what the aesthetic senses are, implies asking what sensible impressions are able to enter into aesthetic expressions, and which must of necessity do so. To this we must at once reply, that all impressions can enter into aesthetic expressions or formations, but that none are bound to do so of necessity. Dante raised to the dignity of form not only the "sweet colour of the oriental sapphire" (visual impressions), but also tactual or thermic impressions, such as the "dense air" and the "fresh rivulets" which "parch the more" the throat of the thirsty. The belief that a picture yields only visual impressions is a curious illusion. The bloom on a cheek, the warmth of a youthful body, the sweetness and freshness of a fruit, the edge of a sharp knife, are not these, too, impressions obtainable from a picture? Are they visual? What would a picture mean to an imaginary man, lacking all or many of his senses, who should in an instant acquire the organ of sight alone? The picture we are looking at and believe we see only with our eyes would seem to his eyes to be little more than an artist's paint-smeared palette.

Some who hold firmly to the aesthetic character of certain groups of impressions (for example, the visual and auditive), and exclude others, are nevertheless ready to admit that if visual and auditive impressions enter *directly* into the aesthetic fact, those of the other senses also enter into it, but only as *associated*. But this distinction is altogether arbitrary. Aesthetic expression is synthesis, in which it is impossible to distinguish direct and indirect. All impressions are placed by it on a level, in so far as they are aestheticized. A man who absorbs the subject of a picture or poem does not have it before him as a series of impressions, some of which have prerogatives and precedence over the others. He knows nothing as to what has happened prior to having absorbed it, just as, on the other hand, distinctions made after reflexion have nothing whatever to do with art as such.

The theory of the aesthetic senses has also been presented in another way; as an attempt to establish what physiological organs are necessary for the aesthetic fact. The physiological organ or apparatus is nothing but a group of cells, constituted and disposed in a particular manner; that is to say, it is a merely physical and natural fact or concept. But expression does not know physiological facts. Expression has its point of departure in the impressions, and the physiological path by which these have found their way to the mind is to it altogether indifferent. One way or another comes to the same thing: it suffices that they should be impressions.

It is true that the want of given organs, that is, of certain groups of cells, prevents the formation of certain impressions (when these are not otherwise obtained through a kind of organic compensation). The man born blind cannot intuit and express light. But the impressions are not conditioned solely by the organ, but also by the stimuli which operate upon the organ. One who has never had the impression of the sea will never be able to express it, in the same way as one who has never had the impression of the life of high society or of the political arena will never express either. This, however, does not prove the dependence of the expressive function on the stimulus or on the organ. It merely repeats what we know already: expression presupposes impression, and particular expressions particular impressions. For the rest, every impression excludes other impressions during the moment in which it dominates; and so does every expression.

Another corollary of the conception of expression as activity is the *indivisibility* of the work of art. Every expression is a single expression. Activity is a fusion of the impressions in an organic whole. A desire to express this has always prompted the affirmation that the work of art should have *unity*, or, what amounts to the same thing, *unity in variety*. Expression is a synthesis of the various, or multiple, in the one.

The fact that we divide a work of art into parts, a poem into scenes, episodes, similes, sentences, or a picture into single figures and objects, background, foreground, etc., may seem opposed to this affirmation. But such division annihilates the work, as dividing the organism into heart, brain, nerves, muscles and so on, turns the living being into a corpse. It is true that there exist organisms in which division gives rise to other living beings, but in such a case we must conclude, maintaining the analogy between the organism and the work of art, that in the latter case too there are numerous germs of life each ready to grow, in a moment, into a single complete expression.

It may be said that expression sometimes arises from other expressions. There are simple and there are *compound* expressions. One must surely admit some difference between the *eureka*, with which Archimedes expressed all his joy at his discovery, and the expressive act (indeed all the five acts) of a regular tragedy. —Not in the least: expression always arises directly from impressions. He who conceives a tragedy puts into a crucible a great quantity, so to say, of impressions: expressions themselves, conceived on other occasions, are fused together with the new in a single mass, in the same way as we can cast into a melting furnace formless pieces of bronze and choicest statuettes. Those choicest statuettes must be melted just like the pieces of bronze, before there can be a new statue. The old expressions must descend again to the level of impressions, in order to be synthesized in a new single expression.

By elaborating his impressions, man *frees* himself from them. By objectifying them, he removes them from him and makes himself their superior. The liberating and purifying function of art is another aspect and another formula of its character as activity. Activity is the deliverer, just because it drives away passivity.

This also explains why it is usual to attribute to artists both the maximum of sensibility or *passion*, and the maximum of insensibility or Olympian *serenity*. The two characters are compatible, for they do not refer to the same object. The sensibility or passion relates to the rich material which the artist absorbs into his psychic organism; the insensibility or serenity to the form with which he subdues and dominates the tumult of the sensations and passions.

George Boas

THE MONA LISA IN THE HISTORY OF TASTE*

The search for aesthetic standards by means of which any work of art can be finally judged would seem to presuppose either that every such work is an unchanging entity, or that, regardless of whether it changes or not, it should always be judged in the same way. Neither of these presuppositions appears tenable to the writer of this paper, who holds, on the contrary, that works of art are not the locus of one value, known as "beauty" or something similar, but are rather multivalent, that certain of their values are experienced by some persons, others by others, and that there is no *a priori* method—except that of fiat—of determining which of the many values are properly "aesthetic." One objection usually raised against this position is that there happen to be some works of art which "the judgment of posterity" has always held to be admirable or "great," and that one has only to examine their characteristics to discover what the distinguishing marks of great works of art are. The Parthenon, the *Aeneid, Hamlet,* and so on, it is maintained, have always enjoyed a high reputation. They are great by almost universal consent; or, if there have been periods when they were not highly esteemed, that is because the people of those periods had poor taste.

* From the *Journal of the History of Ideas*, Vol. I, No. 2, April, 1940. Reprinted by permission of the author and of the *Journal of the History of Ideas*.

It cannot be denied that there are works of art which have almost always been greatly admired. (For the sake of the argument one may neglect those times when they were not discussed at all, having been overlooked for some reason or other.) But having admitted that, one faces the question whether the name, *Hamlet*, or the Parthenon, or the *Aeneid*, has always meant the same thing. Physically, the words or the shapes of stone in which they are embodied have changed little, though the little is not without some importance; but the physical basis of these and other works of art is only a small part of them. More important is what people have looked for in them and either found or not found. Thus the *Aeneid* as a Roman epic differs from the *Aeneid* as an instrument of magic, and *Hamlet* as a chivalric tragedy of revenge differs from *Hamlet* as a Freudian drama. It may be argued that the work of art as the artist intended it is the real work of art, and that we should suspend judgment until we have recaptured it in its primitive state. In most cases such a quest is probably futile, for we often have no way of knowing what an artist intended, and in any event we can, for the most part, only reconstruct what he intended from what we ourselves find. And that is to no small extent dependent upon our education and our original nature. Moreover, to recapture through study an artist's intention is different from reacting directly to a work of art; and the professor of English literature who, having studied Elizabethan language and customs and theatrical practice and the biography of Shakespeare, reads *Hamlet*, is not psychologically identical with the Elizabethan spectator who went to the theater and saw *Hamlet* during what might be called its lifetime. Whatever else Shakespeare may have been up to, he was certainly not producing plays for professors of English to study three hundred years after his death. We may reasonably conclude that to define the work of art as the work intended by the artist gives us only the slenderest clues to appropriate standards for judging it.

The purpose of this paper is to take one of the works of art which have been most admired until recent times, and to examine briefly what critics or commentators of different periods have said about it. From what they said we hope to be able to infer what they were looking for. We are not so much interested in knowing why they admired the work of art as in knowing what they saw in it. It will be found that in at least this one case the work of art was identical with itself throughout history in name only. We have chosen as our example Leonardo's *Mona Lisa*.

II

The *Mona Lisa*, it should be recalled, is usually considered to be a portrait of the wife of Francesco del Giocondo, painted between 1503 and 1506. There is no conclusive evidence that it was intended as an allegory, though the background does not put that beyond the bounds of possibility.[1] No mention is made of it in the artist's literary remains, so that we do not know at what the artist himself was aiming. We do, however, know what he thought the proper fashion of representing women was, and that will be pointed out later.

Leonardo's contemporaries apparently did not consider the *Mona Lisa* his most important work. Several accounts of Italian painting, written during Leonardo's life or a little later, fail even to mention it. This is true of *Il Libro di Antonio Billi*[2] and of an anonymous work written during the forties of the sixteenth century.[3] Paolo Giovio, writing after Leonardo's death, says simply that he painted the portrait of Mona Lisa, "wife of Francesco del Giocondo, which was bought by King Francis I, it is said, for 4000 *scudi*."[4] In the short *Vita* he mentions the *Last Supper* and tells the story of Louis XII's desire to cut it out of the wall on which it was painted, and the *Virgin and Saint Anne*, but does not mention the *Mona Lisa*. There is nothing here, except the unusually high price, which is of interest. The same may be said of the comment of Raffaelo Borghini, made in 1584, that the portrait was such *che non può l'arte far davantaggio*.[5] More to the point is the criticism of Lomazzo, who praises it along with portraits by Raphael and Andrea del Sarto as peculiarly adapted to its subject.[6]

The most influential of the earlier comments on the *Mona Lisa* is that of Vasari, which established a tradition. This paragraph is the best known of the classical statements, and it was apparently the

---

[1] Everything about this famous picture has been disputed. We have accepted the traditional name of the sitter, but A. Venturi in the *Enciclopedia Italiana* maintains that she was Costanza d'Avalos and that the misty background did have allegorical significance. See his section in the article on Leonardo. L. Roger-Milès, in his *Léonard de Vinci et les Jocondes*, 1923, pp. 68 ff., maintains that it is not even a portrait.

[2] See de Fabriczy, *Arch. Stor. Ital.*, ser. V, tom. 7.

[3] *Ibid.*

[4] See Tiraboschi, *Stor. della lett. Ital.*, T. VI, p. iv, lib. iii, c. 7, xxxii (Venice, 1823, VI, 4–5, p. 1602).

[5] See *Il Riposo*, Florence, 1584, p. 370 f.

[6] G. P. Lomazzo, *Trattato dell' arte della pittura*, etc., Milan, 1584–85, p. 434.

source of most of the anecdotes repeated in later times about the picture. It was first published in 1550, some forty-odd years after the portrait was painted. The passage runs as follows:

Whoever shall desire to see how far art can imitate nature, may do so to perfection in this head, wherein every peculiarity that could be depicted by the utmost subtlety of the pencil has been faithfully reproduced. The eyes have the lustrous brightness and moisture which is seen in life, and around them are those pale, red, and slightly livid circles, also proper to nature, with the lashes, which can only be copied as they are with the greatest difficulty; the eyebrows also are represented with the closest exactitude, where fuller and where more thinly set, with the separate hairs delineated as they issue from the skin, every turn being followed, and all the pores exhibited in a manner that could not be more natural than it is: the nose, with its beautiful and delicately roseate nostrils, might be easily believed to be alive; the mouth, admirable in its outline, has the lips uniting the rose-tints of their colour with that of the face, in the utmost perfection, and the carnation of the cheek does not appear to be painted, but truly of flesh and blood: he who looks earnestly at the pit of the throat cannot but believe that he sees the beating of the pulses, and it may be truly said that this work is painted in a manner well calculated to make the boldest master tremble, and astonishes all who behold it, however well accustomed to the marvels of art. Mona Lisa was exceedingly beautiful, and while Leonardo was painting her portrait, he took the precaution of keeping some one constantly near her, to sing or play on instruments, or to jest and otherwise amuse her, to the end that she might continue cheerful, and so that her face might not exhibit the melancholy expression often imparted by painters to the likenesses they take. In this portrait of Leonardo's on the contrary there is so pleasing an expression, and a smile so sweet, that while looking at it one thinks it rather divine than human, and it has ever been esteemed a wonderful work, since life itself could exhibit no other appearance.[7]

There are two important features in this criticism: first, it is Leonardo's skill that is the subject of admiration, rather than the effect of the picture upon the observer, or the "self-expression" of

---

[7] Giorgio Vasari, *Lives of the Most Eminent Painters, Sculptors, and Architects,* tr. by Mrs. Jonathan Foster, London, 1876, II, p. 384 f. It is perhaps worth noting that in the eighteenth century Leonardo was to be blamed by at least one writer for too great fidelity to nature, uncorrected by a study of the antique. See [Dezallier d'Argenville,] *Abrégé de la Vie des plus Fameux Peintres,* 1745, p. 74.

the artist, or a symbol of something called "the times"; second, the painter's skill is supposed to be directed towards reproducing a natural object as faithfully as possible.

To think of the artist as a craftsman who learns and applies a technique is, of course, not unusual in the history of criticism. Even the most fervent admirer of Croce would admit that some artists are more skillful technicians than others. But to focus one's appreciation upon this has been by no means a universal practice among critics. Forgetting, for the purposes of this paper, the past history of such an attitude, as seen, for instance, in the elder Pliny, it is not improbable that technical skill became particularly interesting in the Renaissance, when *homo faber* began experimenting and inventing as he had not done since Alexandrian days.

But one may praise an artist's skill and yet not believe that it was oriented towards a reproduction of "nature." One may admire the exquisite technique of an Odilon Redon, for instance, or a Braque, and say nothing whatsoever about the likeness of its result to anything natural. One may admire the technique of a Byzantine fresco in which the "natural" is almost completely recreated and transformed. The idea that "nature" was of interest and importance in her own right belongs to a period in which men seek to observe facts and record them, and think that observation and record are good in themselves. Vasari, who was himself a painter, is perhaps more sensitive to technical excellence than a critic who has no experience in producing works of art. His own paintings are, like those of most of his contemporaries, admirably skillful in perspective and other tricks of illusion. It is therefore possible, though not probable, that he was simply erecting his own type of skill into a standard for all artists.

It would, however, be sheer pedantry to attempt to prove what everyone knows, namely, that the Renaissance in Italy was marked by an almost religious regard for what later became natural science, and by a delight in the arts which helped man understand the things of nature.[8] The whole matter has been clearly and succinctly

---

[8] As early as 1493 Bellincioni had written a sonnet on another portrait by Leonardo, that of Cecilia Gallerani, the mistress of Ludovico Sforza. The sonnet plays upon the rivalry between art and nature and begins,

Di chi ti adiri? A chi invidia Natura?
Al vince che ha ritratto una tua stella . . .

told by Burckhardt in his *The Civilization of the Renaissance in Italy*, and requires no retelling. But it may be said that the Italians of this period were the first men to rediscover natural beauty, to write biographies again, as the Alexandrians did, to describe in detail the human face and form, to collect strange animals and even strange people. It is in keeping with this taste that the sketchbooks of Jacopo Bellini, of Leonardo, of Pisanello, and of their contemporaries are filled with drawings of animals, flowers, clouds, mountains, and other natural things.

But "fidelity to nature" is a notoriously equivocal formula. The multiple meanings of "nature" and its derivatives have been discriminated by A. O. Lovejoy and we shall not attempt to expand upon his treatment of the subject.[9] But we must notice what the phrase meant to Vasari and earlier to Leonardo. In the passage quoted from the biographer and critic, one observes that the artist is praised for reproducing the likeness of his sitter as Apelles is said to have reproduced the likeness of his grapes. Just as the birds in the classical instance pecked at the painted grapes, so the observer of the Mona Lisa believes the original to be before him, with beating pulses and living eyes. But before the passage is over one finds that Leonardo is praised also for painting the woman with a pleasant and smiling expression, as she appeared when listening to cheerful music or jesting talk; so that "while looking at it one thinks it rather divine than human."

How much literary exaggeration is expressed in these last words and how much they echo a Neoplatonic strain is hard to tell. Even in Leonardo, whose interest in reproducing natural objects led to those amazing anatomical and botanical and geological drawings, there are Neoplatonic elements. If he says, on the one hand, "Wisdom is the daughter of experience," and backs it up with minutely detailed studies of what he observes, he says on the other, "Nature is full of infinite causes which were never set forth in experience."[10] If he says, "O marvellous Necessity, thou with supreme reason

---

(For the whole sonnet, see *Le Rime di Bernardo Bellincioni*, ed. by Pietro Fanfani, Bologna, 1878.) The idea is, of course, a literary commonplace and for that very reason of peculiar interest. The portrait, it may be added, seems to have disappeared. A similar idea is found in the Latin verses on a portrait of Lucrezia Crivelli in *The Notebooks of Leonardo da Vinci*, 1938, II, 394.

[9] See *Primitivism in Antiquity*, pp. 447 ff., and "Nature as Aesthetic Norm," *Mod. Lang. Notes*, XLII (1927), pp. 444 ff.

[10] *Notebooks*. I, 85 and 77, respectively.

constrainest all effects to be the direct result of their causes, and by a supreme and irrevocable law every natural action obeys thee by the shortest possible process," he also says, "Nature being capricious and taking pleasure in creating and producing a continuous succession of lives and forms. . . ."[11] Which of these Natures he saw as he drew his sketches, there is now no saying. But the probability is that most of his contemporaries saw in the sketches after they were drawn the capriciously creative and fertile Nature rather than the mechanistic and purely geometrical.

For a hundred or more years after Vasari there is little or no mention of the *Mona Lisa*. According to the French historian, Lemonnier,[12] Leonardo and his Italian *confrères* who were called to France by Francis I "furent traités avec toutes sortes d'égards et reçurent des appointements en rapport avec leur réputation." There was even circulated the old story that Leonardo died in the King's arms, a story now discredited.[13] But although more of his authentic pictures belonged to the crown—and now to the French Republic—than to any other single collector, most French writings of the sixteenth, seventeenth, and even eighteenth centuries are silent about him.[14] He is not mentioned in the letters of Marguerite d'Angoulême,[15] in the works of Rabelais, Montaigne—not even in his *Journal de Voyage*—nor the Pleiade; the courtiers, who might have seen at least the *Mona Lisa*, say nothing that we have been able to discover of either the picture or its author; even Louis Leroy, whose *De la Vicissitude ou variété des choses de l'univers* (1579) lists the painters whose works have raised his times to eminence, omits Leonardo's name. One possible reason for this is that the *Mona Lisa* belonged to the King and therefore not many people had the chance to see it. But the most famous pictures and sculptures of the time were made familiar to the interested

---

[11] *Ibid.*, I, 253 and 80 respectively. For a denial of the presence of Neoplatonism in Leonardo, see E. Panofsky, *Studies in Iconology*, 1939, p. 182.

[12] In Lavisse's *Histoire de France*, V, i, 316.

[13] See L. Roger-Milès, *op. cit.*, pp. 15 f. The story, as is well known, dates from the time of Vasari.

[14] Though Poussin drew the illustrations for the edition of the *Trattato* which appeared in the middle of the seventeenth century, Leonardo was not so highly esteemed as Raphael, for instance, or even some of the lesser painters. Cf. A. Fontaine, *Les doctrines d'art en France*, 1909, p. 3.

[15] The sister of his great French patron, who, according to Roger-Milès, *op. cit.*, p. 65, is portrayed in Leonardo's (?) *Marriage of Saint Catherine*.

public by engravings, and if Leonardo had captured the imagination of Frenchmen, his works would doubtless have been both known and spoken of, as those of Raphael were.[16]

In the middle of the seventeenth century, Leonardo's name and the *Mona Lisa* emerge once more. Père Dan, who made a catalogue of the works of art at Fontainebleau, calls it the *premier en estime, comme une merveille de la peinture*.[17] In whose estimation it ranked first and why it was considered a marvel are not revealed. Félibien, somewhat later, continues the Vasari tradition.

This is one of the most finished of his works. It is said that he took so much pleasure in working on it that he spent four months on it, and that while he was painting this lady there was always someone near her who sang or played some musical instrument, so as to keep her joyful and prevent her from assuming that melancholy air which comes over one easily when one is inactive and motionless.

Truly, said Pymandre, if I may give my opinion, the time which he put into it was well spent, for I have never seen anything more finished or more expressive. There is so much grace and so much sweetness in the eyes and features of this face, that it appears to be alive. When one looks at this portrait, one would say it was a real woman who takes pleasure in being seen.

It is true, I replied, that Leonardo appears to have taken particular care to finish it well. And Francis I considered this picture to be one of the most finished products of this painter, wished to own it, and paid four thousand *écus* for it.[18]

The excellence of Leonardo's artistry is judged in this passage by its "finish" in the representation of a gentle and sweet woman's face. The time given to the work, four months, becomes a matter

16 The portrait could only have been seen by persons admitted to the "gilt cabinet" at Fontainebleau, which would have required special permission. It was removed to Versailles by Louis XIV, probably after 1694, the last date on which it appears in the inventories of Fontainebleau (See *La Grande Encyclopédie*, XVIII, p. 950). It was not exhibited in the Louvre until after the Revolution. It does not appear to have been engraved until the nineteenth century. For its history in France, see the catalogue of the Louvre by Georges Lafenestre and Eugène Richtenberger, tr. by B. H. Dausseron, p. 56.

17 *Trésor des Merveilles de Fontainbleau* (1642), quoted by Rigollot, *Cat. de l'oeuvre de Léonard de Vinci*, 1849, pp. 652 ff. Cassiano del Pozzo in 1625 saw the painting and commented on its bad condition. See Müntz, *Léonard de Vinci*, 1899, p. 421.

18 André Félibien, *Entretiens sur les vies et sur les ouvrages des plus excellens Peintres anciens et modernes*, 2d ed., 1685–1688, I, 193 f.

of the greatest interest to subsequent critics, who vary it as they will. Vasari had said that Leonardo "loitered" over it for four years—not months—and then had left it unfinished. Lanzi, pointing out the unfinished state of most of Leonardo's pictures, continues by saying that the impression of lack of finish is attributable to the artist's having left certain portions of his pictures less perfectly finished than others. This deficiency, he says, cannot be detected always by the best judges. "The portrait, for instance, of Mona Lisa Gioconda . . . was minutely examined by Mariette in the collection of the king of France, and was declared to be carried to so high a degree of finish that it was impossible to surpass it."[19] Stendhal passes on the story, saying that the artist "never considered it finished."[20] Delecluze reduces the time to three years.[21] The story continues to our own day, through Houssaye, the American Moses F. Sweetser, his contemporary, Mrs. Charles W. Heaton, Gabriel Séailles, Mantz, Edward McCurdy, E. V. Lucas, and Elbert Hubbard.[22]

III

For some three hundred years no one appears to have seen anything mysterious about this painting. It was the portrait of a certain merchant's wife in a cheerful mood, and what was found extraordinary in it was its fidelity to nature. But a merchant's wife is still a woman, and women began to occupy a curious position in many early nineteenth-century minds. They had previously been cruel, coquettish, vain, deceitful, gentle, fickle, tender, weak, but they had rarely been enigmatic. On the contrary, men knew them

---

[19] Luigi Lanzi, *The History of Painting in Italy*, tr. by Thomas Roscoe, new ed. rev., 1853. The history was first published in 1789 and was considered for many years authoritative. It was translated and revised by the Reverend G. W. D. Evans in 1848. In translation the passage appears, "the labor of four years, and, after all, left unfinished." Mariette was the author of the *Abecedario de Pierre Jean Mariette*, which I have not seen.

[20] *Hist. de la Peinture en Italie*, 1817, I, 223 f.

[21] *Léonard de Vinci*, 1841, p. 29.

[22] See respectively, *Hist. de Léonard de Vinci*, pp. 439 ff.; *Leonardo da Vinci*, Boston, 1879, p. 59; *Leonardo da Vinci and his Works*, 1874, p. 51 f.; *Léonard de Vinci*, 1892, p. 140; *Leonardo da Vinci*, 1898, II, 158; *Leonardo da Vinci*, 1904, p. 113; *Leonardo da Vinci*, 1926, p. 9; *Little Journeys to the Homes of Eminent Artists*, 1902, X, ii, p. 46. Elbert Hubbard translated the sum of 4000 *scudi* into eighty thousand dollars. Stendhal had been content with forty five thousand francs.

only too well. But the early nineteenth century introduced a new woman into the history of ideas—*la femme fatale.*[23]

The *femme fatale* emerged with Romanticism. She was all sensation and feeling, as against masculine rationality. She captured men by her apparent passivity, lying in wait like a fascinating serpent for the flitting bird who was the male. Whether the Romanticists knew it or not, she could trace her ancestry back to the Eve of Philo Judaeus. The Romantic critics, whether they were engaged in interpreting paintings or poetry, treated their works of art as if they were hieroglyphs. Each had a hidden "meaning" which only the initiated could uncover. To be one of the initiated, one must have a peculiar kind of sensitivity, an eye that not merely saw the perceptual screen of things but penetrated to something called the reality behind it. Such metaphors in practice meant that the critic was not to record what he saw, but to let his imagination freely play about the work of art and to report what it constructed.

What Vasari was for the pre-nineteenth century critic, Théophile Gautier and Walter Pater became for their contemporaries and successors. Both started a tradition—in apparent independence of each other—which has not died even to-day. Gautier's paragraph was the earlier published.

> Leonardo da Vinci retained the finesse of the Gothic period while animating it with a spirit entirely modern. . . . The faces of Vinci seem to come from the upper spheres to be reflected in a glass or rather in a mirror of tarnished steel, where their image remains eternally fixed by a secret similar to that of the daguerreotype. We have seen these faces before, but not upon this earth: in some previous existence perhaps, which they recall to us vaguely. How explain otherwise the strange, almost magic charm which the portrait of Mona Lisa has for even the least enthusiastic natures? Is it her beauty? Many faces by Raphael and other painters are more correct. She is no longer even young; her age must be that loved by Balzac, thirty years; through the subtle modelling we divine the beginnings of fatigue, and life's finger has left its imprint on this peachlike cheek. Her costume, because of the darkening of the pigments, has become almost that of a widow; a crêpe veil falls with the hair along her face;

---

[23] This is, of course, a commonplace, but see Mario Praz, *The Romantic Agony*, 1933, ch. IV, esp. pp. 243 ff. The reader also would do well to complete what follows in our text by pursuing Mr. Berenson's suggestion of the influence of Lavater and the other physiognomists. See his *The Study and Criticism of Italian Art*, 1916, p. 24.

but the expression, wise, deep, velvety, full of promise, attracts you irresistibly and intoxicates you, while the sinuous, serpentine mouth, turned up at the corners, in the violet shadows, mocks you with so much gentleness, grace, and superiority, that you feel suddenly intimidated, like a schoolboy before a duchess. The head with its violet shadows, seen as through black gauze, arrests one's dreams as one leans on the museum railing before her, haunts one's memory like a symphonic theme. Beneath the form *expressed*, one feels a thought which is vague, infinite, *inexpressible*, like a musical idea. One is moved, troubled, images *already seen* pass before one's eyes, voices whose note seems familiar whisper languorous secrets in one's ears; repressed desires, hopes which drive one to despair stir painfully in the shadow shot with sunbeams; and you discover that your melancholy arises from the fact that la Joconde three hundred years ago greeted your avowal of love with this same mocking smile which she retains even to-day on her lips.[24]

Here simple fidelity to nature has completely disappeared; the eternal feminine has taken its place. The *Mona Lisa* is not the portrait of a young woman; she has ripened through experience. She recalls past lives, stirs up repressed desires, mocks you with her smile. At once a new strain enters into French criticism. Whereas the earlier critics had seen sweetness and gentleness, the later began to see something more troubling. Even Taine, who was scarcely a victim of "the Romantic agony," found the famous smile "doubting, licentious, Epicurean, deliciously tender, ardent, sad," and united it to the smiles of the Saint John, the Saint Anne, and other Vincian smiles.[25] Houssaye, one of the co-authors of Gautier's book, who was interested enough in facts to write a Life of Leonardo, also is captivated by the new mystery. He feels it his duty to bring in her "charm, provocative and ineffable, cruel and divine, sybilline and voluptuous."[26] This diabolical charm appears also, somewhat intensified, in Charles Blanc and Paul Mantz.

Before a painting so wonderful and so admired, the time which was consumed in painting it is explained either by the fact that the artist experienced the fascination which he has so well expressed, and pro-

---

[24] Théophile Gautier *et al.*, *Les Dieux et les demi-dieux de la peinture*, [1863], p. 24 f. The article on Leonardo first appeared in 1858. For further information about it, see Spoelberch de Lovenjoul, *Hist. des oeuvres de Théophile Gautier*, pp. 160, 262 ff.

[25] H. Taine, *Voyage en Italie*, 1902 (1st ed. 1865), II, 409.

[26] Arsène Houssaye, *op. cit.*, p. 125.

longed as far as possible the sweets of conversation with this charming woman, or that he had difficulty in expressing the proud serenity and restrained provocation of this face whose smile, at certain moments, seems satanic and still magnetises us by its long and voluptuous glances. It seems that after having carried the modelling to the point of the most delicate shading, to imperceptible accents, and thus brought it close to us by palpitating truth, the artist may have desired then to withdraw it into the mystery of half-light, to hold it remote from our gaze by shrouding it in a gauze and to make it appear as a dream amid a wild landscape, against an unbelievable background of little mountains, blue, rocky, pointed, cut from crystal, and like stalactites turned upwards towards the skies.[27]

All that was lacking now was an explanation of the mysterious charm of this face. The explanation must lie, according to romantic procedure, in the life of the painter, and it was not hard to find reasons for believing that the original Lisa was the mistress of the painter.[28] Charles Clément told the extraordinary story in full. He noticed, he says, that whereas the men's heads by Leonardo were all individualized, those of the women were all identical. On a panel belonging to the Orleans family was discovered a reclining female whose features were those of *La Gioconda*. In the Fesch Collection and in the Hermitage are two half-length nudes with the same face. The original Lisa was the third wife of Giocondo—so that her husband must have been much older than she. Leonardo was young, witty and handsome when he painted her. The portrait at which "he worked or pretended to work" for four years never became the property of her husband. Finally, it is from the time when he painted the *Mona Lisa* that the other female heads begin to resemble hers.

As a matter of cold fact it requires no deep observation of Leonardo's portrait to see how little it resembles the Saint Anne and the Saint John and the various Madonnas. The one common character is the smile, but the series of thirty or more archaic maidens in the Acropolis museum in Athens have an identical smile, which they share with many other archaic statues of both men and

---

[27] *Hist. des peintres de toutes les écoles. Ecole Florentine*, 1879. See p. 27 f. for the full account. It is typical of writers of this school that they will say, "stalactites turned upwards towards the skies" rather than "stalagmites."

[28] *Michelangelo, Leonardo da Vinci and Raphael*, tr. by Louisa Corhan, (n. d.), pp. 201 ff.; French ed. 1861. A poem on the same theme was produced by M. A. Dollfus and may be found in Houssaye, *op. cit.*, pp. 335 f.

women. Are we to conclude from this anything except that such smiles were the fashion of the times? Leonardo's saints and other supernatural beings do resemble one another; he gave them a certain "ideal" head. But the portraits attributed to him are individualized. The face of the *Mona Lisa* cannot be said to resemble the face of *La Belle Ferronière*, if that portrait be indeed by him. And neither of them closely resembles his saints.

Pater's famous passage on our painting is of course better known to English readers than Gautier's, and was perhaps the source of most later American and English interpretations of it. Pater suggests more than he states, whether from timidity, ignorance, or critical principle, but one may vaguely discern through his poetic prose that, like Clément, he finds a disconcerting similarity running through all the female heads and, like Gautier, a symbol of metempsychosis. The symbolism, he maintains, is not "crude," but the picture has "a subdued and graceful mystery." He believes that the "unfathomable smile, always with a touch of something sinister in it," plays over all of Leonardo's work. "From childhood we see this image defining itself on the fabrics of his dreams; and but for express historical testimony, we might fancy that this was but his ideal lady, embodied and beheld at last." He suggests a fusion of his dream and the real Mona Lisa. And then follows the purple passage which has been reprinted even in anthologies of poetry. In that face "strange thoughts and fantastic reveries and exquisite passions" are "deposited cell by cell" upon the flesh. "All the thoughts and experiences of the world have been etched and moulded there, in that they have of power to refine and make expressive the outward form, the animalism of Greece, the lust of Rome, the reverie of the middle age with its spiritual ambition and imaginative loves, the return of the Pagan world, the sins of the Borgias." Mona Lisa becomes the "fancy of perpetual life," a reincarnation of Leda, Helen, Saint Anne.[29]

Few art critics of the nineteenth century, capable of reading Pater, resisted his musical style, and we find dozens of imitations

---

[29] Walter Pater, *The Renaissance*, 1st ed., 1873. The essay itself was first published in the *Fortnightly Review*, Nov. 1869, pp. 494 ff. Donald A. Stauffer, in an interesting article, *Monna Melancholia* (*Sewanee Review*, XL, 89 ff.) gives reasons for believing that Pater had never seen the original of the *Mona Lisa* and had superimposed Dürer's *Melancholy I* upon it in his memory. For intimations of an influence of Gautier on Pater through Swinburne, called to my attention by Professor Meyer Schapiro, see Louise Rosenblatt, *L'Idée de l'art pour l'art etc.*, 1931, p. 105.

of him in the years that followed the publication of *The Renaissance*. Mrs. Charles W. Heaton, for instance, saw in the portrait, "a
sweet but perplexing poem," and a visible embodiment of "the
words of the preacher, 'vanitas vanitatum.' "[30] Mr. Frank Preston
Stearns, after a passage on the "meaning" of the smile, dwells
upon the sense of mystery in Leonardo's character, which is "expressed without reservation" in this picture.[31] Elbert Hubbard, in
one of his *Little Journeys*, brought in the words of the Preacher,
as well as those of Walter Pater, added Cleopatra to Leda, Helen,
and Saint Anne, and filled three pages with an eloquent description of a smile which he called "ineffable."[32] Mr. George B. Rose
expressed the usual thoughts about the "inscrutability" of the smile,
"a smile that is only on the lips, while in the eyes there are un-
sounded depths. Vainly we question her; like the Sphinx her riddle
eludes us still."[33] Mr. Edward McCurdy, after an analysis of the
details of the portrait, concludes, "Thus, on the very confines of
fantasy, and girt about with suggestions of strange lights and fur-
tive shadows, he has created in this portrait of Madonna Lisa, third
wife of a Florentine official, a myth of the embodiment of which
men dream as of the eternal enigma of womanhood."[34]

I V

From Gautier and Pater, as is clear, runs a tradition which is the
very opposite of that started by Vasari. Whereas the Italian bi-

---

[30] *Leonardo da Vinci and his Works*, 1874, p. 52.

[31] *The Midsummer of Italian Art*, 1895, p. 60. Though the Notebooks had
not as yet been published when Mr. Stearn's book appeared, the *Treatise on
Painting* alone might have shown him that Leonardo was enamored more of
precision and clarity than of mystery.

[32] *Little Journeys to the Homes of Eminent Artists*, X, no. 2, pp. 46-50
(Feb. 1902). Hubbard's opinion of the picture may not seem important; but
he was considered a great authority on "culture" by the general public of his
day. The circulation of his *Little Journeys* was always large and his writings
must have been the source of the aesthetic of many unschooled Americans.

[33] *The World's Leading Painters*, 1912, p. 50. In a similar vein Laura
Spencer Porter conveyed to the ladies of America the "meaning" of the
Mona Lisa in the *Woman's Home Companion*, April, 1914 (XLI, p. 54).

[34] *Leonardo da Vinci*, 1904, pp. 115 f. It is interesting to observe that
James Jackson Jarves, the American collector and critic, who alone of the
writers cited—and many others not cited—knew the Italian painters of the
Renaissance intimately, was almost unique in his time in continuing the
Vasari tradition rather than what we have called the Romantic. See his *Art
Studies of the Old Masters of Italy*, 1861, I, p. 400.

GEORGE BOAS 590

ographer and critic chiefly saw in the *Mona Lisa* a wonderful technical feat, the reproduction of a natural object, the French and English "aesthetes" saw it as a hieroglyph which required not simply contemplation but deciphering. It would appear to have become second nature to think of a picture—at least of this picture— as something of a rebus, a symbol whose meaning could be discovered only by a critic's intuition. That this school of writers attributed their theory of artistry to the artists whose works interested them need surprise no one. Critics are in the habit of reading an artist's mind.

This habit became strengthened when the psychology of Sigmund Freud achieved popularity. The nineteenth and twentieth centuries have been noteworthy, among other things, for a peculiar paradox: a combination of great scientific accomplishment with anti-intellectualism. Early in the former century, Schopenhauer began to argue that the understanding was created by the will to serve its own ends, an argument which he sought to deduce from Kantian principles. These ends, however, were not those of Kant's Practical Reason; they were, on the contrary, purely biological; and it was easy for Schopenhauer's successors to identify them with sexual ends. An artist, according to Freud, is a man whose sexual frustrations are released symbolically in pictures or statues or other works of art. Appetites which would never pass the Censor if expressed in their true nature, are permitted to appear in disguise.

As is well known, according to this theory the fundamental appetite of the human male is his love for his mother, known as the Oedipus Complex. Since incest in most Occidental society is not encouraged, the Oedipus Complex can only be released through art, and hence a Freudian critic will be likely to see in a picture a symbol of the artist's passion for his mother. Here, it will be observed, the critic assumes that the artist is not communicating something to the observer—he is really concealing something from the observer— but unconsciously expressing something of himself. When this something is revealed, it does not mean that the picture will be liked any the more; no standard of aesthetic judgment is implied in the psychoanalysis of a work of art. But it is clear that what mainly interests a Freudian, in any such work, will be the discovery of the unconscious motive. Freud's interpretation follows.

It was quite possible that Leonardo was fascinated by the smile of Mona Lisa because it had awakened something in him which had slumbered in his soul for a long time, in all probability an old memory.[35] This memory was of sufficient importance to stick to him once it had been aroused; he was forced continually to provide it with new expression. The assurance of Pater that we can see an image like that of Mona Lisa defining itself from Leonardo's childhood on the fabric of his dreams, seems worthy of belief and deserves to be taken literally.

Vasari mentions as Leonardo's first artistic endeavors, "heads of women who laugh." The passage, which is beyond suspicion, as it is not meant to prove anything, reads more precisely as follows: "He formed in his youth some laughing feminine heads out of lime, which have been reproduced in plaster, and some heads of children, which were as beautiful as if modeled by the hands of a master. . . ."

Thus we discover that his practice of art began with the representation of two kinds of objects, which would perforce remind us of the two kinds of sexual objects which we have inferred from the analysis of his vulture phantasy. If the beautiful children's heads were reproductions of his own childish person, then the laughing women were nothing else but reproductions of Caterina, his mother, and we are beginning to have an inkling of the possibility that his mother possessed that mysterious smile which he lost, and which fascinated him so much when he found it again in the Florentine lady. . . .[36]

Not only is Freud able to construct a part of the hidden life of Leonardo from the *Mona Lisa*, he is also able to build up the life of the artist's mother. Since she was not married to Piero da Vinci, she was forced to "compensate herself for not having a husband."

In the manner of all ungratified mothers she thus took her little son in place of her husband, and robbed him of a part of his virility by the too early maturing of his eroticism. . . . When in the prime of his life Leonardo re-encountered that blissful and ecstatic smile as it had once encircled his mother's mouth in caressing, he had long been under the ban of an inhibition forbidding him ever again to desire such tenderness from women's lips. But as he had become a painter he endeavored to reproduce this smile with his brush and burnish all his pictures with it, whether he executed them himself or whether they were done by his pupils under his directions, as in Leda, John, and Bacchus.[37]

---

[35] According to Vasari, the smile had to be artificially produced and preserved.

[36] Sigmund Freud, *Leonardo da Vinci*, 1916, pp. 85 ff. There is no objective evidence that Caterina resembled Lisa, in smile or otherwise.

[37] *Ibid.*, p. 91 ff.

The way was now open for further embroidering on this psychological background, and critics were not slow to follow it. Pictures became clues to the subconscious labyrinths of an artist's mind. Regardless of the fact that this particular picture seemed to have been painted as a portrait, which might lead one to suppose that its appearance was to a large extent determined by the attributes of the woman who sat for it, its main interest was now held to lie in what it could tell us about the man who made it. This shift in critical attention was the kind of reversal of opinion best illustrated in the Hegelian dialectic. Whereas in Vasari the picture was considered with reference to its closeness to the objective world of nature, in Freud it is considered as a disclosure of the most intimately subjective world, the so-called Unconscious. But since the world which it reveals can be known only by means of a theory which is applied to the particular object, rather than one which has been deduced from it, the critic has only to make up his mind what was in the artist's Unconscious and then discover it spread out before him in the picture.

One finds a still more remarkable example of this in the volume written on our artist by Rachel Annand Taylor, *Leonardo the Florentine*. For her the *Mona Lisa* is a phase in Leonardo's transition from concealment to avowal of his homosexuality. It is she says,[38] "as if he were afraid to see his Narcissus except in a disguise." Presumably when he painted his Saint John, he was no longer ashamed to see his Narcissus. But even if he were not, it is hardly likely that he painted the picture in order to inform the world that he had conquered his shame. This becomes doubly true if one accepts the Freudian theory that art is always a symbolical rather than a literal satisfaction of repressions.

Happily, we are not engaged in an examination of Freudianism. Our purpose is simply to indicate how it reoriented aesthetic comment on this picture in the twentieth century. A writer now feels it possible to assume that a painter is painting for himself rather than for an observer, and that, if an observer should present himself before a picture, he should find in it what the artist himself concealed in it. But since only initiated Freudians know what is concealed in pictures, the uninitiated observer fails to see what the pic-

---

[38] Rachel Annand Taylor, *Leonardo the Florentine*, 1927, esp. pp. 350–354. Only one who has gone through the whole of this book can get its full flavor.

ture really is, or "means." He is in the position of a European ignorant of Chinese looking at Chinese characters and thinking they are merely patterns.

If the *Mona Lisa* at the present time is considered old-fashioned, that is probably to be attributed more to the writings of the Gautier-Pater school than to those of the psycho-analysts. Leonardo himself is far from old-fashioned; but it is now the scientific and philosophical Leonardo rather than the artistic. This paper is not concerned with the decline of interest in the painting, but we may be permitted to suggest that M. Paul Valéry is probably right in saying that the association of "mystery" with the picture has had more influence than any other one thing in disgusting people with it.[39]

The tendency in the criticism of painting from about 1910 to the beginning of sur-realism has been technical. It has consisted largely in studies of form, color, drawing. Only since Marxian criticism became fashionable has there been much attention paid to subject-matter. But in such criticism little is said of adequacy of representation—fidelity to "nature"; the critic is concerned only with the "social significance" of the work of art. Hence to such critics, the *Mona Lisa* would have no great interest, unless, perhaps, as an illustration of the rise of the middle class, for the lady so carefully portrayed was probably a *bourgeoise*.

It may not be inappropriate to terminate with a celebrated passage from the artist's note-books about the portraiture of women. "Women," Leonardo says, "should be represented in modest attitudes with legs close together, arms folded, and their heads low and bending sideways."[40] The head of La Gioconda is not bending sideways, but otherwise the precept appears to be carried out in the painting. Add to it the memorandum on the importance of painting faces in a nebulous light, and you begin to have a clue to his method

---

[39] See his *Leonardo da Vinci*, 1929, p. 58. For other hostile criticisms of this celebrated picture, see Berenson's *The Study and Criticism of Italian Art*, pp. 3 f.; A. C. Barnes, *The Art in Painting*, 1925, p. 368; P. Dearmer, "Leonardo da Vinci, a Criticism," *Contemporary Review*, Vol. 135 (1929), p. 217. The Italian Futurists, in their campaign to liberate Italian art from the museum-pieces, quite naturally attacked it. A good example may be found in Soffici's *Giornale di Bordo*, 1915, p. 147: "In tram.—Vedo scritto su un muro a grandi lettere bianche su fondo blu: GIOCONDA: ACQUA PURGATIVA ITALIANA. E piu giù la faccia melensa di Monna Lisa. Finalmente. Ecco che si comincia anche da noi a far della buona critica artistica."

[40] *The Notebooks of Leonardo da Vinci*, p. 240.

of portraiture. This will throw no light on what is "expressed" by the picture, nor is that, fortunately, our affair. We know that Leonardo was attracted by chiaroscuro and busy with the means of utilizing it. We may fittingly leave to psychiatrists the problem why such things interested him.

Our purpose in this paper has been merely to show how a given work of art may in different periods have essentially different content—and therefore be admired for different, if not for contradictory, reasons. If this instance is typical, it would appear that works of art which "withstand the test of time" change their natures as the times change. The work of art becomes thus the locus of a new set of values determined by the preconceptions or the predominant interest of the new critic or observer.

Stephen C. Pepper

A REPLY OF EXTREME
RELATIVISMS IN CRITICISM*

Earlier in this book we met an objection to our mode of describing
a work of art to the effect that value judgments were neither true
nor false. We pointed out that this objection was based on an
arbitrary identification of value judgments with commands and
wishes, and that it failed to take account of certain factual relationships constituting the work of art which are as open to description
and to verifiable judgment as any other rather complex factual
relationships. The vehicle, the perceptions stimulated by the vehicle,
the funding process, and the selective systems determining the field
of relevant traits as a dispositional property of the vehicle, are all
matters of fact open to description by a discriminating observer.
By a trick of definition—by defining the aesthetic judgment as a
kind of command rather than a kind of factual statement—the
emotive-judgment school evades this group of facts. The facts, of
course, remain in spite of the evasive definition. And that is why I
believe the tenets of this school will not prove formidable in the
long run. Facts have a way of speaking for themselves.

But there is another objection by another school of aestheticians
which needs to be taken much more seriously, because this one
refers to the facts. This is the objection of the so-called relativists,

* From Stephen C. Pepper, *The Work of Art*, ch. 5 (Bloomington: In-
diana University Press, 1955). Reprinted by permission of the publisher.

who declare that there is no determinate judgment regarding the nature and value of a work of art valid for all men or for all cultures. The nature and worth of a work of art alter from culture to culture, from man to man, possibly even from momentary perception to momentary perception. The relativists of this school do not deny that judgments about the character and value of a work of art may be true. But they are true in some highly-restricted or variable sense.

The initial difficulty with the relativists is to find out just what they mean. One relativist differs from another in the mode of his insistence on relativity. Of course, even the view developed in this book requires some relativity. The judgment of an object of criticism is relative to the existence of a vehicle and the responses of a normal discriminating spectator. In the nature of the factual relationship described these could probably only occur in human society. Our view is thus relative to man. But our view does entail the possibility that a true judgment of the character and value of an object of criticism can be made which would be true irrespective of the perceptual limitations of particular spectators, and irrespective of the failure of the object to conform to the particular cultural pattern of the critic. It is such extreme relativists as seem to deny even this much objectivity of aesthetic judgment who require serious attention before we take leave of the subject before us. Perhaps there is no better way of summarizing emphatically the position taken in these essays than by contrasting it with the position of the more restrictive relativists.

Let us take, then, the view of some prominent relativist in the aesthetic field and examine his arguments and his evidence for them. I can think of no better man for this purpose than George Boas. His brilliant book with the ironic title *Wingless Pegasus* offers an authoritative exposition of a rather extreme form of relativism. Its terminal essay, "The Mona Lisa in the History of Taste," which first appeared some years earlier, has become a sort of classic for aesthetic relativism. I shall restrict my attention mainly to this essay. For here the issue between my position and his can be squarely faced in the treatment of a specific well-known work of art.

He begins his essay with this challenging statement: "The search for aesthetic standards by means of which any work of art can be finally judged would seem to presuppose either that every such work is an unchanging entity, or that, regardless of whether it changes or not, it should always be judged in the same way. Neither of these presuppositions appears tenable to the writer of this paper, who holds, on the contrary, that works of art are not the locus of one value known as 'beauty' or something similar, but are rather multivalent, that certain of their values are experienced by some persons, others by others, and that there is no a priori method—except that of fiat—of determining which of the many values are properly 'aesthetic.' "

To see more specifically what Boas means by "multivalence" we may look at an earlier passage in the book from a section headed "Multivalence": "Not only may a thing or process have both instrumental and terminal value, but it may at the same time have several kinds of each. Eating is both useful for preserving life and also a pleasant pastime. The meal which one eats is a means of a cook's earning his living, or a host's entertaining his friends, of his friends meeting together for conversation, of a series of voluptuous tastes, sights, and smells, and so on. A book, let us say *Pickwick Papers*, may be useful to a reader who wants to know something about manners and customs in early nineteenth century England, who wants to pass an examination in English literature, who has a lecture to give on English humor; it may also and at the same time be very amusing just to read, as indeed it is, and be read for no purpose ulterior to the amusement which is in it. Writing it may have been a pleasant occupation for Dickens, and at the same time an economic necessity. In fact, the inherence of a large number of values in anything would be obvious if theorists had not decided that one must forget most of them. But if one does not arbitrarily excise certain of the values as irrelevant, one is forced to the conclusion that anything may and usually does satisfy several interests."

This second quotation makes it clear that the multivalence Boas has in mind applies mainly to what we have been calling the vehicle of the work of art. No one, of course, could seriously deny that the physical vehicle of a work of art could be used, and often is used, for a great variety of purposes. Boas' list of uses is the merest beginning. A copy of *Pickwick Papers* could make a good paper weight, a source of fuel in an emergency, a weapon of attack if nothing heavier were at hand. But such values are clearly distinguishable from certain other values derivable from a physical copy of *Pickwick Papers*, notably from certain terminal values.

Just previous to the passage quoted, Boas has been at some pains to distinguish terminal from instrumental values. He does not give the impression of regarding this distinction as arbitrary, or a priori, or a matter of mere fiat. It appears to be a distinction forced upon a careful observer by the facts. And when an object formerly valued as an instrument comes to be valued as an end, this is apparently for Boas a notable occurrence. He even slips (if it is a slip) into calling the terminal value "beauty." "But the most impressive evidence of the emergence of terminal from obsolete instrumental values," he writes, "is found in museums, such as that founded in Dearborn by the late Henry Ford, in which people simply look at all kinds of instruments, carriages, sleighs, furniture, lamps, which were all made for use, not primarily for beauty. *Their beauty has arisen from the obsolescence of their utility*" (italics mine). There seems to be nothing arbitrary or a priori in the observation of this distinction, nor in the exclusion of utility value from the value given these objects by visitors to the museum in Dearborn. Nor does there seem to be anything illegitimately arbitrary for Boas, according to this passage, in naming this value "beauty" any more than in naming it "terminal," which Boas never gives any intimation of considering arbitrary. And let me interpolate here incidentally that one of the common conceptions of aesthetic value, or beauty, consists precisely in its identification with what Boas is here naming "terminal value."

If one appreciates the significance of this point—that the distinction between instrumental and terminal values is not a matter of arbitrary fiat but an observation of an empirical difference of fact, and that the naming of the terminal value with the symbol "terminal" or even with the symbol "beauty" is not arbitrary in any sense other than the selection of a name for a class of distinguishable responses—then one can easily see that any other empirical distinctions observed among values will not be arbitrary either. That is, the naming itself is significant evidence that Boas makes an objective distinction here between two kinds of value. Boas himself mentions the possibility of a number of kinds of terminal values also. If a writer elects to name one of these species of terminal value, rather than the whole genus, "beauty," that would be his privilege and would not be arbitrary in any empirically illegitimate sense, either. The only requirement is that the writer recognize the observable relations between the species of value he is attending to at the moment and other species. And the same with any other empirical distinction found among values.

What, then, would be illegitimately arbitrary for an empirical writer in aesthetics? It would have to be something, I suppose, that had the effect of distorting the evidence. An appeal to a priori certainty or self-evidence for some definition of beauty, I would agree with Boas, would be an instance of this, or a dictatorial insistence by personal fiat for a definition of beauty for which no justifiable evidence is offered. I would also agree with Boas that a good many aestheticians in the past have been guilty of these forms of arbitrariness. But what is there of an a priori nature or of irrational fiat in the description of observable distinctions among values and the concentration of interest upon some one distinguishable species of value that can suitably in conformity with usage be called aesthetic? Nothing, of course. So what leads Boas into this false dilemma of positing either no distinguishable aesthetic value and only an indiscriminate multivalence, or else arbitrary fiat and the a priori?

The answer is his failure to carry out first an empirical study of the complex nature of a work of art. In common with most writers on aesthetics he accepts the work of art vaguely as some single object of reference. He does not clearly distinguish between the physical vehicle, the perceptions stimulated by it, and the object of criticism as a dispositional property of it. The first is obviously multivalent like all physical objects in that it is capable of many uses. The second, any one particular perception of the vehicle, is usually univalent. Any particular perception is usually in response to some particular use or mode of enjoyment of a physical object. The third is univalent in the sense that it is generated by a specific sort of selective system which is commonly called aesthetic—such, for instance, as the maximizing of consummatory satisfactions. This mode of selection is empirically observable, as we have seen, and is no more arbitrary than any other natural selective process, no more arbitrary than the flow of water in brooks and rivers forming the drainage system of some valley. The multivalence of the physical object which serves as the vehicle of a work of art is thus quite consistent with the univalence of the object of criticism which determines the aesthetic worth of a work of art.

This statement is somewhat oversimplified, of course, as we know from our detailed study of the object of criticism. The description of the selective system determining the structure and worth of an object of criticism is not as easy to work out as that determining the flow of water in a valley. And a candid observer must concede that there is a lot yet to be learned about the process. There are several alternative theories stressing different factors in the process—one stressing satisfactions, another organicity, another stability, and another vividness. These are different theories about the selective process interpreting the evidence now available in different ways.

It would appear from a number of Boas' remarks in *Wingless Pegasus* that he confuses these alternative hypotheses about the selective process and the resulting nature of the object of criticism with the multivalence of the physical object serving as the vehicle of the work of art. The various instrumental and terminal values which may be attached to the physical vehicle of a work of art are, of course, taken as observed facts, not as a variety of descriptive theories about a fact. But the alternative hypotheses about the selective process generating the object of criticism are precisely this sort of thing—a variety of descriptive theories about a fact. It might be true that there are a number of selective processes generating a corresponding number of distinct objects of criticism. But it would still be important to distinguish among a number of different values as facts and a number of different theories about some one of these values. I incline to believe, however, until more conclusive evidence appears to cause me to change my mind, that there is only one ultimate process of selection of relevant traits for a work of art and that this process generates usually only one object of criticism for a given aesthetic vehicle.

Now, let us return to the essay on the *Mona Lisa*. We have so far found that Boas' opening statement expressing his extreme relativistic view of the multivalence of a work of art is initially plausible only because of its ambiguities and vagueness. In the light of our previous analysis, we can see that he confuses the physical vehicle with the object of criticism, ascribing a multivalence which, with qualifications, does truly apply to the vehicle, also to the object of criticism, to which it does not similarly apply. The physical vehicle can have all kinds of values, instrumental, sentimental, moral, and cognitional, as well as those ordinarily called aesthetic, and still be in its physical properties entirely neutral to them all. But the object of criticism by its very mode of generation is primarily an object of what is ordinarily called aesthetic worth; and, if any other sorts of value attach to it also, these are purely secondary and incidental.

And in Boas' opening statement of the *Mona Lisa* essay there is also implicit another confusion that becomes explicit in other parts of his book—the confusion between a variety of values that can in fact be attached to a single object and a variety of hypotheses that can be offered as descriptions of a single value process.

Let us hold these confusions in mind and proceed with the argument of his *Mona Lisa* essay. After the statement quoted earlier to the effect that "works of art are not the locus of one value, known as 'beauty' or something similar, but are rather multivalent," he calls attention to two objections often raised against his type of theory. The first is the argument from the classics that ". . . there happen to be some works of art which 'the judgment of posterity' has always held to be admirable or 'great,' and that one has only to examine their characteristics to discover what the distinguishing marks of great works of art are." The second is the argument that ". . . the work of art as the artist intended it is the real work of art. . . ." Boas briefly states the difficulties in finding an artist's intentions and the consequent fact that the work of art ". . . gives us only the slenderest clues to appropriate standards for judging it." He then drops the second argument as not worthy of more attention (to which I would on the whole agree), and proceeds to the body of his essay which is a scholarly effort to demolish the evidences for the first argument. In fact, Boas goes further than that. He not only undertakes to demolish the classic but evidently also intends to demolish the object of criticism which would unquestionably be "the locus of one value, known as 'beauty' or something similar," for he emphatically asserts that "works of art are not the locus of one value . . ." etc. Our two views, consequently, clash head on at this point. So let us follow the steps of this argument.

It is an argument from the evidences of men's reports on their judgments of the *Mona Lisa* from the time it was painted by Leonardo between 1503 and 1506 to the present day. It is an argument from the discrepancies of these reports in comparison with one another.

"The purpose of this paper," writes Boas, "is to take one of the works of art which have been most admired until recent times, and to examine briefly what critics or commentators of different periods have said about it. From what they said we hope to be able to infer what they were looking for. We are not so much interested in knowing why they admired the work of art as in knowing what they saw in it. It will be found that in at least this one case the work of art was identical with itself throughout history in name only."

Parenthetically, Boas seems to have overstepped his main thesis of multivalence here, possibly to gain dramatic effect by exaggerating the paradox. He says he intends to leave us only with the *name* of the *Mona Lisa*. Even the physical vehicle is to lose its identity. You will find that *Pickwick Papers* was earlier allowed to be "an economic necessity" and "a valuable source of income," presumably the printed book that was, and is, bought and sold, not *only* the name. I am quite sure Boas does not intend to abolish the physical identity of the vehicle. As he says in one place, "But in general the physical appearance of works of art is fairly stable," which here allows for even a good deal of sensuous identity—the colors, for instance. But there is no question that Boas is demolishing the identity of the object of criticism, and anything similar—that is, trying to.

There appears to be little but the barest factual comment on the *Mona Lisa* till Vasari's enthusiastic report in 1550, forty years after it was painted. Boas points out that Leonardo's contemporaries would not have regarded it as his most important work. But Vasari praises it highly for the technical skill it shows and for its faithfulness to life, its realism. Here is the passage from Vasari quoted by Boas:

> Whoever shall desire to see how far art can imitate nature, may do so to perfection in this head, wherein every peculiarity that could be depicted by the utmost subtlety of the pencil has been faithfully reproduced. The eyes have the lustrous brightness and moisture which is seen in life, and around them are those pale, red, and slightly livid circles, also proper to nature, with the lashes, which can only be copied as they are with the greatest difficulty; the eyebrows also are represented with the closest exactitude, where fuller and where more thinly set, with the separate hairs delineated as they issue from the skin, every turn being followed, and all the pores exhibited in a manner that could not be more natural than it is: the nose, with its beautiful and delicately roseate nostrils, might be easily believed to be alive; the mouth, admirable in its outline, has the lips uniting the rose-tints of their colour with that of the face, in the utmost perfection, and the carnation of the cheek does not appear to be painted, but

truly of flesh and blood: he who looks earnestly at the pit of the throat cannot but believe that he sees the beating of the pulses, and it may be truly said that this work is painted in a manner well calculated to make the boldest master tremble, and astonishes all who behold it, however well accustomed to the marvels of art. Mona Lisa was exceedingly beautiful, and while Leonardo was painting her portrait, he took the precaution of keeping some one constantly near her, to sing or play on instruments, or to jest and otherwise amuse her, to the end that she might continue cheerful, and so that her face might not exhibit the melancholy expression often imparted by painters to the likenesses they take. In this portrait of Leonardo's on the contrary there is so pleasing an expression, and a smile so sweet, that while looking at it one thinks it rather divine than human, and it has ever been esteemed a wonderful work, since life itself could exhibit no other appearance.

Then Boas notes that for a hundred years there is little or no mention of the *Mona Lisa*. The picture was to be sure, in the French king's collection, but, whatever the reason, there is no critical reference to it. In the middle of the seventeenth century it is mentioned by Père Dan in a catalogue of the works of art at Fontainebleau as "premier en estime, comme une merveille de la peinture."

Just a little later comes the following comment by André Félibien (quoted by Boas), still praising the technique and commenting on the sweetness of the lady represented:

This is one of the most finished of his works. It is said that he took so much pleasure in working on it that he spent four months on it, and that while he was painting this lady there was always someone near her who sang or played some musical instrument, so as to keep her joyful and prevent her from assuming that melancholy air which comes over one easily when one is inactive and motionless.

Truly, said Pymandre, if I may give my opinion, the time which he put into it was well spent, for I have never seen anything more finished or more expressive. There is so much grace and so much sweetness in the eyes and features of this face, that it appears to be alive. When one looks at this portrait, one would say it was a real woman who takes pleasure in being seen.

It is true, I replied, that Leonardo appears to have taken particular care to finish it well. And Francis I considered this picture to be one of the most finished products of this painter, wished to own it, and paid four thousand *écus* for it.

Then there appears to be no noteworthy criticism of the picture until the romantics of the nineteenth century, who bring in a new element. ". . . Gautier and Pater . . . ," writes Boas, both started a tradition—in apparent independence of each other—which has not died even today." Pater's passage is so well known that Boas only lifts out a sentence or two, but here is Gautier's description as quoted by Boas:

Leonardo da Vinci retained the finesse of the Gothic period while animating it with a spirit entirely modern. . . . The faces of Vinci seem to come from the upper spheres to be reflected in a glass or rather in a mirror of tarnished steel, where their image remains eternally fixed by a secret similar to that of the daguerreotype. We have seen these faces before, but not upon this earth: in some previous existence perhaps, which they recall to us vaguely. How explain otherwise the strange, almost magic charm which the portrait of Mona Lisa has for even the least enthusiastic natures? It is her beauty? Many faces by Raphael and other painters are more correct. She is no longer even young; her age must be that loved by Balzac, thirty years; through the subtle modelling we divine the beginnings of fatigue, and life's finger has left its imprint on this peachlike cheek. Her costume, because of the darkening of the pigments, has become almost that of a widow; a crêpe veil falls with the hair along her face; but the expression, wise, deep, velvety, full of promise, attracts you irresistibly and intoxicates you, while the sinuous, serpentine mouth, turned up at the corners, in the violet shadows, mocks you with so much gentleness, grace, and superiority, that you feel suddenly intimidated, like a schoolboy before a duchess. The head with its violet shadows, seen as through black gauze, arrests one's dreams as one leans on the museum railing before her, haunts one's memory like a symphonic theme. Beneath the form *expressed*, one feels a thought which is vague, infinite, *inexpressible*, like a musical idea. One is moved, troubled, images *already seen* pass before one's eyes, voices whose note seems familiar whisper languorous secrets in one's ears; repressed desires, hopes which drive one to despair stir painfully in the shadow shot with sunbeams; and you discover that your melancholy arises from the fact that la Joconde three hundred years ago greeted your avowal of love with this same mocking smile which she retains even to-day on her lips.

Nothing said here about Leonardo's skill or fidelity to nature but much about a mysterious charm in the sitter and something deeply emotional if not sinister in her smile. Many other writers of this period discover these characteristics in the *Mona Lisa* or follow the leadership of those who first did. It is also noticed that the same smile is to be found in many other figure paintings of Leonardo, and many writers think they see a resemblance in the faces. Boas fails to see a resemblance in the faces but admits the similarity of the smiles, belittling the observation, however, as no more significant of emotional depth than the identity of the smiles of the archaic maidens in the Acropolis Museum in Athens. "Are we to conclude from this," he suggests, "anything except that such smiles were the fashion of the times?"

The next accretion of interpretations of the *Mona Lisa* in Boas' account comes in the twentieth century with the Freudians, beginning with Freud himself in his study of Leonardo da Vinci. Freud's interest was, of course, not primarily aesthetic but clinical or, rather, in the nature of an analysis of a personality structure. His conclusions are necessarily inferential on the evidence of what is known of Leonardo's life and what has come down to us of his writings and paintings. This evidence is reviewed by Freud in the light of his psychoanalytical experience to reach certain conclusions about Leonardo's character and the drives motivating his production. Since some of the conclusions have to do with the artist's emotions embodied in his works, Freud's statements have a bearing on the aesthetic character of Leonardo's works.

And this leads to the aesthetic pertinence of Freud's comments on Mona Lisa's smile, which he regarded as probably a highly-charged emotional symbol for Leonardo. The emotional charge on this detail—like an emotionally-charged gesture in a heated discussion—would be caught by a sensitive observer as a very significant element in the appreciation of the work of art. The observer would not necessarily know *why* it was so heavily charged with emotion but would feel *that* it was and that it was relevant to the appreciation of the work. This would explain the fascination Gautier and Pater and all the other emotionally-sensitive writers of the nineteenth century found in the smile, and the fact that the smile and the expression of the *Mona Lisa* rarely go unmentioned in any comment on the portrait even by so matter-of-fact a critic as Vasari.

Boas' point, however, is that here is another interpretation added to that of the romantics, and one to be distinguished from that of the earlier critics mainly interested in realism and technical finish.

Boas then notes that lately the interest in the *Mona Lisa* seems to have declined, partly in reaction perhaps to the emotional interpretations of it offered by the nineteenth-century romantics, but mostly because the fashionable criticism of art in the recent decades is either Marxian or nonrepresentational, and the *Mona Lisa* does not attract exceptional attention on either of these scores.

Boas terminates his recording of the four and a half centuries of commentary on the *Mona Lisa* with a sentence from Leonardo's notebooks. "Women," Leonardo says, "should be represented in modest attitudes with legs close together, arms folded, and their heads low and bending sideways." Thus Boas makes a whole circle back to the beginning. And I suppose his insinuation is that Leonardo was a plain, sensible, red-blooded fellow who looked facts in the face with no funny business and, when he was asked to paint a portrait of a merchant's wife, he painted it with proper care and accepted the proper fee. If you want the artist's intention, here it is; and all the rest, from Vasari to Pater and Freud, is froth and has nothing to do with the picture, though it is informative of the temper of the times when Vasari, Pater, Freud, and the others wrote.

And yet you remember that in the opening section of this essay Boas stated that "to define the work of art as the work intended by the artist gives us only the slenderest clues to appropriate standards for judging it."

The concluding paragraph of Boas' paper runs as follows: "Our purpose in this paper has been merely to show how a given work of art may in different periods have essentially different content—and therefore be admired for different, if not for contradictory, reasons. If this instance is typical, it would appear that works of art which "withstand the test of time" change their natures as the times change. The work of art becomes thus the locus of a new set of values determined by the preconceptions or the predominant interest of the new critic or observer."

If this conclusion is taken literally—and I don't see how else we can take it, though I also don't see how Boas can wish it to be taken so—the so-called *Mona Lisa* is a physical locus (a canvas? or a "name"?) which by chance was the locus of a succession of entirely discrete perceptual projections. From 1550 for a century or two it was a structure of meticulous representation and technical finish. Then it ceased to be both of these and around 1850 became the locus of emotional expression. Then it ceased to be any of these and

around 1900 became a piece of clinical evidence and an embodiment
of certain unconscious motivations.

Now, of course, the opposite thesis of this book is that the *Mona
Lisa* as an object of criticism was all of these all the time. All that is
needed to make this clear is a complete analysis of the work of art,
from which the distinctions among the physical vehicle, the perceptions of it, and the object of criticism emerge. Particular perceptions
differ with the mood of the moment, the discriminatory powers of
the spectator, the cultural interests of the time, but the physical
vehicle is fairly stable; and the object of criticism as the structure
of relevant traits that tend to be selected and funded for the object
of criticism on the stimulus of the vehicle is also quite stable. What
Boas fails to take account of is the selective process generating the
object of criticism with the result that the work of art collapses
under his analysis into a heap of unrelated perceptions or cultural
projections.

Of course, from the moment Leonardo finished the *Mona Lisa*,
the picture was nearly all the things the long line of discriminating
critics discovered it was. It was a remarkable piece of realism, a skillful exemplification of artistry, a rich embodiment of emotion, and
quite surely an expression of some unconscious drives. Vasari was
clearly much moved by it. In spite of the emphasis of his time upon
realism and technique, he could not resist remarking that while looking at the portrait "one thinks it rather divine than human." And
it would be hard to believe Gautier and Pater did not recognize the
artistry and realism of the *Mona Lisa* while trying to put in words
the specific emotion it aroused in them through its visual forms and
associations. And Freud, of course, did not ignore Pater but believed
he was amplifying and deepening the understanding of the emotion
Pater found embodied there. And so on from critic to critic. Not but
what there were many irrelevancies, to be shed in the progress
towards the determination of the object of criticism. But the trend
over the centuries has been to amplify and deepen the understanding
of the *Mona Lisa*, not to whittle it away and nullify it.

I wonder if Boas realizes that by his mode of analysis no man
would have a determinate character of his own—not even George
Boas himself—but only his name and possibly his anatomy. Even
the chair upon which I sit would dissolve into a name. For suppose
A describes its color, and B its texture, and C its utility, and D its
artistry, and E its comfortableness. And, to complete the analogy,

let these descriptions be spread out through time so that none of them occurs simultaneously with another. Does that demonstrate that there is a totally different chair for each of these spectators? When C reports on its utility, does that mean that he has no awareness of its color, texture, artistry, and comfortableness? Even if C happens to be color-blind, does that imply that the chair is colorless? Not at all. And, similarly, neither does Boas' collection of varied reports imply that the *Mona Lisa* has not continuously possessed the various properties which the various critics have chosen to stress. The service these critics have done is to show us that for the fullest appreciation we should discriminate them all.

This, I think, is a sufficient answer to the attack on the object of criticism that lies implicit in an extreme form of relativism such as Boas seems to espouse. But the sort of answer I prefer would be a more positive one for a man of such wide and discriminating taste as George Boas possesses. It would consist in observing him carrying out his discriminations in the presence of some excellent work that he admires. Something of this sort happens several times in *Wingless Pegasus*. But I would particularly ask that one read or reread the pages where Boas is describing some of the details he finds in Milton's sonnet on his dead wife. Boas is here expressing his annoyance at a group of critics who try to shut out as relevant to a poem associations which require some knowledge that cannot be obtained entirely from within a poem, such as the knowledge of Milton's blindness. At the height of his indignation over the effects of such criticism, Boas writes: "Since most readers read the sonnet with their whole minds, they will interpret it in the light of all they know, and will not attempt to impoverish its meaning by deliberately and, I venture to say, arbitrarily lopping off *relevance* which is actually there" (italics mine).

And so with the *Mona Lisa* or any other work of art as an object of criticism, I only ask the responsible critic that he shall not attempt to impoverish its meaning by deliberately and, I venture to say, arbitrarily lopping off relevance which is actually there.

Paul Ziff

THE TASK OF DEFINING
A WORK OF ART*

I

One of the foremost problems of aesthetics has been to provide a definition (or an analysis, or an explication, or an elucidation) of the notion of a work of art. The solutions given by aestheticians to this problem have often been violently opposed to one another; e.g., contrast Tolstoi's answer with that of his predecessors. There is no doubt that the problem is a difficult one. But what I should like to consider here is just why it is so difficult. In this way I hope to make clear what is involved in such a definition and what an aesthetician must do, whether he knows it or not, to justify his definition of a work of art.

II

Suppose a child does not understand what a book is, is merely puzzled by people speaking about books. One of the many means at hand to help him grasp the use of that word "book" would be simply to show him a book. But one would not help or try to help him by picking out a pocket book, or a diary with blank pages, or a loose-leaf note book. What is wanted here is a perhaps fat book, but

* From *The Philosophical Review*, Vol. LXII, 1953. Reprinted by permission of the author and *The Philosophical Review*.

not too fat, with a hard cover, perhaps a gold-lettered leather-bound book. If someone doesn't know but wants to know what a table is, to learn the use of the word "table," it would not do to begin by showing him an esoteric table with ninety-six legs, only six inches high. Again one would take a good solid oak table with a modest number of legs, an ordinary, everyday sort of table, not a cabinet maker's nightmare. If we begin with a clear-cut case, one no one would ordinarily be tempted to dispute, we can then shift to the less clear-cut, the disputed, cases. A clear-cut case is a place to start from.

What would a clear-cut case of a work of art be? One is inclined to say a painting like Poussin's "The Rape of the Sabine Women," or Da Vinci's "Mona Lisa," or Rembrandt's "Night Watch," would do here, that no one would want to object. But suppose someone were to say, "No, none of these are works of art." If, when we pointed to an ordinary everyday sort of table, someone were to object, "No, that's not a table," we could and should say he was clearly confused, in one way or another. Maybe he imagined we had not pointed at the table, that we had pointed at a chair; or we might suppose that he supposed the word "table" was only and always applied to multiplication tables; and so forth. Perhaps cultivated confusion at a sophisticated level, but nothing else but confusion, could be the root of a dispute over our clear-cut example of a table; but a refusal to call the Poussin, or the Da Vinci, or even the Rembrandt a work of art, need not be the blossom of a merely blooming confusion. For it is in fact possible to dispute whether any particular painting is a work of art or not, and people do dispute such questions, in a way that it is not in fact possible to dispute whether any particular object is a table or not.

And this is to say simply that there are and can be no such clear-cut cases of works of art in quite the same sense as there can be such clear-cut cases of tables, chairs, and so forth. That this is so stems partly from the fact that there are many uses of the phrase "work of art" in a way in which there are very few uses of the word "table." (For even though the word "table" does have many diverse uses, e.g., one can speak of multiplication tables, dinner tables, table lands, etc., there are very few uses of the word "table" in connection with those ordinary everyday objects that one customarily sits at and eats off of, i.e., tables. But in this sense, there are many distinct and different and even "competing" uses of the phrase "work of art.") And it also stems partly from the fact that among these many uses of the phrase "work of art," some are aptly described as laudatory or eulogistic. The many reasons why this is so will, I trust, become clear in the course of this discussion. For the time being, even though the examples of works of art which I have cited might not or need not be accepted by everyone, they are the clearest cases available, and as such they provide a useful base for our explorations.

In selecting a clear-cut example of a carpenter's hammer, one could choose a hammer with a handle exactly twelve and three-quarters inches long. Perhaps the title of the book we pointed to, the leather-bound book with gold lettering, was *Anna Karenina*. But in describing or talking about the example of a hammer to a child who did not grasp the use of the word, one would not say, "The handle of the hammer is exactly twelve and three-quarters inches long." Instead, one would be much more apt to say, "The handle of the hammer is about a foot long," or something of that sort. In the kind of case we have envisaged, the former statement would, at best, be altogether misleading. Whether a description is liable to mislead depends roughly on why it is wanted. In describing the clear-cut case of a hammer, when we want to help someone understand how the word "hammer" is used, we mention those facts about the object that make it, in fact, such a clear-cut case. That is why we would not say, "The handle of the hammer is exactly twelve and three quarters inches long." This really does not matter; it does not affect and is entirely irrelevant to the status of the example as a clear-cut case. But the fact that the handle is about a foot long is really relevant here. Similarly, we would not mention the particular title of the book, which we were using as a clear-cut case; but the fact that it had a title would be relevant.

Suppose we point to Poussin's "The Rape of the Sabine Women" as our clearest available case of a work of art. We could describe it by saying, first, that it is a painting. Secondly, it was made, and what is more, made deliberately and self-consciously with obvious skill and care, by Nicolas Poussin. Thirdly, the painter intended it to be looked at and appreciated, where it could be contemplated and admired. In short, he intended it to be treated in a way very much like the way that works of art are customarily treated. In saying this I do not wish to suggest that Poussin intended his work to be exhibited in a museum gallery. I do not know, but I would suppose the painting was intended to be hung in some chateau, or something of that sort. So perhaps in this respect the painting is not treated in the way intended by the painter. But there is good reason to believe that the painter did intend the painting to be displayed in an appropriate manner, to be treated with care, and to be preserved for as long as possible. And there is good reason to believe that Poussin did intend the painting to be contemplated, studied, observed, admired, criticized, and discussed by some people, if not by just any people. Fourthly, the painting is or was exhibited in a museum gallery where people do contemplate, study, observe, admire, criticize, and discuss it. What I wish to refer to here by speaking of contemplating, studying, and observing a painting, is simply what we may do when we are concerned with a painting like this. For example, when we look at this painting by Poussin, we may attend to its sensuous features, to its "look and feel." Thus we attend to the play of light and color, to dissonances, contrasts, and harmonies of hues, values, and intensities. We notice patterns and pigmentation, textures, decorations, and embellishments. We may also attend to the structure, design, composition, and organization of the work. Thus we look for unity, and we also look for variety, for balance and movement. We attend to the formal interrelations and cross connections in the work, to its underlying structure. We are concerned with both two-dimensional and three-dimensional movements, the balance and opposition, thrust and recoil, of spaces and volumes. We attend to the sequences, overlaps, and rhythms of line, form, and color. We may also attend to the expressive, significant, and symbolic aspects of the work. Thus we attend to the subject matter, to the scene depicted, and to the interrelations between the formal structure and the scene portrayed. We attend to the emotional character of the presented forms, and so forth. This is, very roughly, what I have in mind when I speak of contemplating, studying, and observing this Poussin painting. (Lest there be any misunderstanding, let me say explicitly that I am not saying that when ordinary people either contemplate or study or observe or attend to or look at or in any way concern themselves with this Poussin painting, they do in fact always attend to or concern themselves with all of the aspects of the painting that I have here mentioned. This is plainly untrue. But it is true that some people, when they look at this painting, are concerned with some of its many aspects that I have mentioned, while other people concern themselves with other of its aspects. And it is true, certainly, that all of these aspects of the painting are attended to at one time or another, and occasionally even all by one very unordinary person at one time.) Fifthly, this work is a representational painting with a definite subject matter; it depicts a certain mythological scene. Sixthly, the painting has an elaborate and certainly complex formal structure. Finally, the painting is a good painting. And this is to say simply that the Poussin painting is worth contemplating, studying, and observing in the way I have ever so roughly described.

It must be clear that whether the Poussin painting does or does not in fact fit the description that I have given is totally irrelevant to what I am saying. For example, it is at least within the nebulous realm of possibility that I am much mistaken in saying it is a good painting. It is even more than merely possible that I have been misinformed about Poussin's intentions. And maybe I have made other mistakes as well. But whether this is so or not does not in the least matter, for I am not trying to show that the Poussin painting is in fact a work of art. Rather I am trying to clarify what may be meant by saying that the Poussin painting is a work of art. What is important here is this: Because I believe the Poussin painting does fit the description I have given, I believe that it is, and I have chosen it as, one of the clearest available cases of a work of art. Our concern here is only with the description and not with whether the description fits the particular case. Each of the various facts mentioned in the foregoing description are characteristic of a work of art; it is these characteristics that concern us.

In order to make clear what the difficulties are in formulating and justifying a definition of a work of art, in the following section I shall present what I take to be an adequate definition based on the preceding account of the Poussin painting. However, I shall not here attempt to show that the definition is in fact adequate.

III

All of the characteristics mentioned in the preceding description of the Poussin painting together constitute a set of characteristics. Several characteristics taken together constitute a set of characteristics if and only if all of the characteristics mentioned are relevant in determining whether something is or is not a work of art and if they are the only characteristics that are so relevant. Anything pos-

sessing all of these characteristics can then be said to be a characteristic case. Consequently, if the Poussin painting does in fact fit the
description given above, it is such a characteristic case.

The set of characteristics given provides us with a set of sufficient
conditions for something's being a work of art. Anything clearly
satisfying these conditions can be said to be a work of art in exactly
the same sense of the phrase "work of art" in which the Poussin
painting can be said to be a work of art. It is important to notice
that I said "clearly satisfying these conditions." The word "clearly"
is crucial here. There is a temptation to say that the preceding
description of the Poussin painting provides nothing more than a
rough schema of what could be said about the work. This is not
quite true, but it is a way of emphasizing the truth that there is a
great deal of latitude in the various details of the description given.
For example, one of the facts mentioned about the Poussin painting
was that it is a representational work. Suppose we now consider
a statue of Praxiteles: are we to say that it is representational? Someone might say that a statue cannot be representational in quite the
same sense in which a painting can be. On the other hand, it could
be claimed that both a statue and a painting can be said to be representational, in the very same sense of the word, but that they are
merely different species of representative works. Again, someone
might say that a sculptor does not make a statue in quite the same
sense in which a painter makes his painting. And again it could be
said that there is no difference in sense but only a difference in species.
And this kind of question can be raised in connection with each of
the characteristics mentioned.

I take it that we are inclined to speak of a difference in sense when
we are impressed by, or wish to stress, dissimilarities. But when we
are impressed by, or wish to stress, similarities, we are then inclined
to speak of a mere difference in species. Now by speaking of a case
that "clearly" satisfies the conditions given above, I mean to refer
to a case in which there is no inclination to speak of a shift in sense
with respect to any of the characteristics listed. Unless this point is
attended to, it might mistakenly seem that we do not have a set of
sufficient conditions, for one can conjure up some curious cases.

Suppose an object were found, satisfying the conditions given
above, but with this one eccentricity: the scene depicted, and consequently the formal structure as well, changed periodically, without
being changed. Imagine an object fitting the description, but having

the peculiarity that, without being moved, it moved occasionally about the room. Thus in a way these odd objects behave somewhat like living organisms. One could be somewhat reluctant to call these things works of art. It would indeed be difficult to know what to say. Shall we say that our set of characteristics does not, therefore, provide a set of sufficient conditions? For we have not mentioned the fact that the object is a stable object, that it does not change or move about periodically of its own accord. This would be a mistake. We should be uncertain whether these odd objects were works of art solely because we should be uncertain whether they did in fact fit the description which we have given. It would be queer to say of an object that it was a painting and that it periodically moved about the room of its own accord. It would be equally queer to say of an object that it was a painting depicting a certain scene and that the scene periodically changed of its own accord. For facts like these cast a doubt on whether the object is a painting in the sense of the word "painting" originally intended, and on whether the painting depicts a scene in the sense of the phrase "depicts a scene" originally intended. But if an object does clearly satisfy the conditions stated, there can be no doubt but that it can be said to be a work of art in the very same sense of the phrase "work of art" in which the Poussin painting can be said to be a work of art.

Although the above set of characteristics provides a set of sufficient conditions, it does not provide a set of necessary and sufficient conditions. No one of the characteristics listed is necessarily a characteristic of a work of art. But a definition in terms of necessary and sufficient conditions is merely one kind of definition, one way of describing the use of a word or phrase. Another kind of definition, and the kind we are here concerned with, is one in terms of various subsets of a set of characteristics, or, in less exotic language, in terms of similarities to what I have called a characteristic case, a case in which an entire set of characteristics is exemplified.[1] The following examples should serve to clarify what is meant by speaking of similarities to a characteristic case.

Suppose we have a naturally formed stone object that has the

---

[1] Let me note that I am deeply indebted to Professor Max Black, both through his published papers and from discussions with him, for many of the ideas in this paper. In particular, I have, I trust, here profited from his account of a definition in terms of overlapping and interacting criteria; cf. "The Definition of Scientific Method," *Science and Civilization,* ed. by R. C. Stauffer (Madison, University of Wisconsin Press, 1949).

shape of a woman reclining. Indeed, it looks as though some sculptor has fashioned it, though we know that this is not the case. What is more, it is worth contemplating, studying, and observing in a way analogous to the way described in connection with the Poussin painting. Further suppose that people do in fact contemplate, study, and observe it, that it is displayed in a museum, and so forth. In virtue of its similarities to the characteristic case, this object can be said to be a work of art. The points of similarity between this object and the Poussin painting constitute a particular subset of the set of characteristics listed above. Imagine this sort of case: we have a nonrepresentational painting, deliberately made by an artist, who intended it to be exhibited and displayed, and who wanted people to contemplate, study, and observe it. But in fact the painting is not worth contemplating, studying, and observing. What is more, no one does bother with it at all. It is not exhibited, displayed, and so forth; rather it is buried away in some cellar. This too, in virtue of its similarities to the characteristic case, can be said to be a work of art. Again, the points of similarity between this work and the characteristic case constitute another subset of the set of characteristics given above.

In each of the preceding examples, when it was said that the object was a work of art in virtue of its similarities to the characteristic case, it was implicitly assumed that the similarities noted were sufficient to warrant the claim that the objects were works of art. No rule can be given to determine what is or is not a sufficient degree of similarity to warrant such a claim. If for one reason or another the dissimilarities become impressive (and what impresses one need not impress another), one is then reluctant to call the object a work of art. For example, a Greek vase is, in many ways, similar to a New England bean pot. Both are artifacts; both were made to serve domestic purposes; neither was intended to stand in a museum; and so forth. Nonetheless, a Greek vase is a work of art while a New England bean pot is not. To see that this is so, consider those points of similarity between a Greek vase and the Poussin painting that are also points of dissimilarity between a Greek vase and a New England bean pot. We do not, in fact, treat a New England bean pot in a way similar to the way we treat the Poussin painting; whereas we do, in fact, treat a Greek vase in a way quite similar to the way we treat the Poussin painting. We set up Greek vases on pedestals; we do display and exhibit them in museums and galleries, and what is more, it is worth while to do so. We do not in fact contemplate, study, observe, admire, criticize, and discuss bean pots in a way that we do Greek vases or in the way that we do the Poussin painting; furthermore, it seems most unlikely that it would be worth while to do so. Unlike bean pots, and like the Poussin painting, many Greek vases are representational. One is inclined to speak, and one does speak, of the formal structure of a Greek vase in a way similar to the way one speaks of the formal structure of the Poussin painting. We do not, in fact, speak of the formal structure of a bean pot, nor is there usually any inclination to do so. Now if one starts, as it were, from the Poussin painting and then shifts to the Greek vase, one begins to feel the strain. For a Greek vase was not (or so we are supposing) intended to be treated in a way similar to the way the Poussin painting is treated. It was designed to fulfill a specific utilitarian function. Many Greek vases are not representational. They were not, in the time of the Greeks (or so we are supposing), set up on pedestals. They were not displayed and exhibited in museums and galleries. They were not contemplated, studied, observed, admired, criticized, and discussed in a way similar to the way in which the Poussin painting is. One begins to feel the strain in speaking of a Greek vase as a work of art. Now if one tries to speak of a bean pot as a work of art, the strain becomes too great. We have reached a breaking point, and one is inclined to say things like, "A bean pot *cannot* be classed as a work of art." It is only a matter of degree.

Finally, neither a poem, nor a novel, nor a musical composition can be said to be a work of art in the same sense of the phrase in which a painting or a statue or a vase can be said to be a work of art. For such things as poems, novels, musical compositions, possess none of the characteristics listed in our set of characteristics. E.g., a poem is not exhibited or displayed; one does not contemplate, study, and observe a poem; a poem is not representational; and so forth. And even though a poem may seem to possess some of the characteristics listed, for one can and does speak of a good poem, the dissimilarities between what is meant in speaking of a good poem and what is meant in speaking of a good painting are sufficiently impressive to warrant our saying it is a different sense of the word "good." All of this, however, does not show that one cannot reasonably use the phrase "work of art" to refer to poems, novels, musical compositions, as well as to paintings. If one wished to describe a use of the phrase "work of art" in which there is such a systematic shift in sense, one could do so in terms of several sets of characteristics. One would take a clear-cut case of a poem and obtain a set of characteristics, then a clear-cut case of a novel and obtain another set, and so forth. Then something would be a work of art, in this use of the phrase, if it possessed some subset of the set of characteristics pertaining to paintings, or some subset of the set of characteristics pertaining to poems, and so forth. This may seen an extremely complex way of using the phrase "work of art," but it is actually often used in somewhat this way by critics who speak of the "art of painting," the "art of poetry," and so forth. Such a "blanket" use of the phrase may be warranted by the fact, if it is a fact, that each set of characteristics is analogous in composition to every other set; e.g., the analogue of contemplating a painting is reading a poem, the analogue of a good painting is a good poem, the analogue of display is publish, and so forth.

There is no need to elaborate this definition any further for the purposes of this discussion. The preceding account is sufficiently explicit to stir up and bring to the surface all the important difficulties that must be noted here.

IV

The definition just given provides a rough description of only one use of the phrase "work of art." But this phrase is and has been used in many ways. So long as art remains what it has always been, something changing and varied, so long as there are artistic revolutions, the phrase "work of art," or some equivalent locution, will continue to be used in many ways. For when such revolutions occur, there is inevitably a shift in some uses of the phrase "work of art." Some understanding of the nature of the disputes that occur over what is and what is not a work of art during such periods of artistic revolution is essential to an understanding of what an aesthetician is doing in offering some one, and only one, definition of a work of art.

When nonrepresentational and abstract painting first attracted attention in the early part of this century, many people complained bitterly that the nonrepresentational and abstract works were not works of art. Thus one critic wrote: "The farce will end when people look at Post-Impressionist pictures as Mr. Sargent looked at those shown in London, 'absolutely skeptical as to their having any claim whatever to being works of art.' "[2] Other critics insisted, with equal vehemence, that the Post-Impressionist paintings most certainly were works of art. If one looks with an impartial eye at these disputes between the traditional and the modern critics, one thing is quite clear. In many cases the parties to the disputes were using the phrase "work of art" in more or less different ways. Indeed, the modern critics, the defenders of the new works, were introducing a more or less novel use of the phrase. To see that this is so, it is necessary to attend to some of the typical complaints that were voiced against modern art by the traditional critics.

In a review of the first exhibition of modern art in America, Mr. Kenyon Cox claimed that

> the real meaning of this Cubist movement is nothing else than the total destruction of the art of painting—that art of which the dictionary definition is "the art of representing, by means of figures and colors applied on a surface, objects presented to the eye or to the imagination." . . . Now the total destruction of painting as a representative art is a thing which a lover of painting could hardly envisage with entire equanimity, yet one may admit that such a thing might take place and yet an art remain that should have its own value. A Turkish rug or a tile from the Alhambra is nearly without representative purpose, but it has intrinsic beauty and some conceivable use. The important question is what it is proposed to substitute for this art of painting which the world has cherished since there were men definitely differentiated from beasts. Having abolished the representation of nature and all forms of recognized and traditional decoration; what will the "modernists" give us instead?[3]

It is often erroneously supposed that traditional critics held representation to be a necessary characteristic of a work of art. This is not true. Such critics did maintain that it was a relevant characteristic, but few insisted it was necessary in that without representation there could be no work of art. What is true is that traditional critics weighted this characteristic enormously, so that it was of paramount importance in determining whether a given work was or was not a work of art. In their reaction against this view, some of

---

[2] Royal Cortissoz, "The Post-Impressionist Illusion," *Three Papers on "Modernist Art"* (New York, Amer. Acad. of Arts and Letters, 1924), p. 42. Reprinted from *Century Magazine*, April, 1913.

[3] "The 'Modern' Spirit in Art," *op. cit.*, pp. 6–8. Reprinted from *Harper's Weekly*, March 15, 1913.

the modern critics have apparently gone to the extreme of suggesting that representation is wholly irrelevant to art.[4] In this respect, our definition would be apt to satisfy neither a conservative traditional critic nor an extreme modern critic. The shift in the notion of a work of art that was brought about through the modern developments was, with respect to the question of representation, primarily a shift in emphasis, and only secondarily a shift with respect to necessary conditions. The point is that representation was of paramount importance in virtue of the fact that "accurate" representation played the role of a necessary condition in determining what was and was not a good painting. This leads us to another point of difference between the traditional and modern critics.

I am inclined to suppose both traditional and modern critics would accept the seventh characteristic listed in our definition, viz., that the work be a good one, as a relevant characteristic of a work of art. (Whether they considered it to be a necessary characteristic is a difficult question that need not concern us here.) But it is fairly obvious that what the traditional critics meant in speaking of a good painting or a good drawing was somewhat different from what the modern critics meant. For example, Mr. Royal Cortissoz, in reviewing the first exhibition of modern art in America, severely criticized Van Gogh's drawing.

> The laws of perspective are strained. Landscape and other natural forms are set awry. So simple an object as a jug containing some flowers is drawn with the uncouthness of the immature, even childish, executant. From the point of view of the Post-Impressionist prophet, all this may be referred to inventive genius beating out a new artistic language. I submit that it is explained rather by incompetence suffused with egotism.[5]

Somewhat later in his review, while discussing Matisse's drawing, Mr. Cortissoz stated that

> whatever his ability may be, it is swamped in the contortions of his misshapen figures. The fact is that real genius in these matters will out. Degas, who has been all his life a disciple of Ingres, uses a magic

---

[4] Cf. Clive Bell, *Art*, pp. 28–30, where such a view is, or seems to be, suggested.
[5] *Op. cit.*, p. 31.

of draftmanship akin to that of his idol, though the style and spirit of his work are wholly his own.[6]

It is, I take it, fairly clear that Mr. Cortissoz' notion of a good drawing, of a good painting, would today be objected to. For he, together with most traditional critics, apparently held that a necessary condition (though not, of course, a sufficient condition as is sometimes naïvely supposed) for a drawing to be considered a good drawing is that the perspective be "true," the form "realistic," and so forth. Few if any critics today would subscribe to this view.

Perhaps the clearest indication of the fact that the modern critics were using the phrase "work of art" in a more or less novel way is to be found in the oft-repeated charge that the new works had broken with tradition. For in claiming that there had been such a break, the traditional critics can be taken as claiming that the degree of similarity between the new works and those accepted in the tradition as works of art was insufficient to warrant the claim that the new works were works of art. The dissimilarities were felt to be overwhelming; the gap was held to be too great to bridge. The modern critics, of course, denied that there had been any such rupture, at least not with the tradition as they saw it; rather they insisted that tradition had been reasonably extended and developed. They repudiated the charge of a complete break by exhuming and pointing to the works of such people as El Greco to justify the modern use of distortion, just as somewhat later the Surrealists were to exhume the works of Acrimboldo and Bosch in an effort to make their own fantasies more palatable to the public. It is for this reason, among others, that the works of Matisse have so often been compared with Egyptian portraits, Japanese prints, and so forth, while the similarities between Picasso's work and practically everything in any tradition have been set forth exhaustively. Whether modern art did in fact break with European tradition is not a point that need concern us. But the fact that the tradition was at least extended cannot be denied and is here relevant. For this is merely another way of saying that there was some shift in the notion of a work or art. Let it be quite clear that I am not claiming to have here *shown* that the modern critics were introducing a somewhat novel use of the phrase "work of art." To show that such was the case, it would be necessary to present

---

[6] *Ibid.*, pp. 36–37.

a great deal more evidence than I have done. But everything about the disputes between the traditional and the modern critics certainly suggests that the modern critics were in fact using the phrase "work of art" in a somewhat novel way. And if the likelihood of this is granted, that is sufficient for the purposes of this discussion.

Once it is realized that the modern critics were most likely using the phrase "work of art" in a somewhat novel way, there is, or is apt to be, a temptation to say that the disputes between the traditional and the modern critics were merely verbal. For one may be inclined to say that in a modern critic's use of the phrase, the new works were in fact works of art, while in a traditional critic's use, they were not. But this is a temptation which we must certainly resist. Even though it may be true that the new works were works of art in a modern critic's use of the phrase, and were not works of art in a traditional critic's use, it would be quite absurd to think that, therefore, the disputes were merely verbal. The disputes, in part, arose from conflicting decisions over the way to use the phrase "work of art," but such decisions were not and certainly need not be thought arbitrary. Decisions may not be true or false, but they can be reasonable or unreasonable, wise or unwise. In effect, the traditional critics maintained that their decision to use the phrase "work of art" in a traditional way was the most reasonable one, and consequently their use of the phrase was the most reasonable use; the modern critics made exactly the same claim in favor of their own somewhat radical use of the phrase. Sometimes these claims were made explicitly; at other times, such a claim is implicit in the criticism, favorable or unfavorable, given to the new works. To understand what is involved in such a claim and what is meant by speaking of a "reasonable use" of a word or phrase, it is necessary to see why it may be important to use a word or phrase in one way rather than another, and what there is that may be worth arguing about.

V

There is no sense in speaking of a "reasonable use" of a word or phrase *in vacuo*. What is or is not a reasonable use depends on the particular context in which the question is raised, on the kind of considerations involved, and so forth. For example, if you want to be understood, you are well advised to use your words in some ordinary and familiar way; but if being understood is not at issue, this advice is not to the point. Not being understood may be one consequence of using a word or phrase in a particular way, but there may be other consequences, and consequences of a different kind. For example, it is, I suppose, no part of the meaning or the use of the phrase "excessive speed" that if a driver of a vehicle involved in an accident is held to have been driving at an excessive speed, he is likely to suffer certain penalties under the law. But even though this may be said to be no part of the use of the phrase, it is nevertheless an important fact which a jurist must keep in mind when attempting to specify the use of the phrase in a court of law. It would be unwise, for example, to lay down a ruling that would constitute a precedent for taking excessive speed to be any speed over posted limits. For a man may drive at a speed greater than the posted limit in an attempt to avoid an impending accident. It would be unreasonable to penalize him for making the attempt if it happened that even so he was unable to avoid the accident.

What I am saying is that once the legal consequences and implications of declaring a person to have been driving at an excessive speed are relatively fixed, we can then, in the light of these consequences and on the basis of certain moral and legal notions concerning the purposes to be accomplished by means of these consequences, say what is or is not a reasonable definition and a reasonable use of the phrase "excessive speed" in a court of law. (One can, of course, reverse this process and argue that once the notion of excessive speed is fairly well fixed in the sense indicated above, it is unreasonable to penalize a man merely for driving at an excessive speed. Thus someone could argue that his use of the phrase in the sense indicated above was reasonable, the consequences that are likely to occur in the course of using the phrase unreasonable. In a sense, the use of the phrase and the significant legal consequences likely to occur in the course of using the phrase each provide a standpoint for criticism. We can criticize either the use of the phrase in terms of the fairly fixed legal consequences or the legal consequences in terms of the fairly fixed use.)

To ask "What are the consequences and implications of something's being considered a work of art?" is to ask an equivocal question to which there can be no univocal answer. We must first know in what context we are to suppose the phrase "work of art" is being used. (Just so one can speak of the consequences of using the phrase "excessive speed" in one way or another only when the context is specified. In a court of law the use of such a phrase may have significant consequences which, in some other context, simply are not forthcoming.) In the context where critical disputes are carried on, there are in fact many significant consequences arising from the fact that a certain type of work is considered a work of art. For disputes between critics are not private affairs. They are carried on in a social context, and they are significant only when set in the framework provided by such a context.

It is, I suppose, no part of the meaning or the use of the phrase "work of art" that if a certain type of work is considered a work of art, works of this type will eventually find their way into a public museum. Nonetheless, public funds will, in fact, be spent on these works. The public will be advised to see and study such works. Books will be written and read about them, and so on. These are in fact some of the present characteristic social consequences of something's being considered a work of art in Western society. The social consequences and implications of something's being considered a work of art have varied in time, and no doubt they will continue to do so. For they are merely an aspect of the particular role art plays in a particular society, and as the character of the society changes, the role of art in the society may also change, together with the characteristic social consequences and implications of something's being considered a work of art in that society. Now although the traditional and the modern critics almost certainly disagreed about the specific characteristics of a work of art, they agreed both in their desires and in their expectations with regard to the characteristic social consequences and implications of something's being considered a work of art. Their agreement in this respect lent substance to their disputes over the use of the phrase "work of art." Indeed, the traditional critics explicitly and with great vehemence maintained that the Post-Impressionist works ought not to be placed in museums; that the public funds ought not to be spent on them; that the public would be ill-advised to spend its time looking at them or reading books about them; and so forth. All of this the modern critics explicitly and emphatically denied. (And this is one obvious reason why it would be quite absurd to call such disputes merely verbal.) Now to determine whether a certain type of work ought or ought not to be placed in a museum, purchased with public funds, and so on, it is necessary to consider what purposes it is to serve when once it has been purchased, when public funds have been spent on it, and so on. And this is to say that in order to determine what is or is not a reasonable use of the phrase "work of art," it is necessary to consider not only the characteristic social consequences and implications of something's being considered a work of art, but also the purposes to be accomplished by means of these consequences—i.e., the various functions of a work of art in society. The role that the functions of a work of art play in determining whether a particular use of the phrase "work of art" is reasonable or not, may be clarified by the following example.

Consider the second characteristic mentioned in our definition of a work of art, viz., that the work be made, deliberately and self-consciously with obvious skill and care, by some person. The traditional view would be that this is a necessary characteristic of a work of art. E.g., in *Art as Experience*, Dewey writes:

> Suppose, for the sake of illustration, that a finely wrought object, one whose texture and proportions are highly pleasing in perception, has been believed to be a product of some primitive people. Then there is discovered evidence that proves it to be an accidental natural product. As an external thing, it is now precisely what it was before. Yet at once it ceases to be a work of art and becomes a natural "curiosity." It now belongs in a museum of natural history, not in a museum of art.[7]

I am very much inclined to object to Dewey's use of the phrase "work of art," but it is most unlikely that such an objection can be made directly on the grounds that his use of the phrase is unreasonable. To see why this is so, it is necessary to see precisely what is at issue here. This may appear to be a relatively trivial point, one hardly worth disputing over; for there may in fact be fairly few natural objects that one is inclined to exhibit and display. What is and what is not excluded from a museum is in this case, however, of only secondary importance. The exclusion of a natural object from a museum of art is primarily of interest when viewed as symptomatic of a particular orientation toward the works that are in fact displayed in a museum. If one adopts a view similar to that of Dewey, there is a tendency to treat the work of art primarily as a "manifestation" of the artistic activity engaged in by the person who produced the object. One is then tempted to look through the

[7] Page 48.

work of art to the artist's "experiences," "feelings," and so forth. Furthermore, one is tempted to say that this "revealing" aspect of the work is essential to its functions as a work of art. Now the relevance of the artist's "experiences" to an appreciation of his work is an extremely complex problem which I shall not even attempt to consider here. But I mention these points in order to stress the fact that such considerations as these are relevant in attempting to determine whether the fact that the object was made by a person is or is not a necessary condition for its being a work of art. To claim that Dewey's traditional use of the phrase "work of art" is unreasonable would, in effect, be to claim that the mere fact that an object is an artifact does not suffice to show that it is thereby incapable of satisfactorily fulfilling the various functions of a work of art. But since such a claim would be made on the basis of a particular view of these functions, Dewey's use of the phrase ought properly to be considered in relation to his own view of what these functions are or ought to be.

There is no doubt but that the explicit disagreements between the traditional and the modern critics stemmed from more or less divergent conceptions of what the functions of a work of art are or ought to be in our society. In writing of the first exhibition of Post-Impressionist works in England, Roger Fry pointed out that the new movement in art "implied a reconsideration of the very purpose and aim as well as methods of pictorial and plastic art."[8] He characterized the purpose of the new art by saying it was devoted to "the direct expression of feeling" and to the making of "images which by the clearness of their logical structure, and by their closely knit unity of texture, shall appeal to our disinterested and contemplative imagination with something of the same vividness as the things of actual life appeal to our practical activities."[9]

What Mr. Fry says here is, of course, quite vague, but he was dealing with an extraordinarily difficult topic. Vague or not, he is quite right in suggesting that modern works serve somewhat different purposes from the accepted works that had preceded them, no matter how difficult it may be to say precisely wherein the difference lies. To consider but one aspect of this enormously complicated question, a traditional view of a function of a work of art

---

[8] *Vision and Design* (Pelican Books, 1937), p. 194.
[9] *Ibid.*, p. 195

was that it was to constitute an object of Beauty, which would inspire, profit, and delight the beholder. Now "Beauty" is not a term likely to be applied to a host of modern works, e.g., to one like Picasso's "Guernica." "Guernica" is no doubt a magnificent, powerful, superbly conceived and executed work, but it is not a thing of "Beauty." It is true that there are many paintings in European tradition to which one would be equally reluctant to apply the term "Beauty," e.g., Grünewald's "Crucifixion" in the Isenheim altarpiece, but it is also true that the obvious religious purpose of the Isenheim altarpiece is something more or less alien to modern art. That modern works do in fact serve somewhat different purposes from the accepted works that had preceded them is perhaps best signalized by the technical innovations introduced and employed by the modern artists. The extent of these innovations must not be underestimated.

It is true that the modern use of distortion has its analogue in El Greco's work among others, but it is also true that El Greco's work was practically ignored until the twentieth century. And of course even his work appears naturalistic in contrast with a work like "Les Demoiselles d'Avignon." To feel the full impact of the modern innovations in the use of color, it is merely necessary to see a work by Miro hung in a gallery alongside works done before 1850. Again one may admit that e.g., Poussin employed intense hues, and Giotto's work must have been quite brilliant at one time; but it is impossible to ignore the fact that many modern painters such as Miro and Matisse employ huge flat masses of color in an altogether new way, a way that is simply incompatible with and wholly alien to the spatial character of a Poussin painting. These and many other such technical innovations all herald the fact that modern paintings are devoted to somewhat different purposes and aims from those of the works that had preceded them. For the widespread adoption of new methods of working in art has, in fact, always been correlative to a more or less radical variation in the purposes and aims of art. (Just so the technical innovations of the monodic revolution in music at the beginning of the seventeenth century, the development of the so-called *stile moderno* or *seconda prattica* with its use of the thorough bass, the introduction of the recitative, and so forth, were the technical correlates of the development of secular music. Indeed, in the eyes of the modern critics of the period, the *stile antico* was seen as the sacred style appropriate to church music.)

Whether the traditional critics' disapproval of the purposes and aims of the new works stemmed from a failure to understand fully what these purposes and aims were, or whether this disapproval was based on a full understanding, is a purely historical question that need not concern us here. That they did disapprove is beyond question, for they voiced this disapproval in no uncertain terms; e.g., in concluding his review of the first exhibition of modern art in America, Mr. Cox adjured his readers to remember that

> it is for you that art is created, and judge honestly for yourselves whether this which calls itself art is useful to you or to the world. You are not infallible, but, in the main, your instincts are right, and, after all, you are the final judges. If your stomach revolts against this rubbish it is because it is not fit for human food.[10]

Most aestheticians today, I believe, would say the modern critics were right in contending that the Post-Impressionist paintings were works of art. Indeed, few people now dare to question the status of modern art as art, and those who do are at once labeled "Philistines" and "reactionaries." But if we say the modern critics were right—and I do not presume to question the matter here—if we say their decision to use the phrase "work of art" in a somewhat new way was a wise one and their use of the phrase was the most reasonable, we must not rashly assume that the traditional critics' use of the phrase "work of art" could be held to be unreasonable when examined on the basis of the traditional critic's own view of what the functions, purposes, and aims of a work of art are or ought to be. On the contrary, it is most likely that when so considered, their use of the phrase would prove to be quite reasonable. Thus an objection to their use of the phrase would most likely have to be made, and no doubt could be made, in terms of a prior objection to their view of what the functions of a work of art are or ought to be. (For one can reasonably dispute over the question of what the functions of a work of art are or ought to be just as one can reasonably dispute over what is or is not a reasonable use of the phrase "work of art.") In accepting the modern critics' decision, we are, in effect, accepting something of their view of what the present functions, purposes, and aims of a work of art are or ought to be in our society.

What then is an aesthetician doing when he offers some one and

---

[10] *Op. cit.*, p. 18.

BIBLIOGRAPHY

I. THE FORM AND CONTENT OF A WORK OF ART

For reservations on the distinction between the spatial and temporal arts, see:

John Dewey, *Art as Experience*, New York, 1934, ch. 10, pp. 214–44.

William Fleming, "The Newer Concepts of Time and Their Relation to the Temporal Arts," *Journal of Aesthetics and Art Criticism*, Vol. IV, 1945–46, pp. 101–6.

For a modified version of Bell, see:

Roger Fry, *Vision and Design*, New York, 1956, esp. pp. 16–38 and 131–77.

The relation of medium to aesthetic effect is discussed in:

D. W. Prall, *Aesthetic Judgment*, New York, 1929, esp. chs. III–XII, pp. 30–299.

George Santayana, *The Sense of Beauty*, New York, 1936, pp. 42–62.

An excellent discussion of various uses of "form" can be found in:

Monroe C. Beardsley, *Aesthetics*, New York, 1958, pp. 165–266.

See also:

Santayana, pp. 63–144.

Some alternative discussions of the relation of form and content are:

Morris Weitz, *Philosophy of the Arts*, Cambridge, 1950, ch. 3, pp. 35–63.

Curt John Ducasse, *The Philosophy of Art*, New York, 1929, pp. 202–8.

Sidney Zink, "The Poetic Organism," *Journal of Philosophy*, Vol. XLII, 1945, pp. 421–33.

See also the debate between Beardsley and Dickie:

George Dickie, "Design and Subject Matter: Fusion and Confusion," *Journal of Philosophy*, Vol. LVIII, 1961, pp. 233–8.

Monroe C. Beardsley, "Representation and Presentation: A Reply to Professor Dickie," *Journal of Philosophy*, Vol. LVIII, 1961, pp. 238–41.

There is a perceptive analysis of aesthetic and non-aesthetic discourse in:

William E. Kennick, "Art and the Ineffable," *Journal of Philosophy*, Vol. LVIII, 1961, pp. 309–20.

II. STYLE AND THE FORM OF A WORK OF ART

A. *The Nature of Period-Style*

The classic and still influential account of Baroque painting is:
Heinrich Wölfflin, *Principles of Art History*, New York, 1954.
See also:
John Rupert Martin, "The Baroque from the Viewpoint of the Art Historian," *Journal of Aesthetics and Art Criticism*, Vol. XIV, 1955, pp. 164-71.
For Baroque music, see:
Manfred F. Bukofzer, *Music in the Baroque Era, from Monteverdi to Bach*, New York, 1947.
Manfred F. Bukofzer, "The Baroque in Music History," *Journal of Aesthetics and Art Criticism*, Vol. XIV, 1955, pp. 152-56.
For the Baroque in literature, see:
Lowry Nelson, Jr., *Baroque Lyric Poetry*, New Haven, 1961.
Mario Praz, *The Flaming Heart*, Garden City, 1958.
Austin Warren, *Richard Crashaw*, Ann Arbor, 1957.
T. O. Beachcroft, "Crashaw—and the Baroque Spirit," *Criterion*, Vol. XIII, 1934, pp. 407-25.
Rene Wellek, "The Concept of Baroque in Literary Scholarship," *Journal of Aesthetics and Art Criticism*, Vol. V, 1946, pp. 77-97.
Helmut Hatzfeld, "The Baroque from the Viewpoint of the Literary Historian," *Journal of Aesthetics and Art History*, Vol. XIV, 1955, pp. 156-64.
For comments on Bukofzer, Martin, and Hatzfeld, see:
Wolfgang Stechow, "The Baroque," *Journal of Aesthetics and Art Criticism*, Vol. XIV, 1955, pp. 171-74.
For the Baroque as a general stylistic feature of the seventeenth century, see:
Carl Joachim Friedrich, *The Age of the Baroque, 1610-1660*, New York, 1952.
Problems of stylistic analysis are discussed in:
Meyer Schapiro, "Style," in A. E. Kroeber, ed., *Anthropology Today*, Chicago, 1953, pp. 287-312.
Thomas Munro, "Style in the Arts: A Method of Stylistic Analysis," *Journal of Aesthetics and Art Criticism*, Vol. V, 1946, pp. 128-58.
Richard C. Kuhns, "Art Structures," *Journal of Aesthetics and Art Criticism*, Vol. XIX, 1960, pp. 91-97.
James S. Ackerman, "A Theory of Style," *Journal of Aesthetics and Art Criticism*, Vol. XX, 1962, pp. 227-37.

B. *Tragedy as a Kind of Style*

For some illuminating remarks about the relation of Aristotle's definition of "tragedy" to Greek drama, see:
H. D. F. Kitto, *Greek Tragedy*, Garden City, 1954, pp. 110-20.
Definitions of Shakespearean tragedy are proposed in:
A. C. Bradley, *Shakespearean Tragedy*, New York, 1955, pp. 15-40.
H. D. F. Kitto, *Form and Meaning in Drama*, New York, 1960, pp. 199-245.
See also:
D. J. Enright, "Coriolanus: Tragedy or Debate?" *Essays in Criticism*, Vol. IV, 1954, pp. 1-19.
There is also Hegel's classic characterization in:
Anne and Henry Paolucci, eds., *Hegel on Tragedy*, Garden City, 1962, pp. 1-96 and 237-366

See also:
A. C. Bradley, "Hegel's Theory of Tragedy," *Oxford Lectures on Poetry*, London, 1950, pp. 69–95, and reprinted in Paolucci, pp. 367–98.
For contemporary discussions, see:
Francis Ferguson, "Oedipus Rex: The Tragic Rhythm of Action," *The Idea of a Theatre*, Garden City, 1953, pp. 25–53.
Robert B. Heilman, "Tragedy and Melodrama: Speculations on Generic Form," *The Texas Quarterly*, Vol. III, 1960, pp. 36–50.
Jerome Stolnitz, "Notes on Comedy and Tragedy," *Philosophy and Phenomenological Research*, Vol. XVI, 1955, pp. 45–60.
Oscar Mandel, *A Definition of Tragedy*, New York, 1961.
And a rejoinder to Quinton in:
Ruby Meager, "Tragedy," *Proceedings of the Aristotelian Society*, Supp. Vol. XXXIV, 1960, pp. 165–86.
For a comprehensive study of the *Poetics* from the point of view of a classicist, see:
Gerald Frank Else, *Aristotle's Poetics: The Argument*, Cambridge, 1957.
For two quite different interpretations of the *Poetics* by philosophers, see:
John Herman Randall, Jr., *Aristotle*, New York, 1960, pp. 287–93.
R. S. Crane, ed., *Critics and Criticism, Ancient and Modern*, Chicago, 1952, esp. the essays by McKeon.

III. THE WORK OF ART AND THE AESTHETIC SPECTATOR

For analyses of works of art in respect of their effect upon a spectator, see:
Kenneth Burke, *The Philosophy of Literary Form*, New York, 1957, esp. "Antony in Behalf of the Play," pp. 279–90.
Cleanth Brooks, "The Language of Paradox," *The Well Wrought Urn*, New York, 1947, pp. 3–21.
For important statements on the nature and value of aesthetic experience, see:
I. A. Richards, *Principles of Literary Criticism*, New York, 1949.
John Dewey, *Art as Experience*, New York, 1934, ch. 3.
Stephen C. Pepper, *The Work of Art*, Bloomington, 1955, ch. 1, and "Further Considerations of the Aesthetic Work of Art," *Journal of Philosophy*, Vol. XLIX, 1952, pp. 274–79.
The relationship of aesthetic object to perception and/or experience is argued in:
Arnold Isenberg, "Perception, Meaning, and the Subject-Matter of Art," *Journal of Philosophy*, Vol. XLI, 1944, pp. 561–75.
Paul Ziff, "Art and the Object of Art," *Mind*, Vol. LX, 1951, pp. 466–80.
Francis Sparshott, "Mr. Ziff and the 'Artistic Illusion,'" *Mind*, Vol. LXI, 1952, pp. 376–80.
For a discussion of the relation of aesthetic object to experience in the context of "expression," see:
Vincent A. Tomas and Douglas N. Morgan, "Symposium: The Concept of Expression in Art," *Science, Language and Human Rights*, Philadelphia, 1952, pp. 127–65.
For different versions of the aesthetic attitude, see:
H. S. Langfeld, *The Aesthetic Attitude*, New York, 1920.
José Ortega y Gasset, *The Dehumanization of Art*, New York, 1956.
Eliseo Vivas, "A Definition of the Aesthetic Experience," *Journal of Philosophy*, Vol. XXXIV, 1937, pp. 628–34.

Curt John Ducasse, *The Philosophy of Art*, New York, 1929, ch. IX, pp. 134–50.

J. O. Urmson and David Pole, "Symposium: What Makes a Situation Aesthetic?" *The Aristotelian Society*, Supp. Vol. XXXI, 1957, pp. 75–106.

IV. TYPES OF EVIDENCE AND THEIR RELEVANCE TO CRITICAL JUDGMENT

A. The Meaning of a Work of Art

For an interesting analysis of meaning and symbolism in American literature, see:

Charles Feidleson, Jr., *Symbolism and American Literature*, Chicago, 1953.

For meaning in painting and architecture, see:

Erwin Panofsky, *Meaning in the Visual Arts*, New York, 1955, esp. pp. 26–54 and 146–68, and *Gothic Architecture and Scholasticism*, New York, 1957.

A classic discussion of symbolism in music occurs in:

Eduard Hanslick, *The Beautiful in Music*, New York, 1957, pp. 20–70.

For a general philosophical investigation, see:

John Hospers, *Meaning and Truth in the Arts*, Chapel Hill, 1946.

The position that art expresses propositions is developed in:

Theodore M. Greene, *The Arts and the Art of Criticism*, Princeton, 1940, ch. 23.

Morris Weitz, *Philosophy of the Arts*, Cambridge, 1950, pp. 134–52.

Symbolism is discussed in:

Charles Morris, "Esthetics and the Theory of Signs," *Journal of Unified Science*, Vol. 8, 1939, pp. 131–50:

Richard Rudner, "On Semiotic Aesthetics," *Journal of Aesthetics and Art Criticism*, Vol. X, 1951, pp. 67–77.

Abraham Kaplan, "Referential Meaning in the Arts," *Journal of Aesthetics and Art Criticism*, Vol. XII, 1954, pp. 457–74.

Susanne K. Langer, *Philosophy in a New Key*, Cambridge, 1942.

For other discussions of meaning and truth, see:

Kingsley Price, "Is There Artistic Truth?" *Journal of Philosophy*, Vol. XLVI, 1949, pp. 285–91.

Manuel Bilsky, "Truth, Belief, and the Value of Art," *Philosophy and Phenomenological Research*, Vol. XVI, 1955–56, pp. 488–95.

Alexander Sesonske, "Truth in Art," *Journal of Philosophy*, Vol. LIII, 1956, pp. 345–53.

Sidney Zink, "Poetry and Truth," *Philosophical Review*, Vol. LIV, 1945, pp. 132–54.

Paul C. Hayner, "Expressive Meaning," *Journal of Philosophy*, Vol. LIII, 1956, pp. 149–57.

B. The Intention of the Artist

For an influential statement on the problem of intention, see:

W. K. Wimsatt, Jr., and Monroe C. Beardsley, "The Intentional Fallacy," in W. K. Wimsatt, Jr., *The Verbal Icon*, Lexington, 1954, ch. 1, and compare with:

Monroe C. Beardsley, *Aesthetics*, New York, 1958, pp. 17–29.

See also:

Isabel C. Hungerland, "The Concept of Intention in Art Criticism," *Journal of Philosophy*, Vol. LII, 1955, pp. 733–42.

Richard C. Kuhns, "Criticism and the Problem of Intention," *Journal of Philosophy*, Vol. LVII, 1960, pp. 5–23.
Henry David Aiken, "The Aesthetic Relevance of Artists' Intentions," *Journal of Philosophy*, Vol. LII, 1955, pp. 742–53.
A critic defends the use of intentional evidence in:
Leslie A. Fiedler, "Archetype and Signature: A Study of the Relationship Between Biography and Poetry," *Sewanee Review*, Vol. LX, 1952, pp. 253–73.
The relevance of historical evidence to criticism is discussed in:
Roy Harvey Pearce, "Pure Criticism and the History of Ideas," *Journal of Aesthetics and Art Criticism*, Vol. VII, 1948–49, pp. 122–32.
For discussions of intention that extend beyond the arts, see:
Karl Aschenbrenner, "Intention and Understanding," *University of California Publications in Philosophy*, Vol. XXV, 1950, pp. 229–72.
J. A. Passmore, "Intentions," *Proceedings of the Aristotelian Society*, Supp. Vol. XXIX, 1955, pp. 131–46.

C. *The Moral and/or Social Properties of a Work of Art*

A classic decision on obscenity in literature was that of Judge Woolsey admitting Joyce's *Ulysses* into the United States. It is reprinted in:
James Joyce, *Ulysses*, New York, 1946.
For a discussion of the relationship of literature to morality, see:
D. H. Lawrence, *Sex, Literature, and Censorship*, New York, 1953.
The relation of art and morality is examined also in:
Clive Bell, *Art*, New York, 1958, pp. 79–85.
Abraham Kaplan, "Obscenity as an Esthetic Category," reprinted in Sidney Hook, ed., *American Philosophers at Work*, New York, 1956, pp. 397–417.
Other classic statements are:
Percy Bysshe Shelley, "Defense of Poetry," reprinted in Mark Schorer, Josephine Miles, and Gordon McKenzie, eds., *Criticism*, New York, 1948, pp. 455–70.
Friedrich Schiller, *On the Aesthetic Education of Man*, New Haven, 1954.
See also:
Delmore Schwartz, "The Vocation of the Poet in the Modern World," and Cleanth Brooks, "Metaphor and the Function of Criticism," in Stanley Romaine Hopper, ed., *Spiritual Problems in Contemporary Literature*, New York, 1957, pp. 59–69 and 127–37.
The Scholastic position as applied to art occurs in:
Mortimer Adler, *Art and Prudence*, New York, 1937.
For discussions of art and society, see:
Kenneth Muir, "The Meaning of *Hyperion*," *Essays in Criticism*, Vol. II, 1952, pp. 54–75.
Christopher Hill, "Benlowes and His Times," *Essays in Criticism*, Vol. III, 1953, pp. 143–51.
T. S. Eliot, "Tradition and the Individual Talent," *The Sacred Wood*, New York, 1960, pp. 47–59.
John Dewey, "Art and Civilization," *Art as Experience*, New York, 1934, pp. 326–49.
Arnold Hauser, *The Social History of Art*, New York, 1957.
Milton C. Nahm, "The Function of Art," *Art: A Bryn Mawr Symposium*, Bryn Mawr, 1940, pp. 312–50.
The Marxist viewpoint can be found in:
Leon Trotsky, *Literature and Revolution*, New York, 1957.

For a much more refined and sensitive Marxist analysis, see:
George Lukács, *Studies in European Realism*, London, 1950.

V. THE NATURE AND USES OF CRITICAL JUDGMENT

For an analysis of different methods of modern literary criticism, see:
Stanley Edgar Hyman, *The Armed Vision*, New York, 1955.
For critics on criticism, see:
Cleanth Brooks, "Criticism, History, and Critical Relativism," *The Well Wrought Urn*, New York, 1947, pp. 215-51.
Richard P. Blackmur, "A Critic's Job of Work," *Form and Value in Modern Poetry*, Garden City, 1957, pp. 339-67.
Allen Tate, "The Present Function of Criticism," *On the Limits of Poetry*, New York, 1948, pp. 3-15.
Murray Krieger, *The New Apologists for Poetry*, Minneapolis, 1956, esp. pp. 182-201.
Rene Wellek and Austin Warren, *Theory of Literature*, London, 1953, esp. ch. IV, pp. 29-37.
R. S. Crane, ed., *Critics and Criticism, Ancient and Modern*, Chicago, 1952, esp. the essays by McKeon, Crane and Olson.
I. A. Richards, *Practical Criticism*, New York, 1929, esp. pp. 255-320.
Critical Relativism is defended in:
George Boas, *A Primer for Critics*, Baltimore, 1937, esp. pp. 138-49.
Curt John Ducasse, *The Philosophy of Art*, New York, 1929, pp. 267-305.
Some representative discussions of the evidential authority and scope of critical judgments are:
Albert Hofstadter, "The Evidence for Esthetic Judgment," *Journal of Philosophy*, Vol. LIV, 1957, pp. 670-88.
Karl Aschenbrenner, "Critical Reasoning," *Journal of Philosophy*, Vol. LVII, 1960, pp. 654-65.
Henry David Aiken, "A Pluralistic Analysis of Aesthetic Value," *Philosophical Review*, Vol. LIX, 1950, pp. 493-513.
Bernard Harrison, "Some Uses of 'Good' in Criticism," *Mind*, Vol. LXIX, 1960, pp. 206-22.
Frank Sibley, "Aesthetic Concepts," *Philosophical Review*, Vol. LXVIII, 1959, pp. 421-50.
Albert Tsugawa, "The Objectivity of Aesthetic Judgments," *Philosophical Review*, 1961, pp. 3-22.
Mary Mothersill, " 'Unique' as an Aesthetic Predicate," *Journal of Philosophy*, 1961, pp. 421-37.
Margaret Macdonald, "Some Distinctive Features of Arguments Used in Criticism of the Arts," in William Elton, ed., *Aesthetics and Language*, Oxford, 1954, pp. 114-30.

VI. THE NATURE AND USES OF DEFINITION

For an extended exercise in definition, see Collingwood's definition of "art" as expression:
R. G. Collingwood, *The Principles of Art*, London, 1938, Intro. and Bk. I, pp. 1-151.
And consult the remarks in:
John Hospers, "The Croce-Collingwood Theory of Art," *Philosophy*, Vol. XXXI, 1956, pp. 3-20.

The necessity of definition is urged and a putatively adequate definition of art is developed in:

De Witt H. Parker, "The Nature of Art," in Eliseo Vivas and Murray Krieger, eds., *The Problems of Aesthetics*, New York, 1953, pp. 90–105.

See also the attempt to provide working definitions of literature and poetry in:

Rene Wellek and Austin Warren, *Theory of Literature*, London, 1953, ch. II, pp. 9–18, and ch. XII, pp. 139–58.

A reply can be found in:

C. L. Stevenson, "On 'What Is a Poem?'" *Philosophical Review*, Vol. LXVI, 1957, pp. 329–62.

Three especially good discussions are:

Morris Weitz, "The Role of Theory in Aesthetics," *Journal of Aesthetics and Art Criticism*, Vol. XV, 1956, pp. 27–35.

William E. Kennick, "Does Traditional Aesthetics Rest on a Mistake?" *Mind*, Vol. LXVII, 1958, pp. 317–34.

Monroe C. Beardsley, *Aesthetics*, New York, 1958, pp. 29–65.

INDEX

INDEX

A Note on the Type

THE TEXT of this book was set on the Linotype in JANSON, a recutting made direct from type cast from matrices long thought to have been made by the Dutchman Anton Janson, who was a practicing type founder in Leipzig during the years 1668–87. However, it has been conclusively demonstrated that these types are actually the work of Nicholas Kis (1650–1702), a Hungarian, who most probably learned his trade from the master Dutch type founder Dirk Voskens. The type is an excellent example of the influential and sturdy Dutch types that prevailed in England up to the time William Caslon developed his own incomparable designs from these Dutch faces.

Composed, printed, and bound by
The Book Press, Brattleboro, Vermont
Typography and binding design by
VINCENT TORRE